David H. Robertson
NORTH TRINITY HOUSE
114 TRINITY ROAD
EDINBURGH   EH5 3JZ

BRITISH HISTORY
1815-1939

HISTORY OF EUROPE, 1450–1660
by P. J. Helm, M.A.
'A very able textbook—exactly right in length, scope and approach for the sixth-former.' *History*

SEVENTEENTH-CENTURY EUROPE
by L. W. Cowie, M.A., Ph.D.
'An admirable survey.' *Higher Education Journal*

EIGHTEENTH-CENTURY EUROPE
by L. W. Cowie, M.A., Ph.D.
'A brisk, tidy, confident account with plenty of facts and apt quotations.' *Times Literary Supplement*

THE FOUNDATIONS OF MODERN
EUROPE, 1789–1871
by M. E. Barlen, M.A.
'Mr. Barlen's coverage . . . reflects the latest research: just what the sixth-former needs' *Times Educational Supplement*

THE EUROPEAN WORLD, 1870–1961
by T. K. Derry, M.A., D.Phil., and T. L. Jarman, M.A., B.Litt.
'An unusually good textbook.' *Spectator*

☆

ENGLAND UNDER THE YORKISTS AND
TUDORS
by P. J. Helm, M.A.
'. . . a worthy addition to the series . . . contains a great wealth of learning reasonably lightly borne . . . highly recommended.'
The A.M.A.

BRITAIN AND THE STUARTS
by D. L. Farmer, M.A., D.Phil.
'The best book on the period written specifically for Sixth Form use.' *History*

HANOVERIAN ENGLAND, 1714–1837
by L. W. Cowie, M.A., Ph.D.
'A valuable survey, packed with information.'
Times Literary Supplement

BRITISH HISTORY, 1815–1939
by J. R. Edwards, M.A.

BRITISH HISTORY
1815–1939

J. R. EDWARDS, M.A.

Deputy Headmaster
Bournville Boys' Grammar School
Formerly Senior History Master
Batley Grammar School

LONDON
G. BELL AND SONS, LTD
1970

Printed in Great Britain by
The Camelot Press Ltd., London and Southampton

PREFACE

THE period covered by this book is one of immense complexity, with an ever-increasing interaction of political, social, economic and international forces. No history of the period can hope to be comprehensive, and in order to provide sufficient detail to give depth to important events, I have concentrated principally, as do most 'A' Level syllabuses covering the period, on political history, though the interaction of other forces necessitates wider information at various stages. The printed material available is very considerable and the period since the First World War, in particular, is one in which minor revisions of a historian's conclusions are constantly necessary in view of the information steadily coming to light as formerly secret material is released by the national archives and as the private papers and memoirs of major figures of the past fifty years are published. Despite this, I hope that the main interpretation of the period I seek to give will remain valid, not only providing the student with sufficient material and ideas for a basic conception but also encouraging further reading.

I have included in the bibliography many of the books to which I am indebted. Those who have taught me and those whom I have taught have unwittingly contributed by helping to shape my ideas. I am also grateful to Mrs. R. Lamb, who typed most of the manuscript; to my colleague Ian Bentley, who has read the proofs and helped with the Index, and finally to my wife, without whose patience and encouragement this book would never have been written.

J. R. E.

CONTENTS

MAPS

I · ENGLAND IN 1815

HISTORY is a continuing process, but in the development of
any country the ends of great wars are usually the best mile-
stones. The war that finally ended in 1815 had been the
greatest and most dangerous war fought by Britain since the
time of the Tudors. It had raised the National Debt to unparalleled heights and had led to the creation of an army
larger and more conspicuously successful in the field than ever
before. Overseas we had greatly expanded our colonial
empire, while at home the war had accelerated the technical,
financial and social changes that are known as the Industrial
Revolution. The greatness of the change was little understood at the time and those who exuberantly welcomed the
defeat of Napoleon little suspected that the coming of peace
would uncover a tangle of problems and a ferment of ideas far
less capable of solution than the threat of French aggrandisement.

(a) THE STRUCTURE OF POLITICS

Since 1810 George III, blind and suffering from porphyria,
had been King only in name. Earlier in his reign he had
attempted, with limited success, to reassert some of the royal
authority lost under his immediate predecessors and the
triumph of his reign had been in 1784 when his right to choose
his own Ministers was vindicated and his skill in electoral
manipulation and in gauging the flow of public opinion was
manifest. But from this date, though his popularity
increased, his power declined through his own physical weakness and the firm and resolute leadership of William Pitt. His
eldest son, the future George IV, now Prince Regent, was extremely unpopular with all classes of society and the English
monarchy could scarcely have survived a successor of his kind.

Monarchy's loss was Parliament's gain, but the King's support still counted a great deal in the parliamentary life of a
ministry. Apart from personal intervention, which certainly
retarded Catholic Emancipation, royal influence in indirect

ways was still very strong and invariably contributed to success in a general election. The large numbers of well-paid sinecures in the government service, though materially reduced by the Economical Reform movement of the late 18th Century, could be used to influence elections and reward the faithful. Many, however, were life freeholds and could, therefore, in course of time turn sour on the donor. A further method of reward had been exploited by George III and William Pitt, who had doubled the size of the peerage and created new orders of chivalry. George III never encroached on the functions of the legislature, nor did he ever attack directly the established constitutional customs which secured the independence of Parliament against the Crown, or even those customs which constituted a perpetual encroachment of the legislature upon functions proper to the head of the executive. The net effect of the reign was that nothing permanent was done to upset the existing tendency to a separation within the executive, unnoticed by Montesquieu, between the agents of the executive, who carried on the actual work of government, and the head of the executive who was by a fundamental principle of the constitution not responsible for the acts of his agents. In a curious way the Tory ideal of a king, superior to the contending faction, whose sole aim was to defend the permanent interest of the entire nation, was actually coming about.

The British Constitution was an intricate balance of functions in which it was impossible to say precisely where power resided. English people of all classes had a passionate love of liberty, although for the poorer people the liberty was far from real, and an instinctive distrust of power, at home or overseas. Only one thing was really certain about English politics: no power could be openly exercised without provoking a reaction, and the greater the power the greater that reaction would be.

Most power lay with the majority in Parliament and the men who controlled it, although the effectiveness of parliamentary decrees was limited by the lack of an adequate Civil Service or a professional provincial administration. The composition of Parliament was in a way a microcosm of the check and balance that made up the Constitution as a whole. This was certainly the long view; the discontented merely saw it as a muddle. The amount of real talent in Parliament was probably not significantly different from today. It might be said that the system produced the right men by the wrong means and from the wrong places.

There had never been any seriously held idea in the past that the British Parliament represented the people. Its apologists claimed that it represented property, the only true basis of law and order, and interests. The chief interest of the country before the Industrial Revolution was agriculture and this was still to a lesser extent true in 1815. Other interests in the long run had to buy their way into Parliament by purchasing land, a system which had worked reasonably well until the rise of the manufacturer, whose interests often diverged from those of the agriculturalist and who was often not in a position to make himself respectable by becoming a landowner. The consequent movement of people to hitherto under-populated areas aggravated the situation.

Apart from the addition of Scottish and Irish representatives, the electoral system had not been changed since the reign of Charles II. Its basis was the Knights of the Shire, two from each county. The franchise was uniform: the forty-shilling freeholder. In some counties, which contained dockyards, naval ports or bonded warehouses, government influence was strong; in others, a great family, such as the Lowthers of Westmorland, was predominant, and elsewhere as in Shropshire, where small freeholders and estates of medium size were numerous, the aristocracy found it more difficult to assert their authority and gentry of moderate means were often elected.

Boroughs had been added to the framework at various stages since 1295 to reward the loyalties of the moment or to increase royal influence in Parliament; the excessive number of boroughs on Duchy of Cornwall land are an instance of this. There were 405 borough members, mostly in pairs; they constituted nearly two-thirds of the House of Commons. Many of the boroughs had never been large, some had dwindled into insignificance or had disappeared altogether. Old Sarum had two electors, Gatton and Bossiney one each. Manchester, Birmingham, Leeds, Sheffield and most of the areas of rising industrial importance were not included in the list. The boroughs were unevenly distributed; Wiltshire and

Cornwall had as many boroughs as the eight northern counties. The franchise varied from place to place, although four or five main types can be distinguished. The thirteen widest were the potwalloper boroughs where all the inhabitants, except those on poor relief, could vote. In Preston the franchise was given to all the inhabitants without exception. The next widest constituencies were the scot and lot boroughs where the qualification was the payment of certain local taxes, and which included the famous Radical constituency of Westminster. Many of these constituencies, however, were decayed towns and had very small electorates, which made them more subject to external influences. Some thirty-seven boroughs voted by burgage tenure, fixed dues to the Lord of the Manor and in cases where one owner gathered into his hands the burgage holdings they formed the sole instances of seats being the absolute property of individuals. More recently created boroughs either restricted the franchise to the corporation, which was invariably co-optative, or to the freemen, who held their position by the accidents of ancient municipal constitutions; for example, in London and Liverpool the franchise belonged to the poor and not to the rich. Hereditary freemen did not lose their vote by moving away from the borough and bringing them to vote could be a heavy expense for a candidate. There were cases when the last-minute creation of honourary freeman altered the result.

The borough franchise was, therefore, not so democratic as that of the counties, but several disadvantages attaching to a system of pecuniary qualification were absent. The Borough electorate consisted of 100,000 individuals, drawn indiscriminately from every class in the nation. In 1815 many European nations were contemplating the adoption of the British parliamentary system, but not a single one would have dared to admit so wide an electorate.

A few boroughs, such as Bishop's Castle in Shropshire, were openly venal and would sell their seats to the highest bidder, but in most boroughs and all counties, though votes were reckoned to have their price, especially after 1832, local influences and patronage were predominant. Voting was open and public, and returning officers, chosen by the local aristocracy, could manipulate the results. A munificent attitude was expected of members and candidates, both in donations to local charities between elections and free beer during them. In many cases the contest was never put to the vote, the local landowners themselves agreeing on the two candidates to be presented; but sometimes revolts would take place, as when Wilberforce defied successfully, in 1807, the traditional division of Yorkshire between the Tory Harewoods and the Whig Fitzwilliams, and when Sir Francis Burdett won Westminster in 1807 without a penny being spent in his favour. Electioneering was usually a ruinously expensive business and members, when elected, were not necessarily faithful to their patrons. Its rewards were pensions, sinecure offices, local influence and sometimes, but by no means always, power. In 1827 Croker estimated that 276 out of 658 seats in Parliament were at the disposal of landed patrons; 203 of these were under Tory control, while eight peers alone controlled 51 seats.

In Scotland the system was even more absurd. In 1831 about 4,000 voters returned all the members for Scottish counties and boroughs; the majority of borough electors were members of co-opted municipal corporations. Ireland presented the same pattern of abuses as England though, as was usual with Ireland, on a magnified scale. Although Roman Catholics had recently been given the right to vote, the system was as much an instrument of the English ascendancy as was the military garrison.

There had been a serious though small movement for the reform of Parliament in the 1780's and the Younger Pitt had actually introduced a bill on the subject, but the French Revolution had brought a reluctance to tamper with the existing constitution lest small concessions lead to great ones. 'Who,' said Pitt, 'would repair the roof of his house in a hurricane?' The new problems brought about by the war and the Industrial Revolution revived the movement for reform, although for the first ten years after the war it was regarded with suspicion by the landed gentry. The Whigs realised in time that the refusal of parliamentary reform might cause the revolution of which the propertied classes were afraid. Its bias on the side of wealth and property was not the only evil; an unreformed Parliament was disinclined to reform the municipal corporations, which was essential to any general improvement in conditions in the great towns; until parliamentary elections ceased to be a form of jobbery there was no chance of

breaking away from the practice of giving official posts as a
reward and of thus securing an effective Civil Service, while
reform in the other great institutions of the country – Church,
Universities, Courts of Law – was improbable until Parliament set a standard by which laxity and corruption in other
spheres could be judged and condemned.[1]

The House of Lords was equal to the Commons in power,
although the practice of exclusive Commons concern with
matters of finance was growing up. In influence the Lords
was probably the greater, owing to the electoral patronage of
many peers; but the Commons was the main forum of national
opinion and, at a time when there were many petitions and
comparatively little legislation, this was important. The
House of Lords had changed considerably following the
peerage creations of George III and Pitt which had made the
dominant atmosphere Tory rather than Whig. By 1815 the
Lords, with a membership of 350, was more equal in numbers
to the Commons and more representative of the nation. Most
of the promotions had been members of noble and gentle
families, but a few were merchants and bankers. Despite this,
the record of the Lords in the 19th Century was a sorry one,
though occasionally they acted wisely by delaying precipitate
reforms. They were an obstacle to changes reasonable in
themselves and demanded by the country as a whole. However, despite this and other shortcomings, the English parliamentary system was the organ of government the most
responsive to popular demands in Europe. The stability of
the country and its institutions impressed foreign travellers.

One of the most important of British institutions was, paradoxically, unrecognised by law. In 1815 the authority of the
Cabinet was of recent growth and the principle of its collective
responsibility was not as yet accepted. The responsibility of
individual ministers was well established in law and carried
with it the sanction of impeachment, but it was scarcely possible to impeach the whole Cabinet. The office of Prime
Minister was also, strictly speaking, unconstitutional. All
Ministers were the King's servants, but the Prime Minister
especially enjoyed the King's confidence, without which,
certainly until the 1832 Reform Bill, the conduct of government would have been difficult. Once it was certain a

[1] See Reform Bill of 1832, p. 80.

Ministry possessed that confidence, timid, independent or
careful men would rally to its support.   It was, however,
becoming evident that no Ministry would willingly be dependent on the royal whim, and that royal confidence could only
be withdrawn when the Ministry fell through other reasons.

The exact relationship of the Prime Minister to the rest of
the Cabinet was still undefined: cabinets continued to meet in
1827 after Liverpool's stroke and later after Canning's death.
Even in choosing the Cabinet the Prime Minister was over-
shadowed by the King; the ideal of George III, as of George
IV, was a 'mixed administration' which would be above party.
'The King could not choose,' as Mr Brock has put it in *Lord
Liverpool and Liberal Toryism*, 'but he could refuse.   The Prime
Minister could choose, but it was difficult for him to insist.'   In
relation to Parliament, however, the position of Ministers was
in some respects stronger than later in the 19th Century; no
Ministry from 1783 to 1830 resigned as a result of a defeat in
the Commons; no Ministry before 1830 resigned on a question
of legislation or taxation.   The precise moment of resignation
was at the discretion of the Prime Minister, who was guided
not by isolated defeats but by the general capacity of the
Ministry to govern.   At the mercy of capricious and independent votes, Ministers were sometimes at their wits' end to
know how to carry on the daily business of the House, but the
overall picture is one of stability.

This very stability was typified by the long tenure of office
of what by 1815 was known as the Tory party.   This was no
party in the modern sense: there was no party discipline or
organisation and on minor matters self-designated Tories
were to be found on both sides of the House, but all agreed that
Jacobinism and, by extension, movements of popular Radicalism and reform, were greatly to be distrusted and if possible to
be destroyed.   In war the Tories had defended English power
and foreign liberty; at home in peace they were pledged to the
defence of property, a view shared by most Whigs, and the
basis of society as they understood it.

Yet it would be wrong to imagine that these were men
pledged merely to resistance to change.   In certain respects,
their resistance was popular, as in their attitude to Roman
Catholic Emancipation; in other matters, particularly those
which could not affect their own position in the State, they

B

were aware that change would be opportune as soon as the
country had recovered its stability.   Hence with comparatively little change of membership the cabinet of repression
before 1820 became the cabinet of liberal Toryism afterwards.

This apparent paradox may be partly explained by the
tremendous influence over the politicians of 1815 of the career
of William Pitt, with whom most had served in their youth.
Pitt had been a reformer who through the threat of war and
foreign invasion had turned to repression, and Liverpool's
Cabinet believed that at every turn they were imitating Mr
Pitt, even when they did not understand him.   Resting as they
did on Pitt's prestige and having, so it seemed, a monopoly of
power, the Tory party had attracted many young men of
talent, some, such as Peel, representative of the men who had
made fortunes from the Industrial Revolution.   Sooner or
later a breach between the old Tories and the younger generation was inevitable[1] but it was not likely to happen so long as
the Earl of Liverpool was Prime Minister.   He was not a
great party leader; though on economic matters he was in
advance of the rank and file of the party, he lacked originality
and breadth of mind.   His importance was that of an expert
committee chairman; his tact, patience and common sense
kept a Cabinet full of strong personalities together.   He had
long experience of administration, having held at various
times all three Secretaryships of State, and in his approach
more closely resembled a permanent head of a Civil Service
department rather than a modern democratic statesman.   He
was honest and conscientious, modest and sometimes awkward, but could be, when occasion demanded, a parliamentary speaker of a very high order.

The key man in the Cabinet after Liverpool was Lord
Castlereagh, Foreign Secretary and leader of the House of
Commons.   His diplomatic skill had formed the Quadruple
Alliance pledged to the defeat of Napoleon, had held it
together despite bitter rivalries and had helped to steer the
Congress of Vienna to a peaceful conclusion.   It was reckoned
that one of his greatest achievements was the condemnation by
the Congress of the Slave Trade.   An honourable man and a
lover of liberty, it was his misfortune to be associated in the
public mind with the despotic rulers of eastern Europe and to

[1] See p. 70.

be, as leader of the Commons, the chief defender of the Cabinet's policy of repression. A man gravely misunderstood, his suicide in 1822 was one of the greatest personal tragedies of the period.[1]

A far less important figure was Lord Sidmouth, who as Addington had been an undistinguished Prime Minister, 1801–4. He was an incapable Home Secretary but was never rated highly enough to blame for decisions of policy. A much abler man was Canning, who held only a minor position. This was at least partly due to his capacity for making enemies; it was only the premature death of Castlereagh that brought him to a position equal to his talents.

Eldon, the Lord Chancellor, was the only member of the Cabinet of really humble origin but at the same time he was the most extreme Tory of them all. A man dedicated to his profession, his idea of humour was to convert the Ballad of Chevy Chase into the style of a Bill in Chancery. In the courts he balanced legal niceties until there was an enormous accumulation of business, yet outside showed great force of character and opposed any relaxation of the severity of the law.

Not yet in the Cabinet, the Duke of Wellington was already a great political figure. In outlook he was a high Tory but he regarded himself as essentially impartial and his overriding principle was that the King's government must go on, as when he carried Catholic Emancipation in 1829 and offered to introduce a moderate reform of Parliament in 1831. His influence over the royal family was important in reducing their power for doing harm.

The Whig party was a shadow of its former self and its weakness and divisions help to explain the long Tory tenure of power. Since 1784 it had had a knack of championing unpopular causes, such as the wish to end the war, and since the death of Fox in 1807 it had lacked an effective leader. The country had repudiated the Whigs, once the incarnation of the country's soul, the moment they had ceased to represent a principle – the defence of the liberties of the people – and had degenerated into a mere coalition of selfish factions. Under the influence of the war many of the great families had changed sides and a feature of the period 1800–15 had been

[1] See p. 54.

the lessening of the parliamentary importance of the aristocratic groups so fundamental to 18th-century politics.   In the
Lords, Grey and Holland carried on the aristocratic traditions
of the past with an almost dilettante interest in reform; in the
Commons Brougham was the best debater but other members
of the party distrusted him and felt he lacked the qualities of a
leader.   The Whigs had little clear policy, although they were
united in Catholic Emancipation; they were more interested
than the Tories in advocating economy, having few recipients
of the financial favours of the Crown; their defence of constitutional liberty had narrow limits, for they approved of suppressing revolutionary literature and accepted what they
called the legitimate influence of the Crown.   Hazlitt
described the two parties as rival stage coaches which splashed
each other with mud but went by the same road to the same
place.

Apart from the many members of Parliament who were
uncommitted to either party, a small group of little importance
at the time but of great interest for the future, had begun to
enter Parliament.   The Radicals were loosely associated with
the Whigs, though they were politically unreliable and were,
in reality, a collection of individuals expressing a wide range
of opinions, some in part acceptable to the ruling classes, others
openly revolutionary.   Their following in the country must
be judged by the steady growth of opinion in favour of
electoral reform.   Apart from Ricardo no Radical member of
Parliament had much authority or was heard with much
respect.

At this stage the real importance of the Radicals lies outside
Parliament, where their views mingled with the older traditions and helped to make Britain a leader of world opinion.
The ideas brought forward by the American and French
Revolution had been absorbed, without the shock of great up-
heavals, into the consciousness of the nation and had mixed
with the great stirring of conscience that was the indirect
result of the work of John Wesley.   Tempered by experience
and moderation they helped to bring about reforms in the
political and the social fields at home, and were a constant
inspiration to would-be reformers abroad.

In 1815 the full impact of the Industrial Revolution that
made these reforms so necessary had not yet been felt.   The

movement for reform was more backward-looking, a demand for a return to the standards of England before the war, which was widely felt, by Cobbett and many others, to have been a better place than post-war England, and a demand for the redress of grievances. But in the opinion of most Radicals the reform of Parliament was the first condition of progress, though the exact form that subsequent progress should take was imperfectly thought out. It was widely held that any large-scale improvement of the material conditions of the masses was impossible, a view given authority by the generally applauded opinions of Malthus.

Malthus believed that mankind had grown up in a hostile environment and was doomed to a never-ending warfare against it, for population tends to increase more rapidly than the means of subsistence. To give charity was merely to aggravate the situation, a view welcomed at a time when the expense of the Poor Law was a matter of general concern. He later produced a second law, the idea of a fixed fund for wages, which claimed it was useless for workmen to agitate for, or for employers to pay, increased wages, since the only result of their succeeding must be to diminish the amount available for wages elsewhere. Malthus deduced from these the need for economic protection; Ricardo, while accepting his main premisses, deduced the need for free trade and provided the economic arguments against the Corn Laws of 1815. Here he was also a disciple of Adam Smith. The *Wealth of Nations* published in 1776, gave coherent expression to the thoughts that had been raised in men's minds by the march of events. In place of the dictates of the State it set the spontaneous devices and actions of ordinary men as the guiding principle. Experience has shown that an industrial society needs a framework of public service if it is to operate without social discomfort, but some of Smith's followers confined the functions of the State to defence and order. These convictions enabled a governing class, essentially humanitarian in its outlook, to overlook the mass of human misery that judicious State intervention, given adequate administrative machinery, might well have mitigated.

The importance of individualism, however, was confirmed in men's minds by the philosophy of Jeremy Bentham. Bentham had been known in England as a prison reformer, on

the Continent as a penologist, but when in the early 19th
Century he met James Mill, who became his secretary and
who recruited to his circle many of the ablest young men in
the country, he evolved the philosophy of Utilitarianism.
This started from the principle that man seeks pleasure and
avoids pain and therefore actions tending to pleasure are
necessarily good.   Every human action and institution should
be judged by the principle of 'utility'; whether it led to the
'greatest happiness of the greatest number' or what changes
should be made to bring about this desirable end.   This could
be easily applied to every aspect of national life and carried a
great authority that was difficult to refute.   Bentham was not
a revolutionary; he believed in action through Parliament.
He wanted reasonable government but not too much of it,
'every law is an evil, for every law is an infraction of liberty',
yet the implication of his ideas was the intervention of
Parliament to prevent the sinister interests of any one class
from encroaching on the general convenience.   The class
most likely to identify itself with the greatest happiness
of the greatest number was, in Bentham's view, the middle
class, and hence Bentham became the champion of parliamentary reform.   His disciples, through experience, accepted
the need for State intervention in social and economic matters.
Utilitarianism had an enormous contemporary influence, and
provided in the years to come a dynamic force of legal, social,
political and economic reform, and a touchstone for all
governmental policies.[1]

   The belief in *laissez-faire*, fathered by Adam Smith and confirmed in essence by subsequent political and economic philo-
sophers, in many cases concealed an admission that the
problems posed by the war and the Industrial Revolution
were, in the framework of the times, insoluble.   It acknowledged that the fund of skill and enterprise was limited and in
the management of their common affairs men would not be
able to find the elasticity and adaptability which they would
in devising schemes for their own self-interest.   The idea of
laissez-faire was anathema to Robert Owen.   Owen was the
self-made man of the Industrial Revolution *par excellence*.   In
the free economic conditions of the time he had, through his
own unhindered enterprise, become a prosperous cotton

---

[1] See especially Poor Law Reform, p. 93.

spinner and, through good management and an opportune
marriage he was by the end of the Napoleonic wars one of the
wealthiest men in the country and ready to devote himself to
the cause of Utopian socialism.   He had become convinced
that the entire basis of the industrial system was wrong, that
competition would necessarily involve misery and that the
remedy was a system of universal co-operation.   He denied
men's responsibility for their conduct and believed that the
way to get good conduct was to provide a good environment.
He urged that the unemployed should be set to useful work in
villages of co-operation, and put forward a new doctrine of
value and exchange, by which he set out to replace money by a
new currency based on the 'labour time' spent by the worker
in production.   The long-term effect of his ideas was considerable, reaching out to the Trades Union movement and
indirectly to Chartism and Marxism; in the decade after
Waterloo his importance lay in the high standards which he
maintained at his village and factory of New Lanark and in
the part he played in campaigning for factory legislation.

This was the intellectual background; other men, and the
growing power of the Press, more directly affected the ordinary
people of the time and brought more conspicuous pressure to
bear on Parliament.

Since the end of the 17th Century the Government had lost
the right of preliminary censorship over printed matter and
opponents of the Court Party saw in it their surest guarantee
against a despotic reaction.   By the end of the 18th Century a
large and important Press was already in existence and
although increase of the Stamp Duty and rising costs had
raised the price of a large daily paper to sevenpence by 1815,
the stirring events of the war had aroused in the country an
insatiable appetite for news, which had enabled journalism to
develop in face of all obstacles, and increase the circulation of
papers already in existence.   Drawing much of their revenue
from advertisements, their political independence steadily
grew.   Parliamentary debates received considerable emphasis
and the motives of politicians were applauded, criticised or
examined.   Steam-operated presses introduced from 1814
onwards lowered costs, and with the better roads distribution
became easier.

Apart from daily newspapers the influence of periodicals was very considerable. The foundation of *The Edinburgh Review* in 1802 began a new era in public criticism. Its tone was Whig to Radical, its circulation over 10,000, and two of its best known contributors were Sydney Smith and Brougham. The Tory answer was *The Quarterly Review* begun with the help of Sir Walter Scott in 1809. *The Westminster Review* was thoroughly Radical. Articles were longer and more serious than had been the case in the previous century and contributors were better paid.

Among weeklies Leigh Hunt's *Examiner* was held in high esteem, while Wooler's *Black Dwarf* (1817–24), Richard Carlile's *Republican* (1819–26) and above all Cobbett's *Political Register* were read with great interest by the working class. They rarely contained news but attracted readers by provocative opinions extravagantly expressed.

William Cobbett was perhaps the most outstanding political journalist of the century. A jack of many trades – farmer, soldier, schoolmaster, journalist and politician – his enthusiasms and prejudices were just as varied. He spoke for the England that was past; he resented and made no effort to understand the results and implications of the Industrial Revolution. His *Rural Rides* give an incomparable picture of the English countryside of his time; his autobiography, *The Progress of a Ploughboy*, is a fascinating account of the effects of his generosity, his pugnacious love of justice and his incurable knack of overstating his case with unnecessary consequences to himself. It is, however, in *The Political Register* that his greatest influence lay; never ambiguous, never dull, reflecting all the Englishman's favourite prejudices, it was read by village schoolmasters and parish clerks to local politicians in alehouses all over the country. His idea of change was to seek to restore the England of the past and his championship of parliamentary reform had this aim in view; his vehemence did harm to the cause and his fine gifts and energy were largely wasted because they were not directed to a single aim. But perhaps his greatest achievement was one completely unappreciated by the government of the day – he, Cartwright and Hunt were all concerned to prevent economic distress from venting itself in violence and to turn the energies of the sufferers to political associations for the immediate purpose of reforming the House of Commons. Cobbett's contribution to the keeping of the peace in the troubled years after the war was a very important one.

Faced with violence, an early 19th Century government was in an extremely vulnerable position. There was no police force and the village constables, unpaid offices held in rotation, were largely ineffectual when dealing with anything more serious than an isolated drunkard. Ultimately the safeguard was the Army, but English love of liberty ensured that in peace time its numbers were strictly limited and over half its total effective strength of about 100,000 was in India or the colonies. Moreover, the Army was an asset of uncertain value: if they obeyed orders and fired, the result could be civilian bloodshed and popular outcry: if they sympathised with the mob, as at the time of Wilkes, the government was left helpless. The penalties for wrongdoing were savage and severe but the chances of apprehension very slight. In the ordered society of the countryside crime was slight, but even in the 18th Century the larger towns had their unmanageable areas and their number had been enormously increased by the movements of population resulting from the Industrial Revolution.

The alarm felt by Members of Parliament at the problem is reflected in the growing severity of the penal code. By 1815 there were some 220 offences punishable with death ranging from murder and highway robbery to injuring Westminster Bridge and impersonating an outpatient of Chelsea Hospital. Its very severity defeated its own ends, for juries very often refused to convict. Sir Samuel Romilly campaigned steadily for rationalisation; he was defeated several times by the Lords when he tried to get the death penalty abolished for the theft of five shillings from a shop. His ideas were eventually to come to fruition in the reforms started by Sir Robert Peel.

In London the only protection of the government in a city of one million people was three regiments of Foot Guards and 1,200 horse, and the London mob could subject Parliament and government to a most unpleasant ordeal. Though the ruling aristocracy had learnt to humour and manage it, they could never wholly ignore it. During the Gordon Riots the mob had London at its mercy; a few resolute leaders, as in France, could have begun a revolution. During the rejoicings for the victory at Salamanca it had terrorised London for three nights, firing in the streets, setting coaches alight and stoning the residences of the anti-war party. Ministers regarded the periodic breaking of their windows and sacking of their houses as an occupational hazard. At every contested election the candidates had for weeks to run the gauntlet of a rough, drunken mob which paraded the streets, surrounded the hustings and pelted speakers. During fairs and public processions packs of thieves swept through the crowds emptying pockets, snatching purses and even stripping men and women of their clothes.

In the countryside violence was less frequent but it found the authorities just as helpless. The Luddite Riots were merely the revolt of misery and want, the incoherent rising of a disorganised and leaderless rabble. They began in Nottinghamshire where the stocking frame knitters had found their livelihood reduced by export difficulties arising from the Continental system and threatened by manufacturers producing an inferior product on wide frames. The actual work of destroying wide frames was entrusted to picked bands with the connivance of the workers as a whole in Yorkshire, Lancashire and Cheshire the movement was far more sporadic and directed against shearing machines and power-looms. It subsided naturally; the united opposition of the propertied classes and the efforts of the Army could hardly affect it.

The riots of 1815 against agricultural protection and consequent high prices were potentially more dangerous, for they were tolerated, encouraged, perhaps even directed, by the leaders of industry. The escape of Napoleon from Elba saved the cause of order, but the riots, although unsuccessful, indicated how with leadership the mob could bring great pressure to bear on Parliament. To many people, however, these opportunities for violence were a guarantee of liberty; 'They have an admirable police in Paris,' commented Lord Dudley, 'but they pay for it dear enough. I had rather half-a-dozen people's throats were cut every few years in the Ratcliffe Highway than be subject to disciplinary visits, spies and the rest of Fouché's contrivances.'

Even had the government wished to repress the people, the means were lacking. The bureaucracy had no political power; the Civil Service was purely clerical and was nominated by the statesmen for whom it worked, who viewed it chiefly as a means of rewarding supporters and providing for younger sons. The Home Office had a staff of twenty clerks; as every document had to be copied by hand, such administrators had no time for regulating people's lives.

The only paid judges were those of the capital. Their independence of the Crown, once appointed, had been one of the principles established in 1688. The British Parliament legislated very little, and a respect for the Common Law, for the general principles of jurisprudence drawn from the accumulated legal decisions of past centuries, formed the sole rule of the three Common Law courts. The dignity of the law in the provinces was maintained by the judge of assize, but in between his visits, the administration of the country, whether legal or executive, had virtually no paid representatives outside London apart from revenue collectors, men much despised.

As Halévy wrote, 'The Central Government did nothing to secure public safety, it provided no schools, made no roads, gave no relief to the poor. With the exception of the postal service, the State performed no function of immediate benefit to the tax payers.' The real rulers of the provinces were the landowners. They had to secure property and privilege for themselves; they learnt to command respect by force of character, courage and good sense. From among them were chosen by the Lord Lieutenant, usually the largest landowner in the county, the Justices of the Peace; recently the Anglican clergy, allied by outlook and usually by blood, also had become Justices in large numbers. Their functions were semi-judicial, semi-administrative. They enforced legislation and customary duties, they punished offenders. Four times a year they met in Courts of Quarter Session which were genuine legislatures engaged in building up from quarter to quarter a new code of law under the pretext of interpreting the old. In this capacity they had put together at the end of the 18th Century, in county after county, a complete poor law, without any interference by the central government. The enforcement of any Act of Parliament or any civil edict of the government depended ultimately on them, but the system worked because it was the landowners who controlled Parliament which in turn controlled the government. Here was no separation of powers; the British Constitution worked because it was the same class that filled every vital function, made laws and implemented them at every level, and this class had a common outlook and, under conditions it understood, a strong sense of justice.   It could govern because in normal times it had the goodwill of the great majority of the people.   It was this basic respect for law and order, stronger in 1815 through the influence of the Evangelical Revival than it had been in the 18th Century, that enabled the country to be ruled by consent and not by force.

Should consent fail, the only force available was the armed forces of the Crown.   In 1689 the Army's existence from the financial and disciplinary point of view had been made dependent on an annual vote of Parliament.   Its importance had been greatly increased by the Napoleonic wars, during which the government had handled far greater numbers of military effectives than had any previous British government, and the victories in Spain and at Waterloo brought to the Army in general and to the Duke of Wellington in particular a great increase in prestige.   Some contemporaries feared the military tendencies of the government – the Duke of Wellington's appointment to the Cabinet in 1818 was held to be a threat to British liberty – but the likelihood that the Army would ever become an instrument of oppression in England was remote.   The Army was used for police purposes in the years following Waterloo but the limits on its use were shown clearly by the widespread protest, from all ranks of society, at the Peterloo incident of 1819.   The Army was essentially in harmony with the other institutions of the nation; its officers were chiefly from landowning families and, if they sat in Lords or Commons, their landowning background was more relevant than their military one.   The part-time army, the English Militia, was officered by landowners and recruited by them; it was a bulwark against tyranny, not an instrument of it, although like the regular Army, it made no pretence to democracy.

Though the Army might be distrusted, the Navy could be safely praised.   In the second half of the war its role was a subordinate one, the unexciting task of policing the seas and ensuring the French fleet kept to its harbours.   But British pride in the sea remained; it was the source of British wealth and greatness.   The Navy was the guarantee of British liberty and by its nature could never oppress it.

In 1815 every aspect of the constitution, executive, legislature, judiciary, at every level, both central and local, was
dominated by the landed proprietor. The business of government was, therefore, in the hands of amateurs, who were men,
on the whole, with a strong sense of duty and justice. Hence
the progress of democratic institutions during the 19th Century
necessarily followed in England a course very different from
that which it was to follow in other European countries which
already had a bureaucracy; in England the machinery of
government itself was to be created. Already, by 1815, the
country was faced with new problems with which the patri-
archal system of the past was not equipped to deal, and the
pressure of public opinion drove the ruling group forward and
carried it further than it would ever have been led by motives
of self-interest. The rule of the landowning classes depended
ultimately on consent, and as the condition of the people
changed, so also would change their view of what was acceptable.

(b) THE ECONOMIC BACKGROUND

In 1815 the main factor for change in the condition of the
people was the Industrial Revolution. This was a revolution
in a particular sense; the system of human relationships called
capitalism was far older than 1760; it attained full development long after 1830. Change is continuous, but in this
period it was accelerated; it was revolutionary partly because
the great manufacturers were daring innovators, revolutionaries in the proper sense of the term, and partly because of the
cumulative effect of these changes on men's lives.

The changes in industry began largely as a result of the
essential stability of the country. The revolution of 1688
terminated the constitutional struggle of the 17th Century and
brought in a period of internal peace. The wars in which we
took part were comparatively distant, their predominantly
maritime nature merely increasing the trade market at our
disposal. There was a growing amount of money available
from the profits of trade for investment. The creation of the
National Debt of 1694 accustomed men to the idea of im-
personal investment, and as the government interest was
progressively lowered, much of the capital available slowly
moved into the industrial field. This coincided with a

remarkable series of discoveries which represented in some cases major breakthroughs in the industry to which they applied. Some of these discoveries were accidents but most depended on systematic thought and were achieved only after repeated trial and error. There was a growing belief in the 18th Century in the possibility of achieving industrial progress by the method of observation and experiment that in England issued from the teaching of Francis Bacon and had been confirmed by Boyle and Newton.

Many of the inventors were men of humble origin, but they could hardly have been successful had they not had trained minds. The Scottish or Nonconformist background of many inventors was not accidental; the Scottish educational system was in advance of that of any other European country at the time, and in England the Nonconformist academies were more progressive in their outlook than other forms of education.

Inventions will only occur when the specialisation of labour in a branch of industry has developed to the point where men devote themselves to a single product or process; this position had already been reached when the 18th Century opened. The Industrial Revolution was in part cause, in part effect, of an intensification and extension of the principle of specialisation.

New inventions worked cumulatively to speed up the rate of change. The use of coal increased the output of iron, the larger output of iron cheapened the cost of machinery, cheaper machines lessened the expense of coal-mining. The greatest change of all, however, was the steady increase of population throughout the period; it provided a growing labour force and a constantly expanding market. In itself it did not of necessity produce an expanding market; Malthus's predictions could well have proved accurate and lower standards of life for all could have resulted. For certain sections of the population, such as the handloom weavers in the early 19th Century, they did; the fact that a raising of standards was possible for the majority was the result of the coincidence of the increase of population with the other changes that made up the Industrial Revolution.

The growing population needed to be fed and this provided an incentive, particularly during the Napoleonic wars when imports of food were greatly restricted, for a great increase in agricultural production. The main features of the period were the adoption of improved methods of cultivation, the introduction of new crops, the reduction of stock breeding to a science, the improvement of implements, better transport facilities and the enterprise and outlay of capitalist landlords and tenant farmers. By 1815 most of the country had been enclosed, the procedure having been cheapened by a General Enclosure Act of 1801. But in the process rural society was convulsed. The divorce of the peasantry from the soil, the extinction of commoners, open field farmers and, eventually, of small freeholders, was the heavy price the nation ultimately paid for the supply of bread and meat to its labouring population.

At the end of the Napoleonic wars the effects of the new inventions and methods were apparent in most British industries. In mining, although methods of production and transport underground remained primitive, the invention of safety lamps, of which Sir Humphry Davy's in 1815 is the best known, helped to protect miners against the dangerous gases and enabled the opening up of deeper seams. The iron industry was steadily increasing its demand for coal, especially since the invention of puddling and rolling by Henry Cort in 1783, which enabled wrought iron to be produced really cheaply. The French war had brought a boom in the industry and after 1815 there was a temporary but acute depression. The coming of railways and the increasing demand for iron by the building and hardware industries led to steady prosperity.

Steam power greatly improved the efficiency of the iron-making process, but had an even more revolutionary effect on the textile industry, changing it from rural and domestic units to urban factory concentrations, a process which, coinciding as it did with enclosures, completely upset the structure of rural England. By the 1790s Crompton's mule had been converted to steam power and cotton spinning rapidly became a factory industry. In 1803 Horrocks of Stockport produced a commercially effective version of Cartwright's power loom and by 1830 there were reckoned to be 100,000 operating in the country. The handloom weavers fought hard to keep their independence; many were to become, in due course, supporters of the Chartist movement. Working conditions in the new factories were for the most part very bad; they employed a large number of children, who were often harshly treated. Wool manufacture followed a similar development to that of cotton, only it changed far more slowly. Fewer fortunes were made and even in the mid-19th Century not more than half the Yorkshire textile workers, still less those of the West Country, had been brought into the factories.

As essential a part of the Industrial Revolution as the new inventions was the immense improvement in communications that took place from the mid-18th Century onwards. Under the old system of road maintenance by parish authorities relying on statute labour, the majority of the roads of the country were neglected and in many parts wheeled vehicles were virtually out of the question, especially in the winter months. Under the auspices of the Turnpike Trusts, established from 1663 onwards, and with government help for a few strategic routes, roads were reconstructed on sound technical principles. This is particularly associated with the names of Telford and McAdam. Telford, one of the great engineers of the 19th Century, a man of immense versatility, advocated a solid foundation, preferably rock, and stressed the importance of proper drainage. McAdam claimed an elastic subsoil was preferable and coated his road with a waterproof surface of small stones crushed and packed together. The rival claims were hotly contested and this kept the need for better roads prominently before the public. By the 1820's the more important routes had been improved out of recognition and this made possible a better provision of public transport in the shape of stage-wagons and stage-coaches.

Before the coming of the railways, however, carrying capacity on land was strictly limited. The first completely artificial waterway was the Duke of Bridgewater's Canal from Worsley to Manchester, built by James Brindley, 1759–61. Its immediate success led to the formation of many canal companies. Canals were invaluable for bulk products, and although the canal mania led to some waste in ill-advised projects, the investment in waterways enabled local food shortages to be easily rectified, and iron and coal to be conveyed in bulk quantities that would have been impossible in any other way. The most important result of the move-

ment was that it developed a new race of engineers equipped
to meet the calls which the age of railways was to make on their
skill, endurance and capacity for disciplined effort. By 1834
England was covered with a network of more than 4,000 miles
of canals and navigable rivers.

Industrial expansion also depended on the availability of
capital. Most of the earliest industrial enterprises started off
as partnerships. Parliament, following the fiasco of the South
Sea Bubble, had made joint stock companies illegal and the
lack of limited liability deterred many people from going into
partnership unless they were proposing to take an active part
in the enterprise. The high profits made by using the new
methods of production were ploughed back into the business.
Additional capital was obtained by mortgaging the factory
buildings. Sometimes loans could be obtained either in this
way or on personal security from friends or men engaged in the
same field of activity. Banks played an increasing part in the
provision of credit and the general furtherance of trade
throughout the 18th Century. They were mostly private ones,
often started by men successful in trade or industry. By 1815
there were some 900 country banks, which had £20 m. of their
own notes in circulation, especially in areas more than sixty
miles from London. A restriction of discounts by the Bank
of England could result in many closing their doors. Together
with the large number of forged banknotes in circulation, the
short lives of many private banks created an atmosphere of
instability. Bankers played a larger part in the extension than
in the creation of industrial firms. They were encouraged by
an act of 1826 which permitted the setting up of corporate
banks more than 65 miles from London. They mobilised short-
term funds and transferred them from areas where there was
little demand for them to others that needed capital. Without
them the extension of industry could hardly have taken place
as rapidly as it did.

The apex of the entire system was the Bank of England,
whose directors were London merchants. The London
bankers used it as a deposit bank and the funds thus placed at
its disposal were used to discount commercial bills. It was for
the governor and directors to display the necessary shrewdness
and to make advances on such a scale as to ensure a satisfactory dividend to the shareholders while not advancing enough

c

to diminish unduly the reserve of the Bank – the final reserve on which the entire currency of the nation was based.   Its greatest debtor was the State.   The Bank had to take care, while allowing the State freely to increase the National Debt, that the public credit was not endangered nor the fiduciary currency depreciated.   The government rewarded this service by depositing its balances with the Bank, especially the Consolidated Fund.   In the interval the Bank was free to put out to interest the enormous capital temporarily at its disposal. By 1815 the Bank, which in 1694 had been a daring innovation, shared the prestige of the system of government.

The National Debt was a source of continual concern to the Englishman of the day.   It seemed that England was being crushed by taxation.   In 1814 nothing whatever was spent out of the proceeds of taxation on poor relief, education, local administration and justice or local police.   Administrative expenditure cost £4 m.; the Navy £20 m.; Army and Ordnance £40 m.; subsidies to allied powers £10 m.; servicing the National Debt £37 m.   The National Debt had been raised by the war from £252 m. to £834 m.   Pitt had organised a Sinking Fund for its redemption, but the scheme of 1786 did not essentially differ from previous attempts.   During the war the government had continued to redeem with one hand, but with the other continued to borrow more rapidly than it redeemed.   As a result of the increase of the Debt there grew up during the period a class of government stockholders, numbering over a quarter of a million by 1830.   Of these over 90 per cent had incomes of under £200 a year.

In 1814 the British wholesale price level was roughly twice as high as it had been in 1790.   By 1816 it was only about one-third above the pre-war price level and after a brief rally in 1818 sank to well below it before 1830.   Falling prices discourage industry, for those that can will wait until prices are lower.   They also raise the real value of all debts fixed in money.   Over this period the real burden of the National Debt likewise increased.

The resources of the government were considerable.   In 1815 a population of fourteen million was contributing £72 m. per year or one-fifth of the national income as compared with the £19 m. paid in 1792 by a population of ten million.   The income tax was producing £16 m. in 1814.   It had been introduced by Pitt in 1799 for the duration of the war and in 1815 the government honoured his promise and abolished it. This meant that the heaviest burden came from indirect taxation, falling on rich and poor alike. Assessed taxes on a bewildering variety of subjects were of increasing importance: male domestics, dogs, licences of coach-builders and horse-dealers, hair-powder, carriages, houses and windows. The burden of tax was made still heavier by local rates. The County Rate covered bridges, justice and police; the Highway Rate, levied by parishes, covered roads. By far the heaviest, however, was the Poor Rate, which increased steadily throughout the period, reaching the total of £8 m. a year by 1818.

The war might have raised the National Debt and increased the burden of taxation, but it had a favourable effect on the economy as a whole. The twenty-two years' struggle had doubled the British export trade and trebled the country's revenue. The carrying trade of the world was in British hands, merchant tonnage had risen from one million to two and a half million tons. Agricultural produce had commanded higher prices than ever before and there had been an acceleration of the enclosed movement; the textile trade had become mechanised to a marked extent and had, directly or indirectly, supplied uniforms to most of the armies of Europe. The iron trade in particular had achieved tremendous prosperity by the demand for armaments. In 1815 wages in manufacturing districts were higher than they had ever been.

At the time of victory this material prosperity seemed the most assured thing in the world; though chequered by spasmodic depressions, sometimes terrible in their intensity, the rise in production of trade had been continuous. It was felt to be deserved and contemporaries were unprepared for any reversal of fortune.

(c) THE SOCIAL BACKGROUND

The dominant feature of the times was the rapid growth of population, which was brought home clearly to contemporaries after 1801 when the decennial census was first introduced. It is estimated the population was around seven million in 1750; by 1811 it was twelve million, by 1821 fourteen million. By 1851 twenty-one million had been reached.

It was not clear at the time why this should be so; the employment of children in cotton mills and the encouragement of
improvident marriages by Poor Law subsidies were suggested
causes. But even in 1830 only one-eightieth of the population
worked in cotton mills and the birth-rate actually fell. The
determining factor as we now know was the fall of the death-
rate; the factory system may have stunted and maimed its
victims but it did not result in their deaths to the extent of
offsetting the sharp decline in infant and child mortality.
Purer water and better midwifery probably accounted for
most of this. Drainage was improved, and water closets
introduced, though these were still far from common.
Cheap cotton clothing was easier to wash than wool and
therefore healthier; the improvement of transport facilities
led to cheaper food and more constant supplies. The
influence of the Evangelical revival led to men becoming more temperate. Bad as conditions of public health
were when Chadwick and Southwood Smith studied them
in the 1840's – and there is reason to believe they had
deteriorated since 1815 – there can be no doubt that in 1815
they were a great deal better in the larger towns than they had
been during the greater part of the 18th Century.

Not only had the population grown; it had also moved and
concentrated. This process continued throughout the 19th
Century, gradually and imperceptibly. In 1831 half of the
population of the country was still getting its livelihood from
the land or from trades closely associated with it. London
dominated the country with a population around one million;
Manchester and Salford grew from 95,000 in 1801 to 238,000
in 1831; Leeds 53,000 to 123,000; Liverpool 82,000 to 202,000.
The new population of these cities including London, came
largely from the neighbouring counties but there was also an
important movement of population from Ireland that brought
with it a very low standard of living. Quite small places grew
rapidly from the establishment of single mills: Dale and Owen
were employing 1,000 at New Lanark; Strutt 1,500 at Belper
and Millford; Horrocks nearly 7,000 at Preston.

Despite the changes affecting many people's lives, the implications of the French Revolution had little appeal to the average Englishman of the time, whatever his position in society.
He believed Englishmen more free than foreigners could ever

be, that his country and its ways of life were superior to those of other countries. He also accepted the established social order and looked invariably to the landed gentry for leadership. Even the radical reformers of the time looked to such men as Sir Francis Burdett and Lord Cochrane to lead them.

The country gentleman, be he duke or squire with a few hundred acres, was at home on the land. There was no absolute monarch to attract people to the capital; Parliament sat for only a part of every year and the country was felt to be the only place where you could live a life worthy of a gentleman. Country houses existed in great numbers and above all else they and their parks were the distinguishing ornament of the landscape; they were often the largest economic units in an area. To the ordinary people the government was an abstraction, associated if anything with the periodic visits of excisemen and the press gang. The reality, to whom respect was given and from whom leadership was expected, was the country gentleman. He dispensed the law as justice of the peace, he told country freeholders how to vote. Most of the people on his land depended on him for their cottages, their work, their relief in times of distress and for the custom which he and his family brought to shops and workshops. Living for the greater part of the year on his estate, coming into daily contact with the governed, he shared their outlook and many of their pastimes. Sport in particular was the great leveller of the countryside. On the hunting field, the racecourse, the cricket field and the boxing ring, rich and poor were united in their enthusiasms.

At his best, the English country gentleman commanded admiration and often affection. Good breeding was not merely a mark of social distinction but a rule for the treatment of others. It made few concessions to the idea of equality, but a gentleman was expected to treat his fellow creatures of all ranks openly and frankly even when it meant sacrificing his interests to do so; a gentleman was under an obligation to be generous.

The essential unity of English society had been commonplace in the 18th Century; by the second decade of the 19th Century fissures were already apparent. The supremacy of the landed classes had in the past been regarded as natural; now there seems to have been felt the need to preserve and enhance it artificially. The movements of population as a result of the Industrial Revolution, the decline of the old order in the countryside aggravated by enclosures and the effects of the Speenhamland system contributed to this. So also did the rise to wealth and prominence of an increasing number of men whose money had come to them not by birth but by business.

Below the gentry in the countryside, the farmers were consolidating their position. The term yeoman covered a great range of wealth and as a class it was fast declining in importance, but in 1815 between a quarter and a fifth of England's farmlands were still owned and cultivated by yeomen. Cobbett on his farm strove to recreate his ideal of the yeoman of the past, living with open-handed generosity to all, both rich and poor. Enclosure of common land, however, was crippling the small freeholder and the intermediate class of the countryside was becoming increasingly the tenant-farmer. The sudden decline in wheat prices at the end of the war and the increases in the burdens on farmers, particularly the poor rate, led to a severe depression in agriculture from 1814 to 1816. Farms were given up, large tracts of land left untenanted and often uncultivated. Agricultural improvements were at a standstill and livestock was reduced to a minimum. It was not until the 1830's that the farmer re-experienced the prosperity the war had brought. This did little to offset the increasing tendency for farmers to emphasise more clearly the gulf dividing them from their hired servants.

The lot of the agricultural labourer had undoubtedly worsened during the previous twenty years. Enclosure acts had deprived him of his right of common pasture in the majority of cases and, being landless, he had suffered from the increased prices for food during the war while the farmer had benefited. The typical labourers of the time were men of great industry and skill, patient, generous, more efficient than any machine, for their exactitude was based on a sensitive knowledge of nature learnt from childhood. Many were farm servants boarded and lodged by the farmers who employed them, though increasingly farmers were finding it cheaper for labourers to live out. The cottages available, built of local materials blending with the landscape, had in the south usually three or four rooms. In the north and west lower standards prevailed and single-room turf cabins were fairly common. The standard of food was higher than on the Continent at the time and a fair amount of meat was consumed, even in workhouses. Even so, all the evidence suggests that the labourer's economic position in every respect was worse than it had been before the war. His wage was supplemented by the earnings of his wife and children, in the fields at harvest time or throughout the year in local crafts such as the making of reed matting in Norfolk and straw plaiting in Bedfordshire, or spinning and weaving in many different parts of the country. But mechanical improvements were making a number of domestic industries uneconomic and thus in this respect too the labourer's family was losing.[1]

Bad though conditions were for many rural labourers, they were at least suffered in the countryside and the fresh air. Those who worked in the towns were not so fortunate. Most townsmen were still following the traditional trades and occupations; for instance in 1829 there were more tailors and bootmakers in London than there were miners in the Northumberland and Durham coalfield, which produced one quarter of the English and Welsh coal mined. Domestic service was still a more common employment for women than factory work. Nevertheless the concentration of employment caused by the industrial changes aggravated the slum conditions of many towns, especially as much of the concentration occurred during the war, when building materials were relatively scarce.

In London itself, which was at the height of its elegance in the West End, the contrast with the East End was considerable. The slums were still what they had been in the Middle Ages, fever-ridden haunts of vice and wretchedness, a maze of alleys, courts and lanes with dirty, tumbledown houses. The streets were unpaved, the houses sewerless. Every old town had its slums but in the new settlements caused by the Industrial Revolution, frequently in remote places, conditions were even worse. Unrestrained by established authority, only the law of the jungle held. Just outside Birmingham was a squalid manufacturing village known as 'Mud City', whose inhabitants were the terror of the neighbourhood, and settlements such as these were to be found wherever the new

---

[1] For the effects of the Speenhamland system, see below, p. 93.

industrial processes had been established. Such places seemed alien and were beyond the understanding of the established authorities. The relationship between dirt and disease was not fully understood and standards that rural isolation made harmless produced severe epidemics in crowded districts. Fever caused more deaths in the industrial towns every year than Wellington's armies had suffered during the Peninsular War, and the severe cholera epidemics later in the century were to bring the first attempts at parliamentary regulation.[1]

The long hours and tedious monotonous labour were as common in domestic work of all kinds as in the new manufacturing enterprises. The mines had always been unhealthy as well as dangerous; it was reckoned, for instance, that half the workers in the Cornish copper mines suffered from tuberculosis. The cotton factories were particularly unhealthy with humid air which clogged the lungs with floating particles of cotton. Workers were fined if they were found to have opened windows. Accidents with the primitive, unfenced machinery were common, and many children, stunted by over-hard labour and by lack of air, inadequate food and sleep from an early age, grew to manhood sickly and deformed.

For many, hereditary skill was counting for less and less, and the filthier the workers' surroundings, the more deadening and brutalising their conditions of labour, the more savage and pagan they grew and the more a race apart. In material matters, however, there were certain improvements. In 1831 the cost of living was 11 per cent higher than in 1790 but urban wages had increased by 43 per cent. The diet of the workers had improved; a greater amount of meat was eaten. An increasing amount of coal was being used domestically and many more people than formerly must have enjoyed regular hot meals. Even before 1834, the large number of 'indigent and distressed' that had worried the government and the local magistrates from Tudor times onwards, had probably decreased in numbers. Against all the evils of the factory system and the new towns should be set the lessening of the strain on those who worked in the heavy trades and the reduction of the sweating of women and young children, the rise in family earnings, the greater regularity of pay and the gain in

[1] See below, p. 138.

welfare that came as industrial work was taken out of the home.

The men who were responsible for these great changes had a range of opportunities that have seldom been equalled before or since. The happenings in France had shattered the equilibrium of 18th-century society and the idea was abroad that anyone had a right to go anywhere or to become anything by the passport of his own energies, talents or superior cunning. The war had been an immense stimulus to economy of all kinds. For the young man of enterprise the conditions of the time were ideal. The government was scarcely aware of the industrial problem and these men were able to a large extent to make the rules of the game. There was no rigid system of patents to prevent an enterprising young man from picking any brains he chose. The regimentation of working class youth by State and trade unions was still far away, while at a higher level the professionalisation of society which limits each man to his own expertise was not there to prevent the versatility of such men as Telford and Brunel or the wealth of ingenuity displayed by the subjects of Smiles' *Lives of the Engineers*. The quick-witted could take their opportunity and be rich men by the time they were middle-aged. Trade and ingenuity earned prodigious dividends. The Bridgewater Canal, which cost £200,000 to build, returned an annual profit of £100,000; and thirty-nine original proprietors of the Mersey and Irwell Navigation made a similar profit for over half a century. In the cotton industry the first Sir Robert Peel, the son of a dispossessed yeoman who invested in a few of the early spinning jennies, left nearly £1 million sterling. These great returns were not secured without hard work and a life of abstinence in the years during which a business was being built up. The history of Walkers' of Rotherham, as recorded by Mr T. S. Ashton, is one of constant self-denial, of dedication that the maximum amount of money might be reinvested in the business.

In their determination to plough as much as possible of the profit back into the business, the employers exacted the same frugality and intensity of labour from their workpeople. The combination was the employees' main defence.[1] As a result of the Combination Acts of 1799 and 1800, which declared

[1] See below, p. 67.

trades unions illegal, there developed the Luddite movement, a form of revolutionary association directly caused by an oppressive legal code, aggravated by the new and oppressive Combination laws. This was class warfare, directed against manufacturers, and the alarm of the governing classes magnified it into a high revolutionary conspiracy. The assassination of a manufacturer called Horsfall by Luddites near Huddersfield caused widespread horror, however, and shows how free from bloodshed the outbreaks of 1812 had been.

On the face of it this was illogical; many of the factors that in France had produced revolution and anarchy were present in England. English political institutions were such that society might easily have lapsed into anarchy had there been in England a middle class with revolutionary inclinations. A system of economic production that was in fact totally without organisation of any kind would have plunged the kingdom into violent revolution had the working classes found, in the middle class, leaders to provide it with a definite ideal, a practical programme. The élite of the working class, however, and the hard-working middle class had been imbued by the Evangelical Movement with a spirit from which the established order had nothing to fear.

Although their theological differences were considerable the sects agreed among themselves to impose a rigorous ethical conformity and at least an outward respect for the Christian social order. Thus freedom of association proved in the end the restriction of individual freedom. Men who were influenced by such beliefs could not be the leaders of revolutions, and even such middle-class champions as the working class had were, although exponents of reform, also believers in order.

Of itself the Church of England had contributed little or nothing to the decisive change of attitude from the 18th Century to the 19th. It was essentially a national church, whose source was the will of the secular government and which faithfully reflected in its hierarchy the social hierarchy of the time. The miraculous element of Christianity was as far as possible ignored and religion was chiefly regarded as a system of humanitarian ethics. Indeed Paley in 1785 in his *Evidences of Christianity* went so far as to describe Christ as the first teacher of the 'greatest happiness' principle.

In the past the clergy had been endowed with opportunities for a larger share of this world's goods than was really compatible with spiritual humility and inspiration, and this had helped to make them in effect a branch of the aristocracy. In 1815 the two archbishops and almost all the bishops were openly supporters of Lord Liverpool's government. Eleven were of noble birth; ten had been tutors or schoolmasters to a prince, duke or statesman. The lower clergy were rarely appointed by their bishops; when they were, the appointments usually went to the bishop's clients or relatives. The patronage of over half the parishes lay with the local landlords. The average priest had little sense of vocation; while there was a war the Army offered a better opening to young men of good birth, but with the coming of peace there was a great increase of ordinands. Services were often dull and uninspiring and the Church was woefully out of touch in most cases with the needs of the people. Men such as Fletcher of Madeley were an exception; most of the new industrial areas had no regular contact with the clergy of the Established Church and, until the voting of £1 m. by Parliament for the building of churches as a thank offering for Waterloo, very few new churches had been erected since the reign of Queen Anne.

The vacuum was filled to some extent by the Non-conforming Congregations. The three Old Denominations, the Presbyterians, the Independents and the Baptists, had democratic constitutions. They enjoyed a system of semi-legal toleration which gave them in practice absolute freedom, although marriages were only legal if performed by a Church of England minister, and some other provisions of the Test Act and the Clarendon Code remained in force. Believing as many did that salvation was the gift of God, the urge to convert their fellow men had been declining since the 17th Century. Another cause of weakness was the independence of each congregation and the position of the minister as a mere agent of the congregation. Often undue power fell to the trustees of chapels, usually the wealthiest and most influential members of the congregation. Thus the old denominations in their way reflected the social pattern of the times.

The force that transformed 18th-century religion was John Wesley. His effect on Dissent was rapid and radical; he took longer to influence the Church of England, but by the beginning of the 19th Century this was already happening. He had had no original intention of founding an independent sect but rather a body whose mission was to complete the work of the clergy and to inspire the Church with a spirit of true Christianity. The attitude of the Establishment and the logical consequence of his actions forced the foundation of a new denomination, in which he imposed a centralised administration, and over which he exercised an undivided and despotic rule. He made no contribution to theological development; his emphasis was on the more practical side of life and above all on the seeking of salvation. His influence, spread throughout the country by his incessant travels and sermons, had first of all a profound effect on the Dissenting bodies. The rationalism and republicanism of the 18th Century was succeeded by an outlook that was orthodox and pietist, and the old nonconformist academies, the educational pioneers of their day, disappeared. There was little intellectual impetus to the movement; the new preachers were often illiterate enthusiasts whose speciality was a popular outcry designed to awaken in their audiences a 'revival' of religious feeling. Nevertheless its influence for good was enormous, even if only in the negative sense of making the older churches take stock of their position. The other nonconformists provided more organisation and centralisation of funds: the Baptist Union was founded in 1812. There was a greater interest in missionary activity, particularly overseas. The Methodists showed their conversion in their everyday lives by discarding vice and extravagance and working hard, virtues that brought them success in business and popularity with their employers. That drunkenness and gambling declined was due very largely to the revived influence of nonconformity. The effects of Wesley's work can be traced in the humanitarian movements of the 19th Century, in the respectability of the British Trades Union movement, in the growth of primary education and above all in the fact that a situation that might have led in the 18th Century to a revolution led in the 19th Century merely to a reform of Parliament.

Several clergymen who were disciples of Wesley and Whitefield, without breaking with the Church, sought to apply their ideals within it. This was the genesis of the Evangelical

Movement, which began at Cambridge under Isaac Milner and Charles Simeon, and through the undergraduates who came under their influence was spread throughout the country. Many persons organised little groups for mutual edification and propagation of religious truth; among these was the Clapham sect, whose most prominent member was William Wilberforce. They planned and undertook the reformation of the Church; the act of 1803 forbidding non-residence unless with the consent of the bishop was part of their work, also that of 1812 which fixed £80 as the minimum stipend for curates. Despite opposition from the majority of clergy, they won many successes and were even more successful when they undertook the reform of the national morality. They attacked Sabbath-breaking, blasphemy, drunkenness, obscene literature and immoral amusements. The abolition of the Slave Trade in 1807 was their triumph; they also attempted to protect working-class children against exploitation; they had an indirect effect on prison reform and the penal code. In every humanitarian reform of the 19th Century the Evangelists constituted an invaluable link between the governing classes and the general public, as represented by the great middle class.

To most Englishmen popery was to a large extent still a symbol of tyranny, associated with the nameless fears that would help to deprive Ireland of Home Rule for over a century. In England and Ireland, Roman Catholics had had several restrictions removed, but complete emancipation still eluded them. Pitt had intended it to be associated with the Act of Union with Ireland in 1800, Fox had proposed wide concessions in 1807, but both had failed through the obstinacy of the King. Several causes, however, made the atmosphere more favourable to emancipation by 1815. The Dissenters, themselves the victims of Anglican intolerance, were now increasingly favouring Roman Catholics, while the anti-religious philosophy that the French Revolution had embodied and which Englishmen regarded with antipathy, meant that any religion became preferable to none. Indeed, if emancipation had not involved the problem of Ireland, it might well have been achieved soon after George III became incapable of discharging the royal functions.

The work of Wesley, the Evangelical Revival, the threat of

armed atheism in Europe, all helped to make the first half of the 19th Century a deeply religious age. The Bible was the daily mentor of millions, its stories helped to mould men's lives, its phrases strayed into men's everyday speech. In many homes it was the only book and a book read with great regularity. It was the last age when a majority of educated people grew up without doubt.

The revival of religion led logically to a greater interest in education. In 1815 the education provided did not touch more than a small number of children outside Scotland. In the years before the Industrial Revolution, 'formal schooling' was, as Cobbett pointed out, unnecessary. Craftsmen are obliged to be resourceful and capable of making decisions as part of their everyday lives. Thereby, as Adam Smith said, 'The mind is not suffered to fall into that drowsy stupidity which, in a civilised society, seems to benumb almost all the inferior ranks of the people.' In other words, schools are necessary when work becomes mechanical toil. Learning and culture, however, were respected by all men and were not yet associated with superior privileges. Great works of literature were genuinely regarded by men from all walks of life as part of the national heritage. In Scotland literacy and education were universal but in many parts of England, especially in country districts, the level of literacy was surprisingly high. This was the reason why during the 18th Century so many celebrated men, engineers such as Telford, political writers like Cobbett, scientists and scholars like Dalton and Porson, had risen from the ranks of the people; that the development of manufactures could draw from the country the necessary staff of engineers and foremen. Wordsworth was the son of a petty yeoman, Keats of a liveryman, Faraday of a blacksmith, Turner of a barber, Chantrey of a carpenter, Lawrence of an innkeeper – to name only a few of the many distinguished men in the literature, science and arts of the period. The effect of the Industrial Revolution with its opportunities for child labour was to reduce considerably the number of children who were taught to read, especially in the large towns.

Compulsory State education at that time would have seemed to many an intolerable invasion of private liberty, although plans were put forward by the Younger Pitt and by Whitbread. Such provision as there was was voluntary, motivated

largely by religion, and haphazard. Its principal supports
were classical grammar schools and craft apprenticeships, but
the S.P.C.K. had endowed some schools for elementary
education, and other children received some instruction at
Dames' Schools or Poor Law Schools of Industry. These
were supplemented by the Sunday School movement started
by Robert Raikes of Gloucester in 1780. By 1820 it was
calculated that they were attended by nearly half a million
children.

From 1808 onwards popular education received considerable impetus from a non-denominational organisation which
became the British and Foreign Schools Society. Its leading
spirit was Lancaster, who reformed discipline, invariably bad
in 18th-century schools, by rational methods of honours and
humiliations, and borrowed from Bell the Monitorial System,
'Steam Engine of the Moral World'. By this a master
instructed a number of senior pupils in a series of questions and
answers; they in turn passed on this knowledge to the other
children. As with the Mechanics Institute, however, the
methods and subjects of instruction resulted not in the training
of the mind but in filling it with a large quantity of unco-
ordinated and therefore largely useless knowledge. Bell, the
originator of the system, became the figurehead of the rival
Anglican National Society, founded in 1811. On these two
societies a national system of primary education was eventually built.[1]

The endowed grammar schools were geared almost entirely
to the teaching of Greek and Latin, to the exclusive teaching
of which many were bound by their foundation statutes.
Many were very small, all offered some free places, most
offered facilities for boarding. There was no rigid line
between them and the Public Schools, into which many of
them developed in the course of the 19th Century. These
represented almost free republics of between a hundred and
five hundred members, governed by unwritten codes of their
own making and whose prevailing morality was that of the
tribe, tyrannical and often barbarous. Bullying was severe,
torturing of fags frequent. It was this type of society that
Arnold and other reforming headmasters, appealing to the
corporate pride of the senior boys, asserting the greater control

[1] See p. 93 and p. 220.

of the masters and elevating the group morality, was to transform into a 'nursery of Christian Gentlemen'.

The Scottish universities were in effect also secondary
schools since they provided a four-year course for boys entering
at fourteen. The emphasis on scientific subjects was far
greater than anywhere else in the United Kingdom. They
also provided further degree courses, which produced many
men of great distinction, in theology, law and medicine.
Alone in the United Kingdom they produced an original
school of philosophy and almost all the great physicians of the
18th Century were Scottish professors. By 1815 they had
become centres of intense intellectual activity.

This was not the case with Oxford and Cambridge which
were temples of pleasure rather than of learning. Oxford was
pre-eminently Tory and every new intellectual movement
tended to be an object of suspicion or abhorrence. There
were, however, some signs of improvement. In 1800 a system
of genuine examinations was organised for degrees, and classes
were introduced in 1807. Very little interest was taken in
science, however. At Cambridge the facilities were better;
lectures in physics, chemistry and anatomy were better
developed. There was a laboratory for applied mechanics,
equipped with a steam engine. However, very little more
interest was taken than at Oxford. Cambridge was traditionally Whig; its Fellowships were less the subject of patronage
and tutors were, therefore, more likely to be competent. The
great majority of undergraduates was deliberately idle and
merely sought to acquire a sufficient veneer of learning to
serve them well in the political and parliamentary life of the
country.

The Inns of Court and the Royal College of Physicians provided little impetus to progress in their respective subjects.
The most important contribution of the period to medicine
was the foundation of the Society of Apothecaries in 1815.
Though apothecaries had a low status and were rated as small
shopkeepers, the Society set up standards for the profession
leading directly to the modern system of medical education.
Some hospitals set up medical schools and by 1830 the term
'general practitioner' was in use.

The education of the middle classes was largely through
books, encyclopaedias and periodicals. Lending libraries

were growing up, that of Liverpool being especially good. In some towns there were literary and philosophical societies; those of Birmingham and Newcastle had a strong scientific bias and that of Manchester was the patron of Dalton the chemist.

Although it was commonly believed that if working men were taught to read they would read only what was blasphemous and seditious, the period was notable for the first serious attempt at working-class adult education, behind much of which Brougham was the leading spirit. The *Penny Magazine*, *Penny Encyclopaedia*, the *Library of Entertaining Knowledge* and especially the Mechanics Institute all made an invaluable contribution. But progress was slow. As late as 1839 33·7 per cent of the men and 49 per cent of the women married in church could not sign their names in the parish registers.

For the majority of people, education could provide little solace, and indeed most of them had little enough spare time. Leisure was believed to be a snare and a danger; hours of work were long because it was more profitable for employers and because 'the devil finds work for idle hands'. Life in the towns in particular was drab even when leisure was available; parks were a rarity, lending libraries were for the comparatively wealthy, serious theatres were expensive, public picture galleries rare.

In 1815 England was in a period of transition more rapid than had been known before. It preserved most of the outward form of the 18th Century, but from within it the new spirit of the 19th was struggling to be free. Many feared the outcome would be revolution; the events of the next few years seemed to confirm the most gloomy predictions.

D

II · THE AGE OF LIVERPOOL

(a) THE PERIOD OF REPRESSION

THE end of a war brings not so much peace as disillusionment. It releases passions which may for a time have slept or have been directed elsewhere. It is a time when the waste occasioned by war has to be repaired, when those who have cheerfully fought or paid higher taxes demand instant relief. War stimulates industries; its ending often produces a slump; this and the discharge of men from the armed forces mean unemployment. The French wars were the nearest approach to total war before 1914. The government, by trial and error, had solved its problems and won the war. A war on such a scale bequeathed unparalleled problems to the peace.

Lord Liverpool proposed no comprehensive measures. He considered he had certain duties; first and foremost the very essence of government, the maintenance of law and order. Apart from this he would withdraw the income tax and so redeem Pitt's pledge when it was imposed as a special war measure; he would reduce the heavy war expenditure and when it was appropriate return to the Gold Standard, while the landed interest would be protected by a Corn Law. Beyond this neither he nor his government appreciated the economic problems of the country, nor did they consider it their duty to attempt to solve them; indeed to achieve any effect something approaching modern economic planning would have been necessary.

The war had left a National Debt of £834 m. The payment of interest on this was a heavy charge and in the circumstances the income tax, producing £14 m. annually, and the war malt duty, producing £3 m. could ill be spared, yet both were abolished in 1816. Both benefited the wealthy classes; the taxes that remained, on items such as food, aggravated the conditions of the poor.

So also did the Corn Law of 1815. Bad harvests and the Continental System had led to a great rise in corn prices and the consequent ploughing up of marginal land. The average

price from 1808–13 was 108 shillings a quarter; a considerable
fall following the good harvest of 1813 and fear of foreign
competition made the landed interest anxious to perpetuate
wartime conditions.   Corn Laws were not new but hitherto
they had imposed a duty on foreign corn; that of 1815 was
unusual.   80 shillings a quarter was then regarded as a
reasonable price and received the blessing of Malthus; until
the home price had reached this figure, no import would be
allowed.   The system was cumbersome as the ports would be
open or shut for a three-month period according to the
average selling price of the previous six weeks.   The law
proved not to be so profitable for them as farmers expected,
partly because less money was available for other foodstuffs.
It had an effect on the distress of the period, especially in 1816
when the harvest was short and the three-month delay
prevented the opening of the ports until November.   As late
as 1820 Huskisson, one of its authors, could declare that it had
saved from destruction the capital of farmers who occupied
inferior soils; it had encouraged the growth of corn in Ireland;
it had relieved us from dependence on other countries.   But
during the 1820's there was growing disillusionment, not so
much with the idea of agricultural protection, although this
was bitterly attacked by the Radicals, as with the way in
which the law operated.   Modifications were to follow in 1828.

The return to the Gold Standard was regarded as the
certain way to ensure a stable currency, without which the
property of fundholders, merchants and creditors was unsafe.
In 1817 the Bank of England, relying on its post-war accumu-
lations of cash and bullion, had slowly returned to cash
payments.   Financial operations on the Continent, however,
caused a drain of gold from the country and the Bank was
restrained by Parliament from further gold payments.   A
parliamentary committee was appointed to investigate and
to reassert the authority of the Commons over the financial
interests of the country. Its chairman was Robert Peel,
recently returned from a successful term as Chief Secretary for
Ireland, and its members included Vansittart, the Chancellor of the Exchequer, Canning, Castlereagh and Huskisson.
Bankers and brokers such as Baring, Rothschild and Gurney
appeared before it, as did the economist Ricardo.   The
experts and the views of Parliament were in favour from the

start of return to the Gold Standard; the question was the technical one of when and how to put that principle into effect. The Act of 1819 provided for a gradual return to gold as the sole currency and from May 1823 the Bank was required to exchange notes for the legal coin of the realm. This act and another passed at the same time forbidding the Bank to make advances to the government without parliamentary authority were the foundations of the British currency system for the rest of the century. The pound having been given a high fixed value, other countries were encouraged to make England a centre of international trade. Too sharp a contraction of the note issue, however, brought a fall in commodity price and widespread unemployment. It would be wrong to underrate the importance of the arguments against return to a currency based on gold and how bitterly many people, especially farmers, attributed all the evils they suffered in the next two decades to this return.

It was the economic ills that were the half-understood consequence of the Industrial Revolution and the economic aftermath of the war that helped to produce the semi-political agitation of 1815-20. Its importance was much exaggerated at the time and, indeed, has been much exaggerated since. To be understood it must be seen with reference to memories of the French Revolution, which to many was a source of fear; the reformers hardly helped their case by the use of phrases such as 'convention' and 'committee of public safety', which to many evoked thoughts of the destruction of privilege and order. In some wilder reformers it inspired irrational and dangerous hopes. Although the economic distress was very real, it vented itself in sporadic rioting and rick-burning; it retained a respect for authority as for example did the miners in 1816 who trundled carts of coal around the country to advertise their willingness but inability to work, or the March of the Blanketeers from Manchester in 1817 to ask the Prince Regent 'why trade was slack'. It was not until 1819 that popular agitation took on a coherent political character and even at Peterloo there were banners denouncing the Corn Laws.

From the foundation of the London Corresponding Society in 1792 working men had taken up the cause of parliamentary reform in the hope that a reformed legislative would remedy their material distress. Under the shadow of the French war the government suppressed all agitation for reform, even though Pitt himself had introduced a reform bill in 1786. Liverpool's government showed no greater readiness to consider the matter, even when the war was over. To them the idea was doubly objectionable: labouring people were insufficiently responsible for a political life, while it was a flagrant contradiction of *laissez-faire* to suggest that Parliament should be reformed in order to remedy economic ills. It was the aim of reformers from 1812 onwards, however, to prevent economic distress from venting itself in violence such as strikes and Luddism, or even revolution, and to harness it to promoting the reform of the House of Commons. It is probable that the reformers exaggerated the willingness to revolt or the ability of the working class to associate for the purpose of reform. The people of England, as the Duke of Wellington remarked, were 'very quiet': Jacobinism and revolution were associated with foreigners and it was believed that England was already the most free country in Europe. There was lacking that massive middle-class support that was to bring success in 1832 and it is probable that the Radical disturbances of 1816–19 retarded rather than advanced the cause of parliamentary reform.

The government suspected the existence of a nation-wide movement and the chief evidence they received for this was the activities of Major Cartwright. This veteran reformer travelled round the country founding Hampden Clubs, modelled on the Hampden Club of London, a group of aristocratic and middle-class dilettante reformers that went out of existence when the movement became popular. Cartwright stressed that these clubs were independent of one another; the law forbade more than twenty signatures on a petition concerned with matters of Church and State, and the idea was that each group should send its petition for parliamentary reform to London and spread support for the movement in its locality.[1] The fulminations of Cobbett gave

[1] *A Hampden Club Handbill:* 'A reform in the Representation of the People in the Commons house of Parliament is the only measure which affords any hope of seeing unnecessary war, with its ruinous expense, avoided; useless offices, sinecure places and unmerited pensions abolished, the Poor Rates considerably reduced and such economy in every part of the State introduced as to enable a virtuous Parliament materially to lessen those taxes which bear most heavily on the growers of corn or on the labouring classes of the community, namely the taxes on candles, soup, salt and leather' (Maccoby: *English Radicalism, 1786–1832*).

added publicity to the movement and many such groups came into existence, with a substantial working-class membership. A reverential attitude grew up towards a mythical powerful headquarters in London which was to prove one of the greatest dangers. Any apparently respectable gentleman with a plausible story coming among provincial workmen in the name of 'The Hampden Club of London' was assured of credence. In 1817 Oliver, a Home Office spy, was able to stir up trouble by adopting such a pose, and he was probably largely responsible for the Pentrich Revolution of that year in which a group of farm labourers attempted to march on Nottingham where they were to establish a 'Provisional Government' which they apparently associated with a full stomach. This use of Oliver, Castles, Edwards and other spies by the Home Office from 1817 onwards was exposed and brought discredit to the government.

The incidents that caused most alarm during the period were the Spa Fields Riots, the 'Peterloo Massacre' and the Cato Street Conspiracy.

A petitioning movement was organised late in 1816 and the resulting petitions were to be presented to the Regent by 'Orator' Hunt, a man of superb demagogic gifts whose tremendous voice and celebrated white top hat never failed to dominate a reform meeting. Hunt was refused admission and a large meeting was called for 2nd December, 1816, at Spa Fields in London to protest. Before Hunt's arrival a disturbance was caused by a certain number of extremists, who believed in land communism and claimed that some of the leading reformers supported them. One of them sought to imitate Camille Desmoulins and urged an attack on the Tower of London. The mob looted gunsmiths' shops and reached the Royal Exchange where three of the leaders were arrested by an alderman and half a dozen constables. By nightfall order was restored but many people read a wider significance into the affair.

In January 1817 artisan representatives from all over England assembled in London and supported Lord Cochrane in presenting a petition with half a million signatures to the Commons. A stone or bullet, however, broke a window of the Regent's coach and the government became very alarmed. Evidence was produced by informers of plots to seize the Bank and the Tower. Habeas Corpus was suspended in March, a Seditious Meetings Act passed the same month and a Home Office circular ordered the seizure of perpetrators of blasphemous and seditious libels, the coupling of the two adjectives being a shrewd move to emphasise the respectability of the government's actions. The main fault of the government was its failure to inquire into the causes of the agitation.

Corn prices were very high in the earlier part of 1817, reaching 116 shillings a quarter, but the harvest was good, corn fell to 75 shillings by September and the postponement of cash payments to 1819 may have contributed to the revival of trade. There was a revival of agitation, however, in 1819 when once again harvests were bad and trade receded. In May 30,000 men met at Glasgow to demand reform and relief, and political agitation gained ground, a meeting taking place in Birmingham, with Manchester the outstanding case of non-representation, to elect Sir Charles Wolseley as their 'Legislative Attorney'. Manchester proposed to follow suit in August by electing Hunt but they were advised it was illegal and decided instead to hold a massive reform meeting on St Peter's Fields. There was a large attendance from surrounding towns, and to prevent looting and disorder men marched into Manchester in an orderly fashion, which, however, added to the alarm of the authorities. Instead of arresting Hunt beforehand, the magistrates waited to see what would happen, perhaps wishing to make a show of authority. The Manchester and Salford Yeomanry were sent through the crowd to arrest him; inexperienced, they failed to keep together and, marooned on their horses in the jostling, heaving, jeering crowd of 60,000, panicked and struck about them with their sabres. The 15th Hussars charged in to rescue them, and the crowd fled in terror, clearing the field in ten minutes, leaving six dead and many injured behind. The magistrates had undoubtedly behaved foolishly; they were unwise to use Yeomanry rather than regular troops, but faced with a huge and well-drilled crowd, with few resources apart from some troops of cavalry and a regiment of infantry at their disposal, and responsible for the security of a large, thriving and disorderly city, they clearly had to take some action. The government at once commended them and indeed had no alternative as Canning pointed out: 'To let down the magistrates would be to invite their resignation and to lose all the gratuitous service in the counties liable to disturbance for ever.'

To many, however, the action of magistrates and government appeared ridiculous. Just as the Duke had triumphed at Waterloo, so had Lord Sidmouth at 'Peterloo'. The Common Council of London sent a long memorial of protest to the Regent, Earl Fitzwilliam resigned his lieutenancy of Yorkshire as a gesture of disapproval, Grey denounced the government's action, while Hunt, prior to imprisonment, was given a royal welcome to London, when, it was said, there were 300,000 spectators in the streets.

The unpopularity of the government in certain quarters was augmented by the Six Acts, which have gained a notoriety which their content hardly justifies. During the Radical agitation Tories had talked frequently of the 'deluded' people and it was the aim of the Acts to prevent the access to the people of those who deluded them. It was this theory, rather than an unconstitutional attempt to rule by force, as the Whigs and Radicals asserted, which prompted the Acts, but the revulsion of feeling at the killing of civilians at Manchester overclouded any impartial examination of the measures, which were not unreasonable in themselves. The Acts were to last for a limited period, a maximum of five years. The first and second prevented drilling and the bearing of arms, the third severely restricted public meetings in size, composition and object, while the fourth, fifth and sixth restricted the freedom of the Press. The government successfully prosecuted Hunt, Wolseley and others for offences connected with Peterloo.

The final episode of the period was the madcap Cato Street Conspiracy of February 1820. It played straight into the government's hands and the spy Edwards was apparently an instigator. The plan was to murder the Cabinet as they sat at dinner at Lord Harrowby's house, to carry the heads of Ministers through the streets on pikes and proclaim Thistle-wood, one of the Spenceans, as 'President of the Britannic Republic' at the Mansion House. The murders could well have succeeded, but Edwards had informed the government and the conspirators were arrested after desperate resistance in a loft in Cato Street.

The government's firm measures had been successful; trade

revived but political agitation was no longer so closely linked with economic distress and the trade recession of 1825 brought no revival of the parliamentary reform movement.

The situation, nevertheless, had been one out of which the Whigs might have made capital, but through lack of leadership they failed to do so. They opposed repressive legislation in Parliament, they exposed and thereby killed the spy system, they denounced Peterloo and maintained that the freedom of speech was essential to the constitution, but they expressed so much aristocratic aversion to the Radicals, even when they were defending their liberties, that they made any union for action between the Whigs and the mass of the people quite impossible. A further opportunity occurred in 1820 over the affair of Queen Caroline, but Grey's qualified support of the Queen's point of view and Brougham's machinations, ostensibly on behalf of the Queen but in reality on behalf of himself, made the King adamant that he would never accept the Whigs as his Ministers. Thus was Liverpool's administration confirmed in power for want of an alternative.

For many years the Regent and his wife had been estranged and Caroline, a lady of indiscreet vulgarity, had paraded round the Continent with a strangely assorted retinue. While Princess Charlotte was alive her cause offered prospects in view of her daughter's chances of the succession and Brougham became her principal adviser. In 1819, however, she was clearly something of an embarrassment to him and he made an offer, without her knowledge, that in return for an increase in her allowance from £35,000 to £50,000, Caroline would give up her title and agree never to come back to England. When George III died, the Queen, unaware of the offer, returned to England while the King demanded that her name be deleted from the Prayer Book, and ordered the government to bring in a bill of divorce, threatening to retire to Hanover if he was unable to get what he wanted. There ensued a crisis which might well have resulted in the overthrow of the monarchy itself. Badly advised, especially by Alderman Wood, with whom she stayed, the Queen interpreted the enthusiasm of the mob, due to dislike of her husband, as evidence of her own popularity. She was represented as the victim of yet another government plot against innocence, the equal of Peterloo and the Six Acts. The government, it was maintained, had imported a swarm of lying Italians to swear the crown off the Queen's head. Popular feeling was high and the Ministers hardly dared to show their faces in public.

The third reading of the Bill of Pains and Penalties only passed the Commons by nine votes, and in January 1821 the Queen accepted the government's offer of £50,000 a year for life. She at once lost her popularity and the crisis was over. The Whigs had failed to exploit it to gain office. Liverpool bought the support of the Grenvillites and brought new blood into the Cabinet.

(b) THE FOREIGN POLICY OF CASTLEREAGH AND CANNING

England in 1815 was perhaps at the height of her European prestige. Her naval supremacy was unquestioned, she had successfully demanded the exclusion of overseas matters from the Congress of Vienna and she had won a new respect from her allies by the considerable achievements of her army. In essence her foreign policy changed little in the century that followed; it was a policy of detachment, which Lord Salisbury termed 'splendid isolation', resting on the maintenance of English naval supremacy and of the balance of power, an ideal rather than a fact as the relative strength and ambitions of each state were constantly changing. But both these principles involved some interference in European and Near Eastern affairs, especially to prevent any power or group of powers from disturbing the balance. This demanded an essentially empirical attitude and changes of alliances as occasion required. 'It is a narrow policy,' said Palmerston in 1848, 'to suppose that this country or that country is to be marked out as the eternal ally or perpetual enemy of England. We have no eternal allies and we have no perpetual enemies. Our interests are eternal and these interests it is our duty to follow.'

England's membership of the Congress system, which coincided with Castlereagh's tenure of the Foreign Office from 1815 onwards, did not depart from this conception. In 1820 Castlereagh stated an unalterable basis for foreign policy, which was accepted by Canning as a text for his own work: 'We shall be found in our place when actual danger menaces the system of Europe but the country cannot and will not act on abstract principles of precaution.'

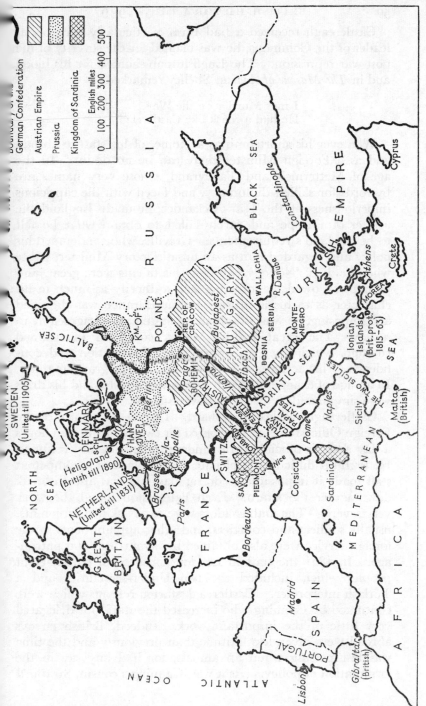

EUROPE IN 1815

Boundary of the
German Confederation

Austrian Empire

Prussia

Kingdom of Sardinia

English miles
0   100 200 300 400 500

NORWAY
SWEDEN
(United till 1905)

NORTH
SEA

GREAT
BRITAIN

DENMARK

Heligoland
(British till 1890)

BALTIC
SEA

RUSSIA

KM. OF
POLAND

REP. OF
CRACOW

NETHERLANDS
(United till 1831)

Brussels
Aix-la-Chapelle
Rhine

HOLST.
SCHL.
HAN-
OVER
Berlin

Prague
BOHEMIA
Vienna

POLAND

HUNGARY
Budapest

Paris

FRANCE

Bordeaux

SWITZ.

SAVOY
PIEDMONT
Nice

LOMBARDY
VENETIA
Ljubljana
Laibach

CARN.

PAPAL
STATES

Rome

ADRIATIC
SEA

BOSNIA
SERBIA
MONTE-
NEGRO
R. Danube
WALLACHIA

TURKISH
EMPIRE

Constantinople

BLACK
SEA

PORTUGAL

Lisbon

SPAIN

Madrid

Corsica

Sardinia

Naples
The Two Sicilies

Sicily

Malta
(British)

MEDITERRANEAN

Ionian
Islands
(Brit. prot.
1815–63)

MOREA

Athens

Crete

Cyprus

SEA

Gibraltar
(British)

ATLANTIC   OCEAN

AFRICA

Castlereagh received a bad Press, particularly because, as leader of the Commons, he was blamed for the severity of the post-war repression. The English mob shouted for his blood and in *The Masque of Anarchy* Shelley remarked,

> I met Murder on the Way,
> He had a mask like Castlereagh.

Whatever his shortcomings at home, of his stature abroad and as a Foreign Minister there can be no doubt. In the age of Metternich and Talleyrand, whose very names are bywords for skilled diplomacy, and faced with the capricious imperiousness of the Tsar Alexander, he made England the arbiter of Europe and rarely failed to obtain what he felt to be England's requirements. Greville, who condemned his policy and regarded him as an unsatisfactory Minister, wrote when he died: 'Nobody can deny his talents were great, and perhaps he owed his influence and authority as much to his character as to his abilities. His appearance was dignified and imposing; he was affable in his manners and agreeable in society. The great feature was a cool and determined courage, which gave an appearance of resolution and confidence to his actions.' He had, indeed, the grand manner. In an age of exaggerated extravagance his tastes and his dress were simple and he had exquisite style.

Castlereagh worked very hard. During his tenure of the Foreign Office 1812–22 he worked for twelve or thirteen hours a day and his official correspondence filled seventy volumes. He found it difficult to delegate and the lack of a competent staff made it impossible to do so; Canning was also to break down under the strain. Even Palmerston found the work very severe. The ambassadors were rarely skilled diplomats, usually soldiers and courtiers, and other appointments in the foreign service were also obtained by favouritism and patronage. In 1821 the staff in London consisted of twenty-eight people, which included the two Under-secretaries and a Turkish interpreter. Castlereagh started reforms which were continued by Canning who increased the staff, but delegated very little of the important work. Indeed, British envoys abroad were given less latitude than previously and the time was fast passing when an ambassador had any say in the formulation of policy. As it was, Canning's cousin, Stratford de Redcliffe, was the last great diplomat of the old school. With the help of Huskisson the Consular Service was over-hauled and consuls were dismissed who did not live up to Canning's high standards.

The war had ended with the First Treaty of Paris, May 1814, which confirmed the restoration of Louis XVIII, the removal of Napoleon to Elba, the limitation of France to the boundaries of 1792, the organisation of Germany as a Con-federacy, the union of Holland and Belgium under the House of Orange, the compensation of Austria with Venice and Lombardy and the division of Italy into independent states, which were all in practice to prove satellites of Austria. The Second Treaty of Paris, after the Hundred Days, reduced France to the frontiers of 1789, imposed an indemnity of 700 m. francs and an allied army of occupation for three years. These were confirmed by the Congress of Vienna, which lasted from November 1814 to June 1815. There Castlereagh secured the exclusion of territories outside Europe from the discussion; Britain kept Ceylon, the Cape of Good Hope (for which the Dutch were paid £2 m. compensa-tion, to be spent on fortifying the French frontier), Trinidad, St Lucia, Tobago, Malta, Heligoland and the protectorate of the Ionian Islands. The principal British interest in Europe was firstly the traditional objective that the coasts nearest to England should not be in the possession of a single hostile power, and secondly the creation of reasonably strong states along France's western frontier. Thus Sardinia-Piedmont gained Genoa, and the Rhineland, which Austria declined to accept, was foisted on to Prussia by the other Great Powers almost as a bad joke. Both interests were served by the union of Holland and Belgium, which logically should have worked; its break-up in 1830 was due more to the folly of the Dutch than to the lack of foresight of the Great Powers. In the treatment of France the British had supported restoration of the Bourbons against solutions put forward by Austria and by Russia both in 1814 and 1815, feeling it to be the solution that contained the greatest chance of permanence and therefore of peace; against Prussian demands for a heavy indemnity of 1,200 m. francs and portions of French territory they urged moderation. Castlereagh realised that if the Great Powers took from France territory she might in the future reclaim, Britain might be involved one day in another war. He could have acquired for his country great accessions of territory and immense financial and commercial advantages but he felt that the long-term interests of Britain demanded security and peace.

It was in eastern Europe, where British influence was unable to make itself directly felt, that Castlereagh met with failure. He strove earnestly for the restoration of Poland in its integrity as an independent kingdom, clearly perceiving that a strong and independent Poland would have served as an effective barrier between Russia and Germany and thus have helped to maintain the European equilibrium. He got little support, however, even from Talleyrand; as Castlereagh wrote to Liverpool: 'His Imperial Majesty intimated that the question could only end in one way, as he was in possession.' The Tsar also occupied parts of Polish territory that before the war had been controlled by Prussia, which now demanded all or part of Saxony as compensation. At one point Castlereagh, Metternich and Talleyrand made a secret agreement to resist Russian and Prussian claims by force but eventually the question was settled fairly amicably with part of Saxony being given to Prussia.

The Congress of Vienna has been heavily criticised as the blatant exercise of power politics and the utter disregard of the principle of national self-determination. In England the transfer of Genoa to Sardinia was especially condemned at the time: Whitbread saw it as 'the compulsory transfer of a free people to a government equally imbecile and corrupt'. Its aim, however, was not so much justice as the maintenance of peace and in this it was markedly successful; there was no war in Europe between the Great Powers until 1854 and apart from the unification of Italy and Germany, and the independence of Belgium, the frontiers of western and central Europe were substantially unchanged until 1914. It was successful in this because it was guided not so much by abstract principles of national justice as by a realistic assessment of the European equilibrium.

The Congress left two legacies that illustrated the problems of maintaining that equilibrium. The Tsar proposed a 'Holy Alliance', an agreement between the rulers of Russia, Austria and Prussia, 'in the name of the Holy and Undivided Trinity' and in which 'the three contracting monarchs will remain united by the bonds of a true and indissoluble brotherhood and would lend each other mutual aid in all future difficulties'. All Christian monarchs were invited to subscribe, including France. It has been suggested that the Tsar had in mind the isolation of the Turks with whom he had been at war when Napoleon invaded Russia in 1812. Castlereagh privately regarded it as a 'piece of sublime mysticism and nonsense' and used the constitutional position of the Prince Regent to prevent an English signature; Metternich regarded the whole transaction with cynical contempt, but that did not prevent him from utilising the Alliance and its author for the promotion of his own policy.

The Quadruple Alliance of November 1815 was Castlereagh's particular contribution and was a straightforward renewal of the alliance that had defeated Napoleon. Castlereagh saw it as a valuable means of preserving European equilibrium and in addition of removing any threats to it by periodic meetings of the Great Powers. The term 'Congress System' is perhaps unfortunate for it suggests something in the nature of an international organisation, a foretaste of the League of Nations. There was no such organisation; there were no arrangements for the preparation of agenda, no rules of procedure. It was merely a continuation of diplomacy by conference and it preserved unanimity as long as France was the principal subject of discussion. The Tsar, however, with the concurrence of Austria and Russia, declared that the *status quo* could only be maintained by the guarantee of all existing frontiers and the ruthless suppression of all revolutionary movements. He proposed a league on these lines at the Congress of Aix-la-Chapelle in 1818 but gave way when Castlereagh made it clear that Great Britain could never accept commitments of this kind and that the plan was clearly impracticable until every state had a government beyond criticism. It was evident, however, that the Tsar and Metternich intended to exploit the Concert of Europe in the interests of repression and reaction, and Castlereagh's position became increasingly a false one.

The Congress of 1818 restored France to full equality with the other great powers, withdrew the army of occupation, which had been commanded by Wellington, and concluded the payment of the indemnity.

In 1819 Metternich issued the Carlsbad Decrees which aimed at limiting the political activities of universities, freedom of political association and the liberty of the Press throughout the German Confederation. When in 1820 General Pepe forced Ferdinand of the Two Sicilies to adopt a liberal constitution, Metternich summoned a Congress at Troppau, where Austria, Russia and Prussia issued a protocol binding themselves, if need be by force, to bring back guilty states to the bosom of the Great Alliance. England and France were invited to agree. While recognising that Austria had a special interest in Italy and was, therefore, entitled to use force if necessary, Castlereagh deplored international action, and in a despatch of great vigour denounced the claim of European powers to interfere uninvited in the internal affairs of sovereign states. The Allies, undeterred, published their protocol and adjourned to Laibach in 1821 where the Italian rulers agreed to the restoration of order in Italy by the Austrian army. Great Britain did not send a plenipotentiary; Charles Stewart, Castlereagh's brother, went as an observer.

In January 1820, Ferdinand VII of Spain was faced with a military revolt caused by his wild plan to reconquer the rebellious American colonies. The insurgents captured the King and forced the restoration of the unworkable constitution of 1812. Castlereagh made it clear that action by the Powers was unnecessary, but he was reluctant to see the end of the Congress System, especially in view of a revolt in Greece which might tempt Russian intervention, leading to the further weakening of Turkey. He, therefore, arranged for a Congress at Verona to discuss the Greek revolt, Italy and Spain. Before it met, Castlereagh took his own life.

Castlereagh had a sensitive nature beneath his cool dignity. He had worked at tremendous pressure during the past ten years and had, as leader in the Commons, borne far more than his fair share of the odium heaped upon the government for the policy of repression. He had additional disadvantages; as Chief Secretary he had suppressed the Irish Rebellion of 1798 and negotiated the Irish Act of Union of 1800; the Irish had not forgiven him. The public had never appreciated the importance of his work as Foreign Secretary and had merely associated his ideas with those of the Tsar and Metternich; the greater the value of a diplomatist's work the less widely does it

tend to be advertised. Castlereagh lacked that ability to
appeal to popular sentiment which distinguished Canning.
The session of 1822 was a heavy one and he was never at his
best as a parliamentary speaker. His death was hailed both
at home and abroad as a triumph for liberty.

His successor in both his offices was George Canning, an
appointment which Canning owed to the support and determination of Lord Liverpool. Canning was a man of considerable ability who had served as Foreign Secretary 1807-9
and might have entered Liverpool's Cabinet in 1812 had he
not made his terms too high. He came in in 1816 in the
minor post of President of the Board of Control, from which
he resigned in 1820 because he disapproved of the Cabinet's
condemnation of the Queen. George IV never forgave him
for this and Liverpool only persuaded the King to agree to the
appointment with considerable difficulty. Although as a
parliamentary manager and a Foreign Secretary he had no
reasonable competitor, it was only through Liverpool's
consistent support that the Cabinet and the rank and file came
to accept him. Everything in his history, method and manner
was calculated to inspire distrust in those who could not
realise that he might also be great. He was self-assured, not
slow to expose the feelings of his seniors, and could seldom
resist criticising with cruel wit. All this might have been
forgiven had he not, with considerable skill, enhanced his
position by using public opinion as an ally.

This asset and the support of Liverpool were necessary to
him when faced with the hostility of George IV. As King of
Hanover, George had a policy and a secret service of his
own with which his British Ministers were not necessarily
acquainted. From 1815 onwards he had been critical of his
Ministers' policy and wished to see Great Britain as an active
member of the Holy Alliance. There developed the 'Cottage
Coterie' which centred round Princess Lieven, the wife of the
Russian Ambassador, and included, in addition to the King,
Esterhazy, the Austrian Ambassador, and Wellington. Its
aim was to circumvent the policy of Canning, which was also
that of the majority of the Cabinet. When the recognition
of the former Spanish colonies was proposed, the group made
a determined attempt to get Canning dismissed. Canning
hinted to the King that he might reveal the King's intrigues

to the Commons and when, shortly afterwards, a coolness developed between Austria and Russia over the Near Eastern question, George submitted with good grace and Hanoverian correspondence was made subject to Foreign Office supervision.

The difference between Castlereagh and Canning was not of policy but of method. If there seems a break in continuity it is because it is always easier for a new Minister rather than an old one to lead his country along a fresh path in international affairs. By 1822 Castlereagh had few illusions concerning the policies of the Tsar and Metternich, he was prepared to recognise the Greeks as belligerents and the revolted Spanish colonies as independent, but he would not glory in flaunting the continental powers, as Canning did, and clung to the form of past association. Although Canning sent Wellington to Verona, he considered that, after the differences revealed there, further international gatherings of this type would do more harm than good; he was thus pursuing more vigorously that policy of detachment which Castlereagh had begun.

The Congress of Verona was principally concerned with Spain. The French had already moved troops to the frontier, on the pretext of establishing a *cordon santitaire* against an epidemic of yellow fever, and in August 1822, faced with the Tsar's suggestion that the French should give passage to his troops and hopeful that the expedition might bring prestige to the restored monarchy, they demanded Europe's moral support for their own intervention. It was granted, but not by Britain, the expedition was successful and Ferdinand was restored. It was dissatisfaction with the outcome, which he blamed on Canning, that drove Wellington into the arms of the 'Cottage Coterie'.

The real importance of the Spanish affair for Britain lay in America. During the French wars the Spanish monopoly of their colonial trade had broken down and it had largely passed into the hands of Great Britain. Powerful elements in the colonies, of which the best known leader was Bolivar, had taken the opportunity to assert their independence and although the royal government received a fair amount of support, Spain was unable to resume control after 1815. Castlereagh had urged the Spanish government to accept the *fait accompli* and was anxious to organise the former colonies as independent monarchies, an idea taken up with such enthusiasm by the French that it was hastily dropped. The situation was further complicated by the French intervention in Spain in 1822 which made a French expedition to the New World seem possible. The United States, afraid that Latin America might become in effect a British possession, recognised the independence of the colonies in the same year, while Great Britain recognised their trading flags. Canning, to prevent United States designs, suggested a joint London–Washington pact guaranteeing the states of South America against military intervention. To this President Monroe's famous message to Congress was in fact a rebuff, but the London Press received orders to represent the message as Monroe's adhesion to Canning's policy. Indeed Monroe was dependent on England for the military and naval strength to prevent the establishment of any new colonies in the New World. Finally in December 1824, Liverpool and Canning forced the Cabinet to agree to the recognition of Buenos Aires, Mexico and Colombia as independent states.

Two years later Canning reviewed the affair in a speech to the Commons. Referring to the failure to intervene in Spain in 1822 he said, 'I sought materials for compensation in another hemisphere . . . I resolved that if France had Spain, it should not be Spain with the Indies. I called the New World into existence to redress the balance of the Old.'

On this occasion Canning was also defending another action, which has been described as his greatest diplomatic triumph. John II of Portugal had sailed for Brazil in 1807 and had only returned with reluctance in 1822. His son Dom Pedro, who had remained behind, declared himself to be independent Emperor of Brazil. When John died in March 1826 Pedro succeeded to Portugal, granted a very bad constitution, and abdicated in favour of his eight-year-old daughter. Canning's sense of humour was delighted by the spectacle of Metternich trying to prove that even a King could not grant fundamental change. In a circular he warned the great powers not to interfere, which they agreed not to do in November.

A new situation arose, however, when the absolutist party under Pedro's brother, Dom Miguel, invaded Portugal with

Spanish help and the government at Lisbon appealed to Great Britain for assistance. With Liverpool's support, Canning persuaded the Cabinet to agree, and three days later troops embarked for Portugal, where their presence had the desired effect. Canning's power of rapid decision and his shrewd diplomatic moves had probably averted a general war. 'We go to Portugal not to rule,' he told the Commons, 'but to defend and preserve the independence of an ally. We go to plant the Standard of England on the well-known heights of Lisbon. Where that Standard is planted, foreign dominion shall not come!'

The Holy Alliance had by now become largely ineffective owing to differences over the Greek revolt. The Turks had begun as military nomads and had basically remained as such. Though they had been encamped on European soil for 400 years they had developed neither political institutions nor civilised traditions, they had submerged, but neither destroyed nor absorbed, their subject peoples. Individually the Greeks had prospered, supplying the Turks with a capable bureaucracy, manning the fleet, making great fortunes in trade and preserving in their religion the great traditions of the past and a sense of national identity. During the French wars Greek merchants had obtained a good deal of the carrying trade in the Mediterranean into which French ships dared not venture, and by these means revolutionary and liberal ideas had flowed into Greece and secret societies had been founded, especially the *Philike Hetaireia* with its headquarters at Odessa. It had encouraged the abortive outbreak of Prince Alexander Hypselantes in the Danubian provinces which acted as a signal for a Greek rising.

The Turkish method of rule was one of prolonged indolence punctuated by bursts of violent activity. One of these occurred early in the 19th Century when groups of free-lance desperadoes were retained by the Sultan to restore the Greek villagers to obedience. The Greek revolt was a generalisation of these local conflicts, invoked by appalling atrocities on both sides, the attention of Europe being particularly drawn to the murder on Easter Day 1821 of the Patriarch and three Greek archbishops in the Greek Cathedral at Constantinople. Russian indignation rose high and the Tsar was in a dilemma. To attack the Turks would be to help the cause of the revolu-

tionary Greeks, but Greeks, although rebels, might assist
Russia in accomplishing her forward policy in the Balkans.
Russia sent an ultimatum, which alarmed the other Great
Powers. Philhellene sentiment had not yet been aroused by
Byron's passionate crusade and Castlereagh successfully urged
the Tsar to be cautious. The subject was to be discussed at
Verona and Castlereagh favoured recognition of the Greeks
when a *de facto* government was established in the Morea,
providing it could be done cautiously and unostentatiously.

Greek delegates were not received at the Congress, but two
events improved their prospects. Although Canning had
little sympathy and suspected that the revolt was instigated
by Russia, he decided that the interests of English trade would
be best served by recognising the Greeks as belligerents, while
Lord Byron's arrival in Greece attracted considerable enthusiasm and sympathy in western Europe. Canning was
convinced that Greek independence was only a matter of
time but refused open support lest it bring repercussions
among the Moslem population of India. He declined to
attend a conference between Austria and Russia on the subject. The views of the two powers proved to be irreconcilable
and the Holy Alliance was at an end. Canning was confident
that sooner or later one or other would seek British support.

The situation was complicated in 1825 by the intervention
of Mehemet Ali, the Pasha of Egypt. Encouraged by the
French, who considered they had inherited a special interest
in Egypt from Napoleon's campaign there, an army was sent
to Greece which efficiently repressed the revolt on behalf of
the Sultan, whose vassal Mehemet nominally was. Unless
the Powers intervened, Greek independence would be lost.

The Tsar Alexander died in December and in April 1826
Wellington was sent to congratulate his successor, Nicholas I,
with whom he signed the Protocol of St Petersburg. This
provided for British mediation leading to Greek autonomy.
The policy of moderating Russian ambitions by becoming
Russia's ally was a new departure for Great Britain which, if
pursued, might have averted the Crimean War and the crisis
of 1877–78.

In 1827 a treaty was concluded between Britain, France
and Russia and a joint fleet commissioned, under Vice-
Admiral Codrington, to patrol the seas round the Morea.

Without orders to engage, this destroyed the Turkish and Egyptian fleet at Navarino. The *Morning Post* considered that without the battle Austria would have settled the affair by diplomacy; it represented a defeat for Canning's policy of avoiding war, but Canning was dead and Wellington had no clear policy. The Sultan's blunders brought about war with Russia over the Danube delta which ended in the Treaty of Adrianople of 1829, which recognised the autonomy of the Danubian principalities, while the independence of Greece was guaranteed by protocols in 1830, after the Egyptians had been expelled by French troops. Fearing Russian influence the Greek State was made as small as possible (in the negotiations Grey played a considerable part) and in September 1832 it was formally recognised with Otho of Bavaria as King.[1]

(c) LIBERAL TORYISM

The affair of the Queen had provided a fleeting opportunity for the Whigs to gain office; their failure on this occasion made Liverpool broaden the support for his government. He purchased the support of the Grenvillites by giving Buckingham, their leader, a dukedom, with generous spoils for other members of the family connection, but more significantly, when Sidmouth's retirement and Castlereagh's death gave him the opportunity, he included in the Cabinet men whose policies would win over moderate reformers and make a Whig government impossible.

The term 'Liberal Toryism' which has been used in recent years to describe this period, was not a contemporary one but is not inappropriate. The High Tories accused the government of 'liberalism', then a suspect and dangerous thing, while the 'liberals' who dominated the Cabinet felt acutely their estrangement from the 'Ultras'. The period is associated with the name of Canning, who was more in the public eye than any other Minister and whose use of public opinion was an asset, but the mainstay of the policy within the Cabinet was the Prime Minister himself. He alone could keep the party together in support of a policy of which many of its members disapproved.

In November 1821 Peel was appointed Home Secretary. The son of a successful cotton manufacturer who had contri-

[1] See p. 190.

buted to the early stages of factory reform, Robert Peel had shown early promise, had taken the first 'double first' on record at Oxford and at the age of twenty-four had been appointed Chief Secretary for Ireland, a post he held from 1812 to 1818. There he could study at close quarters the mazes of the Irish problem, which was to be the occasion of his downfall, and obtain an invaluable apprenticeship in official business. His contribution to the Tory party was a genius for administration and finance and by 1830 he had gathered experience of parliamentary and government techniques unmatched by any other contemporary politician. As Disraeli remarked of him in his later years, 'He played upon the House of Commons like an old fiddle.' He carefully examined public opinion but his opinions tended to be those of the most advanced experts in the various aspects of public life with which he was concerned. In a sense it may be said he originated little: his penal reform was inspired by Romilly, his extension of free trade by the work of Huskisson and Cobden, but by his skill he translated their aspirations into solid achievements.

In politics he was a realist, with a high sense of duty, a lucid and powerful intellect and a strong instinct for leadership. To many, however, he was a cold and unattractive figure, a fact arising from an intense sensitivity and curious self-consciousness and lack of assurance.[1] This made many unsympathetic to him and could help to create unnecessary difficulties, as in the Bedchamber Crisis of 1839.

Peel was essentially a 'government man'. Although he was responsible for adapting the Tory party to the changed conditions of the 1830's, he was never in a fundamental sense a party politician, twice 'betraying' his followers, over Catholic Emancipation in 1829 and repeal of the Corn Laws in 1846. To him national expediency was more important than party programmes and his conservatism was a desire to preserve order and good government in a society where reform alone could prevent revolution.

Nowhere were his qualities more relevant than in the Home Office. The difficulties of preserving order were well illustrated by the severity of the penal code, for whose mitigation

---

[1] It has been suggested that a feeling of isolation in Dublin Society when Chief Secretary may have had a good deal to do with Peel's reserve.

Romilly had long campaigned. Mackintosh had recently presided over a committee of inquiry on whose findings Peel was to base much of his work. It was evident to Peel that the criminal code was defeating its own purpose, for, to escape the consequences of a small crime with a capital penalty, men would willingly commit a murder, while, rather than send a man to the gallows for a trivial offence, juries would often refuse to commit at all. Peel was careful to persuade, and circulated drafts of his bills for comment by judges. In 1823 the death penalty was abolished for over a hundred offences, including theft of all small sums and such bizarre offences as cutting down hop-vines and impersonating Chelsea pensioners. Judges were permitted to withhold formal sentence of death in all capital convictions except murder.

In March 1826 further Acts of Parliament consolidated and codified the criminal laws and improved the operation of criminal justice. All too often in the past, prosecutions had been quashed on purely technical quibbles and defects, and Peel, faced by a rising tide of crime, aimed at making the law at once more effective and more humane.

His work was continued by subsequent Home Secretaries. In 1832 housebreaking, sheep-stealing and coining of false money ceased to be capital offences. In 1841 more statutes were repealed and a proposal that the death sentence should be inflicted only for murder was lost merely by one vote. After 1838, however, no person was hanged except for murder or, up to 1861, attempted murder. Public executions were abolished in 1868.

The men saved from hanging were transported and Peel sought to reduce the length of sentences and their severity. It remained an unsatisfactory system, however, and, as the government did not provide a passage back to England when the sentence was complete, it led to the permanent separation of families. It gave a few men the chance of starting a new life in Australia, but it failed to act as a deterrent and as a rule made bad men worse and weak men into hardened criminals. By 1837–38 it was costing the country about half a million pounds a year. Colonial opinion was restive and convicts were no longer sent to New South Wales after 1840; Tasmania ceased to receive them after 1853 and after considerable agitation in which Robert Lowe, later leader of the 'Adullamites' and Gladstone's Chancellor of the Exchequer, played a conspicuous part, transportation was finally abolished in 1868.

Mitigation of the severity of the law led by the latter half of the century to a decline in the crime rate, but had prison reform been more rapid, the decline might have been even more marked.

Interest in prisons, from the humanitarian and sanitary point of view, was first stimulated by the work of John Howard, High Sheriff of Bedfordshire, in the 18th Century. The situation was chaotic: there was no central control, management was inefficient and there was great variation in standards of accommodation and discipline. It was not until around 1810 that the combined influence of radical enlightenment and evangelical Christianity began to overcome the inertia of the authorities and the resistance of vested interests. The work of Elizabeth Fry and also of other humanitarians continually exposed fresh scandals. Peels' Gaols Act of 1823 was a great consolidating statute which also introduced most of the principles of enlightened prison administration advocated by a generation of penal reformers. Justices of the Peace were compelled to organise a prison on Home Office approved lines in every county and in the major towns, to inspect them three times a year, to maintain them from the rates and to send an annual report to the Home Secretary. Gaolers were to be paid and not to live by fees. In 1824 Home Office scrutiny was extended to a further 150 minor prisons and Houses of Correction. Further administrative reforms followed in 1835 after a committee of investigation. The Home Office could now inspect prisons and could enforce their regulations, while prisoners were to be kept in separate cells and to be employed as far as possible on productive work. It was difficult, however, to find productive work which could be done under prison conditions. In an influential article in the *Encyclopaedia Britannica* of 1823, James Mill suggested the purpose of imprisonment should be 'reform by industry' but most people failed to distinguish between retributive, deterrent or reformatory punishment. On this subject and on the functions of magistrates Peel corresponded with Jeremy Bentham.

The courts themselves were also in need of reform. In addition to consolidating the laws relating to juries, Peel raised the salaries of High Court judges but abolished fees and perquisites. It was a considerable achievement when he secured the appointment of a Royal Commission, in the face of Lord Eldon's opposition, to consider the reform of Chancery, whose equity had almost disappeared under a mass of complicated rules and practices. Its delays and expenses had for some time been a target of considerable criticism. Little, in fact, materialised, but the information so gained was useful to Brougham, Chancellor 1830-34, who simplified the procedure of the High Courts, laid down new rules for the Court of Chancery, abolished many sinecure posts and set up a new court to deal with bankruptcy cases. Private debtors for sums of less than twenty pounds were allowed to go into bankruptcy in 1844 while the establishment of County Courts in 1846 was invaluable to creditors who could now recover small sums easily and cheaply. Imprisonment for debt was finally abolished in 1869.

Peel's best known achievement of this period was the foundation of the Metropolitan Police in 1829, which was to provide, in due course, the solution to the serious problem of maintaining law and order. There were prejudices to be overcome: although in London and the new industrial areas, in the wrecking and smuggling population of coastal districts and in the beggars, gipsies and vagabonds in the countryside there were large social elements that had almost escaped from government regulation, most Englishmen were convinced that this was the price of liberty and equated an efficient police with tyranny.

As Chief Secretary Peel had seen the value of the efficient constabulary set up by Wellington in Dublin in 1808, and in 1814 he had extended it to cover the whole of Ireland. In 1821 he found in London a chaos of police authorities, divided into nine distinct jurisdictions, providing only about 400 regular police to deal with a population of one and a half million. The men themselves were often corrupt and inefficient and could make little contribution to the prevention of crime. The most efficient part of it was the Bow Street Horse Patrol under the Home Secretary's direct orders. Peel made various improvements and, after comparing the situation in London with that in other major European cities, he created, in 1829, a single authority to control an area within a ten-mile radius of St Paul's, with the exception of the City of London itself. The new force was supervised by two commissioners, Colonel Charles Rowan and Richard Mayne, a barrister, whose twenty-year partnership was the basis of its success. Its principal object was the prevention of crime, and good relations with the public were emphasised. There was an establishment of just over a thousand, and to achieve good discipline and a professional attitude, reduced gentry were excluded and recruitment was made from N.C.O.'s of good character. The success of the force was immediate and although there was initial unpopularity and in 1833 a jury returned a verdict of justifiable homicide when a policeman had been killed in a riot, the Metropolitan Police was to be the model and recruiting ground for the various provincial police forces set up in the following years.

Extension was limited by the apathy of authority and the hostility of the working class, though the effectiveness of the system was indicated by the rapidity of the flight of criminals to unpoliced areas when a new force was set up. The Municipal Corporations Act of 1835 empowered the towns concerned to set up police, and permission was granted to counties in 1839. The expense deterred many, but twenty-two had done so by 1853 and forces were made compulsory in 1856. The Home Office had the right of inspection and paid increased grants to local bodies whose police were efficient.

Peel's work as Home Secretary increased his standing in the party and the country and he emerged as the principal rival to Canning in the Cabinet. Huskisson, on the other hand, was Canning's close friend and colleague. He became President of the Board of Trade in 1823 and brought new ideas into the fiscal policy of the government. He had an extensive knowledge of facts and figures and Melbourne pronounced him to be the greatest practical statesman he had known. Inspired by Adam Smith's *Wealth of Nations* and by the writings of Ricardo, public opinion was moving towards the abandonment of the traditional doctrines of Mercantilism. In 1820 the London merchants petitioned against restraint of trade, urging that freedom would enable the capital and industry of the country to exploit the most profitable fields, and the Commons passed a resolution that trade restrictions could only be justified by some great political expediency.

Clearly agriculture and shipping came under this heading, for the prosperity of the land was regarded as the basis of national wealth while a strong mercantile marine would provide an invaluable recruiting ground for the Royal Navy. Parliament refused to accept an income tax so some duties were retained for revenue purposes. Huskisson led the movement towards 'open trade', the substitution of protective for prohibitive duties.

After 1822 it is possible to trace the existence of a small 'economic cabinet' consisting of Liverpool, Huskisson, Robinson, the Chancellor of the Exchequer, and Lord Bexley, his predecessor. The Chancellor was still regarded as the assistant of the First Lord of the Treasury and by virtue of holding this office, Liverpool co-ordinated the activities of Huskisson and Robinson. Robinson was an able man but lazy and often absent from London; his role in financial policy was a subordinate one.

The Budgets from 1822 onwards showed a surplus as a result of the revival of trade and the reduction of the National Debt, and in his first two Budgets Robinson remitted some of the assessed taxes regarded as burdensome by the wealthier classes but which were even harsher on the poor. In 1824 customs duties were tackled. The existing tariff laws were extremely complex, were based on no definite principle and did not correspond to the needs of the new era. The machinery for enforcing them was so inefficient that all too often they were a dead letter and smuggling was carried on in the open. Some of the duties were levied on the raw materials of manufacture, others protected England against non-existent competition. There was no sense in a duty of 50 per cent on foreign cotton goods in view of the superiority of British manufacture. In 1824 the silk and wool trades were regulated. The duty on raw wool was reduced from sixpence to one penny per pound, that on raw Indian silk from four shillings to threepence per pound, while foreign silk goods were admitted on payment of 30 per cent. In 1825 the entire system was revised. On a long list of specified articles the import duties were reduced; for example, cotton goods paid 10 per cent instead of 50 per cent while the duty per ton on iron dropped to £1 10s. 0d. from £6 10s. 0d. Unspecified raw materials now paid 10 per cent and manufactured goods 30 per cent. Tariff barriers between England and Ireland were removed in 1825, while in the same year the colonies obtained unfettered liberty to trade directly with every country, on the sole condition of submitting, like Britain herself, to the provisions of the Navigation Acts. These had been modified by the Reciprocity of Duties Act, which enabled the government to sign treaties, on the model of the Treaty of Ghent with the United States in 1814, providing for the mutual lowering of duties and restrictions. Treaties were signed with Prussia, Sweden, Denmark, Hanover, the Hanseatic towns and the four newly-recognised Latin American states. To encourage the re-export trade Robinson made the bonding system more liberal while Huskisson standardised the weights and measures system.

A parliamentary committee appointed to investigate matters relating to trade and industry failed, in 1824, to get a bill through permitting the export of machinery, but an act of the previous century prohibiting the emigration of workmen was repealed, as its principal result was to prevent skilled men who had gone abroad from ever returning. More important, however, was the repeal of the Combination Acts of 1799 and 1800.

These acts, which represented a change in the fairly favourable view Parliament had had of workmen's combinations in the 18th Century, had been brought in under the pressures of war. They had never been particularly effective. The common law already condemned conspiracy and secret oaths, and compared with the seven years' transportation they could involve, three months' imprisonment under the Combination Acts was a relatively innocuous deterrent. Their principal effect was to drive the movement underground and to enhance the reliance on extorted oaths and physical force towards 'blacklegs' and hostile employers. Ever since 1819 a campaign had been led by Hume in Parliament and in the Press by McCulloch, the economist, for repeal, and the increasing acceptance by informed opinion of the general doctrine of non-interference in economic matters helped to prepare the ground.

After 1822 the rise in the price of foodstuffs in conjunction with a general rise of price rendered an increase of wages an urgent necessity. In consequence illegal combinations multiplied, became aggressive and were frequently victorious.

Hume presided over the Parliamentary committee and witnesses were produced and coached by a tailor of Charing Cross, Francis Place, whose premises had for some years been a headquarters for London radicals. Place was in advance of his time in the art of managing committees and carrying reforms by clever manipulation. He was aware that trades unionists expected repeal to be followed by an appreciable rise in wages; repeal became law because it was supported by liberals who believed that when workers ceased to feel themselves at war with the law of the land they would realise that Combinations were powerless against the operation of the laws of nature and would, therefore, cease to form them.

The outcome was otherwise. Combinations now did openly what had been done in secret; reserve funds were collected, strikes organised, particularly in the cotton industry which was almost at a standstill for five months, while decisions were imposed on the mass of workers by methods of terrorism. Four men were condemned to death by their colleagues in Glasgow, one sentence being actually carried out, and there were numerous acts of violence in Ireland. Demands for a 'closed shop' and restrictions on the use of apprentices and machinery accorded ill with the doctrines of *laissez-faire*.

The purpose of the Act of 1825 was not to make illegal either trades unions, collective bargaining or strikes, but merely to prevent the abuses of collective power and to defend individual workmen and employers. To the offences of 'violence', 'threats' and 'intimidation' were added the more indefinite offences of 'molestation and obstruction'. The penalty was three months' imprisonment and this remained the law until 1871.[1]

The steady upsurge of industrial prosperity which had ensued once the economy had adjusted itself to the changed conditions of peace and to which the liberal policies of Huskisson and Liverpool had contributed, received a temporary setback in 1825.

There had been a wave of financial speculation, much of which had been valuable, but some of which, especially in South America, whose independence had opened a new field for British capital, had lacked genuine security. A large part in stimulating this situation was played by the numerous small banks of the day which often advanced their clients' money without adequate security and issued their banknotes without adequate cover. The government was alarmed by the steady flow of bullion from the Bank of England, and by the autumn the over-strained economic structure began to give way. Sixty or seventy banks of which Pole, Manton and Co. of London was the chief, failed within seven weeks, and many others were on the edge of disaster. Liverpool and Huskisson rapidly consulted with leading bankers and decided to issue as many Bank of England notes as possible to prevent panic.[1]

The government followed this up with two Acts of Parliament designed to ensure that there was no repetition. The issue of notes under five pounds by country banks was forbidden; those already in circulation were to be withdrawn by 1829. The Bank of England was authorised to set up branches in the provinces, while joint-stock banks were authorised outside a radius of 65 miles of London.

The worse sufferers from the depression were the poor; disorder occurred especially in Lancashire where many power looms were destroyed. Although the military forces were strengthened there and some use was made of spies, the attitude of the home department was more humane, and voluntary contributions helped in alleviating suffering. The unrest inevitably brought fresh concern about the Corn Laws. In the face of considerable Cabinet opposition, Huskisson sought to modify them by the introduction of a sliding scale, which would dispense with the worst feature of the existing system, its rigidity. A pivot point of 60 shillings a quarter was selected, at which a duty of 20 shillings would be charged, the duty descending evenly as the price increased. With Liverpool's support the bill, introduced in 1827, might well have passed but Liverpool had suffered a stroke and Huskisson was unable to overcome the hostility of the landowning interest, who were supported by Wellington. In 1828, when Huskisson was no longer in office, Wellington introduced a sliding scale of his own, which declined unevenly to a duty of one shilling at 73 shillings a quarter, a system which tended to encourage speculation and which

---

[1] On 17th December, although the panic was allayed in London it continued in the country and there was neither gold nor notes to send. Fortunately one of the directors of the Bank of England remembered a case of £1 m. of old unused notes in the Bank cellars; they were rapidly despatched and all was well.

failed as signally as its predecessor to keep prices high when the harvest was bountiful.

Liverpool's stroke was not only a disaster for Huskisson's corn law policies; it changed the whole pattern of politics. The Prime Minister had held together a Cabinet of strong personalities and, since 1820, while retaining in Eldon and Wellington the old guard of the Tory party, he had given essential support and encouragement to the progressive elements. The differences, nevertheless, were real, not over trade policy alone, but especially over the question of Catholic Emancipation, which had made for discord in political life since the Act of Union with Ireland.

The choice of Liverpool's successor brought this discord into the open. Canning's claims to the succession were very strong; since 1822 he had been leader of the Commons and he was the greatest orator of his day. His successful foreign policy had made him an international figure and outside Parliament he was the most popular member of the Cabinet. Nevertheless he was unpopular with several sections of the Tories; his long championship of emancipation offended many and raised difficulties with the King; his foreign policy and the personal distrust that many felt for him were other obstacles. The principal alternatives were Wellington and Peel; the former, though favoured by many, was also Commander-in-Chief, but Peel was in a stronger position. The more extreme Tories supported him as a determined opponent of emancipation, but he also had support from the progressives owing to his liberal views on other matters. A resolution of the Whigs to support Canning, whose views on most questions except parliamentary reform coincided with their own, gave him an advantage, and when three dukes violated the royal prerogative by urging the King not to appoint Canning, George summoned him and made him Prime Minister. Emancipation was to be an open question.

Seven Cabinet Ministers promptly resigned, including Wellington and Peel. The latter justified his resignation on the grounds that, in view of his long association with the Protestant standpoint, he could hardly support an appointment that would excite Catholic hopes. Canning had some difficulty replacing them, but when in July three Whigs, including Lord Lansdowne, joined the Cabinet, his team had become a strong one. In order to ingratiate himself with the King, he appointed the Duke of Clarence Lord High Admiral. The traditional pattern of politics was split down the middle; the government was a Whig-Tory coalition, while the less progressive Tories and the Whig leader, Grey, who distrusted Canning, were in opposition. Time was needed to weld these diverse elements together but the support of the Press and the traditional support for the King's Government in the Commons provided this, despite the rejection by the Lords of Huskisson's sliding scale. A new 'liberal system' which might have startling results for the nation's future seemed in prospect. Modification of the Corn Laws and emancipation of the Catholics were planned for 1828 and seemed the prelude of even wider reforms. Canning had been unwell, however, during the preceding months and in August he died. To many it seemed obvious that the coalition he had created would die with him, but its political position was so strong that George, unwilling to undertake again so soon the troubles of Cabinet-making, offered the vacant post to Robinson, who was now Lord Goderich. He had acquired some reputation as Chancellor of the Exchequer and the King believed he could dominate him.

Goderich proved to be a singularly inept Prime Minister. He had inherited Canning's problems but not the qualities which might have helped him to master them. He was 'as firm as a bullrush' and unable to master the discordant elements within his Cabinet. It was these that forced him to resign rather than face Parliament early in 1828: 'a transient and embarrassed phantom', as Disraeli called him.

(d) IRELAND, EMANCIPATION AND THE DECLINE OF TORYISM

Wellington became Prime Minister, but the efficiency of the Ministry depended to a large extent on Peel. Canning's death had left him the acknowledged leader of the Tories in the Commons and on the best of terms with the Tory leader in the Lords. He had been out of office for an honourable reason and he had acquired the reputation of an able and consistent statesman. There was a conscious return to the conception of a central and balanced Ministry, which was the only type that could hope to survive in the independent and undisciplined Commons of the early 19th Century. The prospects, however, were far less promising; four Prime

Ministers in less than a year had destroyed the sense of continuity and stability, and enmity and distrust had grown
among men who otherwise might have worked well together.
Wellington had essentially an unpolitical nature; he had not
the skill to hold together a group of equal and able men as
Liverpool had done, nor did he possess Canning's parliamentary ascendancy. He complained that he was in arrears of
business because his time was spent 'in assuaging what gentlemen call their feelings'. In Parliament Brougham headed
an attack on Wellington as a potential military dictator and
despite his resignation of the office of Commander-in-Chief
it remained a vulnerable point. In his Cabinet Peel returned
to the Home Office and became leader of the Commons, but
of the Canningites, Dudley retained the Foreign Office,
Lyndhurst remained as Lord Chancellor, thus excluding
Eldon, and Huskisson continued to be Secretary for the
Colonies. The King wished for some Whigs, but in the
event none would serve. The problem facing Wellington
was that none of the major issues of the day had been solved
and on none could he expect the unanimity of his Cabinet.
Canning had not settled emancipation nor had Huskisson
the Corn Laws, while in the background hovered the problem
of parliamentary reform.

During the previous ten years this issue had grown in
respectability and in relevance. The panic fears engendered
by the French Revolution had been dissipated by time; many
of the gentry saw the realism of recruiting the rising middle
class of the industrial districts into the political nation as a
bulwark against unrest, while the trade measures of Liverpool's government had emphasised their importance. Three
cases of gross corruption in the less representative boroughs
convinced some of the waverers. The proposal to disfranchise Grampound was raised in 1819 but the political atmosphere was not favourable and it was not until 1821, through
pressure from Lord John Russell and the Whigs, that the seats
were transferred to Yorkshire. A motion urging more general
reform was brought forward by Russell and although defeated,
it was prophetic in that the Whigs voted for it as a party. In
1823 a Norfolk County Meeting, under Cobbett's influence,
passed a resolution in favour of reform and the *Political
Register* was responsible for a steady increase of interest.

Hostility to reform, however, came not merely from the reactionary. Parliament, as has been stated above, was seen as a balance of interests and a move towards democracy would upset that balance. On an earlier occasion Canning had declared that the functions of the Commons 'are not to exercise an undivided supreme dominion in the name of the people over the Crown and the other branch of the legislature, but checking the one and balancing the other to watch over the people's rights and provide especially for the people's interests. . . . Our lot is happily cast in the temperate zone of freedom, the clime best suited to the development of the moral qualities of the human race.'

However desirable the general virtues of the existing constitution its particular vices were hard to defend and the Cabinet was in agreement over the disfranchisement of Penrhyn and East Retford. Huskisson and the Canningite group sought to transfer the seats to Birmingham and Manchester; conservative opinion wished to transfer the right to vote to the freeholders of the hundreds in which the boroughs were situated. A compromise was arranged in the Cabinet, but when the Lords refused to transfer the Penrhyn seats to Manchester, Huskisson voted in the Commons against the absorption of East Retford into its hundred. He then, by way of apology, tendered his resignation to Wellington, who, much to his surprise, accepted it. The Duke's patience was exhausted: the Canningite group had entered the Cabinet as a body, had voted in it as a body, leaving the Prime Minister often in a minority; now they left it as a body. A more supple politician than Wellington might have kept them, but to a man who believed in the virtues of military discipline the essential sympathy with their viewpoint was lacking. Neither Huskisson himself, who was killed in 1830 at the opening of the Liverpool to Manchester Railway, when a reconciliation was to have been effected, nor Charles Grant nor Palmerston nor Lamb, later Lord Melbourne, ever rejoined the Tories. The eventual contribution to Whig talent was considerable, while the foolish action of the Lords did much to provoke in the country the feeling that soon afterwards carried the reform bill.

A further split in the party was occasioned by Catholic Emancipation. The atmosphere of the time was in favour of some modification of the long political ascendancy of the Church of England; Protestant dissenters had been permitted to hold office by the passage of annual indemnity acts since the early 18th Century.   In 1828 Russell introduced a bill for the repeal of the Test and Corporation Acts and despite Peel's op-position on the grounds that repeal might reopen old wounds, the measure was carried.   This inevitably brought to the fore-front the problem of emancipation of the Catholics; the number of English beneficiaries would be few, and a century and a half had proved their loyalty.   It was not to be so simple: the problem of Catholic Emancipation was also the problem of Ireland.

Ireland was a tragic example of the sins of the fathers being visited on successive generations, whether the several English governments seeking to solve its problems or the Irish peasantry themselves.   In Ireland the abuses of England were writ large, in its agricultural and legal systems, its Anglican ascendancy and its electoral corruption.   Many laws had been introduced deliberately as a way of holding down, by subtle means, a potentially hostile subject population.   In matters of land and land-holding, abuses stretched back to the Plantation of Ulster under James I, the reallocation of land by Cromwell and its confirmation and extension by William III.   On top of the complexities of Irish tribal usage which conceded to the Irish peasantry a part ownership of their land had been imposed the more sharply defined English property law with its clear landlord-tenant relationship. There had grown up huge estates whose owners, Protestant, English and frequently non-resident, had few points of contact with a peasantry whom they regarded as brutalised, lawless and completely unreliable.   Their business was in the hands of agents and their aim was to obtain as much rent as possible. Irish leases were long and in the simplest possible form: the landlord contributed nothing by way of property; the tenant acquired no rights in any building he had erected or any improvements he had made.   Both sides lost by this arrange-ment – the scientific agriculture of 18th-century England could make little impact under this system and the soil steadily deteriorated; any attempt by the landlord to keep his farms in hand or consolidate his holdings was strongly resisted by the Irish.

In Ireland land was currency, the payment made for

services and the provider of sustenance. Since the Act of
1793 restoring suffrage to Catholics many forty-shilling 'freeholds' had been created to increase the landlord's electoral
influence. Outside the big towns wage labour hardly
existed; land itself was payment for services and the purpose
of a peasant's land was to produce sufficient potatoes and
milk to feed the man and his family. The population of
Ireland, perhaps owing to the encouragement of the priests,
had grown from around four million in 1790 to nearly seven
million in 1821, a far higher rate of increase than that of
contemporary England, which had the industrial resources
and consequently capital investment in which Ireland was
almost lacking. English trade policy had almost consistently
worked to the disadvantage of such Irish industry as there was.
There was no coal in Ireland, the Irish peasantry had no
purchasing power and there was little to encourage the
would-be manufacturer – for instance, no Dublin factory was
equipped with a steam engine until 1833. Famine was
avoided by the development of the potato as the staple crop.
From the beginning of the 19th Century the introduction of
new strains, more prolific though perhaps more susceptible
to disease, further increased Ireland's chief food supply.
Needing no capital and only unskilled seasonal labour, it
enabled the peasants to marry young and rear large families.
This further aggravated the position, for the custom of the
village partnership demanded that the goods of a deceased
peasant be divided equally among his children, while sons on
attaining their majority and daughters on marriage obtained
a share of the original patrimony. Hence as many as forty
families could be settled on a farm of 150 acres occupied
forty years earlier by a single tenant. The process continued:
tenants gave sub-leases though they did not lease the original
land themselves and left land in their wills though they did
not own it. The farmer, who wished to employ labour, was
forced to grant that labour land. The landlord, whether
improver or absentee, was at the mercy of social usage. There
was no way out through eviction; it was certain to evoke the
savage retaliation of social warfare – threats, physical intimidation and, in the last resort, assassination. The tenant was
at the mercy of brutalising conditions and a chain of rapacious
rent-gatherers. As yet the only emigrants came from the

skilled artisan classes of Ulster, and it was not until the Potato Famine of 1845 cut the Gordian knot that the slow and painful reorganisation of Irish land became a possibility.

In 1828, however, the land question smouldered in the background. The overseas expansion of English interests and the alarming growth of the Irish population, predominantly Roman Catholic as it was, made Englishmen as a whole acutely conscious of the danger of Ireland, without their making any attempt to understand its problems. Many Englishmen had been deeply shaken by the apparent failure of the English colonial empire in the aftermath of the American War of Independence and by the fact that the Irish, led by Grattan, had taken advantage of the English embarrassment to obtain considerable independence for the Irish Parliament in 1783. As British imperial possessions gradually expanded during the 19th Century, so the unity of the United Kingdom itself seemed an essential prerequisite to the keeping together of such widespread and diverse possessions. The French invasion and the Irish rebellion in 1798 highlighted in the mind of the average Englishman, at a time when the populations of the two islands were far more equal than was to be the case later in the century, a second serious danger, that of a potentially hostile country on England's flank that would be a serious embarrassment in time of war. This attitude had prompted the Younger Pitt, by wholesale bribery, to get the Irish Parliament to vote itself into union with that of Great Britain in 1800, a Union in which Irish interests would be consistently outvoted and ignored. To the English this seemed a measure of political necessity against rebels, and the possibility of a threat to English security, however unreal it might be by the end of the century, coloured English attitudes to Ireland and was responsible for much of the intransigence over even moderate proposals of Home Rule. To the Irish the Union was and remained a demonstration of force unsupported by right. Whatever concessions were made to Irish Roman Catholics or tenants, however much British money was spent on rehabilitating Irish agriculture, the English ascendancy was consistently seen as a denial of basic Irish rights. There was no bridging of such a gulf; each side misunderstood the other and from that misunderstanding came increasing bitterness, impatience and violence.

The specific cause of Irish bitterness in the 1820's, and an embarrassment to successive governments, was the failure of Pitt, owing to the opposition of George III, to honour the pledge of Catholic Emancipation he had made when the Act of Union was passed in 1800. In England only a tiny minority, the Catholics comprised six-sevenths of the population in Ireland, and the Roman church retained the form it had possessed in mediaeval days. In the 18th Century the training that priests had received at Douai and other colleges on the Continent had given them urbanity and tolerance, but the French wars had closed this source of education and the college of Maynooth, founded by Pitt and partly subsidised by the government, had helped to produce priests more conscious of their role of defenders of Irish traditions and nationality. Their influence over their flocks was considerable and Protestant landlords would often make use of them to maintain order. They depended exclusively on the voluntary offerings of the faithful, who had also to contribute, by means of tithes, to the wealthy, corrupt and scantily supported Church of Ireland. Members of this church alone could sit in Parliament and hold public office under the Crown, and it was on the removal of this grievance that Daniel O'Connell focussed Irish energy from 1823 onwards. It followed from the propaganda he employed that emancipation, when achieved, neither allayed discontent nor ended the Irish problem.

O'Connell's weapon was the Catholic Association which he founded in 1823. Starting as a small debating society, it grew rapidly to the dimensions of a Roman Catholic parliament, including peers and landowners, priests and people, all, in fact, who felt themselves otherwise unrepresented. From 1824 onwards a voluntary contribution of one penny per month was levied on the peasantry, which became known as the Catholic Rent.[1] The idea was not new but what was new was the skill and success with which the reinvigorated Catholic leadership built up a national organisation for its collection. By March 1825 investments of £13,000 had been accumulated, which provided an invaluable basis for action. More important, it gave the Catholic movement for the first

---

[1] Much of the money came from the towns. In the impoverished countryside collection was difficult; the most productive method was by the priest after Mass.

time a national organisation and O'Connell an exceedingly formidable instrument.

Emancipation bills had been rejected by the Commons in 1812 and 1819, by the Lords in 1821 and 1825, on both of which occasions the heir to the throne, the Duke of York, played a prominent part. Behind the stereotyped arguments of dual allegiance was the very real fear of Irish demagogues at Westminster, of Ireland ruled at the dictation of priests and of English power in Ireland broken for ever. Canning's well-known support for Catholic claims had induced the Association to await events, but the formation of Wellington's government was an immediate signal for action. Meetings were held in most Irish parishes and O'Connell's claim to be master of the Irish peasantry was largely substantiated. He was not a revolutionary but was not averse to brandishing the threat of physical violence. His opportunity came when the Canningites left the Cabinet; Vesey-Fitzgerald, a popular landlord who had frequently voted for emancipation, and member for County Clare, had to seek re-election when he was appointed to the Board of Trade. Normally it would have been a foregone conclusion, but the Association's propaganda and the influence of the priests alienated the voters from their traditional loyalties and O'Connell himself, although as a Catholic debarred from taking his seat, received the majority of votes.

The effect of this result was to render government almost impossible. Wellington could not appoint to Cabinet office or raise to the peerage any Irish member without risking a repetition, while in a general election the Catholics would be almost entirely successful. The Lord Lieutenant warned Wellington that unless emancipation followed, the result would be a rebellion that not even O'Connell could prevent. Wellington proposed the annual suspension of the laws against Catholics, limitation of the Irish County Franchise and payment and control of Catholic clergy by the State. Peel felt this last proposal would cause difficulty with Protestant nonconformists and taxpayers as a whole and urged a complete and lasting settlement. The King refused to commit himself and meanwhile O'Connell asserted that he had more control over Ireland than had the Lord Lieutenant himself. There was some suggestion that Grey should take office at the head of an emancipation ministry; Peel felt that he was in a false position himself in view of his long opposition to Catholic claims. The threat from Ireland, however, demanded resolute action and the leadership of a man whose national prestige would overbear Tory opposition and whose influence over the King would counteract that of the Duke of Cumberland, who warned his brother that he would share the fate of Louis XVI. Wellington alone could do this and in March 1829 the Emancipation Act became law. All civil disabilities were removed from the Catholics though they were not eligible for the Lord Lieutenancy of Ireland and offices influencing the Established Church. The Irish County Franchise was raised to ten pounds, to prevent a proliferation of 'faggot' votes, the Catholic Association was declared illegal and, ungraciously, O'Connell was forced to stand for re-election in County Clare.[1]

Peel's action was regarded in his constituency of Oxford University as a great betrayal. It was rumoured the Pope had ordered a new festival to be inserted in the Calendar – The Conversion of St Peel. On offering himself for re-election, Peel was defeated but was returned for Westbury. But he had not returned to the bosom of the Tory party and although Peel defended his action as one of common sense and the sole hope of preserving peace in Ireland, the affair did permanent damage to his reputation.

The effect on English politics of emancipation was considerable. A further split in the Tory party followed the defection of the Canningites, and made a Whig government a practical possibility for the first time for over twenty years. Perversely some Tories began to favour parliamentary reform on the grounds that a more representative Commons would not have passed the Act of Emancipation. That frequent prelude to political upheaval, industrial and agricultural depression, began in 1829. Petitions demanded reduced expenditure and lower taxation and Wellington found increasing difficulty in asserting his authority in Parliament. Some compared him to Polignac in France and accused him of clinging to power by royal influence and military strength against all opposition. It was clear that although most members did not want a comprehensive reform of Parliament, demand for the elimination of the more corrupt constituencies was growing.

[1] See below, pp. 99, 105.

III · THE AGE OF GREY AND PEEL

(a) THE REFORM BILL OF 1832

UNREST and a desire for parliamentary reform had appeared together after the defeat of Napoleon, but to the political nation reform conjured up visions of Jacobinism and violent revolution. In 1830 another French example changed the atmosphere and convinced many that moderate reform without violence was feasible. From 28th to 30th July there took place three days of rioting prompted by the Ordinances of St Cloud, which sought to reduce the power of middle-class liberals and increase that of the aristocracy and the Church. Charles X left the throne without a struggle and the moderates succeeded in averting the demand for a republic by installing Louis Philippe on the throne as a constitutional king relying on middle-class support. This provided a potent example to English reformers, not only in 1830 but also in the crises of the next two years. To act boldly on behalf of the people did not produce anarchy, as the Tories had argued since 1789. Without this impetus it is possible that returning prosperity might in time have killed the desire for reform.

The death of George IV in the summer of 1830 seemed, at any rate, to have produced a king more amenable to reformers' demands. William IV was an obvious contrast to his brother; simple, at times a little stupid, honest and kind, with few exaggerated ideas of his prerogative but a feeling that his duty was to hold the balance evenly between Whigs and Tories. He was frightened by Radicalism which he equated with Republicanism and his fears were reinforced by those of Queen Adelaide whose German childhood memories were full of the excesses of the French republican armies. His eccentric wanderings through London unattended gave many the impression, however, that he was a democrat at heart. This delusion led to a very general misunderstanding of Grey's slowness about peer-making in the later stages of the Reform Bill[1] struggle; few guessed the difficulties he had with

---

[1] See p. 88.

the King. In fact he treated the Whigs and their bill as fairly as he did only out of an honourable sense of his constitutional duty to his Ministers.

The accession of the new King made necessary a general election at the end of July. Most of the polling took place before the events in France were fully known but they clearly had some result at the end of the poll. It was reckoned the Tories had lost on balance over thirty seats and the 'open' seats in town and country were almost all carried by the opposition. Brougham's return for Yorkshire, with which he had no local connections, seemed to many to herald the coming change.

Apart from its influence on the election, the July Revolution stimulated working- and middle-class interest in reform. Cobbett, who should have known, asserted that the restless labourers of 1830 were aware of the political causes of their misery and of the arch-grievance, the state of the representation. Cobbett's influence was considerable and England owes him a great debt, for in focussing attention on reform, as O'Connell had done on emancipation, he persuaded the poor to seek redress for their wrongs by peaceful and not by revolutionary means. Middle-class agitation also played a considerable part. In January 1830 Thomas Attwood founded the Birmingham Political Union 'to obtain by every just and legal means such a reform in the Commons as may ensure a real and effectual representation of the lower and middle classes of the people in that house'. The Birmingham example was discussed all over the country and was imitated. In July the London Radical Reform Association was founded, consciously copying O'Connell with a Radical rent of one penny. In October it issued an address to the people urging the country to form local societies to promote the cause of annual Parliaments, universal suffrage and the ballot. Movements such as these were to keep reform a burning issue during the constitutional struggle and when it failed to be the expected panacea they were to be the mainsprings of subsequent radical movements.

Many were convinced that change must come but in the autumn of 1830 it was not clear which Prime Minister would direct it. There was no clear majority in the new house against Wellington; the Canningites were in favour of reform and still thought the Duke might supply them with what they wanted. Events in the Lords on the afternoon of 2nd November decided the question; when Grey challenged him on the fact that there was no mention of reform in the King's speech, Wellington replied, 'The legislature and system of representation possess the full and entire confidence of the country.' He felt that it was more nearly perfect than any legislature that had ever been and asserted that he would resist all reform measures of any kind. To the moderates of his party the shock was totally unexpected and it is probable that Wellington spoke more forcibly than he had intended. The effect of this pronouncement was to precipitate more sweeping reform than the moderate Tories wanted. There was widespread unrest in London, a royal visit to the Guildhall was cancelled, the middle classes were furious with the Duke. The government was defeated in the Commons over the civil list proposals and for the first time since 1804 a ministry was driven to resign by a hostile lower house. There followed the first complete change of Ministers since 1807. The King invited Earl Grey to form an administration.

Before he had succeeded to the peerage in 1807 Grey had shown considerable parliamentary talents. Since then he had virtually withdrawn from politics, declaring that he would only take up parliamentary reform when the people of England would 'seriously and affectionately take up the question for themselves'. He had become largely detached from the party; the negotiations with Canning were conducted without his consent, and Althorpe was elected leader in the Commons without his knowledge. Had the Whigs chosen their own Prime Minister in 1830 it seems at least probable that they would not have chosen Grey, but Wellington regarded him as the most reliable of the Whigs and it was on his advice and that of Lansdowne that the King sent for Grey. The Whigs accepted the situation with good grace and he had no difficulty in forming a government.

This, like its predecessors, was in effect a coalition, including Canningites and a few Ultra-Tories such as the Duke of Richmond. Its basis was a consolidated Whig group in the Commons under the leadership of Althorpe. For several years Brougham and Russell had acted as Whig pacemakers but the former never gained the confidence of the party and the latter was too young. Althorpe was an unwilling politician, essentially a countryman, a slow thinker but a man who by infinite pains would come to the right practical decisions. As leader of the Commons in Grey's administration he provided an invaluable bridge between the Prime Minister's lofty eminence and the younger members of the party. In debates in Parliament he was so obviously incapable of soaring above his hearers' intelligence that he won a well-deserved reputation for honesty. Sir Henry Hardinge commented, 'It was Althorpe that carried the Bill. His fine temper did it.' As Chancellor of the Exchequer he was not a success; indeed finance was a weak point of the Whig ministries of 1830–41.

Brougham was more difficult to place. His talents were considerable, his services to reform in the past were frequent. But opinion was unanimous that he was a bad man to work with, and it was no surprise that Althorpe, with his far greater skill at handling men, became Leader of the Commons. It was a minor sensation of the day that Brougham was persuaded to accept the Woolsack where his erratic genius could safely grapple with the tortuous problems of legal reform. Russell was given minor office but, with Durham, Grey's son-in-law and a firm Radical, he had special responsibility for drafting the Reform Bill itself. There was reason in this; they knew what was wanted, they could best supply the need.

Within the Cabinet, Lansdowne and Holland, the son of Shelburne and the nephew of Fox, represented the old Whig traditions, but the principal administrative positions went to the Canningites. Melbourne became Home Secretary, Goderich the Colonial Secretary and, on Lansdowne's advice, Palmerston began his career at the Foreign Office. Grey's achievement was considerable; out of divergent elements he had made a Cabinet superior in ability to its predecessor and thereby he had made a new party. The Cabinet was the most aristocratic of the century, but this was deliberate. Only a government so constituted could hand over some of the power of the aristocracy to the middle class. It was essential to preserve the confidence of the King, of the Whig peers and of the many lukewarm members of the Commons who might easily turn to the Tories through fear of the violent force of revolution at work in the country.

Many assumed that a social crisis was imminent in the

autumn of 1830, but although agitation was widespread it was not unduly violent and few lives were lost. The economic position was undoubtedly bad. Since 1826 the export trade had been depressed. The iron and coal industries had continued to flourish but cotton had been hard hit and much bitterness developed among the handloom weavers whose share of production was steadily eclipsed by that of machinery. The country suffered from over-production but some signs of revival had produced a new agitation for higher wages. Troops at Manchester, however, and warships in the Tyne, helped to ensure that the north remained quiet. But the agricultural unrest of the Midlands and south was more dangerous. The demoralising effect of the Speenhamland systems had reached a dangerous point and it was among the Poor Law gangs that many of the first outbreaks occurred. The immediate cause in many cases was the introduction of the threshing machine, but Ministers noted that outbreaks often followed the appearance of Cobbett and other Radical speakers in country districts.[1] The principal demand was for a living wage and in many cases farmers agreed to an increase and Grey himself suggested a private subscription and a grant from Parliament to relieve distress. Many ricks and farm buildings were burnt and cryptic notes left in the ruins suggested the co-ordination of 'Captain Swing'. But the last labourers' revolt was essentially disorganised and hardly deserved the severe treatment the government meted out to it. That it be clearly understood that a movement towards greater liberty would not involve greater licence, Melbourne suppressed the revolts with a severity that exceeded Sidmouth's. At the Assizes, three were condemned to death, 400 imprisoned and 457 men and boys transported to Australia. A number of successful Press prosecutions followed and in the country the government lost considerable prestige.

This was shortly allayed by the introduction of the first Reform Bill and henceforward to many the life of the Ministry seemed bound up with the continuation of liberty. This first bill was brought in on 1st March, 1831 by Lord John Russell. Drafted by Russell, Durham, Graham and Duncannon, with Brougham, who was anxious to leave some of

---

[1] Cobbett was brought to trial afterwards but defended himself with great skill and the case was dismissed.

the rotten boroughs intact,[1] pointedly excluded, it intended by means of boldness to secure finality. A meagre proposal such as Wellington might have framed would never be accepted as a settlement. Grey wanted a measure which, though radical in form, was conservative in spirit because it would restore stability to the constitution. The extreme Radical idea of universal suffrage was never entertained; Parliament would give the right to vote to those men of substance and respectability who it was expedient should be represented. The only valid reform in Whig eyes was one which attacked the grievances and anomalies which made the existing arrangements unpopular but stopped far short of household suffrage, equal electoral districts and a stiff and rigidly enforced corrupt practices law. The most radical feature of the bill was the abolition of the rotten boroughs without compensation, which was regarded by many as a violation of the sacred law of property and which did much to restore the government's prestige among the people, and the most progressive feature was the substitution of uniform qualifications in borough and county for the varied franchises of the old system. Radicals might lament the disappearance of the universal suffrage of Preston and Westminster[2] but they realised that a standard middle-class suffrage must in time give way to a standard working-class one.

Boroughs with a population of under 2,000 were completely disfranchised; those of between 2,000 and 4,000 were to lose one of their two members. When Russell read the list a contemporary noted, 'As each venerable name was read, a shout of ironical laughter rang from the benches opposite. The general opinion was that the government were mad.' In all, 143 seats were available for redistribution out of a total English representation of 513. Nine large towns and four metropolitan districts were each given two members, eighteen other towns had one member. Sixty-five members were added to the county representation, eight extra seats were allocated to Scotland and five to Ireland. To the forty-shillings freeholders already allowed to vote in the counties were added copyholders, long leaseholders and tenants at will paying £50 a year.[3] In the boroughs a uniform house-

---

[1] See above, p. 3.   [2] See above, p. 4.
[3] Added by the Chandos Amendment, summer 1831.

hold franchise of £10 was introduced. A secret ballot was contemplated, owing to the influence of Bentham, with a higher household franchise, but the Cabinet rejected the idea and the original franchise was replaced. Existing voting qualifications would be retained in the lifetime of their present holders, but in view of the greater numbers, all votes now had to be registered. On the second reading the bill was carried by one vote.[1]

Peel had secured the undertaking that the Ministry would submit to the vote the increase of Irish and Scottish representation at the expense of the English. It was a clever move to exploit English patriotism in a narrow sense and Gascoyne's amendment that there should be no decrease in English representation was passed against the government by eight votes. Grey had the alternative of resignation or dissolution and William IV's fear of provoking a revolution by dismissing his Cabinet finally prevailed over his fear, that dissolution would be followed by an election with revolutionary results.

And indeed it was, only one week later. The Ministry had the bill as its sole programme and everywhere received very firm middle-class support. Many working men at this stage stood apart, believing the bill to be a feeble half-measure, but their abler and more popular leaders adhered to the cause of reform. Traditional loyalties were swept aside and in most counties and in all open boroughs Whig candidates triumphed. In Northumberland, which traditionally returned a Percy, the Duke dared not field a candidate at all. Grey stood directly on the support of the people in a way no previous Prime Minister had done.[2]

After the election in early May the bill was re-introduced. During the summer the bill was thoroughly debated clause by clause, perhaps more thoroughly than any other bill has ever been; the Tories made many suggestions but the government rejected them all. The Radicals were furious at the

---

[1] At 4 a.m. after the division, Macaulay left the House and called a cab 'and the first thing the driver asked was "Is the Bill carried?" "Yes, by one." "Thank God for it, Sir."' These are the terms of the act as finally passed.

[2] Russell, too, was a popular hero. Sydney Smith wrote, 'I met John Russell at Exeter. The people along the road were very much disappointed by his smallness. I told them he was much larger before the Bill was thrown out but was reduced by excessive anxiety about the people. This brought tears to their eyes.'

long delay and Wetherall, the principal Tory spokesman, became the most unpopular man in the country, a fact that was to prove incendiary when he went down to Bristol as Recorder in October. The agitators were tireless in keeping the people up to the mark and were afraid that in the long period of waiting the demand should collapse and so afford to the lukewarm an excuse for dropping their support. In this they were helped by the newspapers which devoted almost all their space to Lords and Commons debates. The middle-class consistently exerted pressure. An element of melodrama heightened the effect. In October the bill was in the Lords, the Tories had taken heart through some victories at by-elections, and after an all-night sitting the bill was rejected by a majority of 41 at 6 a.m. on 8th October. On his bended knees Lord Chancellor Brougham begged their lordships to consider what they had done, and the reformist Press gave the news to the outside world in black-edged editions.

The outburst of dismay was spontaneous. In London the situation was saved by Peel's 'New Police', but the windows of the Duke of Wellington's house and those of other Tory peers were broken. Fury was strongest against the bishops, of whom only two had voted for the Bill; indeed the Established Church was most consistent in its opposition. The Bishop's Palace was burnt at Bristol in serious rioting caused by Sir Charles Wetherall's state entry as Recorder, the prisons were forcibly opened and the Mansion House sacked. Serious rioting also occurred at Derby and at Nottingham where the castle, the property of the Duke of Newcastle, was burnt down. In none of these towns were there strong, well-organised political unions which acted as powerful pressure groups but which were held in check by moderate leaders. Such proved to be more efficacious than troops of horse. Throughout the north, during the winter, there grew up 'low political unions' composed entirely of working men and expecting to fight the Lords physically to secure reform. 'Captain Swing' put in an appearance again and insurance companies reported that the losses exceeded those of the previous year. All over the industrial districts there were strikes, unemployment and violence. Events such as the Bristol Riots, fully recounted in the newspapers, provided a potent example. Fortunately the newspapers also recounted

G

things that helped to restore sanity, such as Canon Sydney Smith's famous speech at Taunton in October, in which he compared Wellington to Mrs Partington and her mop:

> The Atlantic was roused.   Mrs Partington's spirit was up.   But I need not tell you the contest was unequal.   The Atlantic Ocean beat Mrs Partington.   She was excellent at a slop or a puddle, but she should not have meddled with a tempest. Gentlemen be at your ease, be quiet and steady – you will beat Mrs Partington.

The government issued a proclamation in November declaring illegal all political unions with a military complexion, a move which was welcomed by the middle class who feared anarchy.   The bill was reintroduced for a third time in the Commons with several modifications on points of detail, which satisfied some of the arguments used by the Tories against it.   Its fate in the Lords hung in the balance. Only once had there been a mass creation of peers to pass a particular measure, when in 1713 twelve had been elevated to ratify the Peace of Utrecht; but the King considered that such an act exceeded his constitutional obligations to the Whigs, while Grey felt the creation of fifty or more peers would destroy the Lords as an independent and self-respecting body. In January the King finally consented to creations under very stringent conditions, but this proved unnecessary as in April the Lords passed the bill by 184 to 175 on the second reading.

The crisis, however, was not yet over.   In order not to destroy the Bill but to reassert the power and prestige of the Lords, Lyndhurst proposed that the disfranchising clauses of the Bill be postponed until the rest of the Bill was decided. Grey refused to accept it but was defeated.   He and Brougham went to Windsor to ask the King for fifty peers.   William declined to make 'so large an addition to the peerage' and accepted their resignation.   He hoped, apparently, to get the bill passed unaltered by the Tories in order to avoid peer-making.   It was at this point that the country was nearest to revolution.   So successful had been the work of the radical propagandists that the news that Wellington had undertaken to form a government, even though it was proposed to carry a moderate reform, was regarded as the end of liberty and the beginning of military tyranny.   Work was at a standstill and in the provincial towns excited groups awaited the latest news from London and discussed how to make the people's will prevail. Elaborate plans were drawn up to begin rioting in London the moment the Duke took office, in order to tie down troops there and allow revolution to get under way in the country. Francis Place placarded the streets with 'To Stop the Duke, go for Gold' and the Bank of England paid out several hundred thousand pounds in two days.

Wellington regarded it as his duty to serve the King when called upon to do so and to pass a measure of reform, which he had previously opposed, as a matter of national expediency. His attempt to form a Ministry caused a wave of distrust in the Commons, even among the Tories, and it was frustrated by Peel's refusal to co-operate. Peel's later history showed that logically he should have been for the bill. At the time of Emancipation he was already in office, but in 1832 to take office after violent opposition would be an inconsistency he could not accept. Wellington's failure resulted in the King giving Grey a written promise to create peers, but he used his personal influence to persuade members of the Lords to abstain. A half-empty chamber passed the Third Reading and on 7th June the Reform Bill received the royal assent.[1] Reform Bills followed for Scotland and Ireland, that for Scotland providing genuine political representation for the first time.

Seen in its historical perspective the bill was a conservative measure. It enfranchised only part of the middle class; the shilling registration fee, which many did not consider worth paying, and the practice of including rates with rents in many towns reduced the numbers who might have benefited. Great inequality of constituencies persisted and the new boundaries were in some cases drawn up to help Whig interests.[2] Bribery continued and in many cases was more widespread as the traditional methods of influencing votes had been limited by the Act, though it was reckoned there were still some fifty boroughs where the influence of a great land-owner was all-important. There were election specialists who were adept at such arts as the impersonation of voters and the polling of dead men. The bribes were usually smaller, however, and after the Corrupt Practices Act of

[1] For terms see above, p. 85.
[2] For example Eton was deliberately excluded from the Borough of Windsor.

1854, which demanded an audit of a candidate's accounts and defined various forms of corrupt practice, election expenses sank to reasonable levels. Constituencies were still occasionally disfranchised for gross corruption, however. The Reform Act made very little difference to the type of person sitting in Parliament,[1] apart from the inclusion of members of important manufacturing families and a small number of advanced Radicals.

The implications of the Reform Act and the manner of its passing were far more revolutionary. The representative system had been brought into closer contact with the real interests of a country which was undergoing extensive industrial changes. The most significant aspect was the giving of representation to all the major industrial towns. It was the central feature of the long and complex transformation of the rural, hierarchical nation of the 18th Century into an urban and industrial civilisation. It established once and for all that those who had power outside Parliament must have power within it, and despite the Whigs' wish for 'finality' it clearly sanctioned periodic adjustments. The unreformed Parliament had been often responsive to public opinion and had produced much worthwhile legislation, especially during the period of liberal Toryism, but too much was left to chance. Perhaps the happiest chance had been the existence in that Parliament of a party whose leaders had long prepared the minds of the aristocracy for reform. Revolution may have been near, but ultimately it was averted because, whatever its faults, the unreformed Parliament was capable of reforming itself and re-establishing itself once again as a representative forum of public opinion.

(b) THE WHIG MINISTRIES, 1832–41

'There existed a prevalent conviction,' wrote Disraeli, 'that the Whig party, by a great stroke of state, had secured to themselves the government of the country for at least the lives of the present generation'. The Reform Bill had made the Whigs popular but it brought responsibilities, for to many the successful reform of Parliament made the reform of other

---

[1] Tower Hamlets, the largest and dingiest urban constituency in the country, was represented in 1833 by a Whig ecclesiastical lawyer and a wealthy City merchant.

aspects and institutions of the country all the more necessary. Disillusionment and offended vested interests were bound in the long run to set a limit to Whig electoral success. The party, moreover, was an uneasy coalition. The political philosophy of the Whig nobility held that in the long run government should be by consent, but many faced the changes that popular enthusiasm pressed upon them with increasing reluctance. The Radical wing, undisciplined and unreliable, sought to set the pace for the party. Burdett, Attwood and Cobbett were now in Parliament but none were as effective inside as out; Fielden represented another element of Radicalism when he campaigned for factory reform; with Bentham's disciples and O'Connell's 'tail' they made a strange assortment. At various times Durham, Cobden or O'Connell might have appeared as a Radical leader commanding wide-spread support, but personal failings or particular interests always intervened. Relatively unimportant though they might be in Parliament, they represented very important interests outside and, in a House more sensitive to public opinion than before, were listened to with respect.

The Tory party emerged in 1832 at a disadvantage. The spirit of the age was critical of existing institutions and most of the influential periodicals supported the Whigs, but there was a good chance of their revival under a new programme and under the perceptive leadership of Peel. The Carlton Club, founded at this time, set up an organisation in the constituencies to expedite the registration of Tory voters. The Tories represented solid interests; they were not, like the Whigs, hampered by a radical wing with little sense of party loyalty, and their predominance in the Lords gave them tactical advantages.

A wide variety of matters was tackled by the government and a steady stream of petitions, both in support and critical, came from the political unions. Russell wished to provide each session with a bill of capital importance, and owing to Radical influence there was a tendency towards legislation rather than administrative reforms. Among the first was an important humanitarian reform. Since the abolition of the British slave trade in 1807 the movement for the abolition of slavery itself, led by Wilberforce and T. F. Buxton, had steadily grown in strength. Planter opposition was strong;

it was argued that emancipation would mean a shortage of labour and much higher costs of production. The principal secretary at the Colonial Office was James Stephen, a colonial expert and a keen Evangelical, and when Stanley succeeded Goderich as Colonial Secretary a bill was drafted and introduced in March 1833. All slaves were to be freed within twelve months, and compensation, based on the average selling price of slaves, was to be paid. This amounted to £20 m. and was a free gift by Parliament. Slaves in agricultural work were to be apprenticed to their former masters until 1840, an arrangement which worked fairly well to begin with but which was discredited by cases of cruelty naturally exploited by the abolitionists. In most West Indian islands the arguments of the planters were amply justified. Apart from simple humanity, the measure is also important as showing an increased sense of responsibility for the Empire.

The campaign for the abolition of slavery encouraged Oastler, a Huddersfield land agent, to write to *The Leeds Mercury* in 1830 a number of letters headed 'Yorkshire Slavery' and to open a campaign for the relief of the factory children, as a preliminary to getting factory conditions generally improved. There was widespread enthusiasm in the north of England. Sadler, a Leeds banker and an M.P., obtained the appointment of a committee of inquiry. Many landowners, who had their own standards of charity to the poor, were genuinely shocked by factory conditions and had very little sympathy with the mill-owners. Hitherto legislation on this subject had been largely ineffectual; the Health and Morals of Apprentices Act of 1802 had covered only a particular kind of factory worker, whose numbers were diminishing at the time. The Cotton Factory Act of 1819 was of more general application but inspection was left to magistrates who were often either uninterested or unsympathetic. In 1833 Lord Ashley began his long public and humanitarian career by introducing a bill stipulating a maximum of ten hours a day for workers under eighteen. Pressure from the manufacturers resulted in Lord Melbourne appointing a Royal Commission, whose principals were Chadwick and Southwood Smith. The report, framed on Benthamite principles, asked for regulations on factory ventilation, employers' liability for accidents and an efficient system of part-time education for factory children. Education only survived in an unsatisfactory form, but, much more important, although J.P.s retained their right of inspection, four salaried factory inspectors were appointed by the Act, at Chadwick's suggestion. For the first time impartial enforcement was possible. The Act, introduced in the Commons by Lord Althorpe, covered all textile factories, prohibited night work for those under eighteen and any work at all for those under nine. Children aged 9–12 could work nine hours a day, forty-eight hours a week; those aged 13–18 twelve hours a day, sixty-nine a week.

As with factory reform, so in the field of education did a private member's bill prompt government action. In 1820 Brougham had introduced a bill for setting up a comprehensive national system based on a compromise between the Church of England and the Nonconformists, but it was their rivalry and that between the two societies they sponsored, The National Society and The British and Foreign Schools Society, which blocked the way until 1833.[1] In that year Roebuck introduced a bill which was more far-reaching than Brougham's and although the whole House was opposed, a committee of inquiry was established. A grant of £20,000 a year was made for school building, to be shared between the two societies. Preference was given to schools in large towns and the grant was only available when voluntary contributions met half the cost of a new school. The system did not work very satisfactorily and in 1839 a special committee of the Privy Council was appointed whose secretary, Kay-Shuttleworth, a former colleague of Chadwick's, sent inspectors to schools receiving State help. Religious bodies were allowed to set up their own training colleges for teachers.

The statute of this period which attracted the most public attention was the Poor Law Amendment Act of 1834. It was occasioned, in particular, by the mounting expense of the Poor Law administration which had risen to nearly £7 m. a year, and to which the Speenhamland system heavily contributed. This had been introduced in 1795 by the local magistrates meeting at the Pelican Inn, Speenhamland, now a suburb of Newbury, who decided to subsidise wages when the cost of bread, forced upwards in bad seasons by the difficulties

[1] See above, p. 37.

of importing foreign corn, became unduly high. While
avoiding an increase in wages, the system seemed a premium
against the danger of agrarian revolution. The Speenhamland system was widely adopted throughout the south of
England and confirmed by Act of Parliament in 1796. It
added to the confusion of the Poor Law scene, in which, due
to the obscurity of the statutes, in some areas administration
was harsh, in others lax, in some work was expected in
return, in others none.

The allowance paid varied with the price of bread and with
the number of the recipient's dependants. From the first
these allowances delayed the natural rise of wages but until
1813, except for winter unemployment, the system was sparingly used and its evils were held in check. During the
depression, however, farmers were driven to economise and
wages were greatly reduced or even ceased altogether. It
became almost impossible for a farmer to keep a man in
permanent employment at reasonable wages. If he did he
was only saving the rates for neighbours who put their hands
into his pockets to pay their labour bills. Since rates were
paid by occupiers rather than owners of property, the smaller
rate payers were saddled with part of the working costs of
their richer neighbours and were themselves pushed down into
the ranks of paupers. Sometimes the ratepayers in a parish
arranged among themselves to employ and pay a number of
men proportionate to the rateable value of their property;
sometimes the paupers were paraded by overseers on a Monday morning and the week's labour of each individual offered
at an auction to the highest bidder. Sometimes the men were
sent round the farms in chains or gangs, as though they were
serfs. The system robbed men of their self-respect. A visitor
from Jamaica who saw some of these gangs at work considered
that his negro slaves were better off.

Against this mass of subsidised labour, free labourers could
not hope to compete. It was so cheap that men who tried to
retain their independence were undersold. Those who had
saved money or bought a cottage could not be placed on the
poor book. They were obliged first to strip themselves bare.
Thus in the most practical fashion labourers were taught the
lessons that improvidence paid better than thrift, that rewards
did not depend on their own exertions. The more recklessly

a man married and had children, the greater his share of the comforts of life: at Swaffham a woman with five illegitimate children received eighteen shillings a week. Recipients considered they were as entitled to allowances as to wages; their life had attractions once the spirit of independence and self-respect were numbed. Riots were not always protests against the existing system but sometimes means of enforcing its continuance. In one Buckinghamshire village, out of 98 people who had a settlement in the parish, 64 were receiving poor relief and the rates exceeded twenty-four shillings in the pound. Malthusians believed that the system could only lead to disaster. The agricultural distress and unrest of 1830 and 1831 prompted the appointment of a Royal Commission in 1832, of which Nassau Senior and Edwin Chadwick were the most prominent members. The Poor Laws affected the entire administrative and economic fabric of the State and accounted for one-fifth of the total national expenditure. They put a premium on negligence and violated most rules of wise philanthropy. Moreover they had no clear objective and it was this that the Benthamites on the Royal Commission intended to provide.

The investigation was thorough and the unduly lurid picture it painted of the Speenhamland system disturbed contemporaries. The report recognised four categories of paupers: the old and infirm, the orphans, the able-bodied women and the able-bodied men. It recognised that these demanded separate housing and different treatment. It was on the last two categories, however, that the report concentrated, as in this passage referring to the workhouse:

> In by far the greater number of cases it is a large almshouse in which the young are trained in idleness, ignorance and vice; the able-bodied maintained in sluggish, sensual indolence. . . .

It may well be that a high proportion of imbeciles and mental defectives accounted for the last phrase, but in the report the conclusion was clear: that to many to be maintained by poor relief was a desirable existence and in order to promote the greatest happiness of the greatest number – the independent labourers who would be free from pauper competition, the ratepayers whose burden would be lightened, the paupers themselves who by being forced to work would regain their self-respect and realise the virtues of self-help – it was proposed to make the pauper's existence 'less eligible' than that of any wage earner. This presupposed that work was available when, in fact, the Laws of Settlement, which the report wished to relax, made it easier for Irishmen to come to England than for Englishmen to travel about their own country looking for work. In an industrial society, moreover, trade fluctuations put men out of work for periods, and it was failure to appreciate this side of the problem that made the New Poor Law especially unpopular in the north of England.

To promote greater efficiency the report proposed a Poor Law Board, consisting of three commissioners. When it was set up Chadwick was appointed Secretary. It was given an independent political status, in order to prevent jobbery and ensure freedom from party, but the subsequent enormous unpopularity of 'The Three Bashaws of Somerset House' led to its replacement in 1847 by a Board whose president sat in Parliament and was a member of the ministry of the day. Chadwick would have liked a national Poor Law administration levying a uniform rate and acting as a national labour exchange, but this would have been too expensive, and public opinion would never have accepted such centralisation. The Commissioners supervised the work of Poor Law Guardians, who were elected by the ratepayers and were responsible for the poor within a union of parishes. It was hoped that these areas would become in due course of time units of local government. They were used from 1838 onwards for the registration of births and deaths but the unpopularity of the system prevented further extension. It was the duty of the Guardians to refuse outdoor relief to any able-bodied person; the prison-like workhouse with its improving texts, its uniform, its strict rules, monotonous tasks and low dietary scale was intended to be unattractive to all except those who urgently needed it. The fixing of the dietary scale imposed a real problem. Chadwick collected numerous family budgets which showed a scandalously low standard of living. At the maximum the average independent labourer consumed 2,252 calories a day whereas at least 3,500 are needed to maintain an active outdoor life. Inevitably workhouse scales had to be higher and in 1841 a Poor Law inspector had to confess that 'a family could not be maintained in a state of independence out of the workhouse with the same comforts they have within at a less cost than twenty-five shillings per week and this is more than double the general agricultural weekly wage in England'.

To the poor, taken from their familiar surroundings and forced into places which, although both hygienic and well-ventilated, seemed to make their poverty a crime, the 'Poor Law Bastilles' were regarded with horror and were resisted at almost any cost. Riots greeted their establishment in a new area and the Chartist petition of 1839[1] owed a great deal of support to this cause. The clause that imposed the separation of husband and wife aroused the opposition of the humanitarians. Despite the fact that in the long run they benefited financially, the landowners disapproved of the scheme, which was represented in Parliament as a measure of agricultural relief and very scantily debated. It first introduced modern administration to Britain and they resented the interference of government officials with the running of their own counties and parishes. It was all part of the 'botheration' that was to lead to the Tory victory of 1841 and it helped to discredit the scientific Radicals.

Although he was tactless and impetuous, the scheme as it went on the statute book was less than fair to Chadwick. The unpopular side of his work, the imposition of the workhouse test, was adopted; his schemes for the Poor Law as a national organisation curing unemployment, providing schools, hospitals, almshouses, arranging workmen's compensation and raising the general standard of health and housing were too far advanced for a time which saw them merely as a source of jobbery and 'botheration'.

In the north the workhouse test was abandoned in 1840, when some of the other severe aspects of the system were softened; the resistances from an area which had never known the Speenhamland system and the extent of the industrial depression were too great. In the south the poor rate was forced down, the allowance system was slowly crushed out but the wages of the agricultural labourers fell. The sufferings of these men were telling evidence for the Anti-Corn Law League. To supplement wages women and children were driven into the gang system. English farming could only

[1] See below, p. 127.

progress by becoming fully capitalistic and by helping to break the old social obligations of the countryside the New Poor Law facilitated this. Fortunately other work was available from the 1840's onwards in the building of the railways and the expansion of industry, and the workhouses were normally filled chiefly with those physically incapable of work. The rising standards of the age and the increasing sensitiveness of public opinion brought better conditions after 1847; special Poor Law schools came into existence, Poor Law infirmaries were set up in many towns and in 1867 Poor Law dispensaries were established in London.

Grey's Ministry came to an end in a complicated series of events which involved attacks on the position and property of the Established Church and the maintenance of order in Ireland. None of the measures passed since the Reform Bill had been really party measures but these two issues were to raise considerable differences of opinion within the Cabinet.

The success of parliamentary reform encouraged the Radicals and the Dissenters to attack the privileged position of the Church of England. They objected to obligatory baptism, marriage and burial in the parish church, and this was conceded in 1836. They resented the Anglican monopoly of higher education and London University was granted a charter which imposed no religious tests; a bill to permit Dissenters to enter Oxford and Cambridge was thrown out by the Lords. In Ireland resistance centred on the payment of tithe by the whole population to the Church of Ireland whose adherents were only one-seventh of the total. The system was corrupt, much went into lay hands and it often had to be collected by force. By the spring of 1833 tithe was over a million pounds in arrears and the government, in order to restore order, introduced a Coercion Act, a procedure which some of the Cabinet, notably Russell, deplored. Habeas Corpus was suspended, permission had to be obtained for public meetings and a night curfew was imposed. Grey, Melbourne and Stanley, the Chief Secretary, were firmly in favour of it and the result was a decrease in disorder. The tithes, however, could still not be collected and many of the clergy were in considerable distress. The government then proceeded to reorganise the Irish Church by uniting dioceses and appropriating the revenues saved for church building and clergy stipends. From the Treasury bench, but without the agreement of the Cabinet, Russell declared that he would like to see part of the wealth of the Irish Church devoted to other purposes. Stanley, Graham and Richmond all resigned from the Cabinet in protest. Russell and Stanley stood for opposite schools of thought, the one the guardian of Whig doctrines of liberty, the other essentially a conservative. They were also rivals for the leadership of the Commons which would fall vacant when Althorpe's father died, and Stanley's ability and panache made many see him, 'The Rupert of Debate', as the next Prime Minister. Although his action arose from conviction, Russell's move was a shrewd one. Stanley became in due course heir-apparent to Peel and finally leader of the Protectionist Conservatives.

The government's treatment of the Irish Church was the occasion of the publication of the *Tracts for the Times* and the beginning of the Oxford Movement.[1] It claimed that the dogma of the Apostolic Succession had been flouted, and wished to revive the discipline and ceremonies of the mediaeval Church. Its principal effect at the time was to make the government proceed cautiously: in 1836 a Tithe Commutation Act was passed for England which imposed a fixed payment and improved administration. A similar act was introduced for Ireland in 1838.

In the spring of 1834 the Irish Coercion Act came up for renewal. The Irish Secretary, Lyttleton, made a private agreement with O'Connell that in return for concessions he would relax his agitation for the Repeal of the Act of Union, which he had been carrying on since the success of Emancipation. Owing to a misunderstanding, a bill without concessions was introduced, O'Connell made public his side of the unfulfilled bargain and Althorpe decided to resign. Grey, feeling his work was done and lamenting the loss of Stanley, resigned as well.

The next Prime Minister was Melbourne. The King wanted a coalition, but the differences were too great. In a sense Melbourne represented the coalition in his own person. Liberal in many respects and not averse to change as such, he felt as did many of the Whigs, that the country had had enough of reform for a while and his purpose must be to

[1] See below, p. 151.

re-establish that sense of stability on which property depended. He distrusted Benthamism and disdained the agitation and enthusiasm of popular politics. He took office reluctantly but once there his own pride and intellectual interests made him want to hold on to it. He was very loyal to his colleagues and to the young Queen whom, after 1837, he shrewdly instructed in the ways of the British constitution. His Cabinet was a difficult one to keep together in view of his many 'difficulties with respect to men' and he failed to see that a bold programme boldly carried through would have satisfied at least one section of his supporters and put the opposition once more into the position of negative critics. But to Melbourne, as to many other 19th-century politicians, the duty of an administration was to administer, not primarily to legislate.

His first Ministry was very short, for soon after he had taken office, Lord Althorpe succeeded his father and the King refused to accept Russell in his place as Leader of the Commons. Melbourne felt his loyalty to the Crown demanded that he comply with the King's wishes and he accordingly placed all the offices of State at the King's disposal. Wellington was sent for. He proposed Peel, who was in Rome at the time, and during his absence Wellington administered all the departments.[1] Peel formed a Cabinet, and dissolved Parliament in order to obtain a majority. In the Unreformed Parliament, influence and patronage would have made this automatic; that the manœuvre failed was a measure of the change made by the Reform Bill. The election is chiefly memorable for the open letter Peel sent to his constituents at Tamworth. This was to indicate the change from a Tory Party of reaction to a Conservative Party which accepted the Reform Bill as the basis of the political order. He indicated his support for constructive reforms which would lead to the better operation of institutions such as the Church and the municipal corporations. He made it plain that he accepted an equality of civil privileges and would view all problems in this light. He had never been, he stated, a defender of abuses and he summarised his purposes as the maintenance of peace,

---

[1] *Punch*, remembering the Duke's earlier difficulties with his colleagues, showed a Cabinet composed solely of Wellingtons, with the comment, 'Now, gentlemen, at last we are in complete agreement.'

the honourable and scrupulous fulfilment of all engagements
with foreign powers, the maintenance of public credit, the
enforcement of strict economy and the impartial treatment
of all agricultural, manufacturing and commercial interests.
The importance of the Tamworth Manifesto was not the
limited effect it had in 1835 but the basis it laid for the victory
at the polls in 1841. Russell defeated the government soon
after the election on a motion concerned with the Irish
Church; Melbourne returned to office, with Russell as Home
Secretary and Leader of the House. Although the Sovereign
continued to object to certain prospective Cabinet Ministers,
the unwritten law that the Crown accepted the decision of the
electorate passed into the constitution.

Russell's day-to-day attention to parliamentary business,
his reverence for the forms and idiosyncrasies of the House
helped to keep the new government together. He was the
arch-Whig of the 19th Century, a man of firm principles, who
was more concerned with the removal of obstacles to civil
liberty than with the creation of a more reasonable and
civilised society. Despite his advanced views on many subjects he was subconsciously a believer in the divine right of
the Whigs to rule. He was honourable, courageous and
clever, but intellectually and influentially he was a slight man.
This was to be the happiest period of his career, when most
men marked him out as a future Prime Minister. The
government owed much to Peel's constructive opposition; he
treated questions on their merits and aimed at conciliating
'the sober-minded and well-disposed portion of the community'.

The first major question was the reform of the municipal
corporations. They represented as varied and as undemocratic a picture as the parliamentary boroughs. There was
no obligation on them to produce any accounts or, for that
matter, to perform any services. Some took their duties very
seriously and were an asset to their towns, others amounted to
little more than dining clubs. In many instances the work
they could well have performed, of paving and lighting, of
sewerage and the maintenance of law and order, was undertaken by *ad hoc* improvement commissions incorporated by
private act of Parliament. There were 237 boroughs with
corporations and of these 186 had self-elected councils and

26 no councils at all. Where there were elections, the right to vote was limited to freemen who could well be a very small proportion of the whole population. The commission appointed had a Radical bias, which annoyed the House of Lords who held an inquiry of their own and inserted several anti-democratic amendments. Peel, however, saved the main points of the bill. The act set up new corporations, which lost the right to administer religious trusts but received powers to provide for the lighting and safety of the streets. All liable to pay the poor rate could re-elect one-third of the councillors annually, but a quarter of the entire council was composed of aldermen, elected by the council for six years. There was to be an annual audit of accounts. No new corporations were created but ratepayers in towns of reasonable size could petition for a charter. The act was a success and led gradually to an improvement in urban amenities. It broke what was in effect a Tory and Anglican monopoly, as the new town councils fell largely into the hands of middle-class Radicals. The City of London proved too strong to meddle with.

Acts followed for Scottish and Irish municipalities; both tended to be more conservative than the English act, particularly that for Ireland which gave elective councils to only ten boroughs owing to fear of the Catholics.

The same balance of conservatism and reform marked the measures affecting tithes and the rights of dissenters, which have been mentioned above. A significant new departure, however, came in the Durham Report. The Earl of Durham seemed destined to be a great Radical leader and possibly Prime Minister. He was immensely wealthy, extremely popular in the north-eastern colliery district and had earned his name of 'Radical Jack' for his part in promoting the cause of Reform. Melbourne distrusted him and when he made great popular speeches sent him to St Petersburg as Ambassador and then to Canada as High Commissioner 'for the adjustment of certain important questions . . .' and Governor-General. He hoped that this move would placate the Radicals.

Following the precepts of Adam Smith, the Radicals in the early 19th Century had deplored the steady expansion of the British colonial empire which they considered led to the increase of home prices to satisfy colonial needs, as for instance in the case of West Indian sugar; the granting of monopolies such as the East India Company which had a similar effect; the provision of an excuse for maintaining an unduly large army which, if necessary, could crush discontent at home, and the maintenance of an undue number of sinecures for the relatives and friends of Ministers. Bentham had urged the emancipation of colonies and, following his teachings, Radicals had come to see in the colonies an invaluable proving ground for the institutions and methods they wished to see applied in England. Benthamite influence was all-powerful in the East India Company which was now very largely an administrative body, having lost its monopoly of the China trade when its Charter was renewed in 1833. (Monopoly of the India trade was lost in 1813.) The Mills were in its service and they persuaded the directors to appoint Macaulay Law Member of the Governor-General's Council. In India Macaulay introduced freedom of the press, equality of Indians and Englishmen before the law, a legal code based on the principle of Utility and written in everyday language, and played a large part in the foundation of schools. The Durham Report was to be the basis of another important Radical aim, that of responsible and democratic self-government.

Canada consisted of Lower Canada, the original French colony, which however retained no contacts with France and was dominated by the Roman Catholic Church, and Upper Canada, the retreat of the United Empire Loyalists after the American War of Independence over which they retained an aristocratic control. Representative assemblies existed in both colonies but in neither did they have any real power. Strong racial antagonism had developed in Lower Canada while in Upper Canada there was tension owing to the privileged position of the United Empire Loyalists and the tactlessness of the governor. Durham was in Canada for only six months in 1838, but in that time he not only exceeded his powers but also offended both the Canadians and Parliament at home. But what should by Whig standards have been a disgrace, was by Radical effort converted into a triumph. The report has been to some extent overpraised: he proposed union of the two colonies so the French should be

H

outnumbered but, through the influence of Gibbon Wakefield
and other Radicals, he was concerned to make Canada
attractive to emigrants from Britain and he realised that
nothing less than responsible government would satisfy the
colonists. He held that responsible government, far from
loosening the bonds of empire, would preserve its unity by
making it a community of free nations with a national harmony of interests between its various parts. It was the
climax of optimistic liberalism and had close affinities with
Cobden's faith that international harmony and peace would
naturally follow from free trade.

Canadian self-government grew steadily from this point.
The Canada Act of 1840 set up an administration responsive
to public opinion and from 1847 onwards the executive
council reflected the majority in the legislative assembly.
Further progress was made in the British North America Act
of 1867.

The Radicals, notably Wakefield, Molesworth and Charles
Buller, also supported the development of new colonies in
Australia and the foundation of the New Zealand Colonising
Company in 1839.

In the 1840's and 1850's two distinct Radical points of view
developed: that of Wakefield and Molesworth valued the
imperial connection and their propaganda and influence
brought about the granting of elected and representative
chambers to Cape Colony and the Australian colonies in 1850
and to New Zealand in 1852. The contrary view, held by
Cobden, was the traditional Radical opinion that colonies
were wasteful and dangerous politically and in a world of
free trade could have no economic advantage.

The Radicalism of another dependency was of increasing
concern to Melbourne's government and to that of Peel after
1841. After Emancipation O'Connell had turned his
attentions to the repeal of the Act of Union but in 1835 had
made the Lichfield House Compact with the Whigs. O'Connell helped them defeat Peel and muted the repeal agitation.
In return the Whigs promised specific Irish reforms including
a settlement of the tithe question. Steady obstruction from
the House of Lords, led by Lyndhurst, made this side of the
bargain difficult to perform and the arrangement was
unpopular with many of Melbourne's English supporters.

Meanwhile the Lord Lieutenant sought O'Connell's advice on Irish problems and, although violence continued, the Irish administration improved during the Under-Secretaryship of Thomas Drummond (1835–40). He refused to use coercion acts, repressed all dissident groups, both Protestant and Catholic, reorganised the police and reminded the land-owners they had duties as well as rights. After he died of overwork the Irish situation deteriorated and O'Connell became impatient. His Irish group in the Commons had doubled in 1837 and Irish matters increasingly absorbed the House's attention. But the results of co-operation with the government seemed increasingly inadequate and in 1840 he founded his National Loyal Repeal Association, intending to influence Parliament by monster meetings. The Catholic clergy joined him but he was losing control over his younger followers who suspected that at heart he was not a revolu-tionary, and who had formed the Young Ireland movement with a wide programme of national regeneration. O'Connell distrusted Peel but believed he could force his hand without resorting to open rebellion. Impelled forward by his followers, a 'repeal rent' was raised which by 1843 was bring-ing in £3,000 a week. The central committee was able to organise a huge rally within forty-eight hours at any place it chose and several were held during the summer of 1843. The government became alarmed, an Irish Arms Act was passed and when a monster meeting was summoned at Clontarf near Dublin in October, Peel forbade it to take place. This was the crux. O'Connell knew that to proceed would mean bloodshed; he drew back and cancelled the meeting. With this his influence was at an end and lacking his leadership the Repeal agitation began to wane. Young Ireland turned to greater violence.[1]

Two years previously the Whig government had finally fallen. Its last four years had been spent in the reign of Victoria, who succeeded her uncle William IV in 1837. She was only eighteen but tenacious and self-possessed. She was inclined to be a partisan but she brought to the throne a graciousness it had lacked for many years. Initially there were fears of foreign influence over her – from her uncle Leopold, King of the Belgians, from Baron Stockmar and

[1] See below, p. 205.

above all from Prince Albert, her cousin, whom she married in 1840. But although she was influenced it was never unduly and she determined from the start to rule herself and to do her best by her country. A very important influence over her early years as Queen was Lord Melbourne, who himself undertook to be her private secretary and who put at her disposal his long experience of men and affairs. This influence may well have played a part, subconsciously, in the 'Bedchamber Crisis' of 1839 which prolonged his premiership by two years. Disorder in Jamaica prompted the government to suspend the constitution and when the motion was only carried by a very narrow majority, Melbourne resigned. In view of Victoria's Whig partisanship, Peel felt justified in asking for some mark of confidence and requested the dismissal of some members of the Royal Household who were related to members of the former Ministry. This in itself was not unreasonable but Peel argued his case badly: he was 'such a cold odd man she cannot make out what he means'. The Queen took offence, and Melbourne, believing Peel was pressing his case too strongly, offered to resume office. The affair, like William IV's action in 1834, helped to define the constitutional relationship of the Sovereign to the administration of the day. The Whigs were finally defeated on a motion of no confidence in 1841.

(c) FOREIGN POLICY, 1830-46

The earlier part of the period was the one in which Lord Palmerston established his reputation as Foreign Secretary and which marked in many respects his most successful tenure of that office. He was faced at the outset by the first successful violation of the Vienna territorial settlement in western Europe – the Belgian secession from Holland. The Kingdom of the Netherlands established in 1815 should have been successful: economically the two countries were largely complimentary, but differences of race, language, history and religion combined to make the union unpopular. The Dutch from the start assumed they were the governing race, although less numerous, and offended both the Belgian liberals and the Belgian Catholics by their actions. The July revolution in Paris inspired an August revolution in Brussels. Whereas Prussia, Russia and Austria had shrunk from challenging the right of the French people to self-determination, they had no such scruples about Belgium. The French government, on the other hand, was virtually bound to intervene on behalf of the Belgians should the Holy Alliance powers invade and it was widely expected this would result in the annexation of Belgium to France. The change of government in England undoubtedly helped to obtain a peaceful solution, for Wellington had little sympathy with the French and war might well have resulted. Louis Philippe believed Grey and Palmerston might accept an independent Belgium as a compromise solution and Talleyrand was sent to London to further this policy. By skilful negotiation Talleyrand and Palmerston persuaded the Eastern Powers, who were embarrassed by a rebellion in Poland, to accept the situation. Further trouble occurred early in 1831 when the Belgian Congress chose the Duke of Nemours, a son of Louis Philippe, as their King, but once the French were convinced that this, in English eyes, would amount to annexation, the offer was not accepted. Instead Leopold of Saxe-Coburg was chosen. He had lived for many years in England, was the widower of George IV's daughter Charlotte and the uncle of the future Queen Victoria. With remarkable diplomacy he married a daughter of Louis Philippe and under his rule the infant kingdom flourished. The Dutch then invaded Belgium and a French counter-invasion took place, which, with some English help, defeated the Dutch. Both armies were persuaded to withdraw and Belgian independence was finally confirmed by all the Powers in 1839.

The Belgian crisis had been solved by Anglo-French co-operation but this was increasingly lacking during the remainder of Grey's and Melbourne's Ministries. When the troops sent by Canning to Portugal were withdrawn in 1828 the Pretender Dom Miguel had usurped the throne. Dom Pedro of Brazil invaded on behalf of his daughter, Queen Maria, and with British help expelled Miguel. The Portuguese government made an alliance with that of Spain, which had a similar problem, in order to prevent an invasion by the Pretenders with support from the Eastern Powers. This became a Quadruple Alliance in 1834 with the addition of France and England, but the mutual distrust of Palmerston and Thiers prevented a joint expedition to Spain or the intervention of either power by itself. Ferdinand VII of Spain had revoked the Salic Law and left his throne to his daughter Isabella, excluding his brother Don Carlos. Isabella's mother adopted the Liberal cause on her daughter's behalf and received some help from a British legion of volunteers; the war dragged on until 1839 when the Carlist commander deserted to the constitutional side.

Anglo-French co-operation was shaken over the problems of the Near East. These stemmed from the turbulent ruler of Egypt, Mehemet Ali,[1] who had sent troops and his fleet to help his nominal overlord, the Sultan, in Greece and felt he had not received adequate reward. He therefore conquered Syria and marched on Constantinople in 1832. The Sultan appealed to Britain for help but because the government was preoccupied with the Reform Bill and the French favoured Mehemet Ali, none was forthcoming, and when the Turkish army was defeated in November, the Sultan turned to Russia, whose fleet anchored off Constantinople in February 1833. Since 1828 the Russians had decided that a weak Turkey they could dominate would be more advantageous than partition. Palmerston was alarmed by the Russian action which he had not foreseen, and with French help forced the Sultan to give Syria to Mehemet Ali for lifetime. The Russians returned home after extracting payment from the Turks under the Treaty of Unkiar Skelessi of July 1833. This promised mutual alliance and assistance, but in a secret clause, of which the Great Powers soon heard, the Sultan promised, in the event of war, to close the Dardanelles at Russian request, which cut across an agreement made with Britain in 1809.

Mehemet Ali was still far from satisfied and wished for the outright cession of Syria. Encouraged by French diplomats, who believed they had, by Napoleonic inheritance, a special interest in Egypt, he challenged the Sultan, who, confident that the British would in the last resort prevent the break-up of his empire, decided to give battle. Through sheer incompetence[2] the Turks were decisively defeated at Nezib in June 1839. Palmerston felt that British interests demanded action.

[1] See above, p. 59.
[2] Their German military adviser, Molkte, was over-ruled on the battlefield by the Turkish religious leaders.

An Anglo-Turkish trade agreement had just been signed;
Aden had become a British protectorate because its Sultan
feared Mehemet Ali and because of its use as a coaling station
on the way to India. More important, however, was the
realisation that if he did not act, the Tsar would, possibly in
conjunction with the French – and this would result in spoils
for both countries to the detriment of Turkish strength and
English interests. Antipathy between the Tsar and Louis
Philippe helped him and an agreement was signed between
the Great Powers in July 1839 in which Russia was persuaded
to give up the advantages of Unkiar Skelessi. The Turkish
fleet deserted to Mehemet Ali, however, and emboldened
him. Thiers tried to bring about a secret settlement between
him and the Sultan, but without French knowledge the other
great powers agreed to undertake the conquest of Syria.
Thiers publicly stated France would never tolerate this, but
when Syria was overrun easily, he realised he had over-
estimated Mehemet Ali's strength. The French, therefore,
agreed to the settlement made by the other Great Powers.

Throughout the crisis Palmerston had retained the initiative. Melbourne had doubts about his policy and felt it was
unwise to alienate France; Greville had written of him at this
time, 'There is a flippancy in his tone, an undoubting self-
sufficiency and a levity in discussing interests of such tremendous magnitude which satisfies me he is a very dangerous man
to be entrusted with the uncontrolled management of our
foreign relations . . .' and many people were convinced there
was substance in this during his next tenure of the Foreign
Office. Nevertheless he was right in thinking co-operation
with Russia was of the first importance and that safety lay in
working with the power whose independent action he most
feared. The Tsar, however, was disappointed with the
results of his own policy and began to think again of partition.
It was this policy that was to lead to the Crimean War.[1]

When Peel came to power the Earl of Aberdeen became
Foreign Secretary. He was an able man of a very different
stamp from Palmerston. He co-operated closely with the
French Minister Guizot in order to build up a friendship
between the two nations which outlasted him, although
temporarily dissipated by Palmerston when he returned to

[1] See below, p. 167.

power. Guizot felt the friendship of England would allow France a free hand in Algeria and compensate for the coldness of the Eastern Powers. There were rival intrigues in various parts of the world. An amicable agreement was made over the protectorate of Tahiti and the Ashburton Treaty was signed with France and the United States which, in addition to settling the boundary of the United States and Canada, determined the right of search of ships suspected of engaging in the slave trade. The effect of the eastern crisis had been to turn a minor point of procedure into a matter of prestige, which France felt acutely in view of the much greater size of the English fleet. The treaty limited the right of search to ships of the vessel's own nationality.

The French successes in Algeria and the consequent threat to Gibraltar made Aberdeen suspicious when Louis Philippe proposed a marriage between the young Queen Isabella of Spain and his son the Duke of Montpensier in 1843. He persuaded the French to withdraw the proposal and a compromise was arranged whereby Isabella should marry a cousin and, when she had a child, Montpensier might marry her younger sister. Louis Philippe then acted foolishly; ignoring the fact that the Great Powers would never allow his family to inherit the Spanish throne he arranged for the Queen's marriage to an elderly cousin who was believed to be impotent, and the Infanta's marriage to his own son on the same day. It is generally agreed that Aberdeen could have prevented the crisis, which caused fury in England. Victoria wrote Louis Philippe a letter which Palmerston described as a 'tickler' and the coolness between the two countries prevented their intervention in Poland to stop the suppression of the republic of Cracow by the Eastern Powers. Cordial relations were only re-established with France after the 1848 Revolution. Queen Isabella produced a son.

(d) SIR ROBERT PEEL, 1841–46

When the Whigs resigned in 1841 a General Election was held which gave the Conservative party a majority. The conspicuous increase in corruption had told apparently in a Tory direction and the Protestant fervour aroused by O'Connell's influence had worked the same way. Principally there was disappointment with the contrast between Whig talk and

Whig performance; there were many social problems in need of attention and the reforms actually tackled by the Whigs, however necessary they may have been, had left a wake of distrust. It was hoped that a Conservative government would bring more careful administration and more serious attention to duty. The various groups who supported Peel, however, expected different things of him and this was the underlying weakness of his apparently strong position. The country was suffering from a prolonged industrial depression and the export situation was very poor. In dealing with this Peel's hands were dangerously tied, for his majority of members stood primarily for over-protected interests like the home 'agricultural interests' and the colonial sugar and timber interests, and it was hardly to be expected that they would happily support revision of the Corn Laws or the far-reaching customs changes which had been recommended by a parliamentary committee presided over by Hume in 1840 and had been eagerly accepted by the commercial world.

It has been remarked that Peel was in the wrong party but this is to equate Whiggery with Liberalism and to see the Conservative party of Peel's time as that of the end of the 19th Century. Despite their championship of institutional reform, it was the Tories rather than the Whigs who had always shown greater interest in matters of trade, starting with the changes made by the Younger Pitt and continuing to those of Huskisson. It was the Tories, too, who had always shown a greater readiness to accept outsiders, such as Canning and Huskisson, Peel himself and later Disraeli. 'The best brute votes in Christendom' might grumble at their leaders but on the whole showed far greater loyalty than any other political group. This loyalty had a limit as was shown when the break with his party in 1846 revealed the latent aggression. The Whig party of Peel's day, on the other hand, was that of the exclusive great landed families, the divinely ordained aristocracy of 1688. Russell never actually owned Woburn, just as Peel never actually worked in the family firm, but Russell's outlook was territorial and his successes were in the sphere of political institutions; Peel's outlook was that of a businessman and it is no accident that he became a member of a party which believed in efficient administration rather than frequent legislation.

Peel's Cabinet was particularly strong. Among his colleagues were two former Prime Ministers, Wellington and Goderich (now Earl of Ripon), together with Stanley, Aberdeen and, in minor office, Gladstone, all future Prime Ministers. But while, in his view, Melbourne's government had been 'a mere government of departments without a centre of unity', Peel was very much master of his Cabinet. He had detailed knowledge of the work of every department and was always well-briefed at Cabinet meetings. Gladstone, who owed much to him, regarded him as the 'best man of business ever Prime Minister' and felt that the Ministry was outstanding in its financial strictness, its loyal adherence to the principle of public economy, its jealous care for the rights of Parliament, its fair and equal regard for the rights of foreign countries and its single eye to the nation's interests.

In financial matters the Whig governments had been consistently unsuccessful, as Peel himself remarked in 1841 when he commented, 'Can there be a more lamentable picture than that of a Chancellor of the Exchequer seated on an empty chest, by the pool of bottomless deficiency – fishing for a budget?' The deficit had been £3 m. in 1840 and, despite increases in taxes, £2 m. in 1841. The corn situation made Peel's position difficult from the very first, for the price of wheat had reached 86s. a quarter, with distress and pauperism mounting fast. The growth of the Anti-Corn Law League gave additional urgency and after the high bread prices of the winter of 1841–42 Peel decided to amend Wellington's sliding scale of 1828. This had had a high pivot price and the uneven reductions in duty encouraged speculation. Peel started with a pivot price of 50s. on which he placed a duty of 20s. A 10s. duty was reached by even falls interrupted by two pauses until the home price was 63s. Thereafter the duty fell by 1s. as the price rose by the same amount. The change was insufficient to make much difference; it displeased the agricultural interest and it merely whetted the appetite of the Anti-Corn Law League.

Peel was very much more successful with the Budget of 1842, which he introduced himself, although Goulburn, his Chancellor of the Exchequer, was a man of ability. This was the first of an important series which helped to transform the financial situation. The key was the revival of the income tax, for a period of five years only in intention, but in fact permanent, which was levied on every type of income above £150 a year at 7d. in the pound.   Trade was beginning to recover and the additional revenue was to offset the reductions in the customs duties that were to assist that recovery. The raw material duties were not to exceed 5 per cent of their price, in the case of partly-manufactured goods it was 12 per cent and completely-manufactured 20 per cent. Britain's lead over other countries in the Industrial Revolution made these acceptable to the manufacturers and reciprocal trade treaties with a number of countries strengthened the British position.   Prosperity greatly increased the customs yield despite the reductions and in his budget of 1845 Peel removed customs duties on 430 articles and the excise duty on glass.   Sugar duties were reduced although the preference for colonial sugar remained.   In 1846 a further 605 articles were relieved of duty.   Taxation was remitted by these measures at the rate of £2½ m. a year and as many of the duties concerned had been on articles in general consumption, his work helped to relieve distress and to lower the cost of living.   With the surplus that increased trade and the direct taxation of those best able to pay gave him he repaid about £14 m. of the National Debt, lowered the rate of interest on £250 m. of stock and thereby cut the annual debt charge by £1½ m.

Peel also hoped to promote financial stability by the Bank Charter Act of 1844.   The Bank Charter Act of 1833 had encouraged an increase in the number of joint-stock banks which provided expanding credit at a time when the railway boom was encouraging speculation.   There had also been many loans to finance Anglo-American trade.   The expansion had been too fast, however, and brought on a commercial crisis which provided the background of unrest from 1838 to 1843 which nourished both the Chartist Movement and the Anti-Corn Law League.   The situation was blamed on the Bank of England which Ricardo had earlier attacked on the grounds that its two functions, that of a deposit and discount bank and at the same time a bank of issue controlling the entire national currency, were incompatible.   Peel had earlier experience of currency regulation when he had been chairman of the committee which recommended the return to the Gold Standard in 1819 and he became convinced that commercial

crises would not take place if the issue of paper notes, together
with the coin in circulation, never exceeded the amount of
money which would circulate if the currency were wholly
metallic.   By the act of 1844 £14 m. worth of notes constituted a fiduciary issue, backed by government securities;
all other notes issued by the Bank of England had to be backed
by bullion.   The other banks were jointly limited to an issue of
£8½ m., all backed by gold.   The act also separated the issue
and banking departments of the Bank of England, the former
being brought under close government supervision, the latter
being left to the Directors of the Bank.   Creditors could now
be reasonably certain that the value of any paper currency
would be met on demand.   The system was not completely
foolproof, however, and on occasions the government suspended the operation of the act to allow more money to come
into circulation.   Critics of the measure believed the currency
would be more responsive to the economic needs of the
country if issue of currency was at the bankers' discretion.

The year 1844 was prosperous for Peel's government.   The
industrial depression which had resulted from undue speculation had passed, the building of the railways had brought
employment both directly and indirectly.   The Budget
showed that the deficit had become a surplus while the Bank
Charter Act increased confidence and enabled the conversion
of part of the National Debt to a lower rate of interest.   Two
important pieces of social legislation had also taken place, the
Mines Act of 1842 and the Factory Act of 1844.

The Mines Act was the fruit of a Royal Commission
appointed by Melbourne in 1840.   Its report, which was
illustrated with sketches, brought home in vivid terms the
harsh realities of what was to most people an unknown world.
The mines worked on a system of subcontracting and women
and children were employed in many pits by the miners
themselves to carry the coal they won back to the surface.
In some pits ponies were used for haulage and the main shaft
was normally fitted with a winding device, frequently in
charge of an inexperienced person or child.   Elsewhere,
however, the haphazard nature of mine expansion meant that
coalface and pit bottom were connected by low and narrow
passages along which women and children were forced to
crawl pulling small trucks of coal or dragging a bag.   'It is

sad sweating and sore fatiguing work and frequently maims the women,' remarked one of the witnesses. Sometimes the women and girls carried coal on their backs, as much as three hundredweight at a time, and were forced to ascend ladders up vertical shafts. Very young children of five or six were employed to sit in the dark and raise the trap doors on which the ventilation of the pit depended to allow the coal carts to go by. There was no limit to the hours that could be worked, and children who fell asleep were often brutally treated. Brutality indeed was frequent in the pits and so was debauchery. Accidents, often fatal, were a frequent occurrence and it was not until 1881 that the Home Secretary was given the right to hold inquiries. The work stunted the growth of the workers and often left them crippled and distorted. The act, which was introduced by Ashley, forbade the employment of women and girls in the pits at all and boys only over the age of ten. Nobody under fifteen was to be in charge of machinery. Inspectors were appointed who could report on the condition of workers but not, owing to the opposition of Lord Londonderry and other mine-owners, on the condition of the mines themselves. This was added in 1850 after several serious accidents.

The act was a great humanitarian triumph but was opposed by those people it most affected. The mine-owners naturally saw in it a loss of profit and reduced miners' wages. The miners resented the loss of their women's and children's earnings. When their own wages were cut they organised a general strike under Chartist leadership and brought the entire industry of the Potteries to a standstill for lack of coal. When it turned to violence O'Connor[1] ceased to support it and the strike was suppressed by adroit use of troops.

The Factory Act of 1844 was a sequel to that of 1833[2] which had first limited effectively children's hours of work. The 1833 Act had been a disappointment to Ashley and his fellow Evangelicals but the inspectors had proved to be very valuable and their reports did much to instruct public opinion. The Royal Commission into Mines also investigated children's work in the Potteries, in calico-printing works, nail-making and other industries. Their report provided a favourable climate for the introduction of the Factory Bill in 1844. The

[1] See below, p. 128.   [2] See above, p. 92.

purpose of the reformers was to obtain a 10-hour day for all factory workers; their policy, to obtain it by sap rather than by storm. Children's hours up to the age of thirteen were to be 6½ a day, those of women and boys under eighteen were limited to 12 a day. The intention was by this means to limit the hours of men as well, in view of the large proportion of women and children in textile mills, but it was evaded by staggering hours of work. The Ten Hours Agitation continued and came near to success when Fielden, in place of Ashley who had lost his seat, introduced a Bill in 1847 which passed owing to the support of the Protectionists, who saw it as a blow at the Free Traders, and because many mills were working short time on account of a trade depression and the transition would therefore be painless. The act was badly drafted, however, and relay working was still widely practised. After a test case a further act was passed in 1850 which imposed a 10½-hour day and 7½ hours on Saturdays. The operatives considered Ashley had betrayed them, but productivity and hence their pay increased, as their health was so much improved that they could stand the strain of working at higher speeds.

The success of 1844 turned sour in 1845. The summer of that year was a very wet one which caused a disastrous harvest in England. In Ireland there was a serious potato-blight (cf. p. 75) which, in view of the concentration there on this single crop, meant a famine of unparalleled proportions; as Russell remarked, 'a famine of the 13th Century acting upon a population of the 19th'.

After his victory over O'Connell at Clontarf[1] in 1843 Peel had sought to conciliate Ireland. His policy was a twofold one, of increasing the Maynooth grant and improving Irish higher education on the one hand and on the other of investigating and if possible ameliorating the Irish land system.

The wealth and position of the Church of Ireland was recognised by many in both parties as a barrier to Anglo-Irish understanding. It was impossible to make the Roman Church either the Established Church in Ireland or jointly established with the Anglicans because the future of endowments would cause too much bitterness in England. Gladstone's solution was to be disestablishment and partial

---

[1] See above, p. 105.

disendowment, in 1869,[1] but public opinion was not yet ready for such a move. Peel, therefore, allowed the Roman Catholics to build up permanent endowments and appointed a committee of Roman Catholic bishops to administer them, thus submitting the Church to some State control. He also brought forward a Bill to treble the grant to Maynooth, assuming that, in view of the great influence of the Roman Catholic clergy, it would be to the advantage of the English government for them to be well-educated. The grant was only approved with difficulty; there was much bitter opposition in Parliament and in the country many protest meetings; Gladstone, who supported the Oxford Movement, resigned from the Cabinet in protest, and one of the leaders of that movement, J. H. Newman, felt it was an acknowledgement by the Church of England that she did not possess the truth and went over to Rome.

The question of education was equally difficult, owing to the opposition of the Church party in England and also of the Roman Catholic bishops. In 1827 Stanley had set up a Board of National Education in Dublin to establish primary education, the schools being open to both Protestant and Catholic ministers for religious instruction. Despite Catholic dislike, the scheme worked fairly well. Peel wished to extend it by establishing a purely secular University of Dublin, to which the government would contribute, to attract that class which for social and religious reasons was ineligible for the Anglican Trinity College. The scheme, frustrated owing to opposition, was not to be implemented until the early 20th Century. Peel was able to increase the grant for elementary education, however.

The land question was investigated by the Devon Commission of 1845. Its report showed that secondary remedies which did not touch the system of land tenure would neither solve Irish distress nor put an end to agrarian crime. A bill was produced to provide a limited amount of compensation for certain improvements but it was killed by a storm of protests from landowners. Despite his great services to the party Peel had never commanded a warmth of loyalty and he could not afford to alienate the landowner and Anglican interests that contributed so greatly to his strength. It was

[1] See below, p. 206.

the former that was to be the occasion of his downfall in 1846.[1]

The circumstances were the Irish famine. The extent of over-population was such that distress was widespread every summer in normal times, over two million people being unemployed or in want of the necessities of life for an average of thirty weeks a year. Approximately four million people in Ireland lived entirely on potatoes, in addition to nearly two million in Great Britain, and when the potato-blight spread from England to Ireland in the autumn of 1845, famine was inevitable. The 1846 crop again failed and although that of 1847 was good, people weakened by hunger and distress could not resist fevers and other epidemics. The government was at once concerned but the corn harvest was poor in western Europe in 1845 and it was difficult to get increased supplies from eastern Europe and the Levant. Large quantities of maize were bought in America and sold for 1d. a pound in Ireland, where it was nicknamed 'Peel's brimstone'. It was in order to increase the amount of corn available that he decided to suspend the Corn Laws, an intention which circumstances turned into Repeal.[2] £2 m. was voted by the Treasury to provide public works which would bring money into the Irish economy. This was supplemented by a large amount of private charity from England. The scheme was a failure; it needed efficient administration and the administrators were not available. The Irish themselves had no tradition of self-help and were improvident and lawless. Parliament refused to carry into effect Bentinck's proposal that Irish railways should be built with State help; in order to prevent jobbery no works could be undertaken to benefit private landowners, thus a great deal of labour was thrown away on hastily-devised schemes of no use to their localities. In March 1847 with unemployment at 750,000, Russell fell back on the issue of rations in kind. All the prejudices of Free Traders, landowners and businessmen were against the massive State aid and direction that alone could have pre-

[1] In connection with Peel's move to free trade Disraeli protested against the system of appealing to the loyalty of the Tories in order to make them vote for Whig measures: 'The Right Honourable Gentleman caught the Whigs bathing and walked away with their clothes.   He has left them in full enjoyment of their liberal position and he is himself a strict conservative of their garments.'

[2] See below, p. 122.

vented the Irish situation deteriorating; the influence of the landowners was too great to permit the extensive recasting of the land situation which was the basic cause of the disaster. Had Russell been a man of greater vision he might have tackled this – as might Peel had he had the opportunity. In all, the relief measures cost the government £7 m., mostly intended as a loan, but cancelled out against the increase in the Irish income tax in 1853. It was a small sum compared with the £20 m. paid to slave owners in 1833 and slight compensation for the damage done to Irish economic interests in the 18th and early 19th Centuries. Although Russell did his best by the standards of the day, the efficiency of the relief administration declined after the Whig return to power, and there may have been some slight justification for the Irish coroners' juries who returned a verdict of wilful murder against Lord John Russell when men were found dead from lack of food.[1]

The famine solved the problem of over-population. Between 1846 and 1851 one-eighth of the population died as a result of the famine, and another million emigrated, mostly to the United States. Another million followed them in the next ten years, taking with them a legacy of hatred which was another obstacle to the improvement of relations. In Ireland itself the famine was a bitter memory for many generations and was directly associated in people's minds with English rule. For many landowners, already half-ruined, the famine completed the process, and they ejected tenants in order to recoup by creating larger agricultural units. This brought violence which necessitated Coercion Acts. In 1849 an Act of Parliament made the sale of encumbered estates easier and over £23 m. worth of land changed hands, but the new land-lords, mostly Irish themselves, were harsher. A visit by the Queen in 1849, when the violence had died down largely through exhaustion, created a good impression but she went reluctantly and later opposed a suggestion by Gladstone that she should equip and sometimes occupy a royal residence in Ireland.

That Peel decided to solve some of Ireland's problems by a repeal of the Corn Laws was very largely due to the successful campaign of the Anti-Corn Law League.

[1] See below, p. 154.

I

Since 1815 the Corn Laws had been a very sore point – a permanent irritant to the urban, manufacturing and exporting interests opposed to the politically dominant class which had imposed them. Those who argued for their abolition went back to the Free Trade arguments of Adam Smith and claimed that the restrictions on the import of corn hindered the sale of our manufactured goods abroad. The members of the League quoted biblical and other precedents against those who became rich on the hunger of the poor. Cheap bread was a simple and impressive cry which everybody could understand. There was no need for spokesmen to understand the intricacies of agriculture. It was also argued that the policy of high bread prices led to the imposing of rents higher than farmers could meet, and the distress of the agricultural labourers during much of the period was pointed to as evidence that Protection benefited only the very few. The general tendency of the time was in favour of lowering duties and the rights of vested interests were less and less regarded if they happened to conflict with economic theory. The Radicals hoped to rally to an attack on the Corn Laws a wider support than they could expect for any other measure; their repeal would be a greater blow to entrenched privilege than any other reform.

To the Protectionists the Corn Laws were a bastion that preserved the landed power of the gentry. They defended a Protectionist policy on the grounds that it ensured a safe, steady food supply, strengthened the Navy by encouraging British shipping, prevented wages being driven down, and held the Empire together. More specifically they claimed that the campaign was evidence of the greed of the manufacturers who would use the possibly lower food prices to lower wages. Working men were suspicious of the middle-class character of the movement and Chartists believed that many farm workers would be driven to the towns by the competition of foreign corn.

The depression of 1838 and a rise in corn prices provided the opportunity and in January 1839 the Anti-Corn Law Association of Manchester was founded. It was backed by the Manchester Chamber of Commerce and by a number of prosperous manufacturers, such as Strutt of Belper. The principal leader from an early stage was Richard Cobden, who came of yeoman stock but was a cotton manufacturer. He became an M.P. in 1841 and it was his ability and his idealism that gave energy and success to the movement. He was powerfully assisted by another member of the League, John Bright, a Rochdale manufacturer, a powerful orator, self-righteous, but preaching free trade, and the peace he was convinced it would bring, with a religious conviction. Many of their speeches gave a misleading picture of the past and inaccurate forecasts of the future, but audiences who knew nothing of either could understand the implications of cheap bread.[1]

The League's campaign was organised with business-like efficiency. The campaigners were helped by penny postage in 1840 which enabled them to send literature all over the country, by the reduction of the stamp duty on newspapers from 4d. to 1d. and by the extension of the railways which helped their lecturers and principal speakers to stump the country. The first few years were difficult; money was short and opposition was very strong while better harvests from 1842 onwards and Peel's tariff revision, which satisfied many manufacturers, led to a decline in enthusiasm. Very skilful use was made of propaganda and one of the most successful examples was Cobden's conference with the ministers of religion. Many of the ministers were convinced that the Corn Laws were a social evil and contrary to the word of God and they became virtual agents of the League in their districts.[2] After the eclipse of the Chartists in 1842 the League emerged as the principal organised Radical group in the country and it intensified its agitation. Forty-shilling freeholds were purchased and the League obtained some striking successes by manipulating electoral rolls. Parliamentary electors were inundated with tracts, posters and handbills were distributed and several newspapers received cash from the League for supporting its views. In 1844 £100,000 was collected; in 1845 £250,000. At a great meeting in Manchester in December almost £60,000 was promised on the spot. When League spokesmen visited rural areas they were

---

[1] In one of his speeches Cobden described the Corn Law as 'Baptised in blood, begotten in violence and injustice, perpetuated at the expense of the tears and groans of the people.'
[2] One Unitarian minister commented: 'We bind ourselves to the League as to a Covenant.'

greeted by armed labourers who asked if the great day had
come at last. This intimidated the landowners and several
members of the Whig aristocracy, notably the Marquis of
Westminster, began to support the League.

Peel was already convinced by the summer of 1845 that
the Corn Laws would have to be modified. There is no
indication that he was particularly influenced by League
opaganda. He realised that England was not self-supporting, that agriculture was not particularly efficient, and that
wages had not fallen as a result of good harvests. The
crescendo of League activity when the potato famine occurred
made it clear to him that suspension was the only acceptable
remedy and that this was tantamount to repeal, for once
suspended they could never be brought back. When he told
his Cabinet only three members would support him. A
fortnight later, on 22nd November, Russell wrote his Edinburgh letter. In it he accepted the need for repeal and
accused the government of failing in their duty if they
resisted it. He was apparently convinced that it was essential
in order to save the aristocracy. The effect was electric.
Perhaps no manifesto has ever produced quicker and more
far-reaching results. Bright told him that it made the
immediate repeal of the Corn Laws inevitable. Peel resigned;
Russell failed to form a government owing to lack of co-
operation from the Whig aristocracy. Peel, in an embarrassing position, resumed office, Stanley alone failing to rejoin
his Cabinet. There was, indeed, no alternative. The Whig
leaders were, if anything, more divided and neither Stanley
nor Cobden were in the least likely to be able to form a
government.

Peel made the repeal of the Corn Laws part of a comprehensive measure of tariff reform which carried further the
Budgets of 1842 and 1845. Duties on many manufactured
articles were abolished, that on maize went; from 1849 a fixed
duty of 1s. a quarter was intended to be placed on wheat, oats
barley and rye. Until then there was to be a greatly reduced
sliding scale. Landowners' burdens were to be lightened by a
reorganisation of local finance in which the State would
contribute to the Poor Law, the police and the highways.
Farmers were promised credit for land improvement. Radicals were pleased by the care he had shown for the poor by

removing duties from many articles they purchased. This was a statesman-like way out of a difficult situation. Apart from his own preferences, to refuse repeal was to risk serious disorder. He knew whatever he did his party was divided on the subject and opposition might do it irreparable harm in the constituencies. The Protectionists, however, denied there was an emergency and maintained that Peel had betrayed them. They numbered 197 out of a total of 320 Conservatives and would certainly vote against him on the main issue.

The apparent leader of the Protectionist group was Lord George Bentinck, the man behind the scenes was Benjamin Disraeli. Bentinck's rank and dignity reassured those who would have hesitated to follow Disraeli and he showed himself to be a man of greater ability than many expected. Formerly a habitué of the racecourse, he now worked hard and accumulated facts and figures which he then quoted with great violence. He had a hatred of disloyalty: 'I keep horses in three counties, and they tell me I shall save £1,500 a year by free trade. I don't care for that; what I cannot bear is being sold', a sentiment echoed by the aged Melbourne when he commented on the Repeal to the Queen: 'Ma'am, it's a damn dishonest act.' Disraeli too castigated Peel's treachery, comparing it to the Sultan's admiral's defection to Mehemet Ali in 1839: '. . . I have an objection to war . . . the only reason I had for accepting the command was that I might terminate the contest by betraying my master.'

Disraeli had been affronted in 1841 by Peel's failure to offer him office. His wounding speeches had made him many enemies and he had gained a reputation for being an 'adventurer'. He had considerable intellectual powers and wrote several novels in which he ranged superficially over a wide variety of subjects.[1] There was little depth in his work, little real analysis of the problems of England. Yet he had a rococo flair with which he brought colour into what otherwise might have been drab. This in the long run was to be one of the secrets of his success in politics; meanwhile it was to be the seed of much distrust. He had courage, quickness of wit, loyalty and friendship, a capacity for political manœuvring

[1] Notably *Sybil or the Two Nations* which gave a detailed and reasonably accurate description of the life of the poor, and *Coningsby* which reflected some of the aspirations of the Young England Movement.

and, fundamentally, great honesty of purpose. He had been associated during Peel's ministry with a group of young members of landed families who called themselves 'The Young England Movement'. They talked of a revival of chivalry and of a feudal attitude which viewed men as bound by reciprocal duties. They did not hesitate to vote against the Ministry when its attitude was contrary to their principles. Disraeli lent them his debating ability and in return he was saved from isolation and provided with aristocratic links.

Peel's Corn Bill passed the Commons on the votes of the Whigs and Radicals, the majority of his own party voting against him. Peel and those who had followed him were convinced of the rightness of their action. They had placed the needs of the nation and of the labouring poor above purely party loyalties. 'It may be,' Peel remarked, 'that I shall leave a name sometimes remembered with expressions of goodwill in the abodes of those whose lot it is to labour and to earn their daily bread by the sweat of their brows.' It was observed that when he lay dying in 1850, from a fall from his horse, that the poor openly wept in the streets. Peel and his followers also believed that by this surrender they were preserving the aristocracy by averting revolution.

The peers, however, were almost unanimously opposed to repeal but memories of their failure over the Reform Bill induced them to let the bill through.[1] As on previous occasions Wellington put the national interest above his personal preferences: 'I am of your opinion, Sir, it's a damned mess, but I must look to the peace of the country and of the Queen.' By this time Peel was no longer in office; a combination of Whigs and Protectionists had defeated him on a Coercion Bill for Ireland.

Like most objectives of this sort, Repeal of the Corn Laws did not have the results that had been anticipated. At their most extravagant these had been, as forecast by Bright: 'We shall see no more ragged men and women parading our streets . . . but we shall have the people happy – "every man sitting under his own vine and fig tree".' The country in fact could nearly feed itself in years of good harvest and the high

---

[1] Cf.: Halévy's epigram that in 1832 the aristocracy surrendered political to preserve economic privileges and in 1846 surrendered economic to preserve political privileges.

corn duty made little difference; when harvests were bad, ⟋
supply from elsewhere was usually limited and the price ⟋
would have been high anyway. It may have checked the
rise in prices. What in the long run was more important
was that the principle of free trade was firmly accepted by
the majority of the population. The Repeal of the Navigation Laws logically followed in 1849. Many felt that the
League should have continued as an organised group to
secure other Radical objectives; Cobden was urged to lead a
campaign for an extension of the suffrage – but the League
disbanded as it had promised to do. Its legend lived on and
it acquired in the telling complete responsibility for repeal
of the Corn Laws. Its influence was to be a liberal bond for
two generations. Whatever its economic effects Repeal
transformed the political situation, splitting the governing
élite and promoting the creation of the Liberal Party.

(e) Working Class Movements and the Condition of the People

The Anti-Corn Law League had provided a focus for Radical aspirations for several years, but part of its success was due
to the amount of middle-class support it had; it was a 'respectable' movement whose leaders could communicate with the
governing classes and whose aims were acceptable to a large
proportion of them. There were during this period, however,
a number of other movements, coming directly from the working class and developing outside Parliament; their aims were in
conflict with the traditional system; their leaders were not
'respectable' and were regarded with distrust. Much of the
impetus of the movements came from the feelings aroused by
the Reform Bill struggle and from the disappointment with
the act itself felt by many working-class Radicals when the
struggle was over. The grievances of the working class were
difficult to press. They had no direct representation in
Parliament, little money to spend in organisation; if they
pressed their claims too hard they were liable to frighten all
other classes into resistance and might in their impatience
bring the whole force of the State upon their shoulders. They
were more likely to gain success by means of industrial warfare, through the agency of the trade union, but those unions
that did develop were chiefly among highly skilled workers

who were more concerned in enhancing and improving their own position and pay than in leading a revolutionary attack on the middle class.

Lack of support from the skilled artisans, the natural leaders of the working class, was one of the weaknesses of the earliest and most remarkable 19th-century working-class agitation, the Chartist Movement. It followed the failure of a premature attempt to unite the working classes in one great union, an attempt which was inspired by Robert Owen.

Ricardo had inferred that a very large factor in the value of commodities was the amount of labour involved and this was to lead many working men, ignoring the other factors, to question whether they were getting due reward for their labours. Owen suggested an answer by organising co-opera-tive workshops, which would enable the wealth created by industry to be shared among the poor workers. The under-taking was economically unsuccessful as not all the partici-pants were inspired by Owen's high devotion to duty. Owen refused to attack the rich and countenance class hatred. He conceived the idea, however, of using unions as a means of bringing about the reorganisation of industry on a co-opera-tive basis and began a Union of Building Workers in 1832. He extended this into a scheme of enrolling the entire working population for the same purpose and launched the Grand National Consolidated Trades Union in February 1834. His own reputation and the promise of rapid relief from the misery of the times won very wide support, and by direct membership or affiliation a total of half a million supporters was rapidly reached. Lodges spread like wildfire, for every conceivable occupational group, including a Lodge of Ancient Virgins, and the G.N.C.T.U. became indirectly involved in a large number of disputes. The most celebrated led to the trial of six Dorset labourers for taking illegal oaths and the severity of the sentence, seven years' transportation, was indicative of the alarm the G.N.C.T.U. was causing in govern-ment circles. The Loveless Brothers had formed a local lodge of the Agricultural Labourers' division of the G.N.C.T.U. when local farmers at Tolpuddle had promised an increase of wages and then reduced them. They had enforced oaths of secrecy from members in a dramatic fashion which was often necessary at a time when there was no legal

protection of funds. The rules of the lodge forbade drunkenness and violence and the men had not even threatened to
strike, but it was considered to be a test case. The G.N.C.T.U.
held a large meeting of protest in London and later signatures
were collected for a massive petition. The Tolpuddle Martyrs
were reprieved and brought back from Tasmania in 1838.
Five of them settled on farms in Essex.

By this time the G.N.C.T.U. was dead. It had shown itself
unable to support its members' strikes effectively; the reprisals
of employers did their work and dissensions broke up the
union early in 1835. This experience discouraged the highly
skilled trades from hazarding their funds in another similar
movement and made working-class leaders feel it would be
wise to concentrate on getting an extension of the franchise
as a preliminary to other improvements. This group, centred
on London, had founded in 1831 a National Union of the
Working Classes whose voluble advocacy of universal suffrage
had been a factor in preventing the Whig leaders from seeking
a compromise with the House of Lords. They had struggled
for an 'unstamped' Press and in 1836 set up the London
Working Men's Association. Lovett, the principal leader,
described their aim as 'to seek by every legal means to place all
classes of society in possession of their equal political and legal
rights'. Working Men's Associations were founded all over
the country and in 1837 Attwood revived the Birmingham
Political Union and pledged it to similar objectives. The
great unpopularity of the New Poor Law at a time of trade
depression stimulated support and Place and Lovett drew up
the political demands of the working class, which were adopted
as *The People's Charter* in May 1838. The choice of name was
particularly apt and so was the Act of Parliament form in
which it was drawn up. The Preamble concluded,
'. . . Heaven has dealt graciously by the people but the
foolishness of our rulers has made the goodness of God of no
effect.' To remedy this the Charter proposed universal
manhood suffrage, annual Parliaments, a secret ballot, no
property qualification for M.P.s and the payment of members. Equal electoral districts, wanted by the London
Working Men's Association, was objected to by Attwood
because of the preponderance it would give to Ireland.
Attwood's proposal for a petitioning movement in support of

the Charter was also accepted.   The movement was intended to be peaceful and it was represented, in all honesty, to working men that once this objective had been achieved, remedies for social and economic distress would be rapidly forthcoming.   The Charter thus became a symbol for the removal of many grievances, some national, some local.   Dislike of the New Poor Law was an important factor.

It was perhaps over-optimistic to imagine that working men, whose interest in agitation rose and fell in close correspondence with the pattern of harvest and employment, would stop short of violence when it was evident that peaceful agitation fell on deaf ears.   Hence the movement changed hands: the thoughtful, responsible, skilled craftsmen such as Lovett and Place, who distrusted demagogues, giving way to outcasts and adventurers from other parties and classes, men who to keep the confidence of their followers were prone to exaggerate.   In particular Bronterre O'Brien was ready to influence class hatred as part of the campaign and had plans for land nationalisation, while O'Connor helped to alienate any chance the movement might have had in its early stages of Tory support.

Feargus O'Connor had entered Parliament in 1832 as part of O'Connell's 'tail' but after he lost his seat in 1835 he became increasingly concerned about the poor conditions of Irishmen in England.   This led him to advocate a revival of smallholding as an antidote.   Repudiated by O'Connell, he developed his influence in the north of England by attacking the Poor Law and helping to organise trades unions.   He was a flamboyant figure with a powerful voice, a power of rapid repartee and a rough humour.   Although he was never fully identified with the 'physical force' group, many of his writings and speeches were clear incitements to violence.   He spoke of 'flashing swords to the hilt' and 'Come he slow or come he fast, it is but death that comes at last' – phrases that alarmed the London Working Men's Association.   He obtained a powerful instrument in *The Northern Star*, for O'Connor, already emulating Hunt as a great Radical demagogue, now aspired to rank with Cobbett as a great Radical journalist.   It was founded in Leeds in November 1837, coming out weekly at $4\frac{1}{2}d$. a copy; O'Connor had campaigned for subscriptions, guaranteeing 10 per cent interest himself.   At its peak in

1839 it sold 50,000 copies an issue, but it was badly managed, although well written, and was not as successful financially as it might have been. Its readership corresponded with the success or failure of Chartism in the country and it was wound up in 1852. Through it, working men all over the country were able to see themselves as part of a national movement of operatives with similar grievances and similar ideas for their removal. By it, O'Connor was gradually established as the national leader of that movement.

It was in the smaller towns where industry was rarely diversified and where a slump could have a most serious effect that Chartism was most strong. Among the handloom weavers of Barnsley, who particularly suffered, were several hundred Irish immigrants and it was to them that O'Connor first became a political idol. The winter of 1838–39 saw him established as leader of the Northern Chartists with the moderates unable to control him. The ideas of violent revolution gained ground; there were great meetings and processions by torchlight.

Meanwhile signatures were being collected for a National Petition to support the Charter, and a Chartist Convention met in London in February 1839. The moderates were in a majority and urged a delay to collect more signatures in order to convince the government of the weight of public opinion. Melbourne was alarmed, but took a number of shrewd measures. Owen, the Socialist, was presented to the Queen, the Poor Law was relaxed, particularly in the north of England where the greatest discontent lay, a Police Act was passed to enable the Metropolitan Police to be copied in country districts, and General Napier, who had a reputation for courage and liberal views, was placed in command of the Northern District. He invited the Chartist leaders to a demonstration of artillery fire and reported that, despite the sale of six-foot pikes at 3s. 6d. each and cheap copies of manuals of pike exercises and plans to attack troops in their billets at night, he was confident he could handle the situation.

The Convention adjourned to Birmingham in May and began to discuss what to do if the Charter was rejected. A run on the banks, a 'Sacred Month' of abstention from labour and taxed liquor and a refusal to pay rents, rates and taxes were proposed. The wilder elements urged insurrection. A

Chartist riot in Birmingham was suppressed by the Metropolitan Police.

The Charter and a petition signed by 1,200,000 people were presented on 12th July and rejected by the Commons by 237 to 48 votes. Disraeli was one of the few who advocated considering it. The 'Sacred Month' was fixed to start on 12th August but the unions would not co-operate and there was never any real chance of its success. Many workers stayed off work for a few days to take part in processions and meetings, but that was all. The Convention dissolved itself in September, several Chartist leaders were imprisoned and the events of the year were completed by an isolated and abortive rising in Monmouthshire. In gaol, from which harrowing accounts of his martyrdom reached *The Northern Star*, O'Connor built himself up as the national leader of the movement.

Lovett meanwhile organised the National Charter Association which recaptured the enthusiasm of 1839 and built up opposition to the Anti-Corn Law League which it saw as a purely middle-class movement. Lovett hoped he could educate the country into accepting the Charter but hungry working-class Radicals were not prepared to wait so long. In the autumn of 1841 wheat had risen to 86s. a quarter and this brought on mounting distress during the winter which gave encouragement both to the League and to the Chartists. In Sheffield the Poor Rate rose from £142 a quarter in 1836 to £4,253 a quarter in 1842 and by the end of 1841 one-tenth of the whole population of England was drawing poor relief. In Manchester the consumption of provisions declined by one-third and in Accrington families subsisted for days on boiled nettles. Cobden after careful consideration decided not to join forces with the Chartists, who were now more firmly under the leadership of O'Connor. A new Charter was presented, the accompanying petition being signed by 3,300,000 people. Its main feature was a demand for universal suffrage, but there was also an attack on the Poor Law. The 1842 Petition was rejected as that of 1839 had been, but O'Connor would not condone the logical progression to physical force. A number of strikes broke out among coal miners under Chartist leadership, and a movement in Lancashire to remove plugs from machines, known as the Plug Plot, also developed. This was denounced by O'Connor who stated that it merely aggravated the poverty of the workers. Troops under the command of Wellington suppressed the disturbances without difficulty. A number of Chartist leaders were imprisoned.

There the movement might well have ended. It had hovered on the brink of violence, had disappointed the hungry men who had so pathetically placed their trust in it but had alienated any chance it might have had of sympathy from the governing classes. Returning prosperity, the Mines Act, the Factory Act of 1844, all contributed to diminish the hold it had had. O'Connor himself, whose flair for journalism might have made him useful to any political party, remained the leader of the broken and discredited group. He embarked on the purchase of land to establish small-holdings for workers from industry but although he had some success at first, he got into financial difficulties. In 1847 he was elected Chartist M.P. for Nottingham by a freak of the polls, and the following year led Chartism to its disastrous eclipse.

The news of the fall of Louis Philippe and the train of revolutions throughout the Continent – 'France sneezed and Europe caught a cold' – excited the Chartist leaders. The revolutionary situation in Europe disrupted trade in England and provided the raw material of agitation. There were great gatherings in London and riots in the West End, Glasgow was for a time in the hands of a mob shouting 'Bread or revolution'. A Chartist Convention was called in April which showed considerable difference of opinion as to the course of action after the Charter was rejected, as it assuredly would be. The revolutionary group wanted the Convention to proclaim itself the sole legitimate authority; the moderates wanted a memorial to the Queen calling for the dissolution of Parliament and the appointment of Ministers prepared to champion the Charter. A huge meeting was convened on Kennington Common and a procession was to take the Charter in triumph to the Houses of Parliament. The government forbade the procession and enlisted 150,000 special constables. Only 25,000 Chartists turned up and O'Connor consented to the Charter being taken by cab. Like O'Connell at Clontarf, he was unwilling, when it came to the point, to lead a revolution. The petition was claimed by O'Connor to have five million signatures, but there were less than two million. The fact that many were obviously forged should not obscure the fact that it represented an impressive weight of public opinion. Chartism and O'Connor, however, were laughed out of public life. A few outbreaks later in the summer were easily suppressed. Ernest Jones tried to revive the movement, but it was of no avail.

Both at the time and since O'Connor has been condemned and accused of ruining the movement. He was an undoubted egoist who spent too much of his time eliminating rivals, yet movements of this kind need a demagogue to be led effectively. He had little original thought: he stole the movement itself from other hands but of his sincerity, particularly in his later years, there can be no doubt. Violent language is part and parcel of popular movements and Cobden was almost as violent as O'Connor. In the excitement of torchlight meetings, in the tense atmosphere of the crowd, when O'Connor was spurred on by the faces in front of him to even wilder language, there was created an experience and a memory which helped to tide men over the harsh realities of everyday life. O'Connor knew that Parliament would never concede Chartism as a quiet movement; he hoped to frighten them into concessions as the middle class had done in 1831–32. He did not live in vain. Russell was deliberately lenient in 1848; he held that if the Chartists had a real grievance they had a right to express it and that if they had no grievance they would not keep their following. The evidence of real support encouraged him to raise the question of extending the franchise in 1851.[1] All the six points, except annual Parliaments, have in fact become part of the British Constitution in course of time and the conception of a working-class political movement opposed to the middle classes was to find fruition in the birth of the Labour Party. It would be wrong, however, to suggest that the movement was Socialist. Marxism implied that Chartism was the revolt of the operative against the machine by which he was being enslaved, but the majority of Chartists were miners and handloom weavers. The factory operatives were more contented and, through their unions, withdrew at an early stage. O'Connor was a convinced individualist and O'Brien wanted only the public ownership

[1] See below, p. 157.

of land. In a sense Chartism was pre-industrial: O'Connor, like Cobbett, looked back to the old world. It was not a creed but a revolt of hunger and despair. 'By heavens,' said the Chartist, George Harvey, in 1849, 'the patience – or rather, the suicidal apathy of the masses is wonderful and pitiable.'

The revival of trade in 1842 and the great expansion of the railways brought a revival and extension of trades unionism. The Miners' Association of Great Britain was founded in 1841 and had some success in fighting cases of oppression in the courts but it could not survive the depression in coal in 1847–48. Other unions, smaller and more local, gradually built up their strength. They were very largely in the skilled trades and the Webbs considered that they thought more of conciliation and of the closely-related interests of employers and workers than of violent strikes. The atmosphere was certainly more responsible, but it would be a mistake to over-emphasise its pacific aspects. Dislike of strike action was often the result of financial difficulties; it did not mean that a union's hostility to piece work, new machinery or an increase in the proportion of apprentices was any the less. Full-time union organisers were beginning to appear in the larger associations and the larger and more carefully conserved funds meant that unions could meet away from public houses in rooms of their own, with a corresponding improvement in the seriousness and cautiousness of their discussions. In addition to furthering trade objectives, the larger unions offered insurance of tools, Friendly Society benefits and help to emigrants.

The Journeymen Steam Engine Makers and Millwrights Society was particularly noted for its cautious policy and two of its members, William Newton and William Allen, were able to unite 121 small unions covering connected trades to form the Amalgamated Society of Engineers in 1851. By the end of the year it had 11,000 members. The entrance qualifications were strict, it had a national office in London, a high contribution of 1s. a week and other local branches were forbidden to call strikes without the authority of head-quarters. They accepted the view that their purpose was not a social revolution but to obtain the best price on a competitive market for the commodity they had to sell – labour. In their first strike in 1852 they lost but obtained prestige through their high rate of strike pay. In their subsequent history they spent far more on Friendly Society benefits than on disputes.

The advantage of large organisations was also apparent in the 1858 strike of carpenters, masons and bricklayers for a 9-hour day. In 1860 the London Trades Council was formed, quickly becoming a body of national importance to which unions all over the country turned for help in time of crisis. The following year saw the Amalgamated Society of Carpenters and Joiners, which was closely modelled on the Amalgamated Society of Engineers and soon became one of the richest and most powerful of the new type of union. Its general secretary was Robert Applegarth, whom A. J. Mundella, manufacturer and politician, was to describe as 'an ornament to his class and I know some of the best men in the country are proud to call him their friend'. Applegarth saw the trades union as a means to emancipate the working class but laid equal stress on co-operatives, full political rights and education. He was concerned to build up an understanding between working and middle class. He agreed with another key figure in the London union world, George Odger, that 'strikes in the social world are like wars in the political world: both are crimes unless justified by absolute necessity'. Applegarth, Odger and Allen of the Amalgamated Society of Engineers were members of a small policy committee in London which the Webbs have called 'The Junta', and which enabled unions to gain social acceptance. Nevertheless unionism was spreading beyond the aristocracy of labour and there was a growing dichotomy between the respectability of the Junta and the aggressive outlook of some of the smaller unions of less skilled men.[1]

Another important aspect of working-class enterprise was the growth of the co-operative movement. This was influenced by the ideas and schemes of Robert Owen but the movement which started in 1844 made some important innovations. The Rochdale Pioneers, a few poor weavers who provided the original capital of a pound a head, opened a shop at Toad Lane, Rochdale, in that year. They bought wholesale, sold retail – strictly for cash – and distributed

[1] See below, p. 215.

the profits in proportion to the value of the purchases made. To them co-operation was a way of life and in the evenings they met to discuss religion and politics, subjects which were carefully avoided by the Mechanics Institutes.   Within three months the store was firmly established and the idea spread. By 1875 there were 437,000 co-operators in 1,266 stores in Great Britain, particularly in the industrial districts of the north and Scotland.   In 1847 a co-operative building society was established which in the course of the next twenty years spent upwards of £8 m. in providing its members, who were largely from the working class, with freehold houses.   In 1863 the Co-operative Wholesale Society was founded in Manchester which slowly expanded to run its own factories, the first being a biscuit factory at Crumpsall started in 1872.

The movement speedily gained acceptance.   It was given legal recognition in 1846, legal personality in 1852 and limited liability in 1862.   Of all working-class movements its tangible benefits are the most obvious.   By giving good value for money it helped to raise the standard of living and played an important part in the struggle against food adulteration; it helped the Trades Unions to get rid of the last of the Truck Shops, stores run by employers where workers were required to spend part of their wages, against which there were a series of acts, in 1831, 1854 and 1871; the dividend encouraged thrift; and the part ordinary men were called upon to take in its management was a valuable training in practical democracy.

The background to these more successful working-class enterprises was a rise in the standard of living for the more skilled industrial workers and an increased interest by politicians of all parties in what Carlyle called the 'condition of England' question.   Though questions such as child labour first benefited from this interest, the housing and sanitary conditions of the working classes were already beginning to attract some attention.   The increase of population since 1815 and accumulated neglect since then meant that in the more over-crowded areas conditions had, if anything, deteriorated.   These conditions were brought home to the reading public by the graphic accounts of Dickens, by the description of an industrial town in Disraeli's *Sybil*[1] and by Engels' book

---

[1] He gives, for instance, an extremely effective account of the scene at a 'tommy-shop'.

The Condition of the Working Classes in England in 1844 which
gave a picture of the dark mills, narrow streets, bad sewage
and black smoke of Manchester.   Perhaps the most powerful
champion of improvement was Edwin Chadwick,[1] the Secretary of the Poor Law Commission.   He was, to use James
Mill's phrase, 'one of the organising and contriving minds of
the age'.   He was tireless in collecting and digesting great
quantities of evidence but once he had formulated an opinion
he pursued his course with a ferocious conviction that did a
tremendous amount of good but made him many enemies.

The population of towns of over 20,000 in 1821 expanded
greatly.   By 1831 they had absorbed just over an additional
million, by 1841 a further million and a quarter and by 1851
another one and three-quarter million.   The rural population
remained fairly steady, its natural increase finding its way to
the towns in search of work.   For as little as 5*d*. a head,
Irishmen could reach England and Scotland and it was
frequently among them that the worst conditions were found,
used as they were to poor conditions at home.   The work of
sanitary reformers in the late 18th Century was swept away
by the great increase in town populations.   Many of the new
arrivals brought with them very low standards of living.
They aggravated the already overcrowded conditions of
many towns.   Attics and cellars, buildings on every available
space with little or no access to light and air, back to back
rows, court leading to court, all were filled.[2]   A single tap
turned on for perhaps half an hour a day provided water for
the whole street;[3] and in one part of Manchester the number
of privies averaged two to 250 people.   Many yards through
lack of drainage were covered with mud and human ordure
across which the inhabitants had to step on bricks.   The
streets themselves were often open drains.   A high mortality
rate and frequent sickness brought on by the bad conditions
contributed to the wretchedness of the poverty.   'I have
known,' said one investigator, 'instances where the wall of a
dwelling house has been constantly wet with foetid fluid which
has filtered through from a midden and poisoned the air with

---

[1] See above, p. 92.
[2] In Liverpool about 15% of the population lived in cellars in 1831, but in
the new mill towns the percentage was much lower.
[3] At Hyde the poor paid 1*d*. a day to water-carriers for a small supply of water.
It was small wonder that washing was a luxury.

its intolerable stench, and the family never free from sickness'. The East End Poor Law Unions were forced to spend money to remove stinking refuse and stagnant pools that were breeding disease, and it was this that led Chadwick to appoint three doctors, including Southwood Smith, to investigate. They affirmed two propositions which today are commonplace but then were not accepted, that there was a direct connection between certain physical conditions and disease and that diseases were preventable by the removal of these conditions. With the supporting evidence Chadwick persuaded Russell to inquire into public health in 1839. The Sanitary Report of 1841 specially emphasised the importance of house drainage, mains drainage, paving and street cleaning, which were to be considered as integral parts of a single process to be based on a constant supply of water at high pressure. It was only then that a rise in the average town death rate from 2·069 per cent in 1831 to 3·08 per cent in 1841 could be adequately fought.

The refuse of manufacture made conditions worse. Deposits accumulated, rotted and stank. Smoke, heavy and sulphurous, filled the air and helped to make the poisonous fogs which sometimes lasted for days. Brooks and streams were open sewers. Such artificial sewers as there were existed entirely for storm water and it was illegal to connect house drains to them in many areas. In some towns there existed Commissioners of Sewers but their powers were restricted and they were often inefficient and corrupt. Sewers were built without spirit levels and often ran uphill, so the contents oozed back into the lowest levels and stayed there indefinitely. They were tunnels large enough for a man to enter, of rough brickwork, on which filth stuck. Discharge was often into a river from which a water company would draw unfiltered drinking water. To drink beer was certainly safer. Chadwick adopted John Roe's invention of the small egg-shaped sewer through which water would be pumped at high pressure. The water companies, in addition to the sewage commissioners, were a powerful vested interest. Chadwick wanted medical officers to inspect dwellings and report on the action necessary and the Health of Towns Commission of 1843–45 investigated the detailed application of the proposals. A Metropolitan Sanitary Commission of 1847–48 worked on the same lines.

The condition of burial grounds was also a danger to health. Apart from the pathetic custom of keeping the body of a dead member of the family in the already overcrowded house until sufficient money could be accumulated to avoid a pauper funeral, the burial grounds of London in particular were monstrously overcrowded. Fifty-two thousand bodies were added every year to the 203 acres available in the Metropolis. The corrupting bodies poisoned ground and air and menaced their living neighbours. The private cemeteries constituted a very powerful vested interest.

Cholera, spread by the filthy conditions, appeared at regular intervals. There was a severe outbreak in 1848-49 which hastened the setting-up of a National Board of Health which included Chadwick and Shaftesbury as commissioners. It could set up local boards in a Poor Law area on a petition of 10 per cent of the inhabitants or where the death rate was above 23 per thousand. There was much opposition from vested interests and after a struggle London escaped from the Board's control. The prevailing doctrine of *laissez-faire* and the sanctity of private property also militated against them. The Board worked with great zeal and energy and won respect, even though Chadwick's personality and manner made it many enemies. It stressed that the best preventative of cholera was pure water.[1] The policy of flushing the London sewers as a preventative was disastrous, however, and transferred the germs to the Thames. Mortality shot up in the autumn of 1849 and doctors and inspectors met with much opposition from the slum population. When in 1853 the cholera returned, however, the figures showed the value of the Board's work. In London, where it had no control, deaths fell only from 14,789 to 11,621; in the rest of the country, the figure was 12,895 compared with the total of 40,412 for 1848-49.

Although London was slow to move, despite the appointment as Medical Officer of Health for the City in 1848 of Dr John Simon, who was to succeed Chadwick at a reconstituted Board of Health in 1854, other towns showed more concern.

---

[1] There was a striking instance at Mevagissey in Cornwall where 136 had already died of cholera out of a total population of 2,100. The Board's Inspector removed all who would follow him to a tented camp where pure spring water was available. There was not a single case in the camp; all who remained in the town were attacked.

In 1844 Manchester Corporation began to control housing, in 1845 it obtained a Sanitary Improvement Act and in 1848 began to build a large reservoir in Longendale. Liverpool, which opened a public baths in 1842, appointed the first Borough Engineer and the first Medical Officer of Health in the country in 1847. Good work was done by many local health boards.[1] Nevertheless although most people now paid lip service to Chadwick's ideal, the feeling of lack of urgency, a conviction that the accounts of slum conditions were exaggerated, and vested interests and dislike of Chadwick himself, made it infinitely difficult to put his ideals into practice. Chadwick was pensioned in 1854. In 1855 the Metropolitan Board of Works was created which proved to be corrupt and inefficient but which built the Victoria Embankment and completed the main drainage of the capital.[2]

Many Victorians were convinced that the material conditions of the people had improved and were still improving. If the value of money is any indication this was broadly true for the great majority of the population. But wages in the cotton industry averaged just under 10s. a week between 1833 and 1850, while Huddersfield weavers got about £1 a week and London shipwrights' wages also remained steady at around 36s. Building industry wages tended to rise, as did those of mechanics; on the other hand in the cotton industry they fell slightly. The cost of living rose in 1838–42, when the price of wheat was particularly high but was, by 1850, 17 per cent lower than it had been twenty years earlier. It was chiefly the agricultural labourers who had not benefited. Men's wages varied between 7s. and 11s. a week and to supplement them women and children were forced to the fields in gangs, women getting 9d. a day, girls 4d.–6d., boys from seven upwards 2d.–8d. Moreover the standard of farm cottages was very poor: generally they were damp, old and dilapidated. There was, however, some building of model cottages, in which the Prince Consort was a pioneer.

The prosperity brought about by the Industrial Revolution

---

[1] The spread of Medical Officers of Health was slow. Manchester and Leeds made appointments in 1868, but Birmingham, Sheffield and Newcastle all waited until the Act of 1872. Even then part-time appointments were allowed until 1929.
[2] For later history of Public Health see below, p. 238.

in its prime contributed greatly to the more pacific temper of working-class movements and the greater orderliness of the period but there was still a long way to go. Sir James Graham described the lot of many when, in 1847, he spoke of the worker's life as 'Eating, drinking, working and dying.'

(f) THE RISE OF THE RAILWAYS AND THE DEVELOPMENT OF INDUSTRY IN THE MID-19th CENTURY

The building of the railways is, in view of the poverty of the resources, one of the most outstanding material achievements of the human race at any time and certainly one of the outstanding events of the 19th Century. 'Train Roads' of wood with iron where friction was greatest were known in the 17th Century, particularly in colliery districts. The building of canals extended their use as short distance 'feeders' to the canal system. The motive power varied: horses were usual; on very short hauls on inclines use was made of an endless chain – descending full trucks pulling up empty trucks. To get full trucks up a steep incline a steam engine with a winch was introduced before the end of the century while one enterprising railway in South Wales used sails. Murdoch, Watt's foreman, built a model moving engine but the first full-size locomotive to run on rails was built by Trevithick at Merthyr Tydfil in 1804. In 1808 one of his engines, 'The Catch Me Who Can', caused much interest in London. Future development, however, came from the Durham colliery district. In 1813 Hedley produced 'The Puffing Billy' and in 1814 at Killingworth Colliery, where he was enginewright, George Stephenson built the 'Blucher' which could draw eight trucks containing thirty tons of coal up slight slopes at 9 m.p.h. Stronger boiler plates and greater precision led to the building of more efficient locomotives.

Stephenson got his opportunity as a designer of railways as well as of locomotives when he built the Stockton and Darlington Railway, opened in 1825. Steam power was not adopted until the line was half built and the company only catered for goods traffic, private firms running passenger coaches on the line on payment of a toll. The most important of the early railways was the Liverpool and Manchester Railway, which was opened in 1830. It was deliberately intended to break the canal monopoly. Stephenson was the engineer and succeeded in overcoming several difficulties, including the stretch of boggy terrain called Chat Moss. Until 1829 the directors were undecided as to which form of traction to use, but Stephenson's 'Rocket' convinced them at trials held at Rainhill. The line was a fantastic success – not only in the carriage of goods but also of passengers. 256,000 people were carried in 1831. This stimulated a wave of speculation: many companies were promoted. Lines were begun between London and Birmingham and London and Bristol. Euston Station was built with an imposing entrance arch, which a utilitarian age has destroyed, designed as a gateway to the capital. By 1838 500 miles of line had been completed.

The process of railway building was very expensive. A private Act of Parliament had to be obtained, the land had to be surveyed in great detail and then acquired, at a cost of £3,000–£6,500 a mile. Opposition was very strong, from turnpike trusts, from canal companies, from landowners. The line sometimes had to make expensive detours owing to the strength of opposition. Surveyors could often only survey under very difficult conditions – by night or in fog, for instance – to avoid retaliation from landowners. It was maintained that the smoke and noise would kill birds, exterminate pheasants, make cows go dry. It was held that the human frame could not stand the speed and passengers in their open carriages would be suffocated in the tunnels. Justices of the Peace feared the railways would bring bad characters to the countryside.[1] Nevertheless investors were forthcoming for any scheme, several parallel lines were often projected and Parliament, in granting permission, took little account of the final railway network of the country. There were many small investors, who were especially attracted after 1844 when Peel converted the 4 per cent loan to $3\frac{1}{2}$ per cent. In all, the total capital expenditure of the railways worked out at £64,453 per mile compared with £13,000 a mile for the less well built railways of the United States.

The actual construction of the railways was a stupendous task. The navvies showed great physical strength and powers

---

[1] Sunday travel was especially opposed. When a trip to Carlisle was advertised in 1841, the public of Newcastle were warned in 'A Reward for Sabbath Breaking' that passengers would be 'taken swiftly and safely to Hell next Lord's Day by the Carlisle Railway for 7/6d.'

of endurance. The blasting of tunnels could well be very dangerous, but it was the best paid work, fetching around 5s. a day. Wages ranged from at least 2s. 6d. a day upwards. Local men were often employed but a large number of Scots and Irish were attracted to the work. They lived a life of their own, working hard, drinking hard, quarrelling hard, yet generous to their comrades who frequently received no compensation if they were injured at work. They lived under filthy conditions and often terrorised the countryside for miles around.

The second great railway boom started in 1842. The leading promoter was George Hudson, a rough and arrogant York draper who made a fortune by paying dividends out of capital. Before he was disgraced in 1849 he had organised the Midland Railway with its headquarters at Derby, and many shorter-lived combinations. The investing public lost £80 m. by unwise and fraudulent speculation but by 1848 5,000 miles of line had been built, of which 400 were in Ireland. Until 1850 gross receipts never reached 8 per cent on the capital expended and there were still many who considered that horse tramways on public roads were better than railways.

It was, nevertheless, a period of great achievement. George Stephenson and his son Robert built many of the lines, Robert being responsible for the Britannia Tubular Bridge at the Menai Straits, the Berwick Royal Border Bridge and the High Level Bridge at Newcastle-upon-Tyne. Isambard Kingdom Brunel was the engineer of the Great Western Railway, on which the 2-mile long Box Tunnel was opened in 1841. His final work was the Royal Albert Bridge, Saltash (1859), on the extension of the line into Cornwall. The whole G.W.R. was built on a 7-foot gauge, not abandoned until 1892, but after 1846 all other lines had to conform to the 4 feet 8½ inches of the Stockton and Darlington, a width which was the average of the local country carts. The Electric Telegraph patented in 1837 was first put into practical use on the railways.

Parliamentary regulation came with an act of 1844 which laid down certain safety standards and also introduced an important social benefit in ordering a train to be run in either direction over every line every day at a third-class

ENGLISH RAILWAYS IN 1847 AND LOCATIONS OF
CHIEF INDUSTRIES

(With acknowledgement to D. G. Perry, *A Social and Economic History Notebook*,
published by John Murray.)

fare of 1*d.* a mile – the 'Parliamentary Train'. As a result of
this third-class carriages changed from open trucks to a
modest degree of comfort.

The benefits of the railways were innumerable. Further
development of industry would have been most difficult
without them. They opened up new markets, they carried

bulk goods at speeds which were phenomenal at the time and by cheapening the cost of transport they enabled manufacturers to become competitive abroad. They gave a tremendous impetus to the iron, and later the steel, industry. Their reliance on coal led to more pits and greater efficiency in them. In themselves they were a valuable export, for Thomas Brassey and other contractors built railways in France and later in South America. They earned fortunes for many of the middle classes, bringing to large numbers wealth without responsibility. They lowered the cost of living by conveying perishable foodstuffs quickly; they made labour more mobile and by providing cheap transport to such towns as Blackpool they enabled the poor to take holidays for the first time. They provided a better market for the farmer and helped him to get artificial fertilisers and farm machinery cheaply. Finally as we have seen they helped many popular movements such as the Anti-Corn Law League and the Trades Unions by enabling organisers to travel quickly round the country.[1]

Wrought iron was being used for rails from 1820 onwards and the railways used thousands of tons of iron; e.g. the 2,000 miles laid 1847–48 needed approximately 400,000 tons. Neilson's discovery of the greater economies in fuel by using a hot blast in 1828 and the discovery that uncoked coal could be used in furnaces were very valuable aids to production, while Nasmyth's steam hammer of 1840 made the manufacture of large iron bars possible. By 1847 the output of iron was two million tons annually, and this required some eight million tons of coal. In 1856 Bessemer's Converter meant that steel now became cheap enough for widespread use. The mild steel he produced was not of the same quality as Huntsman's cast or crucible steel but, being hard as well as malleable, it was greatly superior to both cast and wrought iron. Another process, the Siemens-Martin open hearth, was invented in 1866. For this gas could be used as the source of heat. Both these processes relied on nonphosphoric ore, which could only be obtained from Sweden and Spain; this was no disadvantage in England where the main steel manufacturing areas were well sited with respect to coal supplies and ports. The same was not true of the Continent and until the

[1] See above, p. 121.

Gilchrist-Thomas process for using phosphoric ores was invented in 1875 Great Britain retained a considerable advantage.[1]

An important development was in connection with engineering proper and the machine tool industry. The main progress in techniques was after 1848: for instance Maudsley's screw-cutting lathe came into general use, while his pupils Nasmyth and Whitworth produced a number of machine tools and pioneered standardised parts.

Steam-ships were also becoming important. The first practicable steam-ship, the *Charlotte Dundas*, sailed in 1803; since then the Dover–Calais steam-packet had started in 1812, and in 1833 the *Royal William* made the first all-steam Atlantic crossing in twenty days. Samuel Cunard got the North American mail contract in 1839 and a regular steam service dates from 1840. Brunel's *Great Britain* was the first iron vessel of any size (3,618 tons) and the first screw vessel to cross the Atlantic. In the same year, 1843, a tug-of-war between a paddle-boat and a screw-vessel showed the advantages of screw propulsion, but Brunel's *Great Eastern* (1858) designed for the Australian emigrant run but never a commercial success and later used as a cable-layer, played safe and had both screws and paddles. Wooden vessels were still used until a fairly late date; the Royal Navy in particular was alarmed by the splintering effects of iron-plate. Many of the tea clippers were composites – wooden walls on an iron frame. Steel came into general use around 1884. In the early steamers fuel consumption was so high that on long voyages they could only carry passengers and valuable freight but between 1863 and 1872 fuel consumption was reduced by half by the invention of a series of compound engines. The tonnage saved from coal was available for large bulk cargoes: the continental market could be flooded with American wheat while the last great sailing vessels were no longer economical to run. The result was a sharp increase in the volume of sea-borne trade, since every steamer could make many more voyages than a sailing ship in the same time.

The cotton industry was largely mechanised by 1830; the woollen industry by 1850. Cotton was our largest single export, India and China being the best markets. Woollen goods were second. Together textiles constituted 60 per

[1] See below, p. 294.

cent of British exports. Coal was also exported in considerable quantities, chiefly to Europe. A very high proportion of exports were manufactured goods, however, and the Victorian boast that England was 'the workshop of the world' was a reality. Imports exceeded exports for the movement towards free trade made Britain increasingly dependent on other countries for many industrial raw materials and an even larger proportion of its food, but the balance was more than made up by a large share of the carrying trade and income from the many British investments abroad.

The Great Exhibition of 1851 tangibly illustrated Britain's primacy. It was the inspiration of Prince Albert, whose enthusiasm prevailed upon an unwilling government, and the expenses were underwritten by private subscribers: it was housed in a gigantic greenhouse, prefabricated and capable of easy dismantling and re-erection, the design of Joseph Paxton, who was in the employment of the Duke of Devonshire In addition to several Hyde Park trees[1] the building contained exhibits from most European countries and the United States and a wide range of British and imperial produce. These still reflected small-scale systems of production, and ingenuity of design and craftsmanship rather than excellence of taste. Financially, the Exhibition made a considerable profit, which was devoted to the construction of the cultural complex in South Kensington, while socially it was a triumph. Widespread disorder had been expected but the people of London and excursionists from the provinces trooped respectfully through the great halls in their Sunday best and took away with them treasured memories that were woven into samplers and fireside tales. The revolutionary crowds of 1848 seemed but an idle dream.

Economically, however, the substance of primacy was not as solid as it seemed. Industry was short of capital, thus keeping units small and many backward. Until 1855 limited liability was hard to come by; either by incorporation under private Act of Parliament or by special and rarely-granted privilege under the Companies Act. Many regarded it as an evasion of responsibility but unlimited liability could bring unmerited suffering to innocent investors and was a powerful

---

[1] Their feathered inmates posed a serious problem. 'Try sparrowhawks, ma'am,' was the Duke of Wellington's advice.

disincentive. Private partnerships, the most usual form of business enterprise, were the greatest sufferers. It was most difficult to dissolve a partnership; partners were suspect who tried to end their responsibility just at a time when their businesses were ceasing to be profitable. Joint-stock companies were in a similar position until an Act of 1837, but this status, and that of the corporation, was difficult to obtain. Many saw limited liability as State interference. Acts of 1844, 1855, 1856 and 1862, however, granted the privilege, for it was realised that not only would very much more capital become available but the small savings of the working class could be given a stake in capitalism.

A rush of new issues followed, averaging £120 m. a year, but after the failure of Overend and Gurney in 1866, the average shrank to £28·8 m. An increasing effect was to divorce ownership from management and although the system was to produce the badly needed cash for technological advance and was to infuse more management skill, it helped to destroy the personal relationship in industry, which had stressed the joint character of the enterprise.

Private banking firms also became limited companies and there was a tendency to amalgamate from 1870 onwards. This made for greater stability, but managers were not prepared to make individual judgments in the way partners had been and it became correspondingly more difficult for a gifted man without capital to forge ahead. Over the whole presided the Bank of England, strengthened by Peel's Act of 1844. The discoveries of Australian and Californian gold in 1849 and 1851 brought more money into circulation; nevertheless it prevented prices from falling as productive efficiency increased. The institution in of 1853 the daily settlement of the London Clearing Banks, by means of cheques on the Bank of England, facilitated greater fluidity and the increased use of cheques meant that gold could be used more economically.

In farming the period was one of increasing prosperity and progress. The virtual completion of the enclosure movement meant that innovations could now be freely applied. 'The age of farming by extension of area had ended,' as Lord Ernle put it, 'that of farming by intension of capital had begun.' One of the most important improvements was better drainage. The invention of cylindrical clay pipes by John Reade in 1843

made possible considerable drainage work, partly financed
by public loans. Clay farmers could get longer seasons, their
speed of operation was increased, their yield improved.
Drainage was the necessary preliminary to efficient manuring
and the German chemist Liebig was responsible for the
development of agricultural chemistry which was to meet the
need for artificial manures. In England increased knowledge
about them was obtained from the experiments of Lawes and
Gilbert at Rothamsted. Nitrate of soda, Peruvian guano,
super phosphates, nitrate of potash and other fertilisers were
available and helped to convince the farmer that his farmyard
manure must not be wasted. Although the scope for
machinery on the farm was limited at this period, agriculture
benefited greatly from the railways, both for obtaining pipes
and fertilisers and for the easy conveyance of crops and stock,
in good condition, to the markets. Knowledge of better
methods and higher standards was spread by the increasing
number of agricultural shows. The first Royal Show was
held in 1838.

From 1850 the profitability of farming steadily increased.
Gold discoveries raised prices; the Crimean War and the
American and European wars of the 1860's restricted competitors; the harvests were good. The increased standard of
living at home meant a greater demand, particularly for
meat. Farmhouses were rebuilt, farm buildings were
constructed to a high standard, though labourers' cottages,
particularly in the south, continued to moulder into
picturesque insanitariness.

Means of communication with which the railways competed decayed. Canals were frequently bought up by railway companies and neglected while turnpike trusts were
gradually wound up and the roads reverted to parish control.
In 1840, however, a schoolmaster, Rowland Hill, had
persuaded the government to adopt his scheme for a uniform
penny post throughout the country, instead of the existing
differential rate based on distance. The scheme which at
first lost heavily (£1 m. in the first year) ultimately justified
itself. The quantity of letters had multiplied ten times in
the thirty years up to 1870. Mailbags were soon conveyed
by rail, increasing the speed and reducing the cost. The
electric telegraph service was taken over by the Post Office

in 1868. By this time too a transatlantic cable had been laid and one to India was completed in 1870.

(g) THE RELIGIOUS BACKGROUND

One of the questions in the Census of 1851 covered church attendance and at the same time a survey was made of the seating of churches and chapels: the former showed a figure for the previous Sunday of just over 50 per cent of the total population of England and Wales while the latter showed considerable inadequacies in the larger towns. The figures were something of a shock to the complacency of mid-Victorian England and illustrated the difficulties of contact with the industrial working class. Nevertheless the prevailing atmosphere of 18th-century England had changed and all classes acknowledged the principles of good conduct and humanitarianism. Occasional riots and distant wars provided an outlet for violence, which also could be enjoyed vicariously through cheap novels and tales of adventure. A strong family life, however, reinforced by a powerful social opinion, laid great stress on the idea of salvation by works and although church attendance was not universal, the Victorian virtues of duty, hard work and self-reliance had very general acceptance.

The foundation of men's self-confidence was the well ordered régime of the Victorian middle-class family. The durable furniture, carefully planned hours, regular Bible readings, appointed visits to relatives, rigid Sunday observance and passion for self-improvement provided the mainspring for many successful business careers and the sense of moral accountancy which was the basis of self-government in the political sphere. Pleasure was pushed into the background, the outstanding popular heroes were religious men and men of serious purpose in life such as Shaftesbury, Bright, Gladstone, Livingstone or Gordon. Literal stress on the Bible, certainty about the existence of an afterlife of rewards and punishments, a feeling that present life was only important as a preparation for eternity, all contributed to this emphasis.

These beliefs, which induced a comfortable complacency, were not without their critics. *Self Help* by Samuel Smiles and books with similar pious titles had large sales, but other books such as Matthew Arnold's *Culture and Anarchy* sought to reveal the basic spiritual disorder of the English people, as expressed in graceless industrial towns, the artificiality of much Christian observance, and its obsession with size, numbers and wealth. In his descriptions of 'Barbarians', 'Philistines' and 'The Populace' he criticised perceptively the established virtues. Dickens, in his novels, showed that the poor could be poor through genuine misfortunes rather than through weakness of character, and helped the middle classes to appreciate their warm humanity. Walter Bagehot, in an essay which reflected Darwinian conclusions, defined 'the cake of custom' as the chief survival factor in society but warned that this could stifle progress and adaptability. Herbert Spencer, on the other hand, tried to connect mental, moral and social development directly with evolution, which he identified with progress. He maintained that the survival of the fittest meant survival of the best. Although he had little immediate influence, he prepared the way for a highly anti-individualistic conception of the State.

Few saw the broader perspectives. The minutiae of religion were almost an end in themselves, and the period saw an increase in the number of sects and in the differences between sects. With the increase of Irish immigration and some well-publicised conversions from Anglicanism, Roman Catholicism became once again a popular religion in England, and the assumption of territorial titles for its bishops caused an outcry which both illustrated the traditional hostility to Roman Catholics and how remote from inter-sectarian violence the country had become. Forms of Dissent multiplied: Methodism split into several branches, as did the Baptists. The Church of Scotland divided in 1843 over the question of lay patronage and the Free Church of Scotland which seceded showed remarkable energy and self-sacrifice in raising funds and building churches. New religious groups sprang up, many of American origin. The 1860's saw the Revivals, associated with the mission and immediate success of Spurgeon, the new development of home missions by Methodists and the first visit to England of Sankey and Moody in 1873. The most notable English group was the Salvation Army founded in 1878 by a former Methodist minister, William Booth (1829-1912). Its music and military paraphernalia struck a romantic chord in many British hearts

0

and perhaps more than any other sect it dedicated itself to taking the gospel to the pagan areas of the industrial towns and to active social work among the destitute and the under-privileged.

Most remote from the realities of the Industrial Revolution was the dissension which rent the clergy of the Church of England in the mid-19th Century, although many individuals inspired by its ideals were to perform sterling work in the slum districts. Hitherto Evangelicalism had been dominant and had permeated people's minds with the ideals of a strict and pious life. Its weakness was on the intellectual side; theology and history had been neglected, the text of the Bible had been interpreted too strictly. A half-way house was the Broad Church movement, a small group for the most part of scholars, whose influence was greater outside than inside the Church, who took the liberal side in the agitation for administrative reform in the Church. Its conception that religion should be an affair of morals and good sense was welcomed by laymen who distrusted the Oxford Movement.

In the privileged and intellectually unreal atmosphere of unreformed Oxford there were many dons who saw the administrative reforms of Peel's and Melbourne's governments as leading to an attack on doctrine. Unlike the great majority of the laity, they felt a sense of emergency against which the Church must assert her position as a divine society. The starting point was Keble's Assize Sermon of 1833 on *National Apostasy*, which was prompted by the proposed limitation of the revenues of Irish bishops; the leader was John Newman, Vicar of St Mary's, a man of considerable intellectual qualities but unduly introspective and self-centred. He was joined by a scholar of distinction, Edward Pusey, the Professor of Hebrew, who fell under his influence. With other associates they published a series of *Tracts for the Times* which aimed at arousing a deeper spiritual life and put forward high claims for the authority of the Church of England. In so doing they became involved with the counter claims of the Church of Rome, and then with proving that they were not mutually exclusive. The culmination was *Tract 90*, published by Newman in February 1841, which sought to prove that the thirty-nine Articles contained nothing contrary to Roman belief. This went too far for the university authorities; the tract was censured and one disciple,

W. G. Ward, was deprived of his degree. In an agony of mind Newman retired to a pseudo-monastery at Littlemore and finally, in 1845, seceded to the Roman Church, of which, late in life, he became a cardinal. Others followed, the most prominent being Archdeacon Manning, later to be Archbishop of Westminster. Despite this the movement continued, though not as effectively. It encouraged a greater care for external order and ceremonial, a deeper conception of the clerical office. It helped to implant in men's minds the Victorian interpretation of the mediaeval conception of the 'beauty of holiness'. Its influence spread to the Free Churches but within the Church of England itself it fostered divisions over inessentials which left it weak at a time when non-belief was becoming far more dangerous than wrong-belief. In the third quarter of the century, however, the Church of England was at least holding its own and greater use of hymns and of a freer and more energetic style of preaching must have made a considerable difference to the value of its services.

This was a great era of church building. The hands of the restorers lay heavy on ancient churches and cathedrals, in many cases ensuring their survival after years of neglect, but often eradicating good work which did not come up to their own standards of purity. Many new churches were erected, especially in the industrial areas, testimonies not only to a sense of pastoral evangelism but to the munificence of local landowners and industrialists. A period of prosperity, such as that of the woollen manufacturers of the West Riding who supplied uniforms to both sides in Bismarck's various wars, was to bear tangible fruit in a crop of over-decorated chapels. Salvation, after all, was by works.

To many, salvation was by temperance. Drunkenness had greatly declined since the 18th Century but was undoubtedly still a social evil and the cause of much misery. The movement, consolidated in the United Kingdom Alliance, had supporters in all parties and religious groups and sought pledges from all candidates at elections. From 1874 onwards, however, following Liberal championship of the Licensing Laws, it became more specifically associated with the Liberal Party and with Nonconformity. Though never reaching the influence and excesses of the United States, it remained an important political and social factor.

IV · THE AGE OF THE PRIVATE MEMBER

(a) RUSSELL AND DERBY, 1846–52

THE fall of Peel ushered in a period of instability in politics
which lasted until the Reform Act of 1867 and Gladstone's
first Ministry. It was the golden age of the private member
when an individual's speech could sway a debate and save or
condemn an administration. Party discipline was very loose
and after an election the state of parties was only known when
the first division was taken. The most important variable
group were the Peelites, small in number but strong in talent
and parliamentary skill; it was fully a decade before most of
them had found a permanent resting place. The Liberal
party was also divided. There were the heirs of the great
governing families, assuming the style and graces of the grand
manner, yet countenancing ideas which undermined the
basis of their intellectual ascendancy. They supported social
reform, providing it was not controversial and did not involve
increases in taxation; they saw it as a way of staving off
Radical agitation and preventing political reform. The
Advanced Liberals were rarely more than seventy in number,
but their influence was considerable. It has been argued
that Cobden at the height of his Corn Law triumph could
have welded them into a powerful party; as it was they suffered
from undue individualism. Many were second generation
manufacturers such as Bass of Derby and Crossley of Halifax,
while others were representatives of that small but continuous
stream of 'gentry' radicalism which has been an important
factor in English constitutional development. Russell established useful links with the advanced Liberals: he needed
their support in his contests with Palmerston while in return
he supported some of their projects, notably the sequence of
unsuccessful reform bills of 1852, 1854, 1860 and 1866.

This situation, particularly in view of the characters and
interests of the Prime Ministers concerned, did not make for
strong government at home. In domestic affairs the greatest
changes took place outside the routine of the party conflict.

Few members realised the cumulative significance of the administrative reforms passed session after session. Parliament was much occupied with abortive debates and many of the crucial questions of the age were not settled while the opportunity existed. The two outstanding failures of the period were the loss of the opportunity, after the Famine, to tackle the problems of Ireland, and the neglect of education, particularly of technical education, which was to have severe effects on the development of British industry towards the end of the century. The liberty of the private member was in this sense the undoing of 19th-century Liberalism.

Lord John Russell, who now became Prime Minister, was not the man to produce strong government in these circumstances, although the division of the Conservative party should have been his opportunity. 'The little personification of Whiggery, an evening at Holland House incarnate', his rise to prominence owed much to his pluck and persistence in the face of physical disabilities, and to his sincerity and force of character. He never spoke a word he did not believe, but intellectually he was a slight man and he lacked that influence over men that was one of Palmerston's greatest assets. His manner was austere and he was not popular on the back benches at a time when the Whips lacked their later authority.

The prestige of the Whigs had not been increased by their support of Repeal. To the Tory gentry they were betrayers of the interests of the class, while the Radicals and the Free Trade Movement generally felt that the purpose of their conversion had been to return to power. Cobden was not offered a place in the administration, the Radical wing was scarcely represented, and the Cabinet of the 'last Whig government' was manned by historic names, including three members of the Grey family and Lord Lansdowne. Apart from the ebullient Lord Palmerston, the Cabinet was too dignified to be effective, a government of departments lacking leadership or resolution.

In Ireland plenty of resolution was needed.[1] The potato crop of 1846 failed utterly and in December cholera broke out. Death stalked the land; in the Skibbereen district one-tenth of the population died in a few weeks; in the whole of Ireland a quarter of a million died. Prompt steps were taken to

------

[1] See above, p. 119.

mitigate the worst features: maize was imported without stint, relief measures were extended and a large private subscription raised. But the relief administration was inefficient and what was lacking was some dramatic gesture of conciliation which would have convinced the Irish that the government really cared. Bentinck's proposal for £16 m. to be spent on building Irish railways might have been appropriate, but Russell relied on Drainage Acts, an Encumbered Estates Court and a reorganisation of the unpopular and largely ineffective Irish Poor Law. He contemplated the endowment of the Catholic clergy in Ireland but could find no way of raising the finance that the Whigs could support. He fumbled with the Irish problem until he fell from power and an opportunity was lost.

The autumn of 1847 saw a financial crisis arising in part from the bad harvests of western Europe. British gold went to Russia and America to buy wheat while the partial failure of the American cotton crop meant that Britain could not sell cotton goods in return for gold. Speculators in the corn market crashed in August, consols fell in price, while railway shares, where speculation had also been rife, plummeted in the autumn. The Bank Charter Act was suspended and the note issue increased, which eased the situation. Industry and the working classes were little affected.

Social questions now assumed unforeseen importance. Against Russell's wishes Fielden's Ten Hours Bill was taken to the statute book in 1847, at a time when cotton factories were on short time and its consequences would be little felt. Strengthened by the act of 1850 its principles were extended to other industries in 1860 when one of its former opponents candidly admitted that the earlier acts 'had contributed to the comfort and well-being of the working classes without materially injuring the masters'. The Public Health Act of 1848 delighted the Manchester School by its implication that bad housing, not factory labour, was the cause of disease. The Poor Law administration was placed under more direct control when it was ruled that the President of the Commissioners was to be an M.P., while some of the more stringent regulations were relaxed. In education an important administrative decision was taken in 1847 when Parliament resolved, despite the misgivings of Dissenters who feared the expense and the turning of schoolmasters into government agents, that extra pay and a pension should be available for teachers considered competent by a government inspector, while new teachers should be attracted by a subsidised apprenticeship scheme.   The scheme paid dividends in the improvement of the quality of teaching.[1]

Russell was a hard worker and a good speaker but one of his greatest failings was a lack of proportion, and nowhere was this more evident when an attempt on his part to turn an ecclesiastical crisis to his own political profit miscarried and started his long decline in public esteem.   In 1847 he had unwisely exposed the difficult relations of Church and State by insisting on the appointment of Dr Hampden, previously hounded by the Tractarians, to the bishopric of Hereford.[2] Many of the Whigs began to doubt his tact and judgment. More doubts were instilled when in 1850 Pope Pius IX issued a Bull restoring the Roman Catholic hierarchy in England and instituting twelve new episcopal sees.   Although the wording of the Bull seemed presumptuous to Protestant eyes it was clearly logical that there should be an Archbishop of Westminster rather than a Bishop of Melipotamus *in partibus*. Russell was concerned about the effect these claims might have on sound Anglicans whose beliefs, he considered, had already been undermined by the Tractarians; while, unsure of the support of the Peelites, he saw an opportunity to rally Protestant England.   Mindful of the success of the Edinburgh Letter, he composed the Durham Letter, addressed to the Bishop of that See, expressing his fears, and intended for publication.   The letter had been written on his own initiative but committed the party; initially it augured well.   It took the wind out of the sails of the Tories, who had seen 'No Popery' as a possible election issue.   An Ecclesiastical Titles Act was passed through Parliament, but remained a dead letter for the 'No Popery' tide was already turning.   *Punch* felt the Prime Minister had made himself ridiculous; the Whigs felt leadership of this sort could well be disastrous. This imprudence alienated the Irish vote and made the Peelites unwilling to serve under him.

It was these misgivings that were to foil Russell's desire to

---

[1] See above, p. 93 and below, p. 217.

[2] When the Dean declined to elect, Russell replied, 'Sir, I have the honour to receive your letter of the 22nd inst. in which you intimate to me your intention of violating the law.'

introduce another Reform Bill, of whose desirability he had been convinced by the orderly nature of the Chartist demonstrations.   He found himself unable to support Locke King's motion in February 1851 for a uniform borough and county franchise as it would increase the number of country voters dependent on the great landowners.   Many Radicals felt this to be hypocritical and the vote went against the government. Russell resigned; no one else proved able or willing to form a government and, somewhat discredited, Russell returned. This experience and the fall of Palmerston in December 1851 set the scene for Russell's own bill in February 1852, of which the main feature was a £5 household franchise in the boroughs. It was killed by indifference.   It has been argued that had Cobden championed suffrage reform, an act might have been passed, but Cobden feared that the Corn Law battle might have to be refought should the Tories return to power.   Radical distrust of Russell and parliamentary preoccupation with the supposed menace of Louis Napoleon proved fatal to the bill.

Russell had the misfortune, throughout his period of power, to be overshadowed by his Foreign Secretary, Lord Palmerston.   Though his first long tenure of the Foreign Office under Grey and Melbourne left, perhaps, the most positive achievements, it was between 1846 and 1851 that Palmerston was to reach the height of his unpopularity in Europe and with the Queen, and the height of his popularity at home.   He was single-minded in his interest in foreign politics and brooked no interference; he worked with unremitting industry.   He knew by instinct that the English were not really interested in foreign politics but in individuals, and he had a knack of exploiting this to strengthen his position at home.   With apparently gay abandon he denounced tyranny wherever it appeared in Europe; he 'gives them all the stomach ache' commented Lord Odo Russell.   It would be wrong to suppose him irresponsible; although his policy might seem to provoke war he was always careful to steer clear of it and would almost certainly have avoided the Crimean involvement had he been at the Foreign Office then.   He was convinced of the need to maintain the European balance of power, which could only be done by constant vigilance.   Cobden challenged the whole conception; he felt that in its defence Britain would acquire dangerous entanglements and that a policy of disarmament and free trade was preferable. But Palmerston was aware of the limitations of British power; and until the rise of Bismarck his instincts served him well. He was, however, the least diplomatic of diplomatists and his language created a distrust of English policy that lasted throughout the century and hardly profited the caused of constitutional liberty. In a sense he was supported by England's past prestige; how well he had called men's bluff was shown by his unexpected failure to prevent Bismarck wreaking his will on Denmark in 1864.

Whatever his diplomatic skill abroad, of his skill at home there could be no doubt. Unlike the other leading statesmen of the day he had the common touch in the lobbies and the ability to make, through the Press, a personal appeal to the public. This was the basis of his position: 'Palmerston is Mamma England's spoilt child,' wrote Bulwer Lytton, 'and the more mischief he does the more she admires him.' In his speeches, with an eye to the Press reports, he tried to put forward some general principle that would be remembered, showing himself to be master of the art of speaking in generalities that would appeal to the great majority of his audience while only alarming his most fixed opponents who could safely be made the objects of his ridicule.

There is a curious parallel between Palmerston's position at home and that of England abroad. He was essentially a nonparty figure in a period of party fluidity, attracting support from all parts of the House. He would have found no place in the more organised parties after 1867. So equally, with insubstantial and varying support, he steered his gunboat through the shallows and whirlpools of the European balance of power. Europe's very disorder was his opportunity, but the rise of Prussian power politics in 1864 was to leave him floundering in deep water.[1]

Palmerston's first foray in 1847 was not notably successful. He failed to understand the real complexity of Spanish politics and mishandled Guizot, with whom Aberdeen had worked amicably.[2] Though his hints at a Coburg candidature for the hand of Queen Isabella were provocative, neither he nor the Queen could excuse Louis Philippe's sharp practice in marrying his son to Isabella's sister before an heir was forthcoming.

The Anglo-French Entente was ruptured and the three Eastern Powers took the opportunity to end Polish independence. In the same year, however, he maintained Swiss independence which was threatened by a revolt of seven conservative and Roman Catholic cantons against the liberal and Protestant majority. He foresaw clearly that France and Austria would exploit the situation and obtained a conference of the Powers where he was able to preserve Swiss interests. The Swiss Federal Union was established.

His main aim, however, was not primarily liberalism but peace; he was convinced that this could be best preserved by persuading rulers to grant moderate constitutions to avert violent revolution. This was the purpose of Lord Minto's mission to Italy in 1847, inspired by the actions of an apparently liberal pope. When revolutions broke out in Italy in 1848, Palmerston considered it vital to make certain that Republican France did not intervene. He saw Piedmont's attack on Austria as preventing this, as bolstering Italian self-confidence and thus making French intervention unwelcome. He failed, however, to mediate jointly with France between Austria and Manin's Venetian Republic and thus was unable to prevent the French from agreeing to the restoration of Austrian dominance in northern Italy.

Despite his Italian sympathies and his earlier share in the creation of Greece and Belgium, it would be wrong to see Palmerston as a champion of nationalism – apart from British nationalism. Peace remained his objective. When revolutions broke out throughout Germany, 'Monarchs running about like a gang of coiners when the police had come among them,' as Carlyle put it, Palmerston was initially sympathetic to the idea of a united Germany that would involve no territorial changes but merely a partial surrender of sovereignty. Soon, however, he was convinced that the attitude of the Frankfurt Parliament was irresponsible, in view of its proposals for an attack on Poland in association with France and its designs on Schleswig-Holstein. This attitude was understandable at the time, though by failing to support the German nation in 1848 he was to open the way to a government far less responsible.

Although south of the Alps he was prepared to see the end of Austrian power, he was firmly convinced of the necessity of

Austria as the basis of stability to the north and did not hesitate to inform Prince Schwarzenberg that he should shape his policy in this way. He showed little sympathy for the Magyar Revolt of 1848–49 and refused to receive Kossuth's envoy. 'If Austria did not exist,' he told the Hungarians, 'it would have to be invented.' This did not prevent his feeling sympathy for the Hungarian victims of the Austrian and Russian reconquest. To the electors of Tiverton, Palmerston joked about the suggestion that he was 'the great instigator of revolution'. He insisted that Britain could state her opinions on any subject of European importance, though to do so might be a continual remonstration against the propagators of 'injustice and wrong'. These ideas were agreeable to the Liberals, while Tory support was forthcoming for their realism.

The Austrian excesses during their reconquest of Italy and of Hungary were very unpopular in England, and Palmerston felt he was quite justified in making a protest. Balance of power considerations also justified British support when the Sultan refused to surrender Polish and Hungarian refugees. This action produced in the British public the first signs of enthusiasm for Turkey, and Palmerston sent the British fleet to Besika Bay, comparing it to holding 'a bottle of salts to the nose of a lady who had been frightened'. With care he made a graceful Russian withdrawal possible; Austria followed reluctantly in 1851. The affair showed that Palmerston had secured French co-operation and that British foreign policy could be most effective where its sea power could be brought to play. In the Schleswig-Holstein affair, where he defended Denmark's traditional rights against the German desire to incorporate their chiefly German population into that of Germany, he failed to mediate effectively or to secure the support of Russia and Sweden. The compromise reached between Prussia and Denmark was fatal to the cause of German liberalism at Frankfurt without permanently settling one of the most complex problems of European diplomacy.[1]

On their return from 'judicious bottle-holding' in Besika Bay in 1850, the British fleet visited Athens. The Greek flag was saluted, the Admiral paid a courtesy call on King Otho, of whose methods of government Palmerston had previously

---

[1] See below, p. 191.

expressed his disapproval, and then seized merchant ships and cargoes as security against British claims which Greece had failed to honour. These included land owned by the historian Finlay which had been seized, and the property and goods of a Portuguese Jew born in Gibraltar named Don Pacifico. He was somewhat disreputable and his claims were exorbitant. Russia and France, co-guarantors with Britain of Greek independence, at once lodged protests. The Cabinet were committed, the Queen was furious and Cobden and his other opponents mounted a powerful attack in Parliament. To many Palmerston at last seemed doomed; but he was fortunate in his time. The British middle class had reached that point when, with economic leadership and naval supremacy apparently assured and nothing to complain of at home, a little foray into foreign politics with the spice of danger but not the risk of war, was just what they wanted. They 'liked his honesty', wrote Trollope, 'they liked his self-asserttion and they did not like it the less because he expressed himself with a hectoring tongue'. His triumph in the Don Pacifico debate was greater outside Parliament than within.

The debate was essentially about the rights of British intervention overseas rather than the correct way of interfering; here Palmerston succeeded in convincing both parties that he had always had the interests of England at heart. He recounted his successes in the past, he proclaimed his position as the reconciler of freedom and law in a Europe shadowed by tyranny and revolution. To make his speech memorable he relied on a striking phrase; just as the Roman of old could say 'Civis Romanus sum' and have the might of the Empire in his support, so might the Briton 'feel confident that the watchful eye and strong arm of England will protect him against injustice and wrong'.

The Greeks gave way; Palmerston's colleagues stood by him, disapproving but aware that he was stronger than they were; one of his frequent and rarely kept promises of good behaviour went to the Palace; while he could be proclaimed as 'the most English Minister that ever governed England'. In an impressive speech Gladstone answered him the following day, maintaining the principle of non-intervention in the domestic affairs of other countries. But Palmerston's position was secure.

The Queen and Prince Albert had long viewed his behaviour with disapproval. Their sympathies tended to the conservative side in European politics and they were frequently embarrassed by letters from brother monarchs and their numerous relatives who failed to appreciate the precise constitutional relationships of England, and irritated by what they felt, unfairly, to be Palmerston's lack of sympathy with monarchies. The Queen complained, with justice, that action was taken in her name without her previous knowledge – and indeed in some cases without the knowledge of the Cabinet. Walter Bagehot was shortly to enunciate the thesis that the Sovereign had the right to be consulted, to encourage and to warn, and it was essentially these rights that the Queen claimed. The boundaries of influence and control, however, are not always clear, and faced with the Queen's formidable personality and Albert's sense of mission, which was often practised in a way that made him most unpopular,[1] it is not surprising that Palmerston was suspicious that the power of England might be used for Coburg aggrandisement. Thoughts of the 'cottage coterie' of George IV came to mind. Even Clarendon, a later Foreign Secretary, remarked, 'The Queen and the Prince laboured under the curious mistake that the foreign office is their particular department and they have a right to control, if not to direct, the foreign policy of England.' Undoubtedly there were extenuating circumstances: pressure of business on the small Foreign Office staff and the Queen's frequent absences at Balmoral and Osborne which might mean dangerous delays. But Palmerston was no respecter of persons, however highly placed, especially when they had been born ten years after his first appointment to office.

Russell found himself in a difficult position. He resented Palmerston's independence and popularity but was aware that his support was necessary to his ministry and, as a true Whig, was suspicious of any monarchical encroachments on policy-making. In August 1850, however, while ensuring the Queen's support for any Cabinet decisions she might disapprove, he persuaded Palmerston to accept a memorandum from the Queen requiring that she should be kept fully informed and that, once stated, policy should not be arbi-

---

[1] It has been remarked that his 'chief crimes were two; that he was a foreigner and not a fool' (J. W. Tilby, *Russell*).

trarily altered or modified. 'To their wishes and remonstrances he expresses the greatest deference,' wrote the diarist Greville, 'and then goes on his own course without paying the least attention to what they had been saying to him.'

Two further incidents earned royal displeasure. When General Haynau who had behaved savagely in Hungary, visited London, he toured Barclay's Brewery and was mobbed by the workmen.[1] Palmerston convinced the Cabinet that a prosecution would make the government unpopular and refused to apologise to the Austrian government, maintaining that Haynau's visit was in itself a provocation. At the Queen's insistence he was more conciliatory. The following year the exiled Magyar leader Kossuth visited England and was fêted by Radical politicians and the Radical Press. Palmerston, who had planned a private reception, desisted at Russell's request, but mentioned his regard for Kossuth to a Radical deputation, which was almost as bad.

Shortly after this, in December 1851, Louis Napoleon's *coup d'état* made him master of France and Palmerston expressed his approval to the French ambassador. The official British policy, as approved by the Queen, was one of strict neutrality towards France. Palmerston, however, had been convinced that the stability of Europe required a strongly governed France and that it would be an act of statesmanship to conciliate the new ruler. No reference was made to Russell or to the British ambassador in Paris, Lord Normanby. Normanby's brother-in-law, Colonel Phipps, was Prince Albert's Treasurer, and the Queen, who had agreed with Russell on a strictly neutral attitude to a *coup d'état* which had caused unnecessary bloodshed, pressed for Palmerston's dismissal. Russell concurred and to public surprise and bewilderment, the 'people's darling' fell from power. Prince Schwarzenberg, the Austrian Chancellor, gave a celebration ball, while in doggerel the Chartist *Reynolds News* prophesied

> Haynau and the Russian Tsar
> Will curse him in their realms afar
> And on their feelings it will jar
> To find old Palmy stronger.

The result was that the French government was not well disposed towards England and a revival of French militarism

[1] He was tossed in a blanket and pursued by workmen with broomsticks.

was anxiously foretold. To alleviate public concern Russell introduced a local militia bill in February 1852. Palmerston carried against the government by eleven votes an amendment reviving the old national militia eligible for service overseas. Sensing that he no longer had a reliable majority, Russell resigned and a militia bill on Palmerston's lines was carried into law by the new government.

The fall of the Whigs brought in the Tories, but they were in no position to rule. Not only were they in a minority but they lacked the leaders to overcome this disadvantage. The career of Stanley, now Lord Derby, had been full of early promise and until he disagreed over policy he had seemed Grey's natural successor as Premier. Then he had drifted to the Tories, becoming a Protectionist in 1846. His reputation made him the natural leader of that party, though he led without enthusiasm. The leader in the Commons was Disraeli, as alien in temperament to Derby as any man could be yet dependent on Derby's prestige to hold the party together and to secure for himself social acceptance. That the two men worked together without serious clash spoke much for their discretion. Initially it was hoped that Palmerston might join, despite Albert's warning that if he did he would make himself Prime Minister, a thought that was the Consort's recurrent nightmare. Palmerston would not accept protection, however, and contented himself with advising the new Foreign Secretary, Lord Malmesbury, who continued a policy of conciliation towards France.

Dependent on the capriciousness of 'majorities collected God knows how and voting God knows why', as Disraeli put it, the policy of the government was bound to be chiefly one of expediency. The *Edinburgh Review* described it as 'the first administration which reduced inconsistency to a system and want of principles to a principle'. Disraeli at times advocated unlikely alliances as with ultra-Whigs such as Lord Grey or with the Manchester School, but the flexibility of the party was in the long run an asset. Immediately, their attitude to protection had to be determined. Disraeli, whom the Queen had accepted with misgivings as Chancellor of the Exchequer, introduced a non-committal budget soon after taking office and at the General Election in the summer of 1852, Tory candidates ignored the question if they could.

It was held that a Tory was 'Protectionist in a county, neutral in a small town, a free trader in a larger one'. In fact, in view of the evident prosperity of the country under free trade Derby and Disraeli had lost their faith in protection yet naturally found it difficult to commit their party to a doctrine they had so bitterly opposed. The new Parliament found Whigs and Tories evenly matched, with the Peelites holding the balance, but drawing towards the Whigs.

In November Villiers' resolution in favour of free trade, which intended to commit the government or force its resignation, was badly handled by Disraeli and the administration was only saved by a conciliatory amendment brought forward by Palmerston. The following month Disraeli's second budget formally abandoned protection, hoping to conciliate agricultural interests by a halving of the malt duty and the increase of urban taxation. Despite his undoubted qualities as leader of the House, where he had impressed all parties by his endurance, tact and readiness of repartee, and amused and reassured the Queen by his unusual accounts of its business, Disraeli was no economist. He sat down after a five-hour speech replete with rhetoric to be confronted by Gladstone, a master of the craft, who tore his economic arguments to shreds and poured scorn on his oratorical devices. It was a battle such as the Commons had hardly experienced since the days of Pitt and Fox, the first of many between the two great parliamentary masters of the age. At a 4 a.m. division, in a tense atmosphere, the Budget proposal to extend the tax on houses to those of £10 rateable value was defeated by eleven votes and the government resigned.

(b) Aberdeen and the Crimean War, 1852–55

'England does not love coalitions', Disraeli declared in his last speech as Chancellor, yet a coalition was the only possible outcome. Russell aspired to be Prime Minister once more but since the Durham Letter the Whigs distrusted him and Palmerston declined to serve under him. Many politicians on the other hand, were unwilling to serve under Palmerston while Derby had neither the political strength nor the will to return to power. In such circumstances the Monarch, constitutionally, plays a prominent role, and the outcome, though seen by some to be the Cabinet Sir Robert Peel would

have formed had he been alive, was more obviously the fruit
of Prince Albert's political ideals.   The new Premier, Lord
Aberdeen, formerly Foreign Secretary under Peel, was highly
regarded by many as a counsellor of the highest distinction.
He had been in politics for nearly fifty years, yet remained
somewhat of a recluse, uneasy in his human relationships and
highly sensitive.   Given a fair passage he might hold together
a difficult Cabinet; given the pitfalls that awaited him he
lacked leadership and control.

The Cabinet was described as a 'Ministry of all the Talents'
and it had general support in the Commons.   The various
elements of this support, however, were unequally represented.
The Radicals had only one representative, the Whigs six,
including Palmerston at the Home Office, where the Queen
considered he would be safe, and Russell at the Foreign Office
with an option to resign it to Lord Clarendon.   The Peelites,
very much fewer in number, also had six Cabinet ministers.
Sir James Graham took the Admiralty, the Duke of Newcastle
War and the Colonies, while Gladstone became Chancellor of
the Exchequer, perhaps inevitably in the circumstances.   It
was a strong team, but it was not agreed on essentials, and a
man who invariably replied to any suggestion of action that
it would break up the Cabinet, was not the man for its captain.

At the Home Office Palmerston showed a capacity for
administration and a modest interest in safe social reforms,
encouraged by his son-in-law, Lord Shaftesbury.   At the
Treasury Gladstone, by his expert management and his
continuation of the free trade policy, gave the ministry its
chief claim to distinction.

Gladstone had always regarded himself as a Conservative,
faithful to the name, policy and ideals of Peel, and it was an
important step in his career when he sat in the same Cabinet
as Whigs and Radicals.   It was also an important stage in the
development of the office of Chancellor of the Exchequer, for
Gladstone's tenure, following immediately upon that of
Disraeli who had also been leader of the House, was to make
it the second place in the Cabinet.   He worked longer hours
than any other Minister and astounded his subordinates by
his capacity.   The permanent officials of the Treasury were
delighted by a chief who penetrated so quickly to the root of
every difficulty.   His spirit of care, caution and economy

permeated the department and lasted well into the 20th Century.   No Chancellor prepared his Budgets more carefully or made more thorough use of every conceivable source of information.   Money was a trust from God, he felt, and it was wrong for the State to require any more from its citizens than it positively needed.   Unashamedly he rejoiced in a policy of 'cheese-parings and candle-ends'.

Public opinion was anxious to get rid of the income tax which had been reintroduced by Peel in 1842.   Gladstone was convinced of the immorality of the tax except in an emergency.   It tempted the individual to fraud and statesmen to extravagance; its demands pressed 'too hard on intelligence and skill'.   He wished to leave money to 'fructify in the pockets of the people'.   He kept the tax, intending to scale it down and out over a period of seven years, a hope which was frustrated by the Crimean War and which has proved illusory ever since.   He removed 123 articles from the customs tariff.   The Cabinet was dubious about the Budget and surprised at its popularity.   He tried to pay for the Crimean War by increases in taxation, the income tax rising to 1s. 2d., but his successor, Sir G. Cornewall Lewis, could not manage without a loan.

Russell's position in the Cabinet was an awkward one.   He remembered perpetually that he had been Prime Minister and was difficult to the last degree.   During his short period at the Foreign Office, he made two decisions that were to have important consequences.   The first was when he decided to send Lord Stratford de Redcliffe back to Constantinople. Stratford personally disliked the Tsar and dominated the Sultan.   His authority at the Porte was immense and no one could equal his opportunities to reform the Turks.   But the Turks had an endless capacity for going back on their promises and Stratford's presence in Constantinople helped to convince them that, right or wrong, reformed or not, in the last resort Britain would save them from destruction.   Russell's second decision was to reject the Tsar's offer of a secret understanding between Britain and Russia for the settlement of the Eastern Question.   This was particularly unfortunate in that both Powers had been basically agreed since 1841 on the desirability of maintaining a weak Turkey,[1] and it was primarily French

<hr>
[1] See above, p. 109.

M

action that aggravated the situation. Both these decisions
can be justified and it is possible that undue Russian influence
might have resulted from an alternative. That they were
crucial is not in doubt.

Russell resigned twelve days after Parliament met and
continued to lead the House without a portfolio. His
successor was Clarendon whose suave and nebulous despatches
hardly clarified the situation.

In 1852, with an eye to French clerical support, Napoleon
III took up the claims of Latin monks to a share in the Church
of the Holy Sepulchre, a right originally granted in 1740 but
restricted by the Turks to Greek monks only in 1808.
Malmesbury had warned the French that this would provoke
the Russians and when the Turks, impressed by a naval
demonstration, made the concession and also, under Austrian
pressure, called off a projected invasion of Montenegro, the
Tsar decided on a diplomatic offensive. He believed this
would obtain the support of Aberdeen, with whom he was
personally acquainted, and he was confident of Austrian
support after the help he had given her in Hungary. In February 1853 Prince Menshikov arrived in Constantinople,
began with insult and then, having impressed the Turks with
his importance, demanded a reversal of the Holy Places
decision and a confirmation of the Russian claim to a protectorate over the Orthodox Christians in Turkey, which was
based on the Treaty of Kuchuk Kainardji of 1774. To ensure
English support, Nicholas hinted at a mutually advantageous
partition of the Ottoman Empire.

Stratford arrived at Constantinople at this point. He had
little difficulty in outwitting Menshikov and persuaded the
Turks to expel the Latin monks but to turn down the Russian
demands for a protectorate, which could in the long run undermine Turkish sovereignty. Menshikov departed in a rage and
to forestall a Russian occupation of the Danubian Principalities of Moldavia and Wallachia, the French fleet, followed by
the British, went for 'judicious bottle-holding' duty outside the
Dardanelles. Napoleon had no wish for war but he was on
the hunt for prestige and was determined on an Anglo-French
alliance, without which revision of the Treaties of 1815 would
be impossible. Nevertheless the Russian armies crossed the
Pruth, ostensibly to counteract Anglo-French influence, and

on 6th July entered Bucharest. Palmerston urged that the British fleet should enter the Black Sea but was overruled by the Cabinet who decided to support negotiations at Vienna.

Diplomacy could indeed, it was felt, easily adjust a matter that Menshikov's behaviour and the Tsar's precipitate action had only complicated. The Powers at Vienna drew up a Note which was thought to remedy Russian grievances without endangering Turkish sovereignty. Turkey would not change the conditions of the Christians without previous agreement with the governments of France and Russia. The Russians accepted the Note, of whose contents they were already aware. The Turks, however, had not been consulted and rejected it on the grounds that it would establish a joint Franco-Russian Protectorate, a view perhaps justified when the Russians announced a similar interpretation. This caused a flurry of withdrawals; war-fever mounted both in Russia and in Turkey, where the Sultan was threatened with revolution.

Mediation was renewed when, in September, Nicholas met Francis Joseph and Frederick William at Olmütz. Count Buol, the Austrian Minister, attempted, with French approval, to reinstate the Vienna Note with explanations that should have satisfied Turkey, but Aberdeen and Clarendon were distrustful and, showing a resolution that should have come earlier and in different ways, ordered the British fleet to Constantinople. Thus encouraged, the Turks could no longer be controlled; they sent an army into the Principalities, and into the Black Sea a light flotilla which was destroyed by the Russian fleet at Sinope on 30th November. Although a perfectly legitimate naval action it aroused a storm of protest in Great Britain.

The country was drifting towards war under Aberdeen's irresolute leadership. If Aberdeen had been master of his Cabinet, he would have made concessions to avoid war; given better support at home Stratford might have restrained the Turks. Palmerston, on the other hand, might have obtained a Russian withdrawal while with almost any Prime Minister but Aberdeen the Russians would not have assumed so readily English neutrality. Napoleon III's bluff that he would act alone was believed and led to the fatal ordering of the Allied fleets to enter the Black Sea. Misunderstandings and misconceptions were rife and permitted the drift to war, though the Russian demands could hardly have been obtained in any other way.   Public opinion, particularly in England, was not blameless.

Encouraged by Palmerston to make moral judgments about Europe, enchanted by Kossuth, whom the Turks had saved from his oppressors, rapidly substituting Nicholas for Napoleon as the ogre of Europe, English public opinion saw the Turks as a plucky little nation oppressed by the enemy of freedom.   Of the fact that the Turks were even more tyrannical and corrupt it was blissfully unaware and, indeed, the densest ignorance prevailed about Turkey as Kingsley Martin has amusingly described in *The Triumph of Lord Palmerston*. Through articles in *The Morning Post* Palmerston urged a strong policy to bring the Tsar to heel and in its turn public opinion urged the government to take decisive action.   The prospect of war was welcomed; it seemed attractive to a generation that had never known its realities.

At this point Russell pledged himself to introduce a Reform Bill; Palmerston made difficulties and resigned from the Cabinet on 19th December, ostensibly on this issue but at a crucial point in the Eastern Question.   The purpose of the manœuvre was not to detach himself from an unpopular Cabinet but to prevent Russell from doing so.   Public opinion at once assumed that the Queen was responsible. When, in response to popular clamour, linked with the public reaction to Sinope, Palmerston was prevailed upon to return, it was widely rumoured that Prince Albert had been sent to the Tower for treachery.   In January the joint fleets entered the Black Sea and popular enthusiasm dreamed of resolute action against the Tsar in Finland, marches deep into the Ukraine and declarations of freedom for Poland.   Aberdeen had always maintained that war was impossible unless Austria was an ally, but this proviso drifted away.   It was impossible to withdraw without disgrace and in March 1854 war was declared on Russia on the grounds that the balance of power necessitated the defence of Turkey.

The will to war was present, but the means were lacking. The Army had stagnated since Waterloo; its administration was inefficient and badly organised; Parliament had kept it permanently short of money.   The low pay and harsh conditions had attracted a poor type of soldier, 'the scum of the earth enlisted for drink'. Clothing was too tight at all times, too hot in summer, not warm enough in winter. Living conditions were if anything worse than those provided for convicts and the mortality rate in a barracks in Britain was far higher than that among the civilians of the locality. In certain foreign stations such as Jamaica and Sierra Leone it reached appalling proportions. Discipline was brutally harsh; in 1850 punishment was restricted to fifty lashes at any one time. Rations were monotonous and inadequate. Commissions and promotions were by purchase, and well-connected officers frequently transferred if their regiment was to be sent abroad. The only true professionals were men with service in India who were rarely promoted to high rank. Military training, apart from the parade ground, was largely neglected. The true triumph of the Crimean War was the courage, devotion to duty and cheerfulness under appalling conditions that marked the British soldier.

Lord Raglan was the British commander. A courageous and sincere man, he had last seen service at Waterloo and lacked the knowledge to make the best use of his troops and of his commissariat. He had the engaging habit of referring to the enemy as 'The French'. The cavalry commander Lord Lucan and his subordinate and brother-in-law Lord Cardigan were on terms of enmity; the latter had his yacht sent out to the Crimea and commanded his brigade from there. Few of the senior officers had any real military ability.

The Navy was little better. Sailors were under no engagement of continuous service until 1853, while many officers had spent years on half-pay. Parliament had kept the fleet short of money and the Navy was slow to adopt steam-power and iron. Most of the admirals were over seventy and out of touch with recent developments: Sir Charles Napier, ordered to take an expedition to the Baltic, encouraged his men with the words, 'Sharpen your cutlasses, and the day is ours.' The Admiralty had little knowledge of Baltic coastal fortifications: most of the ships were too heavy in draught for inshore work and the fleet merely captured a few merchant ships and blockaded Russian ports.

The first base of land operations was Varna on the Black Sea coast, from which an attack was to be made on the

Principalities. Within a week the sanitation had broken down and disease was rife. Meanwhile the Tsar was under pressure from Austria and Prussia to withdraw and finally did so in August. With no enemy to fight it seemed imperative to find the Army some occupation and the Cabinet ordered Raglan to attack Sebastopol, the fortified base of the Russian Black Sea fleet in the Crimea. After a chaotic embarkation at Varna where many valuable supplies and horses had to be abandoned owing to lack of transports, the Allied armies landed at Calamita Bay, north of Sebastopol, for an autumn campaign.

Basically this was sound strategy and Sebastopol should have fallen rapidly. The British troops were transferred too slowly, however, and the Russians had a chance to reinforce. No effort was made to cut off the Crimea from the rest of Russia; and after the victory of the River Alma on 20th September the French refused to collaborate in an immediate attack on the town. Evidence suggests it would have fallen easily. However, the Allies now began a circular investment of the town and thus committed soldiers sent out to a summer campaign in the Balkans to a winter campaign in very different circumstances. Militarily they held their ground despite Russian attempts to dislodge them at Balaclava on 25th October, a battle made memorable by the disastrous and unnecessary charge of the Light Brigade, and at Inkerman on 5th November, where the British artillery did much damage.

The coming of winter meant that the campaign ground to a halt; the appalling conditions were sufficient enemy. Raglan failed to build a road from Balaclava harbour to the lines until the following spring, when a light railway was also constructed. In November a severe gale and blizzard had wrecked ships and ruined supplies. Fuel was short, sanitation inadequate. The men paid with their lives for their commanders' lack of foresight and for parliamentary niggardliness in failing to supply the money for adequate transport and supply services. Cholera, dysentery and malarial fever broke out, the hospital ships were over-crowded and nearly one-tenth of the sick and wounded died on their way to the base hospitals at Scutari. There the complacency of the chief medical officer, Dr John Hall, filth, neglect and bad nursing contributed their toll. The arrival of Florence Nightingale and other intelligent women in November led to a slight improvement.

Her mission had been prompted by the graphic accounts that were reaching England from the numerous uncensored war correspondents, notably W. H. Russell of *The Times*. Primitive photographs of the trenches and sketches in such publications as *The Illustrated London News* made the public, with its growing conception of moral accountancy, less ready to condone the mistakes. Newcastle, the War Minister, was amiable but inept and Russell had urged his replacement by Palmerston in June. But Aberdeen distrusted both men and stubbornly refused to make the change. Public concern, however, was mounting. Delane, editor of *The Times*, ceaselessly castigated the administration. Aberdeen entirely lacked the qualities of a war Premier, at the Treasury Gladstone insisted on ruthless economies, while incompetence in office, at Cabinet level or below, was not met with dismissal. The Radicals in particular were furious; some like Bright had incurred unpopularity by denouncing the war from the start. Roebuck, the member for Sheffield, whose independence was his greatest asset and whose favourite word was 'sham', called for a select committee of inquiry into the conduct of the war in January 1855.

Any chance the government might have had of resisting Roebuck's motion was removed when Russell promptly resigned. 'To escape punishment, he ran away from duty,' as Gladstone put it. He had consistently been a bad colleague throughout the war and this action was fatal to his reputation. Both Russell and Gladstone were aware that the trouble had arisen because the spirit of reform that had permeated elsewhere had not yet reached the War Office, but Gladstone opposed the committee on the grounds that it would increase the confusion. The latest reports from the Crimea told of 18,000 effective troops against 14,000 dead, only one-sixth of which were caused by battle, and 22,000 sick. Against this there could be no defence and the Ministers were beaten by 305 to 148. Silence was followed by derisive laughter. The government resigned.

The only man with a party was Derby and both historians and contemporaries have thought that he should have been able to form a government and would certainly have had the

country behind him.   Disraeli was bitterly disappointed and
was forced to realise that Derby's lack of confidence in him
was partly responsible.   Derby, while believing that the
inclusion of Palmerston and Gladstone was essential, considered that Palmerston's price, the leadership of the Commons, would have made him effectively Premier and was too
high.   Lansdowne explored in vain.   Russell found no one of
consequence would serve under him—except for Palmerston,
who stipulated the leadership of the Commons for himself and
a peerage for Russell.   The Queen refused to consider
Clarendon, whom she felt to be wanting in courage, an odd
objection after Aberdeen. It was evident that Palmerston held
the key and Prince Albert's nightmare became a reality when
the Queen asked him to form an administration. 'I am
l'inévitable', he wrote to his brother.

(c) PALMERSTON, 1855-65

Palmerston had no difficulty in forming a Cabinet, though
Gladstone and the other Peelites resigned out of loyalty to
Aberdeen when Palmerston decided to proceed with the
committee of inquiry.   Gladstone's action was regarded as
irresponsible and unpatriotic.   Russell came in for a while,
Cornewall Lewis went to the Exchequer and Lord Panmure
proved to be little improvement on Newcastle at the War
Office.   Palmerston did not think highly of his new colleagues
but he was loyal, as always, to the aristocratic principle which
Roebuck and his associates hoped particularly to discredit.
The committee's report blamed not individuals but the system
and the government had to agree to an amendment stressing
the need to overhaul the administration and to allow for
promotion on merit.   The Radicals doubted whether 'the
whiskered wonder of seventy years' was likely to save the Army
from the difficulties into which it had been led by 'the
aristocratic system, a system of total incapacity'.   In 1855 an
Administrative Reform Association was set up in London, and
working-class journals asked why it was that the great railway
administrators and contractors were not employed to organise
the supply.   A few concessions were made: the Civil Service
Commissioners were set up to examine the fitness of candidates
and Civil Service pay was increased to attract the career man.
The ordnance was incorporated as part of the War Office, an

improved naval supply service was organised, with a regular shuttle service of ships between the Crimea and Scutari. A Sanitary Commission sent out to the East was invaluable and with its help Florence Nightingale and Alex Soyer, the chef of the Reform Club, were able to make substantial improvements at Scutari. In the Crimea, however, the old obstructionism remained and had Sebastopol not fallen before the next winter, there is no evidence that conditions would have been much better.

Despite his immense vitality and the touching confidence the British public had in him, Palmerston was too old and insufficiently ruthless to be an effective war Premier and to overcome forty years of neglect. He was not prepared to take the gamble urged on him by Granville and to promote comparatively junior officers of talent to high command, as Chatham had done in similar circumstances. His appointment of General Simpson, a man constantly embarrassed by his lack of aristocratic connections, to succeed Raglan when he died in June 1855, was disastrous. Sir Colin Campbell would have been a better appointment. Panmure was an inept War Minister, who was increasingly dominated by his permanent officials. It has been suggested[1] that the Tory Ellenborough would have been a better choice or perhaps Palmerston himself.

The Russians were having some success to the east of the Black Sea but despite this no attempt was made to clear them out of the Crimea or to carry the campaign into the Ukraine. Radical demands for peace had been insistent, reaching their highest point when, in February, Bright made his famous 'Angel of Death' speech. But by allying ourselves with France we had tied ourselves to a government dependent on recurrent military success and until Sebastopol was taken Napoleon would not open negotiations.

Despite Simpson's infectious conviction that Sebastopol would not fall, the town was taken in September, by which time there were ominous signs that British discipline was cracking. The Tsar had died in March, and his successor Alexander II was more disposed to be reasonable. Austrian mediation had already secured Russian agreement to a European guarantee of the Principalities, nominally under Turkish suzerainty, from

[1] By R. Southgate in *The Most English Minister*.

which the independent state of Roumania was to develop, and the navigation of the Danube was to be free to all nations. Both these had been virtually settled by the Russian withdrawal and the Russians also agreed to drop their claim to a protectorate.

The Congress of Paris confirmed these. It was the high-water mark of Napoleon III's European diplomacy and throughout it there was always the risk that a secret agreement between Russia and France would be made. In consequence Anglo-French relations were strained. Britain returned the Aland Islands in the Baltic which had been captured, on condition that they were not fortified. The Russians also agreed that their warships should be exlcuded from the Black Sea and that they would not construct any fortifications on its shores. Lacking any sanction other than Russian good faith this undertaking was repudiated in 1870 during the Franco-Prussian war. In the meantime its removal became the priority of Russian diplomatists: the fact that it could be imposed at all marked the loss of prestige that Russia had suffered from what had been in essence a successful though very limited invasion. Russia had intervened in the 1848 Revolutions; the war ensured that she was not to do so to prevent Italian and German unification. Alexander II embarked on a series of social reforms, including the emancipation of the serfs in 1861. Austria was left isolated diplomatically: the Russians felt she had ill-requited their assistance of 1849. Turkish promises to reform continued to mean little despite Palmerston's hopes; she was saved from outside dictation but it was at the expense of the continued misgovernment of her subject peoples. Neither Polish nor Finnish independence featured in the peace talks and there was no serious discussion of Italian problems, although Cavour of Sardinia, which had sent troops to the Crimea towards the end of the war, frequently raised the subject. To public opinion, which had had high hopes of the war, even seeing it as a Christian crusade against tyrranical government, the terms of the peace were a disappointment and the heralds who announced it were hissed at Temple Bar. No thorough administrative reform had been secured, nor had the Army won victories to restore its shattered prestige, but so great was Palmerston's reputation that it was concluded that peace must be necessary and not discreditable, or he never would have agreed to it.

The lessons of the Crimea were not fully heeded. British inefficiency convinced the Great Powers right up to 1914 that Britain was militarily ineffective, although the wars against Napoleon had not shown this. At home, although there were some improvements, the war produced no outstanding soldier to eradicate the weaknesses. Nevertheless there was greater concern for the private soldier: the V.C. was instituted and opened to all ranks, model hospitals were built at Netley and Woolwich and permanent camps were established. By exposing aristocratic inefficiency, the war tended to enhance the value of democracy.

Many of the troops had to be transferred almost immediately to India where a mutiny of the native troops of the East India Company had broken out in May 1857. Having come to trade and stayed to rule, the British in India in the early 19th Century had become gradually aware that their obligations to the country exceeded the maintenance of law and order. It was recognised on the one hand that the framework of existing Indian law and society should be preserved, and the Act of 1833 which had renewed the East India Company's Charter and virtually restricted it to administration had inferred that native Indians should be employed in administrative positions. On the other hand, to western eyes Indian society was seen to be backward, unjust and inefficient, and it was felt it should give way where it conflicted with the benefits of superior education, technology and law that the British brought. Many of his contemporaries would have agreed with J. S. Mill when he defended the Company's rule as 'one of the purest in intention and one of the most beneficent in act ever known to mankind'.

Nevertheless the Indians would not have agreed. Although from the utilitarian point of view many of the reforms were excellent, they showed little regard for Indian feelings and, in such cases as interference with the laws of inheritance and permitting the remarriage of widows (the custom of *suttee* whereby the widow sacrificed herself on the funeral pyre of her husband had earlier been banned) struck at the roots of Indian custom and society. Both these were decisions of Lord Dalhousie, whose Governor-Generalship from 1848–56 must be regarded as a principal underlying cause of the Mutiny.

Dalhousie was benevolent and progressive. Railways, canals, cheap postage, the electric telegraph, engineering colleges were all introduced. In order to extend the benefits of British rule, he followed the policy of lapse whereby native states without a direct heir fell under British jurisdiction, thus ignoring the long-established Indian custom of adoption. In 1856 he annexed the Kingdom of Oudh, where much of the Bengal army was raised, on grounds of misrule. That British administration was in part responsible is borne out by proclamations issued by the sepoys during the Mutiny which spoke of the *zemindar* or tax-farmer broken by many assessments and the delays of British courts, the merchants restricted to the 'trade in trifles', the upper classes denied their rightful status, the learned who saw Moslem schools and colleges being destroyed. The Indians, they claimed, were promised 'no better employment than making roads and digging canals'.

The victories of Clive and his contemporaries, often against overwhelming odds, had given the British Army a long-lived prestige. But defeats in Afghanistan in 1842 and in the Crimean War had greatly reduced it, and the number of troops in India had been cut to below the level of safety. Native troops greatly outnumbered British, the artillery was almost entirely native and many of the officers were unenterprising and elderly.

In the 18th Century many Englishmen had lived semi-Indianised lives, frequently marrying Indian women. They had taken considerable interest in Indian architecture and culture and had shown an easy tolerance towards the more distasteful aspects of Indian life. The stricter moral tone of 19th-century society brought a greater tendency to criticise while the greater speed of steam-ships meant that tours of duty were shorter and there was less readiness to regard India as home. British wives also appeared and were instrumental in holding the British aloof, with lasting damage to inter-racial relations.

The Army had some specific grievances. The question of caste had been badly handled, high caste soldiers being placed under low caste officers. It was intended to send troops to Burma and a sea passage could entail loss of caste. The land system of Oudh, where many of the soldiers were recruited, was not understood by English officials and some injustice was done. New cartridges, whose ends had to be bitten, were issued, smeared with grease of uncertain origin. The story spread that it was intended to defile the Hindu or Moslem or both and was believed partly because Canning, the new Governor-General, had been preceded by the rumour that he came to persecute the religions of India and force conversion to Christianity. Indian troops who refused to bite cartridges would, it was believed, be disbanded or shot.

Although Indian historians have called it "The Great Revolt" it was never a national rising. Many Indian troops remained loyal and fought on the British side; Indian cooks and grooms continued to serve. Hardly more than one-quarter of the sepoys in the Bengal army took part. There had been mutinies before and this one would hardly have attracted so much attention had it not been for its ferocity and the failure of the senior officers to suppress it rapidly. It spread from Meerut among troops in the Ganges, Jumna and Gogra valleys but by June it was virtually limited to a triangle containing the towns of Delhi, Cawnpore and Lucknow. The Ridge above Delhi was recaptured by a small British force and in September the town itself fell to Nicholson after bitter fighting. Cawnpore was captured by a dispossessed prince, Nana Sahib, who replied to the punishments already meted out to mutineers by killing most of the garrison, including women and children. W. H. Russell, who had arrived in India, was horrified by the brutality on both sides. Many British officers saw the Mutiny as filial ingratitude and wished for vengeance. Cawnpore was recaptured in July.

Nana Sahib then besieged Lucknow with 60,000 sepoys. Lawrence held out in the Residency and its surroundings with a garrison of 2,000 until September, when Havelock reinforced him. In November Sir Colin Campbell finally relieved the town. Its defence and the holding of the Ridge by Nicholson did much to restore British prestige. British superiority, reinforced by the telegraph and the Enfield rifle, ensured a restoration of full British control in 1858 although Canning's order, depriving of their land those of the landowners in Oudh who had helped the rebels, prolonged the trouble.

On the whole, however, 'Clemency' Canning handled the Mutiny calmly; he avoided panic measures and protested against vindictive punishments. Palmerston supported him well, once the Queen had forced him to recognise the gravity of the situation, and he despatched troops efficiently and chose good commanders, particularly Sir Hugh Rose who conducted a brilliant campaign in a disaffected area of central India, taking the town of Jhansi, whose ruler supported the rebels. The effect of the Mutiny, nevertheless, was to exacerbate Anglo-Indian relations. The British tended to become more aloof and more determined to do good, whether their efforts were appreciated by the Indians or not. The Indians turned to religious obscurantism. Materially there were great improvements but a gulf grew between rulers and ruled.

Perhaps unreasonably the East India Company was held to be culpable. Derby's government introduced in 1858 the Government of India Act, which with a carefully worded proclamation guaranteeing religious freedom, abolished the Company and annexed India to the Crown. This in fact meant less parliamentary control, not more, especially as all finance for Indian government was raised in India. When the Charter had come up for renewal there had been at least a reappraisal of British aims and methods. Now that there was government by a Secretary of State there was scant parliamentary interest.[1]

At home Palmerston's ascendancy seemed complete. Party feeling was neither strong nor purposeful. His competitors were neither attractive to the average M.P. nor to public opinion; Derby was inactive, Disraeli distrusted, Russell discredited, while Gladstone, though recognised as a man of talent, had no personal following and apparently no purpose. The government was often defeated but it continued to be supported because there seemed no prospect of an alternative government with a stable majority. 'Conservative ministers working with Radical tools and keeping up a show of liberation in their foreign policy' made effective opposition difficult. In the political field as a whole there was considerable equilibrium, over which Palmerston was well fitted to preside. The middle class on the whole were satisfied with the gains they had made, the sting of Chartism had been drawn while the working classes were growing in prosperity and were not yet ready for political influence. Though

---

[1] For later history of British relations with India see below, p. 235 and p. 506.

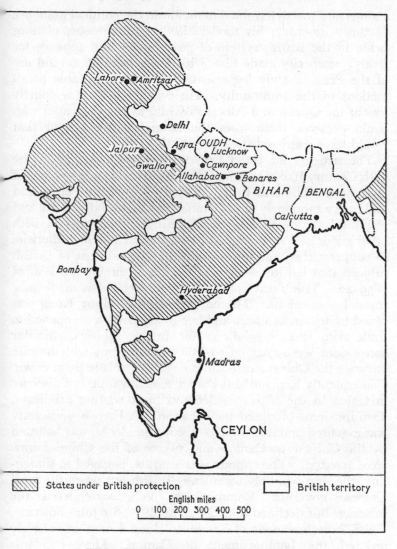

Lahore ● Amritsar

● Delhi

Jaipur ● ● Agra OUDH
Gwalior ● ● Lucknow
Allahabad ● ● Cawnpore
● Benares

BIHAR | BENGAL

● Calcutta

Bombay ●

● Hyderabad

● Madras

CEYLON

States under British protection   British territory

English miles

0   100 200 300 400 500

INDIA AT THE TIME OF THE MUTINY

With acknowledgement to P. Spear, *The Oxford History of Modern India, 1740–1947*
(published by O.U.P.)

Palmerston was determined to maintain the political influence of the aristocracy, his moderation, good humour, obvious pride in the British system of government and concern for British prosperity made him, with the help of his careful use of the Press, a truly 'representative man' acceptable to all sections of the community. He even cultivated a courtly touch; the Queen and Albert saw him as the only man who could preserve them from the administrative reform that would have restricted their prerogative.

The struggle for India between European powers in the 18th Century had made the Chinese particularly suspicious of foreigners. The East India Company had secured entry and had held a monopoly of the China trade, especially in silk and tea, until 1833. Opium was extensively smuggled in with other goods and it was the attempt of the Chinese authorities to suppress this and the consequent ill-treatment of British subjects that led to the first serious clash, the Opium War of 1839-42. The Treaty of Nanking that ended it made substantial concessions. The barren island of Hong Kong was ceded to Britain as a base and five treaty ports were opened to trade with special privileges for British subjects. Similar concessions were granted to other powers but with infinite patience the Chinese authorities began to whittle them down. Consequently England and France took advantage of disorder in China in the 1850's to demand fresh trading privileges. Two incidents provided the occasion. A French missionary was executed and a Hong Kong ship, the *Arrow*, was boarded by the Chinese at Canton and twelve of the Chinese crew were arrested. The captain was a pirate, engaged in smuggling, the ship was only technically British but when the local Chinese governor, Commissioner Yeh, surrendered the prisoners but declined to make an apology, Sir John Bowring, Chief Superintendent of Trade at Hong Kong, impulsively ordered the bombardment of Canton. More incidents followed; the Chinese refused to give way, so did Palmerston.

Cobden prepared a vote of censure. Disraeli was unwilling to support it, but Derby forced him to do so; Russell, Roebuck and Gladstone, whose speech was particularly decisive, helped to produce a majority of sixteen, although there were many abstentions. To the annoyance of the Opposition, who, as Palmerston pointed out, 'so far from looking upon renewed intercourse with their constituents as a punishment, they ought to regard it as a triumph', Palmerston decided to dissolve Parliament. His support for trade won him the votes of the trading interests, but basically he made a straightforward patriotic appeal. He contrasted the innocent English with 'an insolent barbarian . . . [who] had violated the British flag, broken the engagements of treaties, offered rewards for the heads of British subjects and planned their destruction by murder, assassination and poisons.' By implication he inferred that Derby, Gladstone and Russell aimed to 'make the humiliation and degradation of their country a stepping stone to power'.

In a very real sense it was a personal triumph. For the first time since the Reform Bill of 1832 a government had appealed to the country from the Commons and won. Cobden and Bright were both defeated, the Peelites were extinguished as a party. The prosperity of the country brought votes for the government, particularly among the country gentry, who, disillusioned by Derby's failure to restore protection, acknowledged Palmerston's loyalty to the landed interest. It was twenty-two years since the Whigs had controlled so many county seats. Parliament could still be fickle, however, as Palmerston was soon to find.

Matters in China were brought to a speedy conclusion. As soon as troops could be spared from India, in December 1857, an Anglo-French force took Canton and the following spring an expedition to Pekin burnt the Summer Palace. In June came the Treaty of Tientsin which confirmed the earlier concessions and opened five more cities to trade.

By then Derby was Prime Minister, Palmerston having quite unexpectedly fallen from power in February. The previous month Orsini, formerly an exile in England, had failed to assassinate Napoleon III with three bombs made in Birmingham. The French Foreign Minister, Count Walewski, protested, while intemperate French colonels were very outspoken about England. Palmerston felt that, in the interests of good relations with France, it was perfectly reasonable to introduce the Conspiracy to Murder Bill to limit the abuse of asylum in England by foreign anarchists. He was narrowly defeated and many explanations have been offered. Principally he was given a taste of his own medicine;

N

he had acted out of character, although in a statesmanlike fashion. The Press and his opponents dubbed his action as unpatriotic and his majority melted away. Russell, in particular, smelt the chance of power. There were other factors; the recent appointment of the disreputable Lord Clanricarde as Lord Privy Seal had been much criticised, while Clanricarde's brother-in-law, Canning, whom Palmerston firmly supported, was unpopular. The Prime Minister's speech was hectoring and may have alienated some members. The Queen urged him to continue, but although he could probably have secured a small majority on a straight vote of confidence he decided to resign.

Once again Derby formed a government, Disraeli returned to the Exchequer and the leadership of the Commons, and Lord Malmesbury to the Foreign Office. Gladstone declined office, though he continued to sit on the government side of the House. The Tories regarded him as a liability; he was unconventional and unpredictable. He favoured Derby largely because he preferred almost any alternative to Palmerston whom he regarded as irresponsible and extravagant. Nevertheless such was the reputation he had acquired at the Exchequer under Aberdeen that his ultimate political destination was a matter of interest and concern. Bright strongly advised him not to join Derby: 'If you remain on our side of the House you are with the majority and no government can be formed without you. You have many friends here . . . and I know nothing that can prevent you being Prime Minister before you approach the age of every other member of the House who has or can have any claim to that high office.'

However, Gladstone did accept a mission from the Colonial Secretary, Bulwer Lytton, to report on the desire of the Ionian Islands, British territory since 1815, for union with Greece. Gladstone's renown as a Homeric scholar was seen as a fitting qualification. From the start there was a touch of comic opera about the whole affair. He upset the British garrison and the native inhabitants, he was distressed at the few copies of Homer on Corfu, he practised rigid economies, he lectured the assembly on the constitutional virtues. He returned home with little achieved and Palmerston ceded the islands to Greece in 1863.

The government meanwhile was in difficulties over the India Bill but Disraeli skilfully adopted many of the proposed amendments. Ellenborough, President of the Board of Control, quarrelled with Canning over the latter's proclamation on the Oudh Settlement and was forced to resign, but Palmerston was ineffectual as Leader of the Opposition and these difficulties were not exploited.

Palmerston had had to promise the Radicals that he would introduce a reform bill in 1858 but when he fell Disraeli decided to take up the matter in the belief that the Tories had everything to gain from a carefully managed reform. Derby was reluctant and there were two Cabinet resignations. Russell tried unsuccessfully to forestall him. The Bill was very moderate; the country occupation franchise was lowered to £10 and balanced by 'fancy franchise', such as votes for professional people and those with a certain level of savings. Palmerston felt it would be unreasonable to his party and determined to oppose it; Russell and Bright thought it much too moderate. A carefully worded amendment on the borough qualification allowed both Whigs and Radicals to vote against the government which was defeated by thirty-nine votes in the largest House since 1835. The General Election that followed increased Conservative strength by only thirty votes and in June 1859 the government was defeated on a vote of no confidence.

The opposition had unexpectedly found unity on the question of Italy, where the Conservatives tended to favour the Austrian position. In July 1858 Napoleon III and Count Cavour, Prime Minister of Sardinia, had met secretly at Plombières and promised to co-operate in terminating Austrian rule in Italy and the Austrian influence which a bevy of archduchesses had connubially extended among the other Italian rulers. Their motives were different: Cavour wanted Sardinian dominance of northern Italy; Napoleon while sympathetic to the ideals of the Risorgimento wished primarily to replace Austrian influence by French and stipulated Nice and Savoy as the price of his support. Cavour had the task of provoking Austria to declare war, which he succeeded in doing in April 1859. Thus started the train of events which unforeseen and undesired by either party to the pact was to result in the virtual unification of Italy the following year.

The Austrian ultimatum made English public opinion, hitherto uncertain, anti-Austrian. As Palmerston pointed out, Sardinia was a great contrast to the rest of Italy; it was progressive, liberal, free trade and anti-clerical. The events of 1848–49, especially Garibaldi's gallant defence of Rome, had aroused British interest in Italian problems, while the writings of Mazzini, an exile in England and the prophet of the Risorgimento, were influential. Another exile, Lacaita, a professor at London University, had valuable connections with both Gladstone and Russell. Gladstone was entirely convinced of the injustice and tyranny; he had visited Italian leaders of the 1848 Revolution in the prisons of the King of the Two Sicilies and had described the Neapolitan system of government as 'the negation of God', as a result of which he had entered into a correspondence with Lord Palmerston, whom in every other respect he distrusted. In 1854 Gladstone had had long conversations with Manin, who had led the Venetian revolt in 1849. Manin had convinced him that Italian unity was the prerequisite for all effective reforms in Italy. Palmerston was not ready for the complete expulsion of Austria, which he feared, rightly, would have detrimental effects on her position elsewhere in Europe, but both he and Russell were convinced of the need for constitutional reforms in Italy to prevent revolution.

Italy drew the 'two dreadful old men', as the Queen called them, together. The Chief Whip advised a party meeting which was held in Willis's Rooms on 6th June and which may fairly be regarded as the foundation of the Liberal party. A motion of no confidence was passed on 11th June. When the result was known in the lobby where the foreign diplomats were waiting, the Sardinian minister threw his hat in the air and embraced the French *chargé d'affaires*, to the amazement of all around.

Napoleon III expected much of the change of government but in the event Britain preserved a strongly benevolent neutrality tinged with distrust of French ambitions. British diplomacy ensured the survival of the new Central Italian States that had arisen when the Austrians withdrew and stipulated that plebiscites should be held there. British warships were conveniently in the way when the Neapolitan fleet caught up with Garibaldi's two steamers just as he was about to land his men in Sicily, while a personal plea by Lacaita to Lord John Russell prevented the French from intercepting Garibaldi as he crossed from Sicily to southern Italy.

Russell had wished to be Prime Minister, but Palmerston had insisted on his right and his was the directing mind in British policy towards Italy. At Willis's Rooms he had promised Bright a policy of peace and neutrality but he carefully managed Russell who was Foreign Secretary, used him to fly kites and encouraged him to do things which, as official head of the government, he could hardly do himself. Although he strongly disapproved of French designs on Savoy and Nice, he tried to keep on good relations with France and supported Gladstone's and Cobden's negotiations for a trade treaty with France in 1860. He concurred with Russell's despatch of 27th October 1860, which followed Garibaldi's surrender of his conquests to King Victor Emmanuel of Sardinia, in which he supported openly the Italian demand for unity and self-government: '. . . the gratifying prospect of a people building up the edifice of their liberties and consolidating the work of their independence amid the sympathies and good wishes of Europe.' Without British sympathy Italian unification would have been impossible at this time.

The Italian question was of great importance in the history of British politics in that it led, as nothing else would have done, to Gladstone's acceptance of office under Palmerston. The suddenness of his acceptance was much criticised; he was not at Willis's Rooms, he voted with the Conservatives only a week before he became Chancellor of the Exchequer. Like Palmerston in 1852 he joined a government of whose chief he had a low opinion, in the hopes of doing important work, influencing Cabinet policy and himself becoming Premier in due course. In retrospect it was an extremely logical step; his ex-Peelite colleagues, Herbert, Newcastle and Graham, had joined the Liberals while Disraeli evidently barred his way to the leadership of the Tories. His views on many subjects remained Conservative, but in the course of the ministry he emerged as the principal spokesman of Liberalism and democratic views against Palmerston's resistance to reform, particularly after Russell's retirement to the Lords in 1861, where his opportunities for rocking the Establishment boat were more limited. Gladstone, indeed, alone possessed certain qualities that were important at the time. His Oxford background and Whig connections were combined with liberal views on institutional reform, a strong sense of justice and morality that appealed to the middle classes and, as was evident after 1862, a way of speaking that could appeal to and influence the working classes.

Palmerston's last administration 1859–65 brought more stability to politics than had been known since 1846 but it would be wrong to imagine that Palmerston was its absolute master. His Cabinet and consequently its policy was a product of the compromise of Willis's Rooms which had been made for the sake of Italy; when Italy was united the variety of attitudes to home and foreign policy were all too evident. In many respects Palmerston had more in common with his Tory opponents, particularly where the preservation of the power of the old governing classes was concerned, than with members of his Cabinet such as Gladstone or the Radicals Charles Villiers and Milner Gibson. This basic agreement led to quiet, compromise politics. Palmerston's continued popularity was a crucial factor but his tremendous vitality tended to obscure an increasing infirmity.

In his Italian despatch of 1860 Russell had justified rebellion on the grounds of natural right. The government was faced with a similar problem of attitude in 1861 when the American Civil War broke out. Ever since the Treaty of Ghent (1814) Anglo-American relations, despite boundary difficulties and a number of minor problems, had been markedly successful. Although slavery was disliked, the British governing class sympathised with the wish of the Southern States to secede, which had in it an element of poetic justice when the American War of Independence was remembered. There was an excuse for intervention: the Northern States, who had command of the sea, prevented the Southern trade with England in raw cotton, on which Lancashire largely depended. Napoleon III also favoured Southern separation; he had designs on Mexico where, in the event, his schemes were successful so long as the United States was divided. The North had no comparable allies in Europe. While the South could well prove to be economically dependent on Great Britain, the loss of the North's goodwill would be an important factor, particularly as far as relations with Canada were concerned, apart from her value as a market for British manufactured goods. In May 1861 the British government recognised the South as belligerents, while proclaiming its own neutrality, and it was believed that recognition of independence would shortly follow. In a speech at Newcastle in October 1862 Gladstone stated that Jefferson Davis, the Confederate leader, had 'made a nation', which caused Adams, the American Minister, to feel he was shortly to be given his passports. In fact Gladstone had made the statement on his own authority, moved by the distress of the cotton operatives, to many of whom he had given work on his own estate at Hawarden. Recent Southern successes had made him feel it would soon be possible to resume cotton supplies, but he later described his remarks as 'a mistake . . . of incredible grossness'. The government quickly issued a denial that recognition was contemplated and Lincoln's Proclamation of the Emancipation of the Slaves in 1862 hardened British determination to remain neutral.

This was strengthened by the attitude of the Radicals and of the cotton operatives themselves. Bright had markedly more success in rallying working-class support than he had had during the Crimean War. He saw the issue in simple terms of aristocracy versus democracy, and his audiences, many of whose relatives had emigrated to the Northern States, agreed with him. This established his position as the leading popular politician and enabled him to agitate after the war for an extension of the suffrage. Nevertheless there were many practical difficulties in Lancashire. Although the cotton crop of 1860 had been one of the heaviest on record, supplies were very short by 1862 and it was not until 1863 that alternative supplies, which Palmerston had urged the Board of Trade to find, began to arrive from Egypt and the East. By the end of 1862 around half a million people were receiving poor relief, and a fund of £2 m. was raised by a committee headed by Lord Derby.

Certain difficulties, however, arose between England and the Northern States. In November 1861 the British steamer *Trent* was intercepted by a Northern warship, *San Jacinto*, and two Southern agents, Mason and Slidell, who were on their way to get support in Europe, were arrested. This was a breach of international law and British public feeling was strong.

Palmerston sent troops to Canada and the Cabinet drafted a strong protest demanding an apology and threatening the severance of diplomatic relations. The Prince Consort, who was seriously ill and who died a fortnight later, saw the draft and rewrote it in such a way as to give the Americans the hint to reply that the captain had acted without instructions. A letter from Russell suggested that Britain would waive the apology if the envoys were restored and, further influenced by private letters from Cobden and Bright to Sumner, a member of the American Cabinet, President Lincoln took this line of action and thus war was averted.

In an attempt to break through the Northern blockade the Southern government secretly ordered six ships to be built in Britain, making arrangements for armaments to be installed elsewhere. Technically it was no breach of neutrality to do this, although the government had power to arrest a ship if there was a *prima facie* case that it was being prepared for war against a friendly power. Three ships were seized, one was allowed to sail, but did little damage; the other two were *Florida* and *Alabama*, both of which successfully harried Northern shipping. The *Alabama* narrowly escaped seizure; Adams informed Russell of her purpose but there were legal delays and then, incomplete and without a regular crew, she slipped away on 'sea trials' to be fitted out as a warship in the Azores and then to wreak destruction on Northern merchantmen. The Federal government made heavy claims for compensation on the British, naming the equivalent of the British national debt or, alternatively, the cession of Canada. Palmerston refused compensation or reference to a foreign arbiter, holding that in view of international jealousy of Britain's wealth, no arbitration could be impartial, a view Gladstone might well have heeded when he settled the question in 1872.[1]

Three other questions occupied the Foreign Office during this period. In 1862 the Greeks had rebelled against King Otho, and Palmerston, while recognising the right of the Greeks to change their dynasty, was careful not to alienate England's co-guarantors, France and Russia. The Russians had their own candidate, but a Greek plebiscite overwhelmingly elected Afred, Duke of Edinburgh, Queen

[1] See below, p. 227.

Victoria's second son, and then, on his refusal, offered the throne to Lord Stanley. A neutral candidate, a Danish prince, was agreed upon.

Less happy was the treatment of the Polish rising against the Tsar in 1863. Palmerston wished the Russians to restore the semi-autonomy that Poland had been promised in 1815. Napoleon III supported this, hoping to bring about a peaceful revision of the 1815 settlement as a whole. The Russians had, by the Alvensleben Convention, secured a potential ally in Prussia, whose ruling class had extensive Polish interests and although Britain, France and Austria sent notes[1] which hinted at war, the Russians successfully called their bluff. Napoleon was ready for war, particularly one that might acquire the Rhineland for him, but Palmerston, suspecting this, refused to co-operate, even with the holding of a European Congress. Thus Britain had alienated both Russia by protesting too much and France by not protesting enough, factors of considerable importance in the next dispute.

The Treaty of London of 1852[2] had provided that the two Elbe duchies of Schleswig and Holstein, with a predominantly German population, should pass with the Danish crown to Christian of Glucksburg on the death of Frederick VII but that they should remain a separate political entity. It was hoped in this way that German nationalism would be reasonably satisfied, for the duchies had a different law of succession and should technically have gone to a German claimant, while Denmark, of whose territory they formed two-fifths, would still remain strong. In 1863, however, shortly before his death, Frederick had begun to incorporate the duchies. When Christian IX succeeded, therefore, the German claimant, Frederick of Augustenburg, renewed his claim and was backed by Prussia, whose Prime Minister, Bismarck, intended to obtain Kiel and involve Austria. British policy showed inadequate awareness of her diplomatic isolation. Palmerston and Russell talked and wrote agressively, favouring the Danish cause as did public opinion and undoubtedly encouraging Danish intransigence. The Queen favoured German national aspirations and felt it unreasonable for the

---

[1] Russell's language was particularly immoderate and the Queen took him to task.
[2] See above, p. 160.

government to have one policy to the south of the Alps and another to the north. By a narrow majority, the Cabinet decided in June not to enter into a war alone for the sake of the duchies, but by then Bismarck had been able to exploit the situation and in August they were handed over to Austria and Prussia, a joint protectorate that Bismarck was to make the occasion of his war with Austria for the supremacy of Germany in 1866.

It might be argued that an alliance with France might have led to a French conquest of the Rhineland, while one with Russia could only have been obtained by the revocation of the Black Sea Clauses, and that both these would have had a more damaging effect on the balance of power than what actually happened. It is equally arguable that a more cautious policy would have preserved at least Schleswig for Denmark and perhaps limited Bismarck's opportunities. What is certain is that the emptiness of Palmerston's policy was now revealed. It was 'meddle and muddle', Derby criticised, and, as Disraeli had pointed out, he was 'ginger beer and not champagne at all'. Palmerston survived a vote of censure but Europe recognised what had been true, in effect, since 1815, that without an army of continental size of her own and without a major continental ally, British influence on European events was limited. When the British government failed to have any influence on the events of 1870 it was not so much Gladstone's non-interventionism as Palmerston's intervention unsupported by force that was to blame. In the world of Bismarck, Palmerston was out of his depth.

At the Exchequer Gladstone was determined to complete Peel's work. He intended to remove all customs duties except on a limited number of articles for revenue purposes only and if possible abolish the income tax. This demanded rigid government economy and on this question Gladstone and Palmerston were often at breaking point. One of the few passions of Palmerston's declining years was to set the national defences in order, and a complicated series of elaborate and – as it proved – useless forts was planned to defend the main dockyards and naval arsenals. A programme of ironclads was also drawn up for the Navy. In the long run Gladstone won his point but not until there had been some extra expenditure. However desirable Gladstone's attitude from the point

of view of the taxpayers, more money should have been spent
on improving soldiers' unhealthy living conditions.

Gladstone's fiscal triumph was the Budget of 1860. It
incorporated the terms of the Trade Treaty that Cobden, at
the request of Gladstone, had just concluded with France.
The Radicals always maintained that with greater trade, war
was more likely to be averted and the Treaty provided for a
mutual reduction of duties. The Budget proposed no
protective duty on raw produce, food or manufactured goods.
Only forty-eight articles were left in the tariff, for revenue
purposes only. The Chinese war and the armaments
expenditure necessitated another penny on the income tax
but the reductions were paid for by the falling in of some
government annuities. In his speech Gladstone spoke of the
benefits the changes would bring to the working classes: 'You
are enlarging their means without narrowing their freedom,
you are giving value to their labour, you are appealing to their
sense of responsibility and you are not impairing their sense of
honourable self-dependence.'

The Budget greatly increased Gladstone's reputation. His
subsequent Budgets aroused considerable public interest. He
was able to give a certain fascination to their details and his
raising of finance to a moral plane had a somewhat whimsical
appeal. The national expenditure was reduced from £72 m.
in 1861 to £62 m. in 1866 and in consequence income tax
came down from 10d. to 4d., the tax on hops was abolished and
the duties on sugar, cheese and tobacco were sharply cut. In
1861 he encouraged the self-dependence of the working class
by establishing the Post Office Savings Bank, which also
provided the government with a source of loans independent
of the City.

On one item in his 1860 Budget he came into conflict with
the House of Lords. From the beginning of the century
Radicals had demanded the removal of restraints on the
Press. Bentham had prophesied that when this was done, the
editor of a prominent newspaper would become the 'president
of a public opinion tribunal' to which all politicians and public
servants would be forced to render account. This was, as it
turned out, a somewhat naïve prediction but Bagehot had
indicated more recently that with the decline of the Sovereign's power, public opinion as expressed through the Press

was a growing political force. The events of the 1850's and 1860's, particularly the Crimean War, increased this. Journalists acquired a better status and their comments became better informed and more influential on a public that was taking its politics increasingly seriously. The periodicals, so important at the beginning of the century, took second place to the daily newspapers which with steam-driven printing presses and better transport could make a more immediate comment. Owned by the Walter family, *The Times* was in the supreme position. Under its editors Barnes and Delane it was perceptive and influential, but it was difficult always to judge whether it reflected or led public opinion. Sir John Walsh wrote in 1860, 'It leans upon no single class, it represents no exclusive party, it advocates no separate interest. [It expresses] the current opinion of all the intelligent and informed sections of the British community.' At this period its circulation exceeded that of the other London dailies put together. They included *The Morning Post*, over whose editorial policy Palmerston had much influence, *The Daily News* founded in 1846 and whose first editor was Dickens, and *The Morning Chronicle* which had been purchased by the Peelites in 1853 and which was later swallowed by the *Telegraph*. This newspaper was first published in 1855 and was the first penny daily to aim deliberately at as many advertisements and as large a circulation as possible. A vigorous provincial Press followed the same trend, the *Manchester Guardian* becoming a penny daily in 1855 and the *Birmingham Post* in 1857.

There were three burdens on the Press whose removal made possible the decrease in price with the resulting increase in circulation and in influence of papers other than *The Times*. The last Chartist Conference of 1849 campaigned for their removal and an Association for the Repeal of Taxes on Knowledge was formed by Cobden, Bright, Milner Gibson and other Radicals. A tax of 1s. 6d. on every advertisement was removed in 1853. The Stamp Duty of 1d. that every newspaper had to bear went in 1855; it had constituted a major barrier against a cheap Press; even *The Times* was able to decrease its price to 3d. by 1855. The third burden, which was also, as Gladstone pointed out, a burden for educational books, was the duty on paper. To abolish it would mean a loss to the Exchequer of over £1 m. but when he proposed it as part of his 1860 Budget Gladstone was confident he could obtain the money in other ways. Palmerston, however, was reluctant to lose the revenue in view of the difficulty over raising money for defence and, like the Conservatives, he was not anxious to see the newspaper-reading public further expanded. He went so far as to write to the Queen suggesting that if the Lords, encouraged by a small majority in the Lower House, rejected the proposal they would be performing a public service. The constitutional position was somewhat obscure, though conventionally the Lords did not amend money bills. Lord Lyndhurst convinced the Upper House that they were justified in rejecting the proposal. Palmerston, with considerable amusement, passed through the Commons three resolutions mildly denouncing the Lords' action. However, Gladstone was equal to this; all the legislation for the Budget of 1861, including the repeal of the paper duties and the removal of a penny from the income tax, was placed in a single Bill, which the Lords passed. They did not summon up enough courage to reject a Finance Bill until 1909. The affair helped to move Gladstone in the direction of Liberalism and for the first time in his life he became a popular figure. His achievements in promoting prosperity increased this popularity. 'It is a matter of profound and inestimable consolation to reflect that while the rich have been growing richer, the poor have become less poor . . .', he remarked.

A Reform Bill had been submerged by the excitement over the 1860 Budget and the Paper Duties, but the Radicals brought forward an annual motion. Interest in reform had quickened of recent years. Bright had interpreted the American Civil War as freedom versus slavery and hastened to make the appropriate application to England. The loyalty to an ideal and the good order that the Lancashire working class had shown under the strain of the cotton famine was a notable stimulus. Garibaldi's visit to England in 1864 also made a great impression. These events helped to convince Gladstone that the working class was developing qualities for which he had the greatest respect. In the course of a debate on the Radical reform resolution of 1864 he remarked, with many careful qualifications that his hearers and the country as a whole ignored: 'I venture to say that every man who is not incapacitated by some consideration of personal unfitness or of political danger is morally entitled to come within the pale of the Constitution.'

The speech caused a sensation. It appeared to view the franchise as a right, rather than a privilege to be earned and closely associated with a stake in the country which had always been the Whig and Tory view. The Queen was alarmed; hitherto she had respected Gladstone because of the admiration Prince Albert had had for him. Palmerston understood Gladstone's position but cautioned him against committing himself on such issues in advance. He was displeased by the statement and commented to Shaftesbury that there would be strange doings 'when Gladstone has my place'. He was 'a dangerous man, keep him in Oxford and he is partially muzzled but send him elsewhere and he will run wild'. At the General Election in 1865 Gladstone was rejected by Oxford University because of views he had expressed in a debate on the Irish Church establishment. Elected by South Lancashire he came among them 'unmuzzled'. His assertion of the moral fitness of most men to vote, without it being his intention, had taken hold of the popular imagination and Gladstone became the hero of the reformers. Like is attracted by like and Gladstone, never at home in the *milieu* of the Whig aristocracy, found association with Bright and his fellow reformers increasingly congenial. Impatient of the official leadership of his party, he was psychologically in need of a popular stimulus to sustain him. He became 'The People's William' but they as little appreciated his aims as he appreciated and understood their material needs.

It might be argued that even Palmerston understood these better. A number of useful minor reforms had taken place under his aegis – the Children's Commission, extension of the Factory Acts and some useful acts on public health. Palmerston's social record was more impressive than Disraeli's before 1874. He was not prepared, however, to undertake institutional reforms that would loosen the control of the governing class and the frustration of men such as Gladstone with his attitude can well be understood from Goschen's description of him when he asked him about domestic affairs and legislation for 1864. ' "Oh," he gaily replied, rubbing his hands with an air of comfortable satisfaction, "there is really nothing to be done. We cannot go on adding to the Statute Book *ad infinitum*. Perhaps we may have a little law reform or bankruptcy reform, but we cannot go on legislating for ever."'

Palmerston dissolved Parliament in July 1865 and fought the election as a vote of confidence in his premiership as promoting the unity of the country. There were more contests than usual but no clear issues. Reform was scarcely mentioned. Palmerston's prestige ensured an increase in his majority but before Parliament met he had died at Brocket, where Melbourne had died before him. Aged 81, fifty-eight years in Parliament and an active Prime Minister to the end, his death marks an important stage in the development of Liberalism. Now there were 'strange doings', and the Whig aristocracy began its slide, which became precipitous in 1886, into the Conservative party.

(d) PARLIAMENTARY REFORM, 1866–67

By the time Palmerston died, the unrepresentative nature of Parliament was being openly discussed in the great cities. There it seemed that Gladstone's 'Pale of the Constitution' speech had placed on the anti-reformers the onus of disproving the moral fitness of the urban working class. The previous twenty years had seen the steady emergence of an aristocracy of labour, men in skilled trades who increasingly accepted the moral and social outlook of the middle class. In the Trades Union movement the amalgamations formed by men such as Allen and Applegarth represented an attitude of constructive conciliation. The wages of this group tended to be almost twice those of the regularly employed unskilled labourer and although their conditions were still poor and their prosperity precarious, they built up certain standards of respectability which they were unwilling to sacrifice by violence and irresponsibility. Influenced by nonconformist sobriety and by such books as *Self Help*, many saved assiduously. Freehold land and housing associations and the co-operative movement grew up especially where this élite was strongest, in the northern industrial counties. Many joined the Volunteer Movement, revived in 1852, and with a membership of 200,000 in 1868. In addition to being a symbol of English liberty and patriotism it was a valuable social bond.

To men such as these the franchise was seen as a mark of

approval and acceptance.   They felt they had earned a stake
in the country.   The aim was not as yet political power,
although J. S. Mill argued that it was important to have in the
Commons men who could speak for the classes most concerned with the social reforms that were needed.   Most of the
working class élite might grumble periodically about aristocratic privileges but on the whole they accepted the situation
and even secretly liked it.   Bagehot was not untypical of his
age when he argued that the country was most effectively
managed by the 'select few' who had enjoyed 'a life of leisure,
a long culture, a varied experience, an experience by which the
judgement is incessantly exercised and by which it may be
incessantly improved'.   While their prosperity increased and
Parliament showed periodical social concern, most of the
working-class élite imagined the vote would come in time.
It came as a shock when Robert Lowe impugned their moral
worth and the 1866 Bill was rejected.   This provided the
emotional impetus hitherto missing in the Reform question
and the large industrial cities saw working-class demonstrations revolutionary in size but peaceable in intent.

There was no urgency for Reform when Palmerston died
but when Russell succeeded by virtue of seniority it was
evident that he would wish to be associated with some further
extension of the franchise, however moderate.   Since 1846
his career, with the exception of his work for Italy, had been
compounded of frustrations and missed opportunities; now
achievement seemed possible, unshadowed by Palmerston.
Gladstone became Leader of the Commons and many were
dubious of his ability to lead a House elected to support
Palmerston.   He wielded great moral power and had a
magnetic personality but he lacked the finer arts of conciliation
and the easy manner that Palmerston had displayed on so
many occasions.   These were factors of great significance in
determined the course of the bill.

The Cabinet reluctantly agreed to support Russell and
Gladstone and a bill was prepared which made no mention of
redistribution of seats.   The borough franchise was to be given
to the householder who paid £7 yearly in rent, while in the
counties, which were assumed to be less independent owing to
landlord influence, the dividing line was to be £14, with or
without land.   This was essentially a moderate bill which

would perhaps add 400,000 electors. It was evident, however, that a section of the Liberal party was bitterly opposed
and it found a spokesman in Robert Lowe, who had been
responsible for Education under Palmerston. His memories
of New South Wales, where he had been a member of the
Legislative Council, a visit to America in 1856 and his
experiences of mob participation in English elections prejudiced him against democracy. A brilliant man, his
eloquence astonished all, and every speech he made added to
his fame and, in due course, his infamy. His standpoint was
not the self-interest of the gentry but rather the philosophical
and historical conception that government, the highest
expression of the aspirations of an ordered society, was a
matter for the educated and wealthy who alone could consider
policy in a rational, informed and unselfish way. 'If you
want venality,' he remarked in words that aroused much
bitterness outside the House, 'if you want drunkenness and
facility for being intimidated or if . . . you want impulsive,
unreflecting and violent people. . . . Do you go to the top or to
the bottom?' The tragedy of Lowe was that his protest
helped rather than hindered Reform. Bright made him the
butt of his speeches when he stumped the country as he
pictured Lowe and his supporters gathering, as when 'all who
were distressed . . . all who were discontented' had gathered
with David in the Cave of Adullam.

   Disraeli moved carefully. His hold over the party leadership was still insecure but he recognised the opportunity, by
careful co-operation with the Adullamites, to exploit a major
split in the Liberal party. Lord Grosvenor's amendment to
redistribute seats before reforming the franchise was defeated
by only five votes and Russell, supported by those who were
reluctant to see office slip from their fingers, introduced a
Redistribution Bill. In June the Tories moved Lord Dunkel-
lin's amendment to substitute rateable value for rental which
would considerably limit the franchise and even disfranchise
some who already had votes. The government handled it
badly, neither Russell nor Gladstone providing the type of
leadership that was needed and the amendment was carried
by eleven votes. Russell never forgave the Adullamites; he
had never known, he wrote, 'a party so utterly destitute of
consistent principle or of patriotic end'. With a difficult
o

economic situation at home and war threatening between
Austria and Prussia abroad, he vainly sought an honourable
way of continuing in office. Gladstone urged a dissolution,
but the Whig magnates were hesitant to make an appeal to the
country on so Radical an issue. In consequence Russell
resigned, leaving Lord Derby to form his third administration.

In support of the original bill Gladstone had said, 'You
cannot fight against the future . . . great social forces are
against you.' And so indeed it was to prove. Economic
difficulties provided an atmosphere of social unrest. The
harvest of 1865 had been bad and had brought distress while
the collapse of the banking house of Overend and Gurney in
May 1866, arising from speculation following the 1862
Limited Liability Act,[1] had brought on a crisis of confidence
which helped to renew popular agitation against aristocratic
mismanagement. The Reform League, founded in 1865 and
containing both working-class and middle-class members, had
organised a meeting in Hyde Park for 23rd July. In alarm
the Home Secretary, Spencer Walpole, without consulting
the Cabinet, ordered the police at the last moment to close the
Park. Under the pressure of the crowd the railings collapsed
and it was not until the following day that the Park was
cleared by the cavalry, with little ill will on either side. The
League was embarrassed by the rowdyism which damaged
the impression of sobriety they were anxious to convey; nevertheless the riot gave the question of reform an immediacy it
had not hitherto possessed. The Trades Unions, who were
facing a crisis in their history,[2] lent their support to the
agitation and Bright's leadership helped to prevent a degener-
ation into class war. Huge meetings and demonstrations
were held in the provinces, and in London in December an
orderly procession testified to the seriousness of the movement.

In view of the failure of Derby to form a coalition government with the Adullamites which meant that they had no
majority in the House, and in view of the mounting pressure
in the country, it was clearly expedient for the Conservative
government to produce some measure of reform, nor was this
particularly out of character. Disraeli had produced a bill in
1859 and for a year had been friendly with Bright. The
existing franchise had not produced a Conservative majority

[1] See above, p. 147.   [2] See below, p. 215.

since 1846 and there was every reason to suppose that some small and careful adjustments might 'dish the Whigs'. Moreover Derby as Lord Stanley had helped to draft the Reform Bill of 1832 and had always shown social concern. Malmesbury and other Conservatives were firmly convinced that the boldest course was the safest.   Nevertheless it was only to be expected that the Conservative party would have its 'Cave'.   When Disraeli introduced resolutions on reform to test the reaction of the Commons in January 1867, three members of the Cabinet, Lord Carnarvon, Lord Cranborne (the future Marquis of Salisbury) and General Peel (Sir Robert's brother) were opposed.   Cranborne feared that a transfer of political power would lead to a robbing of the rich by the poorer part of the community and that the proposals would weaken Conservative hold on the small boroughs.   In an attempt to satisfy them, Disraeli's bill, based on the resolutions, was withdrawn, and under the Ten Minute Rule a more cautious one introduced.   When it was evident that the majority of the party preferred the original bill, the three Ministers resigned.   That Cranborne did not split the party, as Disraeli himself had done in 1846, owed much to Disraeli's astuteness and expert party management.

In the months that followed, Disraeli's expert management of Parliament itself was shown.   The leader of a minority government, with his own party divided on the issue, Disraeli never lost control of the situation.   Though the outcome was a bill more extreme than anyone had seriously expected, it was for Disraeli a parliamentary triumph of the highest order and firmly established him in the leadership of his party.   It left Gladstone's leadership, on the other hand, seriously questioned.

By adopting Household Suffrage in March, admittedly with careful safeguards of the 'fancy franchise' type that he had adopted in his 1859 Bill, Disraeli prevented a frontal attack by the Opposition.   Thereafter it was a policy of making such concessions as would most divide them.   Although Gladstone made many impressive speeches and kept his popularity in the country, a group of Radicals in the House, known as the Tea Room Party, were enticed away from his leadership by their desire for wider reform.   One considerable difficulty was the question of householders who did not pay their own rates but who compounded rent and rates in a single payment to the landlord. A decision to exclude them would have led to some curious anomalies but Gladstone became entangled in the legal difficulties and failed to give his party a clear lead. After the Easter Recess the Radicals followed a policy of nibbling at the Bill by precise limited amendments. One reduced the residential qualification to one year, a second included lodgers paying £10 a year, while the third, Hodgkinson's, gave the vote to compound householders. This was accepted by Disraeli, who had not made the necessary mathematical calculations, without a division, and it added half a million voters. When Disraeli quietly dropped the 'fancy franchises', Household Suffrage had been achieved. A similar process of erosion made the measures of redistribution more radical.

Disraeli's success in the Commons, though only four of the sixty-one sections of the Bill were actually the work of the government, brought a sense of achievement to the party that stifled discontent, though Cranborne spoke of it as 'a political betrayal which has no parallel in our annals'. The majority of Conservatives hoped it would prove a permanent settlement. When Derby was ill with gout several wrecking amendments were introduced in the Lords, but on his return he showed his complete mastery of the House by forcing their withdrawal. He made a powerful plea for unity and any possibility of a repetition of the difficulties of 1831-32 was averted. 'No doubt we are making a great experiment and "taking a leap in the dark"' he said in August, 'but I have the greatest confidence in the sound sense of my fellow countrymen . . . and that the passing of the measure will tend to increase the loyalty and contentment of a great portion of Her Majesty's subjects.'

When the Bill became law the borough franchise was the householder and the £10 lodger, while in the county constituencies copyholders and leaseholders with property of £5 annual value and the £12 ratepayer were added to those already entitled. The Redistribution Clauses deprived boroughs with a population of less than 10,000 of one seat, and those of less than 5,000 of both seats. Twenty-five new seats went to the counties and fifteen to boroughs including a third member for Liverpool, Manchester, Birmingham and Leeds. Separate acts were passed, on similar lines, for Scotland and Ireland.

The electorate was increased from 1,430,000 to 2,470,000 or almost half the adult male householders in the country. Voting, however, was still open and in the counties, where the majority of the population lived, the vote was still restricted. Some of the boroughs had a very small electorate; thirty-five had less than 1,000. Although the property qualification for M.P.'s had been abolished in 1858 there was no salary until 1911 and few working men appeared in the Commons until 1880. Nevertheless the Act of 1867 was the crucial step in the adaptation of British institutions to the rise of democracy and made the demand for future adjustments irresistible. From the point of view of the Conservatives it was the culmination of the process of adding responsible elements to the political nation. It also recognised that England had ceased to be a predominantly rural country. The representatives of the towns and particularly of the commercial interests came to be increasingly important in Parliament. The extension of the electorate set a premium on efficient party management and a strong party machine. Apathetic electors had to be registered and hustled to the polls, finance had to be raised for this purpose and in consequence M.P.'s became less independent of the Party Whips.

The year 1867 is the watershed of the 19th Century. The dominant thought had been the preservation and enhancing of individual liberty; it was a period when Parliament over-shadowed the electorate, when politics, almost the only news considered important by the Press, seemed more important than it really was. It was a period of economic security and boundless optimism. After 1867 the liberty achieved was slowly but increasingly used to bring about a new social order, a process that has continued into the 20th Century. It was a period that saw, perhaps logically, the decline of the Liberal Party. The power of the executive, supported, as civilisation grew more complex, by an extensive and anonymous civil service, came to overshadow Parliament and interest in politics as such tended to decline. Certain sections of society, notably on the left wing, began to doubt whether politics could provide solutions to the country's problems. Behind it all, only perceived intermittently by the public as a whole, were growing economic difficulties.

V · GLADSTONIAN LIBERALISM

(a) PACIFYING IRELAND

IT was perhaps appropriate that the passing of the Reform Bill should be so quickly followed by the passing of the leadership of the two great parties to two men both of middle-class origin who, in their very different ways, owed their primacy to their own merits and abilities. At Christmas, 1867, Gladstone succeeded Russell, who was to live on until 1878, while in February 1868 Derby resigned through ill health and Disraeli had 'climbed to the top of the greasy pole', as he put it when he succeeded him. The Queen truthfully assured him that only 'his own talent and successful labours in the service of his Sovereign and his country had now earned for him the high and influential position in which he was now placed'. He had overcome ridicule, enmity and distrust in a triumph of personality unequalled in the 19th Century. His misfortune was that it took him too long: at 64 he was a Prime Minister without a majority and he was not to obtain one for a further six years.

At the time of the Reform Bill public attention had been drawn once again to Ireland. The opportunity to pursue a constructive policy of conciliation had been missed in 1846 and although the famine and the subsequent emigration provided that 'clearance' of population which had always been the principal British answer to Irish problems, many difficulties remained. The Encumbered Estates Act of 1849 and the Courts it set up had transferred much Irish land to new owners. These were mainly Irish speculators who lacked even the slender sense of duty of the former landlords. They cleared most of the best land for grazing, the peasants being left with the worst. Nearly 200,000 people suffered eviction and Disraeli estimated that a quarter of the population by 1868 had become helpless paupers.

Those Irish who crossed the Atlantic took with them a sense of bitterness and a determination to remedy matters. Although the great majority contented themselves with making good in the New World, a number conceived it their duty to draw attention to Irish problems by violence. In 1858 a secret society called The Fenian Brotherhood[1] was founded in Chicago, having as its objective an Irish Republic. When the American Civil War ended in 1865 a number of its members, released from the Army, found settling into civilian life difficult and, encouraged by the example of the nationalists of Italy and Poland, began in 1866 and 1867 a series of outrages in England and Ireland. They culminated, in December 1867, in the bomb attack by Fenians on Clerkenwell Gaol in order to release one of their number. They failed but twelve people were killed and 120 wounded. The Fenians had gone too far; the Catholic Hierarchy warned the Irish to keep clear of them. Gladstone, who had thought long and seriously about the problems of Ireland, felt that the moment had come for some measures of reconciliation.

Previously, Gladstone had never taken much interest in Ireland. He had never visited the country, but had become unpopular there in 1853 when he extended to it the income tax, which Peel had withheld. He sought no first-hand knowledge of the problems but once he had convinced himself of the rightness of what he proposed, he became a dedicated man, dismissing objections as factious and ill-considered. He would have bitterly repudiated any suggestion that he was an opportunist, although his enemies detected a greed for office in some of his actions. There were many occasions, however, when he chose an unpopular course because he was convinced of its rightness and this led men to respect him for his integrity. His decision to attack the Anglican Church of Ireland was certainly well-timed, however, and re-established the unity of his party after the humiliations of the Reform Bill.

The rich endowment of the Church of Ireland, which had under 700,000 members in a population of six million, had been declared by Lord John Russell thirty years earlier to be indefensible and most of the Whigs were prepared to take the same standpoint. The Radicals warmed to an attack on entrenched privilege. Soon after Disraeli had taken office Gladstone declared in the course of a debate on the State of Ireland that 'the Irish Church as a State Church must cease

[1] The name was derived from the Fianna, an armed force in Irish legend.

to exist', which his party vigorously applauded. When Disraeli failed to define his attitude, Gladstone introduced a resolution to this effect which was passed by sixty votes. Disraeli saw the cup dashed from his lips and to avoid resignation proposed a dissolution. The new electoral registers were not yet ready and no election could be held before November. With what Gladstone considered an extreme lack of conscience Disraeli continued in office, with Gladstone as virtual leader of the House.

The result of the General Election of 1868 was a surprise and a disappointment to the Conservative party. They had expected gratitude whereas the new electorate merely saw self-interest. Moreover Gladstone and Bright in a series of speeches all over the country educated the voters in the evils of the Irish Church Establishment and in the urban constituencies, with their strong nonconformity, their support exceeded their expectations. The Liberals were returned with a majority of approximately 110 seats.

Disraeli resigned and when Gladstone received the Queen's commission to form a government he remarked, 'My mission is to pacify Ireland' and later noted in his journal: 'The Almighty seems to sustain and spare me for some purpose of his own, deeply unworthy as I know myself to be. Glory be His name.' He was not to lay down his mission, still incomplete, until 1894.

He at once initiated legislation for the Church of Ireland. He had failed to secure its voluntary co-operation and was denounced at diocesan conferences throughout Ireland as a brigand. The Bill passed the Lower House with large majorities. It provided for the disestablishment of the Church and its partial disendowment. The Church retained a capital of £13½ m. and the remainder was variously distributed; some going to Irish hospitals, £2 m. to Irish intermediate education and teachers' pensions, over £1 m. to distress works, nearly £1 m. to cover rent arrears in 1882. In the interests of fairness the Maynooth Grant[1] and the *regium donum* to the Presbyterians were discontinued.

Although there can be little doubt in retrospect that the course taken was the right one, it seemed for a while as if it would cause a clash between the two Houses. Granville was

---

[1] See above, p. 77.

a competent Liberal leader of the Lords but already the flight
from Liberalism had begun and the Lords, hitherto reasonably well-balanced, was becoming increasingly a Conservative
stronghold.   Many peers felt the sanctity of property was
being abused and some, notably Lord Derby, believed,
wrongly as it turned out, that the Act would be fatal to
religion.   In the last speech of his life Derby expressed his
fears: 'Go your ways, Ministers of England; ye have this day,
as far as in you lay, quenched the light of truth in fifteen
hundred parishes.   See if your own Church stand the faster
for that.'   The Queen had little sympathy with Gladstone's
object but she was impressed by his sense of purpose and wrote
to both Derby and the Archbishop of Canterbury that the Bill
ought not to be defeated.   To Derby's disgust, the Conservative peers agreed to let the Bill through, concentrating on
preserving for the Church as much as possible of its endowment.

Of more immediate relevance to Irish distress and discontent
was the land problem.   Apart from evictions arising from the
Encumbered Estates Act, the great pressure on land led to
steady increases in rent and thus to further evictions when
tenants found themselves unable to pay.   Irish farmers were
usually tenants at will, subject to six months' notice and not
entitled to any compensation for improvements, including
buildings, effected to the property.   In Ulster customary
tenant right discouraged eviction if a man paid his rent,
and payment of compensation for improvements was usual.
Gladstone proposed extending this by law to the whole of
Ireland and despite the initial opposition of most of the
Cabinet, succeeded in convincing them that in this matter
England had a moral duty.   The English landowning interest
was sensitive to any infringement of the rights of property;
Palmerston's epigram, 'Tenant's Right is Landlord's Wrong'
was well remembered but it was recognised that the social
bond that smoothed the English relationship was lacking in
Ireland.

As was so often the case with Irish affairs there was imper-
fect knowledge of the problems and in consequence the Irish
Land Act of 1870 was a half-measure that had to be strengthened more radically in 1881.[1]   The end of a *laissez-faire*

[1] A fund was then set up to enable the Irish tenant to purchase his land.

attitude to Irish land and of the landlord's doctrine of his absolute right of property in it were important steps forward but although the act established a species of dual ownership, it failed to define that relationship clearly and to protect the tenant from rises in rents. Since the landlord had to pay not only compensation for improvements but also compensation for disturbance and on a scale that was weighted for the smaller holdings, he now had every incentive to squeeze out the smaller tenants with rent increases and, in case he be charged for what he had done himself, to spend no money on improvements. Thus an act intended to help the peasantry in many cases added to their difficulties. The outcome was an increase in crime and disorder and the government had to introduce a Peace Preservation Act. Irish dissatisfaction with Ascendancy rule increased and a 'Home Government Association of Ireland' was founded in Dublin in 1870.

Although his attention was drawn primarily to other problems, Gladstone continued to be aware of the need for conciliation. He envisaged the Prince of Wales as a Ceremonial Viceroy for Ireland, and asked the Queen to establish a royal residence there and to visit it occasionally. In view of the enthusiasm which had greeted George IV on his visit and the Queen herself when she crossed the Irish Sea, there can be little doubt that more regular contact with royalty would have created valuable goodwill. The Queen, however, was too sunk in her widowhood and too convinced that Gladstone, who tended to regard her office in an institutional light though his loyalty to the throne was unbounded, failed to appreciate her problems. She had little confidence in the character of the Prince of Wales and was unwilling to give him any duties of importance.

Gladstone also failed in his scheme of 1873 to improve the provision of university education in Ireland. There existed the richly endowed and Protestant Trinity College, Dublin, two poverty-stricken non-sectarian colleges and a privately endowed Roman Catholic University. Gladstone's scheme was to unite them all in a new university which was to receive £12,000 a year from Trinity College and substantial funds from Irish Church endowments. To avoid controversy, modern history, theology and philosophy were excluded from the syllabus, although the affiliated colleges might continue religious teaching. Everybody was offended: Trinity College disliked its position in the new scheme; the nonconformists disliked the endowment of denominational instruction in any form; Radicals disliked the restriction of syllabuses, while the Roman Catholics wanted a separate endowment. The Bill was rejected by three votes in the Commons and Gladstone resigned. When Disraeli declined to form a government as he was not yet confident that he would win an election, Gladstone resumed office, but Irish university education had to wait a further generation.

(b) INSTITUTIONAL REFORM

In 1856 Gladstone remarked, 'There is a policy going a-begging; the general policy that Sir Robert Peel in 1841 took office to support – the policy of Peace abroad, of economy, of financial equilibrium, of steady resistance to abuses and the promotion of practical improvements at home with a disinclination to questions of reform gratuitously raised.' It was the tragedy of Gladstone's life that Peel's Conservative party broke up in 1846 for he was thoroughly at home with its brand of progressive Conservatism. He found neither the atmosphere of the great Whig families nor that of the Radical nonconformity, into which circumstances increasingly thrust him, anything like as congenial. The Peelite group brought to the Liberal party a wider outlook and a high standard of intellectual proficiency. Although it had an important aristocratic element the party became in its composition and its attitudes increasingly middle class, using as a definition for this period the group without inherited landed wealth who yet employed the labour of others in some way. It was out of these elements that there came Gladstonian Liberalism whose high water mark was the Ministry of 1868–74.

The Liberal party which swept to power in 1868 with the largest majority since 1833 had as its slogan 'Peace, Retrenchment and Reform'. Palmerston claimed that his foreign policy averted war but it was nevertheless conducted in an atmosphere of belligerency. Now it was maintained that Britain's greatest interest was peace, a view with which Lord Salisbury, who so long dominated Conservative foreign policy, was to concur. Bright and Gladstone formed Liberal thinking on this question. Bright was a Quaker. Gladstone was not a pacifist in this sense but to him war was wasteful and repugnant. He distrusted colonies as leading to expensive commitments and the risk of friction with foreign powers. To him justice was more important than national sentiment. They were supported by a strong vein of idealism in the party and by the relative social isolation of the middle class from the small professional Army.

Retrenchment had always been a Whig-Liberal ideal, dating back to the 'Economical Reform' movement of the late 18th Century. In the Gladstonian period it meant rigorous control of government spending, especially on armaments. It was no accident that the two greatest army reformers, Cardwell and Haldane, were Liberals. Armies were repugnant but if they existed they must give value for money. Liberals also shrank from committing the government financially to social reform and thus increasing the responsibilities and hence the expenses of the State.

Those functions which the State already exercised, however, must be exercised with the maximum of efficiency and justice. Reform in a narrow sense meant extension of the franchise and on this and the fairer conduct of the polls Gladstonian Liberalism had important influence. In a wider sense it meant improvement in the methods of government, selection of government servants by ability and the improvement of institutions for which the government was responsible.

As Prime Minister Gladstone dominated the Ministry. He never ceased to astonish by his parliamentary mastery, his encyclopaedic knowledge, his quickness of decision, capacity for work and powers of concentration. Yet he was not a dictator; he was ready to submit all major matters to his Cabinet and to defer to them if they disagreed with him. He was served by a series of capable private secretaries, of whom the first was Algernon West. To assist him Gladstone had an able team. Clarendon became Foreign Secretary despite the Queen's disapproval. She disliked his views on German unification and his somewhat frivolous references to herself as 'The Missus'. He died in 1870 and was succeeded by Lord Granville, who led the Liberals in the Lords. Indolent, genial and tactful, Granville was as unlike Gladstone in tastes and temperament as possible, but a very warm friendship arose between the two and contributed much to the efficiency

and stability of the Cabinet.   Bright became President of the
Board of Trade and although he proved to be administratively inefficient, like other men who have made their reputation as a popular campaigner, his membership of the Cabinet
was a factor of the utmost significance.   Time had mellowed
society's views on Bright, and the Queen had never forgotten
the moving way in which he had spoken of her widowhood,
but he was quite different from anybody who had ever sat in a
Cabinet before and by this very fact distinguished the new
Liberalism from its predecessors.

It was a mark of great generosity that the villain of the
Adullamites appeared as Chancellor of the Exchequer.
Lowe was a man of exceptional ability who would probably
have been more successful as a Civil Servant.   As a politician
he showed an unhappy touch with a tendency to cause offence
unnecessarily.   In particular he increased Gladstone's difficulties by his Budget of 1871 which proposed a new tax on
matches, a comparatively new article but already taxed by
most foreign governments.   Match manufacture was an
unhealthy and much exploited sweated industry but the House
was much moved by a pathetic demonstration of women
workers and a protest of all parties led to the withdrawal of
the tax and the placing of 2d. on the income tax.   Lowe was
forced to resign in August 1873, with two other Ministers, as a
result of irregularities at the Post Office.   Post Office revenue
and Savings Bank balances had been used for capital expenditure on telegraph services without parliamentary sanction.
Gladstone unwisely took over the Exchequer himself and the
double burden greatly added to the strain of his last six months
of office.

His Secretary for War was an able but elderly ex-Peelite,
Edward Cardwell.   In his reforms of the Army, economy
and efficiency met.   Although the Crimean War had led to
some improvement in the supply services and in soldiers'
conditions,[1] drastic administrative reform was needed to
produce an Army organised to continental standards of
efficiency, a point that the three successful wars fought by
Prussia, particularly the Franco-Prussian War of 1870, drove
well home.   With a Conservative party ready to defend time-
hallowed abuses in the Army and Liberal politicians such as

[1] See above, p. 177.

Gladstone who demanded ever greater economy, the Commander-in-Chief, the Duke of Cambridge, was able to resist all
demand for change from his subordinates and from outside.
Spurred on by public concern at British weakness in 1870,
Cardwell tackled the independent position of the Commander-
in-Chief, the purchase of commissions, the inflexible organisation of the Army and the unduly long and harsh terms of
service.

By an order in council which the Queen reluctantly signed
in June 1870, her cousin, the Commander-in-Chief, was
subordinated to the Secretary of State for War and forced to
move his headquarters from the Horse Guards to the War
Office. He exercised command, subject to parliamentary
supervision, over all land forces of the Crown including the
Militia, hitherto controlled by the Lords Lieutenant and
hence the concern of the Home Office. Equal to the Duke
in status were the heads of two other War Office sections, the
Surveyor-General of the Ordnance and the Financial Secretary. Unfortunately, the Duke remained as Commander-in-
Chief until 1895 to provide a cramping influence on further
development and the consequent failure to organise a General
Staff on the continental model was a crucial weakness in the
South African War. The Adjutant and Quartermaster
branches of the Staff were united.

A Royal Warrant of Charles II of 1683 had started the sale
and purchase of military commissions, which was confirmed
by a legal decision in 1702. Wellington had given it the
approval of his enormous prestige and a Royal Commission
defended the system in 1841. Cardwell saw clearly that it
prevented regimental reorganisation, selection and promotion
by merit, and perpetuated abuses by permitting commands to
be held by men who were untrained and quite unsuited.
The Earl of Cardigan, commander of the fated Charge of the
Light Brigade, may reasonably be instanced as an example
of the system in practice. The opposition, led by its military
members, obstructed to such an extent that, when the Army
Regulation Bill, which included other reforms, had passed
the Commons, Gladstone persuaded the Queen, who appreciated a rare exercise of arbitrary authority, to abolish by
Royal Warrant what after all had been created by Royal
Warrant. On this, Left and Right wing were in complete

agreement; the Left distrusted the royal prerogative on principle while Disraeli called it 'a shameful conspiracy against the rights of the Upper House'. Trick it was, but it served its turn. The Army Regulation Bill had provided generous compensation for purchase money spent on commissions and the Lords, presented with a *fait accompli*, made haste to pass it.

The Army Regulation Act of 1871 provided for an increase of the Army by 20,000 men to 497,000 men and divided the country into sixty-nine infantry recruiting districts. The old numbered regiments of the line had distinguished histories many going back to the 17th Century, but they had no territorial links and were almost all under strength. Each regiment was now given a district, and in most cases a territorial name, the junior regiments of the line being united. Each district had two regular battalions, one at home for training purposes, the other of seasoned troops abroad, and between one and three battalions of militia. The Infantry were rearmed with a satisfactory breech-loading rifle in 1872–74. Cardwell improved the organisation of the Artillery, although the Ordnance insisted on the retention of muzzle-loading cannon for a further twenty years. The Cavalry, an aristocratic stronghold, Cardwell did not touch.

The Army Enlistment Act of 1870 improved conditions of service. Up to 1847 a man had signed on for twenty-one years. In that year it was reduced to twelve but since more than half this time would be spent in tropical climates, men's physique was rarely good enough to make service in the reserve possible at the end of this time. The shorter service of six years with the colours followed by six with the reserve that Cardwell instituted greatly improved military recruiting, which would have been improved even more if Gladstone had been prepared to increase service pay. It also made possible the creation of a reserve of fit, well-trained men. Cardwell abolished flogging in peacetime in 1868 and the withdrawal of many troops from foreign stations helped to make the Army a more attractive career. The successful campaign in Egypt in 1882 could never have taken place but for Cardwell's reforms, yet he left the Army Estimates lower than when he took office.[1]

Liberal reforming zeal also extended to the Civil Service.

[1] For Haldane's reforms see below, p. 377.

The middle-class ideal of careers open to talent was hindered so far as the Civil Service was concerned by the persistence of patronage – the 18th-century conception that public office was a source of income. As with the Army, the Civil Service could never become really efficient until promotion and appointment were by merit, and never truly independent until these were taken out of politics. It was with this in view that Gladstone had appointed in 1853 a Commission led by Sir Stafford Northcote and G. O. Trevelyan which reported that appointment should be by examination. The most that Palmerston would accept was that a Civil Service Commission should examine the fitness of candidates presented by the political heads of the various departments. In 1870 by an Order in Council all positions in the Civil Service, with the exception of those in the Foreign and Diplomatic Service, whose traditions Clarendon successfully defended, ceased to be filled by patronage and were made subject to public competition. High intellectual standards were required for the highest grade, the Administrative Class, and this gave a new stimulus to university teaching.

Further changes followed. A new department, the Local Government Board, was created in 1871 and absorbed the Poor Law Board, the local government section of the Home Office and the medical department of the Privy Council.[1] It inherited the functions of the central Board of Health which had been abolished in 1858. Gladstone was never aware of the crucial importance of local government: it was one of several factors that later led him to fail to appreciate Joseph Chamberlain, and the misfortune of the new department was that from the start it was dominated by the officials and attitudes of the Poor Law Board it absorbed.

The increasing concern of the State with individuals necessitated, to the Liberal mind, an electoral machinery that would more genuinely reflect people's wishes. Although there was little popular demand in the country the government resuscitated in 1872 the Chartist idea of the secret ballot. It was strongly opposed by the Conservatives who feared it would mean the end of control by the old governing class; both parties were firmly convinced that the mass electorate, voting secretly, would always vote for progress and liberty. The Lords

[1] See above, p. 138.

rejected it at first but, when Gladstone bitterly attacked them, let it through.   The effect of the Act was to render comparatively valueless the more obvious forms of bribery, a tendency that was reinforced by the Corrupt Practices Act of 1883, although isolated cases of bribery continued into the 20th Century.   Despite the Conservative fears they won, ironically, the first election under the Ballot Act in 1874; it was only gradually realised that mass electorates tend to be conservative in their outlook.   The revolutionary consequences of the Act were, as no one had foreseen, in Ireland, where it made possible the creation of Parnell's Irish Nationalist Party.

In 1871 the inclusion of the working-class élite in the political nation was demonstrated by the Trades Union Act. Since 1825 the position of Trades Unions had been somewhat anomalous.[1]   The Act of that year had condemned criminal combinations in restraint of trade without defining them precisely, but had approved combinations whose sole objects were the fixing of wages or hours.   Various leading cases had implied that strikes for that purpose would not be criminal, but limitations by Trades Unions of overtime remained dubious and a wealth of uncertainty centred on the application of the words 'violence, threats, molestation and obstruction' in the 1825 Act.   Most Trades Unions had Friendly Society functions and it was believed that the security of their funds was covered by the Friendly Societies Act of 1855.   In that belief, in the case of *Hornby* v. *Close* of 1866–67 the Boilermakers' Society, a respectable craft union, prosecuted its secretary for withholding funds.   In the Queen's Bench it was ruled, to the horror of the working-class élite as a whole, that the Friendly Society Act did not apply and further; although the Trades Union was not exactly criminal it was so far in restraint of trade as to be an illegal organisation.   Disraeli appointed a Royal Commission and it was clear to the Trades Unions that they must justify their existence, a task made more difficult by recent cases of violence involving smaller and less responsible unions.   In particular there had been a series of outrages in Sheffield in which workers who refused to join the local union or were behindhand in paying their subscriptions were subjected to various forms of terrorism.   Sometimes a man's tools were removed or broken, in other cases men had

---

[1] See above, p. 133.

P

actually been killed and in 1866 a can of gunpowder was exploded in the house of a workman who had just resigned from the local Saw-Grinders Union. Confessions made to the Royal Commission established the responsibility of William Broadhead, treasurer of the Associated Trades of Sheffield, who maintained that Trades Unions were entitled to impose what sanctions they chose. The Junta prepared evidence of respectability, seeking help wherever it could, and to mobilise the utmost strength the Manchester Trades Council called the first Trades Union Congress in 1868.

Hughes and Harrison, lawyers and Christian Socialists, were members of the Commission and gave the Trades Unions considerable support. Sober, intelligent workmen were called as witnesses, strikes were disparaged and great emphasis was placed on Friendly Society activities. The Majority Report recommended full recognition of unions and their supervision by the Registrar of Friendly Societies. It proposed certain restrictions on their activities, notably the condemnation of picketing. A Minority Report of three members wanted no restrictions. The Trades Union Act of 1871 gave full legal recognition and protection of funds; the associated Criminal Law Amendment Act forbade picketing and repeated the molestation clauses. The meaning of this was clear when a number of prosecutions followed, including the imprisonment of two women in South Wales who had said 'Bah' to a blackleg. Gladstone became unpopular in consequence in the Trades Union movement and Disraeli repaid the swing of its votes by the Conspiracy and Protection of Property Act of 1875 which legalised peaceful picketing, subject to certain safeguards. A group of men in a trade dispute could now only commit a crime if the same action by one of them acting by himself would have been criminal. The Employers and Workmen Act of the same year put both parties on an equal footing in cases of breach of contract. Hitherto, whereas the employer could be fined, the workman could be imprisoned. Now damages were payable in both cases.

The principal achievement of the last year of the Ministry was the Supreme Court of Judicature Act of 1873, the work of Lord Selborne who had been appointed Lord Chancellor the previous year. The complicated series of courts that existed had frequently been criticised, notably by a Royal Commission of 1867 under the chairmanship of the Conservative Lord Cairns. There were in effect two legal systems side by side, each with a formidable background of case law: the common law in one set of courts, equity which overrode it in another. Both systems were fused; a single judge was to administer law and equity. The Court of Chancery and six courts which in various ways administered the common law – Queen's Bench, Common Pleas, Exchequer, Admiralty, Probate and Divorce – were merged in the Supreme Court which in 1880 was organised in three divisions – Chancery, Queen's Bench, and Probate, Admiralty and Divorce. The old Courts of Appeal – Exchequer Chamber, Appeal in Chancery, House of Lords and Judicial Committee of the Privy Council – were merged to form the new Court of Appeal, whose decisions were to be final. In 1876, however, the House of Lords, or more properly a committee of Law Lords, regained its ancient position as the highest court of appeal in the land. The centralisation of the law continued, however, and, apart from the ancient Chancery Courts of Durham and Lancaster, which survived, all common law litigation above the level of the County Courts, established in 1846, had to be held in London.

(c) EDUCATION

Liberals and all who believed in the freedom of the individual were particularly concerned that the power of the State should not control education. They observed how in France the schoolmaster could be the rival of the priest in swaying the hearts and minds of the people, and they saw the control of education by voluntary bodies, which meant in practice religious bodies, as the best guarantee against undue State influence and interference. Any suggestion of secular education in Victorian England was tantamount to encouraging a lack of faith. The original assumption of the governing classes that education was unnecessary for the poor; that it was prejudicial to their morals and happiness; that it would teach them to despise their lot in life', gave way to the realisation that carefully managed education would promote good order and assist technological advance. The wars of the 1860's seemed to suggest that education was an advantage in battle. The better educated North beat the South in the

American Civil War, while in 1866 Austria was beaten by Prussia, which had the best elementary educational system in Europe, dating back to the beginning of the century. It was appreciated that an educated electorate was better for the country than an uneducated one and the great extension of the franchise brought home the immediacy of the problem. Individual efforts and the extension of State control had already improved the quality and the quantity of education to some extent. Of increasing social importance and influence in the State were the public schools, many of ancient foundation but some established specifically to provide educational opportunities for the rising middle class. Curricula were chiefly classical and invariably narrow; teaching was mostly unimaginative and unproductive; but the chief end of the public schools in mid-century was to produce not men of ability but men of character, a view upheld until the end of the century when a great premium was set on intellectual attainment. Thomas Arnold of Rugby was by no means the first reformer; his predecessor as headmaster had greatly improved the quality and size of the school, while Butler of Shrewsbury (Headmaster, 1798–1836) had introduced modern subjects and tried to create a sense of responsibility among the senior boys, hitherto the ring-leaders in disturbances. Nevertheless, Arnold was enormously influential, not least through the favourable picture drawn by the Radical Judge Hughes, himself an Old Rugbeian, in *Tom Brown's Schooldays*. Arnold did much to stimulate genuine intellectual curiosity, introduced French and Mathematics as regular subjects, civilised the almost traditional atmosphere of hooliganism, secured the co-operation of the Sixth Form and above all through his sermons in the school chapel laid down those moral standards that were to make of the public schools 'nurseries of Christian gentlemen'. Arnold would not have favoured the canonisation of games as character-forming agencies that began in the late 19th Century.

Some of the Proprietary Schools established during the period led the way to better teaching methods and a wider curriculum, notably the school of Rowland Hill, the inventor of penny postage, at Birmingham. He used small rooms for each class instead of one great room where several forms were taught simultaneously which was the usual practice, and encouraged experiments in self-government. There were many private schools, however, of a very low standard, some even as bad as 'Dotheboys Hall'.

The quality of the old endowed grammar schools also varied greatly. Ancient statutes provided salaries so inadequate, in some cases, that it was impossible for a schoolmaster to regard it as his sole source of livelihood. They also invariably restricted the curriculum to classical studies; a case involving Leeds Grammar School in 1805 established that modern subjects were illegal during normal school time. There was no way of ensuring that masters were diligent, and a few schools had no boys at all. As the century went by, however, the old endowed schools were increasingly influenced by public school reforms.

Two Royal Commissions surveyed the position. The Clarendon Commission of 1861 dealt with the nine great public schools; the Taunton Commission of 1864 with other endowed schools. They resulted in The Endowed Schools Act which Gladstone's government introduced in 1869. This appointed three commissioners, whose work was taken over by the Charity Commission in 1874. They were able to revise statutes and to make available to the schools disused charitable funds. This was an impetus to the adoption of new subjects, notably science, although the schools were slow to respond. The first university examining body for schools was set up in 1871 and helped to raise standards of instruction. The Taunton Commission pressed unsuccessfully for the foundation of more secondary schools and for more opportunities for those who could not afford the fees.

If boys' education was inadequate in the early 19th Century, secondary education for girls was virtually non-existent. It was considered neither necessary nor desirable. After 1840, however, there were a number of opportunities. Women were able to obtain higher education at Bedford College, London, from 1846 onwards, while in 1848 the Christian Socialists, Charles Kingsley and F. D. Maurice, who became the first principal, helped to found Queen's College, Harley Street, London, in 1848 as a training college for women teachers. Among the first students were Miss Buss and Miss Beale; the former changed the name of the private school she ran to the North London Collegiate School for Ladies in 1850, while Miss Beale, after serving with Miss Buss, became principal of Cheltenham Ladies College in 1858. They established standards for women's education that have endured, but the Taunton Commission were very critical of what existed in 1864 and it was to meet their criticisms that the Girls' Public Day School Trust was established in 1871. It was not until after the Balfour Education Act, however, that the standards and opportunities of girls' secondary education began to approach that of boys'. In the field of higher education the new universities followed the example of London and provided from their inception equal facilities for women. Newnham College, Cambridge was established in 1871 and Girton was transferred from Hitchin to Cambridge in 1872, although it was not until the end of the century that women were allowed to take Cambridge degrees. Lady Margaret Hall opened at Oxford in 1878.

Elementary education, which was all the overwhelming majority of the working class could hope to aspire to, needed State intervention at an earlier stage. In 1833 the principles of State assistance and concern were established by the granting of £20,000 a year to the British and Foreign Schools Society and the more prosperous National Schools Society, for the building of schools.[1]   The grant was increased in 1839 and as a financial control, a Committee of the Privy Council on Education was set up, with Kay-Shuttleworth as secretary. Inspectors were appointed, a set each for the Church of England, the Roman Catholics and the Nonconformists. There were twenty-one inspectors by 1850 and 4,396 schools open to inspection; grants totalled half a million pounds a year. Training schemes for teachers were being organised by the societies and in 1846 the Committee inaugurated a scheme of apprenticeship at recommended schools which entitled the teacher, when qualified, to a higher salary. Religious jealousies prevented the spending of local rates on education; provision of schools was haphazard with many school-less areas, particularly in the large industrial towns, and many parents were reluctant to send to school children who could be earning. The restriction by law of opportunities for children to earn gradually induced parents to realise that learning was at any rate a harmless alternative.

[1] See above, p. 93.

A Minister, the Vice-President of the Committee of the Council for Education, was placed in charge in 1856. Owing to the influence of the Prince Consort and in view of the rising cost of education, the Newcastle Commission was appointed and reported in 1858. It discovered that only one-eighth of the child population was at school and one-quarter of these were at worthless private schools. It proposed the setting-up of local boards of education with powers to levy rates. The unwillingness of Anglicans to subsidise schools which did not teach the Anglican catechism and the similar outlook of the Nonconformists prevented the adoption of what was ultimately to prove the logical solution. Lowe, who was in charge of education at this period, adopted the Commission's other proposal, payment by results, and applied it in a narrow, mechanical way, basing additional grants to teachers and schools on the number of children who passed an examination set by the inspectors. The system clearly raised the standard of the worst schools but it offered no incentive for the educational development of the brighter children and led to the forcing of the dull ones. Really hopeless children were sometimes despatched to other schools when examination day came round and questions were surreptitiously circulated from school to school. The Cross Commission of 1888 exposed its inadequacies but only modifications were made and the system was not abolished until 1900.

Gladstone's Vice-President was W. E. Forster, a retired Bradford manufacturer with a Quaker background who was Arnold of Rugby's son-in-law. In a subject bristling with difficulties, he evolved an act that has come to be seen as one of the great foundation statutes of the British educational system. Its purpose was not to supersede but to complete previous legislation, but in so doing it made possible the development of a truly national system. The State grant to voluntary schools which were inspected and found satisfactory was doubled. A proposal to pay the fees of needy children at voluntary schools out of the rates was bitterly opposed by Radicals who wanted purely secular education, and Joseph Chamberlain first became prominent by his organisation of the Birmingham League to promote this. His efforts here led to the foundation of the National Liberal Federation in 1877. Forster appreciated that the time was not ripe for the abolition or absorption of the voluntary system, but 2,568 School Boards were created, following existing local government boundaries as far as possible, to build and manage new schools where they were needed. The Boards were elected by rate-payers and could levy a school rate. The question of religious instruction at the new schools was a bitter one and the obvious compromise of the Cowper-Temple clause, whose adoption was secured by Gladstone's personal intervention, pleased neither side. Simple Bible instruction, without any denominational interpretation, was ordered in Board Schools.

The new system had its weaknesses. Payment by results was left untouched. The School Boards themselves were allowed to enforce attendances if they wished and were enabled to provide education up to the age of thirteen. Fees were to be paid where they could be afforded, on the grounds that it was a parental duty to educate their children. The efficiency of the Boards greatly varied but in the larger towns some very striking improvements were made. The London School Board alone built over 400 schools; the Leeds School Board also had a record of efficiency and keen public interest. The new schools were graceless and austere, made of supposedly indestructible materials, but they represented an opening of the doors of education for many to whom they had been tightly closed. Over two and a half million school places were created during the thirty years of the Boards' existence. Mundella's Act of 1880 made education compulsory to the age of ten, although it proved difficult to enforce. The leaving age became eleven in 1893 and twelve in 1899 as better provision became available. But the system proved to be far more costly than had been anticipated.

The compulsory payment of fees was unpopular among the working class and Liberal educationalists hoped to strangle the voluntary schools by making education free in Board Schools only. To forestall this and to acknowledge their debt to the Liberal Unionists Lord Salisbury's government introduced in 1891 a capitation grant of ten shillings to every school which led to the disappearance of fees by 1895.

Extravagant forecasts were made of the results of wider schooling but it was estimated that by 1910 three-quarters of the adult population had been efficiently educated by contemporary standards, leading to improvements in discipline, cleanliness and punctuality. Moreover the compulsory attendance of children at school led to better realisation of the low standards of clothing and nourishment that prevailed in many places. Many School Boards had to start a system of cheap school meals and clothing was presented by the charitable.

After the Great Exhibition, in order to improve Britain's competitive position abroad, the Science and Art Department of the Board of Trade was set up to promote secondary and technical education. It had no official link with the Education Department until 1902. Grants were payable to institutions which taught courses prescribed in its calendar, a system which the Bryce Commission of 1894, appointed to survey secondary education, described as unbalancing secondary education, although its work was on a small scale. A Royal Commission on Technical Instruction of 1882–84, however, criticised provision in England and described the wealth of institutions provided at State expense on the Continent. This caused considerable concern and led to the Technical Instruction Act of 1889, by which technical education was made the responsibility of the newly-established County Councils.

Provision for and efficiency of university education were steadily increasing. As with the public schools they provided ground where the rising middle classes could mingle with the old aristocracy to the benefit of both groups. Royal Commissions had looked into Oxford and Cambridge in the 1850's and acts of 1854 and 1871, with both of which Gladstone was concerned, brought about an institutional reform which improved both their efficiency and their fairness. It was not until 1871 that Gladstone felt sufficiently independent of Oxford to open university examinations to those who would not subscribe to the Thirty-nine Articles. The acts integrated colleges more with the universities and forced them to disburse some of their funds, stipulated that Fellows of Colleges should take on teaching or administrative duties and promoted the foundation of new Chairs. In 1877 Fellows were no longer required to be celibate; few decisions have probably so much changed the atmosphere of Oxford and Cambridge.

The new universities, Durham, founded in 1832 and London, which became a university in 1836, were less expensive and consequently could draw their students from a wider social background. Their syllabuses tended to be more liberal and more responsive to the scientific needs of the age. The Scottish universities also became important centres of scientific progress. Here new elements in the atmosphere, argon, helium, neon, were discovered; the electro-magnetic theory of matter was outlined by Maxwell and Lord Kelvin and developed in detail by J. J. Thomson. Although the study of Applied Science did not progress as rapidly as that of Pure Science the major provincial towns were not slow to see the importance of university education to their industry and, with the help of substantial donations from private individuals, Owen's College, Manchester, founded in 1851, became the nucleus of the Victoria University in 1884 which established tributary colleges in Leeds and Liverpool. It divided in 1903–4. In 1900 Mason's College became Birmingham University; in 1893 the University of Wales, with colleges in different parts of the principality, was created. Women were admitted on equal terms with men and the new universities were largely non-residential, on the continental model.

Attempts were made to provide university-style teaching for those who could not even manage day attendance. In 1871 Cambridge started University Extension Lectures which provided a type of secondary education at this period. Oxford and the new universities followed suit.

(d) Foreign Policy and the End of the Ministry

Foreign policy under Gladstone meant a change of methods, although there is more continuity with Palmerston's aims than appears at first sight. Vigilance was still necessary, firm action on occasions essential. The change in the European power grouping, following the Prussian victories, was a factor of far greater importance in determining British foreign policy than the death of Palmerston. There were two alternatives; involvement which implied an Army of continental size or dignified withdrawal, which amounted to merely lending careful diplomatic support to the settling of explosive issues. In this Disraeli and Salisbury were markedly more successful than Gladstone, although the expansion of colonial commitments led to involvement of a different kind. Great confidence was felt by both parties in the Navy as the ultimate guarantee of British security.

Gladstone maintained that it was dangerous for England 'to

assume alone an advanced and therefore an isolated position, in regard to European controversies; that, come what may, it is better for her to promise too little than too much; that she should not encourage the weak by giving expectations of aid to resist the strong but should rather seek to deter the strong by firm but moderate language from aggression on the weak; that she should seek to develop and mature the action of a common or public or European opinion, as the best standing bulwark against wrong.' Granville, who came to the Foreign Office in 1870, held these views to an even more marked degree than Gladstone.

Hammond, the Permanent Under-Secretary at the Foreign Office, a competent but somewhat blinkered expert, remarked in 1870 that he had 'never during his long experience known so great a lull in foreign affairs.' Almost immediately a crisis developed that profoundly altered the balance of European power. Since 1866 Bismarck had been trying to tempt Napoleon III to some act of aggression that would enable Prussia to cement German unification under her domination. Napoleon never ceased to dream and scheme for territorial acquisitions but the actual occasion of the crisis was one of which he was almost entirely innocent. A Spanish Junta had expelled Queen Isabella and was seeking a suitable constitutional monarch; Bismarck, using the Guelphic Fund, the money confiscated from its King when Hanover was overrun in 1866, promoted the candidacy of a Roman Catholic member of the Prussian Royal House, Prince Leopold of Hohenzollern-Sigmaringen. Not unreasonably Napoleon complained of encirclement, and with considerable adroitness he obtained a withdrawal of the candidature. But he was a sick man and was unable to withstand the demand of the Empress, Gramont the Foreign Minister and other belligerent elements, for a public humiliation of Prussia. The British Government made it clear that Prussia had made every reasonable concession, and King William was quite justified in refusing to promise to the French ambassador that a Hohenzollern candidature would never be renewed. A report of this incident was edited by Bismarck as the inflammatory *Ems Telegram*. Both France and Germany later reproached the British Government for not indicating clearly where it stood, but in fact, after the failures of 1864, both powers had written off

Great Britain as a factor to be reckoned with and it is doubtful whether British diplomatic intervention would have made any difference to the eventual outcome. British public opinion supported Gladstone in his neutral stand. Initially there was sympathy with the Germans, particularly when Bismarck revealed that Napoleon had had designs on Belgium, but after the Battle of Sedan and the fall of Metz, an unparalleled military capitulation, sympathy for the French was predominant, a feeling confirmed when the Germans took Alsace and Lorraine. Gladstone was anxious for a plebiscite in those territories, but Granville persuaded him not to raise the matter in the belief that it would prolong the war. Great concern was felt in England for the starving city of Paris, and London alone sent £80,000 worth of provisions. The dramatic swiftness of the war gave considerable relevance to Cardwell's reforms and there was a temporary increase in the Army Estimates. An anonymous pamphlet, written in fact by a senior officer of the Royal Engineers, *The Battle of Dorking*, brought home to the public the possibility of a German invasion of England.

The weakness of Britain's position in the new Europe was demonstrated when, after the fall of Metz, the Tsar, with German concurrence, announced in October 1870 that he was no longer bound by the Black Sea Clauses, imposed in 1856. With France unable to help and the Turks afraid to act alone, the restriction could only be reimposed by fighting another Crimean War, an action which no serious politician would have dared to justify in the circumstances although the newspapers were speaking of war as imminent. Lord Odo Russell succeeded in persuading Bismarck to take up the matter with Russia, a blatant acknowledgement in itself of Prussia's overwhelming position. A conference held in London declared solemnly the sanctity of treaties and ruled that they could not be abrogated without the consent of all signatories. This done, it hastened to give Russia all she asked for. Granville and Gladstone had probably taken the only sensible course, but to the British public they appeared weak and ineffective. It began to be believed that Gladstone could not be trusted to defend British interests and also that the Russians were treacherous, a factor of significance in shaping public attitudes to the Eastern crisis of 1876-78.

Public distrust of Gladstone's stewardship was increased by his response to the long-standing *Alabama* claims. Palmerston had refused to consider the exaggerated claims the Americans had put forward, but on his coming to power Gladstone felt that the matter would permanently poison relations between the two countries unless a satisfactory settlement were made. Clarendon negotiated an agreement to submit the dispute to arbitration, but the American Senate refused to ratify it, demanding a direct settlement. The Black Sea Crisis made the British Government conscious of its isolation and negotiations were re-opened in 1871, Lord de Grey and Northcote being the British delegates.[1] It was eventually decided to refer the matter to a Court of Arbitration, and the Treaty of Washington, signed at the same time, established important principles in international law concerning disputes between States and liability for damages.

A court at Geneva, consisting of delegates of Britain, the United States, Switzerland, Italy, and Brazil, considered the claims in the light of the Treaty of Washington. Palmerston would have maintained that they could not do so impartially as the foreign delegates would all be jealous of British wealth, a view shared by much of the British public. The Americans, rendered unreasonable because President Grant was seeking re-election, presented a bill for indirect damages, which they had previously agreed not to do, and were only persuaded to withdraw it with difficulty. The award was made in September 1872 and amounted to £3½ m. There was considerable public outcry in Britain at the amount involved, which greatly increased when Gladstone decided to accept it. He described it as 'harsh in extent and unjust in basis' but these considerations were dust in the balance compared with the moral value of the example. He could well have refused and stood on England's national honour, but he considered the long-term good relations of the two countries to be more important.[2] The British public looked wistfully back to the days of Palmerston, and Disraeli, who had behaved with

[1] Telegrams alone cost £5,000. The delegates complained they felt they ought to refer to London to discover whether they should reply to the 'Good Morning' of the U.S. delegates.

[2] At one of the theatres, Gladstone was depicted receiving an embassy from China which demanded Scotland from him. Three replies seemed possible: to yield Scotland at once; to wait a little and end by yielding it, or to name an arbitrator. It was greeted with ironical applause.

impeccable correctness, was cheered for the first time in the streets of London.

An Act passed in 1871 added to Gladstone's unpopularity. The Temperance Movement was strong among the Nonconformist element in the Liberal Party and it had long pressed for a local veto on the sale of alcohol. A very much more moderate measure was introduced in 1871 but hurriedly withdrawn amidst howls of protest from the liquor trade. Much watered down, it reappeared in 1872 and became law. It gave magistrates the right of granting licences, checked adulteration, and limited opening hours. In retrospect it can be seen as a valuable piece of legislation, but the Temperance Movement thought it too lenient while every public house became a focus of discontent which swayed many votes to the Conservative party in 1874 and this Gladstone considered was the crucial factor in losing him the election. From now on the brewers were firmly Conservative, although hitherto they had often been Liberal: Stansfield, the first President of the Local Government Board, was a brewer. Financially this support was invaluable to the Conservatives and they repaid it by extending licencing hours slightly by an act of 1874.

In 1872 Gladstone made two appointments which evaded the qualifications required in a way many felt to be dishonest. His relations with the Queen worsened; he condemned her withdrawal from public life and failed to persuade her to provide useful work for the Prince of Wales; only Granville's tact enabled the forms to be preserved. Many of the great reforms undertaken by the government, notably that of education, had caused great hostility. When he became Chancellor of the Exchequer in 1873 Gladstone became immersed in his passion for economy and in a scheme for ending the income tax. What public opinion wanted, as Disraeli well knew, was a more colourful foreign and imperial policy. Disraeli had not wasted his years of opposition; wisely refusing to take office until Gladstone's cup of unpopularity was full he had carefully built up an efficient party organisation, steadily won by-elections and prepared candidates for every constituency in which the Conservatives had a chance. In an often quoted speech at Manchester Disraeli spoke of a Ministry in decline: 'As I sat opposite the Treasury Bench, the Ministers reminded me of one of those marine landscapes not very unusual on the coasts of South America. You behold a range of exhausted volcanoes. Not a flame flickers on a single pallid crest, but the situation is still dangerous. There are occasional earthquakes and ever and anon the dark rumbling of the sea.'

Gladstone's remaining purpose was to produce a dramatic budget that would abolish the income tax. This would involve the rapid ending of a war being fought against the Ashantis in the Gold Coast and ruthless economies in every department, to which Cardwell, the War Minister, and Goschen, First Lord of the Admiralty, particularly objected. Impulsively, Gladstone, who was perturbed by the Conservative insinuation that he should have stood for re-election when he became Chancellor, decided to dissolve Parliament. The Party was unprepared and without a programme. Chamberlain diagnosed its malaise as leaders without principles and a party without discipline. All the factors that had contributed to Gladstone's unpopularity led to his defeat in the 1874 Election. The Conservatives obtained a majority of eighty-three, forty-eight clear of the Irish party which now, as a result of the Ballot Act, began to emerge as an independent political force. Meanwhile Disraeli could at last enjoy the reality of power, while Gladstone had behind him six years of achievement of which G. M. Trevelyan could write: 'Gladstone did more than any other man to adapt the machinery of the British State and the habits of British politicians to modern democratic conditions without a total loss of the best standards of the older world.'

VI · DISRAELI IN POWER

(a) The Cabinet, the Monarchy and the Empire

In a long period of opposition and minority rule, Disraeli had slowly evolved from the old Tory party of a class, which had rejected Peel because he had gone too fast for them, the new Conservative party of the nation. Essentially a romantic and an idealist, he had shown an excellence in debate which had made him one of the foremost Parliamentarians of the time, and an astute grasp of political tactics which had its reward in 1874 in the first Conservative majority since the repeal of the Corn Laws. Success brought him loyalty; many of his followers had queried the wisdom of the 'Leap in the Dark' which had seemed to some as great a betrayal as Peel's, and these doubts had been apparently confirmed by the General Election of 1868. Now the unprecedented majority seemed a divine dispensation to a chosen people and the Conservatives, looking forward with confidence, saw Disraeli no longer as an adventurer whose genius was tolerated while his authority was contested, but as an object of respect. With a strong majority to lean on and the support of the Queen who welcomed his return with unconcealed delight, he at last had in his hands what all his life he had longed for, Power.

To a friend's congratulations he replied, 'For me, it is twenty years too late. Give me your age and health.' He was now nearly seventy, his health was far from good and only fourteen months earlier he had lost his wife, to whom he had been devoted. His loneliness was very real; his romantic attachment to two elderly sisters, the Countess of Bradford and the dowager Countess of Chesterfield, and his devotion to the Queen, 'The Faery', were at best but make-believe. At a time when the importance and responsibilities of the premiership were steadily increasing, the wonder is not that his performance failed to live up to earlier expectations, but that he achieved as much.

From his 'Young England' days he brought many ideas, subsequently modified by experience, that he now had the opportunity to put into practice. In *Sybil* he had shown the serious divisions in the nation, and he saw as the nation's main hope a greater solidarity and sense of community. Gladstone's reforms had not, in his opinion, reached the main root of the problem, the condition of the people, and it was this that he set himself to improve. Here he had to carry with him his party with its strong property interests, very few of whom supported social reform for its own sake. There was, however, more agreement on his other principles. The Church of England had been a traditional mainstay of the Conservative party and he took over as a government measure a bill introduced by the Archbishop of Canterbury to check the ritual excesses accompanying the Anglo-Catholic movement. The Public Worship Act of 1874 had little effect as a measure, but as a piece of party propaganda it was invaluable.

Like Gladstone, he reverenced the historic institutions that had contributed so much to England's greatness and chief among these, in providing a focus of national and imperial loyalty, he saw the Crown. It had been commonly assumed throughout the earlier 19th Century that the survival of the monarchy would prove incompatible with the march of democracy and the achievement of universal suffrage. Neither George IV nor William IV had been respected, though the popularity of Queen Adelaide had helped the latter, while the Prince Consort's theories of constitutional practice had been so bitterly attacked in the Press in 1854 that the Queen had threatened to abdicate. Since the death of Albert in 1861, Victoria had retired into gloomy seclusion and there was a growing feeling that the monarchy was not giving the nation value for money. In 1867 Bagehot, writing on the philosophy of the Constitution, spoke of the presence in every community of an irrational appetite, emotional or imaginative, which monarchy satisfies and also stimulates – a desire for dignity, serenity, grandeur. He also saw the advantage, even the necessity, of having somewhere in the State a person beyond the competition for office, who would be entitled to be heard on any matter on which he might think it his duty to speak. These, he felt, were the real arguments for monarchy rather than its actual political functions.

Republicanism had received a fillip from the expulsion of Napoleon III and a nation-wide campaign was organised, with Joseph Chamberlain and Charles Bradlaugh as leading members and Sir Charles Dilke as chief orator. In February 1870 the Prince of Wales was cited as co-respondent in a divorce case and although he was quite innocent and his name was cleared, the incident served to highlight a pleasure-seeking way of life, which gave offence in many quarters. He was insulted in the theatre and hissed on the racecourse, while the theme of value for money came uppermost when the Queen, herself parsimonious and reluctant to perform her public duties, asked Parliament for grants for Princess Louise on her marriage and, later, for the Duke of Connaught on his coming of age. In 1871 there was a demonstration in Trafalgar Square against 'princely paupers' and fifty-three members of the Commons voted for a reduced grant. Fawcett and Dilke led a parliamentary campaign to probe the civil list and some fifty republican clubs were set up in various towns. Active republicans, however, were few, although many thoughtful observers felt that the virtues of the wearer would preserve the Crown for one successor, but hardly for more than one.

The new kind of monarchy came into existence with a curiously dramatic change in public opinion. In the autumn of 1871 the Queen was unwell and in November the Prince of Wales had a long and dangerous illness which brought great public sympathy for the royal family. When the Prince made a sudden recovery, the Queen issued a personal letter of thanks to her people and, after Gladstone with great skill and tenderness had persuaded her to do so against her wish, had attended a public service of thanksgiving in St Paul's Cathedral; popular enthusiasm was overwhelming. Two days later an attempt was made to assassinate the Queen and this killed the republican movement in England. Disraeli astutely seized on this revival of royal popularity to make his famous Crystal Palace speech in June 1872, exalting the Crown as the focus of the new imperialism.

It is not until the Jubilee of 1887 that the Queen can be shown, by a study of the Press, to have become generally admired, but from 1872 onwards her prestige and popularity were assured. For Gladstone, Victoria had usually declined to sacrifice her tranquillity and personal comfort for any public duties beyond the scrupulous examination of government despatches on which Albert had always insisted. With greater understanding of the Queen's mentality and greater tact Disraeli, no less convinced that a monarchy that was not seen would not long continue to hold its place in the hearts of the people, succeeded in 1876 in persuading the Queen to open Parliament in person. This initiated a more frequent participation in public events which contributed greatly to the new prestige of the monarchy.

From the personal point of view Disraeli found that the Queen, who by this time had an unrivalled experience of public affairs and had a retentive and faithful memory, was an excellent person to talk things over with, although, except in the matter of the imperial title, he never allowed her to influence the course of events. It was a misfortune that the Queen saw events and Ministers from an intensely personal angle and her happy relationship with Disraeli made her a partisan; Salisbury and Rosebery she favoured, but Gladstone, despite his loyalty to and respect for her person, she could never like.

With the Crown once more brought to the centre of national life, Disraeli had foreshadowed its importance, in his Crystal Palace speech, as the pivot of a great empire. The British Empire had been acquired, to use the famous phrase, in 'a fit of absence of mind' whether as the perquisites of trade or by the accidents of foreign policy. Although much thought had been given to the constitutional development of Canada[1] and other self-governing dominions, no real philosophy of empire had been worked out. The events of 1870–71, in which a major alteration had occurred in the balance of Europe without reference to England, caused to some extent a revulsion from the Continent. England was outclassed as a military power; Russia, Germany and France surpassed her in area and manpower. At present England was 'the workshop of the world' but Disraeli was not deceived, as many of his contemporaries were, by the trade and wealth of Great Britain. All this helped to promote a growing awareness of the Empire, whose existence significantly altered British rating among the powers, and which had the moral virtue of bringing the blessings of civilisation and order to backward and strife-torn communities, a feeling of patronage from which the Liberal Party was not immune. Disraeli attached this growing sentiment

[1] See above, p. 103.

to the Conservative party, although individual Liberals, such as Dilke, Rosebery, Forster and Chamberlain, were perhaps more active imperialists, and had emphasised the importance of British overseas possessions in the election campaign of 1874. In practice, however, Disraeli's active interest was limited to India and the East and he made no contribution to the development of what were to become the self-governing dominions.

Disraeli's first important contribution was the purchase of the Suez Canal Shares. When the canal had been originally proposed, Palmerston had realised what a change it would make in the defensive position of the British Empire and had opposed the project. Largely as a result of this, the canal had been built almost entirely by French enterprise and French money although from the first British ships had been the principal users. In return for the land concession and the labour he had supplied, the Khedive Ismail had been allotted seven-sixteenths of the shares. His financial difficulties, however, were perpetual and as early as 1870 he had offered his shares to the British Government and had suggested, apparently with de Lesseps' concurrence, that the British should take over the whole of what was not yet a paying concern. Gladstone had refused and de Lesseps heavily increased the canal dues. Disraeli had made up his mind that British interests in the canal must be secured and in 1874 sent a private mission to France with this end in view. French public opinion, recovering from the war of 1870, was very touchy and the mission was a failure.

In November 1875 a journalist, Frederick Greenwood, brought to the Foreign Office the news that the Khedive was negotiating with a French syndicate for the sale of his shares. There was a rival syndicate in the field who were making it difficult to raise money in Paris and this delay provided the British Government with an opportunity. Derby was reluctant, but Disraeli managed to persuade the Cabinet to agree to the purchase. De Lesseps urged the French Government to take action but they held their hand, anxious not to alienate the British. An option was obtained on the shares, the Bank of England was unable to raise £4 m. without grave disturbance of the money market and, as Disraeli put it in a letter to the Queen,

Four millions sterling! and almost immediately. There was only one firm that could do it, Rothschilds. They behaved admirably, advanced the money at low rate and the entire interest of the Khedive is now yours, Madam.

The purchase was approved by Parliament without a division and both at home and abroad it was regarded as an act of national leadership. Financially it was an excellent bargain; in the next fifty years the sum was repaid in dividends about eight times over and by 1914 the estimated value of the shares was £40 m. It did not of course give England a controlling interest in the canal and contributed little to securing the route to India; its principal direct benefit was that thereby more reasonable tolls were made possible for British merchant ships which amounted to 80 per cent of the users of the canal. Primarily its value was psychological; coming when it did, it focused attention on the East, and on the need to prevent Russia dominating Turkey and hence the eastern end of the Mediterranean.[1]

From Suez to India is a logical step. Since the East India Company had been abolished in 1858 and the Crown had assumed complete responsibility for the government of India, the matter of a title for the Queen that would emphasise the new relationship had often been contemplated. The Prince of Wales had made a very successful visit to India in the winter of 1875–76, which had brought out the special glamour of the monarchy for the oriental imagination. The Queen took the initiative and Disraeli, who would have preferred to wait a few more years, agreed. The title of Empress of India was not popular in England initially: one speaker remarked that it evoked 'images of conquests, persecution and even of debauchery', while the misfortunes of Napoleon III and Maximilian of Mexico were not a happy augury; but in India, proclaimed in January 1877 by the Viceroy, Lord Lytton, at a great Durbar, it was greeted with enthusiasm. The world understood that a new pledge had been given of the determination of the British Crown to cherish India and it assisted the idea of Indian development parallel with, but not subordinate to, Great Britain. A suggestion that other British territories should be incorporated in the new title was considered but was dropped.[2]

[1] See below, p. 246.   [2] See above, p. 177 and below, p. 506.

For his Ministry Disraeli had formed an efficient team. The Secretary of State for India was Lord Salisbury, who had severed himself from the Conservative front bench in 1867 through his disapproval of Disraeli's reform policy and whose return in 1874 was one of Disraeli's major achievements. Disraeli won confidence by giving it and asked his advice on many matters outside his department. It was not until the later stages of the Eastern crisis when Salisbury succeeded Derby as Foreign Secretary that they really worked well together but Salisbury's successful tenure of this office established his right to succeed Disraeli in the leadership of the party. The fifteenth Earl of Derby, son of Disraeli's former chief, proved a capable Foreign Secretary, despite a tendency to hesitation and procrastination which often afflicted him at critical moments. His Lord Chancellor was Cairns, a progressive lawyer and an invaluable member of the Cabinet; the Duke of Richmond led the Lords, while Sir Stafford Northcote at the Exchequer stood for sound finance and sober respectability. At the War Office Gathorne Hardy showed himself a capable departmental head, who continued the work of Cardwell while showing himself one of the best debaters of the day. Ward Hunt ruled the Admiralty, Hicks Beach showed great ability in administering Ireland while at the Home Office Disraeli placed R. A. Cross, a little-known Lancashire bank director. It was singular chance or an act of rare judgment that gave Disraeli a colleague to realise the aspirations of *Sybil*.

For two years Disraeli ably led the Commons in power as he had led his own party in opposition. He was particularly attentive to his duties, staying long at the House, going out of his way to congratulate his supporters on their speeches, in contrast to Gladstone who barely noticed his supporters at all. Few parliamentary questions or situations could find him unprepared and, rarely speaking away from Parliament, he was completely at home in that assembly. But his high standards of parliamentary attendance and the strains of the premiership, particularly the growing seriousness of the Eastern question, proved too much for his failing health and in August 1876 he accepted the Earldom of Beaconsfield[1] in the hope that in

---

[1] Disraeli had been offered a peerage in 1868; he accepted on behalf of his wife, who became Viscountess Beaconsfield in her own right.

the Lords he might find the strain less exacting.   With Gladstone now making rare appearances, and the growing Irish
obstruction, Disraeli's departure seemed to many to be the end
of the great days of the Commons.   Harcourt, a political
opponent, remarked, 'Henceforth the game will be like the
chess board when the queen is gone – a petty struggle of
pawns.'   Disraeli had few doubts of the wisdom of his change:
'I am dead, but in the Elysian fields.'   He rapidly made as
great a mark in the Lords as he had previously in the
Commons.

The vacant leadership of the Commons devolved upon
Northcote.   Hardy was the member of the Cabinet whose
intervention carried most influence in the House, but the
Whips were afraid his quick temper might land the party in
difficulties, and he was not as attentive as Northcote to the
business of the House.   The latter, though not brilliant,
proved an adequate leader until 1880.

(b) Health and Housing

Sir John Gorst, the Conservative Party organiser, later
defined the principle of Tory democracy as:

> all government exists solely for the good of the governed; all
> who are entrusted with any public function are trustees, not for
> their own class but for the nation at large.   The mass of the
> people may be trusted so to use electoral power, which should be
> freely conceded to them, as to support those who are promoting
> their interests.   It is democratic because the welfare of the people
> is its supreme end, Tory because the institutions of the country
> are the means by which that end is to be attained.

This represents an ideal, but of all periods of Conservative
rule in the 19th Century the work of Disraeli and Cross
between 1874 and 1876 came nearest to attaining it.   Disraeli
was anxious that the Conservative Party's advent to power
should be marked by a policy of generosity.   This was the
moment to put into action the ideas of *Coningsby* and *Sybil*.   If
the inspiration came from Disraeli, it was Cross who with
ability piloted most of the complex acts through the Commons.   Cross was not an outstanding parliamentary figure but
in the torrent of legislation, which included some of the most
important acts of the century, he made a greater contribution
to the well-being of the country than many better-known men.

The idea of the government purely as the good policeman was abandoned with reluctance during the 19th Century. However great the need might be proved to be, the liberty of the subject, which often amounted to a man's right to make a little hell on earth for his neighbours or tenants, was hotly defended. There was great reluctance to introduce compulsive legislation while permissive legislation frequently foundered on doctrines of *laissez-faire*, vested interests and sheer ignorance. All previous legislation dealing with health and housing had been beset with these difficulties and that of Disraeli and Cross was no exception. The Reform Act of 1867, however, in extending the vote to the better paid working classes in the towns, had made them a political factor and hence the ordinary member of Parliament was now more aware of their problems and more disposed to deal with them effectively. Also the sheer bulk of legislation inevitably brought public attention to the matter and helped to create a favourable climate of opinion, which tended to increase the effectiveness of later measures.

The matter of health[1] was brought again to public attention by an outbreak of cholera in 1865–66 and local authorities were temporarily compelled to appoint sanitary inspectors and to undertake provision of sewers, water supply and refuse disposal. Before leaving office in 1868, Disraeli, who showed a concern for sanitation quite exceptional among politicians of the period, appointed a Royal Commission on Sanitary Laws, which reported in 1871. As a result the Local Government Board was set up whose President took over responsibility for the local health boards and the Poor Law guardians. This unfortunate partnership set the pattern of the Board's activities; like the Poor Law Commissioners it aimed at being a watchdog against extravagance and failed to give from the centre the positive stimulus, enlightened guidance and constructive advice based on research that was needed.

But despite this municipal development went forward. The stimulus came gradually through the Reform Act of 1867 which applied the parliamentary franchise to municipal elections. Narrow and corrupt cliques, kept in power at town halls by electoral apathy, could not survive the new public interest. Already in 1847 Liverpool had appointed its

[1] For earlier history of Public Health, see above, p. 135.

own Medical Officer of Health, Manchester had followed in
1869 and in the same year had cleared slum tenements and
laid out Deansgate. The classic example, however, is
Birmingham; in the previous forty years the population of the
borough had doubled and from one of the healthiest it had
become one of the least healthy of English towns. In 1851 the
physical welfare of nearly a quarter of a million people was
supervised by one inspector of nuisances and one medical man
whose office, though unpaid, was on grounds of economy
allowed to lapse. In the diseases which came from dirt and
pollution the borough as late as 1873 held an unrivalled
record. Joseph Chamberlain, Mayor from 1873 to 1876, not
only transformed its civic life but set an example to others.
Birmingham was, he said, 'parked, paved, assized, marketed,
gas-and-watered and improved all as a result of three years'
active work'. The first Medical Officer of Health for the
town was appointed in 1875.

The first great contribution of the Disraeli government was
the Public Health Act of 1875. This was mainly a consolidating statute, incorporating features from over a hundred acts,
many of which were local. For the first time it armed English
municipalities as a whole with most of the powers which had
hitherto proved useful when obtained by some of them under
special acts. Local authorities were now required to provide
and maintain adequate sewerage and drainage, scavenging
and refuse collecting were declared public duties, to be systematically undertaken. Water supply was to be provided
for the area unless this was already provided efficiently by a
private company. Nuisances were to be abated, offensive
trades regulated, infectious diseases were to be controlled;
streets were to be paved, cleaned and lighted. Every municipality or other local government area was to appoint a
medical officer of health, a surveyor and a sanitary inspector.
The act aroused no real controversy, although to many the
State control implied seemed monstrous. Until 1937 it
remained the backbone of sanitary law and it has some claim
on practical grounds to be rated the greatest Act of Parliament
of the 19th Century.

An important subsidiary aspect was the campaign for pure
food. An inquiry run by *The Lancet* had revealed many types
of adulteration, the more sensational of which included alum

in bread and red and white lead in sugar confectionery. An Act was passed in 1860 which empowered local authorities to appoint analysts, but most refused to do so. The Sale of Food and Drugs Act of 1875 at last made the appointment of analysts and the prosecution of offenders compulsory and, despite skilled and prolonged litigation, the grosser and more dangerous frauds began to be stamped out, although such practices as putting salt in beer to create thirst continued.

The inadequacy of housing had long been well known but here the vested interests of landlords were particularly strong.[1] The growing division of towns into rich and poor quarters had led many wealthy people, quite unfamiliar with the dwellings of the poor, to believe the reports to be grossly exaggerated. Alternatively the same attitude of mind that animated the Boards of Guardians prevailed: the conditions were inevitable because they originated in the drunkenness, laziness and folly of many of the poor. The close relationship between adequate housing and health was only slowly understood and the rapid growth of many towns produced problems of overcrowding that have not yet been fully solved.

In 1847 a Society for Improving Dwellings for the Labouring Classes was set up and embarked on a campaign for better houses and the establishment of model lodging houses for the homeless poor. Some government action was taken in Lord Shaftesbury's Acts of 1851 which provided for the inspection of lodging houses but also gave the local authorities power, seldom used, to erect lodging houses of their own. The effectiveness of these acts depended entirely on the efficiency of the local authority concerned, but in the early sixties some progressive municipalities, such as Liverpool and Glasgow, secured under private acts special power to clear and improve insanitary areas and provide alternative accommodation. This rarely meant that the town councils would themselves build the new dwellings; invariably the land would be sold to developers on the condition that dwellings for the poor should be erected. Often this was undertaken by a charitable organisation, like the Peabody Trust in London, but the municipalities could have no guarantee that the standard of the new accommodation would be particularly high. In 1868 the Torrens Act attempted to make this process more general

[1] See above, p. 136.

by empowering local authorities, but not requiring them, to take steps for the improvement of slum areas. The Act was an important step forward in that it recognised the State's right to interfere in the interests of public health with the sacred rights of property. Cross's Acts of 1875, the Artisans' Dwellings Act, was also an important step forward. Local authorities were given wide powers to clear slum areas and rehouse. There was one drawback, however; the Act, like its predecessors, was permissive, owing to the influence of the party's right wing. Disraeli expressed the feeling of the times when he commented, 'Permissive legislation is the character of a free people. You must trust to persuasion and example.'

After the 1875 Act Chamberlain led the way with the most extensive clearance so far – fifty acres of Birmingham slums, which were replaced by Corporation Street. Many other towns undertook smaller schemes while between 1876 and 1884 the Metropolitan Board of Works displaced nearly 23,000 people and arranged for the rehousing of over 28,000. A minor Act of 1879 dealt with excessive demands for compensation, but even so there was a strong feeling that insufficient was being done. A succession of committees and pamphlets followed. Among the latter was *The Bitter Cry of Outcast London*, published anonymously but written by the Rev. R. Mearns, who described housing conditions in East London as too often resembling the middle passage of a slave ship. He pointed out that the Artisan's Dwelling Act, by leading to demolitions, had in some cases made matters worse. A Royal Commission on Housing, with a very distinguished membership, was appointed in 1884. It brought to light once more all the traditional evils, discovered houses built on refuse heaps, drinking water in stagnant tubs, sixteen houses to one lavatory. The long-term result of this was the Housing of the Working Classes Act of 1890 which finally inagurated widespread public intervention in housing, the beginning of a long and difficult undertaking.

In factory legislation Disraeli's Ministry also made a contribution. In 1874 the government remedied the wrong done in 1850 when the Ten Hours Day which Parliament had decreed in 1847 for women and children, was for administrative reasons increased to ten and a half hours. Now the government inaugurated a 56-hour week (10 hours on 5 days and 6 on Saturday) which effectively covered all classes of workers. This was followed by an important consolidation act in 1878 in which the whole intricate series of factory laws was brought under review, improved and codified.

The final act of significance in Disraeli's Ministry was the Merchant Shipping Act of 1876. Here again there was great need for government regulation. The technique, as Chamberlain later described it, was, 'buy your ship as cheaply as you can, equip her as poorly as you can, load her as fully as you can, insure her as highly as you can – and send her to sea. If she gets to the end of the voyage you will have made a good thing out of it; if she goes to the bottom you will have made a better thing out of it.' There was a growing movement in favour of improving this situation, headed by Samuel Plimsoll, M.P. It was in accordance with the social policy of the government and a bill was prepared, but the subject was a thorny one and the government found it difficult to steer a middle course between shipowners and humanitarians. The bill was postponed and Plimsoll lost patience, moved an adjournment, vehemently denounced 'ship knackers', shouted he would unmask the 'villains' who sent seamen to their graves, pirouetted in the middle of the floor, shook his fist at Disraeli and, defying the authority of the Speaker, stormed out of the House. This was in July 1875 and a temporary bill went through in a few days, being confirmed in a permanent Act the following year, which enforced the painting of a safe loading mark or 'Plimsoll line' on ships, and introduced other safety regulations. The example of disorder leading to success, however, did immediate injury to Parliament and was carefully noted by the Irish Nationalists.

Disraeli had given the vote to the artisans in 1867. Gladstone had used the mandate they had helped to give him in effecting great political changes in the institutions of the country and especially of Ireland. Disraeli had sensed that the real demands of the people were nearer home, that it was dissatisfaction with the Gladstone Ministry's lack of achievement in this field that had contributed to the Conservative victory of 1874; the events of 1874–76 show that the Conservatives were not unworthy of the confidence that had been placed in them.

(c) THE EASTERN QUESTION

The attitude of Palmerston in foreign affairs had accurately reflected the growing national pride; the more moral attitude of Gladstone had hardly the same electoral appeal nor did it carry the same weight among the European Powers, particularly after the Franco-Prussian War.   In 1874, however, the diplomatic world soon began to realise that the atmosphere of British diplomacy recalled the time of Palmerston, that observation of European treaties, respect for British rights and consideration for British opinion in matters of European concern were expected and would if necessary be enforced.   From 1876 onwards Disraeli's primary interest was transferred to foreign affairs; Buckle, his biographer, has commented, 'Zeal for the greatness of England was the passion of his life.'   By the time that he fell from office in 1880 England's prestige in Europe and the world had been immeasurably increased.

The testing ground was the perennial problem of Turkey.[1] She had been bolstered up in the Crimean War by Britain and France in the belief that she could be induced to introduce much-needed reforms.   There was no departure, however, from the usual Turkish policy; nothing was done and by the early 1870's her financial position was desperate.   She could neither pay nor properly organise her troops, while her ever-growing taxes, exacted by tax farmers, were a constant spur to local revolts.

Turkish misrule of Christian races could not remain indefinitely a feature of modern Europe.   Greece was independent, Serbia, Roumania and Montenegro were principalities under nominal Turkish suzerainty, but extensive areas, taking no account of racial boundaries, were ruled from Constantinople, a rule which alternated without warning between indulgent laxity and appalling harshness.   Except for the Bulgars all the subject races had brethren living in freedom elsewhere and the Pan-Slav Movement, based on Russia, contributed further to the basic instability of the area.   At the time of the Crimean War the only practical alternative to reform of the Turkish administration had seemed to be the partition of the Balkans between Russian and Austria, with other powers seeking compensation elsewhere.   These two

---

[1] See above, p. 167.

alternatives remained substantially true but the success of the semi-independent states in the Balkans had postulated a third alternative, the development of the Christian races in four independent states with, perhaps, Moslem Albania as a fifth. Gladstone, who saw nations struggling to be free everywhere, hailed the third solution as the right one, but the practical difficulties were enormous: the Christian races hated one another even more than they did the Turks, and the chequered history of the Balkans had intermingled the various nationalities in a way that defied the political cartographers' attempts to sort them out. Neither Andrassy, the Austrian Minister, nor Gortchakov, the Russian, considered this a practical alternative except as a cloak for their own advances, and Disraeli, whose principal aim was the safeguarding of the British Empire, with its immense commercial and territorial interests in the Levant, the Persian Gulf, India and the Far East, from Russian expansion, felt that Britain was inevitably committed to the support of Turkey.

Following a bad harvest in 1874, the Serbs of Herzegovina broke out into revolt against the heavy taxation. Such was the inefficiency at the Porte that they proved unable to cope with even such a minor disturbance as this and the revolt spread to Bosnia. A joint note from Austria, Germany and Russia was presented to the Sultan urging reforms. The Sultan agreed and did nothing. In May 1876 the already tense situation was aggravated by the murder of the French and German consuls at Salonika by Moslem rioters. Under Russian inspiration the three Eastern powers drew up the Berlin Memorandum ordering Turkey to conclude an armistice with the rebels within two months and implement the reforms. Disraeli felt that it would be better for Turkey to give up Bosnia and Herzegovina altogether than to agree to such a slight on her sovereignty and with the unanimous agreement of the British Cabinet he refused to agree to the Memorandum. He feared Russia, distrusted Bismarck, and rightly regarded Andrassy as an intriguer playing a double game. On 24th May, however, in order to restrain Turkish nationalism, the British fleet was sent to Besika Bay. This had the opposite effect to that intended; Turkish nationalism was raised to fever heat, Sultans were changed with bewildering rapidity until Abdul Hamid II, alighting on the throne he was to occupy for thirty-three years, professed a policy of reform and friendly co-operation with England. The Memorandum was withdrawn; Disraeli's policy had prevailed. He was determined that a policy of drift should not draw Britain into war, as in the Crimea.

In May, however, the situation had been further complicated by the rising of armed guerrillas in Bulgaria. The Turks, shamed by their earlier failures, determined to end this as expeditiously as possible and let loose irregular troops called Bashi-Bazouks. They acted thoroughly; in one Bulgarian administrative district it was subsequently calculated that 12,000 Christians perished. At the hill town of Batuk every house was burnt and 5,000 people were slaughtered. Torture, rape, flogging and pillage were the order of the day. The Bashi-Bazouks were rewarded and their leaders decorated.

Information came in slowly from the remote districts and the ambassador, Elliot, lacking official confirmation from the British consul at Adrianople, belittled the stories and Disraeli, misled, minimised them in the Commons. The consul's report, however, got into the hands of the *Daily News*, a well-informed newspaper and particularly devoted to Gladstone, and subsequent confirmation from Constantinople revealed that the atrocities described in the reports were only too true. Disraeli realised that the impression produced in England by these events had completely destroyed sympathy with Turkey and made it difficult for him to support her by war, should that be necessary.

Disraeli's initial denial gave Gladstone his opportunity. He had long been unhappy with Disraeli's Eastern policy, 'the most selfish and least worthy policy he had ever known; Disraeli is the worst and most immoral minister since Castlereagh', and feeling that the government should be attacked with passion such as Hartington could not rise to, he took up his pen and in September published *The Bulgarian Horrors and the Question of the East*. It begins with a calm account of the situation in the Balkans, sharply criticises the British government, examines the reliability of the news and ends in a passionate attack on the Turks. British and French blood and treasure expended during the Crimean War seemed only to have afforded the Turks this opportunity to indulge 'abominable and bestial lusts' and to enact scenes 'at which Hell itself might blush'.   He urged the Turks to carry themselves off 'bag and baggage' and called upon the Concert of Europe, which Disraeli had done his best to disrupt, 'to afford relief to the overcharged emotion of a shuddering world'.   In three days, 40,000 copies were sold and before long 200,000.   With infectious enthusiasm Gladstone went on a tremendous tour of great meetings.   The strength of his eloquence was his massive appeal to elemental humanity and justice; its political wisdom lay in his discernment of and reliance on the spirit of nationality.   To many, Disraeli seemed cruelly cynical in comparison.   Throughout the country meetings were held, clamouring for the expulsion of the Turks, subscriptions were opened on behalf of the crusade.   In Liverpool *Othello* was being played and at the phrase 'The Turks are drowned', the whole audience rose and cheered.

Disraeli was anxious to avoid war but he knew that in Moscow the Pan-Slavs were pressing Alexander II to start a campaign of Balkan conquest under the pretext of philanthropy.   It is possible that the division of opinion in Great Britain may have encouraged the Tsar to seize this opportunity.   In November 1876 he announced that he could no longer remain indifferent to the sufferings of the Balkan Christians.

A conference was arranged at Constantinople, to which Lord Salisbury went as British delegate, which was intended to put an end to the Turkish war with Serbia and to impose a programme of reforms.   The Turks were unenthusiastic, however, convinced that in the last resort the British would defend them, as they had done in the Crimean War.   The Liberals agitated for an army to be sent to coerce Turkey, and Gladstone entreated,

> There were other days when England was the hope of freedom. Wherever in the world a high aspiration was entertained or a noble blow was struck, it was to England that the eyes of the oppressed were always turned.

It was small wonder that the personal following Gladstone had won throughout the country had begun to show itself in pilgrimages to Hawarden.

In April 1877, when the Conference had broken down, Russia declared war on Turkey.   Austria was bought off with the promise of Bosnia and Herzegovina and Gortchakov secured British neutrality by agreeing to respect what Disraeli declared to be British interests: free communication through the Suez Canal, Egypt to be excluded from operations and, most relevant, the inviolability of Constantinople and the navigation of the Straits. Initially the Russians advanced easily, but were later held by the Turks. By January 1878 public opinion, as in 1854, saw the Turks as fighting bravely against an aggressor. The Bulgarian massacres were forgotten. Had Disraeli declared war in support of the Sultan, the country would have been united behind him. In the music halls the Great MacDermott gave the name of 'Jingoism' to the flamboyant patriotism of the hour; it was impossible in London for meetings to be held in favour of peace, and Gladstone, so lately the darling of the people, was constantly the object of hostile demonstrations. The Queen urged war; in the Cabinet there was a widening between Carnarvon and Derby, who desired peace at any price, and those who shared Disraeli's view that the way to save peace and British interests was to show themselves unshrinking.

On 10th January, 1878, the Sultan telegraphed personally to the Queen begging intervention and ten days later the Russians occupied Adrianople. The crisis had come and on 23rd January the Cabinet ordered the Mediterranean fleet to steam through the Dardanelles while Parliament voted £6 m. for military purposes. The Russians advanced until they could see the minarets of Constantinople, and beyond the significant silhouettes of the British fleet. The Queen pressed for war; 'I cannot imagine what you are waiting for,' said Princess Mary of Cambridge to Disraeli at dinner; 'Potatoes, at the moment, Madam,' was the statesman's cryptic reply.

Peace was saved. Russia was exhausted and could hardly face a new war. Disraeli had bluffed and had never intended to make one. The British fleet could have done little more than bombard Constantinople in the event of a Russian occupation, while the lack of a continental ally would inevitably limit the scope of any operations. A truce was concluded, followed in March by the Treaty of San Stefano between the Russians and the Turks. Russia got Armenia and Bessarabia; Roumania, Serbia and Montenegro were declared independent; Austria was given Bosnia and Herzegovina. The most unsatisfactory aspect from the European,

R

and especially from the British, point of view, was the creation
of a greatly enlarged Bulgaria. From a purely Balkan point
of view the idea was not a bad one, although the area included
Serbs and Greeks, but the Bulgars were the least politically
self-conscious of the Balkan nationalities and their language
and liturgy were nearest the Russian. War might have been
made in the name of liberty, but peace was in the spirit of
annexation. Big Bulgaria would be in practice a Russian
satellite and Constantinople, free in name, would in fact be
hemmed in. The Pan-Slavs had won the day.

Andrassy proposed revision by a European conference;
Gortchakov wanted the scope of the discussion strictly limited;
Disraeli insisted that the whole treaty should come under
review. At the end of March, British reserves were called up
and Indian troops were summoned to the Mediterranean.
Derby, whose irresolution had long aggravated Disraeli,
resigned in protest and was replaced by Lord Salisbury. This
convinced the Russians that the British government meant
business and they agreed to negotiate, while Salisbury circular-
ised the European chancelleries with a statement of the British
position, which convinced Bismarck of the need for an unlimited conference.

The Congress of Berlin took place between 13th June and
13th July. It was the most impressive gathering of diplomats
since the Congress of Vienna, with a glittering backcloth of
dinners, balls and royal receptions. It marked the zenith of
Disraeli's career and revealed him finally to the world as a
great international figure, capable of reducing for the moment
the redoubtable Bismarck to a secondary place in a European
assembly held in Bismarck's own capital. 'The old Jew,' said
Bismarck, 'that is the man.'

The real work of the Congress, however, was rehearsed
largely beforehand or off the stage. Salisbury, who many
authorities feel did most of the work, concluded secret agreements: with Turkey, agreeing to the cession of Cyprus as a
base for British military missions in Asia Minor; with Austria-
Hungary, accepting the preservation of Turkish suzerainty
over Bosnia and Herzegovina but to Austrian administration
of the territories; and with Russia, agreeing to the splitting up
of big Bulgaria. All these were agreed to by the Congress.
Bulgaria was divided into three parts. The northern tract,

largely Bulgar in population and between the Danube and the
Balkan mountains, was to be an independent principality
organised by Russia. The central tract, equally Bulgar,
between the Balkan and Rhodope Mountains and christened
by the Congress Eastern Rumelia, became a special Turkish
province under a Christian governor. (A crisis arose over the
right of the Turkish government to maintain troops in the
province when necessary; this Disraeli felt to be a vital issue as
on it the effectiveness of the division of Bulgaria would depend.
He threatened to withdraw from the Congress if it were not
granted; Bismarck, anxious for the success of the Congress,
was convinced he meant business and persuaded the Russians
to agree.) The southern tract, Macedonia, was handed back
to the Turks without restrictions, and subjected a Christian
population, Bulgar, Greek and Serb, to thirty-four years of
misrule, guerrilla warfare and massacres.[1]

The final settlement is open to criticism, quite apart from
the treatment of Macedonia. The Austrian gains conflicted
with Serbian aspirations and were a fruitful source of future
trouble; the whole settlement induced a greater Austrian
interest in the Balkans which led to the fatal clash in 1914.
The division between Bulgaria and Eastern Rumelia was a
purely artificial one and as early as 1887 Salisbury had to
accept their union, although by that time Bulgaria had
asserted its independence of Russia and the principles of the
Congress were therefore preserved. The British acquisition
of Cyprus was everywhere recognised as a telling stroke, well
calculated to restore British prestige in the East, but France
had to be appeased by Britain's secret consent to the seizure of
Tunis, which was effected in 1881 with the encouragement of
Bismarck, who suggested the French build up a colonial
empire in the hope that thereby they would forget Alsace and
Lorraine. The treaty was at best a patching up, not a final
solution, of the Balkan problem, but a final solution was impossible at this date. Disraeli achieved what he had set out to
do; he had reversed the Treaty of San Stefano without a war,
in itself no small achievement; he had broken the alliance of
the Eastern powers, which although it eventually led to the
division of Europe into two armed camps, appeared initially
to give Great Britain a greater opportunity to intervene to

[1] See below, p. 309 and p. 416.

good effect in Europe; he had protected British interests in the eastern Mediterranean, which encouraged Russia to seek her warm-water outlet elsewhere, until the defeats of the Russo-Japanese war and the Anglo-Russian agreement concerning Persia brought her back once again to the Balkans. The Congress did not solve the Balkan problem but it brought to the area, apart from Macedonia, thirty-four years of peace and thirty-four years is a long time.

(d) THE LAST TWO YEARS

On his return to England after the Congress Disraeli was greeted with tremendous enthusiasm. There was a great reception at Charing Cross Station; Trafalgar Square was a carpet of faces, hats and handkerchieves were waved, women threw flowers into the carriage. At Downing Street, all draped with red, Disraeli found an immense sheaf of flowers, sent by the Queen. 'We have brought you back, I think,' he said, 'Peace with Honour.' The Queen wrote to him, 'High and low, the whole country is delighted, except Mr Gladstone, who is frantic.'

Hitherto Disraeli had been the spoiled child of fate and it is often asserted that had he dissolved Parliament in 1878 the Conservatives would have been assured six more years of power. When he decided not to do so, he was ignoring the fickleness of the British electorate. H. J. Hanham, in his recent book *Elections and Party Management* contends, however, that there is no real reason to suppose that a dissolution in 1878 would have secured the Ministry another term of office with a safe majority: the boroughs were still very largely Liberal and the Conservatives had already begun to suffer heavy losses at municipal elections, which became more numerous in 1879 owing to setbacks abroad and economic distress at home. The Home Rulers were stronger than in 1874 and the chances of Conservatives again profiting by Liberal dissensions to slip into Parliament were remote. The Conservatives would probably have kept a majority – their record hitherto deserved that – but it would probably have been a very narrow one with perhaps the Home Rulers holding the balance. Whatever might have happened, the next two years were ones of misfortune for the government.

A government is invariably blamed for economic discontents, even though their chances of remedying them may be slight. In 1870 there had begun an inflation of prices. The Franco-Prussian War, with France and Germany withdrawn from commercial competition, enabled England to increase her exports. The opening of the Suez Canal stimulated the shipbuilding trade, and railway development in Germany and America created an exceptional demand for coal and iron. The expanding trade increased the consuming power of the population and maintained the prices of agricultural produce. In many cases rents were raised – often beyond reasonable limits – and farms were tendered for competition. In 1874 the reaction began, preceded by an orgy of company flotation in Austria-Hungary and Germany, and the demonetisation of silver by the new German Empire and some of the Latin countries which amounted to a contraction of the world's gold supply. Demand returned to normal limits but abnormal supply continued and over-production was the result. The decline of the coal and iron trades, the stoppage of short-time working of cotton mills, industrial disputes, default on the Turkish debt, complications arising out of the Eastern question, all combined to depress every industry. In 1878 the extent to which trade was undermined was revealed by the failure of the Glasgow, Caledonian and West of England banks.

British industry might recover but British agriculture suffered a blow far more serious. The early seventies had been years of tremendous railway speculations in the prairie lands of North America. The boom had collapsed and the United States, like Europe, had suffered a grim depression. Thousands of workless had streamed to the undeveloped prairies encouraged by the railway companies who guaranteed to carry their produce at less than cost for a number of years. Helped by the bounty of virgin nature and by important developments in agricultural machinery, especially the self-binder attached to the reaping machine in 1873, essential in a land where hired labour was virtually unobtainable, the prairie farmer was able to produce wheat at far less than the European cost. Assisted by cheap railway freight rates and the sudden appearance of cheap ocean-going steamer transport, the cost of sending a ton of grain from Chicago to Liverpool dropped from £3 7s. 0d. in 1873 to £2 1s. 0d. in 1884.

Densely populated and highly farmed Europe, more efficient though it was, could not hope to compete, especially as the first impact of prairie wheat arrived at a time when Nature was being particularly unkind to farmers in Europe. Bleak springs and rainy summers produced short cereal crops of inferior quality, mildew in wheat, mould in hops, blight in other crops, disease in cattle and rot in sheep. Normally a poor harvest was compensated for by high prices; now the farmer was faced with the unhappy combination of poor harvests and low prices.

The only answer to this was Protection. France and Germany, valuing their rural populations as a source of conscript armies, introduced it in 1879. Disraeli might have been expected to follow suit, especially as he had split the Conservative party over this very question in 1846. His party had long ago accepted the principle of Free Trade, however, and Disraeli, like most of his contemporaries, believed that herein lay one of the keys to England's industrial strength. A commission of inquiry under the Duke of Richmond was appointed, and, perhaps not fully appreciating the true seriousness of the situation, it recommended that patience, liberal reductions in rent and compensation for tenants' unexhausted improvements would tide agriculture over the difficulty.

This was optimism misplaced. Initially, increased attention was paid by farmers to grazing, dairying and such minor products as vegetables, fruit and poultry. Until 1885 the price of fat cattle was well-maintained, that of sheep until 1890, but foreign competition slowly undermined this branch of agriculture as well. Refrigeration was invented in 1882 and the Argentine began to export meat in large quantities in 1885.

The previous thirty years had been regarded as the Golden Age of British farming. Until 1880 agriculture was still the largest employer. A century of keen practical research had raised its technology far ahead of that of much of the Continent, its breeds were the best, cropping the most scientific, yields the highest. Agricultural wages, especially after the activities of Joseph Arch's trade union, were the highest in Europe. But now wages fell, farmers increasingly went bankrupt or were forced to lower drastically their farming standards. Corn lands were bought by speculators and converted

into sheep lands, private tenants exhausted the land by taking
without giving. Labourers joined the unemployed in the
towns or sought their fortune by emigration. The real basis
of wealth was shifting away from the land.

Disraeli might have been justified in refusing to protect
English agriculture, but he forgot about Ireland. He has
been accused of having no policy for Ireland and of not seiz-
ing in 1874 the opportunity to reorganise its internal government, but one of the causes which produced the Conservative
majority in 1874 was probably resentment at what was felt to
be the disproportionate preoccupation of Gladstone's government with Ireland. Disraeli had not agreed with Gladstone's
measures but felt it was the obvious duty of his government to
give them time to work and to produce all the healing effects
of which they were capable, while maintaining the authority
of the law and assisting social improvements. Ireland had no
industry, however, to maintain her economy during an agricultural depression, and the poor crops and high prices which
had brought ruin in England, brought disaster and tragedy in
Ireland, and undid all previous work of pacification and conciliation. Extensive relief organisation by the Irish government and a large voluntary fund run by the Duchess of
Marlborough did little to check the rise of lawlessness. Withholding of rent was creating a dangerous situation in 1879:
Lord Leitrim was murdered in Donegal and the Irish Land
League was formed with Parnell as president and Davitt, a
Fenian convict on ticket-of-leave, as secretary.

Events in Ireland had an effect on the nature of the Irish
Home Rule party. This had been organised by Isaac Butt in
1870, had gained fifty-nine seats in the election of 1874 and
had introduced an annual Home Rule motion, invariably
defeated by overwhelming majorities. Some of Butt's followers, who preferred more drastic methods, gained the upper
hand and in 1878 Butt resigned the leadership to make way for
them. Charles Stewart Parnell, an Anglo-Irish landlord
who had entered Parliament in 1875, succeeded him, having
previously secured the support of the two leading forces in
Ireland, the Roman Catholic Church and the Irish Republican Brotherhood. Observing the success of Plimsoll's
exhibition,[1] the party had begun an organised campaign of

[1] See above, p. 242.

obstruction, on one occasion keeping the House in session for twenty-six hours. The darkening picture of the slump and obstruction in Parliament at home and of violence in Ireland was worsened by the disasters of Isandhlwana in January 1879 and Kabul in September 1879. Neither was Disraeli's fault: they were accidents caused by unwise subordinates, setbacks inevitable in policies of colonial expansion, but fickle popular opinion, which had praised the purchase of the Canal shares and Disraeli's success at Berlin, now turned heavily against Disraeli's imperialism.

Disraeli's Colonial Secretary, the Earl of Carnarvon, had federated Canada in 1867. This had been successful and he resolved to apply the same policy to South Africa. There was a case for this; four small white communities were threatened by a resurgence of Zulu power. Cetaweyo had at his disposal a highly drilled army of 40,000 celibate, athletic warriors. The history of Zululand was one of incessant wars and aggression. Of the four white communities, Cape Colony and Natal were predominantly English speaking; the Orange Free State was well ordered and, although Dutch in origin, friendly to Britain. The Transvaal was the white man in the woodpile. It was an almost purely pastoral state with a scattered population of 'voortrekkers'. Its internal anarchy was a scandal throughout South Africa and it had a history of bad relations with its coloured neighbours, largely through the kidnapping of Kaffir children. These were virtually used as slaves, although slavery had been forbidden in the Sand River Convention of 1852, by which the Transvaal had obtained its independence. For the defence of the country the insolvent President Burgers hired a gang of unsuccessful gold diggers who were to reimburse themselves by plunder and whose methods were similar to those of the Bashi-Bazouks. Not for the last time in their history, the Boers were sitting on dynamite.

In 1877 Sir Theophilus Shepstone was sent by Carnarvon, with authority independent of Sir Bartle Frere, the British High Commissioner, to discuss confederation with Burgers and to enforce annexation if necessary. At Pretoria he found the situation desperate; a native rising seemed imminent and Burgers had 12s. 6d. in his treasury. Burgers agreed to annexation on condition he and his friends should receive pensions privately, and in public should be allowed to protest against the change. Shepstone, threatened with a request to Germany if Britain would not help the Transvaal, foolishly agreed. Vice-President Kruger and some Boers genuinely objected to the annexation. A further undertaking, made without reference to Frere, was that the Transvaal would be given self-government at an early date. No constitution, however, was granted for two and a half years and then only a Crown Colony administration. Had a free constitution as well as material advantages immediately followed annexation, the Boers might have settled down quietly under British rule.

Frere, the High Commissioner, had also been instructed to work for confederation, but he had become increasingly concerned about the Zulu threat. He had distinguished himself on the North-West Frontier of India and no better choice could have been made if the Ministers at home had determined on a forward policy in South Africa and were prepared for the risks involved. The Cabinet had no such determination, nor were they clear as to the methods by which confederation might be achieved. They had no wish to risk a war and refused to send Frere reinforcements.

Cetaweyo was quite prepared to open negotiations but Frere sent him an unacceptable ultimatum and thus involved England in a war, contrary to instructions. Lord Chelmsford, the commander of the British troops, disregarding local advice and underestimating his enemy, allowed his main force to be lured away from their base camp at Isandhlwana on 22nd January, 1879. Cetaweyo's Zulus then massacred the 800 white soldiers and 500 natives left behind. Only a gallant fight at Rorke's Drift by a detachment prevented the Zulus from sweeping into Natal.

There followed an immediate public outcry at home; the recall of Frere and Chelmsford was demanded but Disraeli defended both, and sent out reinforcements and Sir Garnet Wolseley as Commander-in-Chief. He destroyed the Zulu army at the battle of Ulundi and Zululand was broken up into eight principalities. The removal of the native threat and the failure to grant a liberal constitution made the Transvaalers regret the annexation, which provided Gladstone with a legacy of trouble.[1] The war had a quick effect upon the

---

[1] See below, p. 273.

prestige of the government, especially in view of the conflicting authority given to Frere and Shepstone, while the death of the French Prince Imperial, who was attached to the British Army, gave the affair just that sentimental touch which most surely arouses popular feeling. 'What wonderful people,' said Disraeli of the Zulus; 'They beat our generals, convert our bishops and write finis to a French dynasty.'

Disraeli was not only concerned with the dangers of Russian expansion towards Constantinople, but also the gradual annexation by Russia of areas which seemed to be near the Indian frontier. It has been remarked that if the statesmen of the time had only inspected large-scale maps of the area, their concern would not have been so great, but, be that as it may, it appeared essential to secure the friendship of Afghanistan. The Amir, Sher Ali, had approached the British government in 1873 for a promise of aid in the event of Russian attack; Gladstone's government had refused and from then on Sher Ali gravitated towards the Russians. Lord Lytton, the Viceroy, attempted to send a British mission in 1878 but it was turned back and a Russian mission was given an effusive welcome in Kabul. The British sent an ultimatum, which was ignored and three British armies were sent to Kabul. The Liberals insisted on regarding Sher Ali as a would-be friend whom Lytton had treated badly and there was a strong feeling in England that Lytton was forcing the hand of the government. Sher Ali was deposed and replaced by Yakub Khan, who seemed to be reliable. The British were given military control of the passes and responsibility for Afghan foreign affairs. Sir Lewis Cavignari was installed as Resident at Kabul and the affair appeared to be closed.

However, in September 1879 Afghan soldiers, alleged to be mutinous, massacred Cavignari and his suite. When the news reached England this caused a profound revulsion against Disraeli's policy. General Roberts marched to Kabul, reinforced the British force at Kandahar, and Yakub Khan was replaced by his cousin Abdur Rahman. At this stage Disraeli resigned and Gladstone was left with the problem.[1] The casualties in this war were especially painful to many English people because they could not perceive that the war had any moral justification. It seemed a case of imperial-

[1] See below, p. 274.

ism gone sour, although, owing to the exemplary attitude of Russia throughout, it had no wider complications.

Meanwhile at home the opposition was gathering. Disraeli's government had been more fortunate than its predecessor in by-elections and, as often happens to a party in power, the organisation which had helped to win the election of 1874 was allowed to lapse; on the other hand the New Model Liberal Associations, organised by Joseph Chamberlain and Schnadhorst from Birmingham, were at their maximum efficiency. The drift towards the Liberals was dramatically accelerated by Gladstone's two Midlothian campaigns.

Gladstone was the first major statesman to stump the country. His technique was simple; he directed a series of speeches at the whole country but gave them within comparatively narrow limits so that they acquired a unity of sense and purpose that they might otherwise have lacked. Each series was concerned with one great theme but it was accompanied by a minor or secondary theme to set it off and each speech was designed to cast new light on each of these themes so that the speeches as a whole read together as if they were a course of lectures. The themes were almost invariably the same: the iniquity, injustice and depravity of some institution and of his opponents' policy in supporting it; and, secondly, the financial extravagance of his opponents and their inability to appreciate the principles of good government. The note was always one of high moral indignation and of fervent appeal to the better feelings of his audience.

The two campaigns, in November 1879 and March 1880, were a triumphant success. Their significance is that a man by a direct appeal to the electors made himself not only the leader of his party but the leader of the Ministry, in flat contradiction to all the aristocratic traditions which had hitherto governed English political life. The quantity of the performances is astonishing for a man of 70 and on an enormous range of problems Gladstone had something definite to say. To packed, spellbound audiences, to many of whom hearing Gladstone speak was an experience of a lifetime, he denounced the Government for financial profligacy in pursuit of 'false phantoms of glory. . . . The great duty of a government, especially in foreign affairs, is to soothe and tranquillise the minds of the people,' not 'to encourage the baleful spirit of domination.' The choice was between two moralities, he felt. For five years they had heard nothing but talk of the interests of the British Empire – what was the result? Russia aggrandised and hostile, Europe troubled, India at war, in Africa a broad stain of blood. And why? Because there are other things in this world than political necessities; there are moral necessities. 'Remember that the sanctity of life in the hill villages of Afghanistan among the winter snows, is as inviolable in the eye of Almighty God as can be your own.' Besides this pilgrimage of passion, the election address of Disraeli dealing with the risk of Irish secession, a subject for which the public as a whole had had little preparation, seemed positively uninspired.

Following two by-election successes, which raised his hopes artificially, Disraeli dissolved Parliament in March and the polls were declared in the first week in April. The Liberals swept the board; their majority in the Commons was 137 over the Conservatives; the Irish Nationalists won sixty-five seats as a third party. Gladstone had had no mean adversary. The acknowledged and undisputed head of the powerful Conservative party on one side and the old and solitary warrior who had placed the leadership of his party in other hands and who had in it as many critics as disciples may seem ill-matched. But Disraeli was an aged and sick man and Balfour felt that 'it was personality – in the person of one man – that decided the elections'. In a sense, however, it was inevitable. All governments make more enemies than friends and memories are short in politics. Reverses overseas, industrial and agricultural depression at home, trouble in Ireland joined to Gladstone's tremendous appeal, made the Conservative defeat almost a foregone conclusion. This, it has been said, can be interpreted as the last effort of liberal, detached England, the England of Peace, Retrenchment and Reform, to save itself from the complications and costs of world Empire.

Disraeli died in 1881. Although he died in defeat, his permanent achievements were very real ones, both for his country and for his party. He had presided over the Reform Bill of 1867 and, skilfully adopting amendments which made it a more radical measure than most of his followers wanted, had yet persuaded them to accept it, thus making regular reviews of the franchise an integral part of politics. He had brought attention to a far greater extent than ever before to the bad conditions of many people's lives; in their practical results the Public Health Act and other statutes of the period are among the most important pieces of legislation of the 19th Century. In foreign and imperial affairs he rightly sensed that the public mood demanded a greater emphasis on British rights and needs than Gladstone had always shown. His purchase of the Suez Canal shares, his reversal of the Balkan settlement without a war at the Congress of Berlin, greatly raised the prestige of Britain abroad. His creation of the Empire of India, quite apart from its favourable effects in India, helped to increase interest at home in British overseas possessions at a time when they could provide a valuable economic outlet. If he left two unsuccessful colonial wars to his successor, they should not be seen, as Gladstone saw them, as an express condemnation of his policy, but rather the fruit of the practical difficulties of delegating power. Curiously, a failure of his last year of office was his decision not to protect British agriculture from American competition when his championship of Protection was the issue which helped to split the Conservative party against Peel in 1846.

The tragedy of Disraeli's life was that he only attained power when he was old, sick and a widower. As a Jew, it was many years before he could gain acceptance as leader, and not until 1874 was he followed with pride. For too many years he had to accept the unenthusiastic and often negative lead of Derby; his most frustrating time was in 1855 when, had his personal position been stronger, he could well have insisted that his party took office at the crisis of the Crimean War. Meanwhile, after the split in the party in 1846, the electoral system of the First Reform Act seemed incapable of ever returning a Conservative majority. Had he obtained a majority in 1868, his effectiveness as a practical statesman might well have been greater. For his party, his achievements were no less important. A Radical by origin and instinct he remade the Conservative party, turning a group with a negative policy of reaction into one with a positive policy of social conciliation and imperial greatness. Yet although he ruled the counsels of the party for so long and attracted to it electoral support, it was only within limits that he ever shaped it to his ideas. Salisbury accused him of putting the unity of the party before other considerations, yet by building up the Conservatives as an effective opposition to the Liberals and a sound alternative government, he contributed enormously to the healthiness of Victorian politics, quite apart from laying the foundations of his party's long rule under Salisbury and Balfour. Although, as champion of Tory democracy, his only real successor was Lord Randolph Churchill, the achievements of this concept made a lasting contribution to the health and happiness of the English people. He had real principles and he maintained them; he was a great parliamentary speaker and, in later life, his relations with his fellows and subordinates were exceptionally happy. In his character and career a lasting contradiction to much of what the Victorian age held most dear, he is, nonetheless, one of its greatest figures.

VII · GLADSTONE AND PARNELL

(a) IRELAND AND DOMESTIC LEGISLATION, 1880–85

THE great constructive work of Gladstonian Liberalism really ended in 1874 and if Gladstone had devoted the remainder of his life to religion, as was, he claimed, his intention at that time, English history might have been the poorer but the Liberal party might well have been the stronger. Until 1906 its history was to be one of tensions and differences, secessions and disasters. In proclaiming his mission to pacify Ireland Gladstone had chained his party to an insoluble problem. Ireland was increasingly the reason why Gladstone remained in politics and as he grew older he became steadily more convinced of the moral rightness of his decisions and more autocratic and inconsiderate of his party, where he perceived an alarming growth of material considerations. He was increasingly remote from people who rated imperial interests high or wished to see the State regulate men's lives. His methods of thought and phraseology aroused widespread distrust. Lecky called him 'an honest man with a dishonest mind' and his action in 1885 caused considerable amazement when he went to the polls a supporter of the Union, so far as his closest supporters knew, and only a few weeks later announced, without reference to them, his conversion to Home Rule. His language could often mystify his hearers by the subtle distinctions he made, as when he described Gordon at Khartoum as 'hemmed in but not surrounded'. When he did not wish to commit himself, the ramifications, dexterity and obscurity of his language were unparalleled. Yet among the masses as a whole there remained, except when Gordon died, a tremendous respect and admiration for a man who was the epitome of the finest aspirations of Victorian England, while those who knew him well cherished him more than they knew for his idealism and his unsurpassed mastery of the parliamentary arts.

Gladstone's Second Ministry was as unsuccessful as his first was successful. Cabinet difficulties, hesitations, unpopularity, arose principally from its ideological divisions, which were made worse by Gladstone's growing reluctance to plan or discuss in Cabinet meetings or to quell difficulties between Ministers by strong leadership. Lord Hartington, who had been invited by the Queen to form a Cabinet in 1880 but who had deferred to Gladstone, found him increasingly unintelligible and became, with his Whig colleagues, steadily more aloof. Gladstone's greatest failure, however, was his neglect and lack of understanding of Joseph Chamberlain.

Chamberlain was the son of a Unitarian shopkeeper and had made his fortune as a screw manufacturer. As Mayor of Birmingham 1873–76[1] he had raised the whole tone, competence and public estimation of the municipal service; he was also able to exercise his tireless thirst for action and achievement. His campaign for educational reform led to the formation of a Birmingham Liberal Association and then in 1877 to the National Liberal Federation. Its purpose was to give the greatest possible opportunity for democratic control but in the outcome the Federation was more successful in reducing the personal independence of M.P.s than in putting the rank and file in control, a failure which was to have considerable effect on the relations of the Liberal Party with the working class and its new leaders at the end of the century. The National Liberal Federation contributed very materially to the victory of 1880 and it was as a result of its pressure that Chamberlain, who had only become an M.P. in 1876, was made in 1880 a member of the Cabinet and President of the Board of Trade. His colleagues thought of him as a presumptious intruder; he expressed his views with a blunt frankness and he was by far the most energetic of them all. Gladstone made no attempt to understand him; his background and interests were completely alien to Gladstone's own and Gladstone found it difficult to believe in his integrity. After the victory of 1880 Matthew Arnold had remarked that the Liberal's first concern should be to deal with what Cobbett had called the 'hell-holes of England'. As Sir Winston Churchill put it in his biography of his father:

> Great victories had been won. All sorts of lumbering tyranny had toppled over. Authority was everywhere broken. Slaves were free; conscience was free; trade was free; but hunger and

squalor and cold were also free and the people demanded something more than liberty.

Chamberlain realised the vital importance of social problems. Gladstone, though generous and self-sacrificing[1] with individual social problems in private life, could never see their importance politically. Chamberlain wanted the Ministry to enfranchise the rural householders and adopt land reform and to settle Ireland by setting up democratic local and regional councils. Two men of such ability could have given unparalleled strength to the Liberal Party had they worked together, but their personalities proved to be incompatible.

When Gladstone refused to serve in a subordinate post under Hartington or Granville his accession to the premiership was inevitable. Although the Whig leaders had disapproved of his demagogic methods, it was clear that the great majority of successful candidates had been elected in his name. 'Of course I shall not take any notice of Mr Gladstone, who has done so much harm,' remarked the Queen and she virtually reprimanded him when he kissed hands, but Gladstone was determined to overlook any unpleasantness. He was anxious to conciliate the Whig patricians and gave them eight posts out of eleven. Granville returned to the Foreign Office but faltered under the burden of work and was at sea with an opponent of Bismarck's calibre; Hartington went to the India Office, Spencer was Lord President, Argyll Lord Privy Seal, Northbrook First Lord of the Admiralty, Kimberley the Colonial Secretary. Lord Frederick Cavendish became Financial Secretary of the Treasury. He was Gladstone's nephew by marriage and Gladstone had a high regard for him. He proved invaluable, while he lived, in smoothing over difficulties between the Prime Minister and his brother, the Marquess of Hartington. Harcourt the Home Secretary was Whig by background, but chiefly Radical in outlook; Forster who became Chief Secretary for Ireland had abandoned his Radicalism ten years earlier and was now to be much criticised for his handling of Irish problems. Bright was again included in the Cabinet but was old and no longer the political force he had once been. Gladstone unwisely

[1] One might instance his rescue work with prostitutes in London in which he showed an almost reckless disregard for aspersions that might be cast on his reputation.

s

once again took the Exchequer himself, leading to his undue immersion in detail. Realising the strain was too much he surrendered the office in 1882 to Childers, who moved from the War Office.

The other leading Radicals were outside the Cabinet. Dilke who was at this stage a close political associate of Chamberlain's and who had a large following in the party became Under-Secretary at the Foreign Office. He had considerable parliamentary qualities and had he not spoilt his career by involvement in a divorce, would almost certainly have attained high Cabinet rank. The Queen insisted on his declaring in writing that he had renounced his republicanism. Another able Radical who had made considerable impact in Opposition, G. O. Trevelyan, also filled a junior post.

Great things were expected of so able a team and so large a majority. The majority became disillusioned. Every Ministry, however lofty its idealism, is to a large extent at the mercy of circumstances, and circumstances were more than ordinarily unreasonable in providing problems to which the Liberal government had to take an illiberal attitude: the occupation of Egypt, the repression of popular movements, the need for coercion in Ireland, the mutilation of parliamentary procedure, the Bradlaugh affair.

Parliament was almost immediately discredited by its handling of a question of conscience, a basic question in the Liberal philosophy. Charles Bradlaugh, elected member for Northampton, reputedly one of the most Radical towns in the country, was an avowed atheist. In addition he was an outspoken critic of entrenched privilege including royalty and the House of Lords, and had advocated artificial birth control as the answer to the problems of over-population. He provoked the conflict by claiming the right to affirm his allegiance rather than take the customary oath. The Speaker refused and, when Bradlaugh offered to take the oath in the ordinary way and was forbidden, there developed an involved battle, which was sedulously exploited by a small group of Conservative M.P.s who became known as the 'Fourth Party'. The affair, mishandled, soon developed an importance out of all proportion to its true significance. Bradlaugh was imprisoned in the Clock Tower, refused the right to affirm by the Judges, expelled forcibly by ten policemen, re-elected at Northampton and re-expelled. Gladstone brought in an Affirmation Bill in 1883 on the liberal grounds that it was wrong to make any 'distinctions between man and man on the ground of religious difference' but the Commons, encouraged by the Fourth Party, would have none of it. Bradlaugh eventually was allowed to take his seat after the next General Election and with Conservative support piloted an Affirmation Bill through Parliament in 1888. When he lay dying in 1891 the Commons expunged from the records of the House the resolution of July 1880 which had forbidden him to swear or affirm.

The chief importance of the affair was the damage it did to Parliament's reputation for good sense and the display it gave of party leaders unable to control their parties, in particular the Conservative leader, Sir Stafford Northcote. Northcote had at one time been Gladstone's private secretary and his mind always reverted to those days when he faced Gladstone across the House. Despite his years of conscientious public service, it was increasingly evident that he had neither the authority nor ruthlessness required for successful parliamentary leadership. This was the opportunity of the Fourth Party.

The 'Fourth Party', as they were soon generally called, consisted of four men. It had no policy as such but merely the principle that when one of its members was attacked, the others rallied to his support. By provocative comments and amendments, debates could be spun out for many hours, with the result that Government Bills sometimes had to be abandoned for lack of time. Since all were men of considerable ability, it became a remarkably effective group which supplied some of the deficiencies of Northcote's leadership and galvanised the party as a whole. Wolff had an extensive knowledge of foreign affairs and diplomatic methods and he was shrewd, witty and tactful; Gorst, an able and industrious lawyer, had been largely responsible for reorganising the Conservative party after the defeat of 1868 and believed the new leadership failed to appreciate his talents; Balfour, Salisbury's nephew, a dilettante in philosophy and a promotor of popular concerts, hardly seemed a serious politician, yet had unsuspected energy and ability; finally there was Lord Randolph Churchill.

His way to politics smoothed by aristocratic connections, Churchill rapidly made a mark by his considerable debating skill and his youthful pugnacity which spared neither age nor fame. Though only in his early thirties he rapidly became the most popular Conservative speaker and many marked him out for a rapid accession to the leadership of the party. His political beliefs were in line with Disraeli's ideas of Tory democracy and he often embarrassed the government by adopting a position more Radical than their own. One example will suffice of his effective ridicule. Referring to Gladstone's hobby of felling trees he said: 'Every afternoon the whole world is invited to assist at the crashing fall of some beech or elm or oak. The forest laments in order that Mr Gladstone may perspire and full accounts of these proceedings are forwarded by special correspondents every recurring morning.'

It was not merely the Fourth Party that made difficulties for the government; it was more especially the Third Party and the Irish situation that gave it its *raison d'être*. Its leader was a man of Churchill's age, C. S. Parnell, who was an unlikely leader for a party that owed much of its fuel to agrarian discontent. A member of the Ascendancy class, a Protestant, a large landowner who leased his land, with an English education that had aroused in him no interest in Irish culture and history, he was proud, aloof, masterful and ruthless; it was his tragedy, and Ireland's, that he was betrayed through his own weaknesses. He exploited the Ballot Act and turned the passive and incohesive party of Isaac Butt into the focus of all the elements in Ireland that hated the English. It was his aim to exploit the liberal rules Parliament had inherited from less bitter times in such a way that Ireland alone could be the subject of debate. It should be recognised, however, that in so doing he undoubtedly contained the rising tide of bitterness, supported by American money and, as Gladstone realised, provided an opportunity for a settlement and reconciliation.

The bad seasons that were proving disastrous to English agriculture[1] had aggravated the distress of Ireland. Gladstone's Land Act of 1870, although it had recognised important principles, had caused difficulties by the opportunities it still gave landlords to raise rents and evict tenants. Tenants were dependent on two economic factors: the result of the harvest and the price of agricultural produce, especially potatoes. Since 1878 both had been bad and tenants fell rapidly into arrears of rent. In 1880 over 2,000 families were evicted. Disraeli's sole answer to agrarian discontent had been a Coercion Act; when this lapsed in 1880, the new Chief Secretary, W. E. Forster, who was anxious to mitigate Irish miseries, did not press for its renewal and the government introduced an Evicted Tenants Bill to ease the situation. When this was rejected by the House of Lords, sufferers had no legal redress and took the law into their own hands. Ricks were burned, cattle were maimed. Farmers who took over a farm from which a tenant had been evicted awoke to find graves dug before their doors. There were cases of murder. Crimes of this nature leapt from 300 in 1878 to 2,500 in 1880. Behind them was the Land League, founded by Michael Davitt in 1879 which demanded the 'three F's' – Fair Rents, Fixity of Tenure and Free Sale. Davitt's family had been evicted when he was a child, he had lost an arm in a factory accident; he attacked the Ascendancy with a passionate bitterness but also with an integrity that commanded respect. It was to restrain the extremism of the Land League that Parnell devised, in September 1880, what he maintained to be a Christian alternative to murder. 'When a man takes a farm from which another has been evicted . . . by isolating him from his kind as if he were a leper of old – you must show him your detestation of the crime he has committed.' When three days later Lord Erne's agent, Captain Boycott, served ejection notices on tenants, the method had a name. No one would answer when he spoke, all his workers left him, shopkeepers would not serve him nor would postmen deliver letters. Troops were sent to help him but he was forced to leave the district.

In November Forster initiated a prosecution for conspiracy against the Land League, naming Parnell and thirteen others as defendants, but at a time of political passion the jury system was valueless in Ireland; the jury failed to agree; the Irish hailed it as a triumph. If ordinary law failed, however, coercion became inevitable, despite the opposition in the Cabinet of Bright and Chamberlain who believed that a prompt and generous land settlement would kill Home Rule agitation. Gladstone was insistent that coercion should be linked with some measure of conciliation, although the Queen was convinced that reform would be inappropriate in the circumstances. The Coercion Bill did not become law until March 1881, after the worst obstruction in parliamentary history. At the beginning of February the Commons sat for forty-one continuous hours until Speaker Brand took the division on the first reading 'on my own responsibility' as he put it, amidst a storm of cheering, 'and a sense of duty to the House'. The next day Gladstone initiated a closure resolution which gave the government greater control over debates. The Coercion Act, in force for eighteen months, gave absolute power of arbitrary and preventative arrest. Forster failed to appreciate the bitterness of Irish feelings and thought he could undermine unrest by sweeping several hundred suspected agitators into Kilmainham Gaol. Others took their place.

Given happier circumstances Gladstone's Land Act of 1881 might have promoted better relations. Although he had not thought it necessary to consult either Parnell or Chamberlain, the Act showed a very much better understanding of Irish problems than its predecessor of 1870. In effect it gave the Land League what they had asked for, the 'three F's', and was one more example of disorder leading to success. Any tenant dissatisfied with the rent his landlord proposed to charge could appeal to one of the Land Courts the act set up, which could fix a fair rent, having regard to all the circumstances, for a duration of fifteen years. In practice rents were reduced by the Courts by an average of 20 per cent, which underlines the justice of the tenants' claims. Tenants gained security against arbitrary eviction and the right to sell their leases. The government also made money available to assist emigration and to enable tenants to buy their holdings. The bill was passed by the Lords with great reluctance; they saw it as a considerable encroachment on the rights of property. Although he recognised it as a valuable piece of legislation, Parnell was careful to keep control of Irish extremism by describing it as inadequate, a course which probably obtained better terms for the peasantry from the Courts.

Meanwhile agrarian outrages continued in Ireland. Following the Coercion Act, crimes greatly increased, especially

murder and attempted murder. Gladstone warned Parnell
he would be arrested if he did not mend his ways and in
October he and three other leaders joined the Irish martyrs in
Kilmainham. When Gladstone announced the imprisonment at the Lord Mayor's Banquet he was cheered as though
Trafalgar had been won again. As Parnell had predicted
'Captain Moonlight' took his place and murder and violence
reached a crescendo, although a 'No Rent Manifesto' issued
by the Land League and signed by Parnell against his better
judgment failed because the priests would not support it. The
government then proclaimed the Land League as illegal and
drove its adherents underground.

During his detention, Parnell had frequent information of
the condition of the country and was perturbed by the growth
of irresponsible secret societies. He was temporarily released
in April in order, ostensibly, to visit his sister but in fact to
console his mistress, Katherine O'Shea, on the death of their
infant daughter. His mistress's husband, Captain O'Shea,
who condoned the arrangement, informed Chamberlain that
Parnell would make a bargain. Chamberlain was anxious to
avoid the risk of class war which could lead to a renewal of
terrorism and was eager to become Chief Secretary in order to
put a policy of conciliation into practice. He was ready to
take on full responsibility for the negotiations, but Gladstone
played an important part, although he later denied that there
was an agreement. *Punch* printed a cartoon of the Prime
Minister surreptitiously handing a key in return for the
'Treaty' through the bars of Parnell's prison, with the caption:
'Gladstone committing treason'. The 'Kilmainham Treaty'
as the Fourth Party called it, 'alone in its infamy' (Balfour),
was in fact an agreement whereby Parnell secured his release
and promised to 'slow down the agitation', while the government passed legislation which paid from the confiscated funds
of the Irish Church the substantial arrears tenants had accumulated before the Land Act. The Arrears Act of 1882
cancelled arrears in cases where tenants occupying land worth
less than £30 a year were unable to pay. Its effect was to
reduce the number of agrarian crimes.

Cowper, the Lord Lieutenant, and Forster at once resigned
in protest at a bargain concluded behind their backs. Forster
was a man of great integrity who hated violence but saw no

alternative; he had taken office at a very difficult stage in Irish
unrest and never received from Gladstone the support he was
entitled to expect. Chamberlain felt he was the obvious
successor but Gladstone considered that to appoint him would
be to surrender to a very large extent his own control. He
appointed Lord Spencer as Viceroy, while his favourite
nephew, Lord Frederick Cavendish, went, amidst popular
surprise and derision, as Chief Secretary.

Lord Frederick's abilities were never to be tested. Almost
immediately after his arrival in May 1882 he was walking in
Phoenix Park with Burke, the Under Secretary at Dublin
Castle, when Burke was attacked with long surgical knives by
assassins belonging to a secret society named 'The Invincibles'
who had also plotted to kill Forster. In the affray, Lord
Frederick was also killed. This crime, which Parnell publicly
condemned, aroused particular horror in England and put an
end to immediate hopes of reconciliation between the two
nations. Parnell feared he would be the next victim and
seriously thought of retiring from public life but was dissuaded
from doing so by Gladstone.

Trevelyan, undoubtedly a Radical, was the next Chief
Secretary. A new Crimes Act was introduced which enabled
him to restore order and break up 'The Invincibles', though
not before more murders had taken place, including the killing
of five people at Maamtrasna as they slept, for giving information to the authorities. Parnell, meanwhile, regained his full
authority and founded the National League, which would
promote not the Land Nationalisation Davitt urged, but
Home Rule.

The preoccupation of government and Parliament with
Ireland and with foreign and colonial problems left little
enough time for social reform. There were a number of
minor but useful acts, as for instance the Burials Act of 1880
which removed a long-standing nonconformist grievance; the
Corrupt Practices Act of 1883, which has been mentioned
above, and a Settled Land Act of 1883 which permitted the
break up of ancient estates. Chamberlain was active with
Acts regulating Seamen's Wages and Grain Cargoes in 1880
and a Bankruptcy Act and a Patents Act in 1883 but was
impatient for wider measures. In addition to campaigning
for further franchise reform, which resulted in the Acts of 1884

and 1885, he was preparing a full list of Radical demands, which was to be published as *The Unauthorised Programme* of July 1885 and which was to make Chamberlain, in the eyes of the country, Gladstone's logical heir apparent. Chamberlain was careful, however, to avoid the clash with Gladstone that might have come had he pushed forward his schemes too rapidly. In the meantime he concentrated on the extension of his influence by the part he played in the reform struggle.

Trevelyan, who had annually moved a resolution that the counties should be given the same franchise as the boroughs had received in 1867, and Chamberlain both urged the Cabinet to introduce another Reform Bill. Hartington had accepted the justice of this in principle in 1877 but made difficulties when the matter was discussed. Gladstone, however, overruled him. The bill was prepared and passed the Commons by large majorities. In the Lords the Conservatives, who were aware that the bill would still further reduce the control of territorial magnates over elections, were afraid to reject it but delayed it on the not unreasonable ground that it should be accompanied, as previous Reform Bills had been, by a bill redistributing seats. They suspected the Liberals would so rearrange constituencies that rural voters would invariably be swamped by urban ones and they estimated a party advantage to the Liberals of forty-seven seats. It was naturally hoped that the difficulties aroused by redistribution would delay both bills indefinitely. The Lords further maintained that they had the duty to force an appeal to the people on a measure for which the government had no mandate. The Queen also urged Gladstone to dissolve Parliament, but the Prime Minister denied that there was any obligation.

Chamberlain at once started a campaign in the country with the slogan 'Peers against the People', while John Morley contributed 'Mend them or end them'. Gladstone, however, was anxious to avoid a constitutional crisis and the Queen helped to bring the two sides together through skilful negotiations conducted by her private secretary, General Ponsonby. Many of the problems were settled over tea at 10 Downing Street by Gladstone, Salisbury, Northcote, Hartington and Dilke and only once was a breakdown in discussions likely, but Lady Salisbury saved the day by a personal appeal to Gladstone. In this cosy fashion, which led Gladstone to believe that Irish problems might be dealt with similarly, England obtained her third great Act of Parliamentary Reform, passed by the Lords in December 1884.

It was, curiously enough, an action by Lord Salisbury which gave the Redistribution Act of 1885 one of its most Radical features. He declared unaccountably for single member constituencies. Even Joseph Chamberlain was apprehensive, particularly in view of the effect on his National Liberal Association, which was carefully geared to the existing arrangement. Dilke, President of the Local Government Board, was enthusiastic for the idea and mastered the intricacies of the subject, and although Gladstone insisted on the retention of two members for the universities and towns with a population of between 50,000 and 165,000, the rest of the country was chopped up into 'one horse seats' in a way which blurred the ancient distinction between counties and boroughs. All boroughs with a population of less than 15,000 were disfranchised while those with a population of 15,000 to 50,000 were to have one member only. Counties were apportioned members, as far as possible on a basis of one to every 50,000. The result was greatly to increase the 'swing of the pendulum' at elections and also to undermine the Whig stake in the Liberal Party. Hitherto both wings had been satisfied by running a Whig and a Radical together; single member constituencies increasingly preferred a Radical, and this was one of the reasons why the Whigs tended to leave the party and make their way over to the Conservatives.

The greatest consequences were in Ireland. The Act did not reduce Irish representation to make it proportionate to its population; rather it enfranchised the mass of the Irish peasantry. This situation had been foreseen but Chamberlain and others had conjectured that the greater social contrasts in the electorate would split the Irish party. The outcome, however, was the Eighty Six of '86. Outside Protestant Ulster and Trinity College, Parnell swept the board.

Meanwhile Chamberlain pursued other schemes. He believed that if Ireland could be given a measure of self-government, Home Rule could lose its immediacy, while the extension of self-government to the counties at the same time would end the traditional jurisdiction of the territorial magnates. Though he knew Parnell himself would not be satisfied with anything less than a repeal of the Act of Union he believed that he could obtain his support for a scheme whereby administrative functions could be transferred to a national council in Dublin assisted by county boards. He envisaged a similar scheme for Scotland and even toyed with 'the restoration of the heptarchy' in England, with regional and county councils. The Irish Hierarchy supported Chamberlain's scheme; Gladstone made his approval conditional on the support of Lord Spencer the Viceroy, and Campbell-Bannerman who had become Chief Secretary when Trevelyan retired through ill health. Spencer, who had just obtained a renewal of the Crimes Act, described the Irish as 'unfit for government' although within a year he was to support Home Rule, and the Cabinet rejected the scheme on 9th May, 1885. Chamberlain and Dilke tendered their resignations but had not actually left the government when it was defeated by an unexpected alliance of the Irish Nationalists and the Conservatives on 8th June.

(b) COLONIAL AND FOREIGN AFFAIRS, 1880–85

Gladstone had condemned Disraeli's colonial policy; on coming to power he was to find that many of his views in opposition were difficult to apply in government. In South Africa the Boers expected the restoration of the Transvaal,[1] but the government were hesitant, in view of schemes for federation and other preoccupations and the belief, based on false information, that a majority of the Transvaal population were in favour of annexation. The Boers, on the other hand, their great fear of the Zulus having vanished, felt more confident than ever of being able to defend their independence unaided. It is at least arguable that if full incorporation of the Transvaal had taken place prior to the destruction of the Zulus there would have been no further trouble. However in December 1880 the Boers, disappointed at British treatment, rose in revolt and Colley, Governor of Natal, imagining an easy victory, entered the Transvaal and was decisively defeated and killed at Majuba Hill (February 1881). Only ninety-three British died, but feelings in Britain were outraged; the Queen, the Opposition and the Press urged revenge. Gladstone had a difficult decision to make. If he sought to

[1] See above, p. 255.

avenge the defeat by reconquering the Transvaal, there was a strong risk of the Cape Dutch rising in revolt as well. If, on the other hand, he made peace, this would be a magnanimous gesture which would not only save lives but make future co-operation possible. Nevertheless the government would have conceded to violence what they had refused to reasoned requests – a repetition in theme of their Irish Land Act. As Bryce observed: 'The Boers saw in the conduct of the British government neither generosity nor humanity, but only fear.' The transaction enhanced the arrogance of the Boers and encouraged them to be more intransigent in the negotiations prior to the South African War of 1899–1902. Gladstone believed that both morally and economically it was wrong for Britain to add to her colonial commitments, but both at home and in Europe it was regarded as a display of weakness. The Pretoria Convention of 1881 recognised the independence of the Transvaal but British suzerainty, including the control of foreign relations, was maintained. Unfortunately the word 'suzerainty' was omitted from the confirming London Convention of 1884, probably in the belief that it was already adequately emphasised and this was a central factor in the subsequent difficulties.[1]

Afghanistan was another inherited problem.[2] When Disraeli resigned the British-backed candidate, Abdur Rahman, had been installed as Amir, but in July 1880 a British force under General Burrows was defeated at Maiwand by another claimant and besieged in Kandahar. General Roberts marched victoriously from Kabul to the relief of Kandahar and British prestige was restored. Although no British Resident was sent to Kabul, Britain controlled Amir Abdur Rahman's foreign policy and paid him a subsidy.

Both in South Africa and Afghanistan the government had been careful not to take on additional commitments; in Egypt, to their embarrassment, they had to take on the obligation of suppressing a nationalist movement as well as assuming a heavy military and financial burden. Here again Gladstone's difficulties arose in part from the policy of the previous government which in preventing the weakening of the Turkish Empire and in purchasing the Suez Canal shares had also involved itself in Egypt whose ruler, the Khedive, was nomin-

[1] See below, p. 336.   [2] See above, p. 256.

ally the Sultan's vassal. The Khedive Ismail had acquired a heavy debt which had led to Franco-British supervision of his finances in 1878. French tradition and prestige was bound up with Egypt; since Napoleon I's occupation they had regarded the country as being in a special sense their *protégé* and under the Second Empire a great deal of French money had been invested there, especially in the Suez Canal. Bismarck encouraged the involvement, as a distraction from Alsace and Lorraine and a potential source of conflict between England and France. When the Khedive attempted to escape from the control of the two Powers in 1879, Disraeli would have been glad to go if the French would have gone as well. In view of their emotional and financial commitments, however, the French persuaded the Sultan to depose Ismail and replace him by his son Tewfik.

In opposition to the foreign influence in Egypt a genuinely nationalist movement arose led by Arabi Bey and a group of other army officers who resented the financial stringency foreign control imposed; they were supported by Mohammedan intellectuals. By 1881 they had seized control of the country and an Egyptian repudiation of foreign debts, some £90 m., was anticipated. The Radicals urged Gladstone to come to terms with the Nationalist party, but Gladstone's hatred of financial immorality obscured in his mind any virtues Arabi and his associates might have. Granville followed a devious and evasive diplomatic course; he favoured Turkish intervention in Egypt but the French disparaged this in view of its implications in Tunis where the French obtained a Protectorate in May 1881. It was recognised that a policy of French intervention alone would be fatal to British interests in the eastern Mediterranean, and Granville and Gladstone determined on a policy of co-operation with France in order to restrain her. Gambetta, in his brief ministry, November 1881–January 1882, tried to promote a policy of joint intervention, but apart from British unwillingness Bismarck dampened the scheme for fear it might lead to a permanent Franco-British alliance. After Gambetta's fall, Arabi took firmer control of Egypt, while Granville and the new French Premier, Freycinet, organised a conference of the Great Powers at Constantinople. It was fruitless; the French resisted Turkish intervention, while the other Powers would not contemplate that of any other country. As a precaution against disorder but with strict orders not to land troops the British and French fleets took station outside Alexandria in May. The following month there was extensive Nationalist rioting in which fifty Europeans died; Europeans rapidly began to leave the country and the government was receptive to the plea that British lives were in danger. Arabi restored order and began to build batteries threatening the fleets; an attempt to regain control by international action failed owing to Turkish obstruction.

In July, therefore, on government instructions and with the overwhelming approval of British public opinion, the English fleet silenced the forts after ten hours' bombardment. The French were invited to co-operate, but although he was willing to occupy the Canal Zone, Freycinet was unable to get the support of the French Chamber which, though reluctant to see Britain act alone, was more concerned lest a French involvement outside Europe were an opportunity for Bismarck. Further action in Egypt logically followed and both France and Turkey were invited to participate. The Cabinet as a whole felt it was justified on account of the Suez Canal, but Bright resigned when it was decided to bombard Alexandria. The Conservative Party on the whole approved, but Churchill declared that our interests in the eastern Mediterranean were illusory and that Gladstone was guilty of an act of unnecessary aggression. The invasion of Egypt was a model of military efficiency which demonstrated the value of Cardwell's reforms and greatly raised British prestige. On 13th September Sir Garnet Wolseley destroyed Arabi's army at Tel-el-Kebir and Cairo was occupied without difficulty.

Gladstone shared the national exhilaration and warmly praised the achievements of the Army and Navy but once Britain was established in Egypt, doubts crept in. Although the Queen and public opinion generally were ready for annexation or at least the declaration of a protectorate, and Bismarck urged it in the expectation that it would increase Franco-British estrangement, Gladstone declared that the occupation was only temporary and Britain would leave as soon as order was restored, a promise repeated sixty-six times during the next forty years. During this time the representative of the financial house of Baring who was British Agent and Consul-general expanded a concern for the interests of the British and French bond holders he represented into one for Egypt as a whole, whose ruler he effectively was. It would be wrong to see in Lord Cromer, as Baring became, an agent of imperial expansion but under his supervision Egypt became in fact, if not in name, a British possession. There was, however, an irritating restriction. Feeling that his moral position was weak, and expecting that British troops would withdraw shortly, Gladstone agreed to a Six Power Control Commission to supervise Egyptian finances. Russia and France, who deeply resented the British occupation and hoped for a withdrawal or at least compensation elsewhere, always opposed British suggestions and in consequence Britain became dependent on the Triple Alliance and in particular on Bismarck who was seeking colonial acquisitions in Africa. French bitterness towards England continued for twenty years.[1]

In occupying Egypt, Great Britain assumed the Egyptians' problems and responsibilities. For sixty years Egypt had ruled in the Sudan by violence, brutality and corruption, occasionally relieved when she employed European officials, as for instance General Charles Gordon who was Governor-General from 1877–79. On his return to Britain, renewed Egyptian misgovernment provided the opportunity for a former slave trader and Egyptian official, Mahommed Ahmed, to proclaim himself Mahdi or Messiah and preach a war of liberation from the Egyptians. He obtained widespread support and in 1883 the Khedive prepared an expedition to recover control. Gladstone felt that here was a nation 'struggling to be free' and as a religious crusade it recommended itself to him. Unlike Egypt, there were no European financial commitments in the Sudan and Gladstone took the view that Sudanese affairs were none of his concern. He did not, however, prevent the Khedive from sending an army and when this fell into an ambush and was annihilated in November 1883, which rallied the rest of the Sudan to the Mahdi's support, British involvement became inevitable.

From Cairo Baring urged evacuation of the Sudan. The Queen and Opposition felt that the destruction of the Egyptian

[1] See below, p. 313 and p. 335.

Army, which had had an English general, should be avenged at once, lest Moslem opinion in India be encouraged by the Mahdi's example. The government, however, felt that evacuation of the whole of the Sudan south of Wadi Haifa was the wisest course and the Queen, persuaded by Granville that reconquest would mean heavy British casualties, reluctantly agreed. W. T. Stead of the *Pall Mall Gazette* urged the employment of Gordon to supervise the withdrawal and the Press as a whole supported the demand. Gordon was ready to serve; he persuaded Granville that his personal influence over the Sudanese would ensure a peaceful withdrawal.

In this haphazard fashion Gordon was chosen to perform a task requiring tact and diligence. Salisbury on hearing of the appointment remarked 'They must have gone absolutely crazy' and Gordon in a moment of candour admitted 'I know if I was chief I would never employ myself.' Gordon was a Victorian schoolboys' hero. A man of deep religious convictions, he had an overwhelming sense of mission and a facility for self-deception that exceeded that of Gladstone himself. In addition to serving the Khedive he had soldiered with distinction in China and in Cape Colony. Of his courage there could be no question, of his lack of judgment there was none, except by Baring, who was overruled. Public opinion, to which the government deferred, saw as essentially fitted for an unheroic task a man whom it hailed as a hero and a saint. Gordon's departure from London was royal.

On arrival in Khartoum as Governor-General with secret instructions to withdraw, Gordon had a mystic conviction that he was capable of holding the Sudan. To assist him he commissioned a disreputable slave-trader, Zobeir, an appointment which the government refused to endorse. The Mahdi increased his control of the Sudan while Gordon sent constant telegrams to Baring urging an official change of policy. Gladstone was ill and the government allowed matters to drift, instead of either recalling Gordon for disobeying orders or sending out the reinforcements he required. By May, when the Mahdist forces cut off the main land link with Khartoum, it was evident to most people that, although Gordon's reports of his own position had been optimistic, he was in danger. Hartington, who was War Minister, favoured action. Gladstone, however, was unconvinced; he objected to Gordon dictating his policy and he felt he could leave Khartoum whenever he wished; W. E. Forster commented bitterly, 'He [Gladstone] can persuade most people of most things and . . . himself of almost anything.' The government had lost its freedom of action when it first employed Gordon; now it was in Gordon's hands, and Press and people would not see him perish.

Low water on the Nile made a relieving expedition up the river difficult during the summer and it was not until August that the government decided to take action. As the Mahdist forces slowly closed in on Khartoum, Wolseley's forces cautiously marched south from Wadi Haifa at the beginning of October 1884. On the 21st January contact was made with steamers sent down the Nile by Gordon, who with great ingenuity and courage was defending Khartoum against overwhelming odds; there was an inexplicable delay of three days and when the relieving force arrived at the city on the 28th it was to discover that the garrison and its commander had been massacred two days earlier.

Responsibility for the tragedy was spread among a number of people, especially Gordon himself, but the Queen, who in this case as in so many other ways typified the public attitude, had no doubts. She sent uncoded telegrams to Gladstone, Granville and Hartington: 'To think that all this might have been prevented and many precious lives saved by earlier action is too frightful.' Lord Cromer in a private despatch concurred: 'The Nile Expedition was sanctioned too late and the reason why it was sanctioned too late was that Mr. Gladstone would not accept the simple evidence of a plain fact which was patent to much less powerful intellects than his own.' Gladstone had distrusted the growing emotional 'jingoism' of the masses but his distaste for it and consequent lack of action had led to a disaster for which no apologies were acceptable. Gladstone reached the depths of public execration; the music halls rated him with Pilate and Judas Iscariot. Fourteen votes saved him from parliamentary censure and Rosebery's return to the government after an earlier resignation opportunely bolstered its prestige.

However, in April 1885 Gladstone showed that when required he could act with resolution. A Boundary Commission was about to determine the frontier between Russia

T

and Afghanistan when the Russians seized the Afghan town of Pendjeh. War seemed a distinct possibility and in a speech that added to his reputation Gladstone successfully requested a vote of credit for £11 m. Negotiating from strength and aware that Bismarck hoped to profit from a conflict, Gladstone made moderate proposals to the Russians and trouble was averted. Pendjeh remained Russian but the Afghans kept the more important Zufilkar Pass which the Russians had also wanted.

In general, however, Gladstone's foreign policy during his Second Ministry had weakened rather than strengthened the British diplomatic position. His hatred of jingoism convinced him that any forward policy was *ipso facto* wrong; in consequence he abandoned the Sudan to the Mahdi and failed to appreciate that a better government in the Sudan would have made the better government of Egypt easier. His indecision in Egypt did not prevent the assumption of British responsibility but on terms that rendered Britain especially vulnerable to Great Power pressures, and thus prevented her exerting a detached influence on events. Nevertheless Gladstone was convinced of the moral rightness of his actions and appealed to the masses as the supreme tribunal of Christian morality, but in so far as public opinion as a whole can pass impartial judgments, it saw many of Gladstone's actions as a betrayal of British interests. A generation was coming to manhood whose aspirations the 'Grand Old Man' of politics failed to understand.

(c) LORD SALISBURY'S FIRST MINISTRY, 1885–86

When Disraeli died in 1881 he had no obvious successor and, as had happened with the Liberal party after Gladstone's first retirement, the leadership went into commission. Northcote in the Commons proved ineffectual and the Fourth Party who chafed under his leadership were obliged, in view of Churchill's youth and inexperience, to support the claims to primacy of the leader in the Lords, the Marquess of Salisbury. Salisbury, as Lord Cranborne, had bitterly opposed the Reform Bill of 1867 and had obtained a reputation for being rash and violent in his opinions; the rank and file distrusted him as an intellectual. Disraeli, however, had recognised his talents and he had shown in his handling of the Eastern Crisis and the Congress of Berlin those abilities that were to make him an acknowledged master of diplomacy. In 1880 he stumped the country in answer to the second Midlothian Campaign and showed the ability to make powerful straight-forward speeches. In a sense he did not seek greatness; it was thrust upon him. His career illustrated how an ancient family can produce men of great distinction over a wide spread of generations, yet he had no special belief in the virtues of the hereditary peerage. He had no particular interest in his duties and privileges as a great landowner or in the ancient and beautiful house that was his family home. He proposed the institution of life peerages in 1888 and his opposition in 1867 was not a defence of the landed interest but, like Lowe's, a plea for government by the best. Similarly, in his political life, the longest serving Prime Minister since the Reform Bill of 1832 never particularly liked the office. When in power he was engrossed in foreign policy and had a reliable leader been available would have gladly taken the second place. He twice offered to defer to Hartington and had Lord Randolph Churchill not attempted to assert his authority prematurely, might well have stood down for him in due time. Yet though he allowed free rein to members of his Cabinet he was very much its master and asserted his authority without difficulty in 1887. This authority grew and the strongest forces in the country were gathered round the Conservative banner. He showed great ability in containing a colleague as ebullient as Joseph Chamberlain and ruled the party without embarrass-ment from the House of Lords.

Had Gladstone's Ministry lasted its full term it is conceiv-able that Churchill would have so strengthened his position that he could have claimed the premiership. Since 1880 he had grown increasingly popular both in the party and in the country; in the Commons he had become the pacesetter of Conservative tactics in defiance of the official leadership. The Conservative party organisation, that Sir John Gorst had done so much to create, had declined after 1876; Churchill decided to revive it. He realised the importance of a wide basis of support and believed that this would become most effective if the National Union of Conservative Associations, which was modelled on Chamberlain's National Liberal Federation, became a democratic and representative body.

Thus he developed the conception of Disraeli's Tory Democracy, a democracy which supported the Tory party because it had been taught by experience to believe in the excellence and soundness of Tory principles. In vying with Chamberlain's policy of social reform he hoped to attract the working classes; it is arguable that had he been successful he would have repelled the business interests which increasingly were seeing the Conservative party as their natural home.

Churchill invited Salisbury to lead the Tory democratic movement. When he declined, Churchill decided to obtain control of the National Union himself and then to obtain for it considerable authority. In 1884 he challenged the official leadership, resigning from the chairmanship and being implored to return by the local Conservative Associations. As *The Times* put it, 'The main question at issue between him and the official leaders of the opposition is whether the internal organisation of the party should be for the future established on a popular and representative or a secret and irresponsible basis.' With this success behind him, Churchill's prestige was secured; Balfour reconciled him to Salisbury. He consented to drop the claims of the National Union, but Northcote's leadership of the Commons was doomed.

Churchill played a considerable part in engineering the fall of Gladstone's government in 1885. He made no firm promises to the Irish party but indicated his unwillingness to review the Crimes Act when it expired. In association with Hicks Beach, the Fourth Party then drew up an amendment to the budget which condemned the proposed increased duty on beer and spirits, although the duty on wine was not increased, and declined to add to the duty on real property without relief to the rates. It was considered it would unite the Opposition and secure support from the Irish and the liquor interest. The motion was put at a time of year when majorities tend to be precarious and it was carried by twelve votes. Four Liberals and forty-two Irish voted against the government. Gladstone resigned and refused to resume office although Salisbury was reluctant to have to pass the Finance Bill into law with a minority government. The new electoral registers would not be ready until the winter and Salisbury, on 23rd June, agreed to form a caretaker government with a vague promise of co-operation over the budget from Gladstone.

With Conservative leadership in the Commons in dispute, the invitation to Salisbury to form an administration was accepted without question by the party. It was a measure of Churchill's success that Northcote went to the Lords as Earl of Iddlesleigh and Lord President. The new Leader of the Commons was Hicks Beach, who also became Chancellor of the Exchequer. The Fourth Party was in office: Wolff was sent on a special mission to Turkey and Egypt; Gorst became Solicitor-General; Balfour, President of the Local Government Board where he was not a great success, and Churchill became Secretary of State for India.

At the India Office Churchill immediately displayed considerable administrative ability as well as parliamentary skill. His period of office was marked by the acquisition of Upper Burma, Lower Burma having been conquered in 1824 and 1832. King Thibaw had celebrated his accession in 1878 by massacring all other claimants to the throne; he proved unable to maintain order and alarmed the Government of India by trade negotiations with the French. When he imposed a heavy and unjustified fine on the Bombay-Burma Company, with the intention of awarding their concession to the French, a British expedition was rapidly mounted and it annexed the country with few casualties, although tribal resistance continued until 1889.

The Earl of Carnarvon, formerly Disraeli's Colonial Secretary, became Lord Lieutenant of Ireland. He had been the Minister responsible for the federation of Canada in 1867 and had attempted the federation of South Africa; this experience had convinced him that Irish problems could be solved by giving Ireland a subordinate legislative, and his appointment persuaded Gladstone that the Conservatives probably favoured Home Rule. Carnarvon was given a joyful welcome in Dublin and to keep Parnell's support, the Crimes Act was not renewed.[1] Lord Ashbourne's Act was passed which aimed to spread peasant landownership with State help. On the question of more independence for Ireland, Carnarvon held secret discussions with Justin McCarthy and once, in a West End drawing room dismantled at the end of the season, with Parnell himself. Salisbury gave his full approval, feeling that such a meeting could do no harm, but did not inform the

[1] See above, p. 270.

Cabinet. Carnarvon opened the discussions; by his own account, by stressing that he represented no one but himself; he sought information only and would listen to nothing inconsistent with the union of the two countries. Parnell, nevertheless, assumed from the meeting that Conservative support for Home Rule was a strong possibility.

The Liberal party meanwhile was severely shaken when Chamberlain published his *Unauthorised Programme*[1] in July 1885. This had been prepared for two years; the achievement of Parliamentary Reform was to be followed by intentions that would, Chamberlain hoped, widen still further the breach between the Radicals and the Whigs and secure his own control of the party. Chamberlain believed that Whig domination could not survive into the democratic era; he failed to appreciate that the Radicals had lost to a large extent the confidence of the middle classes who, alarmed by socialism, imperial and industrial difficulties, and by power politics in Europe, were growing suspicious of change. Many hesitated to transfer their allegiance to the Conservatives; men such as Hartington and Goschen, as long as they remained in the party, seemed an adequate guarantee of stability. Gladstone was apparently ready to adopt as much of Chamberlain's programme as Hartington would also accept.

Chamberlain laid great emphasis on the improvement of housing conditions and considered that those who had benefited from the unearned increment of urban land values should make a substantial contribution towards this. He wanted free primary education, the creation of smallholdings, the use of taxation to adjust excessive income differences, County Councils, National Councils in Edinburgh and in Dublin and such long-term objectives as Disestablishment, manhood suffrage and payment of M.P.s. Chamberlain called this socialism but he envisaged it not as helping Marxist socialism but creating a bulwark against it; he was careful to show that it contained nothing new or revolutionary. The Queen, Gladstone and the Whigs were perturbed by the threat to the rights of property and the conception that property had obligations to society as a whole, but Chamberlain had drawn his programme with practical possibilities firmly in mind. Nevertheless it helped the Conservative party to become the

[1] See below, p. 287.

champions of the Established Church and of denominational teaching, the latter question providing a common link with the Irish Nationalists.

As few people could have foreseen, it was not the *Unauthorised Programme* that was to be the decisive factor in English politics during the coming year, but the question of Ireland. To most Englishmen the Union was a tremendously important issue. How could a country with increasing imperial commitments the world over perform them adequately if it was to be split up into small inward-looking nationalities? The 19th-century tendency had been the creation of large units out of small, especially in Germany and Italy; the reverse tendency in the United Kingdom seemed dangerously retrograde. The Sage of Hawarden, cogitating alone, had no intention of weakening his country, but as a sincere Liberal he saw the hypocrisy of helping 'nations struggling to be free' abroad and coercing them at home. Aware that the English claim to govern Ireland rested ultimately on force and the attempts he had made to remove Irish grievances had not diminished the need for that force, he had felt increasingly since the murder of Cavendish that Ireland must be allowed to govern herself. Behind this were his convictions of freedom and of the virtues of self-government. Aware that many in his party did not share his views he kept his own counsel, but subsequent events confirmed his diagnosis. When the Conservatives allied with the Nationalists to overthrow him in 1885 and reversed Spencer's policy, he became convinced, as Spencer was convinced, that Ireland would never be treated satisfactorily as long as it remained the pawn of English party politics. By granting a measure of self-government within the Union the responsible elements in Ireland would be able to restrain those less responsible, a view shared by many highly placed officials at Dublin Castle.

When he had resigned in 1885 Gladstone had seriously contemplated retirement. He was 75 and had found the strain of his Ministry very considerable. His bad relations with the Queen made him unready to be her Prime Minister again. Further, he was aware that Home Rule was an issue which, if he adopted it, would split his party, arouse the resistance of the Conservatives and thus fail in the House of Lords. The new Conservative attitude to Ireland and

Carnarvon's secret meeting with Parnell, of which he had some inkling, gave him grounds for hope. On a controversial issue of this nature the Conservative party alone could control the House of Lords, as had been the case in 1829, 1846 and 1867, and he hoped that Salisbury would perceive his duty – and perhaps split his party in the process as had happened in 1829 and 1846. Meanwhile the Liberal Party would pledge support and remain intact. Silence, he felt, was therefore the best policy and when Hartington in September asked for a party meeting on Ireland and other problems, he declined, abetted by Granville who believed Gladstone alone could ensure the unity of the party. In the preparations for the General Election, however, the Liberals, over-confident of the outcome, gave an impression of discord, with Hartington and Goschen following Chamberlain round the country, contradicting him.

Salisbury was not prepared to undertake the role for which Gladstone had cast him. Theoretically he could see the merits and advantages of Home Rule but he rejected them as practical politics. He had insisted that the government be committed to nothing when Carnarvon met Parnell and the Conservative-Nationalist agreement had not involved any firm promises on the Conservative side. He led a minority government and it was probable his party would still be in a minority after the General Election; he was not prepared to tie the party to permanent dependence on the Nationalists or the Liberals. Moreover his position was insecure and although he set no special store by the premiership, he was aware of the strong feelings of many Conservatives and wished to prevent Lord Randolph or any other aspiring leader from imitating Disraeli's action in 1846 and splitting the party. Gladstone, however, remained optimistic; he urged Salisbury by letter to take action on Home Rule and he personally approached Balfour in December 1885.

By that time, however, the Election had been fought, and in it Parnell's attitude to the two main parties was of vital importance. Via Mrs O'Shea, he had sounded Gladstone on his views, but the Liberal leader did not reply until after the Election,[1] disdaining to bid for Irish support. Accordingly

[1] Herbert Gladstone indicated to the Radical Labouchère, who favoured the Irish cause, that his father was contemplating Home Rule, and it is probable that Parnell knew this.

Parnell decided to favour the Conservative party. He had chosen to misconstrue Carnarvon's views, in which he was encouraged by a pro-Irish speech Salisbury had made in October; he saw Conservative control over the Lords as a great aid to success and he hoped that the Conservatives would be numerically weaker and thus in greater need of his support. In addition to votes in Ireland itself, the Irish voters in English constituencies would do as he directed and on 21st November, two days before polling day, he issued a Manifesto denouncing the inconsistency of the Liberal party, which it was estimated turned the scales in between twenty-five and forty seats. Although many in his party deplored this desertion of Gladstone, the outcome was to make Parnell the arbiter of the Commons.

The Conservative party had increased its prestige greatly by the tenure of office, particularly in the field of foreign affairs where Salisbury had regained the diplomatic confidence that Granville had to some extent lost. This, memories of Gordon, the Conservative cry for 'Fair Trade', a precursor of Tariff Reform, and the Irish vote were to swing the towns against Gladstone. The countryside, in gratitude for the vote and attracted by the *Unauthorised Programme*, particularly the 'three acres and a cow' promised to the rural labourer, swung to the Liberals, particularly in Scotland. In Ireland not a single Liberal was returned; out of eighty-nine contests, Parnell won eighty-five; Ulster elected sixteen Tories. Liverpool returned an Irish Nationalist and this gave Parnell a party of eighty-six, precisely equal to the Liberal majority over the Conservatives. Quite properly Salisbury continued in office although on 14th December the Cabinet privately decided not to introduce a Home Rule Bill. Rumours, in which Labouchère had a part, intimated that Hartington was contemplating an anti-Gladstone coalition and that Chamberlain would pledge Radical support to keep the government in office. Herbert Gladstone felt the party needed a lead and on his own authority he divulged the news of his father's conversion to the Press. On 17th December the 'Hawarden Kite' was airborne.

(d) THE FIRST HOME RULE BILL, 1886

The Queen urged Salisbury that the government should not fall 'into the hands of Mr Gladstone who can persuade himself that anything he takes up is right, even though it be calling black, white and wrong, right'. 'The Hawarden Kite' caused considerable consternation, hasty reorientation of attitudes and a growing conviction that Gladstone was not only an arch dissembler but desperate to return to power. The manner of the revelation was especially unfortunate but the information was overdue.   Gladstone asserted that he had not fully committed himself, but nobody believed him.   In the most unfavourable circumstances possible he now had the task of converting his party.

The announcement united the Conservatives. Salisbury had already decided not to introduce Home Rule and, with a considerable increase in Irish rent refusal and boycotting as his justification, had decided to revert to coercion.   A Coercion Bill had the special merit of freeing the Conservatives from the Nationalists and speeding the reorientation of parties.   The Queen's Speech of January 1886 was intended to force Gladstone's hand by promising one; the Conservative government could then be seen as falling in defence of the Union.   Gladstone's tactical skill did not desert him, however; a Radical amendment on agrarian policy, introduced by Chamberlain's supporter, Jesse Collings, would, it was conjectured, not divide the party and on it the government was defeated on 27th January, 1886, by 331 to 272. Most of the Irish voted with the majority, but many Liberals abstained, while Hartington, Goschen and sixteen other Liberals voted with the government.

On 3rd February Gladstone formed his Third Administration but many of the old names were lacking.   The Whigs had started crossing the House long before: Lansdowne went in 1881 and others followed him.   Now many men of ability went; of his leading colleagues in the Commons only Harcourt was fully committed; the only able peers who stood by him were Granville, Spencer, Kimberley, Rosebery, Acton and Ripon.   Hartington was a great loss; he had all the assurance that came from being the heir to one of the wealthiest and most distinguished dukedoms in the land and in addition he has been described as sharing with Lord Randolph and with Parnell a special quality of 'you-be-damnedness'.   He had a freshness of approach and an eye for practical detail that made him an admirable colleague.   He had suffered much at

Gladstone's hands: but for Gladstone he would have been Premier and but for his interference when he was at the War Office, Gordon might have been saved. He had been shocked by the *Unauthorised Programme*. What Hartington could not tolerate, however, was truckling to Parnell who had requited Liberal co-operation from 1882 onwards by casting Irish votes for the Conservatives.

Now Hartington had gone there was no real reason why the Liberal party should not be reconciled to social reform – Gladstone agreed to something very similar in the Newcastle Programme of 1891.[1] But Gladstone mishandled Chamberlain and lost him as well and the estrangement of the Radical leader was far more fatal to Home Rule and to the Liberal party than that of a Whig aristocrat who would have gone sooner or later. By far the most startling transformation of the century was the metamorphosis of the attacker of the Established Church and the aristocracy, the advocate of land reform, into the trusted colleague of Salisbury and Balfour, Hartington and Lansdowne, in a Conservative Cabinet. Chamberlain himself had proposed a National Council for Ireland but jibbed at the term Parliament. A little concession on Gladstone's part, a greater appreciation of Chamberlain's importance and a realisation that he was worth the appointment to the Colonial Office, for which he had asked and where he would have been preoccupied with the sort of problems that were later to enthral him, might well have kept him loyal. Had Dilke been available to act as an intermediary, all might have been well, but he was fighting a divorce case. Chamberlain grudged the time and effort Home Rule would divert from problems of social reform and considered the proposal had no chance of success. He and Trevelyan agreed to enter the Cabinet providing they were free to criticise the Irish proposals when they were made in detail. Chamberlain took the junior office of President of the Local Government Board, where he performed useful work, in particular sending out a circular calling on local authorities to provide municipal work for the unemployed without the stigma of poor relief, thus admitting social responsibility for men whose unemployment might result from remote economic forces.[2]

[1] See below, p. 318.　　　　[2] See further, p. 367.

Gladstone regarded Chamberlain as an opportunist; Granville, on the other hand, had earned a reward for his loyalty.
A return to the Foreign Office seemed logical, but Granville
was ageing fast and the strain of the work was beyond him; the
Queen, prompted by Salisbury, insisted on Rosebery who
shared Salisbury's views on foreign policy which would ensure
a valuable continuity.   Granville got the Colonial Office, the
post Chamberlain had coveted.   Harcourt went to the
Exchequer and Childers to the Home Office.   Bright refused
to join the Cabinet, Forster was not asked.   Morley, hitherto
a junior associate of Chamberlain, became Chief Secretary
and, for the remainder of his own life, a devoted supporter of
Gladstone's ideals.   No other Liberal politician believed in
Gladstone's form of Home Rule so completely, no other advocated so strongly such close co-operation with Parnell.   For
the rest of the Cabinet Home Rule was a matter of expediency,
which would have as its reward the expulsion of the Irish from
Westminster.

Had Parliament concerned itself initially with other matters,
the Liberal Party might well have consolidated itself.   A dip
into the *Unauthorised Programme* could well have been opportune, but Gladstone was, as Lord Randolph put it, 'an old
man in a hurry'.   Lord Randolph himself was attempting to
stir up opposition in Ireland, where he coined the dangerous
slogan, 'Ulster will fight and Ulster will be right', in a speech
he made at Belfast.   On 13th March Gladstone clarified his
aims in Cabinet and refused to accept Chamberlain's pro-
ferred resignation.   On 26th March Gladstone declined to
include in the Bill four safeguards Chamberlain proposed,
whereupon he and Trevelyan at once resigned and left the
room.   On 8th April Gladstone introduced the Bill in an
impressive three-and-a-half-hour speech.   An Irish Land Bill
to provide a capital sum to buy out English landlords was
introduced on 16th April and was very badly received by the
Radicals who thought it too kind to the landlords and by many
moderates who thought it insufficiently respected the rights of
property.

Later generations cannot doubt Gladstone's sincerity but
the manner of his conversion and bitter memories of Irish
behaviour made it very difficult for the great majority to
judge the Bill impartially on its merits.   Gladstone main-

tained that it would preserve the unity of the kingdom and the Empire. The Imperial Parliament, in which no Irish members would sit, would control defence matters, foreign and colonial policy, customs and excise, coinage, the post office, trade and manufacture. Ireland would contribute one-fifteenth of the revenue for such purposes, approximately £3½ m. It was plausibly argued by the Conservatives that the taxation of Ireland without representation would encourage the Irish to seek full independence. A Parliament in Dublin would be responsible for all matters concerning the country; it would comprise a chamber and senate sitting together over which the Crown would retain the right to veto. The scheme had distinct weaknesses apart from the lack of representation; the Imperial Government might well have to intervene to safeguard the Protestant minority in Ulster or to ensure the repayment of land purchase money.

The Unionist Defensive Alliance gradually took shape. On 14th May Chamberlain and thirty-two followers attended a meeting at Devonshire House which may be regarded as the foundation of the Liberal Unionist Party. Gladstone attempted to split their ranks by conceding Irish representation at Westminster on 27th May and giving hints of other concessions at the committee stage, but under pressure from Morley and Parnell he withdrew. The emotional appeal of a persecuted Ulster, which Gladstone had discounted, was becoming an important factor. Chamberlain spoke bitterly and read a letter from Bright which described the Bill as 'a measure which is offensive to the whole Protestant population of Ireland'. Parnell spoke with studied moderation of the greater stability Home Rule would bring and made the sensational revelation of his conversation with Carnarvon the previous year. The most impressive speech was made by Hartington; he rebuked Gladstone in a way no one else could have done and with all the force of his integrity and prestige denounced the proposals as repugnant to the ordinary Englishman. Finally Gladstone, looking beyond the division that was to follow, appealed on the highest plane to the electorate outside.

> Ireland is at your bar, expectant, hopeful, almost suppliant. . . . Think, I beseech you; think well, think wisely, think not for the moment, but for the years that are to come, before you reject this bill.

At 1 a.m. on 8th June the Second Reading was defeated in a full House by 343 votes to 313. Ninety-three Liberals voted in the majority.

Although many of his party would happily have dropped the bill or resigned, for Gladstone the battle was not yet over. The National Liberal Federation, under the guidance of its organiser, Schnadhorst, had adhered to Gladstone, except in Birmingham. The Liberal leader appealed to the people for a vote of confidence in himself and the policy he had so recently adopted, but the electors as a whole were unprepared for so rapid a change of policy. Gladstone was confident that Home Rule would mean a change of heart in the Irish but most people found this hard to believe with so many recent memories of lawlessness and enmity towards England. The bitterness with which the election was fought led to much foolishness; Gladstone spoke of the battle of 'the masses against the classes', while Salisbury equated the Irishman's talents for self-government with those of the Hottentots and inferred that Ireland needed 'twenty years of resolute government'. Lord Randolph wrote 'The caprice of an individual is elevated to the dignity of an act of the people by the boundless egoism of the Prime Minister.'

In the General Election, fought in July, the new county voters, cheated, in their view, of social reform, swung to the Conservatives. Dissentient Liberals were not opposed by Conservative candidates as far as the party leadership could ensure. With 191 for the Liberals and 85 for the Irish against 316 for the Conservatives and 78 Liberal Unionists, Gladstone's resignation was unavoidable, but he was not prepared to acknowledge the battle as lost. Salisbury invited Hartington to head a coalition government, but he felt the Liberal Unionists were not yet ready for so close an association with their erstwhile enemies, and Salisbury accordingly formed a purely Conservative administration.

(e) Economic and Social Factors

The last quarter of the 19th Century was, compared with the great periods of expansion that preceded it, a period of depression. This was relative, as parts of the economy remained buoyant; statistically trade increased, production of wool, coal and cotton went up; savings grew, the general standard of living improved. Britain, however, was losing the dominant economic position she had earlier in the century; prices consequently dropped and profits fell as well, which exaggerated the feeling of depression for the wealthier classes.

The depression nevertheless was very real. For instance, the price of steel rails which had been £12 1s. 1d. per ton in 1874 slumped to £5 7s. 6d. per ton in 1883 and similar figures could be produced for other commodities. In a Britain unguarded, unlike the rest of Europe, by tariff barriers, foreign competition was becoming serious. Imports increased from £335 m. in 1872 to £363 m. in 1879, while exports dropped during the same period from £256 m. to £192 m., a tendency that increased. Smaller profits meant less money to invest abroad and consequently an important part of those invisible exports that had hitherto redressed the trade balance was also falling off. Pamphlets were written, a Royal Commission investigated, in the hope of finding the answer.

There were many causes, some general, some specific. During the 19th Century, with the brief exception of the Crimean War which had little effect on the economy and on the life of the country, Britain had enjoyed a peaceful existence unique in Europe. Palmerston had provided excitements at small financial cost and the British economy had benefited from the disruptions and divisions elsewhere. With Britain's head start in industrialisation, her economic position was a very strong one. But economies are never static; to be continuously prosperous they need to be constantly dynamic and, lulled by a long period of effortless dominance, the dynamism to a large extent had gone.

This became particularly serious at a time when the political conditions of other countries favoured rapid expansion. By 1870 the period of wars and unification was over; until 1914 the Great Powers maintained peace in Europe and enjoyed their aggression inexpensively, in the Balkans, Africa and the Far East, wherever, in fact, there were weaker nationalities which could yield without destroying the balance of power. This combination of peace at home and expansion overseas was particularly favourable to the growth of indigenous industries in many European countries and applied equally to the United States which by 1870 had recovered from the convulsion of the Civil War.

The United States, long a valued customer of Great Britain, was becoming increasingly self-sufficient economically. Her shortage of labour accelerated the employment of machinery and the adoption of labour-saving techniques; her lack of a well-established iron industry meant a more rapid adoption of the three great steel inventions[1] and she passed Great Britain in steel production by 1890 and in coal production by 1899. Most of this was for home consumption; the great westward moving frontier of the United States provided a constant and insatiable demand, but it meant that Great Britain had lost an important market. The more rapidly expanding population of the United States was constantly replenished by enterprising and often skilled immigrants, and the high tariff walls erected in 1890 gave the country an advantage that could only increase with time.

Germany was in a similar position. The acquisition of Lorraine with its rich iron fields coinciding with the Gilchrist-Thomas invention that enabled phosphoric ore to be used for steel production gave her a great advantage. She had extensive coalfields and the finest technical education system in the world at the time. Her population exceeded that of Great Britain and, like America, she was growing far less dependent on imports of manufactured goods. Higher tariffs were imposed in 1879 and steel production, mostly for home consumption, exceeded that of Great Britain by 1896.

In a world that was rapidly expanding industrially, the growth of the United States and Germany need not in itself have been detrimental to Great Britain; the greater interest in imperial expansion from the 1880's onwards went a long way to counteract British industrial difficulties, allowing new markets to be substituted for those that had been lost; and the discovery of gold in South Africa and new deposits in Australia and the United States helped to push up world prices. Nevertheless there were certain root weaknesses which were only slowly eradicated. British technical education was far behind the best German standards; industry had concentrated too long on learning by apprenticeship which though useful does not lead to detached analysis of processes and techniques. The last quarter of the century saw a great improvement in facilities for technical education, but management remained

[1] See above, p. 145.

suspicious and conservative. Too many firms were controlled by descendants of the founder who were tempted to preserve a *status quo* that provided a reasonable source of income and in many cases lacked the imagination and drive to control an expanding business. A contrary tendency was the growth in the size of firms, as a result of the Limited Liability Acts,[1] which, although it provided an invaluable injection of capital, helped to depersonalise industry. The individual worker no longer had the same sense of identification with the firm, with the result that it was noticed that standards of skill and perfection of finish were already declining. In addition many firms were controlled by managers who had to justify themselves to directors and shareholders by producing high profits, sometimes at the cost of the future development of the business.

Unlike Germany and the United States, British industry had acquired formidable vested interests that tended to resist the new inventions. Much power was wasted. In spite of the Gilchrist-Thomas process non-phosphoric ores were still extensively used. The railways and shipbuilding were slow to adopt steel. Apart from improved transport, coal-getting techniques changed hardly at all during the century and in textiles there were few changes once the initial industrialisation had taken place. British industry was slow to adopt and exploit electricity as a source of power, while vested interests in the coal and gas industries were too strong. In 1884 Sir Charles Parsons had developed the modern turbine to generate electricity but before 1914 Tyneside was the only area where electric power was used on any scale, through the initiative of local factory owners. German output of electrical equipment by this date was three times the British, although all important towns had electrified their tramways and London electrified her underground railway in 1900. Britain was no longer the centre of invention as she had once been; as late as the 1860's, Siemens had considered it logical to build up a steel firm to exploit his invention in Britain, but after him few inventors came. The internal combustion engine, electricity, telephones, were largely developed abroad: British pioneers were imitators not initiators.

In a sense certain British industries in the long run had a detrimental effect on the economic position. A great deal of

---

[1] See above, p. 146.

U

capital was sent abroad, some of which, in the 1850's and 1860's, was invested in railways, which used British iron or steel and which were equipped with British locomotives and rolling stock, replacing with British equipment when the originals wore out.   Early in the 20th Century when investment abroad was helped by the increase of markets and higher prices, British capital revived and helped to build up industrial plant overseas, employing for that purpose much British machinery.   This machinery, however, paid for by British money, made goods which were transported to their markets by British-made railways and which often competed directly with British-made products; a case in point is the cotton industry started in India.

Some industries had specific problems; the shipbuilding industry, for instance, had a series of technical innovations – wood to iron, iron to steel, sails to steam power, which involved considerable and expensive re-equipment in an old-established industry.   Countries starting a shipbuilding industry from scratch had distinct advantages.   In addition steel was a more durable material and the iron and steel industries were particularly affected by the slowing down of the construction of new railways.

Joseph Chamberlain was later to be convinced that British industrial ailments could be cured by erecting tariff barriers;[1] in the last quarter of the 19th Century few dared to go so far. The belief in Free Trade was almost fundamental but there was a suggestion made by the Conservative Party in 1886 that British reprisals should be made against unfair foreign restrictions, a movement known as Fair Trade.   The great expansion of imperial markets and the increasing need for cheap food and raw materials, however, sapped much of its strength and it left only such minor legacies as the Merchandise Marks Act of 1887.

Yet it would be wrong to give the impression that British economy was stagnant.   Between 1893 and 1913 coal output went up 75 per cent, steel 136 per cent, exports of manufactured goods 121 per cent and of raw materials, predominantly coal, 238 per cent.   In 1900 British exports of steel were greater than those of the United States and Germany combined while in 1914 British shipyards were building over

[1] See below, p. 363.

60 per cent of the world's mercantile tonnage. Britain was building up new industries in new materials and new types of products. Nevertheless root weaknesses remained; slowness to adopt and adapt, a far more rapid expansion in other countries, a diminishing share of world markets, a growing dependence on imports and exports that was constantly to place British industry at the mercy of overseas economic situations.

These conditions were propitious for a growth of trades unionism. With a working class on the whole better off than before but with periods of inexplicable depression, the unskilled workers saw the merits of organising themselves on similar lines to the craft unions, but without their emphasis on a policy of conciliation. The new unions were more aggressive and began to question the whole basis of the capital-its society. Hence socialism became a rising political force.

The new unions were growing up during the 1880's. They were encouraged by Joseph Arch's short-lived success in founding a union of agricultural workers at Wellesbourne in 1872, even though its effectiveness was largely undermined by disunity and by the agricultural depression at the end of the decade. Now dockers, unskilled workers on railways, gas workers and seamen founded unions which were not rigorously confined to a particular trade and which demanded very low subscriptions. They were not concerned with the security that Friendly Society benefits provided but rather with ensuring a fixed living wage, which should be a first charge upon industry, instead of wages that fluctuated according to the state of trade. They looked beyond their immediate objectives to amending the law to ensure favourable wage rates, hours and conditions of labour; to ensure a fair statement of their claims, political representation was required, not as a tail of the Liberal party, like the 'Lib-Lab' alliance, but as an independent working-class party.

The term 'socialism' by which this move came to be known had had a specific connotation in Britain in the mid-19th Century. A group who called themselves the Christian Socialists, led by F. D. Maurice, Charles Kingsley and Thomas Hughes, provided a valuable bridge between the working class on one hand and the churches and the rest of the community on the other. They gave working-class movements legal advice, helped with the extension of Friendly

Society Acts to Co-operative Societies and founded Co-operative workshops in the tailoring trade and elsewhere. Although these enterprises failed, the Christian Socialist movement, which hoped for a change of heart rather than a change in the basis of society, contributed greatly to a better understanding of working-class aspirations, and by its legal and practical assistance, helped to set working class movements on a peaceful course.

Continental developments encouraged a great expansion of working-class activities. The French socialist movement after the Commune, the German Social Democratic Party, the books and activities of continental revolutionaries living in exile in England, and particularly of Karl Marx, were all influential. The first strictly socialist organisation, based on these examples, was the Social Democratic Federation founded in 1881 by H. M. Hyndman, an Old Etonian stockbroker. It had local branches, a weekly bulletin called *Justice* and a general council with dictatorial powers of which Marx's daughter Eleanor Aveling was a member, although Marx disowned the movement. It aimed at a complete upheaval of society, for which it sought to prove the necessity by scientific arguments, real and spurious; it naïvely assumed that conditions within capitalism which Marx had so ably analysed would automatically produce its downfall. It had little popular appeal until William Morris, the wealthy poet, artist and craftsman, joined it in 1883, though he left in 1884 to found the Socialist League which opposed parliamentary action and envisaged instead a State built on trade organisations. Another movement, which made no claim to be a political party, was the socialism of Robert Blatchford, author of *Merrie England* and editor of the weekly *Clarion*. He sent round England his red 'Clarion Vans' by which he hoped to make converts to socialism by increasing people's happiness and enjoyment of life. Until the Boer War his influence was very considerable.

Of more specifically political intention was the Fabian Society. Taking its name from the Roman general who, avoiding direct confrontation with Hannibal, undermined his strength by more subtle means, its founders in 1884 wanted to take from English socialism the revolutionary aims and an illusory Utopia to which they believed Marxist ideas and the

Social-Democratic Federation would commit it and by 'the inevitability of gradualness' to work through existing institutions, by careful propaganda and assiduous collection of facts, to bring about improved conditions. It was a small and select society, whose members, Sidney and Beatrice Webb, Annie Besant, George Bernard Shaw, Graham Wallas and others wrote a series of *Fabian Essays* which aimed at revealing bad conditions and convincing co-operators, trades unionists, M.P.s and members of local bodies that for a considerable time they had been practising unconsciously a socialist policy. This restatement of socialism in practical terms with an emphasis on order and planning was valuable, although it alienated liberalism from socialism. The Fabians became influential members of the London County Council and established, with funds left to the society by a wealthy philanthropist, the London School of Economics and Political Science. The Webbs were fascinated by the success of Bismarck's State socialism and in 1895 looked to Joseph Chamberlain to apply it.[1]

The economic situation of the 1880's brought widespread though intermittent distress. The Social Democratic Federation did successful work among the unemployed and in 1886 organised an 'unemployed' demonstration in London, which for a short time got out of hand. It was intended as a counter-demonstration to Conservative speeches on 'Fair Trade'. It increased fear of revolutionary violence and a Mansion House Fund to alleviate distress shot up during the following two days from £19,000 to £72,000. In November 1887 as a protest against police treatment of a crowd at Mitchelstown, County Cork, and to demand the release of the Irish leader William O'Brien, a large meeting in Trafalgar Square was organised by a branch of the S.D.F. which included Home Rule for Ireland among its other aims. It also got out of hand and the area eventually had to be cleared by the Life Guards. In the scuffle two of the crowd received fatal injuries while there were over a hundred casualties. Such demonstrations frightened the ruling classes into taking more positive and humane steps to alleviate distress, and helped to condition the public mind for the trades union successes that followed.

In 1888 a strike of the match girls, whose appalling conditions

[1] See below, p. 327.

of work[1] were exposed in articles written by Mrs Besant, at this stage of her career a Fabian, was unexpectedly successful, which was especially encouraging to the 'New Unionism' of unskilled and general labourers. In particular it led to demands by Ben Tillett, leader of the Tea Porters' and General Labourers' Union, on behalf of the dockers. The dockers were employed as casual labourers and employers did not recognise that they were dependent on the existence of a pool of labour, skilled in the techniques of handling goods and in good health. With low wages and other abuses, men who were fortunate enough to be employed often had to pay themselves off after a couple of hours in order to get a square meal; while they obtained the energy to continue, their job went to somebody else. Although casual labour continued well into the 20th Century, Tillett demanded and substantially secured some positive improvements: an increase from 5d. to 6d. an hour, overtime at 1s. 6d. an hour, employment for a minimum of four hours at a time and to take place at two occasions only during the day, the abolition of piecework and subcontracting. The strike in August 1889 to support these demands, soon involved 30,000 dockers and 30,000 other workers, and paralysed the Port of London. There was a great deal of public sympathy at a time when many thoughtful people were coming to realise how very low working-class standards of life still were. £49,000 was raised in Great Britain and £30,000 in Australia; the money provided strike pay and bribes to other workers not to take the strikers' places. The Salvation Army and Toynbee Hall provided valuable help. 'The whole East End,' wrote John Burns, 'rose and stood up alongside us. We had but to feed the men to the end and the day was ours.' Cardinal Manning helped to mediate, but despite public feeling, the dock owners would hardly have accepted the final terms of settlement but for the pressure of the shipowners who suffered most from the strike and who were well aware that dock charges were high enough to allow for better conditions.

The successful strike marks an important step in the history of working-class organisations. It gave an impetus to the formation of unions among the unskilled and semi-skilled. The Gas Workers and the Miners Federation of Great

---

[1] Many obtained as little as 4s. a week and were fined for a large number of trivial offences.

Britain were established at this time, while the movement spread to the lower middle class with the National Unions of Clerks and Teachers in 1890 and a union for Shop Assistants in 1891. It led to a demand for a uniform eight-hour day, and a great demonstration to draw attention to it was held on 4th May, 1890. The Liberal government of 1892-95 set an example to private enterprise by making an eight-hour day the rule in all workshops under the authority of War Office and Admiralty and all post offices. However, the outcome of the increased confidence of the working class was the foundation of a political party to represent their interests.

There had been two miner M.P.s in 1874 and working-class representatives slowly increased to ten during the next fifteen years. They were in no sense revolutionaries, somewhat awed by their membership of the 'Mother of Parliaments', they were paid and helped at elections by predominantly Liberal money. These were the 'Lib-Labs' and among those supporting them was a young miner called Keir Hardie. He had helped to build up the Ayrshire Miners Union and this experience and his reading of Henry George's influential book *Progress and Poverty* and of Social Democratic Federation literature convinced him that a new non-Liberal approach was needed. He realised and pointed out at the T.U.C. in 1888 that Bryant and May and other harsh employers were pillars of the Liberal Party. He first stood in opposition to the Liberals at a by-election in Mid-Lanark in 1888 and this led to the foundation of the Scottish Labour Party, of which he became secretary. In the election of 1892 three Independent Labour candidates were elected: John Burns, Keir Hardie and Havelock Wilson, the seamen's leader. Hardie arrived at the Palace of Westminster wearing a cloth cap and workman's suit and escorted by a brass band and a wagonette full of his West Ham constituents. He played the leading part in the foundation, at a conference in Bradford in 1893, of the Independent Labour Party. It had similar aims to the Fabians, was suspicious of Marxism and demanded a wide range of social reforms. What it lacked, as did the S.D.F., was money and the I.L.P. did all it could to attract financial support from the Trades Unions. Its influence grew but none of its twenty-eight candidates were elected in 1895; there were, however, successes in municipal elections. The

Fabian Society and the S.D.F. did not support it and, although it had considerable strength in the Yorkshire textile districts, its London support was weak, and it was not until a miners' strike in South Wales in 1898 that the mining community backed it.

The T.U.C. in 1899 was persuaded to organise a conference for the following year to consider ways and means of promoting working-class parliamentary representation. It was encouraged by the performance of the German Socialists in the Reichstag election while the foundation of an Employer's Parliamentary Council to take active measures to oppose the supposed 'weakness' that Parliament was showing towards the Trades Unions indicated that there was no time to be wasted. The conference was held at the Faringdon Street Memorial Hall in February 1900, representing the Trades Unions, the I.L.P., the Fabians and the S.D.F. The Co-operative Societies were invited to send delegates but declined. There were two main points of view at the meeting; the S.D.F. wanted to preach class war, but it was defeated and although it subscribed to the new party for a time, it seceded in 1901. The majority were satisfied with the declaration of immediate objectives. It was decided to promote a group, known as the Labour Representation Committee, which, without being committed to a particular economic theory, would nevertheless be in every respect a politically independent party. This was in keeping with the tactics of the I.L.P. during the previous seven years and was contrived to win the approval of the Trades Unions. Trades Unions were invited to give their support at a rate of ten shillings per hundred members. A journalist with a working-class background, Ramsay Macdonald, later the first Labour Prime Minister, became secretary and performed invaluable work. In the 1900 General Election, two L.R.C. candidates, Bell, who seceded to the Liberals in 1904, and Hardie, became M.P.s. It was not until after the Taff Vale Judgement of 1901 that the Trades Unions would commit themselves fully to support the new venture.[1]

(f) LORD SALISBURY'S SECOND MINISTRY, 1886-92

The Election of 1886, with four parties in the field, seemed to presage a return to the confusion of 1846-59. The signs

[1] See below, p. 367.

were an illusion; the two minor parties were firmly the captives
of the two larger ones as long as the future of Ireland was in
question. The parties were also divided, the Liberals themselves being split over the role of Imperialism, especially as it
was applied in South Africa. At home there were no very
strong issues between the parties, although the Liberals were
tentatively feeling their way towards a Radical policy of social
reform, such as they put into effect after their victory of 1906.
But they lacked the leadership which would have broken loose
from the Home Rule tie and committed the party to causes
which had greater prospects of success and greater electoral
appeal. They lost such a leader in Joseph Chamberlain and
for a long while social reformers looked to him rather than to
the Liberals for parliamentary assistance. Lloyd George
did not enter Parliament until 1890, did not become prominent, through his opposition to the Boer War, until 1900 and
did not obtain office until 1906. At a time when working-
class forces were developing, the policies of the two major
parties were somewhat stagnant and in consequence the working class slowly, and in many cases reluctantly, began to
organise a party of its own.

This could not have been foreseen in 1886. Many
suspected that the schism in the Liberal party would not last
long. It was supposed that Gladstone would soon either
retire or die and the firm commitment to Home Rule would
go with him. Hartington fully expected, to begin with, that
he would resume the leadership of the whole party, and he
was unwilling to become leader of a coalition with the
Conservatives or to enter into any formal agreement with
them; Liberal Unionists supported their policies for the most
part but still sat on the Liberal side of the house, Hartington
on the Opposition Front Bench. The arrangement was
particularly difficult for Chamberlain, who unlike Hartington,
was pledged to a constructive solution in Ireland and wide
measures of social reform. It was only slowly, through his
increased interest in colonial expansion and his fear of
socialism, that he committed himself to the Conservative
party, by which time Balfour had already established himself
as Salisbury's heir apparent. In 1887 he explored the
possibility of returning to the Liberal party if Gladstone
would make concessions over Ireland. A round-table

conference was held of Harcourt, Morley, Herschell, Chamberlain and Trevelyan. The inclusion of Morley was fatal to any progress and Harcourt was not prepared to take a lead in forcing Gladstone into retirement. Trevelyan went back to the Liberal fold, but many Liberals prominent in social and business circles moved over to the other side. In the House of Lords and in English constituencies, except in the landslide victory of 1906, the Liberal party never again had a majority.

Salisbury resumed office in 1886 as of right, although Lord Randolph Churchill, who was becoming an increasingly important figure, was to challenge Salisbury unsuccessfully. Of Salisbury as a leader, Sir Winston Churchill has written: 'In all that concerned the management of individuals Lord Salisbury excelled. No one was more ready to sacrifice his opinion to get his way. No one was more skilful in convincing others that they agreed with him or more powerful to persuade them to actual agreement. His experience, his patience, his fame, his subtle and illuminating mind, secured for him an ascendancy in his Cabinet apart altogether from the paramount authority of First Minister.' These qualities were of prime importance in dealing with Lord Randolph.

Just as the Liberal party had had its difficulties during the Second Gladstone Administration with Chamberlain trying to introduce a more progressive policy than the majority of the Cabinet wanted, so Churchill[1] found himself in a similar position in 1886. Only thirty-seven, his rise to the front rank of politics had been meteoric; no Conservative could compete with him on the platform and he was the principal organiser in the constituencies of the fight against Home Rule. He played a large part in the formation of the Cabinet in 1886 and was its undisputed second-in-command as Leader of the House of Commons and Chancellor of the Exchequer. Hicks Beach had deferred to him as his 'superior in eloquence, ability and influence' and although he was not particularly happy about the proposed coercion policy he had been prevailed upon to take the difficult post of Chief Secretary for Ireland. On Churchill's recommendation an outsider to politics, Henry Matthews, a Midland barrister, who had impressed him when he was campaigning in Birmingham, was brought in as Home Secretary and proved to be a bad

[1] See above, p. 281.

choice. Churchill prevailed upon the Cabinet, against the
better judgment of some of its members, to agree to proposals
which he made in a speech at Dartford in October. He
promised two Royal Commissions to investigate Irish problems, the introduction of the closure in Parliament by a
simple majority, smallholdings for agricultural labourers, a
land bill for simplifying the transfer of land, reorganisation of
local government, reduction of taxation and freedom for the
people of the Balkans. The last comment Salisbury thought
rash and it created a great stir in Europe, while many of the
other proposals aroused some Conservative alarm.

As Leader of the House of Commons Churchill reassured
many of his critics. He showed considerable skill in handling
questions and keeping the House in good temper. As
Chancellor he showed a caution and a passion for economy
that was almost Gladstonian; the Treasury officials initially
suspected he would be reckless, but he proved to be thorough,
ready to listen to advice and patient. He wished to reconstruct the taxation system in such a way that, with £4·5 m.
gained by duties on houses and increased death duties which
would be reorganised on a new scale, income tax could be
lowered from 8d. to 5d., while reductions in tea and tobacco
duties would have popular appeal. He aimed to increase and
reorganise the grant made to local government. Economies
were to be made by reducing the Sinking Fund allocation
(£4·5 m.) and by direct economies of £1·3 m., most of which
would come from Army and Navy Estimates.

Although the Cabinet apparently agreed to the proposals
and Lord George Hamilton was able to make reductions in
Admiralty expenditure, W. H. Smith at the War Office
feared that reductions in the military budget would have a bad
effect on foreign relations, especially with France, where there
appeared to be a revival of militarism associated with the
activities of General Boulanger. Salisbury supported him in
his refusal, in view of the Balkan crisis. Although Churchill
had previously implied that he staked his official existence on
reductions, a compromise, with cuts in spending elsewhere,
could certainly have been reached and his resignation on 21st
December came as a considerable surprise. In his letter of
resignation, Churchill wrote: 'I am pledged up to the eyes
to a large reduction of expenditure and I cannot change my

mind on this matter. . . . If the foreign policy of this country is conducted with skill and judgment our present huge and increasing armaments are quite unnecessary and the taxation which they involve perfectly unjustifiable.' In a second letter he described the domestic legislation of the government as inadequate and its foreign policy as dangerous and methodless. He had burnt his boats by publishing his letter of resignation in *The Times*.

By this action Churchill terminated a promising career and it will always be uncertain exactly why he did it. He probably expected Salisbury to give way and force reductions on Smith; alternatively he may have hoped to repeat his 1884 performance with the National Union and be carried back to power on a wave of popular feeling, but if this was the case he had done nothing to prepare the ground and had resigned on an issue that was unlikely to have much popular appeal at a time when Parliament was not sitting. But even if Salisbury had given way more basic difficulties would have remained: the difficulties of a young and impulsive man who was profoundly – and rightly – convinced of the need for social reforms over which the rest of the Cabinet hesitated, who was at odds over Ireland and foreign policy and whose chief was undoubtedly suspicious of him. Salisbury could only disapprove of a man whose speeches went beyond orthodox Conservative beliefs, who was indiscreet with foreign ambassadors, and whose growing confidence seemed to imply that there was no room in the same Cabinet for both for them. A clash within the party was almost inevitable sooner or later and Salisbury had been expecting it. There were many who felt a profound sense of relief when he went. 'His character,' wrote Salisbury, 'is quite untrained. Both in impulsiveness and variability and in a tendency which can only be described by the scholastic word *vulgaris*, he presents the characteristics of extreme youth.'

Men had resigned from Cabinets before and this need not have been the end of Churchill's political life. Had it not been for the barrier of Home Rule, he might well have ended in the Liberal party. For a while he toyed with the idea of forming a central party with Chamberlain. He attacked the Conservatives, with justice, for their handling of the Parnell letter. He was gaining the experience and judgment that his over-rapid rise to power had not given him, but when he was welcomed back into the Conservative ranks in 1892 he was an incurably sick man and he died two years later.

Churchill probably thought he would be difficult to replace; there is his pathetic comment 'I forgot Goschen.' A Cabinet reshuffle followed his resignation. Goschen, a Liberal Unionist who had been estranged from Gladstone for many years and who had to be found a safe Conservative seat, became Chancellor of the Exchequer on terms which involved the dismissal of Northcote, who was an inefficient Foreign Secretary, an office Salisbury took himself.[1] Goschen was esteemed by the business world and in his Budgets, by more gradual and tactful methods, he was able to achieve many of the changes Churchill had wanted, including reductions in naval and military estimates. In 1888 he reduced income tax to 6d. and in the same year he converted the interest on Consols to 2¾ per cent. As trade improved he found himself in a strong position. W. H. Smith became Leader of the Commons and although a sick man was unexpectedly effective. As Sir Winston Churchill put it: 'A stout-hearted bookseller whose perseverance as Leader was making of his repeated failures a curious but undoubted success.' He showed imperturbability and soundness of judgment. Hicks Beach was losing his eyesight and gave up the Chief Secretary-ship to Balfour.

1887 was Golden Jubilee year and a time of great celebration, when people looked back on fifty years of unexampled progress and prosperity that seemed as if it could only be the prelude to even greater advances. The Queen was now firmly established in the nation's heart, her retirement forgiven, her imperiousness and awkwardness merely enriching a legend. The Jubilee was the occasion of the First Colonial Conference and the Indian princes and colonial Premiers who came to London brought with them the salutory reminder that although Europe might be overshadowed by German strength, the Queen ruled an Empire 'on which the sun never set'.

The government carried the County Councils Act, which

---

[1] Northcote collapsed and died when taking leave of the Prime Minister after his dismissal.

was of great importance, in 1888. The Municipal Corporations Act[1] and the Reform Acts had ensured democratic government in the boroughs but the counties were still governed in traditional fashion by J.P.s in Quarter Session. The 1887 Session had been preoccupied with Ireland and there were good reasons for some striking piece of English legislation. Chamberlain wanted progressive reforms to convince the ex-Liberal waverers that Conservatism could mean progress, and the disorders in London seemed to demand bold reform to distract attention. The Bill was prepared by C. T. Ritchie, President of the Local Government Board, who showed considerable ability with administrative details and he boldly took a number of decisions which otherwise could have produced problems. No attempt was made to force privileged groups of J.P.s into the county administration. The area of London and surrounding counties which was administered by the Metropolitan Board of Works, created in 1855, became the basis of the new County of London but the City of London itself with its ancient privileges was given considerable autonomy. Certain national revenues were apportioned to County Council use and the local electorate was to be democratic, women ratepayers being allowed to vote but not to stand as candidates. One undemocratic element which only narrowly passed Parliament was the creation of county aldermen, initially to provide experience from men who had hitherto ruled the counties. The act left untouched the Boards of Guardians and Parish vestries. It created sixty-two County Councils, large counties having more than one, which took over all administrative functions with the exception of licencing, which the magistrates retained, Poor Law and education. Police supervision was shared by means of a Joint Standing Committee with the magistrates. Following the German example, large towns obtained equal jurisdiction as County Boroughs. The County Councils took a considerable burden of supervising detail from Parliament; later Acts of 1894 and 1899[2] created subordinate authorities. One Act of 1889 extended the system to Scotland and another made technical education the administrative responsibility of the new authorities, a new tax on beer and spirits providing the money for this purpose in 1890.

[1] See above, p. 101.   [2] See below, pp. 324 and 330.

The Board of Agriculture was created in 1889 to co-ordinate ways of meeting the agricultural depression and by the Tithes Act of that year payment was transferred from the occupier to the owner of the land.[1]   In 1891 a further Factory and Workshops Act fixed eleven as the minimum age for the employment of children and extended the 1850 Act to include women employed in every kind of factory.   There was still no legislation directly limiting hours worked by men.[2]

In foreign policy Salisbury was successful in limiting Russian influence in Bulgaria.   At the Congress of Berlin he and Disraeli had secured the division of Bulgaria into three parts; one a principality under the suzerainty of the Sultan but otherwise nominally independent; a second Turkish province, Eastern Rumelia, under a Christian governor; a third section was returned to Turkey in full sovereignty.[3]   It was assumed that Russia would control the principality but under Prince Alexander of Battenburg this proved not to be the case. When in September 1885 the population of the Rumelian capital expelled the Turkish governor and invited Alexander to annex the province to Bulgaria, Alexander, despite Russian commands to desist, responded enthusiastically.   The Tsar demanded that the 1878 Settlement be maintained and a conference was held at Constantinople but it was evident that force alone could divide the Bulgarians, who won military prowess by attacking and defeating Serbia, Austria-Hungary's satellite, who demanded 'compensation' for the unification. Gladstone alone among British statesmen had foreseen in 1876 the possibility of developing Balkan nationalities as an alternative to continued Turkish control or Russian domination and, primed by public opinion, this was the course Salisbury now pursued.   He secured international recognition of the new Bulgaria in April 1886.

The crisis had a second act.   In August 1886 Prince Alexander was kidnapped by Russian agents and forced to abdicate but the Bulgarians were determined to maintain their independence of Russia.   Salisbury co-operated closely with Bismarck; he was particularly anxious to prevent any agreement between Russia and Germany and for that reason had welcomed the Dual Alliance of 1879 between Germany

---

[1] See above, p. 251.   [2] See above, p. 115 and below, p. 381.
[3] See above, p. 249.

and Austria-Hungary. Bismarck used the fear of war, possibly against France which was at the height of Boulangism, to obtain a substantial army grant from the Reichstag in 1887, but refused to back any Austro-Hungarian interference in Bulgaria. To increase co-operation with Bismarck, Salisbury signed a vague alliance with Italy in 1887 while the Triple Alliance of Austria, Germany and Italy was renewed. Notes exchanged with Austria and Italy protected British interests in Egypt and Constantinople. The need for Great Britain always to maintain a favourable majority on the Egyptian control commission provided a constant difficulty. Salisbury had hoped for an agreement with France but again Egypt was to prove a stumbling block and France moved in the direction of an alliance with Russia. Meanwhile Bismarck signed a meaningless Reinsurance Treaty with Russia, not committing himself to any positive action in the case of Bulgaria.

In July 1887 the Bulgarians elected Ferdinand of Coburg, an able and shrewd politician, as their prince, in defiance of Russian wishes. After protracted negotiations a second Mediterranean agreement between Britain, Italy and Austria-Hungary was signed in December, which was a preliminary to possible military action against Russia should she attempt to disturb the *status quo* in the Balkans. To avoid becoming involved, Bismarck publicly stated his confidence in the Tsar and published the text of the Austro-German Alliance to prove that it was purely defensive. The Russians, encouraged by this, asked the Sultan to declare Ferdinand's election illegal in which they were supported by France and Germany. The Sultan did so, but Ferdinand remained Prince and the crisis came to a tame conclusion. Remembering their rebuff at the Congress of Berlin the Russians were reluctant to press their influence in the Balkans and looked instead to Central Asia and the Far East and it was not until the defeats in their war against Japan that they found their immediate interests again in the Balkans. Meanwhile Austria-Hungary had become the dominant power there, with Roumania secretly her ally and Bulgaria and Serbia openly her clients.[1]

Salisbury's diplomacy received the respect of the Powers, although he achieved no obvious political successes. He never took the initiative in European affairs, as Bismarck

[1] See below, p. 412.

usually did, and met situations as they arose. British commitments in Egypt prevented complete detachment from the systems of alliances that were growing up but when Bismarck invited British membership of the Triple Alliance in 1889 he declined as it was directed against France rather than against Russia. He offered as his excuse to Bismarck the vagaries and unreliability of the British electoral system. He was unwilling to commit the country in advance to some unspecified action and remarked to the Queen with reference to the Italian offer of a firm naval alliance: 'England never promised material assistance in view of an uncertain war of which the object and cause were unknown nor could she promise even diplomatic co-operation against any single power such as France,' a view with which Gladstone concurred when he said to General Grey in 1869 '. . . England, come what may, should promise too little rather than too much.'

The greater intimacy of France and Russia posed a serious threat to British ability to send a fleet through the Dardanelles and thus gave an additional reason for the retention of Egypt; it also posed a threat to the British Navy and promoted the doctrine of the Two Power Standard – that the British Navy must be stronger than the French and Russian fleets combined. The strength of the Royal Navy was low and it was inefficient but the Naval Defence Act of 1889 provided for a considerable increase in its size and quality. Regular manœuvres, gunnery practices, reorganisation of the fleet and dockyards were put in hand and very considerable improvements had been made by the time of the Diamond Jubilee Review in 1897 when, without recalling ships from any foreign station, a balanced and modernised fleet stretched for over thirty miles.[1]

In the colonial field, Salisbury concluded a number of agreements that defined and controlled the expansion of the powers. The public in every country was taking an increasing interest in the opening up of backward and unknown regions and the acquisition of territory was seen by many of the powers as a status symbol. The opening of the Suez Canal in 1869 was probably the largest single factor in promoting the opening up of Africa, but Germany and Italy, recently united, were attracted by the acquisition of further territory, while

---

[1] See below, p. 359.

W

in the case of the French, expansion across the Mediterranean served to avert their eyes from Alsace and Lorraine.   Private individuals saw valuable opportunities to tap new sources of wealth.   These rival colonisers tended to set up trade mono-polies which provided an incentive to Great Britain to bring into being large free-trade areas in Africa which would provide outlets for British trade.   The challenge of Africa in itself was an enormous one: to the explorer and adventurer, to the trader, to the missionary, to the humanitarians who saw an opportunity to suppress slavery and introduce better medical knowledge, to those Liberals and Conservatives who conceived, in slightly different ways, that Britain had a mission to bring enlightenment and civilisation to benighted peoples.   The idea of patronage was rarely absent from this; those who co-operated could be rewarded by being appointed to the lower civil and military ranks, chiefs could be honoured.   Anti-imperialist feelings also tended to be based on patronage, by encouraging the enemies of empire and graciously supporting their bid for freedom.   To the subject peoples both types of patronage were suspiciously the same.   Imperial enthusiasm resulted in much distasteful exuberance and delight in acquisition for its own sake, but the pioneers were followed by the administrators, men with long traditions of unselfish work who helped to supply a corrective.

Most of the territory acquired in Africa by the European powers was secured by a more or less friendly arrangement with local chiefs, but the standing in international law was vague and the areas were generally very loosely defined. Britain was often the first-comer and suffered from subsequent agreements and claims made by other powers.   One of Salisbury's principal tasks was to sort out these tangles.   In territories under British control Salisbury was insistent that the tribal system, with its barbarities removed, should be the basis of control and that the British colonial service, with just and humane administration, should maintain the conception of trusteeship.

One considerable problem was German colonial expansion, which was now being encouraged by Bismarck to provide an outlet for German national feeling without disturbing the delicate balance of Eastern Europe.   Germany had come late in the field and was jealous of the large portions of Africa that had already fallen under British control. Gladstone had not prevented German occupation of South West Africa, but the future of East Africa was more difficult. The principal state in the area was the Sultanate of Zanzibar, of Arab foundation, which practised an active slave trade in the interior. British influence secured an ending of the trade, and with the advice of the British consul the Sultan was beginning to build up a more civilised state. In 1884, however, German agents arrived, headed by Karl Peters and began to put into effect the contradictory doctrine of the hinterland, by which, firstly, possessions in an uncivilised country gave a claim to extend indefinitely into the interior and secondly, the process of marching round another country's settlement planting flags, effectively cut off that country from the interior. By means of the second process and 'treaties' made with ignorant chiefs, Peters made extravagant claims in East Africa which were endorsed by the German government. To British discredit, both Gladstone and Salisbury refused to make a stand for the Sultan's unquestionable prior claim and in 1886 British and German spheres of influence were defined, the German being the larger. The British sphere was developed by the British East Africa Company, chartered in 1888. In 1890 Salisbury signed an agreement with the new German Chancellor, Caprivi, which limited and defined the German position. Germany abandoned her claims to Uganda and the Upper Nile, and recognised the British protectorate over Zanzibar. In return the British-owned island of Heligoland was handed over to the Germans, a cession for which Salisbury was much criticised. In his defence it may be said that it would almost certainly have been untenable in time of war.

Colonial relations with France also posed serious difficulties. Salisbury wished to lessen French influence in Egypt and the Nile Valley and hence was inclined to defer to French claims on the western side of Africa. On the lower Niger British and French firms were competing for the palm oil trade but Sir George Goldie consolidated British interests in a single company, chartered as the Royal Niger Company in 1886, and at the Berlin Conference on Africa in 1884–85 the area became British territory, while the French retained the upper Niger. There were constant disputes over frontiers further along the coasts, however, and a treaty in 1890 defined the frontiers of the British colonies of Gambia, Sierra Leone and the Gold Coast; the French recognised the British protectorate over Zanzibar, the British that of the French over Madagascar, to which Britain had some claim. Almost the whole of the Sahara became French territory. Critics considered that British interests had been sacrificed and Salisbury defended the cession of rights over the last territory by describing it as 'light land', for which the French politician Waddington reproached him, 'no doubt Sahara is not a garden and contains, as you say, much light land, but your public reminder of the fact was, perhaps you will allow me to say, hardly necessary. You might well have left us to find it out.' The task of the statesmen was made difficult by the extreme sensitiveness of public opinion over matters of prestige.

Portugal provided a serious problem. Basing their claim on the fact that they had made the first discoveries in the 15th and 16th Centuries, the Portuguese demanded a broad belt across Africa, linking their coastal settlements of Angola and Mozambique, even though they had no settlers there. This clashed with the considerable progress made by Cecil Rhodes whose British South Africa Company was chartered in 1889. Other British explorers and missionaries had penetrated to the north of the Zambesi. Trading on British reluctance to go to extremes, especially in view of the shakiness of the Portuguese monarchy, the government of Portugal was uncooperative but Salisbury remained firm and in June 1891 Britain obtained substantially complete control over the disputed territory.

(g) IRELAND AND THE FALL OF PARNELL, 1886-92

During the 1886 Election campaign Salisbury had remarked that Ireland needed twenty years of resolute government, but there was no immediate return to coercion as the government was dependent on the votes of the Liberal Unionists. Parnell, despairing of Home Rule, suggested that peasants who paid half their rent should be protected from eviction, a scheme the government was forced to accept in August 1887 after the mounting agricultural distress had led to a large number of pitiless expulsions. The tenants' reaction was to apply the 'Plan of Campaign' concocted by William O'Brien and two Irish M.P.s. The scheme was for the tenants collectively to offer to pay a reduced rent and to support any of their number who were evicted in consequence; it was only effective on a limited number of estates and in practice led to the revival of cattle-maiming and 'moonlighting'. Parnell disapproved but was powerless to prevent it. The plan was declared illegal in December. A Closure Act, passed through the Commons in February 1887, enabling a closure to be obtained by a bare majority, meant that Irish opposition to a coercion bill could be overcome easily, but when Balfour became Chief Secretary in March his appointment was greeted with derision. Hitherto he had seemed a dilettante in politics; an Irish newspaper called him 'a silk skinned sybarite whose rest a crumpled rose leaf would disturb', but he proved to be the outstanding member of the Ministry and one of the most effective Chief Secretaries Ireland ever had. In the House he infuriated the Irish members by his coolness, disdain and debating skill; in Ireland he was ruthlessly efficient. He applied Salisbury's policy of firm government followed by relief.

Balfour promptly introduced a coercion bill which was law by July. Under it, trial by jury disappeared and the resident magistrate was given almost unrestricted powers, special punishments of hard labour being instituted for the usual agrarian crimes. A concurrent Land Act reduced the fifteen years fixed rent of the 1881 Act to three and protected the tenant against arbitrary eviction. Coercion was applied in eighteen counties immediately and in August the Irish National League was proclaimed illegal. At Mitchelstown, County Cork, O'Brien incited the peasantry to resist the expected evictions and when he was prosecuted in September, a riot ensued in which the police, ridden down by tenants on horseback, opened fire, killing three. Gladstone bitterly attacked the government when it supported the police but his watchword 'Remember Mitchelstown' aggravated ill feeling. Many of the English working class came to feel that landlords' interests were being protected by the government right or wrong. O'Brien became a martyr through the unwise decision of the government to treat him as a common criminal.

By the autumn of 1889 Balfour's policy had been largely effective. Men such as O'Brien were commanding less support. Many Englishmen regarded coercion with great misgiving but lawlessness had been curbed. An act was passed to facilitate land purchase in 1888; a Railways Act in 1890 to build light railways in western Ireland and to carry out land drainage, and the Irish administration did its utmost to alleviate distress when the potato crop failed in 1889 and during the hard winter of 1890–91. The Land Purchase Act of 1890 set up a Central Land Department, provided for purchase money to be forwarded by the government and repaid over a period of forty-nine years, while in western Ireland a Congested Districts Board came into existence to create viable agricultural units. It began the scientific improvement of livestock and studied the methods of fishermen. Grants were made to factories and women were given training in home weaving.[1] Free Education was introduced in Ireland by an Act of 1892. In October 1891 Balfour succeeded as of right to the position of Leader of the House of Commons when W. H. Smith resigned through ill health.

The Times, whose editor G. E. Buckle strongly disliked Gladstone's adoption of Home Rule, had run a series of articles entitled *Parnellism and Crime* to coincide with the debates in the Commons on the 1887 Coercion Act. On 18th April it produced a great sensation, the facsimile of a letter apparently signed by Parnell which appeared to show that he secretly approved the murder of Burke in Phoenix Park in 1882.[2] Parnell denied the authenticity of the letter but, distrusting the impartiality of a London jury in the circumstances, took no further action, although his enemies tried to get him into the courts. In November, O'Donnell, who had been an Irish M.P. until 1886, considering himself implicated, brought an action against *The Times*, the case of *O'Donnell* v. *Walter*, and Sir Richard Webster, the Attorney-General, who represented the newspaper, produced fresh letters that appeared to incriminate Parnell still further. After a trial on the outcome of which bitterness against Irish violence had great influence, O'Donnell's suit was dismissed with costs in July 1888.

The matter having been thus reopened Parnell asked for a Select Committee of the House to investigate and the government insisted on a Commission of Three Judges, an expensive affair which threatened Parnell with financial ruin. Parnell was defended by Sir Charles Russell and H. H. Asquith; under a brilliant cross-examination by Asquith, Macdonald, the

[1] See below, p. 357.   [2] See above, p. 270.

manager of *The Times*, was forced to admit that no adequate
steps had been taken to verify the genuineness of the letters,
while, under cross-examination by Russell, Pigott, a disreputable Irish journalist who had sold them to the newspaper,
broke down completely. Leaving a full confession that he had
forged the letters, Pigott fled abroad and committed suicide in
Madrid in March 1889. The Commission continued for a
further year, producing a sad tangle of bitterness between the
two nations, but as far as the general public was concerned,
Parnell was completely vindicated. The case cost *The Times*
over £200,000 and greatly damaged its reputation. Although
the government refused to admit its mistake it was evident that
it had no right to interfere in what should have been a matter
for the courts. Parnell was given countless ovations and was
received in state at Hawarden. Gladstone denounced the
government's action in the Commons and was supported by
Lord Randolph Churchill. The general feeling was reflected
in Liberal successes in by-elections.

Matters in Parnell's private life were moving to a climax,
which was to reverse this trend. For many years Parnell had
been living with Mrs O'Shea, a state of affairs condoned by
O'Shea himself who also derived an allowance from Mrs
O'Shea's wealthy aunt, out of deference to whom no attempt
was made to arrange a divorce. In 1889 the aunt died and
O'Shea, whose allowance ceased and who was bitter at
Parnell's success, instituted divorce proceedings in the autumn
of 1890, probably encouraged and financially aided by Parnell's political enemies. For as long as no scandal had ensued,
Parnell's liaison, which was known to all leading politicians
but which was not public knowledge, did little harm politically. That widely respected pillar of integrity, Lord Hartington, for instance, had a similar liaison with the Duchess
of Manchester. Parnell was in a difficult position; he
desperately wanted to marry Mrs O'Shea and a divorce
would make this possible; on the other hand he could perfectly
reasonably claim that O'Shea had connived at the adultery
for years and had profited by it, in which case the petition
would be rejected and the damage to Parnell's reputation
would be less. Parnell wavered between these alternatives, to
the worst possible effect, so that when the affair was public the
average Englishman came to feel as the Queen did: 'Parnell

is shown up not only as a man of very bad character but as a liar and devoid of all sense of honour or of any sort of principle.'

The effect on Parnell's political position was disastrous. Gladstone was inundated with letters and telegrams demanding the repudiation of Parnell and hoped he would have the good sense to retire. Cecil Rhodes sent a telegram with wise advice, 'Resign – marry – return', but Parnell was too arrogant to listen. Gladstone tried to force his resignation but Parnell disregarded him and was re-elected leader. When Gladstone published his letter in the Press, the Irish members realised the full gravity of the situation and the Irish Hierarchy condemned Parnell. After twelve days of bitter debate in a committee room of the House of Commons the Irish party split; twenty-six only, including Redmond, adhered to Parnell; the remainder elected Justin McCarthy as their leader. The two parts only re-united, through sympathy with the Boers, in 1900. Parnell married Kitty O'Shea in June 1891 and died in October, heartbroken and exhausted. The Home Rule Party, as a political force, was dead for twenty years and Gladstone's second bill was drawn up without its help. Like Lord Randolph Churchill, Parnell did not have fully adult judgments; he had encompassed his own ruin. 'A marvellous man, a terrible fall', was Gladstone's comment.

(h) THE SECOND HOME RULE BILL

Gladstone said of himself 'I am as fast bound to Ireland as Odysseus to the mast of his vessel.' Ireland was the sole reason why he remained in public life but it was evident to the party as a whole that it had slight chance of returning to office on this alone. With a large number of his upper- and middle-class supporters alienated, there was additional reason for him to turn to the working class and to the special interests of Wales and Scotland in addition to Ireland. The programme was enunciated in a great speech at Newcastle in October 1891 and represented a new departure for Gladstone. Hitherto he had dealt with great moral issues, now he turned to proposing material gains that might attract votes. He shrank from State socialism or collectivism – there were no proposals to regulate wages, conditions of work or housing, but he moved a long way from the *laissez-faire* policy traditional to the party. There were some who even saw the Liberal party's preoccupation with Home Rule as a blessing in disguise, in that it delayed and perhaps averted the extension of State control.

The programme promised, in addition to Irish Home Rule, a similar independence for and disestablishment of the churches in Wales and Scotland; to please the trades unionists there was to be employers' liability for accidents; for the rural voter popularly elected district and parish councils, land for allotments and smallholdings and better security for tenants; for the Radicals constitutional reforms including the ending or mending of the Lords, the end of plural voting and possibly the payment of M.P.s. It was hoped to attract the temperance vote by a local veto on alcohol. The immediate result was to help the Liberal election prospects but the inability of the Liberal government of 1892–95 to enact more than a fraction of this programme was detrimental in the long run. Furthermore the appeals made were so diverse that the possibility of the party being united on the whole programme was almost inconceivable.

A general election held in the summer of 1892 seemed to suggest that had it not been for Home Rule the Liberal party might have had a substantial majority. As it was there were 273 Liberals, 260 Conservatives, 81 Irish Nationalists and 46 Liberal Unionists, led now in the Commons by Chamberlain, as Hartington had succeeded his father as Duke of Devonshire. The result foretold the futility that was to follow: through the weakness of his own party Gladstone was committed to an immediate Home Rule Bill which would almost certainly be rejected by the Conservative-controlled House of Lords, with the full blessing of the majority of voters in Great Britain. The Ministry provided, all the same, valuable experience of office under the guidance of older men for those who were to be in the forefront of politics in 1905.

The Queen was displeased by Gladstone's return: 'the idea of a deluded, excited man of eighty-two trying to govern England and her vast Empire with the miserable democrats under him is quite ludicrous. It is like a bad joke.' She felt able to impose some conditions on his Cabinet-making which would not have been tolerated on previous occasions. She refused to have Dilke or Labouchère[1] and insisted on Rosebery, whom she would have preferred as Prime Minister, returning to the Foreign Office. Gladstone still showed exceptional vigour, although his eyesight was failing, and he received invaluable help during the Ministry from Sir Algernon West who acted as an unpaid private secretary and liaison officer. The Cabinet was much stronger than that of 1886 and included many men of talent, though they had little unanimity. Harcourt returned to the Exchequer, Morley to the Irish Chief Secretaryship, Campbell-Bannerman went to the War Office. There were two important newcomers: H. H. Asquith became an outstanding Home Secretary, while H. H. Fowler, a Wolverhampton solicitor, was a success at the Local Government Board, although advanced in years. Both were Nonconformists.

The new government went to work with a will. Coercion was withdrawn, greater care was taken to ensure that J.P.s were more representative of their areas, Asquith devised better regulations for mass meetings in London and appointed more factory inspectors, while Fowler set up a commission to consider Old Age Pensions. A labour department of the Board of Trade was formed to obtain accurate knowledge of conditions in trade and industry. Foreign policy under Rosebery's direction followed a similar course to that charted by Salisbury: the Queen had feared a withdrawal from Egypt but this proved impossible and British colonial responsibilities were increased when a formal protectorate was declared over Uganda in 1894, at the request of the British East Africa Company. There were wide legislative proposals for the 1893 Session to prove that the government was not preoccupied with Ireland.

The Second Home Rule Bill in many respects resembled the First; the Parliament at Westminster was to remain responsible for the armed forces, customs (in order to safeguard Free Trade), trade and foreign and colonial policy. Eighty M.P.s from Ireland were still to sit at Westminster but to vote only on imperial matters, an arrangement which would have been largely unworkable. The prospect of their

---

[1] Labouchère had expressed strong views on the Establishment. Gladstone took full responsibility for excluding him and Labouchère, annoyed, sold his shares in the Liberal *Daily News* and coined such epigrams as 'I do not mind Gladstone always having an ace up his sleeve but I do object to his always saying Providence put it there.'

continued presence was very unpopular. The problem of Ulster was still largely ignored but a separate Upper House was to be created in Dublin with strong Protestant representation. The Bill was introduced in an impressive two-and-a-half-hour speech by Gladstone himself and was steered through the Commons with extensive use of the closure, a device which put a premium on 'talking out' and which added to the Bill's unpopularity. Balfour controlled the Opposition tactics and constantly devised some new form of obstruction, while Chamberlain clashed frequently with Gladstone. Whole sections of the Bill were never discussed. Between the first and second readings, a bill disestablishing the Church in Wales was introduced. In September the Home Rule Bill passed the third reading in the Commons by 307 to 267. Salisbury assured the Lords that if they passed the Bill they would be 'untrue to the duty which has descended to you from a splendid ancestry . . . you will be untrue to the Empire of England' and their Lordships obliged by rejecting it by 419 to 41. Many of those who voted with the Noes were former Liberals who owed their peerages to Gladstone.

Gladstone wanted to dissolve Parliament and fight an election on the 'Peers versus the People' issue and there was justification for this in that the House of Lords was openly partisan and continued to reject or mangle Liberal measures. Had a dissolution taken place it would have resulted in a Unionist victory but probably, with the asset of Gladstone's enormous personal prestige, with a much stronger Liberal party than was to result in 1895. The Cabinet, however, telegraphed 'Your suggestion is impossible', dismissing his plans as senile optimism, a decision that seemed to many of the electorate to imply lack of spirit. A few months later, in March 1894, Gladstone resigned over the question of naval estimates. The unfortunate collision of two battleships and the alliance of France and Russia caused considerable alarm in the Press. The expense of naval armaments had greatly increased with evolving ship design and battleships were already costing over £1 m. each. The 'Two Power Standard' that Salisbury had laid down, and England's growing colonial commitments, necessitated a Navy far more expensive than in the days of Peel, but Gladstone, adhering to the earlier standards, refused to be convinced.

Gladstone died in 1898. Although he had failed to achieve the goal of his later years, that of giving Home Rule to Ireland, he had helped to establish the principle of self-determination for nations, notably in Italy and the Balkans. He had played a major role in the modernisation of the major British institutions, blending his conviction in the ultimate accountability of office holders to the popular will with a sound respect for past traditions. In particular the reforms he imposed on the civil service have set enduring standards. He had taken the freeing of trade to its ultimate conclusion and laid down firm principles of economy on which the financial affairs of the nation were conducted. He had firmly supported the extension of the franchise in 1867 and promoted that of 1884; the Ballot Act of 1872 was also his work. His greatest weaknesses were his apparent lack of concern with the living conditions of ordinary people and his failure to realise that in matters of foreign policy the British public was concerned not so much with economy as with prestige. His failure to influence the readjustment of European power in 1870 arose largely from Palmerston's exposure of British weakness when confronted with Bismarck in 1864; more damaging was his reluctance, once he had invaded Egypt, incontestably to assert British authority there; the unhappy compromise of a commission for financial control, of which all the Great Powers were members, created constant difficulties until Britain obtained the firm support of France in the *Entente Cordiale*. After his death, Lord Salisbury said of him: 'He will be long remembered not so much for the causes in which he was engaged or the political projects which he favoured but as a great example, to which history hardly furnishes a parallel, of a great Christian man.' Great masses of valuable legislation are not associated with his name but as a master of the arts of Parliament and of public finance he had no equal. He made and he also helped to break the 19th-century Liberal party, which in a very real sense was the extension of his own powerful moral feelings and his aspirations. He became for many humble men a political ideal, who opposed injustice and oppression in all their forms and who had indicated the moral fitness of the British working class to come within 'the pale of the Constitution'. He was essentially an individualist, whose life was dedicated to setting individuals and nations free but who feared that socialism, while perhaps freeing individuals from want, would deprive them of their initiative and weaken their moral character. He feared that imperialism would pervert the masses from their function as the highest and most disinterested tribunal on earth. Both in socialism and imperialism he had come to be at variance with the times in which he lived, but the quality of his example in politics is an undying memorial. His respect for the good sense of the ordinary elector, his conviction that liberty is the best guarantee of progress, his conception of the moral accountancy of those in public life were all factors of the utmost importance in the development of parliamentary democracy.

(i) LORD ROSEBERY, 1894–95

There was no obvious successor to Gladstone. He had been grieved by the coolness of the Queen's leave-taking and by her failure to ask him for his advice on who should be the next Premier. He would have proposed Lord Spencer but it is extremely questionable whether such a choice would have been acceptable to the party. The obvious successor was Sir William Harcourt. He had a Whig background but a Radical outlook: he would have been happy, for instance, to see the House of Lords abolished. He had considerable talents and experience but an unfortunate manner, a blend of wittiness and rudeness which succeeded in upsetting most of his colleagues, especially the sensitive Rosebery, and Morley. Rosebery felt later that it would have been better for Harcourt to have attempted to form a government; as it was he remained bitter, showed the greatest scorn for Rosebery and publicly announced that, though Leader of the Commons, 'I am not a supporter of the present government.'

Lord Rosebery was specifically the Queen's choice. She had been greatly impressed by his grasp of diplomacy and his understanding of Bismarck. As Foreign Secretary he had continued Salisbury's work with a belligerency that Salisbury deprecated. Fortune had showered her blessings on him from an early age; he had succeeded to great estates, he was eloquent, he was popular. He had been an energetic first Chairman of the London County Council, he had been a successful conciliator in the coal strike of 1893, and in Scotland he was well liked. He declared that he had three wishes, to marry an heiress, to own a Derby winner and to be Prime Minister of England. All were granted but all brought unhappiness. His wife, a Rothschild, died young; his three Derby successes made him unpopular with the Nonconformist supporters of his party and his premiership was transient and inglorious. The support of the Queen, the Liberal Press and the Cabinet, who preferred him to Harcourt, made him Prime Minister, but it was clearly absurd for him to lead the Party from the Lords where he had only forty-one supporters. He did not share some of the party's most sincerely held convictions; its dislike of aggressive imperialism, its dissenting fervour against horse-racing and gambling. As a Prime Minister who had never been a member of the House of Commons he had little understanding of the problems there and annoyed the Irish, on whom the government depended, by infering that Home Rule was impracticable.

Under these conditions the prospects were hardly auspicious. To the general public the Cabinet seemed ineffective once Gladstone had left it and the hostility of the House of Lords increased the impression of futility. Welsh Disestablishment and Harcourt's attempt to control the liquor trade by a series of local vetoes were both rejected. A bill to give help to evicted Irish tenants went the same way and an Employers' Liability Bill was deprived of its effectiveness. The government's contention was that they were 'filling up the cup' by proving to the public the irresponsibility of the Lords in obstructing useful measures, but the Press increasingly maintained that the Liberals were 'fanatics' and 'faddists'.

One important act was passed, the Parish Councils Act of 1894. The creation of parish councils in villages with a population of over 300 logically followed from the County Councils Act of 1888.[1] It pleased Nonconformists because it gave to democratically elected councils many of the functions hitherto exercised by churchwardens and vestries. An opposition amendment limited their expenditure to the product of a penny rate. District councils were set up above parish councils to act as the local sanitary authority and, it was hoped, succeed the Boards of Guardians, a role of which they were deprived owing to the Conservative fear that it

[1] See above, p. 308.

would lead to an increase in rates. Even so the act was an important step forward in the democratisation of government.

In 1894 Harcourt introduced an important Budget. The increased naval expenditure was met by 1*d*. on the income tax, while the liquor interests were defied by 6*d*. on a gallon of spirits and 6*d*. on a barrel of beer. Death duties were rearranged so that they applied equally to all forms of estate and were charged on a graduated scale from 1 per cent on property up to £500 to 8 per cent on property over £1 m. The very poor were exempt. The duties were bitterly attacked by the Conservatives but they shrank from rejecting the Budget in the Lords.

A deterioration in international relations made a stronger government necessary. China had been defeated by Japan and seemed to be on the point of collapse; a scramble for spheres of influence seemed highly probable. The government was defeated in June 1895 in a thin House for having failed to provide the Army with sufficient credits, a misfortune which followed the success of the War Minister, Campbell-Bannerman, in securing the resignation of the Commander-in-Chief, the Duke of Cambridge, who had long obstructed reform. His successor, Lord Wolseley, would hold office on ordinary service conditions and was to be a member, with the other heads of military departments, of an Army Council responsible to the Secretary of State.[1]

An attempt to reconstruct the government seemed hopeless and Rosebery, not unwillingly, resigned. In the General Election that followed the Liberals were handicapped by their own disunity, the unending quarrels of the Irish and the numerous I.L.P. candidates who helped to split the 'progressive vote' so effectively that some Liberals suspected they were financed by the Conservative party. The Conservatives obtained 340 seats and the Liberal Unionists 71, making a total of 411 for the new government. The Liberal Unionists kept their own party organisation and whips, but to all intents and purposes from now on they were part of the Conservatives. The artificial distinction made it impossible for Chamberlain to become Leader of the House of Commons or in due course to succeed as Prime Minister.[2] The Liberals got 177 seats and the Irish 82.

---

[1] See above, p. 212 and below, p. 359.   [2] See below, p. 352.

Rosebery continued as Liberal leader until 1896 when
ironically Gladstone himself dealt him the *coup de grâce*,
emerging briefly from his retirement to preach a crusade on
behalf of the massacred Armenians;[1] to a man as sensitive as
Rosebery it seemed as if even the dead were rising up against
him and he decided to resign, for which he had probably
been waiting for an opportunity. For a while the Liberal
Opposition seemed stronger under Harcourt's leadership but
he found himself increasingly at variance with the national
enthusiasm for imperialism and resigned in 1898. Asquith
was offered the leadership but declined on financial grounds
as the work involved would necessitate giving up his lucrative
practice at the Bar. Campbell-Bannerman became Leader
and proved, despite the initial lack of enthusiasm the party
felt for him, to be a happy choice. An indifferent speaker
and by no means an intellectual, he was genial and good
humoured, able to handle men well, successful as Chief
Secretary in Ireland and at the War Office, very shrewd and
sufficiently a Radical to weld the party together.[2]

[1] See below, p. 333.   [2] See below, p. 370.

VIII · CHAMBERLAIN AND THE EMPIRE

(a) LORD SALISBURY'S THIRD MINISTRY, 1895–1902

Joseph Chamberlain was the member of the new Cabinet most in the public eye and he almost had the status of a co-premier. By 1891 he had put aside any thoughts of returning to the Liberals, not so much because of Home Rule but because he was deeply concerned with the new forces of imperialism and socialism. There was at this time some confusion of terms: Chamberlain still thought of himself as a socialist in the former sense of being concerned with social welfare; what he feared was Marxism, or, as he called it, Collectivism. The Webbs saw the latter term as standing for an organised as opposed to a libertarian society, as much an aspect of the nation's state as imperialism and hence a bulwark against the class war tenets of Marxism. To socialism in the Marxist sense, which seemed to many at this time a menace of terrifying proportions, imperialism provided a safe alternative, stressing the unity of the nation with the conception of service throughout society and a respect for traditional virtues. The middle class in particular saw security in the return of the Conservatives and believed that they would bring in cautious social reforms that would avert socialism. The movement of the moneyed and propertied classes away from the Liberal party seemed to deprive it of the stamina required to take a firm line of action, a crucial factor in Chamberlain's own adhesion to the Conservative party. He believed strongly in harmony between classes; socialism seemed to imply class war, at a time when every working-class agitator denounced wealth and property.

Before the election Chamberlain had drawn up an alternative programme to socialism. Its keynote was not State help but State encouragement – of thrift, foresight and self-reliance. An Old Age Pension Scheme should be introduced which would be contributory and operated by the Friendly Societies – in contrast to the socialist theory that they should be provided to all out of State funds. He wanted local

authorities to advance loans for house purchase by the
working classes, compensation for industrial injuries, courts
of arbitration for industrial disputes and labour exchanges.
Reforms of this nature seemed safe; and safety was of crucial
importance in a world that was, for the British elector,
growing unstable economically. There was considerable
unemployment and a trade depression in 1895; Britain was
maintaining a favourable trade balance only by exporting
those commodities that in the long run would turn its present
customers into future rivals, while with every increase in
foreign colonies or spheres of influence yet another area would
be closed by high tariffs to British trade. There was much in
this thought that was alarmist but it conditioned the attitudes
of the time, producing that kind of tension that found its
release on Mafeking night. More specifically it resulted in
three matters, to which Chamberlain and Balfour were to pay
considerable attention: the need for military strength, for
better education and training to make economic revival
possible, and for the development of the Empire both as an
outlet for British trade and as a strategic asset. To many of
the electorate these were priorities ahead of social reform.

The Cabinet was a strong one. In 1895 Salisbury enjoyed
undisputed authority, and hence could afford to give Chamberlain and Balfour a wide discretion. In a time fraught
with difficulties where the risk of war was very real he maintained peace with the other Great Powers with considerable
diplomatic skill. However, he was Foreign Secretary as well
as Prime Minister and this, with his membership of the Upper
House, tended to make him preoccupied and remote from
many of his colleagues. Later he became an ailing man and
spent every winter in the South of France. This made
Balfour's role crucial. With a Prime Minister who did not
always recognise his own Ministers when he saw them the
Leader of the Commons had the special task of ensuring the
smooth running of the routine of government. He was an
enigmatic figure who varied between great charm and energy
and aggravating nonchalance. He had the confidence of
many of those Tories who felt that Chamberlain went too far
and he was able to ensure harmony despite the deep-lying
rivalry between himself and the former Radical.

Chamberlain had asked Gladstone for the Colonial Office

in 1886. He had been sent on a mission to Washington by Salisbury in 1887 to settle a dispute with Canada and had become greatly interested in colonial questions. He found a considerable affinity with the leaders of the self-governing colonies who were men more like himself than Salisbury or Hartington. The great expansion outside Europe gave room to manœuvre and clashes between the Great Powers in the colonial field were so frequent that the Colonial Office was virtually a second Foreign Office. Only five years younger than Salisbury who, with much achievement behind him, was thinking of retirement, Chamberlain was a man of frustrated ambition. The control of the department most closely associated with the rising spirit of the age at last gave him the scope he needed. There was surprise when he turned down the Home Office and the Exchequer and accepted what had hitherto been a minor department; he made it the key one in the government.

Hicks Beach, now recovered, took the Exchequer which Goschen had declined. He was the only true Conservative in the front rank apart from Salisbury and Balfour. Former Liberal-Unionists held other important posts: Goschen took the Admiralty and Lansdowne the War Office. A distinguished ex-Governor-General of Canada and Viceroy of India, Lansdowne's talents were diplomatic – as befitted a descendant of Talleyrand – and he was better placed as Foreign Secretary from 1900 onwards than at the War Office where considerable administrative abilities were required. The Duke of Devonshire was Lord President of the Council and hence nominally in charge of education, for which Sir John Gorst had the practical responsibility. The Cabinet contained eight peers at a time when the peerage was very popular.

Had Chamberlain gone to the Home Office there might well have been further social reform. The most important measure was the Workmen's Compensation Act of 1897 which was a better bill than that rejected by the Lords in 1894. It did not go so far as the German measure and demand that employers take out insurance against accidents but it made it clear that full responsibility lay upon them. Seamen, servants and farmworkers were not included until 1900. A clause excluded the worker from benefiting if his wilful misconduct had caused the accident, and this gave rise to court cases that limited the effectiveness of the act.

The possibility of Old Age Pensions had come to the fore when Bismarck introduced them in Germany in 1889. Charles Booth, a wealthy and philanthropic Liverpool shipowner, whose investigations in London were revealing much neglected distress – he estimated that nearly one-third of the population were living below the poverty line – drew up a non-conributory scheme and was a member, with Chamberlain, of the Aberdare Commission of 1892–93, which exposed many of the difficulties of the aged poor but took no positive action.   In 1896 Chamberlain appointed a committee under Lord Rothschild which examined several schemes and another committee of 1899, chaired by Henry Chaplin, drew up a scheme and recommended a reform of the Poor Law as well.   The Chaplin Committee wanted a 5s. pension payable at 65 for those with less than 10s. a week other income. Bismarck had rightly commented that it was unfair to pension soldiers while allowing 'the veterans of industry to die in misery' but when the committee reported, Chamberlain was too involved in South African problems to take action and the Cabinet was deterred by the expense in time of war.   The government failure to act was legitimately held against them by the Liberals, especially as the New Zealand government introduced a scheme based on Booth's idea in 1898.

Two other pieces of legislation seemed specially designed to protect Conservative interests.   One half of agricultural rates was remitted to help farmers and landowners over the depression.   The London Government Act of 1899[1] was intended to check the growth of socialism in the Metropolis. The Progressive party in the L.C.C. led by the Webbs had gained control and was attempting to increase its authority. It had failed to take over the City of London in 1894 and now aimed at absorbing the functions of the numerous *ad hoc* bodies, untouched by the 1888 Act, which dealt with public health, maintenance of streets, and gas and water.   The Act of 1899 continued the privileges of the City of London and created sixteen metropolitan boroughs to succeed the *ad hoc* bodies.   This would limit 'socialist extravagances' by the County Council and would frustrate 'municipal socialism' in

---

[1] See above, p. 308.

that the wealthy boroughs would not be rated to provide better amenities for the slum districts.

Chamberlain realised that the expense of social reform was a paramount factor in preventing its adoption and when the South African war was over his Tariff Reform campaign had as one of its objects the provision of some of the money that was required.

At the Colonial Office, Chamberlain was extremely active. He introduced a number of measures that considerably aided the Crown Colonies, particularly the British West Indies whose sugar industry he helped to revive. He encouraged the study of tropical agriculture and founded schools of tropical medicine in London and Liverpool. He floated loans for the building of harbours and railways in the West Indies and West Africa and gave similar encouragement to protectorates and associated states. To him the colonies were 'underdeveloped estates' and he departed considerably from the *laissez-faire* attitude hitherto prevalent.

One matter that particularly affected the self-governing colonies was the question of imperial defence, in which Balfour took considerable interest. There had been many commissions and committees concerned with the War Office, the Admiralty and their relations with the Treasury. In 1895 Devonshire, who as Hartington had presided over the last such commission in 1888, was made chairman of a defence committee, but there was agreement on neither its membership nor its role. Lansdowne and Lord Wolseley increased the size of the Army and a considerable amount of money was spent on manœuvres and accumulating military stores. The work of building up a stronger Navy also continued and this was of paramount importance if Great Britain was to continue in isolation. A dispute with the United States which began in 1895 suggested that Britain could still afford to do so. The enormous increase in American economic strength encouraged the American government to assert its claim to be the protecting power of the Western Hemisphere. President Cleveland was standing for re-election and judged that a little anti-British belligerence would be opportune. The occasion was an extravagant claim made by Venezuela to a large part of British Guiana. Secretary of State Olney asserted that the Monroe Doctrine applied and that he would support

BRITISH HISTORY 1815–1939

Venezuela. Salisbury hoped the matter would blow over particularly as the Venezuelans had made their case worse by occupying some of the disputed territory. Salisbury then pointed out that the Monroe Doctrine was quite irrelevant, the matter was no concern of the United States and he would not in any case assent to the transfer of British subjects to a country as disorderly as Venezuela. He was prepared for arbitration over some areas of gold-bearing land. Cleveland, in a message to Congress, stated that he would impose the findings of an American Commission on Great Britain, if necessary by war. This message, which was completely unwarranted, served to indicate British isolation and encouraged Germany to take an attitude hostile to Britain in South Africa. The effect of the war scare on American business however, helped to restrain the country and Chamberlain, who had useful connections through his American wife, was able to ease the tension. An Anglo-American Commission with a Russian chairman was appointed and substantially confirmed the boundaries Salisbury had proposed in 1899. Balfour had made a notable speech of conciliation at the height of the crisis and spoke in terms of a loose Anglo-American Federation; the effect of this and of Salisbury's restraint was to increase understanding between the two countries.

The condition of China after its defeat by Japan in 1894 seemed to foreshadow a scramble for concessions, spheres of influence and territory by the Great Powers. The Germans were the first in the field and as a reprisal for the murder of two missionaries extorted a ninety-nine year lease of the port of Kiao Chow in 1898 as a Far Eastern station for its rapidly growing Navy. Emboldened by this the Russians obtained a lease of Port Arthur two months later as an ice-free terminus of the Trans-Siberian Railway, which had recently been completed with French money. The French obtained a port in Southern China. Britain had about 80 per cent of the Chinese foreign trade and Salisbury saw that to prevent other powers obtaining an advantage he would have to obtain a corresponding lease for Britain: 'It will not be useful and it will be expensive but as a matter of pure sentiment we shall have to do it.' Wei-hai-wei in the north came into this category but the acquisition of land on the mainland adjoining Hong

Kong increased that Crown Colony's viability. To prevent further annexations Salisbury secured the division of China into spheres of influence.[1]

In securing co-operation of all the Powers Salisbury hoped to blur the sharpness of the rival alliances of France and Russia on the one hand and Germany, Austria-Hungary and Italy on the other. Although in the Far East he had success and set an example of joint action which was followed in 1900, the eastern Mediterranean was an area of greater difficulty. The Sultan of Turkey had ordered massacres of Armenian Christians, on the grounds that they were revolutionaries, in 1894, 1895 and 1896. Lord Kimberley, Rosebery's Foreign Minister, tried to organise a Great Power protest and when that failed proposed single-handed intervention, a course that Gladstone supported in his last public speech, at Liverpool in 1896. Germany was establishing her influence in Constantinople and the Kaiser visited the Sultan in 1889 and again in 1898 when he went to Damascus and Jerusalem, proclaiming as he went the might of Germany and her friendship for all Moslem peoples. Her support for the integrity of the Turkish Empire, Russian fear of encouraging Armenian independence since she had Armenians of her own and the seizure of the Ottoman Bank in Constantinople by Armenians, the occasion of further massacres, now led to the complete failure of Salisbury's hopes of Great Power intervention. He was more successful, however, over Crete, where the British fleet could influence matters directly. Cretan Christians rebelled against the Turks and appealed to Greece for help in 1896. The Greek invasion led to a Turkish declaration of war and the occupation of Thessaly by the Turks. Great Power intervention, initiated by Salisbury, stopped the war but the murder of British sailors in Crete led to the Powers, less Germany and Austria-Hungary, forcing the Turks to evacuate Crete which effectively passed under Greek rule in 1898. Salisbury felt increasingly that in the past 'we had put all our money on the wrong horse' and even reverted to the Tsar's proposal of 1853 that Russia and Britain should combine to end Turkish rule in Europe.

The growing strength and influence of Germany was causing increasing alarm. German Navy laws of 1898 and 1900

[1] See below, p. 335.

greatly extended the size of the German fleet, while in Turkey
Marschall, the German ambassador, was beginning to occupy
a similar position to that of Stratford de Redcliffe fifty years
earlier. German money and expertise were behind the
scheme to build a railway from Berlin to Baghdad, which
could lead to a further extension of German influence, though
probably in rivalry with Russian. To Chamberlain, an
agreement or alliance with Germany seemed a logical way of
ending British isolation and counteracting French colonial
acquisitiveness and supported by Devonshire but with little
enthusiasm on Salisbury's part, he opened negotiations in
1898. The Kaiser applauded the British seizure of Wei-hai-
wei and Kitchener's Sudan campaign, which only confirmed
Salisbury in his belief that the Kaiser's aim was to embroil
Britain with France. An agreement was reached with
Germany in August 1898 over the future of Portuguese African
territories, but this was after the Germans had frustrated the
British attempt to purchase Delagoa Bay, the port which
provided the sole non-British link for the Boer Republics with
the rest of the world. Another attempt at negotiations in
1899, when Balfour made a firm offer, came to nothing when
the Chancellor Bulow pointed out that the English government could not bind future administrations and therefore
English support was not reliable. The effect of these advances
was to make the Kaiser feel that Britain felt insecure.

The growth of armaments, however, was causing concern
elsewhere and a Peace Conference was held, at the Tsar's
instigation, at The Hague in May 1899. The Russians may
have suggested it because they were finding the pace of
rearming a strain. No measure of agreement could be
reached on a five-year limitation but the establishment of the
Hague Court of Arbitration was a valuable outcome.

The other Great Powers were ready to take advantage of
British involvement in South Africa. The Russians increased
their influence in Manchuria and Persia; the Italians planned
the acquisition of Abyssinia; the French and the Spaniards,
who had just been defeated by the United States in the
Spanish-American War, began to infiltrate Morocco. The
Russians proposed intervention in South Africa, but the Boxer
Rising in China made the Germans unwilling to co-operate
and no plans were made. National feeling had been aroused

in China by the acquisitions of foreign countries and a group calling themselves the 'Fists of Sacred Harmony' murdered foreigners and native Christians. In June 1900 the German Minister was killed and European diplomats took refuge in the British legation. The Germans organised an international force, which could only reach China by sea by using British coaling stations, and the rising was suppressed, the leading Boxers being punished. The Germans maintained, despite their earlier help to the Boers, an attitude of benevolent neutrality to the South African war, while the Kaiser's conduct at Queen Victoria's deathbed created a very good impression in Britain and helped to undo much of the harm that the pro-Boer German Press had done.

French attempts to extend their power in Africa had in 1898 received a marked setback at British hands. The upper waters of the Nile, as yet unoccupied by a European power, were still in the hands of the Mahdi's successor.[1] Despite a British warning, Captain Marchand started on a long journey across Africa in July 1896 to explore the area and claim it for France. Chamberlain, who considered that Salisbury was too ready to make concessions, had already urged the reconquest of the Sudan as a fillip to British self-confidence and prestige; Salisbury was concerned not to give any impression that the expedition was aimed against France but saw merit in the extension of Christian and humane government in the area. Moreover he had considerable confidence in Kitchener's discretion.

France and Italy through the Control Commission refused to sanction the raising of a loan by Egypt for the reconquest, so it was financed entirely by Britain. Both Egyptian and British troops took part, under Kitchener's command. The expedition was a triumph of careful organisation; a railway was built to provide rapid communications and great care was taken to keep troops free of disease. At the battle of Omdurman, the Sudanese, commanded by the Khalifa in person were completely defeated and Khartoum was occupied, the Mahdi's tomb being symbolically destroyed. On his arrival, Kitchener opened sealed orders, which had been kept secret in case the French had tried to exploit the situation, to go in search of Marchand, who three days later was reported as

[1] See above, p. 277.

having raised the French flag at Fashoda, a small town further up the Nile. Marchand refused to evacuate, although the only way in which he could receive supplies or communicate with his government was through Kitchener. The French had some substance in their claim in that they had always declared their interest in the area and in 1885 Granville had limited British interests to Egypt itself, but neither Russia nor Germany were prepared to support them and the French administration was divided over the Dreyfus Case. Marchand was forced, very politely, to withdraw. For a moment war had seemed distinctly possible, with public opinion aroused in both countries; but now Salisbury did his utmost to soothe French feelings and even renamed Fashoda. The Sudan came under the joint sovereignty of Britain and Egypt in 1899. Salisbury's prestige and moderation had been very effective and when Paul Cambon came to London as ambassador relations between the two countries began to improve.

(b) THE SOUTH AFRICAN WAR

The Convention of Pretoria of 1881[1] had granted the Transvaal independence subject to British suzerainty and control of their foreign relations; the Convention of London, confirming it, had omitted the word 'suzerainty'. Nevertheless Britain regarded herself as the paramount power in South Africa and as such bound to take such action as would prevent the interference of European rivals. Zululand was annexed in 1885 and later Tongaland to prevent the Boers obtaining access to the sea, while Bechuanaland and Pondoland came under British influence. The Chartered Company, pushing up into Rhodesia, obtained a strip of land along the Transvaal frontier to extend the Capetown–Kimberley railway. The Boer republics might still have continued in the state of isolation they desired had it not been for the discovery of gold at Johannesburg in 1886, which brought a rush of prospectors and later mining experts from the United States and from Europe. These men, called by the Boers the 'Uitlanders', were an affront to everything the Dutch Reformed Church had taught the Boers to value with their pleasure-seeking lives and their lack of religion, and the growth of their numbers made the Boers feel that they would shortly

[1] See above, p. 274.

no longer be the masters of their own country and their small pastoral society would be destroyed forever. It was, a Cape politician commented, 'Monte Carlo imposed on Sodom and Gomorrah'. However, the Uitlanders could be taxed and the proceeds swelled the hitherto empty Transvaal Treasury. The government revenue rose from £154,000 in 1886 to over £4 m. in 1898 but none of this was used to improve conditions of life in the Rand. To maintain independence, President Kruger was unwilling to allow the Uitlanders votes in the Volksraad elections nor would he set up a municipality for Johannesburg which, under Uitlander control, would become virtually a rival government.

The great increase in wealth made Kruger ambitious. He engaged Dutch civil servants who strengthened the anti-British bias, he built a railway through Portuguese territory to Delagoa Bay and he made contacts with Germany who began to supply him with arms. In 1894 he refused to trade with the British across the Vaal and wished to limit his trade contacts to Delagoa Bay. Chamberlain insisted, when he took office, that trade was resumed. Meanwhile the Uitlanders felt increasingly maltreated by the Boers; by then they outnumbered them two to one and paid nine-tenths of the taxes. When Kruger rejected a petition in August 1895 carrying 30,000 signatures, the Uitlanders seriously contemplated rebellion. In this they were encouraged by the Prime Minister of Cape Colony, Cecil Rhodes, whose brother Frank was a leading Uitlander.

Rhodes had made a fortune in the Kimberley diamond mines and he was managing director of the Chartered Company. An idealist as well as a successful businessman, he aimed at the extension of British power in South Africa by reconciliation of the British and the Dutch. The Dutch of Cape Colony trusted him and their support made him Premier; he saw the attitude of Kruger as merely out of date obstructionism. He spent £260,000 organising the Uitlander plot, which he believed would be immediately successful on the Rand, but to prevent a counter-attack from the country districts he mobilised a small force of Chartered Company police with instructions to move in once the rebellion had started. They were commanded by Dr Starr Jameson who had had a striking success against the Matabeles in 1893. President Cleveland's message[1] reflected doubts of British strength and this led the American and German Uitlanders to call the rebellion off. Chamberlain was aware of the scheme and although it would have given an opportunity for the British government to intervene, he was also aware of its dangers.   His only contact with Rhodes was through the High Commissioner in South Africa, Robinson, who sympathised with the Boers.   When Jameson decided to invade on his own initiative in December 1895, to try to start a rebellion, Rhodes exclaimed that Jameson had ruined his plans while the British government sent repeated telegrams to the small force to desist.   Chamberlain sent a telegram to Kruger repudiating the Raid.   Jameson, who had triumphed with ease over the primitive weapons of the Matabeles found the German rifles of the Boers more than a match for him and he was easily captured.   The prisoners, through Chamberlain's pressure, were released for punishment in London.   An all-party committee which reported in 1897 examined the question and severely censured – but did not punish – Rhodes, who had resigned as Premier of the Cape. It cleared Chamberlain and the Colonial Office of complicity but did not compel the production of all the telegrams between the Colonial Office and the Chartered Company, which gave to the Boers the impression that the British government had planned the affair.   From what is now known of the telegrams it is evident that it had not, but some would have given a bad impression if they had been printed at the time. From now on, however, there was open hostility in the Transvaal between the Boers and the British Uitlanders, who looked to their mother country to help them.

The Boers, on the other hand, looked to Germany.   On 3rd January, 1896, the day after Jameson's capture, the Kaiser had sent a telegram to Kruger congratulating him and followed it by despatching ships and troops to Delagoa Bay. The Portuguese refused transit and a British squadron discouraged further action, but the impression created in Britain was a very adverse one, as Germany had been regarded hitherto as a friendly power and had been indulgently treated in the colonial field.   It is possible that the Kaiser, who was almost in a state of hysteria at the time, may have been prompted to this action by annoyance with Salisbury.   The

French refusal to assist German intervention helped to smooth things over, but an unfortunate impression was created abroad by the enthusiasm with which Jameson and his accomplices were greeted in London, even though they were properly sentenced. The Queen soundly rebuked her grandson, the Kaiser, but he and Admiral Tirpitz were able to use the affair to obtain from the Reichstag the money necessary for expansion of the German fleet. The Cape Dutch were becoming suspicious of British intentions and in the Orange Free State a pro-Kruger candidate, Steyn, became President in 1896.

After the Raid the Chartered Company was deprived of its armed forces and in February 1897 Sir Hercules Robinson was succeeded as High Commissioner by Sir Alfred Milner, Chairman of the Board of Inland Revenue and formerly under-secretary of finance in Egypt. A Liberal Imperialist, he was a first class administrator but less confidence could be placed, as it proved, in his diplomatic gifts. He arrived determined to conciliate the Cape Dutch but at once denounced Kruger as the cause of tension.

The Jameson Raid was Kruger's excuse to step up his armaments. Arms poured in, mainly from Krupps. Two large forts were erected at Johannesburg bristling with guns which were kept permanently aimed at the houses of suspected Uitlanders. German artillery officers trained the Boers. No attempt was made to redress legitimate grievances. When asked the purpose of the brave array, Kruger is said to have replied, 'Oh, Kaffirs, Kaffirs and such like objects.' The British government knew that time was on its side, though Kruger had now assumed almost dictatorial powers and sooner or later there would be trouble from the Uitlanders. The British were treated by the Boers with some of the arrogance and contempt with which they treated the natives; it was this at bottom which produced an intolerable situation.

The occasion was the acquittal of a Boer policeman who had killed a British workman, Tom Edgar. 21,000 British subjects in the Transvaal sent a petition to the Queen requesting protection in March 1899. This posed a dilemma for the government. If they declined the petition, loyal subjects everywhere would feel the government had abandoned the 'Civis Romanus' principle; on the other hand acceptance could well entail war. Milner urged the government to support the Uitlanders and they decided to do so in May. There ensued five months of negotiations which culminated in war, as Kruger possibly intended they should. Meanwhile Chamberlain was concerned to convince the public that there was no question of 'bullying' a small nation but that the position of the Uitlanders was impossible[1] and that every opportunity had been given to the Boers to improve it.

The first attempt to negotiate with the Boers was a conference at Bloemfontein in June between Kruger and Milner. The Colonial Office did not expect success but believed it would publicise the matter. The two principals were strangely contrasted and no accord could be established between them; there was Kruger's interminable obstinacy on the one hand and on the other the scintillating intelligence and lack of patience of Milner. It was a not unreasonable Boer contention that Uitlanders were birds of passage; they wanted a seven-year residence and renunciation of British citizenship before a vote was granted. Kruger claimed that Great Britain was no longer the 'paramount power' in the Transvaal and that under the Conventions the Boers had the absolute legal right to determine franchise matters. Milner wanted five years' residence only and broke off the conference; a cable from Chamberlain urging him not to do so arrived too late. Milner had proved not to be as moderate as Chamberlain had believed and Kruger had won the first round. Chamberlain was anxious for a settlement and when on 18th July the news reached London that the Uitlanders had been granted seven years' retroactive franchise and five new constituencies had been created in the Rand, he felt that the crisis was at an end. Selborne, the Colonial Under-Secretary and Milner, on the other hand, did not; they felt there were inadequate guarantees and the offer was merely a pawn in Kruger's game which had complete independence as its objective. Balfour pointed out the difficulty that if Britain insisted on a second conference to finalise details and Kruger refused on the grounds that franchise was a domestic matter, the government would have had a diplomatic rebuff.

Chamberlain decided to offer a Joint Commission to investigate the situation; if Kruger refused he would set up a

[1] Milner compared them to the Helots of ancient Sparta.

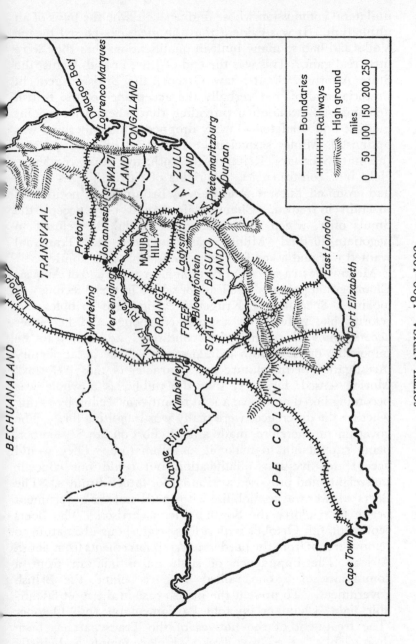

SOUTH AFRICA, 1899-1902

(With acknowledgements to R. C. K. Ensor, *England, 1870-1914*, published by O.U.P.)

unilateral commission whose findings could be the basis of an ultimatum. It was evident that the measures passed by the Volksraad had so many built-in qualifications that they were little real gain. This was the end of July; in mid-August the State Attorney, Smuts, saw Greene, the British Agent in Pretoria, and offered verbally the acceptance of the British demand at Bloemfontein providing that schemes for a joint inquiry and conference were dropped. Chamberlain was optimistic, Milner suspicious. An official offer came from the State Secretary, Reitz, on the 19th: five years' residence, eight new constituencies, full rights of citizenship, as Smuts had promised, but a renunciation by Britain of her position as suzerain in return. Chamberlain would only accept the Smuts offer, which so infuriated Reitz that he refused to negotiate further. Milner was convinced the Transvaal wanted war and asked for troops to be sent to its frontiers.

Meanwhile in a speech at Birmingham at the end of August, Chamberlain provided the lead for which imperial feeling was looking. Speaking of Kruger he said, 'He dribbles out reforms like water from a squeezed sponge and he either accompanies his offers with conditions he knows to be impossible or he refuses to allow us to make a satisfactory investigation of the nature and character of those reforms.' Morley sensed, however, that the public as a whole was becoming bored and gave a lead to anti-war feeling by asking whether the differences were really worth fighting for.[1] The government, therefore, made a final effort on 8th September, being careful not to make it an ultimatum. They would accept the five-year qualification but could not concede sovereignty and proposed a tribunal for future disputes. The Boers' answer was to mobilise with speed and the government began to reinforce the South African garrison. The Boers replied on 9th October with a forty-eight-hour ultimatum to remove troops from the borders and reinforcements from South Africa. The impudence of such an ultimatum from a community of 63,000 rallied support behind the British government. To present the British case in the most favourable light, Chamberlain told Parliament on 19th October 'The treatment of the natives of the Transvaal has been disgraceful . . . the Great Trek took place mainly and chiefly

---

[1] Many of the Boers felt the word 'sovereignty' was the real point at issue.

because, in their own words, they wanted to wallop their own niggers.' He felt that this was the most apt reply to those who saw the Boers as a harmless pastoral people who were being bullied by imperialists and 'Randlords' because they happened to be sitting on a gold-field. Even Morley considered the treatment of the Uitlanders unjust and supported a five-year franchise qualification; where he differed with the government was over the use of war as an instrument of policy.

This was the measure of Chamberlain's success. Since May the speeches he had made and accounts of negotiations he had issued had helped the public to appreciate the important issues at stake. Milner was convinced that Kruger's aim was Boer domination of South Africa, and Kruger's actions both before and during the war give some substance to this. The Cape Dutch were in a very difficult position and were a moderating influence on both sides. It is true that the atmosphere of aggressive imperialism that emanated from parts of the British Press and public, particularly after Omdurman, made the Boers not unreasonably suspicious of British actions, and they remained convinced that the British government was behind the Jameson Raid. On the other hand their own aggressive element encouraged their belief that an opportunity had come to fight on favourable terms and to win. Certainly the war started at the time of year most suitable for the Boers, as Ensor has pointed out. Their last action, the Ultimatum, was to perform for the British government an inestimable service, for, by presenting the Boers as the aggressors, it consolidated support for the government's actions both in Great Britain and in the self-governing colonies.

Despite the great reforms undertaken by Cardwell and Lansdowne's additions to the Army, Britain was not militarily prepared. There was no general staff, no plan of campaign. It was a long time since the Army had had to fight a foe of equal calibre, armed with equal weapons and misleading reports from South Africa had left them ignorant of the fact that the Boers were in this category. The Boers on the other hand believed they could win the war by swift action while they still had local superiority of numbers. They were highly mobile, mainly mounted, and able to cross the rolling grasslands of the veldt with great speed. Well armed, in many cases with the Krupps rifle which was superior to the British, they had a high standard of marksmanship. With the assistance of the Orange Free State they had 50,000 against 15,000 British, many of whom were quickly isolated in Lady-smith in Natal and Kimberley and Mafeking on the Capetown–Bulawayo railway. The Boers made the mistake of besieging these towns instead of sweeping down into Cape Colony, which would have secured for them the support of many of the Cape Dutch. The main British army under Sir Redvers Buller was split into three, and each part was defeated by the Boers.

There was great indignation in London and Balfour decided on rapid action. Buller was relieved of his command and Lord Roberts, perhaps the most respected British general, was sent out to replace him. Kitchener went as his chief of staff at Salisbury's insistence, although Balfour saw weaknesses in his character that were fully confirmed in 1914. The military situation was at once transformed. Kimberley and Ladysmith were relieved in February and with one large force Roberts advanced between March and June through Bloemfontein, Johannesburg and Pretoria. Mafeking was relieved on 17th May, when London went wild with joy. The main Transvaal army under Botha was defeated by Roberts at Diamond Hill in June and the last organised force on 27th August. In September Roberts proclaimed the annexation of the Transvaal, although it was still largely unconquered and Kruger fled to Europe to seek assistance. Although he was fêted by the French, the Kaiser refused to see him in view of the help he needed from Britain to suppress the Boxer rebellion. He died in Holland in 1904.

With the war apparently over, the Cabinet decided to hold a General Election to take advantage both of the elation that victory brings and of the divisions within the Liberal party. The Liberals complained of foul play, although the seven-year duration of Parliament was more honoured in the breach than the observance. It was not unreasonable to have an election before proceeding to a settlement but in the excitement of the moment other matters tended to be forgotten and hence the swing against the Conservatives was considerable in 1906. Meanwhile the government could exploit the patriotic enthusiasm the war had brought. Recruits had poured in and the cost of equipment had often been met by private contributions. The colonial governments showed their confidence and their loyalty by sending troops. The Liberal party was in a quandary. The Liberal Imperialists led by Rosebery, who held himself pleasantly aloof from politics, fully supported the war; they included able politicians such as Asquith, Grey and Haldane, who had links with the Webbs. Campbell-Bannerman, the leader of the party, was slightly to the left of centre and endeavoured to maintain its unity, working for a generous settlement once the war was over. The pro-Boer element found their champion in Lloyd George, who now came to the forefront of politics. As a Welsh Radical he was convinced of the rights of small nations and denounced the war as a capitalist plot. His powers of oratory and his reckless energy gave him prominence. On one occasion, at the risk of his life, he challenged the authority of Chamberlain by addressing a meeting in Birmingham. A riot ensued and he had to be smuggled out disguised as a policeman.

In a special sense it was Chamberlain's election, just as to the popular mind it was Chamberlain's war. While Salisbury fully supported the war, he had his doubts about the election but had been overruled by the rest of the Cabinet. Chamberlain was ceaselessly active, sending telegrams, including the famous one 'Every seat lost by the government is a seat gained by the Boers,'[1] and making a dozen decisive speeches. It was Chamberlain's record that the Liberals combined to attack. The result was a slight decrease in the government's majority from 152 to 134.

The financing of the war was in the hands of Hicks Beach, who was a Gladstonian in money matters. He was under pressure from his party to balance increases in direct taxation by increases in indirect taxation but he considered that the cost of the war should be met by taxation rather than by loans, although four, totalling £135 m., were issued. In 1901 he introduced two mildly Protectionist duties which caused considerable controversy, the one on refined sugar and and the other, of a shilling a ton, on exports of coal. These were followed in 1902 by a nominal duty of 3d. per cwt. on imported corn and 5d. on flour. It was defended as a revival

---

[1] The unauthorised abbreviation was 'A vote for the Liberals is a vote for the Boers.'

of the nominal duty left by Peel in 1846 and abolished in 1869, but Campbell-Bannerman attacked it as a transparent device to introduce imperial preference. The total cost of the war was £217 m. and it added over 20 per cent (£149 m.) to the National Debt.

When Roberts left South Africa in September, 1900, handing over the command to Kitchener, few could have foreseen the eighteen months of guerrilla activity that lay ahead. With no hope of ultimate victory, fighting without uniform, travelling light over Cape Colony as well as over the annexed republics, the Boer commando swooped on the long British lines of communication and ambushed patrols. Every farm was an intelligence centre and a supply depot. Kitchener cleared the whole country systematically, erecting block-houses and barbed wire entanglements, demolishing outlying buildings. The inhabitants, rounded up, were concentrated into large camps which were badly managed, resulting in a mortality rate of 117 per thousand and among children of 500 per thousand. Miss Emily Hobhouse exposed the conditions, the Liberal party raised an outcry, a relief fund was organised and the Colonial Office took over direct responsibility for the camps, which led to a great improvement.

In March 1902 the Boer leaders contacted Kitchener and offered peace on the basis of the British annexation. The Queen of Holland helped to get negotiations going. The terms were otherwise mild; the British government had found this type of war both expensive and inglorious and were anxious to finish it before Edward VII's coronation. Peace was signed at Vereeniging on 31st May, 1902. Though the republics became Crown Colonies, it was with the promise of eventual self-government. The Boers were not required to surrender their arms and a grant was made of £3 m. to enable them to rebuild their farms. Reconciliation began, making a more permanent settlement possible in 1906.

While the dreary second stage of the war was in progress, the Queen had died, on 22nd January, 1901. She had been optimistic throughout the war and had been active in visiting wounded soldiers, decorating heroes and comforting widows. She had become a legend in her lifetime, perhaps all the more respected for being rarely seen. She could be both amiable and kindly, and sombre and awe-inspiring. In a curious way she was a representative figure: 'Her prejudices and convictions were so exactly those dominant in her age that she seemed to embody its very nature within herself,' as Kingsley Martin has written. During her reign loyalty to the person of the monarch became more important than loyalty to the institution of monarchy, and thus she helped to evolve a new function for the Crown. She was not a constitutional monarch; she expected to play her part in the workings of government and the formation of cabinets. She never appreciated the value of the party system and her ideal government was a coalition, but friction between Crown and Ministers was considerably less than it had been under her uncles. By the latter part of her reign she had acquired an incomparable experience of State affairs and her advice was often valuable. As Salisbury put it after her death: 'No Minister in her long reign ever disregarded her advice or pressed her to disregard it without afterwards feeling that he had incurred a dangerous responsibility.' She had considerable common sense and knew what her country wanted – particularly the middle class, whose firm morality and desire for improvement she so faithfully mirrored, which was, as Lady Longford has observed in her recent biography of the Queen, the secret of her people's affection for her. 'Every ounce a bourgeoise and every inch a Queen.' For despite her domesticity and her sentimentality she had a matchless dignity. When they heard of her death, her people felt, as is usual on such occasions but with far greater conviction, that an age of greatness was also passing.

(c) THE DOMINIONS

To many who were concerned about Britain's weakening position in the world the great increase in British overseas territories was a reassurance. Colonies had been habitually despised by the Manchester School and many Victorian statesmen had publicly doubted their value.[1] The expansion of what has been called by C. R. Fay 'the informal empire' of trade, investment and influence was felt to be of far greater value than the mere acquisition of territory; nevertheless spheres of trade and influence often led to 'dominion', whether to prevent occupation by another power or to maintain

[1] See above, p. 102.

conditions of law and order favourable to trade. Once a
territory had been acquired, few statesmen were willing to
surrender it. Quite apart from the popular Press, investors,
trading concerns, missionary societies and a small section of
Radicals saw them as valuable acquisitions, although their
interests, especially those of missionaries and trading concerns,
frequently clashed. Gibbon Wakefield and his fellow Radicals saw the merit of systematic as distinct from haphazard
colonisation, with planned colonial land policies, organised
emigration and opportunities for social and economic
development. They had considerable influence on the
colonising of Australia and New Zealand.

Emigration became an important social factor during the
19th Century. It was an outlet for discontent, particularly
among the Irish, and an unrivalled opportunity for advancement away from the more stratified society at home. In 1815
less than 2,000 left Britain but by the 1850's the yearly
emigration figure had reached a quarter of a million. Large
numbers returned, but between 1815 and 1870 the net loss
of population was around seven million, of whom half went
to the United States, one and a half million to Canada, and
one million to Australia. Few received government assistance
although there were a large number of private schemes to aid
emigration.

In the middle years of the 19th Century the predominant
feeling among M.P.s was that colonies should not become a
financial burden and their advancement to self-government,
where this was possible, was in line with this. The experience
of the thirteen American colonies and the recommendations
of the Durham Report had indicated that the conferring of
responsible government was, in fact, the only certain way of
preserving as assets these British communities overseas. The
British North America Act of 1867 conferred the status of a
new, federal and almost completely self-governing dominion
on Canada. Meanwhile the transportation of convicts to
Australia was dying out, although Western Australia continued to accept them until 1867 and the growth of the free
population made possible Russell's Australian Colonies Act
of 1850 under which New South Wales, Victoria, South
Australia and Tasmania established democratic government.
In 1885 the Australasian Federation Act was passed but in

view of the unwillingness of New South Wales, a Free Trade colony, to co-operate with its Protectionist neighbours, only a very loose form of federation was established. Pressures for the achievement of a greater degree of unity were strong, however. It seemed evident that Australia, as a united continent, would become more conscious of its nationality and better able to resist potential aggression from the French in Tahiti and the Germans in Papua. The tropical north of Australia also presented problems of a magnitude that could only be dealt with by the co-operation of all the settled areas. The great distances involved made a considerable degree of self-government by the states necessary, but Enabling Acts passed by the State legislatures in 1895–96 led to a federal convention in 1897–98, which drafted proposals. These were eventually passed by referendums in each of the six colonies and the Commonwealth of Australia was constituted by the Parliament at Westminster in 1900. Certain defined powers were surrendered by the constituent members to the new Parliament established at Canberra, which was opened by the future King George V in 1901. Its constitutional relationship to the United Kingdom was similar to that of Canada except that there was no appeal to the Judicial Committee of the Privy Council.

New Zealand had achieved responsible government in 1852 and became a pioneer in various social and constitutional reforms, such as votes for women and Old Age Pensions. Despite difficulties with the Maoris, its development was smooth and it developed important economic links with Britain when cold storage shipments began in 1882. It was formally granted dominion status in 1907.

The conception of the dominions as members of a free brotherhood of nations gradually developed by means of a series of conferences. The first colonial conference was held in London at the time of the 1887 Jubilee. Lord Knutsford, the Colonial Secretary, remarked that 'there is on all sides a growing desire to draw closer in every practicable way the bonds which unite the various parts of the Empire'. The meeting chiefly discussed defence and New Zealand and the Australian colonies contributed, in consequence, to a strengthened naval force in the Pacific. A second meeting held at the instance of the colonies themselves in 1894 at Ottawa discussed preferential trade within the Empire, but British adherence to Free Trade was a considerable obstacle. It was, however, useful in leading to the improvement of imperial communications. The third conference was occasioned by the Queen's Diamond Jubilee in 1897 and was attended only by Ministers of self-governing colonies. It discussed ways in which the Empire could be united: political, military and naval, and commercial. Chamberlain wanted a Council of Empire, but the colonies valued their own independence. With greater understanding Balfour relied on 'Silken bonds of sentiment' rather than a rigid constitutional form. The Admiralty wanted a united fleet but it was evident that the special local concerns of the colonies made this unwelcome. Increased contributions to the expense of the Navy were made, however. British free trade made a genuine imperial preference impossible but the colonies agreed to modify their tariffs so as to discriminate in favour of British goods. It was decided that the conference should meet at regular intervals in future.

A feeling of mutual responsibility was increased by the contingents which the self-governing colonies sent to South Africa during the latter stages of the war but the fourth Colonial Conference of 1902 also stressed the equality and independence of the dominions. The Canadians decided to establish their own fleet, although the other members continued their contributions to the Royal Navy. Each member showed its growing concern with the protection of its own industries but a readiness to adopt imperial preference. The conference gave the British government the strong hint that it should impose duties which it could remit to members. The fifth conference in 1907 which adopted the title 'Imperial' showed the progress of nationalism when Australia decided to form her own Navy but co-operation was shown by the decision to create an Imperial General Staff for military matters and to co-ordinate laws on trade and naturalisation. Once again a resolution was passed favouring imperial preference, Britain alone dissenting. A defence conference in 1909 was held in response to the potential threat from Germany, which was also the main feature of the Imperial Conference of 1911. This reflected the growing pattern of the Commonwealth to be, one of consultation and co-operation without the sacrifice of the several national autonomies. The Great War showed how real that co-operation could be but at the same time it enhanced the dominions' sense of their national pride and distinctness.[1]

(d) BALFOUR'S MINISTRY, 1902–5

It had been a Hanoverian tradition to distrust the heir to the throne and in this Queen Victoria had been no exception. She had refused suggestions that Edward should deputise for her in London or perform useful work by taking up residence in Ireland. His indiscretions on one or two occasions had led the Queen to debar him from seeing major State papers until 1892, with the result that when he came to the throne he had little experience of the machinery of government while his exclusion from serious public duties had pushed him towards a life of pleasure. He lacked the Queen's application and industriousness and also her ability, but in a different way he enhanced the standing of the Crown and was as successful a sovereign. The power and influence of the monarchy decreased during the reign but it came far more into the public eye. He was expert in pomp and publicity, dignified, had an excellent memory, charm and exceptional tact. His unself-conscious pursuit of pleasure was for many a refreshing contrast to the stuffy atmosphere of his mother's court. The most international of English monarchs – he spent three months abroad every year – his interests and attitude to life were distinctively English. He had little influence on politics and Balfour had a low opinion of him, but his personal interest helped Fisher's work in the Navy while for the Foreign Office he was an ambassador beyond compare in his state visits, although it would be wrong to attribute to him any influence on foreign policy. Not least among his services was his departure from tradition in the happy relationship with his son and heir.

A change was also in process in the 'elective monarchy'. Salisbury was finding the pressure of both the premiership and the Foreign Secretaryship too much, and he was persuaded to hand over the latter post to Lansdowne, who was eager for an escape from diplomatic isolation, preferably by means of an approach to Germany. Balfour was virtually in

[1] See below, p. 445.

control, supporting Chamberlain when it was suggested that his business interests had profited from the war, and the Service Ministers against the economies which Hicks Beach wanted. His brother Gerald Balfour was now a member of the Cabinet as President of the Board of Trade, making, with Salisbury's son-in-law, Selborne, at the Admiralty, four Cecil relatives in the Cabinet and Cranborne, Salisbury's son, as Under-Secretary of Foreign Affairs, just outside. To criticisms of the 'Hotel Cecil' Salisbury replied that relatives 'cannot be treated as a class apart who can be employed but not promoted'.

Salisbury had always regarded an alliance with a great European power as potentially embroiling Britain in difficulties which were not her proper concern; he concurred, however, with an approach to Japan, which was prompted by the fear of losing the China market in view of increased Russian and German interest there. Following the Boxer Rising in 1900 the Germans maintained Chinese integrity by the Yangtse Agreement but it was clear by the following year that they would not prevent Russian encroachment. Lansdowne and Chamberlain made a further approach to Germany in the spring of 1901 but the German condition was that Britain should underwrite Austria-Hungary, a condition probably intended to be unacceptable. There is no evidence that a British alliance was considered either necessary or desirable in Berlin, where Britain was seen as the principal obstacle to the extension of German influence. Agreement between Britain and Japan was reached, and an alliance was signed in January 1902. The *status quo* in the Far East and the integrity of China were to be upheld but Japan was recognised as having a special interest in Korea. The Germans hoped it would lead to difficulties with Russia and gave it every encouragement.

In July 1902 Salisbury resigned. He died thirteen months later. Balfour was invited to form a government and accepted when he had visited Chamberlain, who was unwell. Chamberlain had been touched by Balfour's loyalty to him during the war and co-operated with him willingly; moreover his position as a Liberal Unionist and the fact that he still occasionally evinced Radical opinions made him unacceptable to the Conservative back benches. It is always intriguing to speculate what might have been the outcome if Chamberlain had become Premier, but it was not really practical politics. Balfour succeeded his uncle, whom he resembled in many ways, with the general consent of the party.

As Prime Minister, Salisbury, as Hicks Beach remarked, 'did not exercise the control over his colleagues either in or out of Cabinet that Lord Beaconsfield did . . . he frequently allowed important matters to be decided by a small majority of votes even against his own opinion and left his colleagues very much to themselves, unless they consulted him'. He did not produce a constructive programme of domestic improvements but preferred that he and his colleagues should deal with matters as they arose. The few important reforms he promoted all had become virtually inevitable. He was not a 'backwoodsman', however, but merely a believer that politics was the art of the possible. Balfour's outlook was very similar, although he was more susceptible to the increasingly democratic atmosphere of the age. Both had a curious failing: Salisbury could never remember faces, Balfour facts and figures. Neither was popular; both were regarded with respect. The Duchess of Marlborough said of Balfour in 1902: 'Both mentally and physically he gave the impression of immense distinction and of transcendent spirituality.' As a Prime Minister, Balfour is usually accounted a failure; he lost in the course of his Ministry almost all the key members of his Cabinet through resignation, yet it was a period of important achievements, to all of which he made a crucial contribution. His deficiency was as a manager of men; he was not well-fitted by temperament to lead a political party. He had a certain aloofness that tended to make him unsympathetic to human problems – Neville Chamberlain considered he had a heart of stone – and his philosophic detachment tended to make him see both sides of any political problem, to the detriment of his enthusiasm as a partisan. At times it made him show dangerous indecision.

Hicks Beach resigned with Salisbury; he had found himself out of sympathy with recent trends. A man of his calibre as an administrator and in debate was difficult to replace; the ponderous and importunate Ritchie was an inadequate substitute at the Exchequer. It has been argued that Balfour should have pressed Chamberlain to take this post;

such a course might well have avoided the Cabinet split on
tariff reform.[1]

The first important measure for which Balfour was responsible was the Education Act of 1902, an unpopular but logical
settlement of a complex problem.[2]   Neither Salisbury nor
Chamberlain was enthusiastic, but Balfour was convinced of
the need, studied every aspect and steered it through Parliament with unfailing tenacity.   His objective was to unify and
improve secondary and primary education, which it was
generally recognised was markedly less effective than that of
Germany.   Reformers felt that as an essential step secondary
education should be as free as primary and the chaos of
administrative responsibility should be superseded by a logical
system.   The Charity Commissioners were not connected
with any government department; the Department of Science
and Arts was now controlled by the Education Department
but it had considerable independence.   Since 1889 the Board
of Agriculture had had power to make educational grants and
the same year responsibility for technical education had been
given to the County Councils.   In the hands of some of them,
notably London where Sydney Webb was chairman of the
responsible committee, this also became a form of secondary
education.   The School Boards, with the encouragement of
the Department of Education, had started a number of courses
beyond elementary standard.

Religious difficulties resulted in a division of responsibility in
primary education.   Since 1870 the Nonconformists, who in
numbers were losing ground in the last quarter of the 19th
Century, had regarded the new Board Schools with their
simple religious instruction based on the Bible, as especially
their preserve.   The Anglicans, regarding these new schools
as almost agnostic, were finding the maintenance of their
schools a heavy burden, even though there was a State grant,
and wished for rate support like the maintained schools, a
suggestion bitterly opposed by the Nonconformists.   Whatever decision Balfour took was bound to be unpopular with a
substantial section of the voters.

Gorst was placed in charge of education in 1895 and the
following year introduced a Bill which transferred complete
control to County Councils over secondary education but leav-

[1] See below, p. 364.   [2] See above, p. 217.

ing intact the School Boards, which Chamberlain supported. It aimed to increase State support for voluntary schools. The Liberals talked it out but Balfour pushed through legislation in 1897 which raised the grants to voluntary and poor Board Schools. He introduced better pensions for teachers, abandoned payment by results and raised the school leaving age to 12 in 1899. In the same year the Board of Education was created which absorbed the Science and Arts Department and established regular co-operation with the Charity Commission. Attempts to provide a satisfactory unified control at local level failed and matters were complicated by the Cockerton Judgment of 1901, a frankly political test case involving the London School Board, which ruled that its funds were not to be used for secondary education. The situation was legalised for one year and in March 1902 a Bill was introduced to provide a permanent solution.

Its principal originator was a remarkable official of the Board of Education, Morant, who later in the year became Permanent Secretary. He had reorganised the educational system of Siam while still in his twenties and was an enthusiast for centralised and uniform organisation. He was one of the most remarkable men of his day, the founder not only of the modern educational administrative system, but also the first director of Lloyd George's National Insurance Scheme and the first permanent secretary of the Ministry of Health in 1919. He gradually acquired considerable influence over both Balfour and Devonshire and played a decisive part in the final negotiations. Like Chadwick he was no sufferer of fools and all critics tended in his eyes to come into that category.

Morant was determined that the School Boards, which he felt to be wasteful and inefficient, should go and although this was unfair to most of the urban boards, it was undoubtedly true of many of the rural ones. Their functions were taken over by County Councils and County Boroughs, which now became the local authorities for all types of State education apart from the universities and enjoyed a large measure of autonomy. A compromise set up 'Part 3 Authorities', namely the councils of boroughs with a population over 10,000 and urban districts with over 20,000, which assumed responsibility for primary education within their areas, an

arrangement which lasted until 1944. The Voluntary Schools
were saved and the Nonconformists much embittered by the
payment of their current expenses by the rates, the managers
providing the buildings and appointing the teachers. The
Cowper-Temple clause[1] was retained: only undenominational
religious instruction was to be given in provided schools.

The long-term effects of the act were all that its drafters
could have wished but it had passed only with difficulty and
was greeted by an outcry. Within the Cabinet Chamberlain,
who had first come into prominence over the question of
denominational education, assented to it only with reluctance.
Asquith called it a piece of 'reactionary domestic legislation',
and huge public meetings agitated against it. It was felt that
the new authorities would not be as democratic or as responsive to public opinion as the old Boards, which the Liberals,
who had created them, valued greatly. There were particular
difficulties for Nonconformists in areas where there was already
a Church of England school and the population did not justify
another. Rural Wales, with its predominantly Nonconformist
population, was particularly affected and Lloyd George's
speeches brought him into increasing prominence. He
revealed all the resentments felt at the privileged position of
the Established Church and the devastating social jealousies
fomented by the advantages which 'Church' enjoyed over
'Chapel' in the field of education. In Wales there was
massive refusal to pay rates and Dr John Clifford, a senior
Baptist minister who was the chief opponent outside Parliament, and other leading Nonconformists had their goods
distrained upon rather than pay. The Welsh County
Councils refused for some time to take up their duties and
only agreed to do so when Welsh education was removed from
Morant's control.

Subsequent criticism of the Act came from Conservative
back benchers who saw it not only as potentially expensive but
also as a dangerous act of State socialism. Its social effects,
however, were slow. The new authorities were allowed to
build their own new secondary schools; they charged low
fees but provided scholarships from the elementary schools.
They were also able to integrate into the system the old
endowed grammar schools. It was the middle classes who

[1] See above, p 222.

chiefly benefited, for the number of working-class children affected was relatively small. Nevertheless it greatly increased opportunities for the reasonably able. The Education Act was extended to London in 1903.

Social justice of a different kind was served by the Irish Land Purchase Act of 1903, which was the work of the Chief Secretary, Wyndham, and Macdonnell, a distinguished Irish Roman Catholic who had become Permanent Under-Secretary in 1902.[1] The Ashbourne Acts had introduced a scheme of land purchase which operated from 1885 onwards but insufficient money was available and William O'Brien founded the United Irish League to speed up the process. Lord Dunraven assembled a conference of landowners which co-operated with O'Brien and Redmond, the leader of the Irish Nationalist party, in bringing pressure on the government. The outcome was the Act of 1903 which provided large cash contributions from the Exchequer to bridge the gap between what the landlords could afford to accept and the tenants to pay. Allowance was also made for arrears of rent. Repayment was to be over sixty-eight and a half years, a scheme honoured until the Irish Free State repudiated it in 1932. Under the act a large portion of Irish land changed hands and in association with Balfour's earlier measures it did much to transform the face of the country.

As part of his policy of 'killing Home Rule by kindness' Gerald Balfour had set up Irish County Councils by an Act of 1898 which in particular conferred powers to help Irish agriculture. These worked well and after the Land Act the Dunraven Conference became the Irish Reform Association, in order to promote a degree of devolution. In association with Macdonnell a scheme was worked out to which Wyndham through carelessness gave his tacit approval. Extreme Unionists smelt Home Rule by the back door and Wyndham publicly repudiated the scheme and then was forced to resign in March 1905 in a way which was discreditable to the Prime Minister. Macdonnell, however, continued, and so did the policy of conciliation.

Another important piece of legislation, which like the Education Act lost votes for the government, was the Licensing Act of 1904. Throughout the 19th Century there was

[1] See above, p. 316.

constant agitation to prevent over-indulgence in drink by means of reducing the number of public houses. This was increasingly associated with the Liberal party, for the non-conformist lower middle class was particularly intolerant of working-class vices, and 'local option' without compensation became part of its programme. There was considerable doubt as to whether the holders of redundant licences were entitled to compensation, the Temperance Movement maintaining that the annual grant of the licence contained no guarantee of renewal. In *Sharpe* v. *Wakefield* of 1891 the Lords decided against compensation but it was not until 1902 that the brewers became unduly alarmed. Balfour felt that if it was public policy to reduce licences, this should not be linked with injustice; compensation should be paid not from the Exchequer but from a fund levied on the trade, on the grounds that reductions enhanced the value of the remaining public houses. The act although unpopular with those who hoped to eradicate drinking, was a common-sense measure and led to a gradual reduction in the number of licensed premises.

Balfour's clear grasp of problems and his foresight were shown in his reorganisation of the Committee of Imperial Defence. Before the South African War there had only been a small and largely ineffective committee, in which Salisbury had taken little interest. The deficiencies exposed by the South African War and the critical report of the Elgin Commission led to its reconstitution in 1903. It had no fixed membership; the Prime Minister who was ex-officio Chairman could invite whom he pleased and the Canadian War Minister was a member for a period. Its purpose was to study problems of strategy and new technical advances and to offer advice. Unlike the Cabinet it had a permanent secretariat which minuted its proceedings. Balfour showed particular concern for it and stayed in office during 1905 in increasingly difficult circumstances to round off the revision of British strategy with the Anglo-Japanese treaty and to give the new committee a reasonable breathing space.

Brodrick the War Minister projected a reorganisation of the Army with a total of 600,000 men but this was attacked on all sides on the grounds of expense. A committee under Lord Esher investigated the organisation of the War Office and reported in 1904 in favour of the abolition of the post of Commander-in-Chief and the creation of an Army Council on the lines of the Board of Admiralty. This was adopted and an improved system of appointment to the higher ranks was worked out, but nothing was done about a general staff.[1]

A key figure at the Admiralty since 1902, Sir John Fisher became First Sea Lord in 1904; he worked closely with the First Lord, Earl Cawdor and received the firm support of the King in bringing about a rejuvenation of methods, a redistribution of squadrons and the creation of a new monster ship, the *Dreadnought*. He had a profound conviction that the Navy was the best guarantee of Britain's safety and considered that Tirpitz's German fleet had the sole purpose of attacking Britain. This necessitated a concentration of the fleet in home waters, the scrapping of redundant vessels and the keeping of ships on police duties in distant parts to a minimum. He gave a new status to the engineer branch, improved methods of entry and insisted on rapid promotion on the basis of merit instead of merely upon seniority. He made the reserve fleet created in 1900 more effective, set up a Naval War College at Portsmouth and instituted a service of fleet auxiliaries. He was bitterly opposed by many, especially Admiral Lord Charles Beresford, who considered he had misinterpreted the fleet's role. He rode roughshod over all opponents and controversy forced him to resign in 1909,[2] an event which momentarily eased naval tension with Germany.

The *Dreadnought* was launched in 1906. It was larger than any ironclad previously built and was better armed and swifter. With its flexible gun mountings it threw a weight of broadside which could utterly overwhelm any rival of a former design. In 1904 the range of the biggest guns was 4,000 yards, by 1914 it was 12,000. It was supported by the *Invincible*, a new, fast and heavily armed cruiser. Hitherto Britain had not been an innovator in naval matters; now all other fleets would be out of date as soon as a sufficient number had been built. It was proposed to lay down four a year but the Liberal government reduced the number and thus gave

[1] See below, p. 378.
[2] When given a peerage Fisher took as his motto 'Fear God and Dread Nought.'
z

the Germans a chance of catching up. A new German Naval Law was passed two months after the launch and work was put in hand. A serious obstacle was the need to widen the Kiel Canal, which was not completed until 1914, when, as Fisher correctly prophesied, war broke out.

It was the government's aim to avoid such a war by diplomacy and Salisbury had been active in eradicating points of colonial friction by agreement. The Entente with France in 1904 was in the same tradition, but it promoted an understanding that was to be the germ of something more and was to re-establish the equilibrium of Europe that the weakness of Russia, demonstrated by her defeat in the war with Japan of 1904–5, had upset. In no sense was it intended on the British side as an alliance against Germany but rather as an escape from an isolation which, in view of Egypt,[1] was becoming increasingly embarrassing. On the French part there was a clear choice; reconciliation with Germany would have been relatively easy and in the long run would have averted the sufferings of the Great War; but a tentative alliance of Western democracies had a closer affinity to the ideals of 1789. British relations with France had been strained since 1882, although since the end of the Fashoda crisis the French Foreign Secretary, Delcassé, had been ready for an improvement. An additional difficulty had arisen when the French began the active occupation of Morocco where Britain had trading interests. When the question of Alsace and Lorraine was taken up again by the French government in 1902, Balfour and Lansdowne saw their opportunity and the failure of negotiations with Germany led to the opening of those with France. Understanding was reached in March 1903 and in May the King's visit to Paris helped to adjust public opinion in both countries to the new arrangement. A number of minor issues were settled and the French agreed to support Britain in Egypt, while Britain supported French intervention, in association with Spain, in Morocco, which was rapidly becoming disorderly.

The definitive Treaty was signed in April 1904. It assured Britain of a firm majority on the Egyptian Control Commission and terminated the influence that Germany formerly had brought to bear in this connection. Further matters

---

[1] See above, p. 277 and below, p. 509.

helped to make co-operation closer. With the British fleet being concentrated by Fisher in home waters it was necessary partly to entrust Mediterranean security to the French fleet. During the Russo-Japanese war France and Britain were allied to the opposing sides and close co-operation was needed to prevent embroilment. Russia was unpopular with the British public who regarded her as a cruel, tyrannical power and distrusted her expansionist policy in Asia, while the Russian government believed the British alliance had encouraged the Japanese to fight. A large British ship was sunk accidentally in the Far East and a potentially disastrous incident occurred in October 1904 when Hull trawlers on the Dogger Bank were fired on at night by the Russian fleet proceeding to the Far East. The Russians were 30 miles off course and assumed the trawlers were disguised Japanese torpedo boats. The British attitude was conciliatory and the Russians, prompted by France, made amends.

An even more serious crisis arose in March 1905 when the Kaiser visited Tangier and proclaimed the freedom of the Sultan and posed as the defender of international commercial interests in Morocco. The Tsar was temporarily under German influence and the Kaiser saw the opportunity to split the Entente and obtain further colonial compensation. Ports in north-west Africa would be valuable for the German Navy. The French Foreign Secretary, Delcassé, was forced to resign and a Conference met at Algeciras in January 1906. Grey, the new Foreign Secretary, promised to follow Lansdowne's policy and secret military conversations with the French government were initiated and continued until 1914; most of the British Cabinet were unaware of them until 1912. At the Algeciras Conference bluster and mismanagement spoiled a good German case; only Austria-Hungary supported her ally and the failure of the Kaiser's attempt to smash both the Entente and the Franco-Russian alliance was complete. France and Spain obtained mandates to police Morocco, under a Swiss Inspector-General.[1] The British government made an approach to Russia, which resulted in a Convention in 1907,[2] but every effort was made to maintain good relations with Germany, to strengthen which the King paid a state visit to his nephew at Kronburg.

[1] See below, p. 414.   [2] See below, p. 412.

In August 1905 a reciprocal treaty of alliance was signed with Japan which enabled her to accept more moderate peace terms at the Treaty of Portsmouth, arranged under United States auspices in August 1905. The Treaty of 1902 had marked the decline of British influence in northern China, and the Alliance showed British concern at Russian infiltration of Afghanistan and Tibet. British policy in India was in the hands of the Viceroy, since 1898 Lord Curzon. A clever, pushing young man he had been Under-Secretary at the Foreign Office in 1895 and had been promoted to the Viceroyalty while still under forty. Initially his enthusiasm for reform was wholly beneficial but power went to his head and he became resentful of advice and criticism. He had obtained the appointment of Kitchener as Commander-in-Chief of the Indian Army but when the Cabinet took Kitchener's side in a dispute over military administration, Curzon quarrelled violently with the government at home, which resulted in his resignation in 1904. He had at times made assertions that 'would raise India to the position of an independent and not always friendly power'. He had wished to tighten up relations with Afghanistan to prevent Russian infiltration, but the government insisted on a less harsh approach. In 1903 he had sent the Younghusband Mission to Tibet, and the government feared that he wanted annexation. The Mission exacted harsh terms at Lhasa, some of which the Cabinet refused to implement. In general his relations with the home government caused Balfour to hold a low opinion of Curzon's stability and this may well have been decisive when he was asked to recommend a successor to Bonar Law in 1922.

Meanwhile Balfour's own position was seriously weakened by the Tariff Reform dispute.

(e) TARIFF REFORM

The fourth Colonial Conference of July 1902 urged the extension of imperial preference and requested the British government to facilitate this by some slight abandonment of Free Trade principles. This made a great impression on Chamberlain and when he visited South Africa in the winter of 1902–3 to arrange a customs union between the four colonies and to promote reconciliation, he became more than ever convinced of the need to strengthen trade links as a

gesture of imperial unity. In 1903 the industries of Birmingham and Lancashire cotton were depressed and the fundamental reason was the growing competitiveness of foreign
industry, itself protected by tariffs. The practice of 'dumping' or selling goods at prices low enough to undermine the
native industry was beginning to do serious harm. Some
policy of protection seemed to make sense, particularly as
Canada had recently imposed import duties to counteract the
McKinley Tariff of 1897 in the United States. If Protection,
which was thenceforward called Tariff Reform to avert the
evil eye, was linked with Empire Free Trade, however, there
were difficulties. British industry wanted foreign industrial
products excluded; the dominions and colonies were chiefly
exporters of primary products and raw materials and any
scheme to satisfy them would involve a tax on food imported
from outside the Empire, in return for which they would give
preference to British manufactures and machinery. It could
therefore be argued by the Liberals that any scheme to satisfy
both would be of much greater benefit to the colonies and
industry than to the people as a whole, a dilemma which the
Unionist party did not succeed in solving.

There was, however, an even more fundamental consideration. Free Trade had been seen in the mid-19th Century as
a valuable way of checking government extravagance; now,
however, there was an increased pressure for social reform
although the Old Age Pension scheme had been abandoned
due to difficulties of financing. The Unionist party was
pledged not to increase direct taxation, which fell chiefly on
the rich, and Chamberlain, believing like Bismarck that socialism could only be averted by the provision of State-subsidised
social security, sought to widen the basis of indirect taxation to
provide the necessary funds. He had proposed this as early
as 1894. That the Free Trader Hicks Beach had had to
resort to temporary low import duties to finance the Boer
War[1] illustrated the very real difficulty the government were
having in meeting financial estimates which even in peacetime
were topping the £100 m. mark.

To discourage Canada from taking a completely independent line on trade matters, the Cabinet, Ritchie being the
sole dissentient, appeared to favour in August 1902 the

[1] See above, p. 345.

remission of the Hicks Beach corn duty for the dominions and colonies only. In Chamberlain's absence Ritchie appealed to Free Trade sentiment within the Cabinet and incorporated the complete removal of the corn duty in his 1903 Budget, a decision which Balfour had endorsed as he feared the effect of the opposition's 'Bread Tax' clamour on by-election results. Chamberlain was justifiably annoyed and, tired after his visit to South Africa and depressed by the secessions from the Liberal Unionists over the Education Act, decided he must launch his great scheme of fiscal and social reform without delay. Balfour had promised an inquiry but Chamberlain announced his belief in Imperial Preference and a return to tariffs in an important speech in Birmingham on 15th May,[1] views he later repeated in the Commons. There he admitted the working class might have to pay three-quarters of the cost of preference but he asserted that the equivalent value of the new tariffs would be returned to them in social reforms. The Cabinet was seriously divided; although not a single prominent figure supported Chamberlain a majority were chiefly concerned to hold the party together, which was Balfour's main aim. Devonshire and three others supported Free Trade within the Cabinet; outside Hicks Beach organised a Free Food League, to which fifty-four Unionist M.P.s gave their support. They included Lord Hugh Cecil and Winston Churchill who felt that Chamberlain's purpose was to lead a Protectionist party; in consequence they were ready to work with the Liberals, whom Churchill shortly joined. Meanwhile Chamberlain was having considerable success in converting the constituencies.

In September Balfour put forward a compromise which would empower the government to try to force down foreign tariffs by retaliatory duties. It did not commit the country to a general tariff and did not tax food, but on the other hand it did nothing for the Empire. It pleased neither side. Devonshire was convinced it would be swept away in favour of pure protection at the first opportunity. Chamberlain offered to resign in order to concentrate on the campaign; this was not in any sense a severence with Balfour as his son Austen remained in the Cabinet. There then followed an

---

[1] Chamberlain's speech in Birmingham coincided with Balfour's announcement to a Protectionist delegation that the time was not yet ripe.

involved series of misunderstandings which resulted in the dismissals of Ritchie and Balfour of Burleigh, and the resignations of Hamilton, Devonshire and Chamberlain; the Duke's resignation, in view of his great prestige, was regarded by some to be the worst blow of all. From then on until his own resignation in 1905 there was hardly a month when the Cabinet did not threaten to dissolve. Each side felt they had been tricked.

Balfour now accepted the fiscal question as one on which the party could agree to differ. His new appointments reflected this; with Austen Chamberlain at the Exchequer and Victor Cavendish, Devonshire's nephew and heir, as Financial Secretary to the Treasury he could keep in touch with both sides. To Chamberlain, however, Tariff Reform was a crusade: he hoped not only to counteract socialism but to provide a dynamic creed that would consolidate the unity of the party and compensate for votes lost by controversial legislation. The Tariff Reform League provided funds and spread branches into the consituencies; a Tariff Commission produced facts and figures based on a survey of industry, from which Chamberlain's support came. In 1904 he replaced Devonshire as Chairman of the Liberal Unionist Association and the Conservative Press as a whole supported him. His speeches increasingly became pleas to save particular industries but the Liberals were able to make great play with the fact that food prices were certain to rise. Balfour could not make up his mind whether to support Chamberlain and he was opposed to the democratisation of the party which the campaign entailed. Although he saw merits in the Tariff Reform case he was perturbed by the steady Unionist losses at by-elections.

The Liberal party was still recovering from its split over the South African war. At the end of 1901 Rosebery had attempted to recover the leadership and had declared his opposition not only to the Boers but also to Home Rule; in February 1902 he repudiated Campbell-Bannerman's leadership and founded the pro-imperialist Liberal League, of which Asquith, Fowler, Grey and Haldane were leading members. It was intended to capture the party, not to split it, and a certain measure of unity was achieved in the fight against the Education Bill. The Tariff issue, however, was a gift beyond compare; it was one in which the Liberal party had the support of all the established economists and to which they had all the answers; they were fighting on old ground and they did so with zest. Chamberlain's hope that the Liberal Imperialists would be attracted to his scheme for the sake of the Empire proved illusory; Asquith in particular was outspoken in his criticism. For two years there ensued a remarkable debate both in the Press and between hundreds of orators. Asquith followed Chamberlain round, refuting his arguments, disproving his facts, exposing the fallacies. The Liberals pointed out that there was no place for British India in the system, yet its economic development directly threatened Britain; that there was no guarantee that the colonies, whose interests differed widely and with whom the trade was under half that with the rest of the world, would continue to give Britain favours equal to the sacrifices she was making by surrendering Free Trade. Chamberlain's slogan 'Tariff Reform means work for all' made less sense in 1905 when British trade began to recover from the uncertainties following the South African War and Russo-Japanese War. The Liberals knew many of their supporters and their Labour allies preferred to raise revenue by the direct taxation of the rich and they rightly assessed the power of the free food cry, the effective comparison of the big and little loaf. Campbell-Bannerman's hold on the party strengthened, although it was still not certain whether the Liberal Imperialists would serve under him.

Meanwhile Balfour sought to reunite his party. Although the Free Food League had secured the presidency of Devonshire it had collapsed in 1905. In a speech at Manchester in January, he proposed retaliatory duties and a colonial conference to discuss closer commercial union, but promised that proposals would be submitted to the electorate before action was taken. After a delay Chamberlain accepted but the reunion of the two leaders was not convincing. Fears about the future of the economy seemed very real, however, and two measures were passed in 1905 to alleviate unemployment. The Alien Immigration Bill was intended to counteract the influx of Jews whose readiness to work for any wage and whose acquisitiveness seemed to deprive British workmen of work, although many Jews developed new industries and expanded employment prospects. Restrictions were imposed but the right of political asylum was safeguarded. An act of enormous significance, although its actual achievement was slight, was Walter Long's Unemployed Workmen Act.

1905 saw hunger marches and demonstrations of the unemployed. Long, the President of the Local Government Board, realised that the established remedies for dealing with poverty were inadequate to help the man who was temporarily out of work through no fault of his own. Poor Law treatment was degrading and undermined morale. 'We were making paupers of men,' said Long, 'who were willing and anxious to be self-supporting citizens.' Difficulties were increased during the winters when many manufacturers laid off men they did not need. Owing to lack of information the reserve force of industry was much larger than was necessary and many men were chronically under-employed, working only spasmodically, a state of affairs which was intensely demoralising. Long held a conference in 1904 on relief of casual unemployment in London and the following year the scheme was extended to the whole country by the act. It was very cautious; there was not to be any disbursement of public funds except for registering the unemployed, establishing labour exchanges and assisting emigration and removal. Local Unemployment Committees could not be compelled to undertake these functions, but they were expected to make public appeals for funds to support those who were out of work. £125,000 was raised by the end of the year; in 1906 under the Liberals Treasury contributions were forthcoming. The significance of the act was the acceptance of responsibility by the State. As Beveridge put it to the Poor Law Commission, 'it is one of the most revolutionary departures of modern times. The Tories don't realise what they have let themselves in for'.[1]

The poor, however, were soon to have their own champions in the House. The Trades Unions had regarded the new Labour Representation Committee[2] with little enthusiasm, until a dispute with serious implications occurred in 1901. The Taff Vale Railway was brought to a standstill by an unofficial strike and the company sued for damages the Amalgamated Society for Railway Servants, whose members

---

[1] See below, p. 381.   [2] See above, p. 302.

were implicated.   Hitherto it had been taken for granted that the Trades Union Act of 1871 gave absolute protection to union funds, but the court held the Society was liable.   Although the Court of Appeal reversed the decision, the company carried the case to the House of Lords where they secured a favourable verdict.   The Society had to pay £32,000 in costs and damages.   At once the movement saw the likelihood that any strike, even if successful, might ruin the union that ran it.   At the same time the case of *Quinn* v. *Leatham* weakened the effectiveness of the Act of 1875 by questioning the right peacefully to picket and boycott employers using non-union labour.   The fact that both these were decisions of the House of Lords added to Trades Union annoyance. Balfour reluctantly appointed a Royal Commission but the Labour Representation Committee was the workers' hope. Its membership more than doubled and several by-elections were won.

Working-class movements and the Liberal party were both horrified and alarmed by the Chinese labour scheme in South Africa.   The mines of the Rand had run down during the war, and, failing to secure the limited supply of Kaffir labour at cheap rates, the owners persuaded the government to agree to the temporary intake of indentured Chinese labourers. To ensure they worked for long enough to cover the cost of transport and to meet local objections the Chinese were housed in compounds to which they were confined even when they were not working.   There was no evidence that they were badly treated but there were justifiable humanitarian and moral objections to the system.   It smacked of slavery; it treated labour as a mere commodity; it showed little regard either for the feelings of the self-governing colonies or of the British workmen, who saw a serious threat in the profuse and povery-stricken labour of the East.   The affair demonstrated how little real contact the Conservative party as a whole and Balfour in particular had with the feelings of the working classes.   Although the scheme was economically profitable, vice and punishment were predominant in the compounds and humanitarian feeling was outraged.   It was undoubtedly a significant factor in the Election of 1906.[1]

Towards the end of 1905 Balfour, who had held his Cabinet

[1] See below, p. 372 and p. 374.

together with difficulty since 1903, decided to resign. His leadership of the party appeared to be challenged when in November the annual conference of the National Union adopted Chamberlain's resolution in preference to Balfour's own. He believed, however, that Liberal dissensions were greater and hoped to profit by them. Spencer, whose leadership had seemed an acceptable proposition to both wings of the Liberal party, had retired in September. Campbell-Bannerman in a speech at Stirling in November proclaimed a 'step by step policy' towards Home Rule, a scheme immediately repudiated by Rosebery at Bodmin who declared he would not serve under Campbell-Bannerman. Balfour expected a Liberal split would follow, but unknown to him Asquith and Grey had privately given their assent to the Home Rule policy and the principal effect of the Bodmin speech was to exclude Rosebery from office. Despite Chamberlain's advice to the contrary, Balfour decided to force the Liberals to take office in the hope that the divisions of the party, its 'little England' foreign policy and the prospect of a government shackled once more to Home Rule would bring the electorate to its senses before Parliament was dissolved. Campbell-Bannerman agreed to form an administration on 5th December.

IX · LIBERAL SWANSONG

(a) ACHIEVEMENT AND FRUSTRATION, 1905–9

SINCE he assumed the leadership in 1898, Campbell-Bannerman's stature had steadily grown. None of his rivals had the shrewdness, determination and devotion to the party to an equal extent. But he was old and not in the best of health and many assumed he would go to the Lords. Three Liberal Imperialists, in the so-called 'Relugas Compact', undertook to join the Ministry only if he did; they also demanded the Exchequer and Leadership of the Commons for Asquith, the Foreign Office for Grey and the Lord Chancellorship for Haldane. Campbell-Bannerman overcame this obstruction; he refused to go to the Lords and he persuaded Asquith to accept the Exchequer and deputy leadership unconditionally. Grey proved intransigent and the Foreign Office was offered to Lord Cromer; only when he refused did Grey consent to take it providing Haldane was in the Cabinet. Reid, the last Liberal Attorney-General, became Lord Chancellor; Haldane, whom the Prime Minister disliked, was given the War Office. Despite the failure of the Relugas Compact, the Liberal Imperialists had obtained important posts and Asquith was given a private assurance that a Home Rule Bill would not be introduced during the lifetime of the new Parliament. Some Liberals were disappointed by Rosebery's absence but it was recognised that his Bodmin speech made this unavoidable. Out of deference to him his son-in-law, Lord Crewe, a quiet, competent and moderate man, became Liberal leader in the Lords.

There were other eminent men in the new Cabinet, which greatly impressed contemporaries. Morley took the India Office, a difficult post when India was full of anti-European agitation. He was fussily old-maidish, pitying younger men who had not lived in Gladstone's golden days and overestimating his own importance. John Burns, the London labour leader, became President of the Local Government Board, an appointment greeted with great public enthusiasm.

Burns had, in fact, lost touch with working-class aspirations, and his vanity and stubbornness stood in the way of important reforms in his department, under the influence of whose permanent officials he fell. The combination of the Board's responsibilities was unfortunate; the Poor Law was essentially a deterrent service and the Board had obtained a reputation for obstructing thorough and expensive improvements of Local Authority health services. Burns did nothing to overcome this and the important measures of social reform were initiated by other Ministers.[1]

In particular they were promoted by two younger men who were anxious to make their mark politically. As President of the Board of Trade Lloyd George received a reward for his skill and prominence as a debater, particularly over the Education Bill. Of humble origin he had been brought up in an atmosphere of opposition to the Anglican landed establishment in Wales and he had become devoted to the cause of social reform. He had great powers as an emotional speaker, a thrusting and creative mind, fertile in political expedients, and was almost unequalled as a manager and user of men.[2] At the Board of Trade he was a great success; he undertook a census of industry and showed exceptional skill as a negotiator in industrial disputes. When Asquith became Prime Minister in 1908, Lloyd George was promoted to the Exchequer and became a political force in the country almost equal to Asquith himself. The two men, working together, were a formidable combination. Lloyd George's definition of his aims in comparison with those of socialism was, according to Churchill, 'Socialism attacks Capital, Liberalism attacks Monopoly.'

Winston Churchill, Lord Randolph's son, was, like Lloyd George, somewhat of an outsider and worked closely with him. Initially Under-Secretary for the Colonies, where, as his chief Lord Elgin was in the Lords, he had to act as spokesman for some of the government's most important policies, he moved in 1908 to the Board of Trade. He had left the Conservative party out of his devotion to Free Trade and for this he earned their hatred. He was unpopular in the Cabinet and reluctant to suffer fools, chief among whom he rated John Burns. He had an immense exuberance and loved the excitements of politics; he craved for great causes

---

[1] See below, p. 383.   [2] See below, p. 441.

and tended to disdain the routine. In his early thirties he had still much to learn and was not too proud to do so.

Immediately on taking office Elgin suspended the Chinese labour scheme and Parliament was dissolved. The Election was held in January 1906. The campaigns reflected the controversial actions of the Unionist government; the Liberals pointed out the difference between the 'Big and Little Loaf' and aged workmen who claimed to remember the Hungry Forties testified to the horrors of Protection. The Conservatives regarded as a dirty trick without parallel the Liberal exploitation of the Chinese labour scheme; posters were displayed of manacled Chinese slaves in attitudes of piteous supplication. The outcome was the delayed result of the late 19th-century franchise extensions and of the natural swing in politics that had been temporarily checked by the excitements of the first part of the South African War; for the first time the working class effectively voted for a more Radical policy. The decline of the Conservative party organisation since 1901 was an important factor. The Liberals obtained 377 seats, which gave them an overall majority of eighty-four; the Unionist M.P.s fell to 157; Balfour lost his seat in Manchester; only in Birmingham did the Unionists actually gain votes and the majority of the new M.P.s were Tariff Reformers, which suggested that their views were not a fundamental cause of the defeat. The Editor of the *Observer*, J. L. Garvin,[1] called for an end of 'the Byzantine theory of Unionist leadership, the theory of speechless loyalty to an hereditary succession' and although Balfour got back at a by-election, Chamberlain might have seriously contested the party leadership had it not been for his paralytic stroke in July 1906.[2] The Irish Party, now more strongly organised under Redmond, won eighty-three seats.[3] The real sensation, however, was the emergence of a new Fourth Party. The Labour Representation Committee obtained twenty-nine M.P.s and received the invariable support of twenty-four others elected with Liberal help. The new Labour party still remained a special interest group and, lacking clear leadership, not a particularly effective one. To show its complete independence of the

---

[1] An admirer and biographer of Chamberlain.
[2] Probably attributable to his exertions during the celebrations of his seventieth birthday. Through his son Austen he continued to exert considerable influence and died in 1914.   [3] See above, p. 318.

government it sat on the Opposition benches. Its members received a salary of £200 a year. They were not revolutionaries; mostly moderate men, they were flattered by their membership and their courteous reception, but to the other parties they were seen as a portent and even the Conservatives appreciated that their grievances must be taken seriously or votes would be lost to them at the next election.

The new Commons was a great contrast to its predecessors. It had fewer rich men, fewer Anglicans, over 300 new members, many of whom were intellectuals, journalists and university lecturers. They came full of hope and Campbell-Bannerman encouraged them and trained them far more effectively than Asquith could have done. The new Premier quickly asserted his mastery of the House and humiliated Balfour, which as a leader of a divided party before the election he had never been able to do. But the new members were aware of a growing sense of frustration, which was to do the Liberal party lasting harm. They saw the need of convincing the electorate that the Liberals were the party of progress, for only in this way could a slide to socialism be averted, but firmly in the way stood the Conservative-dominated House of Lords.

The constitution theoretically assigned to the Lords the function of a moderating and revising chamber; Balfour himself had described them as a theatre of compromise. Since 1892, however, they had been remarkably one-sided, wrecking Liberal bills and passing Conservative ones without demur. Their action may have been justifiable in 1892-95 when the Liberals were dependent for their majority on the Irish and when many of the bills put forward could be claimed as being undesired by the electorate. In 1906 there was no doubt where the electorate's sympathies lay, but in a speech at Nottingham during the election Balfour warned that 'the great Unionist Party should still control, whether in power or whether in opposition, the destinies of this great Empire'. He believed the Lords would be strengthened by the course he proposed they should follow. Measures were chosen with care; bills sponsored by the Labour party or of obvious social value passed untouched, even when revision might have been desirable; bills dealing with land or designed to help a particular Liberal interest group were mangled or rejected. The outcome was frustration for the Liberals and a growing impression that they were ineffectual, but remarkably little bad feeling in the country where the prestige of the peerage, whose wealth was now increasingly fortified by business interests or American heiresses, remained high. In retrospect the action of the Lords seems short-sighted; they were creating a situation that no government worthy of its salt could find tolerable and they were fortunate in that they confronted so essentially moderate a man as Asquith. As Ensor has indicated, Balfour and Lansdowne, convinced that Britain owed her greatness to patrician rule and that the true function of the lower classes was to support the governing families, could only regard with alarm the type of person who was now sitting in the Commons and even in the Cabinet. To the Conservative leaders it seemed unlikely that they could have the disinterested approach and the breadth of vision that was necessary for the collective exercise of sovereignty. In so using the powers of the House of Lords they felt that they were merely exercising their customary and legal privileges.

Meanwhile, despite difficulties in passing legislation, the Liberal Ministry was proving it could govern effectively. Although many of its members were opposed to imperialism, it could not escape from imperial problems. Asquith argued successfully for the honouring of existing Chinese labour contracts but no fresh recruitment was allowed; the Transvaal when it secured self-government expelled all Chinese labourers. The Boers were dissatisfied with the constitution granted by the Conservatives in 1905; in a forceful fifteen-minute speech Campbell-Bannerman convinced the Cabinet that the former republics should be given complete self-government and dominion status. Universal suffrage was granted for the white population; English and Afrikaans were given equal status as languages in the Transvaal; although the English were more numerous than the Dutch, they tended to support Dutch politicians such as Botha and Smuts who reciprocated the government's attitude of reconciliation. An even bolder experiment in 1907 was the granting of self-government to the completely Dutch population of the Orange Free State. The government's moderation paid; the Boers showed readiness to unite all four colonies, under Milner's guidance, into a single State. Delegates met at Durban in 1908 to devise a

constitution, which the four legislatures enacted in 1909 as did
the British Parliament. Union came into force in 1910.
There can be little doubt that the settlement was a wise one,
even though it proved impossible in 1910 to insist on rights
and privileges for the non-white population. It ensured that
South Africa remained faithful to Britain during two world
wars. At the time, however, the granting of self-government
to the Boers was bitterly criticised by the Conservative party:
Balfour spoke of it as 'the most reckless experiment ever tried
in the development of a great colonial policy'.

The Lords passed the Trade Disputes Bill of 1906 which in
effect reversed the Taff Vale and *Quinn* v. *Leatham* decisions,
in accordance with the report of the Royal Commission which
Balfour had appointed.[1] A very complicated bill had been
introduced in the Commons which the Trades Union M.P.s
rejected as too involved and introduced a measure of their
own, exempting the Unions from all actions for tort arising
from strikes and redefining peaceful picketing. It even
sanctioned the breaking of a contract by a strike. The
lawyers were horrified but the Prime Minister decided that
the Trades Union measure should be adopted, which won
him warm Radical support. It was believed that the Unions
would use their exceptionally privileged position with
moderation, a belief on the whole justified. When there were
a number of serious strikes in 1911, however, the Liberals were
blamed for a dangerous and irresponsible piece of demagogy.
This was unfair for the Conservatives had had the opportunity
to amend the Bill in the Lords but judged it expedient to let
it through unscathed.

Balfour urged drastic treatment of the Liberals' Education
Bill of 1906[2] which aimed at forcing the surrender of the
majority of the voluntary primary schools by forbidding
denominational teaching in schools receiving government aid.
In practice the 1902 Act had not been as favourable to the
Anglicans as the nonconformists asserted it would be and the
new bill was clearly a piece of partisan legislation which
aroused little interest in the country. The Lords distorted it
by cleverly-worded amendments and the government had
to admit defeat and withdrew it. Campbell-Bannerman
asserted 'a way will be found, by which the will of the people,

[1] See above, p. 368.   [2] See above, p. 356.

expressed through their elected representatives in this House will be made to prevail'. Believing the Lords would only dare to reject one per Session, a bill to abolish plural voting at elections was sent up but returned on the grounds that it ought to be accompanied by a redistribution of seats. It was difficult to arouse enthusiasm on this score when the fact that the Trade Disputes Act had become law suggested the responsiveness of the present franchise to people's wishes. In 1907 four Bills dealing with land reform in the three kingdoms were rejected or mangled by the Lords. The Liberals were furious; Lloyd George made his famous remark that the House of Lords was not, as the Conservatives claimed, 'the watchdog of the Constitution, but Mr Balfour's Poodle', and the Commons passed resolutions to restrict the Lords' veto to the duration of a single Parliament. The Lords continued as before and it became increasingly evident to the Cabinet that a conflict must be provoked on an issue calculated to arouse national feeling. The comparative poverty of many Liberal members made them reluctant to risk a dissolution until they were reasonably certain of victory. The sole alternative was 'filling up the cup'.

Lloyd George meanwhile had been promoting some useful and non-contentious legislation at the Board of Trade. The Workmen's Compensation Act of 1906[1] extended Chamberlain's act of 1897 to include all fully-employed manual workers, and loss of work through industrial diseases entitled a worker to benefits in the same way as did accidents. A Merchant Shipping Act of the same year was prompted by the large numbers of foreign seamen in British service. Pilots' licences were confined to British subjects and higher standards of food and accommodation were stipulated in the hope that more British would be attracted. Foreign ships using British ports had to comply. The Patents Act was also protectionist. Many foreign firms took out patents in England which they had no intention of working there in order to prevent British firms from copying their methods and machinery. New patents had to be worked within three years or they lapsed. In 1908 Lloyd George created the Port of London Authority to take over the work of the large number of small private concerns operating the port, which had restricted its develop-

[1] See above, p. 329.

ment. He conducted the difficult negotiations with skill.

There was considerable concern at this period over the 40 per cent of the volunteers during the South African war who were rejected on the grounds of physical unfitness. An Inter-Departmental Committee on Physical Deterioration, set up in 1904, painted a depressing picture of the health of the nation. Low wages and large families and the consequent inadequate food and bad living conditions resulted in a mortality rate among young children as high as fifty years earlier, and in the wretched physical conditions of many of the survivors. Local authorities provided milk depots in poor districts from 1899 onwards, health visitors were appointed in many areas and school meals were being provided by charitable organisations. This last service was given statutory recognition in 1906 when authorities were permitted to spend not more than the product of a halfpenny rate on providing meals. The service expanded rapidly and by 1910 more needy children were being fed in London by the education committee than by the Poor Law. In 1907 the medical inspection of schoolchildren was authorised and although treatment was left to parents it marked an important stage in the assumption of State responsibility. Herbert Samuel, Under-Secretary at the Home Office, was responsible for introducing Borstals in 1907 for the treatment of young offenders and for the institution of the Probation Service. He consolidated existing legislation in the Children's Act of 1908 and extended it to cover not only cruelty but also negligence. In these ways the responsibility of the community as a whole for its children was at last recognised.

Haldane at the War Office was responsible for the second great series of Liberal Army reforms.[1] His post was one of particular difficulty in Liberal Cabinets committed to retrenchment and on principle indifferent to the Army, and Campbell-Bannerman believed he had entrapped a colleague he disliked, having suffered himself in the same position. His own considerable influence over the left wing of the party alone could have induced a change of attitude at a time when the need for an efficient and expanded Army was vital. Like Cardwell, however, Haldane saw the financial restrictions as a challenge. Although Lord Roberts advocated conscription on the continental model, most Englishmen, especially

---

[1] See above, p. 213.

Liberals, found the idea repugnant and Haldane hoped to make it unnecessary by a great expansion of the trained reserve.   The Territorial and Reserve Forces Act authorising this was passed in 1907 and by appointing Lord Esher, a close friend of the King's, as chairman of the committee to organise the new Territorial Army, he secured Edward VII's valuable social and personal influence.   The landed gentry were linked with the new regiments, compounded of Yeomanry and Volunteers with engineer and artillery units, and transport and supply services, by means of County Associations under the presidency of the Lord Lieutenant.   It was the skeleton of a real army, organised in divisions and brigades and capable of rapid mobilisation and expansion in time of war.[1]   The ancillary O.T.C. Movement in public and grammar schools was also a great success.

The Territorial Army formed the second line.   In the regular Army some reorganisation took place, although the Cardwell system was preserved on the basis of seventy-two infantry battalions at home, with appropriate support from other arms, and seventy-two abroad garrisoning the Empire, especially India and Egypt.   The troops at home formed an expeditionary force ready for rapid mobilisation which was a key factor in stemming the German advance in 1914.   The best generals supported Haldane's schemes and he was able to implement them despite much Commons criticism.   There was all-party support, however, for the creation of a General Staff which helped to standardise forces and equipment throughout the Empire.   Asquith, once he became Premier, gave firm support to the Committee of Imperial Defence,[2] whose membership included Esher and Balfour.   It appointed numerous subcommittees which gave scope to the professional members and enhanced the value of the secretariat.   Although the Navy could have been larger, it is untrue to suggest, as was alleged in 1914, that Britain entered the war unprepared.

At the Treasury Asquith proved efficient.   He inherited a department cast in a Gladstonian mould that regarded as its prime duty the enforcement of economy on other parts of the government.   In his 1907 Budget he distinguished between

[1] Kitchener condemned the new force as a mob of playboys who would fail in the hour of danger and contaminate the morale of regular units.   He refused to use it as the basis of his new army in 1914.   See below, p. 424.

[2] See above, p. 358 and below, p. 415.

earned and unearned income for the first time for tax purposes, 9d. being levied on the former for taxpayers with less than £2,000 a year and at the existing rate of 1s. on the latter. All his Budgets showed cuts in naval and military estimates, producing surpluses that were used to reduce the remaining food taxes and to accelerate debt redemption. His 1908 Budget, introduced after he came Prime Minister, included Old Age Pensions, a matter more than due for settlement.[1] They were the first relief payments to be made directly by the government and their object was to withdraw all but the destitute aged from the Poor Law. Those over 70 who had an income of less than £21 a year were to receive 5s. a week, 10s. if married, and a reduced amount was payable for incomes up to £31 a year. On both sides of the House it was described as inadequate but as Churchill pointed out, 'We have not pretended to carry the toiler on to dry land; what we have done is to strap a life belt around him.' It had been imagined that such a measure would discourage the poor from saving but it was evident from the unexpected number who came forward to claim the new pensions that there was, as Lloyd George observed in 1911, 'a mass of poverty and destitution in the country which is too proud to wear the badge of pauperism'. Flora Thompson's Lark Rise spoke of the effect of the new pensions:

. . . life was transformed for such aged cottagers. They were released from anxiety. They were suddenly rich. Independent for life! At first when they went to the Post Office to draw it, tears of gratitude would run down the cheeks of some . . . and there were flowers from their gardens and apples from their trees for the girl who merely handed them the money.

Asquith had succeeded to the premiership on 6th April. Campbell-Bannerman's health had been failing for some time and as deputy-leader Asquith had had to deal with many of the details of running the party and the government and doing so with such skill that he was the inevitable and unchallengeable successor. The party had been losing in by-elections and it was widely felt that stronger leadership was required. Campbell-Bannerman died later in the month. He was a popular figure; every section of the party, as well as the Irish and Labour members, all trusted him and the King had found

[1] See above, p. 330.

him far more agreeable than Balfour. He was tolerant, warmly sympathetic with the crusade against poverty and was able to secure the smooth running of a government containing almost too many talents. It is unlikely that Asquith would have managed as well and the success of the Campbell-Bannerman administration was an almost essential prerequisite to that of Asquith's own.

Of Yorkshire nonconformist background, Asquith had become a reasonably successful barrister who had rapidly impressed the party when he entered Parliament and who had become a distinguished Home Secretary in 1892, when still in his early forties. He had shown exceptional administrative ability, distinguished parliamentary powers, precision, shrewdness and soundness of judgment that flourished best when he was in office. His natural gravity was lightened when he married in 1894 the gay and brilliant Margot Tennant who carried him into the social whirl of high society. His work since 1905 had confirmed and strengthened his talents and now at fifty-five he was destined to hold the premiership for the longest continuous period since Lord Liverpool. His ability to transact business swiftly and almost effortlessly enabled him to survive a series of crises that would have killed lesser men; he did not provide dynamic leadership but tactful and effective co-ordination of day-to-day business.

The spark of genius which gave the government not merely distinction but dynamism was provided by Lloyd George who succeeded Asquith at the Exchequer and was in practice the second man in the government. He balanced Asquith's moderation with his own Radicalism and although his elevation was regarded by the working class as a pledge of progress he had impressed the business community by his conciliatory reasonableness. The Cabinet was also strengthened by the promotion of Churchill to the Board of Trade, Runciman to the Board of Education and McKenna, a first-rate administrator who promised to co-operate with Fisher, to the Admiralty. Apart from Burns the only weak member of the Cabinet was Herbert Gladstone at the Home Office, who embarrassed the government by his handling of an important Roman Catholic procession and was persuaded to go to South Africa as the first Governor-General in 1910, when Churchill took his place.

At the Board of Trade Churchill was responsible for the eight-hour day in the mines, the first statutory limitation of the hours of men apart from those associated with safety restrictions on the railways, a measure attributable to working-class pressure in Parliament. Trade Boards were established to enforce, by negotiation with employers and employed, just minimum wages in the 'sweated trades.' The evils had been exposed by Beatrice Webb in the 1880's but government reluctance to intervene was not overcome until the *Daily News* organised two revealing exhibitions. The first trades covered were tailoring, the making of paper boxes, of lace and of chains; the system was extended in 1913.

In 1909 a Housing and Town Planning Act laid down for the first time standards that contributed to the improvement of the national health. Hitherto housing acts had been chiefly concerned with destruction; this act aimed at creating a better environment, though the higher amenities were invariably lacking. Large local authorities began to establish municipal housing estates and by-laws governed the activities of private enterprise.

One great public service remained unreformed during the period. Much prized in the early 19th Century as an antidote to revolution the Poor Law was still permeated with the Utilitarian doctrines as interpreted by Chadwick.[1] The workhouses had an evil reputation among the poor although conditions had greatly improved, especially since the appointment of men such as Crooks and Lansbury of the Labour party and numerous women as members of Boards of Guardians. Books and toys were allowed in 1891; in 1892 the men were given tobacco and in 1894 the women tea. The treatment of children had much improved although pauper children continued to be educated in 'barrack schools' rigorously separated from the rest of the community, in some instances up to 1929. Boarding out began in 1867, sometimes in institutions such as Dr Barnado's. A revolution had taken place in the treatment of the sick. Not until 1864 were Guardians permitted to supply cod liver oil and quinine which were regarded as too expensive for paupers, but a severe cholera outbreak in workhouses in 1866 led to the creation of Poor Law Infirmaries in London and the larger towns, in effect an embryonic national hospital service. Their facilities

---

[1] See above, p. 93.

were open to all-comers in 1883. With the better understanding of disease and the great advances in surgery made
possible by anaesthetics and then antiseptics, the new hospitals
were in urgent demand for the growing population and they
were virtually State hospitals by 1905. Environmental
improvements had largely eliminated typhoid and cholera
but T.B. had taken their place as 'the most pauperising of all
diseases' and was responsible for about one-seventh of the
total cost of the Poor Law. For the most part, however,
dislike of the Poor Law, even of its medical service, resulted
in a reluctance among sufferers to seek early treatment and
consequently increased the risk of infection. The Poor Law
Commission proposed that district medical officers should
seek out cases of serious sickness among the poor and when Dr
Newsholme became Chief Medical Officer at the Local
Government Board some progress was made. He held that
'disease more often causes poverty than poverty disease'.

Several investigations towards the end of the 19th Century
indicated that the Poor Law was the dreaded though inevitable resort of a large number of people through no fault of
their own. The University Settlement of Toynbee Hall in
Whitechapel, started in 1884 with the admirable aim of
helping the rich to understand the poor, enabled a number of
men later to be prominent in social reform, such as Beveridge,
Morant, Tawney and Attlee, to obtain invaluable experience
which stood them in good stead. A social inquiry of enormous
importance was made by Charles Booth and published as the
seventeen volumes of *Life and Labour of the People of London*
between 1886 and 1903. He established, by careful analysis,
that one-third of the population of the capital, about a million
people, were on or below the poverty line which he set at £1
a week. He showed that the proportion of paupers among the
elderly advanced rapidly with age and that in addition to large
families, intermittent or casual employment was a fundamental cause of poverty. Rowntree's *Study of Town Life*,
a survey of York published in 1901, strikingly confirmed his
conclusions. He proved that the death rate among the
poor was double that of those who were better off.[1]

Public concern mounted and Balfour appointed a Royal
Commission on the Poor Law just before he resigned. Its

[1] He supplemented his original study by surveys in 1936 and 1950.

immediate occasion was the conviction of the responsible civil servant, J. S. Davy, that it had departed from the guiding principles of 1834, but the Commission ranged over the whole background of life and labour of the poor and aimed at establishing how public relief could best improve matters. Under the chairmanship of Lord George Hamilton and with a membership that included, in addition to civil servants, Octavia Hill, Charles Booth, Beatrice Webb and George Lansbury, it interviewed hosts of witnesses and conducted valuable surveys. In 1909 two Reports were produced. The majority wished to patch up the existing structure, renaming it Public Assistance, urging complete separation of the various types of paupers and improvements in the treatment of the sick, the children and the aged. It was to be administered by County Councils; the old Boards of Guardians were to go – reforms that were largely implemented in 1929.[1] The Minority Report, largely the work of the Webbs, was a revolutionary document. The whole structure was to be broken up and the country's resources were to be so organised that no one could fall below minimum standards of life. Detention colonies would take care of the idle and public works programmes were to come into effect in times of unemployment.

The failure of Burns to adopt either report was the greatest 'non-event' of the period. Prejudice died hard, the calm self-confidence of the Webbs' Report alienated many sympathisers, while the distractions of Pensions and National Insurance – both invaluable measures which removed the fear of the workhouse from many – the Constitutional Crisis, Home Rule and War left little enough time to mobilise public opinion. Burns claimed he could do all that was necessary and improvements took place in the care of children, who had to be boarded out after 1915, in the opportunities to take outdoor relief and in the institutions themselves. But much remained for criticism: the workhouses were the 'gaol as well as the goal of poverty' as Lloyd George put it and too much of the spirit remained that Lansbury had detected when he had first visited Poplar Workhouse as a Guardian in 1892, '. . . everything possible was done to inflict mental and moral degradation . . . of goodwill, kindliness, there was none.'

---

[1] See below, p. 502.

(b) THE CONSTITUTIONAL CRISIS, 1909–11

The British Press and public had periods of intermittent concern about Britain's defensive position and the identity of possible aggressors. Tirpitz's naval preparations, themselves partly spurred on by Britain's own, made many people afraid of Germany, although a growing number, encouraged by such books as Norman Angell's *The Great Illusion* (published 1910) were convinced that war, even if victorious, would be disastrous to the economy and that every effort should be made to prevent the further growth of tension. It is possible that Fisher's departure from the Admiralty in 1909 may have temporarily reduced it. The Liberal reduction of the Cawdor programme[1] in 1906, however, had deprived Britain of her great lead in Dreadnoughts over Germany and in 1908 McKenna asked for eighteen over the next three years. He was opposed by Lloyd George and Churchill and in order to justify a smaller number the Ministers had to state publicly what was known of the German position. This caused serious alarm; the Opposition demanded that eight battleships be laid down at once and in the music halls the chorus was taken up 'We want Eight and we won't wait.' The hysteria lasted well into the summer and has been attributed to various causes. The government gave in; eight ships were built at once and five during each of the next two years. They were to provide the basis of Jellicoe's Grand Fleet but the irony was that many of them were never, ironically, to fire a shot in war. Fisher's concentration on Dreadnoughts meant the Navy was starved of smaller convoy ships; fortunately Tirpitz had had the same lack of foresight.

The increased naval expenditure and the unexpected costliness of Old Age Pensions which had been introduced without any accurate idea of the numbers involved,[2] meant that £15 m. had to be found in 1909 by extra taxation. Lloyd George saw the opportunity to introduce taxation changes of a truly radical nature which in themselves would constitute an important measure of social reform and which, as part of a finance bill, it was expected the Lords, according to tradition, would not reject. Liberal frustration with the

---

[1] See above, p. 358.
[2] It appeared, possibly through dishonesty, that 1 in 25 of the population of Ireland was over 70, whereas the figure for England was 1 in 88.

Lords was mounting to dangerous heights; their main measure
of the 1908 Session had been a carefully framed Licensing Bill
which had received much non-party support. Its aim was
to accelerate the effects of Balfour's Act of 1904 but a Conservative party meeting in the Lords had caused it to be
rejected out of hand. The Government had completed
almost all their non-contentious programme and were faced
with the certainty of the Lords' obstruction on measures such
as Home Rule and Welsh Disestablishment which they had
promised their supporters. Unless the Lords' veto could be
broken the government would become ridiculous and it is
difficult to see how anything but the rejection of a finance
bill could have brought matters to a head. As Jenkins has
established in *Mr. Balfour's Poodle* there is no real evidence that
Lloyd George framed his Budget as a deliberate trap, although
the land clauses were certainly provocative. As Conservative
opposition mounted, however, he saw the opportunity,
remarking to Masterman, 'I am not sure we ought not to
hope for its rejection. It would give us such a chance as we
shall never have again.'

Lloyd George described it as a 'War Budget' 'for raising
money to wage implacable warfare against poverty and
squalidness', and he introduced some new measures that were
intended to be the beginning of the campaign. To provide
work for the unemployed and to save the roads from further
deterioration under the weight of the new motor traffic he
instituted the Road Fund, provided from a new tax on petrol
and from motor licences. To help the unemployed to find
work and to assist the better deployment of labour, a national
system of labour exchanges[1] was to be set up and the economy
of the countryside was to be helped by a new Development
Commission which was to promote forestry, experimental
farms and agricultural education. Income-tax payers with
less than £500 a year were to receive an allowance of £10 per
child under 16. The additional money necessary was to be
raised by increasing tobacco, spirits and liquor licence duties
(the latter a pious gesture to Liberal traditions); by the
increase of income tax to 1s. 2d. in the pound, a clear indication

---

[1] They were originally the idea of the Webbs and Churchill persuaded the
Cabinet to accept them. They were an effective test both of the need and the
willingness to work, and promoted the flexibility and fluidity of labour. Working
men were initially suspicious but soon came to value them.

that it was now accepted as a fundamental tax rather than a temporary expedient, by the introduction of Super Tax on incomes over £3,000 and by a large increase of the Stamp Duties. Increases in direct taxation were always regarded as objectionable by the Conservatives but the proposed new land taxes were particularly a fighting matter, as Lloyd George possibly hoped they would be. To the old governing classes land was peculiarly sacrosanct as the most fundamental type of private property, respect for which was the basis of the Englishman's traditional liberties; on the other hand to the Radicals the great landowners had alienated part of the birthright of the people as a whole, for whose benefit land ultimately should be held in trust. In particular it was held that the value of land had frequently been enhanced as a result of industrial development and if only part of the 'unearned increment' had been devoted to the provision of amenities urban conditions would have been greatly improved. It was now proposed to place a 20 per cent duty on the increase in site value when land changed hands, to levy a duty on land held back from development until a high price was reached and to tax landowners' mining royalties and way leaves. These taxes would involve a complete valuation of all land in the country, a process which landowners would find exceedingly troublesome. Their yield was small, the cost of collection high and Lloyd George himself discarded them in 1920 but their value as political irritants was enormous. They ensured bitter opposition from the Conservatives who also feared the Budget would remove the revenue motive for a tariff and would lead to more dangerous Socialist measures. They held it to be a confiscatory measure actuated by class hatred and spite.

In the Commons the Budget was fought bitterly; divisions were frequent and old Fourth Party techniques[1] were adopted to spin out debates. Balfour particularly condemned the illegality of inserting a Valuation Bill into a Bill for raising revenue.[2] Outside the House a Budget Protest League was formed and another league to defend it. Although many members of the Cabinet were unhappy about the Budget, Asquith supported Lloyd George and the government's determination held firm. Much of the landowners' protest

[1] See above, p. 265.   [2] See below, p. 392.

could be readily represented as that of rich men attempting to dodge their fair share and Lord Rothschild was so ill advised as to figure prominently in meetings and petitions. Lloyd George conducted a tremendous campaign in the country, skilfully concentrating on the landowners, whom he designated 'the Dukes', and ridiculing them with such telling effect that the general public knew exactly whom to blame when the Budget was rejected by the Lords. At Limehouse in July he pointed out 'a fully equipped duke costs as much to keep up as two Dreadnoughts; and dukes are just as great a terror and they last longer', and on the possibility of rejection he asked, 'Should five hundred ordinary men, chosen accidentally from among the unemployed, override the judgment, the deliberate judgment of millions of people who are engaged in the industry which makes the wealth of this country?' Such remarks seemed to be deliberate taunts.

The Lords' right to amend money bills had been declared null in 1689 but they had often made use of their right to reject them before 1860. In 1861 Gladstone had incorporated all financial measures in a single bill[1] and since then it had been virtually accepted that the Lords left financial matters entirely to the Commons, merely signifying their assent to Budgets as a matter of form. Even in the autumn Asquith thought it inconceivable that the Lords would so upset the established balance of the constitution as to reject it but Balfour and Lansdowne had already decided that the Budget was so revolutionary and unprecedented that the government should be forced to obtain a specific mandate from the people for it. They apparently thought it unlikely that the government would so upset the constitutional balance in return as to curtail the powers of the Lords. An appeal by the King to exercise restraint fell on deaf Conservative ears.

On 4th November the Budget left the Commons after a final division of 379–149 and was rejected by the Lords on the second reading by 350 votes to 75 on 30th November. Two days later Asquith passed a resolution through the Commons 'That the action of the House of Lords in refusing to pass into law the financial provisions made by this House for the service of the year is a breach of the Constitution and a usurpation of the rights of the Commons.' Parliament was dissolved and a

___

[1] See above, p. 193.

General Election arranged for January 1910. Asquith approached the King on the question of creating peers to swamp the Conservative majority in the Lords, but the King, following the precedent of the first Reform Act, would not commit himself until after a second General Election, particularly as a very large number of creations would be involved.[1] Lloyd George had been in the forefront hitherto, now Asquith was in his element defending with all his legal precision the traditions of the constitution and the rights of the Lower House.

Balfour had hoped to fight the election on Tariff Reform *v.* Socialist finance but the issue on the platforms inevitably became the Lords' veto on which it was difficult to make out a disinterested case that would hold water. Only a sweeping victory at the polls could really justify the rejection of a money bill. The election results suggested that had the crisis not occurred the Conservatives would probably have won the next normal election and would have been able to reverse the contentious measures perfectly legally. From a formidable majority over all parties in the old Parliament, the Liberals now had only a majority of two over the Conservatives and were really dependent on the eighty-two Irish and the forty Labour members. The Labour party's hopes of independence seemed doomed and many M.P.s cast votes reluctantly to keep the Liberals in power. The Irish had not liked the whisky duty in the Budget but they stipulated an immediate attack on the Lords, followed by a Home Rule Bill. The Conservatives claimed that Government actions were henceforth wholly determined by this bargain, which they held to be immoral. They maintained that neither of the parties who gave the Liberals their majority were loyal or responsible and both represented sectional rather than national interests. These beliefs were responsible for the growing bitterness of party politics. However, the unqualified success of Campbell-Bannerman's grant of self-government to the Transvaal had convinced many Liberal waverers that similar action would be successful in Ireland.

It was difficult to know how best to proceed.[2] It was generally though inaccurately assumed that the King had

[1] See above, p. 88.
[2] It was at this time that Asquith, parrying a question on what the government was going to do, made his famous reply 'We shall have to wait and see' which his enemies later alleged typified his whole attitude of mind.

agreed to the creation of peers, while Grey and others maintained that the composition as well as the powers of the Lords should be reformed, an idea later taken up by Lord Rosebery. Anxious to act speedily Asquith concentrated on the question actually at issue and promised reform of composition in the future. On 3rd April three resolutions were passed through the Commons suggesting absolute Commons control of money bills and a maximum duration of five years for Parliaments to prevent the Commons abusing their new privileges. The Budget was again passed through the Commons and the Lords, having made their protest, let it through without a division on 28th April.

The dispute came to a halt when the King died very suddenly on 6th May. Superficially he had been very popular; he had excelled at the ceremonial functions of monarchy, he had been accounted a good Liberal though in reality his outlook was as conservative as any elderly clubman's. He had been too much of a good European to be a truly English King, a role which his son and successor suited much better. George V had already visited the dominions and had unsophisticated middle-class tastes and habits. He created at once an impression of goodwill and impartiality, which helped to make him a symbolic father figure during the war. Then he made himself by his good sense and moderation a source of stability for the country, refusing party demands that he thought might harm the country and visiting areas that showed signs of unrest. In 1917 he emphasised his Englishness by adopting the surname of Windsor and insisting on the renunciation of German titles by those of his relatives who were resident in England. After the war his popularity, enhanced by effective tours and broadcasts, steadily increased and the example of his happy family life raised the monarchy to a place in the nation's hearts from which not even the abdication of Edward VIII could shake it.

Although George V had been acquainted with State papers during his father's reign and was well aware of the problems at stake in the constitutional crisis, Asquith's decision not to confront the new King with very delicate decisions immediately met with general approval. Liberal militants deplored it, but Asquith decided to proceed by means of a Constitutional Conference which met at Downing Street in mid-June.

Asquith, Lloyd George, Crew and Birrell faced Balfour, Austen Chamberlain, Lansdowne and Cawdor. The Irish and Labour members protested about their exclusion. Both sides were really the prisoners of their own extremists and there was no real chance of compromise. Balfour was prepared to go a very long way but ultimately he felt there were certain fundamentals in the constitution that must be safeguarded from whims of majorities; these should be submitted to a referendum. When the Liberals refused to include Home Rule among these, the Conservatives broke off negotiations, although Asquith had proposed a scheme whereby in the event of a dispute the two Houses should vote together, which in view of the huge Conservative majority in the Lords would mean the Liberals could only get their way when they had a large Commons majority. Some Conservatives were ready to settle the Irish question by negotiation to clear the way for tariff reform but Lansdowne, who had large estates in southern Ireland, was obdurate; recent Irish history held too many bitter memories for him.

Lloyd George in particular wanted compromise and suggested in August a coalition to settle a number of problems of national importance, including the powers of the Second Chamber, Home Rule, the remedying of social evils and an impartial inquiry into the fiscal system. He was willing to stay outside a coalition government if it would facilitate matters. For a moment agreement seemed possible but the Conservative back benchers were unhappy and Balfour would do nothing to split his party. During the negotiations, however, he formed a high opinion of Lloyd George which was possibly a decisive factor in the latter being able to form a government in 1916.[1]

Balfour had privately intimated to Lord Knollys, the King's secretary, that he was willing to form an administration to prevent the King being coerced into the creation of peers – which the Conservatives maintained put the Liberals morally out of court. Knollys fortunately did not pass Balfour's offer on and thus saved the monarchy from a possible act of constitutional folly that might well have imperilled its future.

The King meanwhile insisted that Asquith's Parliament Bill should be presented to the Lords before a dissolution took

[1] See below, p. 440.

place. It proposed that money bills as certified by the
Speaker would be passed by the Commons only; other bills
would be subject to a two-year suspensive veto by the Lords,
during which time they must be passed by the Commons in
three successive sessions; and, as proposed in Asquith's resolutions, there should be a five-year limit to Parliament. This
was to be the form of the Act when it finally passed. The
Lords placed the bill aside and Lansdowne introduced one
of his own which included certification by a joint committee
and a joint sitting after one year to determine contentious
bills, while matters of major importance should go to a referendum. The Liberals rejected the last proposal on the grounds
that it would deprive Parliament of its sovereignty and it was
difficult to convey the complexities of legislation to the
electorate. In practice the Liberals doubted whether the
preponderant English electorate would favour Home Rule.

The Lords also passed resolutions by Lord Rosebery which
aimed at reforming its composition by adding certain office
holders and life peers to representatives of the hereditary
peerage, but they cut little ice. Balfour in particular
thought a more representative Upper House would want more
power, not less. Meanwhile Asquith secured a promise of
peers from the King by threatening, if refused, to fight an
election on 'The King and the Peers versus the People.'
Asquith doubted the wisdom of another dissolution and feared
the matter was growing stale in the public mind. Indeed,
though political excitement was intense and bitter partisanship even spread into the London drawing rooms, the country
was a long way from revolution. A large number of people
had disliked one or other part of the Budget and did not view
the Lords' action as unduly scandalous. After a campaign
dominated by Asquith during which the Conservatives played
down Tariff Reform and the Lords Veto and fought on the
Home Rule issue, the result of the December General Election
was, with half a million fewer voters, almost an exact repetition of that of the previous January. Both sides were disappointed, but the public as a whole felt the question had
been decided. The Parliament Bill passed triumphantly
through the Commons and reached the Lords in May. A
long committee stage ensued during which numerous drastic
amendments were carried.

The revelation that the King had agreed to the creation of peers led to a sharp division in the Conservative party. Balfour, Bonar Law, Lansdowne and Long favoured surrender to avoid the creations; they became known as the 'Hedgers'. The 'Ditchers', vowed to 'no surrender', were originally organised by Lord Willoughby de Broke and attracted the support of Austen Chamberlain, F. E. Smith, Selborne, Salisbury and the octogenarian ex-Lord Chancellor, Halsbury, who was cheered to the echo at a banquet in his honour in July when he denounced compromise or capitulation. Only his family saved him from being drawn in triumph in his carriage through the West End.

The final debate in the Upper House in August was one of intense drama with the result in doubt until the end, even though Morley and Lansdowne warned that there would be a creation of peers and the King sent Knollys down to remove any possible uncertainty. The bill passed by a majority of seventeen. The act was a decisive one, establishing that the British Constitution is ultimately unicameral; since then the Lords have rarely rejected but have concentrated on amending legislation. Ironically it appeared evident that the Lords were fully justified in resisting the 1909 Budget because under the procedure of the new act it could not have been certified as a money bill, and to clarify the position the Budget in 1913 was divided into two parts, one purely financial, the other, which could be rejected, affecting general legislation. Asquith and most of the Liberals were glad no peer creations were necessary, although a list was drawn up containing many excellent names; as Churchill pointed out, they would have aided their legislative programme immensely. It had been a classical contest fought in a way that had greatly enhanced Asquith's reputation.

A constitutional matter of lesser importance but not without significance was the growth in the numbers and power of the Civil Service. It numbered 162,000 in 1911 against 50,000 in 1881 and the growing complexity of statutes meant that the filling in and interpretation of details largely lay with officials. Individual civil servants were in fact more makers of policy than were their responsible Ministers, for instance Morant in Education or McDonnell in Ireland while Llewellyn Smith and Sir Ernest Aves organised the details of labour exchanges and Trade Boards respectively. In a sense these men had greater power than most of the conspicuous political figures of the time.

(c) THE TIME OF TROUBLES, 1911–14

The Constitutional Crisis triumphantly over, Asquith and his colleagues might well have expected a smooth passage ahead, but troubles gathered about them. The Lords' last-ditch defence of their privileges, though not unconstitutional, had encouraged others to believe they could loudly assert what they felt to be their rights, even to challenging the fundamental basis of law and order without which no civilised society remains civilised. Strikers and suffragettes, Orangemen and Irish Nationalists all helped to promote an atmosphere of disorder so much reported on in the Press that foreign dangers crept up almost unobserved.

The slowness of Liberal social reforms, only one of which, Trade Boards, had dealt with wages, and the apparent ineffectiveness of the Labour party, led to a movement away from parliamentary action and towards strikes. This tendency was aggravated by the Osborne Judgment. W. V. Osborne, Secretary of the Walthamstow branch of the Amalgamated Society of Railway Servants, sued his union in 1908 for contributing to the Labour party out of its funds. Osborne denied that he was financed from capitalist sources although the Webbs asserted that he was. The case went to the House of Lords who declared, basing their judgment on the Act of 1876, that all political action by Trades Unions was illegal. This took the movement completely by surprise and was opposed by many distinguished lawyers. Sixteen M.P.s lost the salaries paid by their unions in consequence and the Labour party had to fight the 1910 Elections on a very tight budget which forced them to become largely dependent on Liberal financial support. An attempt to raise a voluntary fund from Trades Union members failed dismally. The Labour party pressed for legislation to cancel the Judgment, but the government did not make time until 1913. It should be added that in 1911 Labour M.P.s particularly benefited from the payment of an annual salary of £400 to all members.[1] The Trades Union Act of 1913 restored the right of unions to

---

[1] This was to ensure their support for the National Insurance Bill.

support political parties financially but under certain safe-guards. Political funds were to be kept distinct and a levy was to be made only if members agreed by secret ballot; any member who wished could contract out without suffering any disability. These safeguards were resented but made little difference to the amount of money actually received by the unions.

In the period 1910-14 Trades Union preference for direct action came to the surface. Apart from disappointment with the lack of parliamentary achievement, imperialism, which had absorbed and distracted, attention, had brought disillusion-ment, prices were rising although wages were stationary and the unions themselves were permeated by those ideas originat-ing in France, and owing much to Marx, called Syndicalism or Industrial Unionism. The function of Syndicalism, as James Conolly, the Irish Labour leader, put it, was 'to build up an industrial republic inside the shell of the political state in order that when that industrial republic is fully organised it may crack the shell of the political state and step into its place in the scheme of the universe.' The stuggle was a class war in which sympathetic strikes, lightning strikes and various forms of industrial sabotage would lead to a general strike. Many of the strikes of the period were straightforward wage demands but many owed much to an underlying spirit of discontent and to Syndicalism, and it was these in particular that prompted many of the union amalgamations that took place during this period.

The railways were an important area of strife. The com-panies would only negotiate with unions when directly ordered to by the government and their position was a particularly crucial one as the sole effective means of inland transport, just as the mines held a similar position as the sole effective source of power. Dislocation of these two industries would in the long run hold the country up to ransom. In 1910-14, a railway strike, in particular, could undermine the authority of the government itself and restrict its ability to maintain law and order. When a general strike eventually broke out in 1926, both industries had lost their paramount position.

An unofficial railway strike in the north-east during July 1910 was followed by trouble with the seamen and a com-pletely irresponsible strike in the Lancashire cotton industry over the precise work of a single grinder. The employers retaliated by lock-outs. In November a large strike, again over a trivial matter, occurred among the South Wales miners which exploded into violence at Ton-y-Pandy when a mob looted and terrorised the village for three days. Local police were unable to deal with the situation and after firm warnings Churchill, now Home Secretary, reluctantly sent troops from Salisbury Plain, an action whose violent consequences the miners greatly magnified and which they held against Churchill for a long time.

A seamen's strike in June 1911 which resulted in increased wages stimulated other unions to try their hand. There ensued a dock strike which paralysed the Port of London for a fortnight and led to savage rioting in Liverpool. Vans collecting essential goods for hospitals and children had to obtain passes signed by Tillett or Mann but Churchill provided a military convoy for anybody who wanted it. The greatest crisis came with the railway strike in August, which took place during a heat wave that increased the irritability of both sides. Asquith refused to permit negotiations because of the risk of war arising from the Agadir Incident, but foolishly did not explain this to the union leaders who ordered the strike to take place. Lloyd George stepped in and by appealing to the patriotism of both sides and by persuading them that he understood and was sympathetic to their respective positions, he brought the strike to an end on acceptable terms within forty-eight hours. Nevertheless a general strike seemed very near and everybody was alarmed and puzzled by the sudden disorder. One employer felt 'It is a revolution – the men have new leaders, unknown before and we don't know how to deal with them.'

Unrest continued into 1912 though it seemed to be past its peak. In March the miners were out on strike for a daily minimum wage, but the unity behind it was destroyed when the government suggested district minima, together with a joint negotiating board with a neutral chairman to settle disputes. This was embodied in the Wage Machinery Act of 1912, which proved to be of considerable benefit. A dock strike organised by Tillett and Mann's new National Transport Workers Federation was defeated by the organisation of a non union labour service by the Port of London Authority and the Conservative Press made great capital out of a light-ning strike of 6,000 railwaymen over a colleague's dismissal for drunkenness off duty. It was, they said, 'a strike for the right to get drunk'. There ensued a lull but in 1914 it was evident that the difficulties were beginning again. In 1913 J. H. Thomas had succeeded in uniting into the National Union of Railwaymen three out of the four railway unions, and his union with the transport workers and the miners formed the Triple Alliance later in the year whose aim was to synchronise the expiry of agreements and disputes. The railwaymen secured the support of their colleagues in what would be an unparalleled piece of intimidation if their demands were not met by December 1914.

The strikes embarrassed the Liberal party, as they made it quite clear that they were no longer the party of the people. However, they were not without remedies for the more glaring social evils and their most impressive contribution was the National Insurance Act of 1911. Ramsay Macdonald guaranteed the support of the Labour party, of which he was now leader, in return for the payment of M.P.s. The act represented an important advance towards collectivism although it was prompted by the complete inadequacy of the provision that the majority of the community could make for themselves. Those who could afford it, impelled partly by their dislike of the Poor Law, joined Friendly Societies, which had been recognised as early as 1793 and which, by acts of 1846 and 1875, had obtained legal status and a central registry. They were an essential part of Victorian life providing not only security but also good fellowship and colourful cere-monial. Their regular dues, however, were frequently too much for the casually employed and although by the beginning of the 20th Century they had some six million members and funds of over £40 m., less than half of the working population were even moderately covered against the effects of illness, and fewer than one in ten against unemployment, as Lloyd George pointed out in 1911. A pauper burial was seen as a mark of shame and other types of 'collecting societies' were in existence to guard against this, of which the largest were the Liverpool Victoria, the Royal Liver and the Scottish Legal. In addition burial insurance was part of the business of com-panies offering 'industrial assurance' of which the largest was the Prudential, which, founded after the cholera epidemic of 1848, was expanding at a time when many of the smaller societies were defaulting. In forming a State scheme the government was careful to take Friendly Society and similar schemes into account.

The scheme was based on that working in Germany since 1889. It was contributory: flat rate payments for flat rate benefits. Although some elements in the working class felt it should be free, like Old Age Pensions, the contributory principle removed the stigma of accepting charity and overcame the reservations of the wealthier half of the community. Compulsory contributions of 4d. per week were collected from each employee, to which his employer added 3d. and the State 2d. – hence Lloyd George's claim that the worker was obtaining 9d. for 4d. This provided the sick with doctoring, medicine and maintenance at ten shillings a week. It was crucial to obtain the full co-operation of the medical profession and although the British Medical Association was opposed and Lloyd George had to wear down many suspicions and guarantee the doctors' professional freedom, this was eventually secured. Under the supervision of local insurance committees a greatly superior service was provided, although hospitals were not included, and the average doctor obtained a much better income. The State had long taken some responsibility for environmental health services; this inclusion of personal medical services was of crucial importance and may be reasonably taken as the starting point of the Welfare State. It justified Lloyd George's claim in his 1909 Budget, that he was taxing 'the pleasures of the few in order to spare the sorrows of the myriad' to which Churchill had added that Liberalism was 'the cause of the left-out millions'.

The Friendly Societies, Trades Unions and insurance companies providing similar benefits had to be treated with care and most were brought into the scheme as 'Approved Societies'[1] to administer the maintenance benefits, though the doctors with their memories of contract service under them in the past demanded exemption. The organisation of the scheme was a great undertaking and the Ministers and civil servants responsible did not spare themselves. One of the

[1] They were required to have a minimum membership of 10,000 which excluded most Trades Unions.

junior members of the team called it 'A very exciting time . . . with something of the feeling of enthusiasm of one who has taken part in a sort of Charge of the Light Brigade.'

Health Insurance was specifically Lloyd George's contribution; the second part of the Act, insurance against unemployment experimentally for two and a quarter million men in the building, mechanical engineering, shipbuilding, ironfounding, vehicle construction and saw-milling trades, was the work of Churchill. $2\frac{1}{2}d$. per week was to be contributed by employer, employee and the State, in return for which men were to be paid $7s$. from the second to the fifteenth week of unemployment. Many believed the scheme would be heavily in debt, but before the Great War it had already made a handsome profit. Most other manual workers were included after the war.

Subsequent history has shown how very valuable the scheme, which Lloyd George saw as only a step towards fuller State responsibility, was to be, but at the time it was strongly criticised. It seemed to submit the citizen to a degree of bureaucratic control and interference which was trivial by present-day standards but in that less regimented age was regarded as iniquitous. Dislike of Lloyd George's triumph was an important factor in stimulating Conservative opposition, aided by the sensationalism of the popular Harmsworth newspapers. Lord Northcliffe, who was essentially a businessman and often used his enormous influence irresponsibly, tended to over-dramatise events and he had considerable influence in the Conservative party. Every popular prejudice or professional concern about some item of the scheme was fastened upon; deductions from wages were described as a monstrous oppression and duchesses urged the public not to 'lick stamps' (contributions were collected by means of stamped cards). The Act was passed but the behaviour of the Conservative party influenced others less responsible.

A substantial element in the Conservative party, particularly the Halsbury Club, as those who had resisted the Parliament Bill to the 'last ditch' called themselves,[1] was becoming discontented with Balfour's leadership. Three successive elections had been lost and with the next election not due until 1915, by which time in all probability the

[1] See above, p. 392.

government's popularity would have risen as a result of a successful settlement in Ireland, many foresaw Conservative exclusion from power for many years to come and in consequence felt frustrated and bitter. As was inevitable, Balfour was made the scapegoat; it was argued that Tariff Reform was the obvious vote winner for the party and he had failed to exploit it; it was argued that he had failed the party during the Parliament Act, although in retrospect he pursued the most sensible course. It might well have been argued that he should never have allowed the Lords to have got themselves into the position where their humiliation became necessary. Balfour maintained that his resignation in November 1911 was not influenced by the 'Balfour Must Go' campaign and that he could have clung to the leadership had he chosen, but despite his Fourth Party apprenticeship he was a man who, like Asquith, flourished more in office than in opposition and disillusioned by recent events was glad of the opportunity to depart. He remained in public life, 'by universal consent', as Aquith said, '. . . the most distinguished member of the greatest deliberative assembly in the world.'

His resignation came as a surprise and he had no obvious successor. Austen Chamberlain was a strong candidate, a man cast in his father's image (even to the eyeglass) but lacking his father's essential ruthlessness, without which no politician can rise to the top. 'He always played the game and always lost it,' as Churchill unkindly said of him. He was honourable, progressive and enlightened but as a Liberal Unionist difficult for the die-hard Conservatives to accept. An alternative candidate who commanded much support was Walter Long, ten years older, 'pure Squire Conservatism', not particularly intelligent, inclined to be impulsive, but widely respected as an ideal representative of those honourable members of county families who were the traditional backbone of the party. But his support came mainly from the back benches and it is therefore probable that had Chamberlain been ruthless enough he could have forced himself into the leadership. Neither candidate was particularly anxious for an open fight and the consequent weakening of the party during the Annual Meeting of the National Union of Conservative Associations, which was due the following week, but neither would withdraw. This provided the opportunity for a third candidate, who had been persuaded to come forward by Max Aitken, an able and wealthy young Canadian with a gift for political intrigue and journalism who had recently come to England.

Andrew Bonar Law was the son of a Presbyterian minister of Ulster origin who was serving in Canada. He was sent to Scotland to be brought up by relatives and in due course became a partner in William Jacks and Company, a prosperous firm of iron merchants. An M.P. in 1900, he soon established himself as an able debater, with a mastery of facts and figures and an adeptness in clinching his arguments. He was one of those speakers who was able to convince his audience that he had merely put into words their own thoughts. In the country he was hardly known at all in 1911 and he had never held Cabinet office. Nevertheless he impressed those who knew him: Lord Derby said of him to the King 'He has all the qualities of a great leader save one – and that is he has no personal magnetism and can inspire no man with real enthusiasm', but he almost certainly led the party more effectively than Chamberlain or Long could have done. Chamberlain feared that Long would intrigue against him if he were elected and he therefore proposed they should both stand down in Bonar Law's favour, to which Long reluctantly agreed. Perhaps the most curious and unlikely choice of leader the Conservative party has ever made, Bonar Law proved himself to be devoted to the party and a man of considerable administrative and parliamentary abilities. Asquith's jibe, that he was 'The Unknown Prime Minister', was less than fair. In 1911, however, he was very inexperienced and undoubtedly made mistakes that Balfour would have avoided; he found it necessary, to keep the party united, to run more with the extremists than his predecessor would have done, but he showed resolution and caution which made his position unchallengeable by 1914.[1]

The growing atmosphere of violence in politics was intensified by the actions of the Suffragettes. During the late Victorian period women had gradually asserted their equality

[1] As a widower who disliked social life he left the social side of Conservative politics to 'Lady Londonderry, a great hostess and, so the malicious averred, an unfailing political barometer. Austen Chamberlain once said he could always tell the state of his political fortunes by the number of fingers (2 to all 10) she gave him when they met.' (R. Blake: *The Unknown Prime Minister*.)

with men in rights and opportunities. The Married Women's Property Acts of 1870, 1882 and 1893 had given them full legal control of property they inherited or acquired; their educational facilities increased with good private schools and secondary education on equal terms with boys after 1902; the universities opened their doors – in the case of Oxford and Cambridge reluctantly – and they won their way into the medical and legal professions, and teaching. One privilege yet eluded them, the right to vote in parliamentary elections. J. S. Mill had introduced an unsuccessful amendment proposing female suffrage in 1867, but in local elections they made progress. If they were ratepayers they could vote for School Boards in 1870, for County Councils in 1888, for District Councils in 1894. They could be members of County Councils and Borough Councils in 1907 and most people assumed parliamentary franchise would follow in due course.

Progress was too slow, however, for the Women's Social and Political Union, founded in Manchester in 1903. Under its leader Mrs Emmeline Pankhurst and under the tutelage of Keir Hardie it forced itself into prominence in 1905 by violently interrupting a meeting addressed by Sir Edward Grey. The movement grew rapidly in numbers and militancy, its members specialising in interrupting Cabinet Ministers and padlocking themselves to fixtures. Its influence on the suffrage was initially favourable – hence the Act of 1907 – but after a while the public reacted against the violence of its tactics. In 1909 the women tried hunger strikes when in prison to force the authorities, who replied with forcible feeding through tubes, to release them. This was the signal for greater violence in 1911 and 1912. The King was roughly addressed by unknown women who denounced him as Tsar and Torturer even in Buckingham Palace itself. Asquith was a particular target – Lord Weardale, mistaken for him, was whipped at Euston; Redmond, in a carriage with Asquith in Dublin, was wounded in the ear by a hatchet, while on the golf links at Lossiemouth a group of women began to tear his clothes off him until his daughter intervened. Christabel Pankhurst organised crime and arson: letters in pillar boxes were ignited; empty houses, pavilions, grandstands were burned to the ground at various times; bombs were exploded and exhibits in picture galleries damaged. To counteract hunger strikes, as public opinion was unhappy about forcible feeding, McKenna, now Home Secretary, introduced the Cat and Mouse Act in 1913 which allowed women on hunger strike to be released and re-arrested when they had recovered their strength. On Derby Day, in the same year, Miss Davidson died from wounds received when she threw herself in front of the King's horse and such fanatic devotion made the authorities fear that sooner or later a murder would be committed. At a National Union of Teachers meeting in 1914 a woman declared that 'The Power of Tyranny is tempered by assassination.' It is difficult to know what the outcome would have been had not the war intervened, during which the women earned their vote by their devotion and self-sacrifice. Asquith was increasingly repelled by the women's tactics, as were most people, and although he introduced a suffrage motion on a free vote in 1912, he made no attempt to pursue the matter when it was rejected.

It was against a background of such extraordinary events that the government tried to fulfil their pledge to the Irish and thus began a sequence of events quite as extraordinary and a good deal more dangerous, during which the whole fabric of constitutional government was threatened and civil war seemed imminent. Men essentially reasonable apparently took leave of their senses when they crossed St George's Channel; Cabinet Ministers prepared for war, Privy Counsellors urged rebellion, the House of Lords contemplated dissolving the legal basis of the forces of the Crown, high-ranking officers divulged secrets, the mostly loyal Irish were refused what had been granted to the Boers of the Transvaal. The Ireland of 1912 was much better fitted to govern itself than it had been in 1886: it had had county councils since 1898 and successive acts had largely solved the agrarian problem. Time, however, was short. Redmond was a model of constitutional rectitude but his party, softened as most extremists are by the atmosphere of Westminster, was losing control over Irish opinion. The younger generation in Ireland was not prepared to accept half measures; some, such as Sinn Fein,[1] were openly hostile to the Irish Nationalists and wanted complete separation. Unless Home Rule was granted

[1] The name means 'ourselves alone'.

quickly, Irish resistance would become violent and Redmond could no longer afford to make concessions.

The opponents of Home Rule were sincerely convinced it was an unworkable proposition. Irish lawlessness was not now a serious objection but the feeling that granting it would be fatal to the integrity of the British Empire remained; if Ireland went, India would follow and the process could only mark the end of England's greatness. More specifically there was the problem of the ascendancy class, even though much Irish land had passed from their hands. Those who remained – and they included Lansdowne and many others prominent in the Conservative party – were convinced that their expropriation, probably without compensation, would follow Home Rule. It seemed unreasonable to abandon the loyalists to the tyrany of 'Papist peasants'. Balfour and Lansdowne believed the Union must be preserved but as the struggle ensued it was generally realised that, as Lord Randolph Churchill had seen in 1886, 'the Orange card was the one to play'.

The Irish Nationalists believed in the mystic unity of their country and also considered it would not be economically viable without its prosperous north-east corner, which had a quarter of the population and paid three-quarters of the taxation. This view was also shared by the Ulstermen themselves, who, encouraged by the Conservatives, saw the chance, by remaining part of the United Kingdom, to wreck the practical operation of Home Rule and make it impossible. Here was an unbridgeable gulf; Protestant, of Scots descent, different in character and outlook, a thriving industrial community, the Irish of the Belfast area were a tremendous contrast to their southern neighbours. Redmond was prepared to offer them anything short of complete exclusion; Ulster would accept nothing less.

In April 1912 the government introduced three contentious bills. The Female Suffrage amendment necessitated the withdrawal of a Plural Suffrage Bill and it was not reintroduced until the following year. The Welsh Disestablishment Bill followed the Home Rule Bill on its wearisome circuits; it detached the Welsh dioceses from the Church of England, allowed them to set up a representative governing body and transferred a proportion of their funds to the University of Wales and the County Councils. It was a symbolic gesture that gladdened the hearts of Welsh nonconformists. The Home Rule Bill was envisaged as the beginning of a federalist scheme which would provide a similar arrangement for other parts of the United Kingdom. The Parliament at Westminster was to deal with matters of imperial importance with a reduced Irish representation (42 against 100), while a new bicameral Parliament in Dublin would deal with home affairs, subject to the veto of the Lord Lieutenant. A complicated financial arrangement would last for so long as Ireland was unable to pay its way. There is little doubt that such a scheme would have been administratively feasible; the present constitution of Northern Ireland is very similar to it. The government held itself free to amend the Bill if necessary, which in practice meant, if the views of Ulster had to be accommodated.

Just how strong those views were was now to be made clear: the Ulstermen had acquired a leader of unlikely antecedents but of dynamic personality. Sir Edward Carson, a southern Irishman of Italian origin, had been Solicitor-General 1900–5. He was an eloquent and exceedingly prosperous barrister of great personal charm who was as unlike his followers as Parnell had been unlike his. A superb actor, he gave the impression of being a man of iron who would stop at nothing though in fact he was a good deal more moderate than many Conservatives or Orangemen. It is impossible to know what he would have done if Home Rule had been implemented in 1914. In September 1911 he had announced in a speech at Craigavon that in the event of Home Rule 'We must be prepared ourselves to become responsible for the government of the Protestant province of Ulster.' With the blessing of the magistrates, a Volunteer Force was organised and just before the Bill was introduced in the Commons 80,000 marched past him, Bonar Law and Walter Long at Balmoral, in Ulster.

Bonar Law committed himself to Ulster, in the belief that it was the only way to save the Union and to preserve the unity of his party. Of Ulster descent himself he was emotionally involved and this helps to explain such bellicose words as his speech at Blenheim in July 1912 when he said '. . . I can imagine no length of resistance to which Ulster can go in which I should not be prepared to support them and in which, in my belief, they would not be supported by the overwhelming majority of the British people.' Such words appear irresponsible on the part of a Privy Counsellor, but in Bonar Law's defence it may be said that true democracy is not only a question of majority decisions but also of minority rights: by the whim of a parliamentary majority the Ulster Protestants were to be delivered into the hands of their hereditary enemies. The Conservatives maintained that the issue had not been fairly presented in the December election of 1910 and it was, therefore, their duty to force a dissolution, as they would have been able to do had the Lords' veto still been intact. They were confident the English public as a whole did not want the coercion of Ulster. Bonar Law, therefore, more sensitive to his position in the party than his reputation in the country, spoke of the Irish policy as 'a conspiracy as treacherous as ever has been formed against the life of a great nation'. Balfour supported him: had he still been leader he would probably not have identified himself so much with the extremists but nobody could have prevented the mounting tide of bitterness.

Meanwhile the Bill proceeded on its first two circuits, with large majorities against it in the Lords. The Irish Nationalist leaders continued to maintain that the behaviour of Ulster was mere bluff; Asquith was inclined to agree and believed in the long run that the minority shared his own respect for the Constitution and would bow to the will of the majority. He made no firm attempts to start negotiations, refused to take up the Agar-Robartes Amendment of June 1912 to exclude permanently the four Protestant counties, nor would he exacerbate matters by prosecuting those who spoke or behaved seditiously (who in the former case could reasonably include the leader of the Opposition). From one who laid such emphasis on fighting within the framework of Parliament, the arrest of Bonar Law could well have alienated many powerful people and institutions in the country, from the King downwards. Asquith's policy was to 'wait and see', believing that in due course an opportunity for effective intervention would come. He was convinced of the logic of Ireland's continued unity and in any case was dependent on Redmond. Most contemporaries thought Redmond obstinate and unreasonable, believing his hold on Ireland to be the equivalent of Parnell's, but in practice he had no room for manœuvre. The failure of an Irish Transport Workers Union had led to

the creation of the Irish Volunteers under the auspices of Sinn
Fein, to keep the strikers out of mischief. The Irish Republican Brotherhood and the Irish Citizen Army also watched him
with vulture eyes, ready to swoop at the first sign of weakening.

At Westminster bad feeling was aroused when the Marconi
Scandal occurred in 1913. Lloyd George and Rufus Isaacs,
the Attorney-General, had speculated in the shares of the
American Marconi Company, of which Isaacs' brother was a
director at a time when the parent English Marconi Company
had tendered successfully for the contract to complete the
imperial wireless chain, a matter which was public knowledge
but not yet approved by Parliament. Isaacs denied in
Parliament having shares in the English company but made
no mention of his American interests. Without Bonar
Law's prior knowledge Carson and F. E. Smith accepted
briefs to defend the accused Ministers before a Select Committee and this prevented him from exploiting actions which if
not dishonest were imprudent to say the least. Lloyd George's
career was saved, but the affair increased party bitterness.

By the autumn of 1913 the exclusion of Ulster was being
seriously talked of by both parties, though neither Redmond
on one side nor Lansdowne on the other were prepared to
agree. Asquith began secret negotiations with Carson to see
if he would accept entrenched safeguards. The King urged
compromise, feeling that whether he gave his consent to the
Bill or not, he would offend half his subjects; Asquith assured
him the Royal Veto was out of date and it was his constitutional duty to stand by his Ministers, which led him to rebuff
the Conservative demand that he force a dissolution. Lloyd
George suggested the temporary exclusion of the Protestant
counties, which he hoped would allow both sides to adjust
themselves, but neither would contemplate it. This became,
however, the firm basis of a proposal made in March 1914 and
reluctantly acquiesced to by Redmond that counties could opt
out by a simple majority for six years, which of course could be
extended indefinitely if the Unionists won the next election.
But this, while less than fair to the substantial Protestant
minorities of Fermanagh and Tyrone, was, as Carson put it,
still 'a sentence of death' and the proposal was violently
rejected. Asquith may be criticised justifiably for not braving
Nationalist wrath and insisting on permanent exclusion, which

Bonar Law and Carson, more moderate than many of their followers, could have accepted. By allowing matters to drift, violence only became more inevitable.

If violence did occur, how reliable was the Army? Its officers were predominantly Unionist and a great number belonged to the Anglo-Irish ascendancy class, in particular the Director of Military Operations, Sir Henry Wilson, who was secretly advising the Ulster Volunteers and openly took the view that the Army must not be used to coerce Ulster. To prevent its use at all Lord Willoughby de Broke brought forward the idea, incredible in view of the international situation, that the Lords should refuse to pass the annual Army Act, on which military discipline depends. Bonar Law and Lansdowne seriously contemplated it but Balfour pointed out that it was a dangerous precedent in view of Labour unrest and wiser counsels prevailed. The government suddenly became alarmed, however, although it is still uncertain exactly why; the Unionists believed its actions to be deliberately provocative. Churchill, the First Lord, and Seely, the War Minister, concerted plans to undermine Ulster resistance. Part of the Navy took station off the Isle of Arran and General Paget, Commander-in-Chief in Ireland, was recalled for consultations.

On 16th March, 1914, Carson made a melodramatic departure from the Commons, amidst a standing Unionist ovation, ostensibly to form a provisional government in Belfast, while Paget returned to Dublin, with orders to prepare for the seizure of strategic points and with the promise that in the event of a march north officers domiciled in Ulster might stay at base. With incredible stupidity Paget distorted and publicised the latter instruction in such a way that senior officers received the impression that the government planned an immediate offensive and that their resignations were required forthwith unless they would comply with government instructions. On the evening of 20th March, Paget telegraphed that many officers, including Brigadier-General Gough, his three colonels and all but twelve of the officers of the Third Cavalry Brigade 'prefer to accept dismissal if ordered north'.[1] This was the 'Curragh Mutiny'. Asquith

---

[1] There is no doubt that some officers were coerced by their colleagues into offering their resignations.

tried to impress on Gough, summoned to London, that it was
a misunderstanding but Gough, supported by Wilson, was
adamant and refused to withdraw the resignations until he
received, through the folly of Seely and Morley, a written
promise that the Army would not be used to coerce Ulster.
Asquith handled the matter badly, and there was a considerable outcry in the country.   Seely and two generals resigned,
though Wilson, who had behaved with extreme partiality,
remained in office.   To restore confidence Asquith took the
War Office himself.   As A. P. Ryan has put it: 'The soldiers
trusted Asquith; his massive common sense and refusal to be
stampeded into the excitement of the moment proved
invaluable.'   But Ulster had won a victory and the example
was not lost.   J. H. Thomas announced in the Commons, 'If a
strike breaks out in November . . . I shall advise the men to
arm.'

Ulster was arming.   On 24th April, defying a government
proclamation, their stock of weapons and ammunition was
enormously increased by supplies purchased in Hamburg
in the 'Gun Running of the Larne'.   Many Ulstermen
seriously wondered whether William II might not imitate his
Orange namesake and free them from the Catholic yoke.
This galvanised the Irish Volunteers into action; it soon
exceeded Carson's force in numbers and in June, Redmond,
with some reluctance, took personal command.   In July the
force organised its own gun-running at Howth, when more
German arms were unloaded in broad daylight with the
authorities powerless to intervene.   As the Volunteers
marched back into Dublin in triumph, a foolish Assistant
Commissioner of Police sent for troops.   When they arrived
they were stoned by the crowd and, at Bachelors Walk, opened
fire, killing three civilians and injuring thirty-eight.   This
was felt to be most unfair discrimination; the Larne had been
condoned, but Howth was answered with massacre.   Thus a
trivial incident inspired the Irish with complete distrust of
the fairness of the government in London and helped their
extremists to get the upper hand.

By the end of June, when the Lords mangled the Bill on its
third circuit and the two-year time limit had expired, Asquith,
at a loss to know how to implement the Bill when it became
law, agreed to reopen negotiations on the basis of the exclusion

of a specified area for a specified time. This was at the Buckingham Palace Conference of 21st–24th July, under the chairmanship of Mr Speaker Lowther, in which Asquith and Lloyd George, Redmond and Dillon faced Lansdowne and Bonar Law, Carson and Craig. The time limit was never discussed; the conference lost itself, as Churchill put it, in 'the muddy by-ways of Fermanagh and Tyrone'. The Howth gun-running followed on 26th July. Civil war seemed inevitable. On 4th August a reunited country was at war with Germany.

(d) Prelude to the First World War

The years preceding 1914 were ones of tension in foreign affairs although in that year the general atmosphere was calmer than it had been for some time. Many of these tensions were economic – intrigues for concessions in the less-developed parts of the world and for territorial acquisitions in Africa and elsewhere – but by 1914 most of these had been settled peacefully. They had arisen in part from the need felt by most European statesmen to distract their peoples from tensions in Europe which basically resulted from the lack of approximation of political frontiers and racial boundaries to the east of the Rhine. Non-Germanic populations occupied Alsace and Lorraine, Slesvig and Prussian Poland; Russia ruled harshly a large part of Poland; Austria-Hungary was composed of eleven different nationalities many of which had kinsmen across the frontiers. Nine of them were subjected to a greater or a lesser degree by the Germans and the Magyars. Ultimately the subjection of all these areas and peoples depended on force and the uneasiness created by this fact, in view of the growing consciousness of national feeling, led to the building up of armaments and the forging of alliances, both of which contributed further to the increase of tension.

These alliances were something new in European affairs. Traditionally alliances had been concluded at the beginning of a war with the limited purpose of bringing that war to a successful end. When peace came they seldom endured. An attempt to keep the victorious alliance of the Napoleonic Wars in being to supervise the peace ended in discord after seven years. The alliances concluded after 1870 were not directed to any specific war, they were ostensibly defensive. Nevertheless they had serious implications. It was only too easy for Europe to be split into two hostile camps, thus greatly increasing the serious consequences of any local differences of opinion. Bismarck, who began the system in an attempt to isolate France and to justify to the Reichstag a substantial military establishment, was well aware of the dangers once France acquired allies of her own. When her major ally was Russia, Germany was faced with the possibility of war on two fronts. As a result she was bound more closely than ever to the fortunes of Austria-Hungary as her sole certain supporter, Italy being unreliable, as was clearly shown in 1914 when she remained neutral, entering the war in 1915 as Germany's enemy. It would be wrong to speak of the certainty of any alliance functioning as its makers intended; in practice there were major contacts between nations which cut across the frontiers of the military alliances. Almost every country was divided as to whether support for an ally should go as far as the call to arms. Had the Kaiser and the Chancellor possessed greater authority in Germany in 1914, support for Austria might not have been so unqualified; had President Poincaré of France not been in St Petersburg, he might not have pledged so readily the support of his country to Russian championship of Serb rights; without French support, Russia would probably not have mobilised. Above all, had the Germans not invaded Belgium, Britain might well not have fought alongside France. The alliances had serious international implications and contributed to the building up of tension; in a crisis they predisposed one party to support the other but they did not make that support certain.

The subtle balance of alliances arranged by Bismarck could only be maintained by the master himself and after his fall in 1890 Europe rapidly coalesced into two armed and potentially hostile camps; Germany tied to Austria-Hungary, with Italy as an uncertain third party, on the one hand; Russia and France, who concluded an alliance 1891-95, on the other. Within Germany itself Bismarck had balanced the civil and the military power but none of his successors as Chancellor managed to do so and the Army grew progressively more independent. By 1914 it was virtually conducting a different foreign policy from that of the Chancellor, Bethmann-

Hollweg, which led the Austrian Commander-in-Chief to query appositely: 'Who rules in Berlin?' The Kaiser should have done. He had considerable political gifts and was more farsighted than many of his advisers, but he was inclined to be impulsive and irresponsible and was too often tempted to play the sabre-rattling war-lord while shrinking from the consequences of violence. In this way he weakened his position and the Chancellor, Bülow, dealt him the final blow in 1908 and imposed on him the limitations of a constitutional monarch. In that year, in England, he had given an interview to the *Daily Telegraph* in which he patronisingly declared that his intervention alone had saved England during the South African war from a general war on behalf of the Boer republics. In addition he was England's friend in a hostile Germany. Such indiscretions caused bitterness in both countries and the Kaiser became powerless to influence later events or to restrain the German military leaders. The Chancellor rapidly found himself in the same position.

Britain stood apart from the system of alliances, although the Anglo-French Entente and the secret military and naval conversations which began in 1905 committed her to some extent. Owing to the influence in the Cabinet of the Liberal Imperialists and Grey's own enthusiasm for an agreement with France, British foreign policy during the period had remarkable continuity. Sir Edward Grey, Foreign Secretary 1905–16, was probably one of the most constantly honourable men in politics. A complete contrast to Palmerston in character, interests[1] and methods, he shared his profound belief in the maintenance of the balance of power and devoted himself to preventing Germany from forming an alliance against England. His frankness as well as his disinterestedness brought him a very high reputation both in England and abroad.

Grey's aim was to remove as many causes of tension as possible and following the Algeciras Conference[2] a determined effort was made to placate Germany by proposing naval disarmament, as a result of which the Cawdor programme was cut down, but a conference at The Hague obtained nothing tangible. On the other hand relations remained good. State

---

[1] He shunned social life and had a passion for ornithology.
[2] See above, p. 361.

visits were exchanged and Haldane was a guest at the German Army manœuvres.   An approach to Russia was more success-ful.   There were potential sources of trouble in Tibet, Afghanistan and Persia and the Anglo-Russian Convention of 1907 largely eradicated them.   Both countries promised not to interfere in Tibet nor to negotiate with it except by means of China, the nominal suzerain.   Curzon had urged the strengthening of British control of Afghanistan but the government had felt such a move unnecessary and agreement was reached with Russia on the basis that Britain would in no way change the political status of the country, in return for which Russia would have political relations with the Amir only through Britain.   Persia was more difficult; its decay had reached an advanced stage and the Russians, anxious for a warm water outlet, had already established a powerful influence in the country.   Britain's interests were the strategic ones of keeping Russia away from the Persian Gulf and the frontiers of Afghanistan and Baluchistan.   The Shah's sovereignty was upheld but Persia was divided into two zones of influence, with a neutral area in between.   This was nowhere near as comprehensive an agreement as that with France in 1904;[1] the question of the Dardanelles was deliber-ately avoided and the Radicals disliked the idea of too close an association with the reactionary government of Russia; the Russians for their part, until the Bosnian crisis, wanted to keep Germany's friendship.

The effect of the Convention on Russia joined with that of the unsuccessful war against Japan to centre her attention once more upon the Balkans, where since 1897 there had been considerable co-operation with Austria-Hungary, although Russian economic penetration of the Far East and Persia continued.   Since 1903, however, when the pro-Austrian King of Serbia, Alexander Obrenovich, had been assassinated and replaced by a rival dynasty, the Dual Monarchy had become aware of the desire for national unity of the Southern Slav people, some of whom were within its boundaries, while outside were others, like the Serbs who, it was unrealistically believed, might play the part Piedmont had done in Italy.[2] This could have only two possible long-term consequences: the absorption of all the Slavs within the Monarchy, possibly, as

---

[1] See above, p. 360.   [2] See above, p. 185.

the heir to the throne the Archduke Franz Ferdinand envisaged, with a fair degree of autonomy, or their unification outside the Hapsburg Empire, which would lead to similar movements elsewhere and hence in all probability to that Empire's complete disintegration.

In July 1908, to the great surprise of foreign governments, the Sultan was forced to grant a constitution by a group of Army officers known as the Young Turks, who believed there was a plot for the dismemberment of Turkey. An event so unlikely as Turkey reforming itself caused immediate consternation and while there was yet time, Aehrenthal of Austria and Iswolsky of Russia – the latter on his own authority – made a private bargain whereby Austria would assume sovereignty of Bosnia and Herzegovina, which she had ruled since 1878,[1] while Russia would obtain the opening of the Dardanelles to warships. The Russians intended to consult the Great Powers but before they could do so the annexation of the two territories was proclaimed by Austria on 5th October. Prince Ferdinand of Bulgaria, nominally a Turkish vassal, declared his country's complete independence while Crete, also nominal Turkish territory but ruled by a Greek prince since 1898, demanded incorporation in Greece.

The British Press was outspoken about these blows to the prestige of the new Turkish régime and Grey demanded a conference, which Austria refused. This refusal was backed by Germany, who, although she had extensive interests in Turkey, did not wish to alienate her one firm ally and saw an opportunity to humiliate Russia, who had now declared her support of Slav interests. In January the difference between Turkey and Austria was settled by a cash payment and the return of a small piece of territory, the Sandjak of Novibazar. While Bosnia and Herzegovina with their Slav populations had remained nominally Turkish, the Serbs had hoped to incorporate them and secure an outlet to the sea; now this appeared to be permanently barred and King Peter looked to Russia to help him.

Germany meanwhile concluded a dispute with France in Morocco which had arisen when a German deserter from the French Foreign Legion was harboured by the German Consul at Casablanca; Germany recognised France's

[1] See above, p. 248.

preponderant political position, while the French recognised Germany's commercial interests. Believing Edward VII's state visit to Berlin had resulted in an Anglo-German agreement on the Balkans, the French decided they could not support Russia in a war there and Russia consequently decided it could not help Serbia. The Austrian Foreign Minister, Aehrenthal, now had Serbia at his mercy but shrank from annexation in view of insoluble policing problems that would ensue; he demanded an acknowledgement of the Bosnian-Herzegovinian annexation instead; the Germans, appearing, as the Kaiser put it 'in shining armour' at Austria's side, demanded and obtained a similar one from Russia.

The South Slav problem was far from solved; merely exacerbated. Serbia became increasingly hostile; the Russians began to overhaul their armed forces. The Germans, on the other hand, began to regret their unqualified support of Austria-Hungary in view of the many German economic interests in Russia and Bülow was forced to resign as Chancellor; he later claimed he told the Kaiser not to repeat the Bosnian affair.

Europe had been near war and Grey and Asquith were increasingly convinced that the responsibility was that of Germany who was seeking supremacy in Europe by breaking the existing alliances and understandings. Further alarm was caused by the Agadir Crisis of 1911. Morocco was collapsing into civil war and in October 1911, informing the Algeciras Powers in advance, the French sent an army to occupy Fez and protect European residents. Supposing annexation would follow, Kiderlen, the German Foreign Minister, despatched the gunboat *Panther* to Agadir apparently to protect German residents and interests[1] but in reality to force a new Moroccan settlement and obtain compensation for Germany. Grey had formal obligations to support France over Morocco under the Entente, wished to avert a further Franco-German agreement to which England was not party and suspected that the Germans coveted an Atlantic naval base. There was no real substance in this, the Kaiser deprecated further intervention in Morocco and Kiderlen accordingly pressed the French government for 'compen-

[1] There were no Germans at Agadir so the nearest one was ordered to go there to be protected; he had some difficulty in attracting the *Panther*'s attention as the warship had been ordered to stay off shore.

sation' in the French Congo. To ensure British participation in any agreement Lloyd George, with Grey's and Asquith's approval, warned, in a speech at the Mansion House in July, that Britain might well be forced to fight if her interests were endangered. That the arch-enemy of costly naval expenditure should speak of war made a considerable impression. The speech ended all chance of a Franco-German agreement and for a while there seemed a serious possibility of an Anglo-German war until September when Kiderlen, against the background of a financial crisis in Germany, opted for modest compensation in the French Congo in return for an acknowledgement of the French protectorate over that part of Morocco accorded them as a sphere of influence in the Act of Algeciras.

The imminence of war aroused British concern about defence. A subcommittee of the Committee of Imperial Defence drew up *The War Book* which detailed procedure for each department should war occur, and which was revised regularly until 1914. A meeting in August revealed the disparity of Army and Navy plans and Churchill was sent to the Admiralty as First Lord to form a naval staff in view of McKenna's unwillingness.[1] The Naval War Staff which resulted, however, was in no sense the equal in effectiveness of the Army General Staff. It was in 1911 that the Cabinet as a whole were first acquainted with the secret naval and military conversations with France, and this caused particular concern among the Radicals. To appease them and have a freer hand to oppose resumed Russian activity in Persia, Grey opened negotiations with Germany on the limitation of naval strength, to which Bethmann-Hollweg responded; they failed because Germany set her demands of British neutrality too high and because the Chancellor could not prevent Tirpitz from publishing a new and greater naval programme. Hence French and British co-operation became closer and although no firm undertakings were made, it was mutually agreed that the majority of the British fleet should be concentrated in the vicinity of the Channel, while the bulk of the French fleet stayed in the Mediterranean.

Although the Russians still dreamed of control of the Straits and perhaps of Constantinople itself their more immediate

[1] McKenna took Churchill's place at the Home Office.

objective was to ensure their continued domination of the
Black Sea which the closing of the Straits to warships secured,
although preventing their own fleet from entering the Mediterranean. By 1912, however, Turkey seemed on the point
of collapse; the Young Turk Revolution had not produced
any improvement, and the passage of merchant ships was
interrupted. This was a matter of crucial importance as 50
per cent of Russia's foreign trade and 90 per cent of her grain
exports went through them. Free passage which meant in
effect preventing the domination of another Great Power in
Constantinople where German influence was already strong,
was now the primary Russian interest in the Balkans and her
support of Slav nationalities there had been aimed strictly
at creating a barrier. Under Russian patronage Serbia and
Bulgaria signed an alliance and prepared to attack Turkey,
the Serbs hoping for Bulgarian support against Austria later.
The French, reacting from Agadir, gave Russia encouragement, which they had refused to do at the time of the Bosnian
crisis; Poincaré did not want war but he wished to assert the
French position as a Great Power. Germany would have
supported Austria, but Berchtold the new Foreign Minister
had no certain policy. His principal aim was to keep the
Balkan States weak if possible.

In October 1912 all the states in the southern Balkans
declared war on Turkey and all were successful. Austria had
missed the chance of propitiating the Serbs who secretly
feared they would be submerged if a Southern Slav State was
formed, and stood helplessly watching the triumph of Balkan
nationalism although she co-operated successfully with Italy
in limiting Serbian expansion by the creation of an independent Albania.

Russian fears of the capture of Constantinople by Bulgaria
were not realised and the Great Powers co-operated in bringing about a peace conference in London. This had to accept
the division of the spoils and their re-apportionment in
August 1913 when the other states deprived Bulgaria of some
of her gains, but Grey tried to make of it a demonstration that
Triple Alliance and Triple Entente could co-exist peacefully;
the Germans urged conciliation in the hope of detaching
Britain from the Triple Entente but were nevertheless convinced that a war with Russia was sooner or later inevitable.

An Army law was passed which greatly increased the German armed forces and made a capital levy, which could hardly be repeated. Meanwhile Austria was restrained from attacking Serbia, which had increased greatly in size. The wars asserted Balkan independence and largely eradicated Great Power influence there; they gave an example of swift and decisive battles which impressed on the Great Powers the crucial importance of striking the first blow should the war, which none of them sought, occur. In England, however, Lloyd George tried to get the naval estimates reduced in 1914 but Asquith stood quietly but firmly by Churchill and the suggestion was withdrawn. A measure of agreement, however, was reached by Harcourt, the Colonial Secretary, on a partition of the Portuguese African colonies with Germany, and British industrial interests were quite prepared to see Germany strengthening her economic hold on the centre of the Turkish Empire providing the fringe areas were left inviolate. The Russians were very sensitive to the increase of German control, however, particularly when, at Turkish invitation, the German general Liman von Sanders began to reorganise the Turkish Army in 1913. Hitherto France had been more conscious of the value of their alliance than Russia; now the Russians tried to strengthen the Triple Entente rapidly and attempted unsuccessfully to arrange a firm alliance with Britain, although Anglo-Russian naval talks took place to please the French. As the Tsar put it, 'we need the guarantee that the Straits will not be closed to us', but the Germans were too deeply committed to draw back, disregarding Bismarck's warning that south-eastern Europe was 'not worth the bones of a Pomeranian grenadier'.

Despite all this, in the summer of 1914 war seemed remote. In England Lloyd George was urging a fresh approach to Germany; in France the three-year conscription which Poincaré had introduced was proving bitterly unpopular and a Radical Ministry had come into power. The Germans had doubts about committing themselves too deeply to Austria; they had little sympathy with her fear of nationalism. The network of alliances was unstable; there was no guarantee that in the event any power would act according to the letter of its agreement. In Germany, however, there was no clear ruler, only conflicting pressure groups: the army leaders wished to destroy the French Army; Tirpitz saw the British navy as the menace; businessmen and democratic elements were suspicious of Russia, a view shared by the official policy-makers; Conservatives tended to think a war of any kind would restrain socialism.   Lack of a single policy involved Germany in being surrounded by a host of potential enemies.

The occasion for war was the murder of the Archduke Francis Ferdinand on 28th June when visiting Sarajevo, the capital of Bosnia, on Serbia's National Day.   The visit was envisaged as a challenge to Slav Nationalism but there is no evidence that the Serbian government, whose army had not yet recovered from the Balkan wars, was in any way implicated.   It was easy to make out that they were, however, and Berchtold saw the opportunity for an easy war which would restore the fast waning prestige of the Monarchy and which at the same time, providing it had German backing, would restrain the growing independence of Count Tisza, the Hungarian Prime Minister.   Had an ultimatum been sent immediately, the sympathy of the Great Powers would have been almost entirely on Austria's side, but delay was fatal and by the time it was sent on 23rd July, the Germans having almost casually given their approval, the Russians were determined to uphold Serbia as a buffer state to safeguard the Straits.   They thought in terms of a conference, however, but when Austria ignored the conciliatory Serbian reply and declared war on Serbia on 28th July the Russians, assured of French support, began to mobilise as a diplomatic measure.

In Germany the Kaiser and Bethmann-Hollweg had had second thoughts and for a moment contemplated co-operating with Grey's proposal for a conference when the Austrians had occupied Belgrade; it has been argued that a visit by Grey to Vienna and Berlin at this point might have tipped the scales, but Moltke, the German Chief of Staff, telegraphed a message of full support to his opposite number in Vienna and went ahead with German mobilisation, which occurred on 1st August.   As the Russians were not ready, Moltke's plan was to knock out France rapidly first and, having declared war against Russia on 1st August the Germans manufactured an incident with France and declared war on 3rd August.   Had this not occurred the French would have hesitated; the strength of the Alsace-Lorraine frontier was such that comparatively few German troops could have held it, and the horror of the German strategists, a war on two fronts, could well have been avoided.

Britain had no inescapable commitments except her guarantee of the neutrality of Belgium under a treaty made in 1870 with France and Prussia. Although the Conservative party as a whole was ready to stand by France, the Cabinet was very divided on the matter, Morley and Burns resigning when war was imminent, while many in the party thought war should be avoided at all costs. Grey, aware of this uneasiness, could only warn the Germans not to rely on British neutrality, but on the other hand he would not in any way commit the country to the support of France and Russia. As a precaution, he warned the Germans that their navy would not be allowed into the English Channel, but Moltke had no interest in the German navy and had not planned for its participation. Grey was subsequently accused of not making clear to Germany where Britain stood over Belgium, but the Germans went into Belgium with their eyes open – they had no other plan – and believed the war would be over before the British Army, whose military value they rated low, could arrive. Any threat of force made by Britain before circumstances made it essential would have been extremely unpopular in the country and would have seriously split the Liberal party. Grey and Asquith had neither the personalities nor the opportunities to educate the public in the need for war as Chamberlain had done successfully in 1899.

When the Germans violated Luxemburg on 2nd August and a twelve-hour ultimatum was sent to Belgium demanding the passage of troops, the Cabinet decided British action would be necessary. When he rejected the German ultimatum on 3rd August, King Albert appealed to George V for support and the Cabinet decided to intervene on behalf of both Belgium and France. Grey's and Asquith's reputations and popularity were at their highest point. Bonar Law pledged the support of his party; Redmond with considerable courage in view of his uncertain hold over his followers and the fact that Home Rule was not yet settled, promised Irish support.[1]

[1] In 1916 James Stephen commented on this: 'He took the Irish case, weighty with eight centuries of history and tradition, and he threw it out of the window.'

Macdonald, unsupported by most of his party, bitterly criticised Grey's secret diplomacy which had, he claimed, entangled Britain with inescapable commitments to France. An ultimatum was sent to Germany demanding she respect Belgian neutrality and when it expired on 4th August, the two countries were at war. Parliament gave its approval on 6th August. Few imagined the war would be long, that England's involvement would disrupt the even tenor of her life, or that the war would bring revolution, social or political, in most parts of Europe. Grey spoke truer than he knew when, looking from the Foreign Office windows and seeing the lamplighters in St James's Park, he remarked to a friend, 'The lamps are going out all over Europe; we shall not see them lit again in our lifetime.'

X · THE FIRST WORLD WAR

(a) 'Business as Usual', 1914–15

The War Book procedure[1] had been set in motion on 29th July and once war broke out proclamations were issued which requisitioned merchant ships, forbade trade with the enemy and controlled the movements of aliens. The Treasury issued paper money and the Government took over the railways, guaranteeing them the 1913 dividends. For reasons of economy no naval manœuvres were held in 1914; the substituted trial mobilisations were in progress when the international situation became tense and the ships were at battle stations when war broke out, twenty dreadnoughts facing thirteen German equivalents across the North Sea. Lord Chancellor Haldane, temporarily in charge of the War Office, mobilised the army. There were a quarter of a million men in all with the colours but only 100,000 were immediately available. The Government contemplated keeping them at home to form the nucleus of a large army, but Balfour, Lansdowne and Sir Henry Wilson successfully insisted they should go to France where they took up position on the French left and had to fit into the French strategy, a lack of independence that basically continued for the remainder of the war. Very highly trained, a factor which would, it was hoped, outweigh its smallness, the army was short of machine-guns and mechanised transport and had no field telephones nor wireless until later.

Asquith was Secretary for War as well as Prime Minister and, believing that none of his colleagues were suitable for the former post made an appointment which, whatever its long-term consequence, greatly reassured the public and at a stroke – without the embarrassment of a coalition – gave the Government a 'national' character. Lord Kitchener had had a long, distinguished and uniformly successful career as a soldier in different parts of the Empire and the public

---

[1] See above, p. 415.

had enormous confidence in his ability.[1] He was convinced, unlike most people, that the war would be a long one and planned accordingly. Whatever his success in raising troops, however, his limitations soon became apparent. He had been out of England for forty years, serving mainly in wars against badly armed and ill-disciplined natives, and he had no experience or knowledge of the technique of modern warfare against a foe of equal calibre. Almost the whole of the General Staff went to France, so no expert advice was to hand, even if he had been willing to take it. He relied on flashes of inspiration which at times were both apt and effective. He was a bad administrator, unable to delegate authority, disliked by the generals, particularly Sir John French, the Commander of the British Expeditionary Force, and ill-equipped for the essentially political nature of his office.[2]

Following the timetable of the Schlieffen Plan the Germans, with five million trained men under arms as opposed to the four million on whom the French could call, advanced steadily. The appearance of the B.E.F. on the French left flank helped to interrupt it and a reasonably successful battle was fought at Mons, though the B.E.F. had to follow suit when the French continued to withdraw. By 5th September, the Germans were within 20 miles of Paris but at the Battle of the Marne, which seemed a miracle to contemporaries, the advance was stopped by French troops, rushed to the front in some cases in taxicabs, and the Germans wheeled northwards to secure the Channel ports. Churchill went with a force of Marines to hold Antwerp but the Belgians were unable to assist him and he was forced to withdraw. His presence at the front in person, and indeed the whole episode, was criticised, Balfour being one of the few Conservatives at that time who retained any respect for him as First Lord of the Admiralty.

By October, the Schlieffen plan had failed; the German Chief of Staff, Moltke, was replaced in operational command by the War Minister, Falkenhayn, an organiser of ability, but he could not prevent the war of stagnation and attrition that ensued and the armies faced one another along a line

---

[1] His appointment was strictly for the emergency; in Cabinet meetings he sat on the Prime Minister's right hand and he drew three salaries at once.
[2] See below, pp. 425–435.

stretching from near Ostend to a point 50 miles north-east of Paris and then east and south-east to the Vosges Mountains. The stagnation was illustrated in the first Battle of Ypres, in October and November, which although perhaps decisive in containing the Germans who were trying to turn the Allied flank, resulted in heavy British casualties that effectively destroyed the Expeditionary Force as an entity. Meanwhile on the Eastern front the Russians after being routed at Tannenberg in August had penetrated Galicia.

The Antwerp affair led to the First Sea Lord, Prince Louis of Battenberg, a cousin of the King, being unjustly suspected of German sympathies and he was forced to resign. Churchill decided to recall Lord Fisher in his place; initially there was accord between the two determined men, although the appointment was a very controversial one for Fisher, despite such expressions of regard as 'Yours till hell freezes over', was old and cantankerous and no match for Churchill's energy and powers of argument. Meanwhile the German fleet remained chiefly in harbour where the British were able to plot its movements with ease as the German naval code was captured by the Russians early in the war and obligingly handed over to the British. Jellicoe kept his own fleet in safe anchorages and was criticised for being unduly cautious. It is arguable that if Beattie had been in supreme command he would have adopted a more daring policy and possibly shortened the war; on the other hand he might have brought about disaster. A major naval defeat for Germany would have been inconvenient; for England, dependent on sea-borne trade, such a defeat would have been a catastrophe.

At home, few adjustments in the government were regarded as necessary. Fighting was considered to be a departmental matter, and Asquith who had survived so many difficulties in the past, expected in the future to solve them by the same methods and constitutional procedures. A War Council replaced the Committee of Imperial Defence, to be replaced in its turn by the Dardanelles Committee, but the Cabinet retained supreme control. Although the Conservatives wished to fight more ruthlessly than the Liberals were prepared to contemplate, differences were kept in the background. Welsh Disestablishment and Home Rule both became law, but were not to operate until the war was over. There was

DI

no decision over Ulster and on this question party bitterness was restrained only with difficulty.

Patriotic feeling ran high. Kitchener, featured in a famous and effective poster, with finger pointing and the caption 'Your Country Needs You', appealed for 100,000 volunteers, and impelled by their enthusiasm and in some cases by the pressure of older men and employers, two and a half million men flocked to the colours up to March 1916, adding greatly to Kitchener's prestige. Training facilities were overloaded and Kitchener disdained to make the Territorials the basis of his 'New Army'. Discrimination in Ireland continued; the Ulster Volunteers went to France but Kitchener would not accept the Irish Volunteers as such and fresh battalions had to be formed from them. Kitchener was not effective on the supply side and by the end of 1914 his strategy was felt to be a failure. The prospect of indefinite stalemate in France prompted the Cabinet to think of other lines of attack. This would depend largely on the Navy and Fisher put forward his long cherished scheme of forcing the Baltic and landing troops in Pomerania. The Cabinet regarded it as impracticable and were persuaded, despite French misgivings at the diversion of effort, to adopt a plan of Churchill's. This involved capturing Constantinople, which it was hoped would induce the Turks, who had entered the war on Germany's side in October 1914, to make peace. The supply line to Russia would then be open; the Balkan states would come over to the Allies, and it was hoped, somewhat unrealistically, Germany would be so weakened that she would seek peace.

The plan was feasible but it was hamstrung from the start by difficulties. Churchill exuded self-confidence and believed the Navy would capture Constantinople single-handed if necessary. Kitchener said no troops were available and although some were freed in due course, they were inadequately trained and ill prepared.[1]

Asquith gave his consent but insufficient backing to ensure success; Fisher apparently concurred but was obstructive. A premature bombardment warned the Turks of the British plans and when troops eventually landed on the Gallipoli peninsula, in itself a dubious move, they found the Turks

---

[1] The War Office had no detailed maps of the area until some were acquired from Turkish prisoners.

prepared. Available reinforcements were insufficient, British leadership was poor, and the two sides settled down to trench warfare under conditions that eventually made the British evacuation necessary.

In France entrenchment was the order of the day. A well-planned British surprise attack at Neuve Chapelle in March 1915, prepared with aerial photographs, models and large-scale French maps, pierced the German line. A German offensive in April and May, the Second Battle of Ypres, although held, resulted in heavy British losses. To the south, with their 400 miles of front against the British 40, the French also stood firm. The Germans were distracted by the Russian successes against Austria-Hungary and the Western Allies were given a breathing space to build up their strength.

There was little fundamental rethinking, however, of the problems of stagnant warfare and men were too often committed, with appalling loss of life, to taking and retaking the same area of mud in the same way. The generals, conscious of their failure, blamed the shortage of shells. This principally arose from the lack of appreciation that it was a new type of war on an entirely different scale; at Neuve Chapelle British guns shot off as much ammunition as was used in the whole South African war but even so had insufficient to make use of the initial success. Kitchener followed peacetime administrative and production methods.[1] The Press took up the matter; its influence was unparalleled at a time when the political parties, despite considerable misgivings, especially on the part of the Irish and Labour members, were bound by a vow of silence. Northcliffe worked up the scandal in the *Daily Mail* and although public regard for Kitchener was unshaken it enabled Lloyd George, in close contact with the newspaper world, to come forward as the champion of popular but drastic improvisation.

It was being gradually realised that the economic adjustment of the nation to a struggle that was proving longer than most people had anticipated was essential. The shell shortage highlighted the whole question of the shortage of labour in the munition factories, largely caused by restrictive practices. The Trades Unions were very sensitive on this

---

[1] Lloyd George found women at Woolwich Arsenal 'tediously filling shells one at a time with ladles by hand from cauldrons of seething fluid'.

matter; prices were rising and wages were at a standstill, yet many employers were making substantial profits. A vague statement on wages by Asquith in February 1915, caused considerable annoyance and led to an unofficial strike on the Clyde. Lloyd George took up his pre-war role as industrial conciliator-in-chief and in the Treasury Agreement of March 1915, confirmed by legislation, the Trades Unions accepted dilution for the duration in return for the restriction of profits and a share in the direction of industry through local joint committees. The last promises were not kept and it proved impossible in practice to enforce arbitration in wage disputes, as had also been envisaged in the agreement. Lloyd George's reputation was greatly increased by the arrangements and in April, after a fierce row with Kitchener in the Cabinet, he became Chairman of a Munitions Committee which did not include the War Minister.

In May there began a chain of events that further increased Lloyd George's reputation and his control over the war effort. Fisher had resented increasingly his subordination to Churchill and saw no reason why he should not occupy a position comparable to that of Kitchener. On 15th May, although he had countersigned and ostensibly agreed to every order affecting the Dardanelles, he suddenly reacted against the sending of more ships and wrote a letter of resignation. He sent a copy to Bonar Law whom he hoped would assist him in view of the intense Unionist dislike of Churchill and departed for Scotland, whence Asquith ordered him to return 'In the King's name'.

On receipt of his copy Bonar Law went straight to Lloyd George and offered two alternatives: either a public debate on naval administration and the shell shortage or a coalition. Lloyd George backed the latter proposal and Asquith reluctantly agreed, on his own terms. He had little respect for Bonar Law's ability or character and gave other Conservatives higher positions. Law was refused the new Ministry of Munitions, for which his business background would have been an asset, because Lloyd George wanted it, and the Exchequer, because he was a Tariff Reformer – it went to McKenna. He accepted the Colonial Office.[1] Conserva-

---

[1] He was in a weak bargaining position because although he was not personally implicated, his firm, William Jacks & Co., was being prosecuted over a munitions contract.

tive pressure resulted in Churchill being transferred to the Duchy of Lancaster and Haldane leaving the Cabinet entirely because he had been hounded by the popular Press over remarks made many years previously when, speaking of philosophy, he had acclaimed Germany as his spiritual home, but no Conservative received a key post apart from Balfour. Curzon was given high status but little work as Lord Privy Seal. Nobody was prepared to incur the odium of sacking Kitchener. Arthur Henderson, leader of the Labour party since Macdonald had resigned through his dislike of the war, entered the Cabinet with responsibility for Education. Redmond was also offered a Cabinet post but Asquith, misguidedly, would not give him the Irish Secretaryship which he wanted. The Irish were very annoyed by the appointment of Carson as Attorney-General.

Balfour went to the Admiralty at Churchill's suggestion. His long membership of the Committee of Imperial Defence and the War Council equipped him for this, and his prestige was desirable in view of the disruption of the department. A technical expert, Sir Henry Jackson, became First Sea Lord and he co-operated well with Balfour, especially after the creation of the Department of Invention and Research, which, among other things, made valuable experiments in sound ranging.

(b) ASQUITH'S COALITION, 1915–16

With the exception of Lloyd George and his new Ministry Asquith's new team was no more dynamic than his old. The Ministry of Munitions gave an unparalleled opportunity for brilliant improvisation and Lloyd George was equal to it. Cost was secondary to production; as far as he was concerned, 'What we stint in materials we squander in life. . . . What you spare in money, you spill in blood.' In June 1915, he discussed requirements with the French in a conference at Boulogne and this helped him to keep well ahead of the unduly modest demands of the War Office, although not until 1918 was there actually a surplus of ammunition. He requisitioned raw materials that were needed and gave manufacturers costs of production plus a reasonable profit, a practice that led too often to unduly large profits which, however, the Government were frightened to touch. Royal Ordnance Factories and later the Ordnance Board, responsible for design, were

brought under his control. New 'national factories' were
built, chiefly in rural areas, and new weapons were developed
and manufactured, notably the tank, which Churchill had
pioneered at the Admiralty, and the Stokes light mortar.
Many contracts were placed abroad. By the end of Lloyd
George's first year, the country was producing more eighteen-
pounder gun ammunition in three weeks than it had formerly
produced in a year.

Relations with labour were less successful. The Ministry
contained able businessmen and economists, but no trades
unionists, and labour relations continued to be dealt with by a
number of different Government departments. The Labour
movement dreaded the thought of industrial conscription,
and when a system of leaving certificates for munition workers
was brought in, it was so unpopular that it was withdrawn in
1917, after which the sole sanction was the threat of call-up.
The national shortage of labour was alleviated by the widespread employment of women in jobs normally held by men;
in July 1915, the suffragettes held a large demonstration in
London to demand 'the right to serve'. There were difficulties with shop stewards, many of whom were syndicalists
and, after 1917, Bolshevik sympathisers, but the influence of
patriotism was strong and working days lost as a result of
strikes were only a quarter of those lost before the war. A
significant factor may well have been the very much larger
wages most working-class families were receiving as a result of
overtime and the large number of women at work.

The employment of women and the building of new factories
in rural areas involved the extension of the Ministry's responsibilities. Seebohm Rowntree became head of the Welfare
Section and on his advice factory canteens and washrooms
were introduced, and factory Welfare Officers were appointed.
Reduced absenteeism was the result. Lloyd George became
convinced that drink was undermining the worker's strength
and in consequence stricter licensing hours were introduced
and beer weakened. As a pilot scheme for the nationalisation
of the industry, State ownership of public houses was introduced in the Carlisle area where there were many munitions
factories. George V made 'The King's Pledge' not to touch
alcohol until the Germans were defeated, but his example
was not widely followed.

It is always a temptation during wartime to raise loans, which, though more expensive in the long run, share the burden of the war with future generations who also benefit from the victory, or so it is said. McKenna made an unrealistic distinction between wartime and peacetime sections of the Budget; the latter balanced, the former did not, the limitation being McKenna's decision that taxation should cover the interest on the loans and the sinking fund of the National Debt. The most important loan was War Loan, paying 5 per cent, an unduly high rate of interest which had inflationary consequences. Throughout the war less than 30 per cent of national expenditure was covered by taxation, a quarter of which came from the duty on excess profits made in contracts for war equipment and materials, which reached 80 per cent in 1917. Income tax was raised to 3s. 6d. in McKenna's Budget of September 1915, and reached 6s. in 1918. Despite the affront to Free Trade import duties of 33⅓ per cent were levied on various luxury articles. The National Debt rose alarmingly from £265 m. to £7,809 m.

There was a steady rise in prices throughout the war, and they had reached three times the pre-war figure by 1919; wages as usual were slow to follow although they had reached parity by the end of the war. The high interest rates contributed to the price rise, as did the absorption of much industrial capacity by the demand for munitions, which forced up prices of the limited supply of other products. Until the last year of the war Britain's international trade position was favourable; of the £1,825 m. lent to Allies, principally Russia, France and Italy, £1,000 m. came from loans raised in America. After the war the repayment of these loans became a highly complex problem that brought much bitterness. The American position was an anomalous one; she helped to finance and furnish supplies for the war effort, a function that went far to turn her from a debtor nation into the world's greatest creditor, yet 90 per cent of her population wished to keep out of the war. German submarine activity made this difficult.

Fisher had prepared for a gigantic naval confrontation; the country was quite unprepared for the submarine activity which crippled British trade and for a time brought about an acute shortage of shipping. In February 1915, the Germans

declared the Western Approaches to the British Isles to be a
war zone which neutral vessels entered at their peril.   A
submarine commander had no men to seize ships or for prize
crews and therefore was strongly tempted to sink unexamined
and without warning, actions which brought the strongest
moral condemnation, especially when the *Lusitania*, which
was admittedly carrying munitions, was sunk in May 1915.
It was also carrying some American citizens.   Repeated
protests from Wilson put an end to unannounced sinkings
during 1916; but the decision to start them again brought
America into the war.[1]

The British also imposed a blockade, though not by such
means: it included food as well as potential war material and
in addition to a complete prohibition of trade with the enemy
there were restrictions on trade with neutral countries adjacent
to Germany.   The Germans had understood total war as
little as anybody else and deliberately respected Dutch
neutrality in 1914 so that she could provide an outlet for
German trade.   The British blockade was extremely effective
and contributed substantially to the German defeat.

Real defeat could only come on land, however, and there
slight progress was made.   The Dardanelles campaign made
little headway[2] and Sir Charles Munro, sent out to relieve
Hamilton, the existing Commander, sent back a gloomy
report, indicating that the campaign was not worth fighting –
as Churchill put it, 'He came, he saw, he capitulated'.
Bulgaria had come into the war in September and an attack
on Serbia was projected.   An important group in the Cabinet,
including Law and Lloyd George, wanted to transfer the
Gallipoli troops to Salonika, to stiffen Greek support for the
Serbs; the weight of army opinion, with some Cabinet support,
wanted concentration on the west alone.   There an Allied
offensive, of which the British share was in the Loos area, was
inadequately planned and resulted in casualties two and a half
times those of the Germans.

Dissatisfaction with the conduct of the war boiled over in
the Cabinet.   It was evident that recruitment, supply, and
the direction of strategy was too heavy a burden for Kitchener,
particularly with his unwillingness to delegate.   Sir John
French, Commander of the B.E.F., who resented his sub-

[1] See below, p. 445.   [2] See above, p. 424.

ordination to Kitchener, was dismissed. Kitchener and Haig, French's Chief of Staff, had intrigued frequently. When Kitchener showed eagerness to investigate Munro's report, he went out to Gallipoli with the Cabinet's blessing, while Asquith took personal control of the War Office and in four weeks reorganised the running of the war. The over-large Dardanelles committee which succeeded the War Council in June went and was replaced by a new War Committee with a membership of six. Churchill and Curzon, the leading opponents of evacuation, were excluded; Churchill, restless to fight, resigned the Duchy and took command of a battalion in France. Haig was appointed Commander-in-Chief in France and, most important of all, Sir William Robertson became Chief of Imperial General Staff with full responsibility for strategy. On his return, Kitchener was furious that he was confined to supervising supply and wished to resign, but Asquith convinced him he should remain as 'the symbol of the nation's will to victory', 'the great poster' as Margot Asquith put it. Despised by his colleagues, he soldiered on.

Robertson and Haig rapidly established a harmonious relationship with one another and with Kitchener and consequently, though Bonar Law and Lloyd George had won the Cabinet conflict to reorganise control of the war, Cabinet influence over military policy was probably weaker in 1916 than at other stages of the war.

Robertson was a rarity in the British Army, a Field-Marshal who had risen from the ranks. He was straightforward, penetrating to the roots of problems and with a great capacity for detail. He was, however, suspicious of civilian control,[1] suspicious of the French and determined to manage personally the strategy of the war, which he was convinced should only be fought in the west. Haig was more tactful; he was at one with Robertson in disliking political interference, and had the skill to prevent Lloyd George from dismissing him. His career had been a model of military success and he was held in high esteem in the army; his stature grew in the last year of the war, when his determination to conclude matters before the end of 1918 gave his generalship a resolution that brought him into the first rank. Both men, however, must take

---

[1] His characteristic retort to suggestions was 'I've 'eard different'.

responsibility for the uncertain leadership and muddled strategy of 1916 and 1917.

Robertson's dislike of engagements outside France led to a skilful evacuation of Gallipoli in December and January and as far as the war against Germany was concerned there was now an exclusive commitment to the Western front. Two hundred thousand British troops and double that number of French were kept at Salonika, although Serbia had now been occupied, and imperial concerns took a great many more, a division of effort that nearly jeopardised the war in France. Asquith noted in March 1915 that he and Grey were the only two members of the Cabinet who believed that Great Britain should not expand the Empire in the peace settlements. Kitchener wanted Alexandretta in the Persian Gulf and personally supervised the Sykes–Picot Agreement of January 1916, a Franco-British partition of Asiatic Turkey. A collateral agreement promised Constantinople to Russia.[1] A quarter of a million men, originally based in Egypt to protect the Suez Canal, advanced through Sinai into Palestine, occupying Jerusalem in December 1917, and then moving north to take Damascus. Its Commander was Allenby and Lawrence won an unparalleled reputation in encouraging and helping to lead the revolt of the Arabs against the Turks, which was of considerable assistance to the advance of the British troops.

The Government of India committed 300,000 men to a campaign in Mesopotamia to prevent Turkish attacks on the Persian oil wells. At Kut 10,000 were forced to surrender in April 1916. Although the officers were reasonably treated, more than two-thirds of the British other ranks were dead by the end of the war as a result of the appalling conditions under which they were imprisoned.

This diversion of effort, whether successful or not, did nothing to end the war against Germany and public opinion became increasingly anxious for resolute action. The French Government had urged conscription at the beginning of the war and it first became a Cabinet issue in May 1915. Irish opposition was very strong and so was that of the Labour party, which regarded it as incompatible with elementary

---

[1] These secret treaties caused considerable outcry when they were revealed by the Bolsheviks.

human liberties and remembered how the French had broken rail strikes before the war by calling up men for compulsory service. Kitchener was unenthusiastic although an appeal from him would have led to the country accepting it without question; voluntary recruitment still brought the army more men than it could equip and it is questionable whether compulsory service made any real difference. Lloyd George and the Conservatives in the Cabinet pressed for it and to appease them Asquith brought in the Derby Scheme, named after the Director-General of Recruiting, which the Liberals persuaded themselves would make conscription unnecessary. Unmarried men who attested their willingness to serve would be called up first, then married men. The outcome was that large numbers of married men came forward, confident they would not be needed, but comparatively few bachelors. This led to the conscription of unmarried men being instituted in January 1916 after a Cabinet crisis which resulted in Simon's resignation as Home Secretary in protest. Universal military service came in April during the patriotic fervour that followed the Easter Rising in Dublin, but Asquith was discredited by the way he bowed to Conservative pressure and seriously contemplated resignation.

Conscription brought the problem of conscientious objectors. It was evident that many of those who claimed 'conscience' did not have genuine religious scruples and unless they passed rigorous tests, of which membership of the Society of Friends was the most prominent, they were treated as non-conscientious and sentenced to penal servitude for the remainder of the war if they would not accept non-combatant service, for example as medical orderlies. Sixteen thousand men refused combatant service, of which 1,300 went to prison. They were openly criticised by Lloyd George who was increasingly finding more affinity with the Unionists over the running of the war.

The Easter Rising served to enhance the growing rivalry of Asquith and Lloyd George. When Redmond had pledged Ireland's unconditional support in 1914 and the Home Rule Bill had been placed on the Statute Book and then promptly bundled into cold storage, there were many extremists who grew openly more contemptuous of the war, which they felt to be no affair of Ireland's, and who saw in it an opportunity to obtain independence, with German assistance if necessary. The Germans encouraged such hopes, using as their intermediary Sir Roger Casement, formerly a member of the British consular service. He was captured on Good Friday shortly after landing in Ireland from a German submarine with instructions to prevent the rebellion the Germans had planned for Easter Sunday and which they now found themselves unable to support. A small extremist group of activists acting alone, however, seized the Dublin General Post Office on Easter Monday and declared Ireland to be a republic, under the presidency of P. H. Pearce. Four days of fighting ensued with fatalities on both sides.

Public opinion in Ireland shrank from the violence but the situation was an extremely delicate one for the British government. It was evident to most leading politicians that the Dublin Castle system of government had broken down and that there was an opportunity for a more acceptable settlement. On the other hand the undertones of treason and the stresses of war made magnanimity difficult; a subtle balance was necessary if Irish goodwill was to be retained – and the goodwill of America – yet with the permanent prevention of such acts of irresponsible violence. It was a time for statesmanship and leadership, a challenge to which Lloyd George might well have risen. Asquith did not.

In the first flush of indignation the British Military Commader, General Maxwell, was left to wreak an arbitrary vengeance. The seven signatories of the Declaration of Independence and all the participating commandants of the Irish Volunteers, except De Valera, who was a United States citizen by birth, were shot. Three thousand were arrested, many of whom had nothing to do with the rebellion, and two-thirds of them were interned in a disused distillery in Merioneth. In London Casement was hanged, although Asquith tried to establish his insanity. The effect was deplorable; a few squalid revolutionaries became martyrs.

Characteristically Asquith, failing to induce Lloyd George to take over from Birrell who had been Chief Secretary since 1907 and who now resigned, took temporary charge in Dublin himself. In the hope of reassuring the Irish party he decided Home Rule should be implemented at once, contradictory impressions of his Ulster solution being received by both sides.

Lloyd George, partly on his own initiative, began negotiations and reached an agreement with Carson and Redmond whereby Home Rule should be granted at once but the six disputed counties should remain part of the United Kingdom until after the war, when a conference would be held. At some cost to his prestige in the party, Bonar Law concurred but the plan foundered on the opposition of Lansdowne and the other Anglo-Irish magnates who had never been wedded to the Ulster cause and who felt that such a concession, extorted by force in time of war – or so it would appear – would be disastrous. Asquith was not prepared to overrule them and a further blow was dealt to his prestige in the party and in the country.

Such a fiasco was additional fuel to the extremists' fire. With the old system of government continuing to operate, with H. E. Duke as Chief Secretary, the Irish foreswore constitutional methods and Sinn Fein, grown from a society for the revival of the Gaelic language into a national movement, replaced the old Nationalist party as the focus of Ireland's aspirations.

With Parliament virtually silent and the Press vocal, Lord Northcliffe through *The Times* and the *Daily Mail* exerted great influence in the country with his attacks on Asquith. Increasingly, by contrast, Lloyd George was depicted as the man with the ruthless efficiency essential to solve the nation's problems and he seemed to the public mind the natural and logical successor to Kitchener and perhaps to Asquith himself. War exertions were severely straining Russia and were producing those conditions which were to lead to revolution early in 1917, and the government decided to send Lloyd George and Kitchener on a mission of encouragement. In the event Lloyd George was preoccupied with the Irish negotiations and Kitchener went alone on 5th June. Not far from Scapa Flow the cruiser *Hampshire* struck a mine and practically all those on board, including Kitchener, were drowned. In a sense it was at an ideal moment for his contemporary reputation; his great work of raising volunteer armies had been done; his inadequacies were hidden from the public by his enormous reputation and prestige.[1]

[1] For many years the more credulous refused to believe in his death; mythical explanations were produced for his disappearance.

As his successor the generals wanted the pliable Derby,[1] who at that time had a great though largely unfounded reputation. Bonar Law and Lloyd George, in a discussion at Sir Max Aitken's home, decided that Lloyd George's own claim to the office should be pressed on Asquith by the threat of ending the coalition, although there is no evidence that the Prime Minister had anybody else in mind except possibly Austen Chamberlain, a promotion Bonar Law was determined to prevent. Lloyd George initially would only accept if he had greater control over strategy than Kitchener had had, but eventually accepted office on very much the same terms. He found Robertson, whom Asquith supported, a difficult man to work with and in consequence, later in the year, developed the scheme of a council with supreme power to run the war and thus produced the crisis that led to Asquith's resignation.[2]

Lloyd George's conviction that the war was being misdirected was confirmed by the Battle of the Somme, a four-and-a-half-month campaign that resulted in over 400,000 British casualties and gained virtually no ground, though French morale was increased by important gains in the Verdun area and Ludendorff, who had succeeded Falkenhayn as commander in the West in August, admitted in his *War Memoirs* that the Germans had been fought to a standstill.

Though materially and morally the Somme was probably the turning point of the war, the army Kitchener had created was virtually destroyed in it. There were 57 divisions in France in July (compared with 95 French and 117 German) fighting with tremendous spirit though with insufficient technolgical support, especially of machine-guns, which in the hands of the Germans did untold damage. Joffre insisted on a combined operation, concentrating particularly on the Somme area which was the junction point of the two armies; this entailed a massive frontal attack whose preliminary bombardments warned the Germans of the heavy infantry attack that was to follow. An attack on the northern flank might have led to a more mobile campaign; as it was the November mud that brought the attacks and counter-attacks temporarily to an end found the armies in much the same positions though with three British soldiers lost for every two

---

[1] He was likened by Haig to a feather pillow, in that he bore the impression of the last person who had sat on him.   [2] See below, p. 438.

Germans. It is not surprising that the patriotic idealism of the war poets was replaced in their writings by a deep appreciation of the harsh conditions of the trenches, where the remorseless nature of the fighting was enhanced by the use by the Germans of poison gas.

Another apparently inconclusive battle, though like the Somme significant in retrospect, was fought off Jutland at the end of May. A few minutes' conflict at sea was the inglorious conclusion to the years of rival preparations that had caused difficulties at home and embittered international relations.[1] It was provoked by the tightening British blockade which caused Admiral Scheer to bring his fleet out to destroy at least part of the British Grand Fleet. In the brief interchange the British losses were heavier but the Germans retired under cover of darkness and a British opportunity to intercept them as they returned to port was missed.[2] They made occasional forays during the next two years, but morale steadily dropped through long idleness in port and the drafting of many of the best officers and men to submarines, on which the Germans now concentrated. 'From the point of view of Grand Strategy,' remarked Hankey, who became Secretary of the Cabinet at the end of the year, 'Jutland was as sweeping a success as Trafalgar.' Hitherto the concept of 'business as usual' had largely obtained at home; sartorial standards remained high, food reasonably plentiful and although the Zeppelin raids caused a fair amount of inconvenience, their actual damage was very small. Apart from the service departments and the new Ministry of Munitions, the machinery of government functioned normally. The intensified submarine campaign, however, brought home the realities of war to the civilian population and made it clear that the traditional conception of administration and restraints on government activity would have to be abandoned if the war was to be fought to a victorious conclusion. In particular comprehensive economic controls, including rationing, would be necessary to make effective use of valuable shipping space.

The only possible alternative was a negotiated peace, for

---

[1] See above, p. 359 and p. 384.
[2] It should be remembered that the British possessed a copy of the German signal code.

which President Wilson had worked earlier in the year through his trusted emissary, Colonel House, and which the new Austrian Emperor, Karl, aware of the progressive disintegration of his domains, also sought. In November Asquith sounded his Cabinet's views on the next phase of the war and the most explosive contribution came from Lord Lansdowne who warned that a continued war would create lasting damage to the economics and civilisation of Europe, views which became public when published in the *Daily Telegraph* a year later.   There is no evidence that the Germans would have accepted a return to pre-war frontiers, but the idea was still-born at a time when the British public probably concurred with the views expressed by Lloyd George in an interview for an American newspaper in September when he spoke of a 'knock-out blow', a fight to a decisive finish.

Thomas Jones, assistant secretary of the Cabinet and Lloyd George's most perceptive biographer, quotes a senior civil servant as remarking in 1916: 'Lloyd George had a passion to win the war which none of the other members of the Cabinet seemed even to understand'.   The conception of Lloyd George, the man of 'push and go', contrasted with Asquith, the man of 'wait and see', was sedulously cultivated by Lord Northcliffe, who controlled almost half the circulation of the London Press.   The lack of progress in winning the war, the enormous casuality lists and the growing shortages inevitably served as fuel.   Lloyd George himself was basically loyal to Asquith but wanted a War Council of three with himself in the chair and free from Cabinet control, to direct strategy, organise munitions and adjust the nation's economy, a task for which he believed his previous experience well fitted him.

Asquith had been Prime Minister for nearly nine years and was inevitably weary and in consequence irresolute at times. With his judicial mind and his intense respect for constitutional forms and practice, he was not ideally fitted to be a wartime leader.   He was intensely loyal to his colleagues and most of his Cabinet reciprocated that loyalty.   In the Commons he was the dominant figure, and although his public image as represented in the Press, for which he had great disdain, was not flattering, he was still widely respected in the country.   Lloyd George's original proposal for Asquith to remain as Premier conducting the ordinary routine of government might well have worked and would certainly have saved the Liberal party. On the other hand the position would be anomalous, with the Premier as parliamentary spokesman for a colleague with greater executive powers than himself.

The key to the situation was initially the attitude of Bonar Law. He suspected that Lloyd George was a self-seeker but he was perturbed by the growing hostility to the existing arrangement among the Unionist back benchers, over whom Carson, who had now resigned from the government, seemed to be gaining a greater control than he had himself. As over the Home Rule crisis, Carson seemed to convey a sense of resolution and dynamism in contrast to his real executive abilities about which Asquith then, and Lloyd George at a later date, had no illusions. On 8th November he put down a motion censuring the government over the handling of German assets in Nigeria, phrased in such a way as to detach Conservative votes. Aitken, of whose advice and great powers of persuasion Bonar Law was highly appreciative, was able to bring the conflicting prejudice and beliefs of Lloyd George, Bonar Law and Carson into harmony. Although he had little confidence in Asquith as leader it was some time before Bonar Law would give Lloyd George the support without which he was powerless against the Prime Minister.

On 1st December, Lloyd George submitted his scheme to Asquith who insisted on presiding himself and subordinating the new council to the Cabinet. Bonar Law privately promised Lloyd George his support. On the 3rd an article in *Reynolds News*, purporting to be an interview with Lloyd George, stated that he would resign, with Unionist support, unless his scheme was accepted, and would appeal to public opinion against Asquith's incompetence. This brought a confused reaction among the Conservative Ministers, many of whom were very annoyed. The '3 Cs' (Chamberlain, Curzon and Lord Robert Cecil), professing loyalty to Asquith, stated that they would resign to bring the dispute into the open. Bonar Law informed Asquith of Conservative views, possibly inferring that they were solidly against him, and in consequence an agreement was reached between Lloyd George and Asquith in the evening which gave the War Minister the substance of what he wanted.

EI

The situation was dramatically changed, however, by a *Times* leading article the following morning. Its editor, Dawson, was uniformly hostile to Asquith and in close contact with Carson on whose information he probably based his inspired description of the previous day's events which he interpreted as a complete surrender by Asquith. To most people, however, Lloyd George seemed the probable source, a hypothesis given apparent substance by the visit of the newspaper's proprietor, Lord Northcliffe, to the War Office the evening before.

The Liberal members of the Cabinet, not hitherto aware of the developments of 3rd December, promptly urged Asquith not to give way to Lloyd George; feeling his support to be stronger than he had expected and despite a warning from Bonar Law, Asquith wrote to Lloyd George repudiating the agreement, justifying his action by quoting *The Times* article. He also called on the King and told him that he was going to reconstruct his Cabinet completely. He must have been aware of the risk but believed it was preferable to a complete surrender of power.

Lloyd George resigned on 5th December, Bonar Law inferred he would go as well while the '3 C's' made it clear they could not continue to support the government if it did not include both men. Asquith was most shaken, however, by the resignation of Balfour, who believed that Lloyd George was about to control the war effort and would have no place for him. Asquith regarded Balfour as a kindred spirit, like himself a gentleman in politics, and the true leader of the Conservative party. A.J.P. Taylor sees Asquith's own resignation as a manœuvre to rout his critics, prompted by the belief that no one else could form a government; Asquith's biographer, Jenkins, considers he had insufficient support to continue.

Asquith's misappraisal of Balfour was shown by the latter's part in the council negotiations that followed. At bottom his influence in the Conservative party was greater than that of Bonar Law, whose handling of the Irish question earlier in the year had earned Lansdowne's particular dislike; to the country as a whole Balfour's membership of any new administration was almost a guarantee of its soundness and respectability. At the King's request he conducted on 6th December a meeting at the Palace of Bonar Law, Lloyd George, Asquith and

Henderson, the Labour leader. Bonar Law was only prepared to form a government if Asquith was a member, but Asquith was aware that the tone of any new administration would be set by those who were most distrustful of his leadership and judged he could have more influence and better preserve his control over the party from outside. It was this decision, and not any act of Lloyd George's, which really split the Liberal party. Bonar Law, as previously agreed, then deferred to Lloyd George.

On 17th December, Lloyd George secured the support of the Labour members, who were prepared to follow anyone who looked like winning the war; Addison gathered in about half the back bench Liberals while Bonar Law pledged the support of his own party. The other Unionist Cabinet Ministers, apart from Lansdowne, were committed when Curzon, who had previously assured Asquith, 'I would rather die than serve under Lloyd George', hastened to accept office. Balfour's acceptance of the Foreign Office was a crucial achievement. The Liberal ex-Cabinet Ministers stayed out to a man. It is a moot point whether the new government was really an improvement, but the general public, tutored by Northcliffe, had few doubts and for a government in wartime public confidence is the one essential.

(c) WIZARDRY IN ACTION

Lloyd George was now at the height of his powers. He was a man of striking appearance, short and stocky but with a fine head and a great mane of white hair. He had a beautiful speaking voice, a perfect use of words, and a strange sort of magnetism, a personal projection, which gave him a great hold over his audiences. He was so skilful in catching the mood of his listeners, whether a single individual or a great meeting, that many contemporaries, notably Keynes, were quick to conclude that he had no principles. He was, however, strongly patriotic and loathed oppression. 'The volatility of his methods,' wrote Harold Nicholson, 'concealed the rock-like immobility of his aims', while Churchill remarked, 'He was the greatest master of the art of getting things done and putting things through that I ever knew; in fact no British politician in my day has possessed half his competence as a mover of men and affairs.'

With a quicksilver mind, tremendous energy, and great courage and gaiety even in adversity, he provided an impetus which drew out the best in men even though they might dislike him. He had little military knowledge, which led him to make serious mistakes, notably his undue confidence in Nivelle in his zest for rapid victory, and he was nervously intolerant of opposition, aware that he led no party and that his position depended on preserving a chance combination of circumstances. He used men and their ideas ruthlessly, casting them aside when their usefulness was finished. Much about his conduct of public affairs and his private life was questionable and his deviousness was a byword in political circles. Yet he was essentially the right man in the right place at the right time and there was no one else who possessed his peculiar talents and his prestige in the country to an equal degree.

His coming to power has been rightly described[1] as not merely a change of government but a British-style revolution. He rarely attended the Commons, dispensed with the historic Cabinet and ruled dictatorially through a small War Cabinet of Curzon, Milner, Henderson and Bonar Law, who alone had departmental responsibilities as Chancellor of the Exchequer. It met daily with the purpose of determining grand strategy, assisted by an efficient secretariat to keep minutes and to ensure the implementation of decisions by the departments concerned. This was an important innovation led by Hankey, the former secretary of the Committee of Imperial Defence, who had a flair for interpreting Lloyd George's intentions, sometimes with an admixture of his own ideas. A further staff for the Prime Minister grew gradually, housed in huts in St James's Park and nicknamed 'The Garden Suburb'. War Cabinet committees dealt with matters of detail and controlled the subordinate Ministers, though Balfour and the service Ministers had greater independence. The two latter, Carson at the Admiralty and Derby at the War Office, were much influenced by their professional subordinates.

Bonar Law was the Prime Minister's *alter ego*. Baldwin called it 'The most perfect partnership in political history.' His caution and common sense, exercised with tact, ideally balanced Lloyd George's volatile flashes of inspiration. Over

[1] By A. J. P. Taylor.

the Commons he exercised a subtle mastery which has been rarely equalled and without which Lloyd George's dictatorship could hardly have been exercised. He had an extremely clear mind with an excellent memory, particularly for figures, which enabled him to make complicated speeches without notes. As a person, despite his melancholy disposition, he was simple and kind.

Through a number of new Ministries, of which only that of Labour was intended to be permanent, the economy and manpower were slowly adapted to the needs of war. They took some time to function effectively and the year 1917 was in consequence one of particular suffering and, in places, real discontent; Lloyd George appointed commissions of inquiry which led to substantial pay increases for government work. The new Ministers were businessmen, not politicians. Maclay, who was in charge of shipping and who refused to enter Parliament in either House, requisitioned all British merchant ships. Lord Rhondda the food controller worked closely with County Agricultural Committees which ensured the farmers' co-operation and he introduced a system of rationing covering principally meat, butter and sugar, which worked reasonably fairly though it proved quite impossible to check the large numbers of 'coupons'. Bread was not rationed but its price was kept down by means of a subsidy. It was, indeed, by controlling prices that the new Ministries operated most effectively; for instance, rent control was introduced in selected areas following a pilot scheme in Glasgow as early as 1915. Following the precedent of the Ministry of Munitions much production was commissioned on a 'cost-plus' basis which, while delivering the goods, did nothing to eradicate wastage and inefficiency and still led to excessive war profits in some cases.

There was extensive control of staple British industries. The mines were temporarily nationalised though with no attempt to reorganise the industry and make it more efficient. To save shipping space, cotton production was limited to 60 per cent of its pre-war level; sections of the industry laid off were compensated by a levy on the remainder, a system which was repeated in the nineteen-thirties and which discouraged the redeployment of the redundant labour.

Neville Chamberlain, who had just completed a successful

term as Lord Mayor of Birmingham, was a failure as director of National Service, a task which required prodigies of improvisation. Lloyd George himself took insufficient interest in the crucial matter of manpower, which resulted not only in shortages in France but also misdirection of skilled men into the army when they were urgently needed to produce munitions. Many Trades Unions continued to resist controls or demanded higher wages in the name of the freedom for which men were dying in France. Not until August 1917 was manpower treated as a whole and even then anomalies continued.

The German submarine offensive[1] of 1917 rapidly made nonsense of government controls. In April they sank one ship in four and British ships accounted for two-thirds of the million tons lost: home reserves of wheat were down to six weeks' supply. Carson, prompted by Admiralty convictions that merchant captains had neither the skill nor the delicate instruments needed for keeping station, refused to introduce a convoy system until Lloyd George and Curzon suddenly arrived at the Admiralty on 30th April and issued the necessary orders. It was a dramatic success; the escorts, to which both Japan and the United States contributed ships, forced the enemy to discharge torpedoes at long range and the merchant ships, weirdly camouflaged, zigzagging in formation, presented an uncertain target. The system made possible the development of effective anti-submarine devices and less than 1 per cent of the ships convoyed were lost, which meant that by the end of the war all the shipping losses had been replaced. It serves as the best example of Lloyd George's dynamism.

Elsewhere Lloyd George was less successful and in particular in his support of Nivelle, who had recently become French Commander-in-Chief and whom since he distrusted Haig, he placed in command of the British troops as well. The collapse of Roumania, whose great resources of corn and oil fell into German hands, provided an increased sense of urgency. Nivelle had great self-confidence and shared Lloyd George's passion for a short-cut to victory. A series of almost ludicrous accidents and indiscretions[2] combined dangerously

---

[1] See above, p. 430.
[2] Detailed plans of attack for the whole of the French 5th Army fell into German hands but Nivelle, though he knew this, did not issue fresh orders.

with lack of co-operation by his subordinate generals, both French and British. The offensive, begun in February 1917, was insufficiently swift and the Germans skilfully withdrew to a much stronger position. British casualties were particularly heavy at the Battle of Arras in April where the Canadians distinguished themselves in the taking of Vimy Ridge.

Though Nivelle's offensive was not disastrous by contemporary standards, the victory he had promised remained as elusive as ever and with the French armies on the edge of mutiny he was replaced by Pétain in May, though Haig and Robertson prevented any attempt to retain a supreme command. The French difficulties were kept secret and Pétain, with unshakeable calm and prompt attention to grievances, gradually restored confidence, while the burden of holding the line fell on the British.

Valuable support to Britain was coming from overseas. Troops from the Dominions and from India distinguished themselves on the battlefield and although the ultimate effect of this experience was to make the Dominions more conscious of their own separate nationhoods, the co-ordinating organisation necessary gave an illusion of greater imperial unity. In March 1917, the Dominion premiers met in London and formed the Imperial War Cabinet which Lloyd George wanted to develop into an imperial executive but for which he obtained no Dominion support. General Smuts, however, became a member of the British War Cabinet.

In the hope of starving out Britain before American patience was exhausted, the Germans renewed unrestricted submarine warfare in January 1917. To distract the United States they encouraged Mexico to recover the lands she had lost in the eighteen-forties and news of the proposed alliance coupled with the sinking of American merchantmen precipitated the United States declaration of war in April. Balfour crossed the Atlantic to cement the alliance and all trade leaks to Germany were stopped, although it was a year before American troops appeared in France in significant numbers.

Meanwhile Haig was preparing for a decisive stroke in Flanders to win the war if possible and to distract German attention from the French weakness. It is known as the Third Battle of Ypres or, from its last phase, Passchendaele. Unfortunately the preliminary bombardment, during the

wettest August for many years, destroyed the drainage system
of the Flanders plain and Haig's plan never got past its initial
stage.   Lloyd George had misgivings about the campaign
from the planning stage onwards; some of the generals were
also doubtful but did not venture to disagree with Haig openly
and the consensus of the Commons, as reported by Bonar Law,
was that he should be supported.   In view of Haig's prestige
Lloyd George did not feel strong enough to remove him but
openly condemned as a misuse of manpower what he described
as the 'Battle of the Mud'.   There is no doubt the campaign
caused heavy German casualties and prevented an attack on
the French, but Haig refused to call off the offensive, which
advanced four miles in three months, until conditions became
quite impossible in November.   As a result there were no
reserves available to follow up the tank break-through at
Cambrai later in the month.

Tanks had been devised by an Engineer officer, Sir E. S.
Swinton, and were developed by Churchill at the Admiralty,
as the War Office showed no interest.   Although the Germans
knew of them in 1916, they never copied them and were unable
to prevent a mass break-through at Cambrai, on the higher
and firmer ground, when they rolled back the German line
with surprising ease.   Troops were lacking to follow up, however, and the opportunity was wasted.   Lloyd George became
increasingly cynical about Haig's ability to use troops and
kept him short by diverting some to Palestine and retaining
over a quarter of a million in England.

Victory was still in the balance at the end of 1917 and
through controls and rationing the war was having a far
greater effect on the civilian population than any previous
struggle.   It was desirable to make it clear what was the
purpose of the war, in which British participation had expanded so enormously from the limited intervention envisaged
on behalf of Belgian neutrality in 1914.   A number of secret
treaties, which had made rash promises prompted by the
exigencies of the moment, had followed.   In April 1915, for
instance, Italy, an ally of doubtful value, had been induced to
declare war on Germany and Austria in return for certain
Austrian territories, to which her own claims were slight, and
the promise of colonial expansion.

In the Middle East incompatible promises were made to

Arabs and Jews. A German hint at a Jewish state in Palestine, under Turkish supremacy after the war, prompted
British action in the same direction, which had the added
advantage of keeping the French, who under the Sykes–
Picot Agreement had a zone of influence in Syria, as far away
as possible from the Suez Canal. Balfour was impressed by
the claims made by Dr Chaim Weizmann and his fellow
Zionists on behalf of their countrymen and although many
prominent Jews felt that they should identify themselves completely with their countries of residence, the Cabinet agreed to
the Balfour Declaration of November 1917, which stated that
the British Government viewed with favour the establishment
in Palestine of a National Home for the Jewish people, subject
to safeguards for the existing population. The declaration
aroused great enthusiasm among Jews in Allied countries and
especially in the United States. A year later, however, an
Anglo-French statement promised Arab independence.

President Wilson's offers of mediation in 1917 had led to a
general adoption by the Allies of the idea of self-determination,
which not only committed them to these objects for which they
had entered the war but greatly extended them to include the
reshaping of eastern Europe and western Asia. The Russian
revolutions of 1917, leading to an armistice with Germany in
November,[1] seemed to make such possibilities infinitely remote
and Lansdowne renewed, this time publicly, his plea for a
compromise peace, while Milner saw the virtues of a strong
Germany as a bulwark against Bolshevism, an idea promoted
in the thirties by many who had formerly sat at his feet.

The Bolsheviks published the secret treaties, which discredited Allied war aims and made drastic rethinking essential. In December 1917, the Labour party and the T.U.C.
jointly repudiated secret diplomacy and urged reconciliation
with former enemies, echoing the idea of Ramsay Macdonald
and the Union of Democratic Control which had been founded
by left wing dissidents in 1914. In return for the promise of
T.U.C. co-operation in the further mobilisation, Lloyd George
largely endorsed their aims, after obtaining the approval of
the King, the Dominion governments, and Asquith and Grey.
Full reparation and independence were promised to Belgium,

---

[1] This was followed by a wholesale surrender of territory by the Russians at
Brest-Litovsk in March, 1918.

Alsace and Lorraine would go back to France, independence would be granted to Poland, and self-government to the constituent nationalities of Austria-Hungary, while an international organisation was to settle international disputes.

The Labour party itself was doing some drastic rethinking. The demand of the Russian workers for an idealistic cause to fight for after the overthrow of the Tsar was very influential and Henderson resigned from the War Cabinet after a visit to Russia, in order to reconstitute the British Labour party and broaden its influence.   His action serves to indicate that there was not at this time the sense of national unity so evident in the Second World War.   Barnes took his place in the War Cabinet as Labour party representative.

Henderson's intention was to establish a national party rather than an interest group.   Its aim, as Sidney Webb stated in the party programme, was 'To secure for the producers by hand and by brain the full fruits of their industry and the most equitable distribution thereof that may be possible, upon a basis of the common ownership of the means of production and the best obtainable system of popular administration and control of each industry and service'.   The detailed programme had four specific aims: the universal enforcement of a national minimum standard of livelihood, by means of social security and the maintenance of full employment by public works; the democratic control of industry or nationalisation; a revolution in national finance by means of high taxation of the rich and a capital levy; and finally, the apportioning of surplus wealth for the common good.   Much of this had a socialist ring but the party's feet were kept firmly on the ground by its continued financial dependence on the Trades Unions.   They could see full employment being maintained by State regulation in wartime; they could see no reason why this should not be equally possible in time of peace.

For its foreign policy the party adopted the ideas of the Union of Democratic Control, which brought into the party a number of Radicals who did not necessarily concur with its domestic aims.   It also entailed the return of Macdonald who had been estranged since the beginning of the war.   His outspoken condemnation of it won far more public hatred than did out-and-out pacifists such as Snowden and Lansbury; it also gave him a misleading reputation as a man of extremist views.[1] The superficial similarity to communism of many of the ideas put forward by the Labour party was to prove an electoral and social disadvantage for some time though in reality the reconstituted party was a barrier against extremism.

It was as yet far from clear what would be the pattern of post-war political practice. Asquith and his followers in theory gave the government independent support but Asquith in practice looked for opportunities to discredit Lloyd George, a policy that never failed to ensure Unionist support for the Prime Minister. A potentially powerful critic of the Government was Churchill, whom Lloyd George brought back to political life as Minister of Munitions, an appointment which so annoyed the Conservatives that for a short while the Government's existence was precarious. To ensure support for the future Lloyd George created the Ministry of Reconstruction under Addison.

The new Ministry undertook comprehensive surveys into many aspects of national life and although little came of them, the fact that they occurred at all was an important recognition of the wide responsibilities now assumed by the State. One of its few positive results, based on the earlier work of a committee appointed by Asquith in 1916, was the last great reform of the franchise, itself a recognition of the crucial services performed in wartime by men and women in all ranks of society. The existing householder franchise only gave votes to three men out of five and the register on which it was based was seriously out of date. Property owners could have an unlimited number of votes, though only one in each constituency. Although its passage was delayed by the Lords and many Unionists disliked it, the Representation of the People Act became law in June 1918. All men over twenty-one were given a single vote, though a second vote might be cast for a university candidate or on account of business premises, a privilege which was abolished in 1948. The dangers of extending the vote to women were safeguarded by restricting it to those over thirty with certain property qualifications held personally or by their husbands. Voting was now to take place on a single day and frivolous candidates were discouraged by a £150 deposit.

Meanwhile, little progress was being made in the war. The

submarine campaign, although it was being mastered, still caused a widespread popular fear of food shortage. There were also demands that the German air attacks should be repaid in kind, though most experts believed that planes could best be used in co-operation with troops at the front. Smuts thought that the Germans could be bombed into surrender and after a bitter struggle within the Cabinet and the steady opposition of the Army and the Navy, who shared control of air policy and operations, a third service, the Royal Air Force, was created in 1918, with Rothermere as the responsible Minister. It made no significant new contribution.

Virtual deadlock continued on the Western front and Robertson and Haig wanted the troops in the Near and Middle East,[1] where Jerusalem was taken in December and control of the oil wells was secured. In October 1917, the Germans reinforced the Austrian Army which broke through the Italian lines at Caporetto; Lloyd George wanted Allied reinforcement of the Italian armies to see if more success could be obtained in a fresh theatre of war. He organised a Supreme War Council of Allied Premiers and military advisers, with a secretariat led by Hankey at Versailles in November. It was valuable in co-ordinating shipping and finance but was militarily ineffective owing to the mutual suspicion of British and French generals. Robertson, in particular, was obstructive and despite the powerful support he had from the King and others, Lloyd George successfully called his bluff and forced his resignation in February. His successor was Sir Henry Wilson, who had played a not altogether honourable part in the Curragh Mutiny.[2] Haig was retained, at the insistence of General Smuts.

It was too late to exploit the initiative which the Allies had had throughout 1917; the Russian Armistice had released many German troops for the Western front and Ludendorff was aware that time was short. Great strikes in Germany in January 1918 collapsed before the resolution of the authorities but they served as a warning indicative of the demoralising effects of the British blockade. Moreover the arrival of American troops was clearly imminent.[3] Ludendorff hoped

---

[1] See above, p. 432.   [2] See above, p. 407.
[3] A year earlier German naval officers had jeered that the only way they could cross the Atlantic was by swimming or flying.

to roll back the British line by a flank attack in Flanders, distracting attention by a bluff advance on the Somme, at the junction of the French and British armies. Haig, though warned of the German intentions, was inadequately prepared and when the Germans attacked in thick fog on the Somme on 21st March, the Allied troops were taken by surprise and were driven back forty miles within a few days, helpless in a mobile warfare so different from that to which they had become accustomed.

On 23rd March Lloyd George moved into the War Office, replaced Derby by Milner and rushed over to France the troops that had been kept in England through distrust of Haig. American troops in England were also used. With the Germans driving a wedge between the French and British armies, Haig accepted a unified command and in April Foch became Allied Commander-in-Chief though without an effective staff. Foch was to be largely instrumental in saving the situation in the crisis of 1918 and in successfully co-ordinating the operations that followed. Meanwhile valuable stores were lost to the Germans and over a thousand field guns; by late May they had crossed the Marne and by mid-June were within forty miles of Paris. The Allied line, however, remained unbroken and the German advance increased their front by one third, bulging out with dangerously exposed flanks. They had inadequate transport for their lengthening lines of communication while the numbers of British and American troops in France were increasing.

At home the age of conscription was raised to fifty and, in response to a back bench outcry and against the best advice, conscription was extended to Ireland. In 1917, Lloyd George had once again tried to solve the Irish problem, not with any real hope of success but chiefly to impress overseas opinion. Ulster was privately promised that nothing would be done without its consent and a Convention at Dublin, which Sinn Fein refused to attend, broke up a year later with nothing achieved. The threat of conscription that followed, even though Lloyd George promised it would only apply when Home Rule had been granted, played into the hands of the extremists, and the Irish Nationalists, with Redmond dead, left the Commons and joined Sinn Fein. On 23rd April there was an Irish General Strike, except in Belfast, and the consequent arrests of Sinn Fein leaders threw the movement into the hands of wilder men. Lord French was sent as Viceroy, to rule by force.

Lloyd George had to rely on the generals in Ireland; in France his distrust of them nearly proved fatal to his government. On his appointment to the War Office Milner dismissed Sir Frederick Maurice, Director of Military Operations and a close friend of Robertson's. On 7th May Maurice wrote to *The Times* a letter, which was a breach of military etiquette, accusing Lloyd George of lying in April when he had told the Commons that there were more British troops in France in January 1918 than a year previously. In fact, as Lloyd George showed, these figures had been supplied by Maurice; he had subsequently corrected them but it is uncertain whether the Prime Minister knew this. For a moment a back bench rebellion under Carson seemed likely but the Conservatives rapidly came to heel when Asquith, sensing the chance of revenge, took up the matter. Lloyd George was aware that the whole control of war strategy was at stake and that he was liable to be censured for all the disasters since 21st March. But in moving the establishment of a Select Committee of Inquiry, Asquith failed to rise to the occasion and Lloyd George was able not only to destroy his proposal and discredit both Maurice and Asquith in the process but to initiate a personal dictatorship by making criticism of the government's military leadership tantamount to sabotage of the national effort. In the only division against the government during the war he received an overwhelming vote of confidence which permanently split the Liberal party.

Throughout Europe a split seemed to be growing between the rulers and the ruled. In England the patriotic enthusiasm of the workers was fading; the summer of 1918 saw frequent strikes against various aspects of government policy with shop stewards stealing the initiative from the official union leadership. In Germany there was growing dissatisfaction, intensified by the candid memorandum of Prince Lichnowsky, the former German ambassador in London, in which he blamed the outbreak of war chiefly on his own government, and by the skilful propaganda of the Ministry of Information under Sir Max Aitken, later Lord Beaverbrook. Lord Northcliffe, brought in to help, enthusiastically committed the government to the League of Nations and national self-determination; firm promises for instance were made to Poland and Czechoslovakia.

In France the Germans had overreached themselves and were checked at the Second Battle of the Marne in mid-July. A counter-attack followed in which British, French and Americans worked smoothly together, the last, though inexperienced, showing considerable promise. The German centre was pushed back in August but the shorter line actually left them in a stronger position. Both sides were exhausted; a compromise peace seemed a likely outcome. Moderate and influential Germans were urging the opening of negotiations and a German Crown Council in August decided in favour of doing so. On the German home front the sufferings of the poor were very severe.

The picture suddenly changed. Allenby's advance northwards from Palestine led the Turks to seek an armistice; the Allied troops so long inactive at Salonika advanced into Bulgaria, which also sued for peace. When German troops failed to hold the Hindenburg Line, Ludendorff lost his nerve[1] and on 29th September told the German government they must seek an armistice at once by opening negotiations with President Wilson on the basis of the Fourteen Points which he had issued in January 1917,[2] believing they would get easier terms from an idealist. Wilson was not prepared to make concessions, but he believed that if the Germans accepted the Fourteen Points, the Allies would morally be obliged to do so. The French, in particular, were perturbed by the three weeks of United States–German negotiations and wanted stiffer terms but Lloyd George was aware that the goodwill of the United States must be preserved and believed that most of the Points were sufficiently widely drawn to permit of a variety of interpretations.

In Germany there was hope of a last-minute stroke to get better terms. There was talk of a *levée en masse* but in Berlin there was a grave shortage of fuel and food and an influenza epidemic was virulent, which also caused many deaths in England and India. It was beginning to be felt that the Allies would be less harsh if the Kaiser was deposed. There

---

[1] He may also have had a paralytic stroke.
[2] Four more than 'le bon Dieu', as Clemenceau put it.

was a plan for the German High Seas Fleet to intercept British communications with France and force an action with the Grand Fleet, but the spirit of the sailors had deteriorated through long inactivity and pacifist propaganda and crews mutinied rather than put to sea, securing control of Kiel on 4th November and raising insurrections in the major north German towns during the next few days.

The German government accepted the Fourteen Points on 23rd October and they were discussed by the Supreme War Council on 4th November. Both British and French representatives made reservations, but faced with the threat that the United States would negotiate a separate peace, the German offer was accepted, the actual armistice terms being determined by the field commanders.

It was evident that the French wanted harsh terms; President Poincaré suggested that Germany should be invaded and some territory laid waste. Clemenceau, the Prime Minister, did not agree but on Foch's insistence the Rhineland was occupied. Haig was quite prepared for merely a German withdrawal from foreign territory but he insisted on the surrender of the German fleet. With only sporadic fighting continuing once negotiations had opened and the French invasion of Lorraine imminent, the Germans had little option but to accept the Allied terms and on 9th November the Kaiser abdicated, fled to Holland and a republic was proclaimed in Berlin.

The terms were agreed at 5 a.m. on 11th November and came into force six hours later. The German Army was to retire behind the Rhine, within a month a large quantity of equipment and the bulk of the fleet was to be surrendered, as were looted valuables and gold. In the East the Treaty of Brest-Litovsk was to be cancelled[1] and German troops were to retire behind their 1914 frontiers. Although the German armies still occupied strong positions, revolution had broken out at home and the will to fight had gone. Germany, as Cruttwell says, 'came to the end of her endurance and it is doubtful whether any other country would have endured so long'. In England the rejoicings lasted for three days.

---

[1] See above, p. 447.

XI · THE SEARCH FOR NORMALITY

(a) AFTER THE WAR, 1918–20

'OUR blood-stained stagger to victory' as Lloyd George put it, with three-quarters of a million dead and double that number permanently affected by wounds or gas, had been made possible by unprecedented exertions, expenditure on a scale thought impossible before the war and a social and economic upheaval whose effects could never be eradicated. Lloyd George's masterly improvisations had brought fuller employment and higher wages than the working class had ever known and had submitted industry to State management or control. The Budget of 1918 stood at £1,000 m., five times that of 1914; ten times those of the late 19th Century.

Victory was costly. Moral values had been debased; victory had been acclaimed as an end in itself and iron determination in a fight for freedom was the obverse of propaganda designed to arouse unthinking and unjustified hatred of the Germans. On the material plane although the losses of shipping were largely replaced, 610,000 new houses were needed, the railways required extensive repairs and re-equipping, the mines had been worked with little regard to future operation and no attempt had been made to rationalise the industry during its temporary nationalisation. The war had led to the expansion of the shipbuilding and steel industries beyond peacetime needs while the treatment of the cotton industry had tended to fossilise a pattern that even before the war did not correspond to economic needs. Little, however, had been done to encourage the modern growth industries, especially that of mechanical transport.

The end of the war released a flood of peacetime orders which created a short-lived boom in 1919; this led to much unwise investment in the old staple industries and the real weakness of Britain's economic position was concealed. For some time the idea persisted that Germany could be made to pay for the war, and the well-established right of the victor to exact an indemnity became entangled with the conception that the payment of reparations was an admission of guilt. Germany's economic difficulties precluded any large-scale payments, quite apart from the practical difficulties of the form in which such very large sums were to be transferred. Closely linked with this was the settlement of inter-Allied war debts, for neither Italy nor France was able or willing to settle with their creditors until money was forthcoming from Germany. Following Pitt's practice, Britain had become once again the paymaster of Europe, though using American gold as well as her own. Including transactions with the Dominions, £1,825 m. had been lent and £1,340 m. borrowed, of which £850 m. had come from America. Had all these debts been written off much trouble and ill-feeling might have been avoided, for the pre-war sanctity of contract had been eroded and there was a growing feeling among the debtor nations that the United States might contribute money to that common cause to which they had given blood and sweat.

There was a heavy internal debt, for only 28 per cent of the cost of the war, £9,000 m., had been met by taxation, some 80 per cent of it direct as opposed to 54 per cent before the war. The heavy reliance on borrowing, with high interest rates for the wealthier classes, was inflationary and created a National Debt fourteen times that of 1913, whose service took half the national revenue and hence, especially when the government's economy drive started, precluded costly social reforms.

The post-war boom led to a rise of prices until they were nearly three times the pre-war level in March 1920 and they fell rapidly when the boom collapsed, wages following a similar pattern. The boom temporarily concealed the problems of returning to the pre-war world, which particularly to the older men represented that ideal of economic and social stability of which the war had been merely a tragic interruption. The war, however, had occurred at an unfortunate stage of British economic development when considerable readjustment was necessary; the great imperial expansion had temporarily saved the British economy but it was no longer as valuable an asset as it had been. Many markets had been lost during the war, when foreign customers had had to find other suppliers, with the result that exports were 43 per cent less in 1919 than in 1913. Again much foreign investment had been lost and also part of the carrying trade. Until 1929 it was firmly believed by most people that a return to pre-war conditions would in the long run be possible; it needed the great depression to bring home with a shock Britain's fundamental economic weakness.

Meanwhile there were more immediate political concerns and before the government could proceed to their settlement it was desirable to hold a general election, which was overdue by three years and which in any case would have been desirable as a result of the great changes in the franchise. Lloyd George's own position was the key to what followed; not a party leader himself, the continuation of the coalition in some form was his sole hope of remaining Prime Minister. The Labour party would not stay. He tried hard to induce Asquith and his principal colleagues to join the government, but Asquith still resented his treatment in 1916 and would not accept the Lord Chancellorship, an appointment of great dignity for which he was well qualified. Balfour thought it would be most undesirable to resume party controversy at this stage but Bonar Law was only prepared to continue providing Lloyd George gave several safeguards. He accepted imperial preference but without food taxes; although Home Rule was to remain on the statute book, Ulster was not to be coerced while there were to be some financial adjustments in the Welsh Church Disestablishment Act. Meanwhile close co-operation continued with Lloyd George who relied heavily on his advice; on numerous occasions a word from Bonar Law led the Prime Minister to abandon an impetuous idea.

The Unionists were confident of a sweeping victory and Lloyd George's Liberal Whips had to strike a bargain that Unionist candidates should not run against 150 Liberals. Nothing could be done to save those Liberals who followed Asquith. Without this agreement, known as the 'coupon', far fewer Liberals would have been elected. It has often been suggested that votes cast in the Maurice Debate[1] determined the apportionment of the 'coupon' but the facts do not bear this out; for instance twelve who voted against Lloyd George on that occasion were endorsed and no official candidate was put up against Asquith, although he was defeated by a rebel Unionist who would not withdraw. It has also been

[1] See above, p. 452.

alleged that the coalition parties demanded a much harsher peace than Asquith and Labour, but in reality there was little to choose between them. Lloyd George saw the need for moderation, but public opinion, fanned by the newspapers,[1] ran high, leading him to speak strongly, to his embarrassment when he pleaded for moderation later. Both Lloyd George and Bonar Law should have done more to discourage the vindictive feelings of their audiences, which were especially promoted by Lord Northcliffe who had a personal vendetta against Lloyd George. There is, however, no evidence that this question significantly affected the election result.

The election was principally a vote of confidence in Lloyd George, in his capacity to provide inspired leadership in peace as he had done in war, a forecast that his previous record seemed to justify. It seemed possible that he might be able to create a 'fit country for heroes to live in'. On a low poll, of just over 50 per cent, the coalition obtained 474 seats, of which 136 were Liberals. Only twenty-six Asquith Liberals were returned, without Asquith himself whose defeat appeared to many to be a disgraceful lack of appreciation of his distinguished services.[2] All the other Liberal ex-Ministers lost their seats and the party considered disbanding but held together under Sir Donald Maclean. The real opposition was the Labour party with a strength of fifty-nine. Macdonald, Henderson and Snowden were not elected and all but one M.P. was a Trades Unionist. Adamson was the leader until 1921, then Clynes.

No women took their seats, the first, Lady Astor, appearing in 1919. More significantly the seventy-three Sinn Feiners would not come to Westminster but constituted themselves an independent Assembly, the Dail, in Dublin.[3] The M.P.s who sat have been stigmatised by Asquith as the worst Parliament he ever knew and by Baldwin as 'hard faced men who had done well out of the war'. There was a higher percentage of businessmen and trades unionists, as well as new members, than usual but it would be wrong to infer from this any sinister responsibility for the character of the years that followed. With many of the best of the younger men still in France,

---

[1] The *Daily Mail* published in a box on the front page each day the totals of British casualties.
[2] He returned, at a by-election, in January 1920.
[3] See below, p. 469.

numbers of their elders were able to entrench themselves before the next election.

Much of the government reorganisation of the last two years of the war remained. The War Cabinet stayed until October 1919, meeting rarely and even then Lloyd George seldom took the ordinary Cabinet into his confidence but relied on outside advice and implemented it by means of the 'Garden Suburb'.[1] Parliament was treated with disdain by Lloyd George but was expertly managed by Bonar Law, who had the major say in all the government appointments. He gave up the Exchequer to Austen Chamberlain, who was shrewd and supremely loyal. Balfour, 'the most extraordinary *objet d'art* that ever embellished statesmanship', became Lord President after the peace conference, when Curzon succeeded him at the Foreign Office. F. E. Smith, who had risen rapidly since his entry to Parliament in 1906, became Lord Chancellor at the early age of forty-six as Lord Birkenhead. Long took over the Admiralty from Churchill who received both War Office and the new Air Ministry as compensation. Public opinion as a whole was disappointed that there was not a greater reshuffle.[2]

Some new Ministries were set up or carried over from the war years. The Ministry of Labour controlled not only labour relations but also Exchanges and unemployment insurance. Health insurance was logically grouped with the Local Government Board to form the new Ministry of Health, under Addison. The need for a single control was emphasised by the great influenza epidemic of 1918–19 and by the revelation that only just over 30 per cent of the conscripts were perfectly fit and healthy. Morant was the first Permanent Secretary; his sudden death in 1920 meant that its work proved to be less constructive than it might have been. The new Ministry of Transport also controlled the electricity supply industry. As a consequence of these new Ministries and the great extension of government activity the civil service numbers went up from nearly 58,000 in 1914 to 116,000 in 1923 and 120,000 in 1930. The individual was increasingly looking to the State to satisfy his needs, and force of circumstance, especially the teachings of the war and the compulsions of the

[1] See above, p. 442.
[2] Beaverbrook left the government and bought the *Daily Express*. He proved to be an outstanding journalist.

economic depression, was to lead politicians of all persuasions to promote collectivist tendencies.

With the Unionist party capable of forming a government in its own right, Lloyd George's position was inevitably precarious and it was essential for him to ensure real successes and to make them personal ones. His role at Versailles was essentially such. He was in effect a free agent and could conduct, with Clemenceau and Wilson, the main themes of the conference. Balfour did valuable work in impressing on the conference and its numerous sub-committees a sense of urgency.

The Conference was principally concerned with the future of Germany, that of the former Turkish and Austro-Hungarian empires being discussed elsewhere though the same principles on the whole were followed. Unlike previous great settlements it was a dictated peace in which Germany had no part and which was imposed on her in circumstances that were in due course to suggest, even to the victors, that it might not be morally binding. It inherited from the 19th Century the conceptions of the Concert of Europe, that European statesmen should meet regularly to discuss common problems and avoid war, and of the Balance of Power, that there should be collective action against an over-strong potential aggressor. Instead of war and armaments, the peacemakers envisaged a new instrument of international justice and security, the League of Nations.

The Covenant of the League was written into the treaty and owed much to the work of Smuts and Lord Robert Cecil. President Wilson, who was believed in Britain at the time to have the nobility of soul and profound historical understanding that were needed to bring about a lasting settlement, put much confidence in it. From the start a general consensus as to its purpose was lacking; Britain and the United States thought of it as an instrument of conciliation, the French as primarily a guarantee of their own security. The League was at the same time the bulwark of a territorial settlement constructed on extremely nationalistic lines and the instrument of the new internationalism. The democracies of the inter-war years, concerned with their own prestige or economic difficulties, failed to think of the international implications of their actions and thus precipitated further trouble. One example was Japanese expansionism, occasioned by such actions as the

British return to the gold standard and similar policies which brought about a shrinkage of the world market and by the closing of valuable outlets for Japanese goods in the Ottawa Agreements. There was a failure to appreciate both at Versailles and later at Geneva that politics and economics were inextricably intertwined. The greatest failure was on the part of America who conceived it possible to become the leading nation economically and yet contract out of international politics.

The territorial settlement was forged in a power vacuum in eastern Europe. For the first time since Peter the Great Russia was no longer an effective force and several boundaries were drawn that vanished with the revival of Russian power towards the end of the Second World War. Many of the successor states to the fallen empires, drawn as far as possible to correspond with ethnic boundaries, were neither militarily nor economically viable, while President Wilson's insistence on the virtues of republican government saddled many of them with régimes alien to their experience and their historical traditions.

With the German fleet interned at Scapa Flow and the former German colonies safely bestowed as trust territories or mandates on Britain or her dominions, Lloyd George could afford to act as mediator between American idealism and French realism. Alsace and Lorraine were returned, but the French judged this insufficient and wanted a Rhine frontier, although this would have meant including five million Germans. 'This is not peace – but an Armistice for twenty years' was Foch's prophetic comment when his country was forced to accept merely the demilitarisation of the coveted area and a phased withdrawal of Allied Forces from it over fifteen years, during which time France could also occupy the Saar with its valuable coal mines.[1]

The French wanted a strong Poland at Germany's expense in the east, but this was also prevented. At Lloyd George's insistence a plebiscite was held in Silesia, and Danzig with its German population became a free city under League of Nations auspices instead of part of Poland. It would have been logical to allow the German element of the former

[1] The French tried to build up separatist movements in the areas they occupied.

Hapsburg Empire to become part of Germany but at French request and to help Czechoslovakia, which had a very mixed population including Germans, this area became the economically barely viable state of Austria. The French were promised an Anglo-American guarantee against the German aggression, but when the Senate refused to ratify and the English part of the agreement lapsed in consequence, the French not unreasonably thought they had been cheated. Over the next few years they constructed an elaborate system of alliances with Belgium and the new eastern European states.

Despite considerable pressure from the public Lloyd George realistically saw that no precise figure for reparations could be set until it could be gathered exactly what Germany could afford. Her liability was stated in the Treaty and a Commission set up on which the French were preponderant after American withdrawal. They were determined to exact to the full. The German army was restricted to a hundred thousand men, the navy according to a reduced scale, while submarines, military aircraft and heavy artillery were banned. It was inferred that a general disarmament would follow.

The Peace Treaty has been much criticised. The influence of President Wilson, who knew little of Europe, led to some potential problem states, but most of the decisions made were to a great extent inevitable. Some of the frontiers which were drawn may have been the occasion of future difficulties,[1] but the growth of Nazi power, in particular, arose from far deeper and more complex questions. Far more relevant was the failure of the great powers to think and act internationally, through the League of Nations, or through conferences of which there were twenty-three between 1920 and 1922. Lloyd George constantly advocated conciliation; for the French security was paramount. The United States defected from the start, through the obstinacy of Wilson who refused to accept the Senate's reservations over preserving the territorial integrity of members of the League. In Britain a sense of isolationism was creeping back and, although Lloyd George returned triumphantly, before long he was blamed for its clauses by the left wing. Keynes in the *Economic Consequences of the Peace* spoke of the need to restore Germany to her former economic strength as a prerequisite to the prosperity of

---

[1] See below, pp. 556-566.

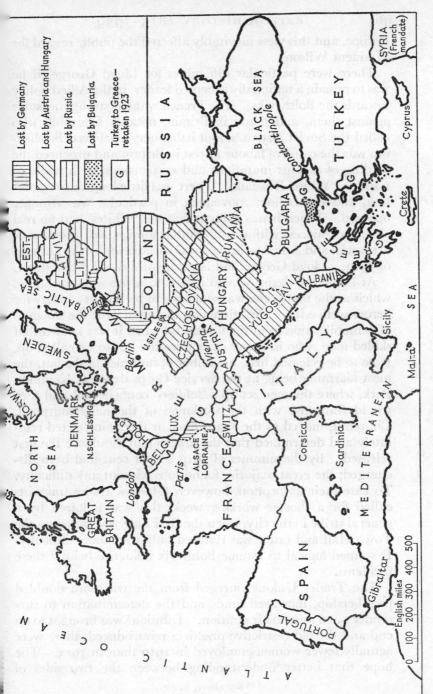

EUROPE AFTER VERSAILLES

Lost by Germany

Lost by Austria and Hungary

Lost by Russia

Lost by Bulgaria

G Turkey to Greece—retaken 1923

Europe, and this view inevitably affected the public regard for President Wilson.

There were particular difficulties for Lloyd George, if he was to remain a nationally accepted leader, in the Allied policy towards the Bolsheviks. The French wanted strong measures against them, and many in Britain, notably Churchill who called the Soviet system 'a foul baboonery', believed Bolshevism was the cause of labour unrest in Britain and procured the sending of surplus munitions and even troops for a while to assist the 'White' Russians. There was little long-term resolution, and the Labour movement in particular was strongly opposed. When it was evident that the 'Whites' had no real chance of success without substantial foreign aid, war weariness set in and Allied assistance was withdrawn by the autumn of 1919. Lloyd George had been unenthusiastic throughout.

At home the desire was to return to a pre-war normality, which at the same time was somehow to be 'the fit country for heroes to live in'. Dissatisfaction mounted over the slowness of demobilisation from the forces and when it was known that skilled men, who in many cases were the last to be called up, were to be released first, a number of mutinies broke out, the most alarming being at the Service Corps depôt at Kempton Park, where the men set up a 'soldiers' council' and said they would fraternise with the workmen of the neighbourhood. Churchill, moved to the War Office at this point, acted resolutely and determined that the first to join should be the first released. By the summer of 1919 80 per cent had been discharged; the great majority found jobs without any difficulty. To ease their absorption, however, Glasgow trades unionists called for a shorter working week; this was followed by a general strike in the city, when the Red Flag was raised on the Town Hall and order was restored only with some difficulty. It seemed logical to assume Bolshevik influence behind these incidents.

The Trades Unions emerged from the war with doubled membership, increased funds and the determination to surrender not a jot of their position. Dilution[1] was brought to an end and the old restrictive practices reintroduced; there were actually fewer women employed in 1919 than in 1913. The hope that better understanding between the two sides of

[1] See above, p. 426.

industry might be engendered proved illusory; a National Industrial Conference set up for this purpose collapsed under the weight of suspicion and the depression of 1921. A system of Whitley Councils, called after the Deputy Speaker of the Commons, was introduced to provide the opportunity for the joint consultation of employers and union representatives but survived principally in the government service. A permanent but not compulsory court of arbitration was set up in 1919.

Everybody hoped the high wartime profits would continue, with the world allegedly gasping for British goods. Speculation was rampant, much financed by the banks who were themselves by now largely consolidated into the Big Five. Amalgamations took place in almost every industry and prices rose rapidly, the employers making little effort to resist the wages claims that inevitably followed. During 1919 there was an average of 100,000 men on strike every day, and that year saw police strikes in both London and Liverpool. To add to their strength, many union amalgamations took place, forming notably the Amalgamated Engineering Union of 1920, the Transport and General Workers Union of 1921 and the General and Municipal Workers of 1924. The Transport and General Workers was organised by Bevin who had gained his reputation and his nickname of the 'Dockers' K.C.' by his skilful championship of the dockers' rights. He and J. H. Thomas of the N.U.R., who revived the Triple Alliance in 1919,[1] were a new and more constructive type of union official. The T.U.C. became a more influential body in its own right with the setting up of a General Council permanently in session.

Thomas had a particular success when Lloyd George settled a strike against a proposed reduction of wages in the autumn of 1919 on the railwaymen's terms; this put them in a very favourable position, which they were reluctant to jeopardise by further striking. The miners, whose industry, like the railways, was still government controlled, remained dissatisfied. In an industry in which it could be reasonably argued that the owners of royalties contributed nothing to productivity, class bitterness was real and there was little attempt at understanding by either side. 'I should call them the stupidest men in England,' said Birkenhead of the miners, 'if I had not

[1] See above, p. 396.

previously had to deal with the owners.' The Sankey Commission was set up in 1919 to try to deal with this impasse.

Presided over by a judge who was later to be a Labour Lord Chancellor, it consisted of three owners and three businessmen on the one hand, three miners and three economists favourable to them on the other. Four reports were issued but seven members favoured nationalisation, a course which Lloyd George rejected. The miners on their part would accept nothing else, feeling they had been betrayed. With 3,000 pits owned by 1,500 firms, reorganisation of some sort was overdue. The only results were the reduction of the working day to seven hours, temporary limitation of profits and the establishment of the Miners' Welfare Fund, which spent money on pit-head baths and similar amenities. With Europe still disordered, sales of coal ran at record levels and in October 1920 the miners struck for higher wages. Though offering a temporary settlement on the miners' terms, Lloyd George took advantage of the situation to acquire for the government, in the Emergency Powers Act of 1920, dictatorial powers to settle industrial unrest.

Two incidents that summer had shown the use of strikes or the threat of strikes for political purposes. This appeared to onlookers to have a suspicious affinity with the aims of the Communist Party of Great Britain, set up in July 1920 and disowned by the Labour party. With the Poles mounting a campaign in the Ukraine against Russia, dockers in London refused to load munitions for Poland on to the *Jolly George* in May. In July when the French wanted to intervene after the Polish defeat Bevin presented an ultimatum to prevent Lloyd George from co-operating with them. In both cases the government gave way, aware that public opinion was against further involvement.

(*b*) THE DECLINE AND FALL OF LLOYD GEORGE,[1] 1920–22

In the winter of 1920–21 the post-war honeymoon ended abruptly and although Lloyd George continued in office for a further two years it was in a period of growing disillusionment. There had been unwise investment and expansion, for Europe had not yet recovered from the post-war turmoil while British industries were not efficient enough to recover the markets

[1] The title of a fascinating book by Lord Beaverbrook.

lost during the war. There was too much shipping and primary products were being over-produced, a state of affairs that prevailed until the Second World War. In 1919 and 1920 industry had absorbed men as quickly as they were demobilised and there was practically no unemployment, but after December 1920 it rose rapidly, reaching two million by the summer. As long as the boom persisted the government was generous – even extravagant – in its distribution of public funds.

An example of this was the government's housing policy. The shortage of houses, with the wartime halt to building and neglect of repairs aggravating the inadequacies of the past, was fully appreciated by Lloyd George and Addison, his Health Minister. Instead of the government setting up its own agency, however, the local authorities were instructed to build as many houses as they could and let them at low rents. They were expected to spend the equivalent of a penny rate from their own resources; the government supplied the rest. Nearly a quarter of a million houses were built in this way although at an unduly high cost and public responsibility for this most basic of health services was fully established. With the depression the government took fright, reduced the subsidies and then stopped them altogether in 1922 with the result that, with a lower marrying age after the war, the housing shortage was as bad as ever.[1]

The hopes of peacetime achievement were particularly great in education. The department, now a Ministry, under the historian, H. A. L. Fisher, was responsible for the Education Act of 1918 which raised the leaving age to fourteen, greatly restricted the employment of schoolchildren and aimed at providing for the continuation of education after the leaving age. Like the other social services, it was curtailed as a result of the depression, but Fisher's work helped to improve the status of the teaching profession.

The State insurance system was overhauled and extended. The limit was raised to £250 a year and rates of contribution and benefit for Health Insurance were increased. Although it was recognised that the existing operation through approved societies was unsatisfactory, it remained untouched.[2] An Act of 1920 extended unemployment insurance to nearly twelve

[1] See below, p. 487.   [2] See above, p. 397.

million workers, offering weekly benefits of fifteen shillings (twelve shillings for women) for short periods of unemployment; longer periods were covered, with family allowances, in 1921. As a self-supporting system it was wrecked from the start by the rapid growth of unemployment, before it had had the chance to accumulate funds. To keep the unemployed from the Poor Law and to save the poor rate from strain in hard hit districts 'uncovenanted' and 'extended benefits' were introduced, popularly known as 'the dole'. No distinction was made after 1927 but the name persisted. Whatever its associations, the dole may well have prevented revolution or widespread disorders.

In shipbuilding, the unemployment rate in the winter of 1921–22 was as high as 36·1 per cent and in iron and steel it was 36·7 per cent. In Northern Ireland 25 per cent of the insured population was unemployed, in Scotland 21 per cent. Some towns were very severely hit; the Hartlepools had 60 per cent and parts of Glasgow 59 per cent. Relief works were only sparingly resorted to; an opportunity to reinflate the economy by extending the house-building programme was neglected. Government expenditure in general was sharply cut, by means of the 'Geddes Axe', to save £50 m. a year and to enable a shilling to be dropped from the income tax. This was in response to a campaign in the popular Press; the reductions merely aggravated the situation.

To reduce government responsibilities the railways and the mines were decontrolled; some reorganisation took place in the former which were grouped in four large companies, operative from 1923, but the mines were handed back to their pre-war owners at the end of March 1921 at a time when export coal prices sank from 115s. to 24s. a ton and home demand was shrinking with industries going on short time. The owners proposed a wage cut and the abolition of the national wage rate introduced during the war; the miners were not prepared to accept the arrangement whereby wages were related to the richness of the seams on which they were working. The reduction in the weekly wage was as high as 49 per cent in South Wales. A lockout was prepared for 1st April and the government, fearing communist influence behind the miners and, as was suspected by the working class, anxious for a showdown, mobilised the armed forces. Lloyd

George was ready for a temporary subsidy but the miners' cause became hopeless when the other members of the Triple Alliance which they had invoked refused, at the last minute, to strike in support on 15th April, a day known in Trades Union history as 'Black Friday'. The weakness which this incident demonstrated had always been present in the Triple Alliance. By its terms, one of the three unions could commit the others to sympathetic action without surrendering its un- divided control over negotiations, which in this case the miners' executive had refused to reopen by a majority of one. Moreover, moderates such as Thomas[1] felt that potentially revolutionary actions of this nature were playing into the hands of the government; the new role of the unions should be one of partnership.

The miners remained on strike until the beginning of July when district agreements were imposed and a temporary subsidy given. They could have obtained better terms in March. Wage reductions followed in other industries and were on the whole tacitly accepted. There was in fact much less unrest during the slump than during the boom.

Working-class confidence in Lloyd George, however, was largely shattered while other actions of his were to undermine the willingness of the Conservative party to continue to sup- port him. He had promised Bonar Law in 1918 that he would consider some tariff reform and in 1921 'key industries' were 'safeguarded' against foreign 'dumping', words that in themselves it was hoped, would avert Liberal wrath. What it really implied was the protection of certain home industries against cheap foreign competition and it deceived nobody. The result was a fissure between the Liberal and Conservative supporters of Lloyd George.

The Dominions, now virtually sovereign states, were unwil- ling to make such concessions as would have brought about Empire Free Trade.[2] It was chiefly sentiment that tied them to Britain, stimulated at this time by a series of successful tours by the Prince of Wales, whose popularity was at its height.

Conservative loyalty was severely tried by the handling of Ireland. Sinn Fein candidates elected in 1918 had

---

[1] For his part in the affair J. H. Thomas was compared to Judas by one news- paper, against whom he won heavy damages in a libel action.
[2] See below, p. 505.

constituted themselves the Dail and had appealed unsuccessfully to President Wilson for mediation. Events from 1914 onwards had convinced them that the English could not be trusted to honour their promises and would readily resort to the use of force; consequently they regarded force rather than peaceful persuasion as the most sensible course.

A massive boycott was tried initially. The Dail appointed an executive committee under De Valera, whose American citizenship had saved him from execution in 1916, which assumed the functions of government, levied taxes, established courts of justice and issued instructions to local officials. It was hoped that the British administration would wither away through disuse. The Irish Republican Brotherhood, with an ancestry as a secret society going back to the Fenians of the 1860's, insisted on speedier measures and under its influence the Volunteers became the Irish Republican Army. It was directed by Michael Collins, an excellent organiser who inspired great devotion and who discovered every British move in advance from the mainly Irish employees of the Dublin Castle administration. His troops were summoned secretly for a specific task and, that completed, they melted into civilian life. With comparatively few active at any given time they were able to keep occupied many times their number of British troops and police. They were paid by Sinn Fein funds, constantly replenished from the United States.

The Royal Irish Constabulary was a particular target. Its members were ambushed and had to be withdrawn from outlying posts. It was demoralised even more by social ostracism, which led to its members who were chiefly Irish, resigning in large numbers. To replace them men had to be recruited in England, largely from demobilised N.C.O.s and, later, officers. They were issued with surplus khaki uniforms and black webbing and were dubbed the 'Black and Tans' after a well-known pack of hounds in County Limerick. An auxiliary division, the 'Auxis', was formed from among them and authorised to undertake reprisals, which, though often effective, caused far more outcry among the British public than the outrages which occasioned them.

The year 1920 was decisive from the military point of view. It became abundantly clear that only a full-scale reconquest would make the exercise of British power possible. When

Home Rule was already on the statute book, this was flying in the face of reason. The Tory party had little sympathy with Irish aspirations and strongly advocated the use of force, a policy which Lloyd George's favourite military adviser, Sir Henry Wilson, also advocated. Trouble occurred chiefly in south-west Ireland and in the cities of Cork and Dublin, where on 4th April the I.R.A. excelled itself by destroying all the income tax records, an example repeated at branch offices throughout the country. Appalling examples of violence occurred on both sides, the Black and Tans on occasions sacking villages and behaving inexcusably. Martial law was proclaimed in the south-west and Tans and Auxis did much damage in Cork in December 1920. The authorities seemed powerless to control them.

To persuade public opinion, particularly that of the United States, that the government had some policy apart from repression, the government of Ireland Act was passed in 1920. It superseded Asquith's Act and, at Bonar Law's insistence, set up one parliament with limited powers for the Six Counties and one for the rest of Ireland. They could be federated by means of a Council of Ireland some time in the future. Ulster, which had wanted to remain part of the United Kingdom, was forced to accept self-government; when the Dail forbade trade with the North in January 1921 Ulstermen became prouder of their unwanted privilege. In the south a similar proposal was outstripped by events.

The impasse was broken by George V's speech when he opened the Ulster Parliament in June 1921 and proposed dominion status for the rest of the island. The idea was Smuts' but it was evident to Lloyd George that the country would not support the indefinite continuation or extension of the present coercive policy, while the Irish were known to be ready for negotiations. As a preliminary a truce came into operation in July 1921; the I.R.A. did not surrender its arms, which would have been impossible to enforce in any case, but once stopped, the war became steadily more difficult to restart.

The conference consisted of five Irish representatives, of whom Collins was the most outstanding, and five British Ministers, led by Austen Chamberlain and Birkenhead, who acquired a high regard for Collins, which was reciprocated. They met in secret session. For reasons of defence it was desirable for the Irish to remain within the Commonwealth and Lloyd George tempted them if they would agree, with control of Ulster for a trial period. This was forbidden by Bonar Law, now in retirement, and a renewal of the war seemed likely. Lloyd George called Irish bluff, promised to rig the boundary commission so that Ulster would not be viable and finally issued an ultimatum – sign, or war within three days. The Treaty was signed on 6th December and approved by Parliament ten days later, when a speech by Bonar Law prevented a Tory back bench revolt.

The Dail concurred by a narrow majority. The minority included De Valera who resigned as president and a government was formed under the more conciliatory Arthur Griffith, the founder of Sinn Fein. Authority was officially granted them on 16th January.

Deep divisions remained in Ireland. The Treaty was conditional on the holding of a General Election, which showed a majority of 72 per cent in favour, an unreal percentage, because an electoral pact between Griffith and De Valera gave the latter's supporters more seats than they would have won otherwise. De Valera encouraged intransigence by forceful speeches. In April, I.R.A. irregulars under Rory O'Connor seized the Four Courts in Dublin, from which they were not dislodged until June with British help. British participation followed the murder of Sir Henry Wilson, who was wearing Field-Marshal's uniform, on the doorstep of his own house in a busy London street in broad daylight. The government was bitterly criticised by the right wing, who claimed this was the consequence of the Irish concessions, of 'shaking hands with murder'.

The British intervention led to an open civil war between the new Irish government and its intransigents, in which atrocities worse than those during the Troubles and considerable physical destruction took place. Collins was killed in an ambush in August while Griffith died of a heart attack, though poison was suspected. Seventy-seven executions and 11,000 internments took place before peace was restored. The constitution of the new Irish Free State was finally approved in December 1922, with W. T. Cosgrave as Premier and T. M. Healy, an ageing and respected former M.P., an imaginative choice as Governor-General. This was technically a royal appointment but the only other restrictions on Irish independence were an oath of loyalty for members of the Dail and the retention by the British Navy of three treaty ports, together with one in Ulster. There was no mention of the Southern Unionists in the new Constitution, but they were in no way discriminated against. The Boundary Commission failed by 1925 to settle a division between the two parts of the island which would be agreeable to both sides, so it remained that of the Six Counties, which was undoubtedly unfair to the Roman Catholic districts of Fermanagh and Tyrone. The Irish had, to recall Gladstone, stood at the Bar for the last time,[1] but the rejection of 1886 had implanted a sense of bitterness that had grown with the years; now that liberty was achieved, it was too late for Ireland to be reconciled.

Lloyd George had brought a settlement to a perennial problem and that was no mean achievement: it was a piece of opportunism that was well justified. But British history had been strewn with the bones of politicians whose careers had been ended or blighted by the intractable island and Lloyd George's was no exception. The left wing could not forgive the use of the Black and Tans, the right found it hard to accept the breaking of the union, especially when the Civil War confirmed all their beliefs in Irish irresponsibility. Measures of retrenchment always made a government unpopular and by-election results were adverse from 1919 onwards. The Coalition's big majority in Parliament was hard to control. Many in politics were concerned about future political alignments; little except thoroughgoing protection now divided Conservatives and Liberals and the logic of events suggested a fusion in opposition to socialism, which was increasingly stealing Lloyd George's former Radical thunder. Fusion was much discussed in the spring of 1920 but the rank and file on neither side were enthusiastic.[2]

In the spring of 1921 the stability of the Coalition received a severe blow when Bonar Law resigned on account of ill health; during his tenure of office his reputation had steadily increased and Chamberlain, loyal to the Coalition though he was, had not, as Leader, the same control over the Conservative party. He carried them with him over the Irish settlement but too many feared their principles would be compromised or their

careers blighted if the Coalition became permanent. A cata-
logue of accusations could be mustered against Lloyd George
to justify such an attitude: his dictatorship, his rare appearances in the Commons, his sale of honours,[1] to name only a
few. In February 1922 he offered to resign so that Chamberlain could form a purely Conservative government, but
Chamberlain was too loyal or too wary to accept and in any
case Lloyd George may not have been serious.

It was in the field of foreign affairs, where Lloyd George had
a high regard for his own talents, that he hoped to find salvation, but in fact drove the final nail into his coffin. Under
Dominion pressure he sent Balfour as British representative to
a Naval Conference at Washington (November 1921–
February 1922) where Britain accepted naval parity in battleships with the United States while Japan agreed to keep in
service only three-fifths of the British number. The British
wish to ban submarines was opposed by the other participants.
Thus the only ships really restricted were those which were
largely out of date. Britain gave up the Anglo-Japanese
Alliance but the *status quo* in the Pacific was guaranteed by a
four-power treaty. Lloyd George was more closely involved
personally at the Genoa Conference of April and May 1922;
he hoped to bring Russia and Germany back to equal status and
close trading contacts with other nations, but the United States
blighted the prospects by refusing to attend and France would
only co-operate if given firm and specific guarantees of military
support in the event of difficulties with Germany. The only
outcome was a Russo-German pact at Rapallo.

Turkey was even more a scene of failure. The Treaty of
Sèvres signed with the Sultan in 1920 had provided for the
occupation of parts of Turkey for five years. The Greeks,
with Allied blessing and notably the encouragement of Lloyd
George, invaded western Turkey, where the coastal towns had
a Greek population and penetrated far into the interior until
brought to a standstill by feuds between royalists and republicans in Greece itself. This gave an opportunity to Kemal,
who was building a national Turkish State; he drove back the

---

[1] This was unreasonable, as the Conservatives took a half share. The other
half became the Lloyd George Fund. There was a recognised scale: a gift of
£50,000 led to a barony. So many were awarded after the war that, for
instance, Cardiff became known as 'the city of dreadful Knights'. A Royal
Commission later looked into the matter.

Greeks, captured Smyrna on 9th September and appeared to threaten the neutral zone, especially the town of Chanak on the edge of it. Alarmists saw an invasion of the Balkans to follow. Lloyd George saw the opportunity to resist aggression and rally national opinion behind him. Without consulting Curzon, the Foreign Secretary, he and Churchill drafted a flamboyant communiqué talking of the 'Turkish menace' and the risk of war. The French, who had been selling munitions to Kemal, were annoyed and withdrew their troops from the neutral zone; most of the Dominions resented an action which seemed to involve them in an unnecessary war, a view shared by public opinion in Britain. The Conservative party, traditionally pro-Turk, felt the danger was exaggerated. The British Commander in Chanak fortunately delayed taking action until the danger was past. On 11th October at the Pact of Mudania the Turks agreed to respect the neutral zone.

The Chanak Affair brought to a head distrust of Lloyd George on the Conservative back benches, a distrust shared, in retirement, by Bonar Law. It was almost ironical that it was, as Lord Boothby has put it, 'The last occasion on which Great Britain stood up to a potential aggressor before the outbreak of the Second World War.' Expecting that the Conservative Party Conference meeting on 15th November would vote against the Coalition, the Cabinet decided on 10th October to fight a general election as a Coalition again, Baldwin, President of the Board of Trade, alone dissenting. Chamberlain who felt that the party had used Lloyd George in the past, considered it disloyal and dishonourable to throw him over when he was no longer needed, a view shared by other leading Conservatives. He was confident that the back benchers, without a leader, would come to heel, but at the request of the Chairman of the party, Sir George Younger, he agreed to hold a meeting of M.P.s at the Carlton Club on 19th October to secure official approval.

Two men bore perhaps equal responsibility for the outcome. Baldwin had a passionate loyalty to the party, which he believed reflected all that was best in the country. He distrusted Lloyd George as a political schemer and was shocked by the irregularity of his private life and his cynical use of the honours system. He feared the effects of his dynamism, as he said at the meeting: 'A dynamic force is a very terrible thing.

It had disintegrated the Liberal Party and was in progress of disintegrating the Conservative.' Baldwin's principles gave him considerable influence over the ordinary back benchers; they also gained him the ear of Bonar Law, to whom he had formerly been Parliamentary Private Secretary.

Beaverbrook has been his own biographer but it would appear that Baldwin's part in persuading Bonar Law to come forward was as great as his. He felt that as long as Lloyd George remained in power his aim of Empire Free Trade would never be achieved. On 18th October Beaverbrook stayed with the former leader until midnight and would not leave until he had agreed to come to the meeting. Both men realised that Bonar Law was the only man who could entice the naturally loyal Conservatives away from the official leader of the party at such a meeting. Bonar Law was reluctant; ageing and not in the best of health he had no particular wish to return to active politics; moreover he had enjoyed a long and mutually profitable partnership with Lloyd George which had immensely benefited the nation. To the last he hoped Lloyd George would resign in Chamberlain's favour. Even on the morning of the 19th he was still reluctant; only the last-minute persuasion of Sir George Younger finally convinced him the future of the party was at stake.

The morning of the meeting brought the news of the Newport by-election in which an Independent Conservative, supported by Beaverbrook, defeated unexpectedly the Coalition Liberal. It may have swayed the last-minute doubters. Bonar Law's speech was decisive: 'The feeling against the continuation of the Coalition is so strong that if we follow Mr Chamberlain's advice our party will be broken and a new party will be formed.' By 187 to 87 the Conservatives resolved to fight the election independently. It was not a reactionary intrigue; as McKenzie has put it, the meeting was 'a thoroughly healthy manifestation of internal party politics'. On hearing the result Lloyd George promptly resigned.

Most prominent politicians were still under the Lloyd George spell at a time when disillusionment with his policies had largely broken it in the country. By 1922 Lloyd George was strangely out of date; he and his party had been almost too successful in promoting social reform and smoothing the way to greater democracy; the forces they unleashed consolidated themselves behind a Labour party which was prepared to go much further; the forces that feared such changes naturally coalesced behind the Conservatives and in the circumstances Lloyd George's cardinal error was in failing to conciliate the Conservative back benchers. Had Lloyd George and Asquith, two of the finest minds the Liberal party ever produced, not bitterly distrusted one another, the outcome might have been different, but in the long run probably not. When he failed to weld the Coalition into a permanent party, as Balfour and Chamberlain had done a quarter of a century earlier, Lloyd George had no political future. Unlike Joseph Chamberlain he was not a man of apparent principle nor a man who inspired trust. He had held the highest offices continuously for nearly seventeen years, an unparalleled record in modern times in Britain. He never held office again.

(c) Two Unknown Prime Ministers

The resignation of Lloyd George brought in a period of Conservative dominance that effectively lasted, with a slight interruption at the end of the twenties, until 1939. The Parliamentary System depends on the effective clash of political interests; before 1931 the Liberal party had virtually died, although slight signs of revival were discernible in 1929, but the Labour party was still too untried and incohesive to take its place as a real alternative government. The Conservatives were firmly entrenched in power, disguised as the National Government, from 1931 onwards.

As he left Westminster Abbey after Bonar Law's funeral, Asquith unkindly remarked that the unknown Prime Minister had been laid to rest close to the Unknown Soldier. Bonar Law's premiership was short and undistinguished but few men were more widely respected in political life; the description was more apt if applied to his successor, Stanley Baldwin, to whom the temporary alienation of the most distinguished Conservative gave the unexpected chance of power.

Bonar Law sought election as Leader of the Conservative party before accepting the premiership. For his Cabinet he had few established men to draw on, for all Lloyd George's Cabinet, apart from two, refused to accept the Carlton Club decision. Although the breach was healed in 1925, the under-secretaries established themselves in power and complacent and pedestrian management took the place of leadership. Heads of great families–Salisbury, Devonshire, provided ballast; Curzon continued as Foreign Secretary; disgruntled after Chanak he jumped after the main chance but missed the dukedom he aspired to in Lloyd George's Dissolution Honours. Bonar Law gravely doubted Baldwin's capacity for the Chancellorship but appointed him when he failed to attract McKenna who though he hated Lloyd George, preferred the security of the chairmanship of the Midland Bank. Such a dearth of talent was dubbed by Churchill as a 'government of the Second Eleven'; Bonar Law saw it as a caretaker administration.

The new Prime Minister's aim was tranquil and normal government, thus reflecting the probable wishes of most voters. The premiership was to revert to its traditional role and in consequence he disbanded the 'Garden Suburb' whose work had often cut across the functions of the departments. The Cabinet Secretariat under Hankey, which had already proved itself invaluable, was retained and became an important and indispensible part of the machinery of government.[1] In the General Election campaign Bonar Law, whose personal triumph it very largely was, played down controversial issues including protection, which he promised would not be introduced before the next election. The Labour party had an extremely controversial matter, a capital levy to eliminate the war debt, as the main plank of its election programme but it was discarded during the campaign as it was so evidently a liability. Many voters, however, distrusted the party's doctrinal rigidity and it was widely believed to be tainted by communism.

The outcome confirmed the Conservatives in power with 345 seats and an overall majority of seventy-seven. There were 117 Liberals in all, split fairly evenly between the followers of Asquith and those of Lloyd George. Churchill was among those who lost their seats. The Labour party was no longer the substantially trades unionist party of former Parliaments; with 142 members it contained a considerable minority from middle-class backgrounds, many of whom were attracted to the party by its abandonment of the traditional

---

[1] See above, p. 442.

THE SEARCH FOR NORMALITY

foreign policy, which was held to have been responsible for the war. The Independent Labour Party represented the most socialist element, although both Macdonald and Snowden were nominated by the I.L.P. Twenty-nine of them, the 'Clydesiders', elected from the Glasgow area, believed profoundly in social revolution and included Kirkwood, Shinwell, Wheatley and Maxton, who rapidly became one of the most popular figures in the House but had little power of leadership. The party as a whole was not revolutionary but principally wanted acceptance and imagined that a policy of social reform would lead almost inevitably to the socialist ideal. Politically the party was immature though it gained strength from genuine idealism and the solid support of the Trades Unions. Its association with Bolshevism in the public mind was a constant embarrassment; the party firmly repudiated any connection though Russian achievements continued to exercise a fascination.

The first task of the Labour party was to elect a leader. The outgoing leader, Clynes, who had been Minister of Food at the end of the war, was a moderate trades unionist, shrewd, straightforward and unassuming. Although most of the leading men in the party, apart from Henderson, supported him, he was beaten by five votes by Ramsay Macdonald, whose pacifism, suggesting, quite wrongly, extremist views, made him attractive to the Clydesiders.

Macdonald was the illegitimate son of a peasant girl and assumed his father's surname. Brought up in poverty, he became interested in socialism when he came south but until 1894 expected that the Liberal party would fulfil working-class aims. Attracted to the I.L.P., he was elected secretary of the Labour Representation Committee in 1900 and an M.P. in 1906. He played a major part in the foundation and early years of the party and was enabled to do so by the acquisition of a private income on his marriage to Margaret Gladstone, a relative of the Prime Minister, in 1896. In appearance he was very distinguished, with the tastes of a cultivated man of leisure but an ability in his speeches to make emotional appeals which gave the impression that he was a man of high principle. His real personality was strangely elusive; few political leaders have been less understood or have stood more detached from their followers. Churchill's jibe that he was 'the boneless

wonder' had an echo in the experience of his own colleagues who found it hard to pin him down, to extract
practical propositions from a cloud of wordy generalities.
Beatrice Webb described him as 'a magnificent substitute for
a leader.   He has the ideal appearance . . . but he is shoddy in
character and intellect.'   Lord Elton called him 'a moderate
with the equipment of a fanatic'.

Although he professed socialism, Macdonald was not a
supporter of concrete socialist proposals. He was romantic
and benevolent in his aims, essentially moderate in his actions.
Though elected by the Left, he aligned himself with the Right,
a factor which led to his party failing to establish a positive
identity. Nevertheless he was probably the best leader for
his time. The most skilful parliamentarian the party had, he
was an established national figure and in himself a guarantee
to the public at large that here was no wild and revolutionary
force. With the help of Baldwin, whom in many ways he
resembled, he established the Labour party as a genuine
alternative government and, despite his failures, retained the
respect of those whom he led, although he was supersensitive
to criticism. He was an able chairman of the Cabinet, skilful
in negotiations and a capable Foreign Secretary whose actions
set the tone of much of British inter-war diplomacy.

He was supported by Henderson, an efficient organiser who
thought his parliamentary talents essential. Snowden, who
twice served him at the Exchequer, was able but with a biting
tongue, and despised him for his vanities and his vagueness.

Bonar Law's brief Ministry contained few events of importance. The Germans were defaulting on their reparations
obligations, fixed at £6,600 m. in 1921, owing to a currency
crisis and in January 1923 the French occupied the Ruhr,
which produced 85 per cent of German coal and 80 per cent of
her steel and pig iron. The British view was that Germany
must be restored to financial prosperity before reparations
could be collected and that they should be limited to what the
receiving countries owed in war debts. The government
failed to prevent the French action which resulted in German
passive resistance and lack of co-operation which caused the
mark, twenty to the pound in 1918, to fall to 22,300 million to
the pound at the end of 1923. Curzon sent a stiff note in
August which restored some confidence in Germany.

Anglo-French relations had been strained by the Chanak Affair, but Curzon handled negotiations with skill at the Lausanne Conference that followed. He not only secured the great prize of the Mosul oil wells for Britain but he reestablished British prestige in Europe and conciliated Turkey. His success raised his standing in the government though Bonar Law found him difficult to work with.

Baldwin was sent to Washington to negotiate a settlement of the war debt of £987 m. In August 1922, Balfour, temporarily in charge of the Foreign Office, had issued a Note maintaining that British debt settlement should be related to what she received herself from others. It was not well received in America and when Baldwin arrived with instructions to settle on this basis, Mellon, the U.S. Secretary of the Treasury, offered a firm repayment programme over sixty-one years with interest at $3\frac{1}{2}$ per cent. Montague Norman, Governor of the Bank of England, who accompanied Baldwin, was a financial purist who did not wish Britain's position as the centre of the international money market, which he wished to restore, to be damaged by any hint of default. Baldwin felt honest Englishmen should pay their debts. Without reference to Bonar Law he settled for interest at 3 per cent for ten years, then $3\frac{1}{2}$ per cent, on a reducing debt for the remaining fifty-one. On arrival at Southampton he told the Press it was a fair settlement and thus made it difficult for the government to repudiate it. Bonar Law seriously considered resignation; Keynes maintained – correctly – that the settlement would be a hindrance to British and world recovery, particularly as the exacting of payments from Germany continued to be necessary. Both Italy and France obtained more generous arrangements from the United States later, but the British settlement was not revised.[1]

Baldwin's mishandling of the war debt question made him on the face of it an unlikely successor to the premiership when Bonar Law resigned in May 1923 on being informed that he had incurable cancer of the throat.[2] Most of the leading Conservatives were temporarily estranged by the Carlton Club decision and the only politician of stature in the Cabinet was Lord Curzon, who desperately wanted the premiership. Bonar Law regarded his succession as inevitable but had little

---

[1] See above, p. 456 and below, p. 530. [2] He died in October.

confidence in him.   He had recently received a letter from
him which suggested a dangerous lack of proportion, while
Curzon's facility to jump the way the wind was blowing suggested a lack of principle.   Beaverbrook, indeed, called him 'a
political jumping jack'.   Such behaviour was contrasted with
his overwhelming sense of grandeur and almost insufferable
pomposity.   Despite his prestige and his brilliance most men
in public life knew in their hearts that Curzon would not do.
Bonar Law had not committed himself, but his secretary, Water-
house, consulted by Lord Stamfordham, suggested Baldwin.
    Balfour's advice in particular was sought.   He had had
misgivings about Curzon for a long time and felt he should not
benefit from his last-minute desertion of Lloyd George.   More
vitally, he believed that recent developments in British politics,
particularly the rise of the Labour party which as yet was unrepresented there, made it undesirable to have a Prime
Minister in the House of Lords.   To Curzon's intense annoyance, the King summoned Baldwin: 'Not even a public figure,'
as he put it, 'a man of no experience, of the utmost insignificance.'[1]   This was not an independent exercise of the prerogative as is sometimes suggested, but of great constitutional
significance in that it was now apparent that the premiership
must be held by a member of the House of Commons.
    Baldwin later wrote to Asquith: 'The position of leader came
to me when I was inexperienced, before I was really fitted for
it, by a succession of curious chances . . . I had never expected
it; I was in no way trained for it.'   His previous career had
not been distinguished.   Taking his father's seat when he died
in 1908, he was a retiring back bencher until he became
Parliamentary Private Secretary to Bonar Law in 1916 when
it was hoped his wealth would enable him to do the entertaining the latter disliked.   He became Financial Secretary to the
Treasury in 1918, giving up a fifth of his private fortune to
help the country's financial difficulties, an action that was
much admired but little imitated.   As President of the Board
of Trade in 1921 at the age of 53, he was respected both by the
business community and by the Commons.   Nevertheless
when he became Prime Minister in 1923 he was almost unknown, a man without a political past despite his prominent
part in the downfall of the Coalition.

[1] These views did not prevent him from continuing as Foreign Secretary.

He was soon to show that he was Bonar Law's logical successor. As was Bonar Law's, the keynote of his policy was 'Tranquillity'. He felt that he was 'chosen as God's instrument for the work of healing the nation' and that the main purpose of his political life was 'the binding together of all classes of our people in an effort to make life in the country better in every sense of the word'. His bitter dislike of Lloyd George, who adopted Keynesian ideas,[1] may have prejudiced him against using the resources of the State to prevent unemployment, but in the political field Baldwin probably played a more important part than Macdonald in integrating the Labour party into constitutional life and making it possible for it to be a genuine alternative government. In industrial disputes he was more conciliatory than most Conservatives and his handling of the General Strike, once it had begun, was masterly. The Labour M.P.s invariably listened to him with unfailing respect.

His conception of class conciliation, which he derived in part from an idealised recollection of relationships at his family's steelworks in Worcestershire, was tempered by his loyalty to the Conservative party which he held to be the repository of the fundamental morality and honesty of the nation. When public opinion deprecated great armaments, he avowedly hid his knowledge of Germany's position lest his party's electoral chances be damaged. Churchill called him 'The greatest party manager the Conservatives had ever had.' Unlike Lloyd George, he never neglected the back benchers. He sat for hours in the Commons and was acutely sensitive to its atmosphere. He rarely took an initiative, even in the Cabinet, but in a subtle way influenced the course of events which usually worked for him. Frequently he realised the best policy was to leave well alone.

In the nation as a whole he was trusted for much of his career as few other politicians have been, precisely because he did not seem to be a politician. Shy, nervous, clever, he presented to the world an immense personal charm, a plain countryman's common sense, a stolid adherence to those principles that had made the Old England great and which exactly matched the nostalgia of the man in the street, bemused by the problems of the inter-war years. Sucking his

[1] See below, p. 504.

pipe, contemplating his pigs, he seemed a rock of reassurance. 'In personal contact he gave an impression of deep and unforced sincerity.'[1] His mastery in Parliament was matched by his supremacy in the new art of broadcasting; unlike Lloyd George and Macdonald he had precisely the ability to chat as the fireside friend. These apparently effortless performances were tremendous works of art whose creation exhausted him. They encouraged him to move in generalities; like Macdonald he was not primarily a man of action, but he was a man of much greater ability.

Chosen though he was almost by accident, the perpetrator of serious errors whose frank acknowledgement invariably restored his popularity while he was still in political life, Baldwin never had a serious challenger as leader of the party. Perhaps for this reason he made no attempt to reinstate Austen Chamberlain until 1924. Neville Chamberlain, who held a key position in all his Ministries and who often resented his inaction, was never a serious competitor.

Neville Chamberlain had followed his father's steps in local government and had been Lord Mayor of Birmingham in 1916. A failure as director of National Service, he had entered the Commons in 1918 at the age of 50. Baldwin made him Minister of Health in 1923, the office most suited to his talents. His Housing Act was designed to restart the housing programme after the expiry of the Addison Scheme; it offered a small subsidy to private builders building for sale as well as to local authorities. The former chiefly benefited from it and although nearly half a million houses were built under the scheme, representing a further step by the Conservatives towards collectivism, the housing problems of the very poor were still unresolved. Chamberlain was promoted to the Exchequer when Baldwin failed to secure McKenna.

Chamberlain showed himself to be an administrator of ability with a great capacity for detail. Resolute and strictly business-like, but with high ideals, he accomplished valuable reforms in the running of the social services. In personality he was a complete contrast to Baldwin, lacking his breadth of vision and his mastery of the Commons. In the Cabinet he was dictatorial, unready to accept advice and impatient of criticism. As an administrator of the social services he lacked

[1] Sir Colin Coote.

the human touch; he shrank from co-operation after 1925 with Churchill who wished to dramatise the problems of the neglected in a great campaign. He was, Sir Arthur Salter said, in manner 'glacial rather than genial'. Where Baldwin conciliated, he antagonised.

Baldwin's first Ministry was short lived, although it settled down well. The problem of the unemployed, of whom there were still over one million, remained perplexing and inevitably many, including, it was rumoured, Lloyd George, felt Tariff Reform would help the situation. In a speech at Plymouth in October, Baldwin suddenly announced, in a way that almost suggested he was thinking aloud, that he must be free to introduce protection, though he promised that there would not be any food taxes. He subsequently claimed he wished to steal a march on Lloyd George; he may have believed such a campaign would establish him firmly in the leadership or that he was implementing the resolution of the Imperial Conference of 1923 in favour of preferences.[1] What it certainly did was to introduce a division of principle between the Conservatives and the other parties and bring the dissidents of the party back to the ranks. His Cabinet colleagues thought the announcement, for which the country was in no way prepared, extremely ill-advised and after the General Election in December 1923 which Bonar Law's pledge made necessary, Baldwin acknowledged to a party meeting that Tariff Reform was a mistake and should be laid aside.

The two Liberal groups also came together again and Asquith and Lloyd George jointly signed a Free Trade Manifesto. Election expenses were met by the Lloyd George Fund and the reunited party gained forty seats, making 159 in all. The Labour Manifesto rejected tariffs as being no remedy for unemployment but only an aid to profiteering. They won fifty seats, making a total of 191, of whom only half were trades unionists. Although the largest party with 258, the Conservatives no longer had a majority, and in view of the election issue could hardly expect the support of another party. Paradoxically Baldwin was not ejected from the leadership; his public image was if anything enhanced – a man who put his principles before his party – and his party remained united.

[1] See below, p. 505.

Parliament did not meet until 21st January when the government was predictably defeated on a Free Trade amendment to the Address. In the previous month the country gradually accustomed itself to the prospect of a Labour government which many believed would undermine the fabric of the State. It was suggested that Asquith should head a Liberal-Conservative coalition to avert the danger or even that McKenna should lead a civil service government of 'national trustees'. Asquith and Baldwin wisely appreciated that nothing should be done to sour the Labour party, and a Labour minority government, with general Liberal support but not membership, would be a useful, safe and probably short-lived experience. Asquith had little freedom of action; a coalition with the Conservatives would have been unworkable in the circumstances and at best he could hope for a reversion of the premiership when Macdonald failed. On 22nd January, 1924, the first Labour Prime Minister kissed hands.

(d) LABOUR IN CHAINS

Although he was without ministerial experience, Macdonald, who became Foreign Secretary as well as Prime Minister, had been for many years balancing the various groups within the Labour party and was to show ability in muzzling the left wing and in performing routine administration. Macdonald kept himself aloof from his colleagues both in the making of appointments, which largely excluded the left wing, and afterwards. He was advised on constitutional practice by Haldane who became Lord Chancellor, despite great misgivings, chiefly because he wanted to supervise the revived Committee of Imperial Defence. Henderson, who also had Cabinet experience, was only included at the last moment as Home Secretary. A number of peers, whose connections with the party were tenuous, sat in the Cabinet. Snowden, the most distinguished figure in the movement after Macdonald, whom he disliked, got the Exchequer. The Ministry of Health went to Wheatley, the only Clydesider in the Cabinet and, as it turned out, the most effective Minister. The majority relied heavily on their civil servants, a factor which did not make for revolutionary measures.

The Executive Committee of Labour under the Chairmanship of Lansbury, a prominent left-wing M.P., attempted to summon Ministers before it to answer for their shortcomings, but this awkwardness was overcome, also such problems as the wearing of court dress or the accepting of invitations from the capitalist classes. The most important legislation was Wheatley's Housing Act[1] which aimed at restoring the main responsibility to the local authorities. He negotiated carefully for an expansion of the building trades and promised that the scheme would operate for fifteen years. The houses were built to rent, but the rents were often beyond the means of the very poor. At the Board of Education Trevelyan gave greater scope to progressive education authorities, increased the number of free places in secondary schools and revived State scholarships to the universities. Following the aims laid down in Tawney's *Secondary Education for All* he commissioned the Hadow Report which recommended the raising of the school leaving age to fifteen with a break at eleven, and the 'senior school' for the less intelligent older children who failed to get to grammar schools. In due course these proposals were implemented.

At the Exchequer Snowden soon showed he was cast in a Gladstonian mould. The McKenna duties[2] were abolished apart from a few kept purely for revenue purposes which were reduced. Rigorous economy was practised, although £28 m. was spent on public works to alleviate unemployment, which, with the export trades still depressed, obstinately persisted. The party was aware it should have the answer but failed to find it. Industrial peace might have been expected, but Macdonald handled Trades Union leaders ineptly and at one time the government even considered using Lloyd George's Emergency Powers Act.

The Union of Democratic Control, and hence the Labour party, had asserted that it was better qualified than the other parties to promote international understanding but its approach tended to be insufficiently economic and Macdonald in particular was anxious to appear a moderate. He had three specific aims in 1924: to improve Anglo-French relations, which would involve a settlement of the reparations question and the evacuation of the Ruhr; strong support of the League of Nations; and negotiations with Russia.

[1] See above, p. 467.   [2] See above, p. 429.

Macdonald revelled in his role as a world statesman and showed a talent for diplomacy, and an ability to appear a man of principle even when proposing a purely expedient solution. Despite his professed impartiality, he regarded the French as potentially more dangerous than the Germans and with skill persuaded them to withdraw from the Ruhr within a year, at the London Conference in July.

A committee under the United States general, Dawes, had been appointed as a result of Curzon's efforts to get reparations restarted. It proposed a sensible scheme and the establishment in Germany of a permanent international transfer committee. Macdonald's skill assured the acceptance of the Report by France and Germany and he organised a preliminary loan to Germany, which began to attract considerable American investment. The Dawes Scheme functioned smoothly for five years.[1]

To make the League more effective Macdonald put forward the Geneva Protocol. As the Covenant stood members were not under any obligation to implement policy decided by the League as a whole or to oppose aggressor countries. The usual British view was that the League existed for discussion and conciliation; the French, supported in England by the League of Nations Union, felt that all nations should be obliged to go to war against an aggressor. Macdonald's proposal was that signatories should accept arbitration, agree to disarm gradually and promise mutual support in cases of unprovoked aggression, an eventuality he did not expect. The French ratified but Baldwin's Conservative government discarded it as a dangerous blank cheque.[2] Nevertheless the ideas behind it and Macdonald's conciliatory approach to Germany defined British attitudes for several years.

As was only to be expected the Labour government promptly recognised the new Russian régime. However, the pre-war and wartime debts of the Tsarist government posed a problem, for the Bolsheviks would only consider honouring them if the British government would guarantee a Russian loan, a course which the Opposition refused to allow. A general treaty made no mention of the Russian debt but included a modest commercial treaty, which the Opposition parties bitterly opposed. It may have been to avert further

[1] See above, p. 480 and below, p. 511.   [2] See below, p. 491.

trouble over this that Macdonald, with modest achievements behind him and probable difficulty from frustrated left wingers ahead, chose to dissolve over the Campbell Affair.

This also had communist undertones. Campbell, an avowed communist, was charged with incitement to mutiny for urging soldiers, in a news-sheet he edited, not to allow themselves to be used in industrial disputes. The Attorney-General then discovered what he should have found out at the beginning that Campbell had a good war record and decided not to proceed. There had been back bench protests, however, and the Conservatives at once denounced interference with justice. In the vote of censure, which Asquith tried to avert by his favourite device of a Select Committee, the government was defeated by 364 to 191, the majority of Liberals being tired of supporting a government whose members denounced them as class enemies, little better than the Tories. Macdonald mishandled the affair but he was in a highly nervous state owing to his supersensitiveness to criticism.

The suggestion of communist influence in the Labour party which the Campbell Affair had inferred seemed confirmed by the publication of the *Zinoviev Letter* just before polling day. This was allegedly signed by Zinoviev, the President of the Communist International, and gave plans for a class war, in which the Labour Party was unwittingly to play a part. Its publication by the Foreign Office, and so presumably with Macdonald's authority,[1] accompanied by an official protest to the Russians, gave it verisimilitude. The Foreign Office issued it in good faith because another copy was in the hands of the *Daily Mail* which threatened publication It was almost certainly a forgery, although this has never been definitely established. Macdonald could have handled the matter better.

The *Letter* may have brought more voters to the polls and pushed the waverers over to the Conservatives, but it had no real effect on the result as Labour had a million more supporters than in the last election and the substantial Conservative success was chiefly due to its winning of Liberal votes,

[1] It was in fact authorised by Sir Eyre Crowe, Permanent Under-Secretary, and Macdonald, who was somewhat in awe of him, subsequently accepted his explanation.

who, with Tariff Reform now renounced, were chiefly concerned to get the Labour government out. Asquith lost his seat and at the King's personal invitation went to the Lords; Lloyd George led the remnant of forty in the Commons. Labour got 151 seats; the Conservatives 419. Stronger than ever before though in fact he had played around with his followers' principles, Baldwin took office in November 1924.

The first Labour government was largely a disappointment even to its more moderate followers but its lack of a majority made any socialist legislation out of the question. To Macdonald this was almost an asset; his concern was to prove the respectability of his party and its fitness to govern in the traditional manner and on the whole his Ministers proved their capacity, despite their failure to function as a team. Macdonald's own contribution in foreign affairs was particularly important. In the inevitable post-election disillusionment there was serious talk of replacing Macdonald but, as with Baldwin, although he did not precisely match up to the aspirations of his followers, there was no one else who had the respect of the country and thus the ability to win elections to an equal degree. Henderson and Clynes stood loyally beside him. Snowden made no secret of his disapproval but was not prepared to come forward; moreover he could not arouse enthusiasm. Above all Macdonald was saved by the *Zinoviev Letter*, which could be represented as a capitalist plot. In such circumstances responsibility for the defeat was clear; there was no need to re-examine Labour's role in politics or to change the leadership. Blinded by its dogma, defeat in such circumstances confirmed all the party's traditional propaganda.[1]

(e) BALDWIN'S SECOND GOVERNMENT

Between 1924 and 1929 the belief that a return to pre-1914 normality was possible reached its high-water mark. This was particularly true of foreign and economic policy and in both cases it was based on the false diagnosis of some factors and the ignoring of others. Austen Chamberlain, probably miscast as Foreign Secretary, conducted foreign relations in a gentlemanly and trustful manner and promoted the spirit of conciliation. Macdonald's more dangerous commitments,

[1] See also p. 519.

the Geneva Protocol and the Russian Treaty, were scrapped: later, relations were broken off with Russia, which was suspected of fomenting trouble in India after a raid on Arcos, the Russian trade delegation in London in which nothing incriminating was found. The Treaty of Locarno of 1925 applied the principle of the Protocol to the relations of France and Germany. Other potential difficulties, at the suggestion of Stresemann, the first post-war German politician to become a European figure, were ignored, especially that of Germany's Eastern Frontier. Those between Germany, France and Belgium were guaranteed by Britain and Italy, but although this could well be a hazardous commitment, especially in view of the alliance and undertakings accumulated by France with Germany's eastern neighbours, no preparations to meet it were made until the spirit of Locarno was outstripped by events.

As an earnest of new-found confidence in her, Allied troops were withdrawn from a third of the Rhineland and Germany became a member of the League and of its Council, even though she was not fulfilling the disarmament clauses of the Treaty of Versailles. The Allied Control Commission that had been set up to supervise disarmament was disbanded. Reparations were paid regularly and were more than covered by the money, principally from America, which was enjoying an unprecedented prosperity, which poured into Germany and helped to create the most modern industrial plant in the world. Stresemann averted eyes from this by talking peace; Briand of France and Austen Chamberlain hung upon his words. In the Kellog Pact of 1927–28 all nations of the world renounced war except in self-defence, although British lack of co-operation foiled a scheme for naval disarmament. It was assumed that pre-war security now prevailed.

If Austen Chamberlain deluded himself he was pursuing the right policy the same was also true to some extent of the Chancellor of the Exchequer. Baldwin had made a surprising appointment that was much criticised in the party and came as a surprise to Churchill himself.[1] He had changed parties while out of Parliament during the previous two years and Baldwin rightly rewarded his parliamentary skill and zest for

[1] When he was offered and accepted the Chancellorship he believed, so he said, that it was that of the Duchy of Lancaster.

politics, though almost any other Cabinet office would have suited him better. Churchill's first major decision, the fruit of much discussion since the war, was, in April 1925, not to renew the Act of 1919 which had suspended the gold standard. This was largely a matter of prestige. Reputable economists held that gold was the only sound basis for a currency and the occasion seemed favourable because the pound and the dollar appeared to be close to their pre-war rate of exchange. Norman, Governor of the Bank of England, believed that only such a step could restore the City's prestige as the principal money market of the world, which, following the pre-war analogy, he held to be essential for British prosperity and economic stability. It was also felt that if the return posed temporary difficulties for British industry, in the long run the effect of the keener competition would be wholly beneficent.

Almost the only economist to condemn the move was Keynes, who believed that the discrepancy was 10 per cent and therefore a return at the old parity would necessitate the reduction of prices by that amount, at the cost of unemployment and strikes. Although his figure may not have been correct, his general prediction was right. The international position of the City, now that Britain was no longer a creditor nation, could only be maintained with foreign deposits and much of this proved to be 'funk money' that fled rapidly from 1929 onwards.[1] The overvaluing of the pound priced many British exports, especially coal, out of foreign markets and thus hampered British trade recovery. The optimistic idea that industry would adjust itself proved illusory; neither capital nor labour was sufficiently flexible or adaptable. The consequence was wage reductions, a miners' strike and then the only general strike in British history. Churchill later admitted that the return to pre-war parity was a blunder, but the economic experts, Norman, and the Cabinet as a whole must share the responsibility. Other major countries stabilised their currencies by devaluation.

The adverse effects of the return to the gold standard worked on an economy that was already weak. Exporters had not recovered markets lost during the war when alternative suppliers had been found or a home industry built up. The old staple industries on which Britain had relied so profit-

_____
[1] See below, p. 516.

ably for so long were no longer in a commanding position. Indian home production of cotton increased steadily during the inter-war period as well as imports from Japan; Lancashire was the loser, although the finer cloths based on Egyptian cotton continued to find ready markets. In iron and steel the old markets had shrunk; France, for instance, had recovered Alsace and Lorraine with their valuable iron industry while Italy's demand had decreased. Coal was particularly affected: reparations were paid partly in coal and Germany was using lignite to reduce imports: Italy was taking more coal from Germany and developing hydro-electricity; Russia was formerly a valuable customer but her economic dislocation and political difficulties stood in the way of trade; South America changed to oil fuel. Only around half the world's shipping was now coal-fired as opposed to 96 per cent before the war. Of the million unemployed, over three-quarters were in the old staple industries.

Although the position was to some extent offset by the rise of new industries, the volume of exports was 20 per cent down on 1914. Imports on the other hand were 20 per cent up. Britain imported four-fifths of her wheat and flour, three-fifths of her meat, all her raw cotton, nine-tenths of the wool and timber she needed and one-third of her iron ore. A potentially disastrous situation was mitigated by a change in the terms of trade in which the price of primary products fell relatively to the price of manufactured goods, which constituted Britain's main exports. But the advantage was to some extent illusory for the primary producers were too poor to buy British exports to the extent they had in the past; the consequent unemployment at home further reduced the available market. As previously, invisible exports produced a favourable balance in the Twenties except in 1926, but with the decline in world shipping and less money available to invest abroad their value as a factor declined.

By 1929 world trade was 133 per cent above that in 1913, but the British share of it had been reduced. Germany's on the other hand had increased, with better industrial plant and greater adaptability. In Britain the consumer goods and service industries expanded, but her products made insufficient appeal overseas. There was not enough readiness to study customers' requirements and, aggravated by the rate of exchange, British costs were unduly high. Their dependence on electricity rather than coal meant that the new industries could be set up in the Midlands and the south, away from the areas of declining industry and so could not relieve the unemployment there.

Two important inquiries, the Balfour Committee of 1924 and the Macmillan Committee of 1929,[1] uncovered the nature of the problems but in 1925 employers were convinced that the answer to unduly expensive exports was to reduce wages. Baldwin took the same point of view: 'All the workers of this country have got to take reductions in wages to help put industry on its feet.' It was later realised that such a policy adversely affected industry by reducing consuming power. Baldwin's statement amounted to a challenge to the Trades Unions, many of whose leaders were willing to join with employers in redeploying industrial resources for the good of all. Wage reductions, however, suggested inequality of sacrifice and peace in industry once broken, more extreme leaders came to the fore, notably A. J. Cook, the Miners' Secretary.

The coal industry had suffered particularly from post-war fluctuations. The dislocation of 1919[2] and the French occupation of the Ruhr in 1923-24 had brought boom conditions; in 1921-23 and after 1924, the reverse was the case. Apart from South Wales, the industry was organised in small units and owing to slowness in mechanisation British increase in output lagged far behind that of most continental pits. Royalties were a heavy charge, around £5 m. a year, and particularly annoyed the working class who felt that they were in no way earned. Underground transport was particularly inefficient and many poor seams were being worked, though in the eastern half of the country the seams were thicker and the industry on the whole more prosperous. As the largest industry in the country, and with a product, which, as A. J. P. Taylor has pointed out, was easily recognised as 'black', it was well fitted to be the testing ground of the government's policy.

In May 1924, partly as a result of pressure from the Labour

---

[1] The chairmen were not the politicians of those names but, respectively, a steel magnate and a judge.
[2] See above, p. 466.

government, the miners had received an increase in wages, but almost immediately the French withdrew from the Ruhr and the recession in coal exports began, aggravated by the return to the gold standard. The miners, wrote Keynes, were 'the victims of the economic juggernaut'. The owners demanded a decrease in wages and an increase in hours. The leaders of the Miners' Federation were obdurate; there must be no concession. The President, Herbert Smith, tough, kindly and given to brevity, stated that there was 'nowt doing'; A. J. Cook, the Secretary, who described himself as 'a humble follower of Lenin', presented the uncompromising attitude of the members. They were unwilling for the T.U.C. general council to handle the negotiations and merely wanted unconditional support. The Triple Alliance was dead; Cook believed he could persuade other unions into declaring a sympathetic strike which they did not really want.

At the end of June 1925 the owners gave a month's notice that they were ending the 1924 wages agreement, announced reductions of between 13 per cent and 48 per cent but offered better terms if the miners would accept an eight-hour day, instead of the seven hours imposed after the Sankey Report. A lock-out was promised for 31st July unless their proposals were accepted. A government committee found in favour of a fixed minimum wage for the miners and when the T.U.C. general council announced an embargo on all movements of coal if the lock-out took place, Baldwin unexpectedly offered a temporary subsidy for nine months.

31st July was Red Friday, on which, in contrast to Black Friday which had broken the Triple Alliance,[1] Trades Union solidarity seemed to triumph. Baldwin defended his action by reference to the suffering such an embargo would cause and to the public's lack of preparedness for it. He may merely have wished to buy time, for the months of the subsidy were spent by the government in making preparations for such an emergency. Meanwhile the difference between the owners' offer and the old wages was made up by a government payment of £23 m. The miners pinned their faith on a Royal Commission appointed to look into the efficiency of the industry. It proceeded in a businesslike manner but none of its members, Samuel, a former Liberal Home Secretary,

_____
[1] See above, p. 469.

Beveridge of the London School of Economics, Lawrence of Glyn Mills and Lee of Tootal, Broadhurst, Lee Ltd. had any first hand knowledge of the industry. The majority of the T.U.C. general council were opposed to plans that might seem to challenge the government, although the unwillingness of the transport and railway unions to shoulder the burden of sympathetic action alone led to plans for a national strike. In the meantime the output of the mines reached record levels.

Anderson, Permanent Under-Secretary at the Home Office, planned an emergency system of transport and supplies based on the organisation originally prepared by Lloyd George in case Black Friday had been Red. Stocks of food and fuel were built up and ten civil commissioners were appointed to assume absolute power in their regions if contact with London was broken. Communists were believed to be influential in the unions and the best known ones were arrested prior to the strike for 'incitement to mutiny'. A private concern, the Organisation for the Maintenance of Supplies, which the unions suspected of having fascist connections, provided a cover for the government's serious preparations.

The Samuel Commission made its report in March 1926. It proposed the nationalisation of royalties, the amalgamation of smaller pits by compulsion if persuasion failed, improved arrangements for research and distribution, better working conditions, but an immediate reduction of wages. Baldwin would have been wise to have imposed it on the industry but instead he invited both sides to criticise it. Both did so; the miners in particular would accept 'Not a penny off the pay, not a second on the day', as Cook put it. Complete deadlock ensued; the Parliamentary Labour Party deprecated a strike, the miners were unwilling for the T.U.C. to make a bargain on their behalf. Baldwin did not make any proposals but declared a state of emergency on 30th April, the day the nine-month agreement expired. A lock-out began on 1st May, when a special Trades Union Conference authorised a National Strike for 3rd May, telegrams calling for the strike being sent out to all the branches concerned.

Hitherto Baldwin's actions seemed provocative to many trades unionists but under the threat of the strike he presided over negotiations on 2nd May during which agreement seemed very near. T.U.C. delegates were continuously at

Downing Street. Although the Cabinet felt that the sending of telegrams was itself highly provocative, the final straw came thirty hours later. Marlowe, the editor of the *Daily Mail*, had written a provocative leader condemning a general strike as 'a revolutionary movement intended to inflict suffering on innocent members of the community and put constraint on the government'. At midnight the compositors refused to set it; Marlowe telephoned the news to the Cabinet and although they were denounced by the leader of their own union, some Ministers, notably Churchill and Neville Chamberlain, demanded an immediate breaking off of negotiations on the ground that an 'overt act' had been committed. Threatened by resignations, Baldwin acquiesced, although Birkenhead was confident the T.U.C. could be persuaded not to support the miners. To the bewilderment of the T.U.C., who deplored the government's 'precipitous and calamitous decision', discussions came to an end.[1] The miners accepted the decision enthusiastically; they hoped to extort an indefinite subsidy.

The National Strike began at midnight on 3rd May; the term 'General' by which it is usually known, with its associations of syndicalist revolution, was given it at an early stage by Churchill, whose attitude set the government's demand of unconditional surrender. The first line only came out: transport and railway workers, those in heavy industry, building and the public utilities. Other industries were held back until later. The inclusion of printers in the first line was a mistake: the attempted suppression of the Press helped to prejudice the public against the strike while depriving the strikers of the chance to present their case to the nation as a whole. In two senses only was the strike general: the workers called out were almost unanimous in their action while the cessation of work which resulted in key industries and services largely paralysed the ordinary life of the nation. The strikers asserted that this was not their intention; for most of them the strike was an act of self-sacrifice and generosity to secure a living wage for the miners. There was, in

---

[1] Baldwin informed the T.U.C. delegates personally that in the government's view the strike had in effect started. The trades unionists discussed his statement, prepared an answer, only to find that the Cabinet room was in darkness and everybody had gone home to bed. The Cabinet had, however, waited for some time, expecting a more rapid reply.

consequence, no attempt to interfere with the maintenance of essential services by volunteers; at Newcastle the Strike Committee helped with the distribution of food.

The strike coincided with a period of good weather; for the strikers it was almost a holiday, while for the rest it introduced an element of excitement and a foolproof excuse for being late for work. Some achieved the ambition of a lifetime by driving trains, with the added attraction that there were no penalties for mistakes. The technical operation of the railways was beyond most volunteers, but although trains were few and unreliable there were surprisingly few mishaps. Undergraduates worked in the docks, while the dockers stood by and jeered at their reactions to the unaccustomed toil. The electricity and gas supplies were maintained by using naval ratings in the power stations. Buses were the chief target for strikers' retaliation and most London buses were windowless after the first day or so. The road transport industry, particularly the small, family haulage firms, carried all essential supplies according to plans made by the government.

On the whole remarkably good humour prevailed. The general council were anxious to appear moderate and responsible and were embarrassed by the offer of Russian support. Sparing use was made of troops, although some authorities consider that Churchill displayed them provocatively in London. He was also the editor of the government newssheet, the *British Gazette*, which referred to the strikers as the 'enemy' and tended to be distrusted. Many people, including many employers and some members of the government, saw the chance of a 'showdown' with the unions. The B.B.C. news was listened to with confidence although Reith only preserved the independence of his company by suppressing news the government did not like. The radio industry – in addition to the road transport industry – greatly benefited from the strike. Most daily newspapers were able to bring out a single sheet of news after the first few days. The Trades Union publication, *The British Worker*, was dull, moderate and had little influence on the public as a whole.

Relations between strikers and the police remained good: at some places Police *v.* Strikers football matches were held. The special contempt of the working class was reserved for the large numbers of special constables, mostly of middle-class

background, who were enrolled. Had they been used extensively, serious violence might have ensued, which could have
easily turned the strike into a revolution. As it was, there
was a considerably tenser atmosphere during the last few days.

Baldwin from the start represented the strike as a challenge
to the Constitution; he refused to consider conciliation, which
was proposed by Lloyd George and the Archbishop of Canterbury among others, and declined to restart negotiations until
the strike was called off. In view of the government's attitude
and the adverse effect on public opinion a long dislocation of
this kind would have, the forces they had unleashed were
becoming almost an embarrassment to the moderate members
of the T.U.C. and they sought some formula for ending the
strike that would not seem to be a surrender.

It was at this stage that the suggestion was made by Sir
John Simon, the former Liberal Home Secretary, that the
strike was illegal; it was almost immediately refuted by other
lawyers and probably was not decisive in frightening the
T.U.C. into surrender, as has been suggested. Nor was the
threat that union leaders would be arrested and funds im-
pounded a factor. Such actions would have created martyrs
and encouraged violence and George V in particular deprecated such steps. Far more relevant was the T.U.C.'s concern at the heavy expense of the strike and the adverse effect
on public opinion. Unofficial negotiations went on continuously, particularly after a notable broadcast by Birkenhead on
8th May. Samuel put forward the idea of a National Wages
Board which would impose wage reductions when the other
proposals of his report were implemented. When Baldwin
promised in a broadcast that the government would do all it
could to ensure that the strikers were reinstated, the T.U.C.,
led by J. H. Thomas, took up Samuel's idea and, although the
miners refused to co-operate and they received no government
assurances, they called off the strike on 12th May so that
negotiations might begin.

In strike headquarters and working-class homes throughout
the country the sudden ending of the strike, which had been a
tremendous display of solidarity, was a shock. When employers tried to exploit the situation and force the men back on
adverse terms, the strike broke out again with great bitterness
and Baldwin hastily redeemed his broadcast promise by

insisting on a return to pre-strike conditions. The railway-men, who had joined in reluctantly, had a hard struggle for reinstatement. Baldwin offered to implement the Samuel Report, with a short-term subsidy, if both sides would accept it first. The miners refused; for them the struggle was half political. 'If the British Constitution makes a man work underground for less than £2 a week it is about time that Constitution was challenged,' said one of their number at a meeting. The government then disclaimed further responsibility. Parliament surrendered the seven-hour day for five years; the owners insisted on district agreements and lower pay, but on the basis of the eight-hour day the majority of miners received a shift pay similar to that of the 1924 Agreement. By July even Cook was urging the miners to accept, but although some men drifted back to work, the majority stayed out until driven back by starvation and the cold in November 1926. The longer day created a pool of unemployment which ensured that the owners kept the whip hand. The long-term effects on the prosperity of the mines were adverse, however; twenty-eight million tons of coal exports were lost and some markets were never recovered; £42 m. had to be spent on importing German and Polish coal. Even so half a million men were laid off in other industries owing to the coal shortage.

His handling of the strike, even though he might have averted it, raised Baldwin greatly in public esteem. His attitude seemed to convey magnanimity and a spirit of con-ciliation. Their brief experience of manual labour made many members of the middle class understand more easily working-class attitudes; conversely the working men respected those who took on manual tasks with enthusiasm, if somewhat ineptly. After the General Strike, which seemed to have the elements of revolution and demonstrated working-class solidarity to an impressive degree, the risk of class warfare in Britain was at an end. Even direct actionists admitted 'the era of effective strikes has passed'. In the unions, whose membership fell to its pre-war figure, more conciliatory men came to the front, notably Bevin and Thomas, who, in view of his responsibility for the capitulation of 12th May, was for-tunate to survive as a politician. The influence of industrial leaders such as Sir Alfred Mond of I.C.I. helped both sides of industry to understand the need for greater teamwork. Employers seemed to have learnt a new respect; there were few wage reductions, even during the period of the depression. The healing of the wounds was interrupted by a further failure of leadership on Baldwin's part, which lowered his prestige and contributed to the Labour victory of 1929. Several Conservative M.P.s, including some members of the Cabinet, saw an opportunity to curtail the influence of the unions and that of the Labour party as well. Baldwin should have withstood them; instead he allowed them to take the initiative. The resulting legislation, forced through by means of a closure, was the Trade Disputes Act of 1927, subsequently repealed in 1946. It made general strikes or strikes 'designed to coerce the government' illegal; civil servants were not allowed to join unions affiliated to the T.U.C. while in future men had to contract into the political levy, reversing the 1913 procedure. It was expected that this last measure would greatly restrict the funds available to the Labour party.[1]

The first clause has never been invoked although some activists proposed there should be a general strike against the forbidding of general strikes. Most trades unionists quietly acquiesced to an act which they knew to be condemned by moderate opinion and which would therefore be repealed when the time was propitious. The attack on Labour party finance led to an immediate reduction in contributions but in the long run made little difference.

One of the most resolute opponents of Trades Unions was also the author of the government's social achievements. On appointment as Minister of Health Neville Chamberlain immediately presented twenty-five measures to the Cabinet, all of which were in due course passed into law. 'Our policy,' he said, 'is to use the great resources of the State not for the distribution of an indiscriminate largesse, but to help those who have the will and desire to raise themselves to higher and better things.' In particular he devoted himself to the improvement of local government, ensuring that the standards of services provided were uniform throughout the country. This involved the condemnation of what was known as 'Pop-larism' from the action of Lansbury and the Poor Law Guardians of Poplar who made widespread use of Poor Law funds to help the poor and unemployed. Chamberlain had no

[1] See above, p. 394.

sympathy with such exceedings of the statutory requirments, whether prompted by emotional concern or a desire for social justice. He received special powers to curtail it in July 1926. In co-operation with Churchill the Widows, Orphans and Old Age Pensions Act of 1925 was introduced. Like Health Insurance it was based on the contributory principle and fixed at a level which would not discourage, as Chamberlain put it, 'those virtues of thrift which have done so much for the country in the past.' 9d. a week, shared equally between the employer and the employed, entitled the latter and his wife to an old age pension of ten shillings a week over the age of sixty-five; his widow to a similar pension at any age, with children's allowances, and an orphan to seven and sixpence weekly. Pensions technically continued under the old scheme[1] after the age of seventy. The scheme was extended to clerical workers in 1937. Although of substantial benefit to individuals, it was regressive in the sense that, providing flat rate benefits for flat rate contributions, it made no distinction of need.

The increased provision of pensions combined with an extension of unemployment benefit to reduce temporarily the impact on the Poor Law. Unemployment benefits were not raised but the strict insurance principle was abandoned in 1928; providing a man had worked for thirty weeks in the previous two years and was genuinely seeking work, he received payments indefinitely. The organisation of the Poor Law had remained substantially unchanged since Burns had declined to implement either the Majority or Minority Reports of 1909.[2] The rates charged by unions varied from a few pence in the pound in the prosperous areas up to fifteen shilling in areas of heavy unemployment. It was to call attention to this injustice that Poplar Council protested in 1921 and were imprisoned for contempt of court.[3] They won their point, however, and rate relief was made available for the hardest hit districts. Most unions, however, still made little effort to provide specialised treatment for the various categories of inmates.

By an act of 1929 Chamberlain transferred the functions of the old Poor Law Guardians to Public Assistance Committees

---

[1] See above, p. 379.   [2] See above, p. 383.
[3] They purged their contempt by resolution of a special council meeting held in Brixton Prison.

of County and County Borough councils, thus further consolidating social services under a single local authority. This enabled the cost to be more widely spread although the impact still remained heavy on some county boroughs. The result of this and associated legislation was to grant outdoor relief as a general rule to all who had accommodation and to give local authorities the right to assume responsibility for a child when the parents were deemed unfit. On the whole Public Assistance was distributed in an increasingly humane manner, but the Curtis Report of 1946 showed that the conduct of workhouses (or poor law institutions) left much to be desired.

Sixty-two counties and eighty-four county boroughs now became responsible for a far greater range of services than in most countries. Two-thirds of their income came from block government grants, calculated according to a complicated formula, and special grants for education, police, housing and road expenditure. Education was now taking 2·2 per cent of the national income, twice the pre-war figure. 100,000 houses a year, at an annual cost to the Exchequer of £4 m. by 1939, were being built by local authorities. The Treasury made a special grant of £24 m. a year to offset the exemption of agriculture from the payment of rates and the reduction of rates on railway land by three-quarters, in return for the reduction of freight charges on coal and steel.

Chamberlain's other legislation covered milk, smoke abatement, patent medicines and asylums. It helped to make him a national figure and increased his self-confidence and egotism. He remained loyal to Baldwin, unwilling to take part in intrigues against him, particularly those of younger Conservatives such as Macmillan, Boothby and Stanley who advocated increased use of the State's power to help industry and working men. Soon after the election Beaverbrook began a Press campaign for Empire Free Trade, although it was evident to most people that the Dominions were unlikely to give preference to British manufacturers if they competed with their own. Beaverbrook wanted another Conservative leader; Baldwin skilfully mastered the challenge by making Neville Chamberlain, his only possible rival and an avowed Protectionist, chairman of the party and thus tied closely to him. As late as March 1931 pressure was put on Baldwin to resign but he skilfully aroused public dislike of the Press lords by accusing them of wanting power without responsibility, 'the prerogative of the harlot throughout the ages'. He was vindicated by a by-election success over an Empire Free Trade candidate and was not challenged again.

In its outlook the party as a whole had changed little. Its organisation was a balance between central office and constituency parties, each to a certain extent independent of the other. All the traditional forces of the State were grouped on its side: universities, chambers of commerce, the Civil Service, the armed forces, the Church of England. The great majority of the newspapers were Conservative. The Labour party might sing *The Red Flag*, even if insincerely, but the Union Jack was always prominent on Conservative platforms. In the General Election which Baldwin arranged for May 1929 the Conservatives offered 'The mixture as before' and called it 'Safety First'.

The Labour party had become more authoritarian, emphasising the need for loyalty, which was of increased importance now Labour controlled many local councils and had had experience of national government. Although it had middle-class members, it was still basically a working-class party for which many working men and women voted as a matter of course. It had an efficient local organisation; there was little unity of aims, however. The I.L.P. wanted a drastic approach to the country's problems and denounced the official manifesto, *Labour and the Nation*, as inadequate. Even its modest proposals were too socialist for Macdonald who explained it away as a long-term programme. Both Conservative and Labour offered a safety-first policy; neither had any relevant ideas to offer as a solution to Britain's economic difficulties.

The Liberals believed they had. When Asquith resigned as leader in October 1926, shortly before his death, Lloyd George took his place and promoted inquiries, inspired by Keynes and financed by the Lloyd George Fund, into economic problems of the day. These suggested the abandonment of the balanced Budget which had been the traditional Liberal pride and the using of the State's resources to conquer unemployment and reinflate the economy. He proposed the building of a national system of trunk roads, including new bridges and ring roads at a total cost of £99 m., capital schemes for improving the railways, a larger housing programme and a greatly increased provision of electricity. Many of these ideas were the bread and butter of Roosevelt's New Deal and would almost certainly have been effective in Britain but Keynes had not yet reached the point where he could prove that men receiving good wages instead of unemployment benefit indirectly helped the employment of others by increasing their own expenditure. To most people the increase of government expenditure could only bring disaster and would make the individual poorer rather than, by preventing unemployment, on the average better off. The Liberals made little impact on local government and although the Lloyd George Fund was used to field over 500 candidates, making 1929 the only truly three-cornered election in English history, their programme was too new and Lloyd George too little trusted for them to poll many votes. The other parties virtually ignored unemployment.

An act of 1928 introduced an element of uncertainty. To honour a promise made by Joynson-Hicks, the Home Secretary, votes for women were introduced on equal terms with men, though it is uncertain which party benefited from this in 1929. This and natural increase provided seven million more voters. The Conservatives obtained slightly more votes than Labour but were harmed by the increase in Liberal candidates and the relatively small populations of some of the traditionally Labour seats in the north. They obtained 260 M.P.s against Labour's 288. The Liberals, firmly in third place, won 59 seats and two million extra votes. Baldwin promptly resigned.

(f) COMMONWEALTH AND EMPIRE

The period between the wars saw considerable changes in the position of British overseas possessions. The Dominions were, by 1918, virtually sovereign states with divergent economic interests but tied to Britain chiefly by sentiment. In 1923 the Imperial Conference passed a resolution in favour of preferences but Baldwin's defeat in the election of that year led to only modest adjustments being made when he returned to power. The Conference of 1926 avoided the topic; at Canadian insistence it devoted itself to defining dominion status as:

Autonomous communities within the British Empire, equal in status, in no way subordinate one to another in any aspect of their domestic or external affairs though united by a common allegiance to the Crown and freely associated as members of the British Commonwealth of Nations.

More precise definition followed at the Conference of 1930 and the Statute of Westminster of 1931 gave force of law to the agreed position as far as it was possible to do so. The British Parliament ceased to be sovereign over the Dominions and the government in London no longer had any authority there. A special department with a Secretary of State was responsible for Commonwealth Relations. Governors-General, nominally representing the Crown, were appointed on the recommendation of the Dominion government concerned and acted in effect as independent constitutional monarchs. Visible links were maintained by royal visits; the Prince of Wales was particularly active in this respect after the Great War.

India remained a possession of the British Crown. Towards the end of the 19th Century Indian intellectuals, influenced by the ideals of Western liberalism, became increasingly interested in the possibility of parliamentary self-government. In the way stood the steady conviction of most Englishmen that they could govern India better than the Indians, which prevented modest concessions at an early stage. The Indian National Congress, which first met in 1885 and which included representatives of all classes and religions, only turned to non-co-operation, passive resistance and civil disobedience when its first moderate demands were refused. The Indian Councils Act of 1892 included Indian members in the Viceroy's and Provincial Legislative Councils but they were to be nominated, not elected, in most cases.

Curzon's attitude to Indian aspirations, towards the end of his Viceroyalty,[1] caused considerable discontent and large protest meetings were held in the main towns. Much disorder was occasioned by his partition of Bengal, in itself a perfectly reasonable act. The reverses suffered by the Italians at Adowa and the Russians in their war with Japan were damaging to European prestige and the consequent activity of many intellectuals in Press and platform agitation was calculated to embarrass the government. Morley, with

[1] See above, p. 362.

some courage, offered to become Secretary for India in 1906; he was aware that some of the younger Indians were now demanding complete autonomy. The Morley–Minto Reforms of 1909 were still governed by the belief that India was not fit for self-government, but their main feature, the Indian Councils Act of 1909, was a considerable advance on that of 1892. The powers of the legislative Councils were increased, as was their Indian membership, which was now elected. The Councils had no powers to eject the executives if they disapproved of them, however. Ordinary constituencies were not introduced for the elected members; special representation, weighted in the case of minorities, was given to the various religious groups, which, while strengthening the position of the government as the arbiter between them, also increased communal tensions, particularly between Hindus and Moslem. Hitherto the British administration had made no religious distinctions; this special representation was a highly mischievous concession made to a Moslem deputation headed by the Aga Khan. It encouraged the two main groups to see themselves as distinct from one another and led ultimately to the unhappy partition of 1947.

The great majority accepted the reforms as the prelude to further concessions. Indian contributions to the war effort encouraged Congress to demand in 1916 dominion status for India, and in 1917 the Government promised increased Indian responsibilities. The hardships of the war and the influenza epidemic caused considerable Indian discontent, which was increased by the Amritsar Massacre of 1919 when General Dyer ordered troops to fire on an unarmed crowd, killing 379, in retaliation for the murder of four Europeans. Although Dyer was severely censured, for many Indians this was the parting of the ways. The Montagu–Chelmsford Report of 1918 advocated a substantial advance in parliamentary, though not responsible, government. The Government of India Act of the following year set up dyarchy in the provinces, with Indian elected representatives controlling all executive functions except justice, police and finance. At the centre there was a bicameral legislature, of whose members a majority were elected, but certain powers were retained by the Viceroy and his executive Council which included some Indian nominated members.

The effect of these reforms was offset by the Rowlatt Acts which gave the government increased powers of arrest and summary trial of political suspects. Gandhi, who had come to prominence in the first place as the champion of the rights of the Indian community in South Africa, organised a campaign of non-co-operation, which included refusals to trade and the withdrawal of students from schools. Although Gandhi stressed the value of moral force some acts of violence were committed and Gandhi himself was imprisoned. Many Indian leaders took part in the new administrations nevertheless and some were promoted to high executive position.[1]

In Britain most political leaders were prepared for further transfer of power, although there was little sense of urgency. In 1926 Baldwin appointed Edward Wood, created Lord Irwin and later Earl of Halifax,[2] as Viceroy. He succeeded Lord Reading, a far more eminent man, because he seemed to Baldwin to have noble if undefined aspirations and a mind above party politics, a view which was endorsed by the public when he was criticised by the Conservative Right wing. But it was his decision to exclude Indians from the parliamentary commission chaired by Sir John Simon which finally reported to the Indian Constitution in 1930; and as a result the Commission had considerable difficulty in obtaining co-operation from the Indians. Irwin anticipated the report by promising dominion status in 1929.

The result of this declaration was to encourage the Indians to greater disobedience; Gandhi led a procession to the sea to violate the government salt monopoly by boiling sea water and the first civil disobedience campaign spread rapidly over the country, leading, to the horror of the Labour back benchers, to the imprisonment of 50,000 Indians. The Simon Report proposed full responsible government in the provinces and indirect elections to the central legislature; the precise future of India was to be determined by Conference. It was held in London in 1930 and Congress refused to send representatives until Gandhi was persuaded by Irwin to attend in return for the release of political prisoners and other concessions. Churchill, in particular, denounced this agreement and resigned from the Shadow Cabinet in January 1931 over the

---

[1] Notably Lord Sinha, Governor of Bihar. It was sheer blindness to exclude him from the Simon Commission. [2] See below, p. 554.

policy of conciliation in India, an act which estranged him from his party and discredited him in advance when he sounded the alarm over Germany. His warnings of the bloodshed that would follow Indian independence were vivid and in the event fully justified.

At the second Round Table Conference, which Gandhi attended, the communal question dominated all others. Gandhi maintained that Congress alone represented political India and that Hindus and Moslems could live together without special safeguards; coming without advisers, the failure of the Conference to some extent discredited Gandhi, whose place as Congress leader was taken by Nehru in 1933. Macdonald made his own Communal Award in August 1932 and a third Round Table Conference settled the details of the Government of India Act of 1935. This confirmed the end of dyarchy and introduced responsible government at the centre, except for defence and foreign affairs. The latter covered the princely states as well and would only come into force when a majority of them assented. Complicated safeguards at all levels limited the real transfer of power. Under its terms the new provincial governments took office in 1937, when Congress, contesting elections for the first time, won eight out of eleven provinces. The war came before they had had a fair trial. Central government was not transferred until full independence was granted in 1947. Although they participated in it, Congress leaders denounced the scheme as inadequate from the start. It was the last and most tragic of the missed opportunities.

When war broke out in 1914 Britain assumed control of Egypt to ensure defence of the Suez Canal. A satisfactory settlement after the war was prevented by nationalist feeling; in 1922 Britain unilaterally recognised Egyptian independence but British troops were kept in the country and joint control over the Sudan was retained. When the Governor-General there was murdered in 1924, British military control was tightened. In 1930 Henderson forced Lord Lloyd, the High Commissioner, to resign and tried to get agreement, but his efforts failed because Britain was unwilling to surrender the sole control over the Sudan it had exercised since 1924. The British remained in Egypt until after the Second World War.

By the Treaty of Versailles Britain received Palestine as a

mandate with the responsibility of establishing a National
Home for the Jews, while at the same time allowing the free
development of the indigenous Arabs, a virtually impossible
combination. The Jews who arrived intended to turn the
National Home into a National State and in October 1930
further Jewish immigration was restricted until the Nazi
persecutions began. This increased Arab alarm about the
future and in consequence the Peel Commission of 1937
recommended partition, with a British mandate of Jerusalem
and Bethlehem. The proposal had a poor reception and in
1938 the partition commission reported that it was impracticable as the lands occupied by the two communities were intermingled. In May 1939 the government gave way to Arab
violence and agreed to restrict further Jewish immigration.
By the time the war was over both sides were intransigent and
Britain surrendered the mandate to the United Nations.

In these three areas, India, Egypt and Palestine, Britain had
assumed responsibilities in good faith and, in different ways,
had overstayed her welcome. In Africa most of the British
colonial possessions had not proved to be the great assets
which was predicted at the high tide of imperialism and they
were increasingly regarded as 'sacred trusts' where the interests
of the native population should be paramount, although they
were administered autocratically. The chief exception was
Kenya, where it was discovered that white men could live
permanently in the highlands; many settlers arrived who
created a dream world where their money went further than
at home and where domestic and farm labour was plentiful.
Kenya also had an Indian population who were ready to
exploit the natives but resented subordination to the Europeans. The white settlers were refused responsible government in 1923 and again in 1927, it being considered, probably
rightly, that they would obstruct the Colonial Office aim of
trusteeship. Southern Rhodesia was taken over from the
Chartered Company in 1923, having voted against incorporation in the Union of South Africa, and was granted self-
government subject to certain safeguards for the coloured
population.

XII · THE HUNT FOR SECURITY

(a) THE SECOND LABOUR GOVERNMENT, 1929-31

THE second Labour government provided no solutions to the country's economic problems, whose seriousness it failed to appreciate until sudden realisation brought on the extraordinary events of 1931. It received fairly firm Liberal support, which Lloyd George justified by claiming that the election had really endorsed the Liberal programme. As a result, the Liberals tended to be held responsible for Labour's failures and Lloyd George's hold over the party, which often split three ways, was weakened. Macdonald returned to the premiership, Snowden to the Exchequer, while Henderson insisted on a suitable reward for his services to the party and was given the Foreign Office, where he was a success. Sidney Webb as Lord Passfield became Dominions and Colonial Secretary while Margaret Bondfield, Minister of Labour, became the first woman to reach Cabinet rank. Wheatley was excluded; the sole spokesman of the Left in the Cabinet was Lansbury. Macdonald made no attempt to pursue a Socialist programme or to cure the country's economic problems – apart from the appointment of J. H. Thomas as Lord Privy Seal with the task of ending unemployment.

The Conservative government had substantially continued the policy of conciliation in Europe which Macdonald had initiated. A conference was held at The Hague in August 1929 to produce a final settlement of German reparations.[1] Snowden's plain speaking caused some difficulties but the outcome was the Young Plan by which payments were arranged over a period of fifty-nine years and were related to Allied debt payments to the United States. When the arrangement was finally agreed in 1930, the last Allied troops left German soil. When Stresemann, the ablest and most peaceable of inter-war German statesmen, died in October 1929, Henderson became the dominant figure at the League of Nations and obtained the rare position of enjoying the

[1] See above, p. 488.

511

confidence of both French and Germans. His genuine goodwill and informality led to his election as president of the World Disarmament Conference which met in February 1932 when he was no longer Foreign Secretary.

Conciliation also involved the settling of other differences. Diplomatic relations were re-established with Russia, despite Russian lack of enthusiasm.[1] A naval conference was held in London and broke the deadlock of the Geneva Conference of 1927 when Britain refused to accept a reduction of cruisers. This was now agreed to as well as a five-year suspension of the building of large ships. A ratio of 5:5:3 for the United States, Britain and Japan was agreed though it was in practice unenforceable. France and Italy could not come to any agreement and remained outside the pact.[2]

At home the successes were not so substantial. As a minority government, the administration was dependent on Liberal tolerance though it was not prepared to take up Liberal ideas. It hoped by means of public corporations and regulating legislation to introduce some order into capitalism without transferring economic control either to the State or to the workers. On the model of the Central Electricity Board, set up by Baldwin's government in 1926, Morrison created the London Passenger Transport Board in 1931, which came into operation eventually in 1933. Addison's Agricultural Marketing Act of 1931 led to the setting up of boards of producers which would fix prices and collectively market their products. A similar move against the interests of the consumer was the Coal Mines Act of 1930, which reduced the working day to seven and a half hours and aimed at producing stable prices and thus guaranteed wages. Of greater value was Greenwood's Housing Act of 1930 which, while endorsing Wheatley's Act, granted greater powers of slum clearance. Other legislation failed, whether through Liberal refusal to support it, or, in the case of Trevelyan's Education bill, by its being rejected by the Lords. They justified their act by claiming that the country could not afford the extension of the school leaving age to fifteen, which it proposed. In his resignation speech Trevelyan remarked that the crisis in trade required 'big socialist measures' in which the government seemed to show less and less belief.

[1] See above, p. 491.   [2] See above, p. 474.

Since the Dawes Plan, which had restarted reparations, and the substantial loans arranged for Germany, a great deal of American money poured across the Atlantic which was used for the modernisation and re-equipping of German industry and in effect for the payment of reparations themselves. In 1928 American lending slackened off and, encouraged by the apparently solid prosperity that had prevailed during the presidency of Calvin Coolidge, American stock exchange prices steadily rose, attracting considerable amounts of money from Europe. On 29th October, 1929, there was sudden panic on the stock exchange and within a week 240 securities had declined in market value by $15,984 m. This affected investment and trade all over the world, although its effect in Europe would have been more immediate if it had been realised how utterly the whole structure of reparations and Allied debt payments depended on the willingness of the American investor and speculator to send dollars across the Atlantic.

There were some immediate repercussions on the British economy. The price of primary products, the bulk of British imports, had increased in a time of high consumption but now fell heavily; this turned the terms of trade 20 per cent in Britain's favour but the producer countries were ruined as markets, ceasing to buy British goods, whose prices remained comparatively high, and hence reducing their use of British ships. Britain maintained her normal level of imports at less expense, to the advantage of real wages and of the balance of payments. We exported considerably less, however, and in consequence unemployment steadily mounted, though not as rapidly as in Germany or the United States.

The American crash unleashed many other factors that international confidence had hitherto kept comparatively dormant: the lack of balance between primary produce and industrial output; the post-war instability of the economies of many countries; the British return to the gold standard at an unduly high figure; the world wide increase in tariffs, particularly those of the United States which made it difficult for foreign nations to earn American currency. Moreover war debts upset the normal pattern of trade, while consumption was unable to increase sufficiently to absorb the rapidly increasing production. The gravity of these problems, disturbing the pre-war economic structure, was not realised by most bankers, industrialists and politicians. Not least in failing to comprehend them was the Labour government. It could not hope to solve them because they were international problems, but it should have been able to do something to mitigate their effects. Socialists had for years been prophesying the collapse of capitalism but when it appeared to have come they proved to be so influenced by traditional economic conventions that they were capable only of half measures. As far as tackling the problems of the economy was concerned, the second Labour government was a futile interlude.

With light-hearted enthusiasm J. H. Thomas led a committee of Lansbury, Mosley and Johnston to cure the depression. Spending of public money was deprecated by Snowden at the Treasury. The most challenging proposals came from Sir Oswald Mosley, Chancellor of the Duchy of Lancaster, a comparatively recent recruit to the party. He envisaged sweeping government control of the economy. This would involve the reintroduction of tariffs – a view shared by bankers, the Federation of British Industry, the T.U.C. and even the Manchester Chamber of Commerce. He wanted bulk purchasing agreements with overseas producers, the systematic use of credit to finance development through the public control of banking. Pensions and allowances were to be increased not only to enlarge purchasing power but to encourage earlier retirement from industry. It seems probable that these proposals, most of which are common currency today, would have cured unemployment more effectively than those made by Lloyd George but like his they were too new and revolutionary for public acceptance and were moreover condemned by Snowden. Mosley's plans were rejected by the Cabinet and their author resigned in May 1930.

Mosley hoped to take up the fight outside but the Parliamentary Party decisively rejected his ideas. He was nearly successful at the party conference and on the strength of this founded the New Party in February 1931. Like Lord Randolph Churchill he believed that he had a real party following but only four M.P.s joined him. Others withdrew, suspecting his autocratic tendencies, and the Labour party expelled him. In so doing they lost a man of undoubted talent who henceforth devoted his energies to extremist organisations; any vigorous plans for combating the depression tended to be suspect in the Cabinet. Thomas took refuge in clichés and platitudes; no effective steps were taken.

Churchill had balanced his Budgets by raiding the Road Fund and reducing the Sinking Fund; with Snowden strict orthodoxy returned. Income tax was raised to 4s. 6d. in the pound in 1930 and other taxes were increased; even so a deficit was likely in 1931 and Snowden appointed in February a committee under Sir George May, who had retired as Secretary of the Prudential, with two representatives of labour and four of the business community, to establish the need for rigid economies. Pending the Committee's report, a temporary budget was introduced in April. Unemployment, meanwhile, failed to decrease in the spring as was usual and reached 2,700,000 by June.

The government had appointed the Macmillan Committee on Finance and Industry in 1929 and it reported in the summer of 1931. Its chief impact on the current situation was to reveal the full extent of the City's short-term indebtedness for the first time and to indicate the influence of the depression on Britain's international balance of payments. This caused some public concern, but the public was quite unprepared for the impact made by the May Report, published at the end of July. This was an inept document which painted an unduly gloomy picture of the country's financial position and hence helped to undermine international confidence. It demanded rigid economies notably at the expense of the unemployed; relief should be cut by 20 per cent and the insurance fund should be made to pay its way. In the interests of orthodoxy the Sinking Fund was not to be touched and largely through devious accountancy a deficit of £120 m. was produced (£170 in a full year). It was, wrote Keynes, 'the most foolish document I ever had the misfortune to read'.

Many, however, took it very seriously, especially when it was not offset by any official statement of reassurance. The international money market was already in a very nervous condition and since 15th July the Bank of England had been losing gold at the rate of £2½ m. a day. This was connected with a financial crisis in central Europe that had begun in May when the Kreditanstalt of Vienna failed through the depreciation of its holdings and a flight of French money perturbed by the growth of Nazi influence in Austria. The Bank of England advanced £4,300,000 to the Austrian National Bank which was guaranteeing the Kreditanstalt's foreign liabilities. German banks had heavy investments in Austrian industry and were affected by the crisis; the Reichsbank lost heavily in gold and foreign exchange and abruptly curtailed its credits with the result that the two largest German commercial banks closed their doors. Short-term loans from foreign banks to Germany were hastily recalled, particularly French money deposited in London which had been re-lent to Germany. The Germans could no longer pay reparations, nor could the French and British pay interest on war debt. President Hoover in due course proposed a year's moratorium on all payments.

The London money market was in an embarrassing position; it lost short-term balances, much of which was 'funk' money taking flight at the slightest rumour, while British foreign credits, in any case depreciated by the general depression, were either still in Germany, where they had been left to give an element of stability, or could be withdrawn only at the risk of extending the crisis. This was hardly the government's fault alone; many merchant banks, equally blind, had lent unwisely. The Bank of England might well have managed to preserve its own resources and hence the gold standard but the price would have been the failure of several British merchant banks. Despite new credits from France and the United States at the beginning of August, the drain continued and Macdonald was recalled to London on 11th August.

Ultimately this was a crisis of confidence. Britain's financial position was basically sound and, had movements of funds out of London had been blocked, the crisis might have been overcome, though in the long run it might have been the end of London as the world's financial centre. There was a fear that if the gold standard was suspended this would lead to galloping inflation of the post-war German type although this had not occurred in the 19th-century crises. According to Chamberlain, the bankers informed Macdonald that measures of a different type were essential. They considered that the country was on the brink of disaster, the main reason for this being the lack of confidence that foreigners had in the government's economic measures. The remedy they proposed, which foreign bankers supported, was a carefully balanced Budget brought about by strict government economies. Their particular target was, like that of the May Committee, unemployment benefit, whose extension in 1930 had caused some alarm abroad. A general reduction of wages, it was thought, would follow.

In the circumstances the government had no alternative but to accept their proposals. Financial confidence was essential and the Labour government, at odds within itself, with the Left wing pressing for more generous treatment of the unemployed and Macdonald making no attempt to influence either the Cabinet or the T.U.C., possessed neither the confidence of the City nor the resolution to conduct an unorthodox policy. It deliberated in an atmosphere of tension, as Lord Ponsonby has pointed out: 'headlines, crowds, hectic movements, day and night meetings, the door of Downing Street loosened on its hinges by the constant passage of leading figures of all three parties as they hurried by the ever present battery of photographers'.

On 20 August the T.U.C. general council refused to accept the need for the economies; on the 21st the Opposition leaders told the Prime Minister that the agreed economies were quite inadequate and that they would support him in proposing more severe ones. But they would not support the other cuts without a cut in the dole. At the height of the crisis a telegram from the government's New York brokers stated that the prospects of an American loan would not be good without strict economies. The Cabinet was split; nine including Clynes and Henderson said they would resign rather than acquiesce.

The outcome seemed obvious: a Conservative–Liberal coalition to enforce the economies which even the Labour dissidents realised would have to come. In the event this was what occurred, disguised as a government of national salvation with the unlikely twist of Macdonald as its leader. Lloyd George was temporarily out of politics owing to a severe operation, and his deputy Samuel made the suggestion of an all-party government to preserve some element of Liberal independence. The key role, however, was taken by the King, who had the constitutional duty in such a crisis to get the strongest government he could as quickly as possible. He admired Macdonald and when the latter reported to him the disunity of his Cabinet, invited him to remain as the head of a temporary, all-party administration. He suggested that Baldwin and Samuel serve under him, which Macdonald could hardly do himself. Without consulting his Cabinet but assuming that at least a hundred of his party would acquiesce, he accepted with alacrity on 24th August. When the crisis and the party truce were over he foresaw no difficulty in taking his place at the head of the Labour Movement once more.

Baldwin also committed his party without consulting them but received their firm support. More sensitive than Macdonald to trends of opinion he realised that the abrupt worsening of the depression with the consequent increase in unemployment had brought about an overwhelming sense of insecurity to a large proportion of the population and a yearning for some sense of national purpose. The creation of a national government seemed to provide this; it made internecine party strife seem almost immoral. Its actions were accepted uncritically and it became in effect a dictatorship. Due to Baldwin's foresight this emotional wave placed the Conservatives firmly in power.

To the Labour party Macdonald's action seemed a betrayal of the worst order. He was accused of plotting the crisis by arranging publication of the May Report after Parliament had risen; rumours of a coalition had been rife earlier in the year and he had hinted to Lord Passfield (Sydney Webb) a drastic reconstruction of the government in the autumn; he showed throughout a lack of sympathy with his colleagues' point of view and a closer affinity to the Opposition; he parted from them without regret and spoke bitterly of them thereafter; he was flattered by the thought of leading a more socially acceptable government. These were half-truths; it is probable that Macdonald, muddle-headed and short sighted, genuinely believed that the decisions he took were the best ones for the nation and perhaps for his party as well.

A Cabinet of ten was formed: Snowden remained at the Exchequer, Thomas and Sankey were also members. The Conservatives were represented by Baldwin, Neville Chamberlain, Hoare and Cunliffe-Lister (later Lord Swinton); Samuel and Reading represented the Liberals. Only four former

Labour Ministers and eight back benchers supported Mac-donald. In practice the National Government marked the end of the slight Liberal revival but it only superficially split the Labour party, though it weakened it. Henderson became leader, though he lost his seat in the General Election, but it was a reversion to the pre-1922 style of leadership. As Citrine put it:

> The Labour movement could reasonably complain of dictation. Never again would a Labour Prime Minister or a Labour Chancellor of the Exchequer be permitted to exercise such auto-cratic power.

The rank and file tended to see the crisis as yet another capitalist swindle and saw no need to reappraise the Labour party's position or to accept its responsibility, through inept government, for the turn of events.[1]

Parliament met at the beginning of September and amidst such demonstrations of patriotism as cancelled war bonds and savings certificates sent to the Treasury Snowden introduced the severe budget he had planned in the spring. The annual payment to the Sinking Fund was cut by £20 m.; income tax went up to five shillings in the pound. Economies of £70 m., only £14 m. more than the Labour Cabinet had been pre-pared to accept, were produced by a 10 per cent cut in salaries paid by the State and in unemployment benefit,[2] which was granted on stricter conditions. Police salaries were only reduced by 5 per cent, balanced by those of teachers which were to go down by 15 per cent.

Any hope that the run on the pound might be checked proved illusory, especially when, owing to government inepti-tude and the unduly harsh treatment of some long service ratings, there was a lower deck mutiny in the Atlantic fleet at Invergordon. It procured fairer treatment for the Navy, while teachers were promoted to the standard 10 per cent reduction, but although nervous foreigners might assume a naval mutiny meant Britain was on the verge of collapse, it probably only advanced the exchange crisis by a few days.

By 19th September the French and American credits arranged in early August were exhausted and two days later the government began to manage the currency, which earlier

---

[1] See above, p. 490.
[2] It was reduced, for men, from seventeen shillings to fifteen shillings a week.
KI

had seemed almost immoral. The Gold Standard was suspended with the result that the exchange rate fell abruptly from $4.86 to $3.40 to the pound. The Bank rate was raised from $4\frac{1}{2}$ per cent to 6 per cent. Had this been done in early August, the whole crisis might have been avoided. Public confidence in the National Government remained high:

> 'It had been formed,' writes Lord Francis-Williams in *A Pattern of Rulers*, 'in the wrong way for the wrong reasons to apply the wrong remedy to the wrong disease but it had given the British their moment of high drama and they loved it with all the force of their romantic natures.'

(b) Social Background

In his *English Journey* of 1933 J. B. Priestley discerned several distinct Englands co-existing. The old agricultural England superficially had changed little. The villages whose building materials so perfectly blended into the countryside, where good taste seemed instinctive, still slumbered in the reflected light of the twin suns of squire and parson. Most Englishmen, though they shrank from employment on the land, liked to think that they were countrymen at heart and that there was a superior quality of civilisation in the timeless patterns of rural life. In fact agriculture had never completely recovered since the depression in the last quarter of the 19th Century,[1] although there was a temporary increase of prosperity during the Great War. The farming population steadily declined in numbers as young men sought easier alternatives to such arduous and poorly paid employment, though conditions began to improve with the Agricultural Wages Act of 1924 and the increasing use of machinery.

Up to 1914 such revival of farming as there was arose mainly from individual efforts to find new sources of profit. The supply of dairy products and eggs to the big cities, market gardening, and prime quality meat production were reasonably profitable. Scientific research, sponsored by the Ministry of Agriculture (upgraded in 1919 from the Board set up in 1899), helped to control the worst agricultural pests and diseases and ensured the high quality of fertilisers and artificial feeding stuffs. Additional uses were found for agricultural produce and the canning industry stimulated the

---

[1] See above, p. 251.

growing of vegetables and fruit.   These tendencies continued
in the ninteen twenties, with additional land utilisation by the
development of the sugar beet industry and the activities of the
Forestry Commission, set up during the Great War.   Prices,
however, were falling and much land reverted to rough
pasture.

The National Government began to reverse the trend
though it has been argued that, with a surplus of food in the
world as a whole, the country's resources could have been
better applied.   At a time when other depressed industries
were being assisted and food preferences for the dominions
were being arranged, it seemed unreasonable – and unwise
politically – to exclude British farming.   Quotas were
imposed for imported foods; the British farmer was encouraged
to supply the remainder by acreage subsidies to growers of
cereals and higher and steadier prices for a variety of products
whose distribution was controlled by Marketing Boards.   Of
these milk, established in 1933, was the largest, one of the
most successful and one of the most beneficial in that it made
possible the distribution of milk at subsidised prices in
depressed areas.   Food prices to the consumer remained
relatively stable due largely to the low cost of imported food
but British agriculture was subsidised to the tune of
£100,000,000 a year by 1939, made up of derating, direct
subsidies and the additional cost of raising at home what
could have been produced more cheaply abroad.   Output
increased by one-sixth from 1931–39; many tractors and other
machines appeared on the farms.

The squires in reality were going fast.   High taxation,
particularly death duties, was breaking up the great estates
and depriving small farmers of the advantages that a tenancy
in a large progressive landholding can bring.   A few large
country houses were erected but it was much more usual for
old ones to be demolished or to pass into the hands of institutions, as, for example, the palatial residence of the dukes of
Buckingham which became Stowe School.   The growing
difficulty of obtaining domestic service cut down the scale of
those establishments that remained.   The illusions of gentility
were maintained by upper middle-class families who retired
into the countryside or commuted from the country to the
towns.

The country parson suffered from the decline in church-going which was becoming most usual in middle-class suburbs. All denominations were affected, the Roman Catholics with their stricter discipline probably least, but most made determined efforts to refurbish their image and keep in tune with the times. Considerable interest was aroused by the parliamentary storm in 1928 over the revised Prayer Book of the Church of England, which was designed to permit the greater use and acceptance of Anglo-Catholic practices and beliefs. Though accepted by the Lords, it was twice rejected by the Commons where non-churchgoers predominated. The debates were an oratorical feast that the mundane and complex nature of most legislation rarely produces. The Convocations illegally sanctioned use of the Book pending parliamentary approval.

Priestley also described a second England, that of the old industrial areas, chiefly in the north. They remained grey and forbidding, often narrow and closed communities where the paternalism and inward-lookingness that had been derived from the countryside survived more strongly than in rural societies. They preserved the traditions of local custom and self-reliance in entertainment more strongly than anywhere else. Priestley's fourth England, that of the unemployed, was, in fact, an invariable constituent of these communities, especially in the Welsh mining valleys and in the north-east. At Tow Law in County Durham unemployment was 80 per cent, at Shildon very nearly 100 per cent. In these areas hope had almost gone, dereliction and despair prevailed. Priestley wrote of Stockton-on-Tees: 'The real town is finished. It is like a theatre that is kept open merely for the sale of drinks in the bars and chocolates in the corridors.' Often it was only the cinemas and the pawnshops that prospered.

The dole was subject to an often humiliating means test which bred an atmosphere where informers flourished but it helped to keep people alive, even though they might come to feel that nothing they did was worth while. Men hung around apathetically, women struggled, often heroically and at considerable personal sacrifice, to maintain reasonable standards. The dole became a way of life, as Walter Green-wood's book, *Love on the Dole*, illustrates. Voluntary organisations, particularly the Quakers, did what they could to make

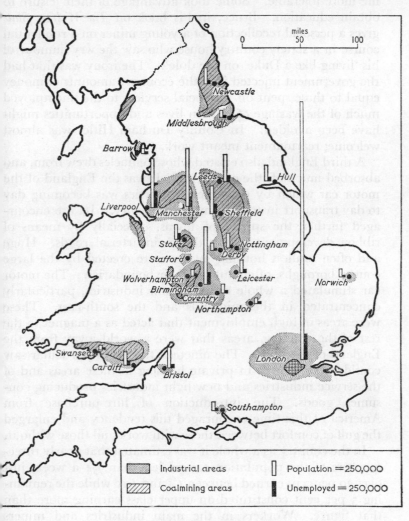

miles
0   50   100

Newcastle

Middlesbrough

Barrow

Leeds   *Hull*

Liverpool   *Manchester*   *Sheffield*

Stoke   *Nottingham*

Stafford   *Derby*

Wolverhampton   *Leicester*   *Norwich*

Birmingham
Coventry

Northampton

Swansea   *London*

Cardiff

Bristol

Southampton

▨ Industrial areas	▯	Population = 250,000
▨ Coalmining areas	▮	Unemployed = 250,000

INDUSTRIAL ENGLAND, 1931

(With acknowledgements to A. J. P. Taylor, *English History 1914-45*, published by O.U.P.)

life more tolerable.   Some took advantage of their leisure to obtain education.   Bruce, in his book on *The Welfare State* gives a personal recollection of a young miner on a residential course in a stately country house who saw the wry humour of his 'living like a Duke, on the dole'.   The irony was that had the government injected into the economy amounts of money equal to those spent on the social services to the unemployed much of the wastage of human lives and opportunities might have been avoided.   In County Durham Hitler was almost welcome; rearmament meant work.

A third England also existed whose tentacles drew from, and absorbed much of, the other two.   It was the England of the motor car which by the nineteen thirties was becoming day to day transport instead of merely a luxury.   Its use encouraged further the spread of towns, especially by means of ribbon development, along the main arterial roads.   Huge and often soulless housing estates were erected by the large county boroughs, often outside their boundaries.   The motor car stimulated a whole range of new industries, particularly concentrated in the midlands and the south-east.   These were areas of high employment that acted as a magnet to the rest of the country, areas that were a world away from the England of the dole.   The nineteen thirties in particular saw considerable growth in private housing in these areas and of the service industries and new light industries producing consumer goods.   The introduction of hire-purchase from America at this time encouraged this tendency and enlarged the gulf of comfort between those with work and those without.

In the country as a whole it was estimated that nearly three-quarters of the population earned less than £4 a week; just over 20 per cent earned between £4 and £10 while the remaining 5 per cent constituted an upper class earning more than that figure.   Workers in the main industries and miners brought home an average weekly wage of 49s., while in the textile industry with its large number of women workers the average was 36s.   In 1935 the working class was paying for 79 per cent of the social services.   By no means all benefited; self-employed workers were excluded from the unemployment schemes, as were farm workers until 1936 and domestic servants until 1938.   Women, unless working, were only provided for when child-bearing.   It was reckoned that one-

third of the families below the poverty line, of which the level
was set higher than in the surveys at the beginning of the
century, received no help from the public social services at all
and had to rely on haphazard voluntary assistance. Eight
million families, it was reckoned, had no reserves of savings
and had to borrow money to meet any unusual expense.
Perhaps because of this the amount of betting grew during the
period, especially on horses. A weekly subscription to the
football pools, the popularity of which steadily increased,
seemed to many a form of insurance with prizes beyond the
dreams of avarice.

Seebohm Rowntree repeated his survey of York in 1936[1]
and found that 17·7 per cent of the total population were
below the poverty line which he set higher than in 1899. A
similar survey in Bristol produced a much lower figure in 1937.
Unemployment, old age or unduly large families would result
in half the working class knowing poverty at some stage of
their lives. It was reckoned that four and a half million
people had an inadequate diet but in general the health and
cleanliness of children was improving. The latter factor,
especially, helped to break down class barriers. There was
considerable ignorance, however, of the right sort of diet.
Housing accommodation had improved; for instance almost
every house in York had its own water supply and lavatory
while one-third had baths. Housing conditions in Scotland
were the worst in the country. By 1939 the great majority
of people in need could receive free medical treatment.
There were nearly 60,000 beds in 400 hospitals under public
health control and around 77,000 in voluntary hospitals.

Patterns of recreation had changed. The music halls that
have come to typify the lighter side of the Victorian age were
closing their doors; the cinemas were opening theirs. They
offered to the lonely, the poor and the unemployed a world of
illusion into which they could escape. The spectator
instinct was increased by the development of professional sport
on a large scale. The radio brought professional entertainment into the home and though thereby helping to unify
family interests and decrease drunkenness, made the average
citizen less of a participator. Dancing in various styles, on
the other hand, was very popular.

---

[1] See above, p. 382.

A group of radio manufacturers had promoted in 1922 the British Broadcasting Company, which was given an exclusive licence by the Post Office with little thought about the principles of competition and free expression involved. Its manager, Reith, was a man with a mission who considered informing and instructing more important than merely entertaining. His influence was if anything strengthened by the establishment in 1926 of the British Broadcasting Corporation, created by royal charter, of which he was the first Director-General. Formed to prevent a repetition of the indirect influence the government had exerted during the General Strike, it imposed programmes governed by firm standards of morality and a dislike of disturbing controversy. It extended knowledge of classical music, particularly by sponsoring such occasions as the Promenade Concerts. Its news broadcasts had the unrivalled advantage of immediacy and obtained considerable reputation for fairness and accuracy.

Radio had a stimulating influence on newspapers, which did their best to compete and provide counter-attractions. The most important figure in Fleet Street was Lord Beaverbrook, whose ideas of subject matter and presentation, though not his politics, had a very wide influence. Advertising was an increasingly important source of revenue particularly for the 'quality' papers. There were circulation wars, with the *Daily Express*, with a sale of over two million copies a day, maintaining an easy lead. The majority of the newspapers were Conservative in politics; the sole Labour representative, the *Daily Herald*, became more successful when Bevin took charge of it in 1927 and secured the support of Odhams Press in 1929. The literary tastes of intellectuals and the ordinary people diverged more than they had done in the 19th Century, though both could appreciate the cult of detective stories and the delightful escapism of P. G. Wodehouse.

Many benefited from the general introduction of holidays with pay in 1938 and the practice of taking an annual holiday away from home grew steadily with the corresponding growth of favoured seaside towns. Despite the misfortunes of the unemployed, the great majority of people enjoyed a richer life than ever before. Although the economies of 1931, when only one in five got secondary education, delayed the raising of the school leaving age to fifteen, the Hadow Report was gradually implemented and opportunities for secondary education increased. The Spens Report of 1938 was concerned with technical education and first suggested the idea of offering various types of education within a single school, a conception, now known as 'comprehensive', which has been proclaimed as a great social unifier, whatever its educational virtues.

The events of 1931 helped to change men's attitudes. It was gradually accepted that pre-war normality was unattainable, as well as socially undesirable in many respects. Though a higher degree of security at home had been obtained, even for the unemployed, international security seemed more elusive and the means set up to ensure it more ineffectual. Most people shrank from the implications of rearmament but were quick to denounce alternative measures when they failed; they shrank from facing the problems of politics in the pious hope that the country would muddle through and things would somehow turn out for the best. Politicians also deluded themselves; Macdonald and Baldwin combined to avoid awkward problems and to create an illusion of national unity and well-being. At home the National Government was tolerably successful, though events worked in its favour; abroad its avoidance of basic problems brought in the end disaster.

(c) HOME AFFAIRS

Events conspired to make permanent a government formed as a 'committee of public safety' to meet an emergency financial situation. The Budget of September 1931 and the devaluation of the pound removed the immediate pressure but the problems that had brought the crisis about remained and it was believed that a truly national effort might find solutions. In practice the dominant party in the government, the Conservatives, had only one to offer, their traditional one of a tariff, and within the government they put strong pressure on Macdonald to have an election to sanction it. In Parliament Churchill pointed out that it was essential to make the government really national by basing it on a popular majority. Macdonald had little option but to give way; rejected by Labour he was the prisoner of the Conservatives. For the

Liberals it was more difficult. If they accepted Protection they would be virtually indistinguishable from the Tories and there would be little chance for them of an independent political future; some knew, nevertheless, that the National Government was their sole chance of political office and Samuel gave way to Tory pressure. Lloyd George was opposed. It was 'the most wanton and unpatriotic election into which the country had ever been plunged'. The Liberals took little notice, but the Lloyd George Fund was closed to them.

The election repeated many of the features of the 'coupon' election of 1918.[1] Each element of the coalition presented a few distinctive ideas of its own under a general request by Macdonald for 'a free hand', 'a doctor's mandate' to apply whatever remedies, including tariffs, that might seem appropriate. No mandate was sought for Protection as such. In such confusion and vagueness, the election was a vote of confidence in the government that had stood up to the crisis compared with the one that had abandoned its responsibilities. Surprisingly, in view of the fact that he presided over both and himself held a prime responsibility for the turn of events, Macdonald was the hero of the hour. Rallying round a man whose speeches were growing so vague and general that he seemed all things to all men, the people yielded to a comfortable emotional sense of national unity. The government's supporters were united only in their vilifications of Labour, in which Snowden in particular joined with gusto. He described as Bolshevism run mad their programme of maintaining free trade while planning the economy. A scare was started that a Labour government would confiscate savings bank deposits to pay for the dole. 'Tomorrow', said one Conservative Minister on the eve of the election, 'there will be a new England or no England'.

The election, on 27th October, brought the National parties 60 per cent of the vote and 521 seats; the Liberal dissentients won thirty-three, the Labour party fifty-two. Mosley's New Party was swept away; Lloyd George and three members of his family formed an independent group entrenched in Welsh affection but without a future. It is probable that the Conservatives would have won a clear majority had they

[1] See above, p. 457.

fought alone and the government increasingly took on a Conservative character. Baldwin as Lord President was clearly its real leader; Samuel and the Free Trade Liberals soon resigned, though Simon who was Foreign Secretary and those who were ready to accept Protection remained. Macdonald's prestige rapidly disintegrated; his son Malcolm was the only valuable Labour recruit. Neville Chamberlain was the dominant figure in Home Affairs and succeeded Snowden, who went to the Lords, as Chancellor of the Exchequer. His determination, interest in social questions and high principles made him the pace-setter of the Cabinet; had he been easier in personal relationships the quality of his work might have been more appreciated and he might have been readier to take advice.[1]

His views on the depression were firm and narrow. He deprecated interference with private enterprise and assumed the system would right itself if public expenditure was curtailed. The alternatives of encouraging industrial expansion through government guarantees or reinflating the economy by a large-scale public works programme which could be of great social value, were not seriously considered. The one positive interference with an unfettered economy was the abandonment of free trade.

After a cursory inquiry by a Cabinet Committee and despite the fact that Cabinet agreement was lacking, Chamberlain and Runciman, President of the Board of Trade, introduced an Import Duties Bill in February 1932, which imposed a tariff of 10 per cent on all goods except raw materials, most foodstuffs and imports from the Empire. An advisory committee was set up under Sir George May which made various proposals during the next three years. In conjunction with the Ottawa Agreements there was evolved a comprehensive but moderate tariff which was to leave a quarter of all imports duty free and half paying duties of 10 per cent to 20 per cent. It reduced the number of imports and protected home industries, formed a useful additional source of government income and allowed a system of imperial preferences and reciprocal reductions with other countries to be constructed. It did not produce the economic miracles that had been hoped for. Foreign manufacturers fiercely competed

---

[1] See above, p. 484 and below, p. 552.

with British goods overseas to sell those products excluded from Britain; the fewer manufacturered goods Britain imported led to the reduction of exports to the richer, producing, countries. In the long run imports of essential foods and raw materials could not be much reduced; the principle effect of tariffs was to reduce exports.

The Ottawa Conference, held in July and August 1932, was the last act of the illusion that Great Britain and the Dominions had common economic interest.[1] No member wanted to damage her trade relations with countries outside the Commonwealth. Twelve separate agreements were signed that in practice made it more difficult for Britain to make reciprocal reductions with foreign countries. Snowden resigned as Lord Privy Seal in protest: 'I cannot go on sacrificing beliefs and principles bit by bit until none are left.' Samuel and his section of the Liberal party left the government but did not go into active opposition until over a year later. Seventeen trade agreements were signed with foreign countries between 1932 and 1935 which arranged quotas for the import of meat, butter and other natural products in return for concessions to British exports.

Unhappy about these tendencies, Macdonald sought to escape by promoting what was to be the last great international meeting of the inter-war years, the World Economic Conference at South Kensington. Resolutions were passed deprecating tariffs, exchange restrictions and unstable currencies, but most of the countries who sent representatives were pursuing purely nationalistic policies and Britain was no exception. American refusal to co-operate in any constructive policy precipitated a failure that was probably inevitable.

British policy further exacerbated this tendency. The Lausanne Conference of June 1932, meeting during Hoover's moratorium on international debts, ended German reparations with a final token payment which it was tacitly agreed should not be made and which Von Papen construed as absolving the Germans from 'war guilt'. An agreement in December 1932 further removed the restrictions on German armament. The end of reparations meant that the French and other debtors refused to resume their repayments to Britain, which inevitably opened the question of British

[1] See above, p. 505.

payments to the United States. Although in theory independent they had in practice become linked with the honouring of other international obligations and moreover had been incurred in a common war. The high United States tariffs made payment difficult while the stability of the pound was endangered by the transfer of gold. Although President Roosevelt was willing to make some concessions Congress would not agree and after 1933 the British government defaulted.

At home unemployment reached nearly three million, 23 per cent of the insured population, in January 1933. Production was down 15 per cent during the depression years but by the end of 1933 it was above the 1929 level; exports recovered slowly and were only 83 per cent of the 1929 figure in 1937. Britain averted a balance of payments crisis by the continued fall in the prices of raw materials. Compared with other industrial countries recovery was relatively swift. The rise in real wages that a falling cost of living brought about released money mainly invested in private housing, which performed the same role in the British recovery that the public works programme of the New Deal did in the United States. The continued growth of the consumer industries and of private spending assisted, as did developments in a variety of industries, old and new. There were signs of another depression by 1937, but it was averted by rearmament.

It is the misfortune of governments to be blamed for depression; their stock rises with increases of prosperity. In reality government measures contributed little. The effects of the tariff policy have been outlined above. Devaluation gave a temporary advantage to British exports but when others, particularly the United States, followed suit, the advantage disappeared and to bring about some stability a pseudo-gold standard was operated with France and the United States from 1936 onwards. Taking advantage of the low return on industrial stocks, the government converted 5 per cent War Loan to 3½ per cent in 1932, a measure which with conversions of other funds in due course reduced the National Debt by one-fifth. To facilitate this, the Bank Rate was lowered to 2 per cent and thus, by accident, a period of cheap money was inaugurated. The government subsequently claimed that it had cured the depression, but money was not invested to any extent until it was clear that the markets had recovered. The most that might really be claimed was that the very fact of a Conservative rather than a Labour government in office in itself restored business confidence. Deficits were incurred in 1932 and 1933 but the government was not willing to indulge in large expenditure, which would have been a valuable contribution to recovery, until the economy had recovered through its own efforts.

With foreign competition reduced by tariffs and quotas it was hoped that British industry could put its own house in order. It was intended that this should be voluntary, the government stepping in only as a last resort. On the model of the wartime reductions the cotton and shipbuilding industries lowered their productive capacities. The doubling of Indian cotton production and the increase of Japanese exports led to the destruction of six million spindles in Lancashire. In shipbuilding, British yards were not well equipped for oil-burning and motor vessels and the decline of world trade in the depression reduced the demand. Berths of over a million tons building capacity were empty or closed, creating serious unemployment in some towns. At Jarrow, the worst hit, it reached 72·9 per cent. The employers would accept no responsibility nor would the government, and it was largely saved by the voluntary effort of the county of Surrey, whose Sheriff, Sir John Jarvis, founded a metal and engineering works there. In 1935, with the economy recovering, the government gave subsidies to tramp shipping under the Shipping Assistance Act, following the practice of most foreign governments, and inaugurated a 'scrap and build' scheme. Government loans helped to launch the *Queen Mary* whose building had been halted by the depression. Although this gave an impetus, British yards were only responsible for one-third of the world's launchings in 1938 as opposed to 61 per cent in 1910–14.

Recovery of the coal industry was slow; 41 per cent of the miners were unemployed in 1932 and by 1937 exports were still only half the 1913 figure. The age of many British pits and awkward seams made mechanisation difficult and 43 per cent of all the coal produced was still cut by hand in 1937. Government proposals for reorganisation or planned reduction of productive capacity met with little response; mining royalties were finally nationalised in 1938, however.

The iron and steel industry was relatively prosperous. Costs of manufacture were high owing to much old fashioned plant and later the expense of reconstruction. Some amalgamations and closures took place, under the auspices of the Iron and Steel Federation founded in 1932, but there were also important expansion schemes such as John Summers between Chester and Flint, Stewarts and Lloyds at Corby and Richard Thomas at Ebbw Vale. The revival of large-scale engineering and shipbuilding, the demands of new industries, especially motor cars, assisted recovery but by 1937 exports had only reached 59 per cent of the 1929 figure. It was rearmament which in due course greatly increased production.

The most important of the newer industries was the making of motor cars. There had been comparatively little progress before the Great War compared with the United States and Germany but after the war the adoption to some extent of American mass production methods helped to raise output from 32,000 cars a year in 1920 to 182,000 in 1929. There was even greater expansion in the nineteen thirties when British car exports obtained a larger share of the world market than the Americans. At home buses and lorries began to compete seriously with the railways. Roads were classified, the 20 m.p.h. restriction on vehicles removed in 1930 and licences were only granted after a driving test. Some new by-passes were constructed and important capital works such as the Mersey Tunnel, but the opportunity to give Britain a comprehensive trunk road system during the Depression years was missed.

Car manufacture gave a great boost to the engineering industry; leather, rubber and non-ferrous metals also benefited. The electricity supply industry expanded rapidly, giving an important market for electrical appliances. Industry based on new materials, mainly synthetic, steadily came into existence. Courtaulds, a silk firm established in Essex in the 18th Century, were the British pioneers in rayon. I.C.I., formed by amalgamation in 1926 was, with a total capital of £56 m., the largest industrial organisation in the Empire and produced a wide range of goods, particularly in the field of synthetic fibres and plastics. All these helped to increase the prosperity of the country, particularly its southern half.

The nineteen thirties also saw a remarkable boom in house construction, mostly without government assistance. The Wheatley scheme[1] ended in 1932 as a result of government economies: slum clearance under the provisions of the Greenwood Act began in 1934 and overcrowding became a legal offence in 1935. Such was the problem that, despite Chamberlain's concern, only half even of the declared slums had been cleared by 1939. Building costs fell during the Depression and much was done at cut rates by men who camped out in the half finished houses they were constructing. Nearly three million houses were constructed by private enterprise in the thirties; with interest rates low money was readily available and building houses to rent was a profitable investment. The better-off section of the working class was able to afford the new housing and their standard of living tended to rise, particularly in the south. One-third of all existing houses in England and Wales in 1939 had been built since 1919.

In his 1934 Budget Chamberlain announced that the country had left *Bleak House* and might now begin *Great Expectations*. Income tax came down to 4s. 6d. in the pound and the cuts in salaries paid by the Government or local authorities were restored then or in the Budget of 1935. But despite industrial recovery, unemployment remained. It fell below the two million mark finally in July 1935; a year later it was 1·6 million. Many men over forty-five did not expect to work again, many young men had never worked. They benefited little from the subsidised services such as housing or education. The unemployed were principally concentrated in certain districts designated special areas in 1934 and given limited government assistance. South Wales, with unemployment at Merthyr Tydfil at 61 per cent in 1934, for instance, was hard hit, as was west Cumberland where the unemployment rate at Maryport was 57 per cent. The Tyne–Tees area, industrial Lancashire, the tin-mining districts of Cornwall, Northern Ireland, and industrial Scotland were seriously affected, the situation in the last giving rise to the Scottish Nationalist movement. In contrast the 1934 unemployment figure for Birmingham was 6 per cent and for High Wycombe 3 per cent.

[1] See above, p. 487.

The provision of funds for the unemployed caused considerable controversy. The principle of insurance collapsed when men were out of work for years and in 1931 the government imposed a means test, which was regarded by the working class as highly unreasonable and which the Public Assistance Committees of those local authorities controlled by Labour would not operate. To counteract this Chamberlain set up a non-political Statutory Committee by the Unemployment Act of 1934 which operated a scheme based on insurance principles but allowing for longer periods without work. The national rates proposed caused an outcry when it was found that they were less than those in operation in some distressed areas and the new scales were not imposed until 1937. By then the Unemployment Assistance Board had assumed responsibility for the long-term unemployed and the links with the old Poor Law had virtually withered away. This was a very real achievement but the way in which it came about increased Labour dislike of Neville Chamberlain.

Among individual politicians on both sides of the House there were many who believed that the State could plan the economy and thus reduce unemployment. Some spoke in extravagant Marxist terms that aroused the distrust of their Labour colleagues, and trades unionists feared that planning might entail the direction of labour. The writings of Keynes, particularly his *Treatise on Money* of 1930 and *The General Theory of Employment, Interest and Money* of 1936, were very influential. He believed that employment was determined not by the level of wages but by the two rival motives in each person, the propensity to consume and the propensity to invest. There was no need for investment to be in useful goods or to promise a high rate of interest but if the supply of money and credit should be low the propensity to consume and the propensity to invest are both lowered and unemployment rises. From this he drew four conclusions: that the State should control the policies that influence credit and investment; that when employment declined interest rates should be lowered; that public works should be used to stimulate investment and, finally, that income should be more equally distributed to increase consumption and hence employment. The drawback to these ideas, which worked well in America, was that in England they did not take into account the problem of the

LI

declining staple industries.   Moreover it could be added that
greater equality of incomes tends to give a smaller surplus for
investment.

The National Government's popularity naturally declined
from the high water mark of October 1931.   Baldwin in
particular was shaken by the result of the East Fulham
by-election of October 1933 when the Labour candidate
captured a seat with a 5,000 majority that had been won by
the Conservatives with a 14,000 majority in 1931.   He concluded that it was a victory for pacifism and it so influenced
him that he shrank from presenting the need for rearmament
to the electorate in the General Election of 1935,[1] and admitted
in November 1936 in a speech to the Commons of 'appalling
frankness' that he had put the interests of his party first.
There is no evidence that Baldwin was right; Neville Chamberlain attributed the by-election defeat to the means test and it
is probable that housing conditions were also a major factor.
Labour won 200 boroughs in November of the same year and
captured the L.C.C. in 1934.

In June 1935 Macdonald and Baldwin exchanged offices.
The powers of the former were waning fast and he was
becoming a somewhat pathetic figure, still convinced he was a
socialist, a view hardly anyone else shared.   There was a
Cabinet reshuffle with Simon, discredited by his handling of
Japan's invasion of Manchuria, going from the Foreign to the
Home Office and being succeeded by Hoare who had Eden
as his coadjutor as Minister for League of Nations Affairs.
Malcolm Macdonald became Colonial Secretary.

Lansbury had been elected leader of the Labour party
when Henderson had resigned following his defeat in the
General Election of 1931.   When he resigned himself following the split of his party over attitudes to the Italian invasion
of Abyssinia, Baldwin dissolved Parliament to take advantage
of the confusion of his opponents and a General Election was
held on 14th November, 1935.   In the campaign both parties
really affirmed their support for the League of Nations and
for any sanctions short of war.   Fearing an undue emphasis
would damage the government's prospects, Baldwin played
down the need for armaments, as he admitted in the Commons

---

[1] He obtained additional evidence to support this decision from the results
of the 'Peace Ballot' in the summer of 1935.   See below, p. 545.

a year later. He said to the Peace Society during the election campaign: 'I give you my word there will be no great armaments.' It may be said in his defence that few appreciated the dangers that lay ahead and it would be unjust to speak of sharp practice at a time when the public firmly backed the support of sanctions. Housing, unemployment and the problems of the special areas were the main questions of the day and the low poll suggested a lack of controversial topics. It was a vote of confidence in Baldwin and his government which was Conservative in all but name; certainly one of no confidence in a Labour government. The Conservatives won 432 seats, Labour 154, while the Liberals were reduced to twenty plus Lloyd George's group of four. There was a solitary communist. The two Macdonalds were both defeated but returned at by-elections, Ramsay for the Scottish Universities after strenuous canvassing of Conservative voters by Baldwin who said of him: 'He floats around like a wraith.'

After the disastrous election of 1931 in which the Labour party lost many working-class constituencies and most of its front bench, Lansbury became Leader of the party with Attlee and Cripps, junior Ministers in Macdonald's second government, as his principal subordinates. The party became more obviously socialist than before, the events of 1931 being seen as the consequence of compromising with Capitalism. Left wing intellectuals were dominant, some of whom were inspired by the idea of Russia's Five Year Plan which had begun in 1928. Strachey and others contemplated association with Mosley[1] who founded the British Union of Fascists in 1932 after a visit to Mussolini, whose conception of the Corporate State with liberty subordinated to State service, greatly impressed him. For a while Mosley's movement seemed to have a future but a meeting at Olympia in 1934 displayed a violence which shocked the public and it gradually declined, especially when fascism abroad became conspicuously ruthless and inhumane. Also in 1932 the Independent Labour Party broke away from the main movement which it found too moderate, but some ultra-progressives remained within the party in the Socialist League, which advocated dictatorial means, if necessary, to put into operation a socialist programme. It was, however, expelled for

[1] See above, p. 514.

association with the communists in 1937 and then dissolved.

A substantial element in the party, including Lansbury and Cripps, believed that the League of Nations, which Cripps described as an 'International Burglars Union', was unduly aggressive in its treatment of the Abyssinian question. At the party conference in October 1935 Lansbury, a sincere pacifist, made an impressive speech but his cause was outvoted in a motion supporting the policy of sanctions put by Bevin, who in this represented the realism of the Trades Unions. Morrison, Clynes, Dalton and other former Ministers were returned in the election, but members of the 1931-35 Parliament had been impressed by Attlee's abilities as deputy-leader and he was elected to succeed Lansbury. It was felt initially that he was a stop-gap choice but his unassuming qualities made him more generally acceptable than a more dynamic leader would have been. Roy Jenkins has written:

> Attlee as Labour leader was partly the product of the reaction to Macdonald. . . . Better a pedestrian speaker who meant what he said than a spell binder who bemused himself with his own words; better a middle class man with no social ambitions than a worker who was trying to rise, better a self-effacing modesty than a self-destroying vanity.

Under his leadership the party found greater unity and sense of purpose and became for the first time a majority government in 1945.

In May 1935 the Silver Jubilee of George V as King was celebrated. It was an unprecedented occasion and a deliberate evocation of the past. The King, almost a living embodiment of the Victorian virtues, had become through his genuine concern for people, his visits to various parts of the country and his effective broadcasts a father figure, and he and Queen Mary had raised the monarchy to a place of affection in the hearts of its subjects. There were remarkable demonstrations of loyalty in the poor and distressed areas. When he died in January 1936 the nation mourned a king whose reign had so firmly established the modern constitutional monarchy that it survived the shock of an abdication only ten months later.

Edward VIII, who had become very popular as Prince of Wales, was a bachelor when he came to the throne. He found the rigid constitutional role his father had built up somewhat restricting and believed that the monarchy should move closer to the people and help to initiate more adventurous policies. This attitude might, in due course, have brought about difficulties with his Ministers had not a more pressing problem intervened. He had fallen in love with a witty and attractive woman who had the drawback that she was an American and a commoner and the serious disadvantage for a monarch who was Head of an Established Church, which held that the marriage vows must be binding for life, that she already had two husbands, one divorced and one about to be. As long as there was merely a friendship, although the foreign Press might speculate, the Government could take no action but when Mrs Simpson obtained her second divorce on 27th October, 1936, the question came to a head.

The King had not expected any difficulty, believing he could keep his private life distinct from his public functions; he thought he could marry Mrs Simpson and remain on the throne. When objections were made, he contemplated a morganatic marriage, which had worked satisfactorily with various German princes, but the Dominions were unanimously against such a proceeding. The course of events was determined by Baldwin, who had overcome the inertia he had shown in the spring, when his position as Premier had seemed threatened. He handled the matter with tact but firmness, insisting on a prompt decision out of the public eye in order to preserve the position and prestige of the monarchy.

It was not until 1st December that the affair became public and some effort was made to create a 'King's Party' to prevent coercion by his Ministers. Its main supporters were Beaverbrook, Rothermere and Churchill, whose attitude caused some public resentment and further emphasised his isolation since his quarrel with Baldwin over concessions to India.[1] Public opinion as a whole wanted the matter quickly and quietly settled; indeed any drawn-out struggle might have prejudiced the future of the monarchy itself. The King accepted the position; he abdicated on 11th December, making a farewell broadcast that night, and went into exile as Duke of Windsor. He married Mrs Simpson in 1937.

[1] See above, p. 508.

His brother and successor, George VI, was better suited to the constitutional role. Shy and frail, he showed great courage and devotion to duty, especially in wartime, and gave a similar display of happy family life to that which had contributed so powerfully to his father's popularity. The monarchy had been shaken but by the Coronation in May 1937 its magic had returned.

The Kingmaker also had his hour of glory. It was generally felt that Baldwin's handling of the affair was beyond reproach and he had expressed the sense of fitness and decency of the British people as a whole. Like Macdonald in 1931 he fleetingly assuaged that desire for a national leader whom men could admire. He resigned at the Coronation amidst public adulation, while at the same time Macdonald crept away to die a few months later at sea. But the laurels withered on Baldwin's brow and he was given much of the blame for Britain's military unpreparedness in 1939, a responsibility he shared with his successor, Chamberlain, and with the unwillingness of the nation as a whole to face unpleasant facts.

The abdication had an unexpected side effect in Ireland. De Valera, who had opposed the Treaty from the start,[1] had become Prime Minister in 1932 in succession to the more moderate Cosgrave. He carefully removed the restrictions on Irish sovereignty, declaring a separate Irish citizenship under the terms of the Statute of Westminster, removing most of the powers of the Governor-General and appeals to the Judicial Committee of the Privy Council. His unconcealed aim was a republic and in retaliation the British government imposed a 20 per cent tariff on imports from Ireland to which the Irish replied in similar terms. The British had no case except over the sanctity of treaties and the trade restrictions were removed gradually from December 1934 onwards. When Edward VIII abdicated, De Valera, instead of recognising his successor as did the other Dominion governments, deleted the monarchy from the Constitution, for which he obtained only a narrow majority. The Northern Irish were more than ever determined to preserve the partition. Malcolm Macdonald conducted the negotiations which clarified the relationship of the two countries in 1938. Free trade was

[1] See above, p. 473.

virtually established, the three naval bases were handed back
and the Irish paid £10 m. in settlement of the land annuities
and other claims.

(d) REARMAMENT AND ILLUSION

In the nineteen twenties both Labour and Conservative
parties pursued similar policies on defence. It was a time of
security, particularly after the Treaty of Locarno which
seemed to have healed the sores of the war, and politicians
were unanimous in the belief that great armaments were not
required. The Committee of Imperial Defence was revived
under Haldane's tutelage but the idea of a Ministry of
Defence, to co-ordinate the plans of the three services, was
killed by their mutual jealousy accentuated by the development of the Air Force as a distinct entity. It had proved it
could act by itself when it suppressed a revolt in Iraq.

Arms expenditure declined to $2\frac{1}{2}$ per cent of the national
income in 1933. Most money was spent on the Navy which
was the best prepared of the services for war, although aircraft
carriers were neglected. The R.A.F.'s dispositions were
shaped by Lord Trenchard, Chief of Air Staff 1919–29, who
saw aeroplanes as long range artillery to devastate enemy
cities and neglected air defence. The Army really existed
for an internal security role in the various British possessions
and money was spent on providing it with reasonable living
conditions rather than mechanising it or providing it with
superior arms and equipment.

It was the profound hope of the British people as a whole
that such weapons would never again be needed. Baldwin,
in particular, shrank from facing up to the reality of German
rearmament and represented a popular tendency to look
away from European problems. Many felt that Britain's
greatest contribution to world peace was to behave peaceably
herself, which was, probably, the point which the majority
who voted against fighting 'for King and Country' in the
Oxford Union debate of February 1933 were trying to make.
Both Conservative and Labour were much in agreement,
although Labour was more faithful to the idea of collective
security. Baldwin in theory supported the League of Nations
but failed to take much interest in it in practice.

An international attempt to reduce the size of armaments,

made at the instance of President Hoover in February 1932, might well have brought the United States into co-operation with the League of Nations. Henderson had been elected Chairman.[1] The British attitude was cautious, in the belief that only they could be relied on to keep their promises. They believed that conciliation was still possible. The real difficulty arose between France and Germany. Germany wanted parity of armaments with France; France would only agree if Britain would guarantee her security by real military preparations. It was British refusal to do this which led to the failure of the conference, which was brought to an end when the Germans walked out on 14th October, 1933, leaving the League of Nations a week later.

Although the government had not committed itself to great armaments, Samuel and his Liberals and the Labour party condemned its attitude and pressed for disarmament as the main element in its foreign policy. The service chiefs, however, were becoming convinced that rearmament was necessary, being particularly alarmed by the Japanese invasion of Manchuria in September 1931 and by the appointment as Chancellor in January 1933 of Adolf Hitler who had made no secret of his great-power ambitions for Germany. The government gave cautious approval in March 1932 but while plans were being made, arms estimates remained low. Baldwin's interpretation of the East Fulham result as a victory for pacifism gave point to his vague hope that armaments on a large scale would remain unnecessary.[2]

Whether they were or not clearly depended to a very large extent on the effectiveness of the League of Nations. By its Covenant any nation which resorted to war without giving the League an opportunity for arbitration should be regarded as a common enemy. It had no powers to reinforce this viewpoint: it could only recommend its members to declare war and if a majority voted in favour of sanctions, the minority could not be made to co-operate. Most people believed that sanctions, in effect an economic blockade, would succeed. The British view of the Covenant was that it imposed obligations that could not be fulfilled and it ought therefore to be revised. France and her allies, and in Britain the League of Nations Union, wanted a firmer undertaking on the part of all

[1] See above, p. 512.   [2] See above, p. 536.

members to co-operate with which side the League declared to be in the right.

The effectiveness of the League was tested by its reaction to the Japanese attack on Manchuria in September 1931. China, which nominally controlled Manchuria, was in a state of considerable anarchy and the Japanese excuse was that their trading interests had suffered. The Japanese aggression was prompted to a large extent by international economic policies which tended to deprive her of her trade and the Ottawa Agreements of 1932 were a further incentive. Any effective reaction by the League would to a large extent depend on the attitude of Britain, the only member apart from China and Japan with a major stake in the Far East. The crisis came just after the National Government had come to power and when it was preoccupied with other matters. No steps had yet been taken to build up Singapore as a major naval base and in view of the local naval supremacy given Japan by the Washington Treaty, effective action would have been impossible without American co-operation which was not forthcoming. Britain was anxious to preserve good relations with Japan in view of her financial and commercial interests in the Far East, and saw the League as a means of conciliating her by engineering a graceful Chinese acceptance of the position. The war broke out in Shanghai in 1932, where the British and United States consuls secured a truce but there was no co-operation between the powers at Foreign Secretary level and the Japanese were able, without challenge, to set up the puppet state of Manchukuo in the territory they had conquered. The Lytton Commission appointed by the League at British request was sympathetic to many of the Japanese grievances but deprecated her use of force and proposed that Manchuria should become an autonomous state under Chinese sovereignty. The Japanese refused to accept the Report and withdrew from the League at the end of 1932. The use of sanctions, which would have been meaningless without American co-operation, was not considered and the Japanese dictated a settlement with China at the Treaty of Tangku, which left Manchuria completely in their hands. The effectiveness of the League even as a means of conciliation was severely shaken. It was an invitation to return to power politics.

The proceedings were carefully noted by Hitler and his conclusions were confirmed by his own experience. When in October 1933 he left the Disarmament Conference and then the League he had expected immediate consequences: a French invasion of the Ruhr, a Polish invasion of East Prussia. Nothing happened: it was the first trial of strength, in which he won an easy victory. He made no secret of his methods: he had many of his former associates murdered in June 1934 and Chancellor Dolfuss of Austria a month later. The French were reasonably alive to the possible dangers; they maintained a high level of armaments and constructed from 1930 onwards the Maginot Line along their German frontier, which was believed to be then so impregnable that it promoted a false sense of security and, contrarily, made them readier to appease Germany. A vigorous Foreign Minister, Barthou, strengthened the French alliances and began the discussions which led to the Franco-Russian Alliance of 1935. Hitler had no illusions about the danger that Barthou represented to his plans and Nazi support was given to the plot which assassinated him and King Alexander of Yugoslavia in Marseilles in October 1934. The French were displeased but powerless when the Saar was returned to Germany in March 1935 after a plebiscite which voted 90 per cent in favour of this course.

British attitudes to Hitler were more complicated. Most people had a feeling of guilt about the way in which Germany had been treated at Versailles, which skilful German propaganda and British distrust of the French attitude encouraged. Many Conservatives initially saw Hitler as a desirable alternative to communism and for a while excused his methods as temporary excesses. Even when it was evident that they were all too permanent, there was failure to grasp the depths of deceit, the brutal ruthlessness, and the complete inhumanity that were essential facets of the Nazi régime. They found it hard to believe the Germans could allow themselves to be led into a second major war. The Labour party deplored his dictatorship but maintained that Germany's legitimate grievances had brought about his rise to power. They put their faith in collective security with which they believed disarmament was compatible. The government pursued several policies inconsistently: they contemplated a defensive alliance;

they began to rearm; they hoped the necessity for both would be removed by judicious appeasement.

An important development in the second policy occurred on 4th March, 1935, when a White Paper, the *Statement relating to Defence*, was published. It was produced by senior service officers and civil servants on their own initiative and while defending past policy insisted that the time had now come when considerable extra expenditure could no longer safely be postponed. The needs of each service were discussed. The proposals only received gradual public acceptance and the government hesitated to endorse them fully. Hitler replied by repudiating on 14th March the clauses in the Peace of Versailles banning German conscription and announcing he would raise an army of half a million men.

There was considerable alarm in France; the League Council denounced Hitler's action in April, but did nothing further. Churchill, who had advocated rearmament since 1932, maintained that France, Britain and Italy should have reoccupied the Rhineland and its bridgeheads, but the most the three powers could bring themselves to do was to sign the meaningless Stresa Front against aggression in April 1935. In answer Hitler promised that he was still bound by the Treaty of Locarno, which Germany had freely signed.[1] In order to undermine the loyalty of France's allies he promised Mussolini that Austria would be an Italian sphere of influence, signed a non-aggression pact with Poland and negotiated a Naval Agreement with Great Britain on comparative naval strengths (June 1935). France was not informed of the agreement in advance and it caused considerable mutual distrust between her and Britain. In this way, by bilateral treaties, Hitler undermined collective security.

The pacifist movement was at its height in Britain in 1935, where a spate of books and plays about the Great War had revived the post-war feeling of disillusionment. It was at this point that the League of Nations Union organised a house to house canvass, the 'Peace Ballot', with the loaded questions usual in such cases but impressive in that eleven and a half million votes were cast. The results were overwhelmingly in favour of international disarmament and collective security through the League. The questions were mischievous in

---

[1] See above, p. 491.

that they seemed to imply that the League of Nations had reserves of power independent of the co-operation of its members and failed to face up to the problem of what should be done to meet an aggressor if peaceful methods failed. The results nevertheless helped to confuse government aims when confronted by Italian aggression in Abyssinia.

The conclusions of the ballot more or less coincided with the Labour view of foreign policy. The government played with two alternative policies: support of collective security through the League up to the point of economic sanctions; rearmament and agreements outside it with the aggressors to limit their activities. It was this last policy which was later called appeasement.

Abyssinia had been an Italian sphere of influence for many years and in view of the unsettled state of the country the interest of a European power should have been beneficial. In 1928 it had joined the League of Nations with Italian support and a pact of friendship had been signed between the two countries. But the Italians had prepared plans for incorporating Abyssinia from 1933 onwards and provoked a clash on the border with Italian Somaliland at the end of 1934. The government was at first unwilling to prejudice economic relations and solidarity against Hitler, and Eden was sent to Mussolini to offer him part of Abyssinia, which would be compensated by receiving an outlet to the sea through British Somaliland. When this was rejected, the government, surprised by public hostility to the Italian action – Abyssinia was seen as a 'little black Belgium' – tried to present a face-saving formula. Hoare, the Foreign Secretary, made a speech to the League which aroused great enthusiasm in Britain. He promised that Britain would announce her complete support for collective security if all other members of the League would make similar promises. If this worked the government would receive the credit and the League would have 'teeth'; if it failed the way was clear for Britain to rearm and the responsibility for the failure of collective security would not be hers.

The League quickly decided on the imposition of economic sanctions although three members continued to trade with Italy, and the United States, who was not a member, imposed no restrictions. Sanctions at first caused Italy fairly serious economic difficulties although some of the banned articles were ones of which she had an ample supply. They were not serious enough to deflect Mussolini from his chosen policy. In proclaiming the League as 'the keystone of British foreign policy' Baldwin seriously embarrassed the Labour party whose policy he had to a large extent stolen. Lansbury who wanted the party to take up a more clearly pacifist standpoint resigned when Bevin's motion in support of the sanctions was carried at the party conference, and at the General Election which Baldwin held in November to take advantage of Labour difficulties, the government promised that there would be no wavering in its support of collective security.

By the time the election was over it was evident that the sanctions applied were not producing the desired effect. Chamberlain urged oil sanctions; Labour spoke of blocking the Suez Canal, but many politicians were having second thoughts. The French, counting on Italian support against Germany, deprecated further action and if the League decided on the use of force, Britain would be its sole agent. The Foreign Office pointed out how disastrous an Anglo-Italian war would be in view of the potential threat from Germany. In consequence Hoare and Laval, the French Foreign Secretary, made a private offer of the greater part of Abyssinia to Italy, even though the Italians had conquered very little of the territory to be ceded.

A public outcry of almost unparalleled proportions denounced the Hoare–Laval deal when its details leaked out and Hoare was forced to resign. There was some pressure on Baldwin to follow him but he was able to turn Attlee's imputation of his honour to good account and rally support in the party. Eden, who was highly regarded by the public, became Foreign Secretary, but the sincerity of the government's support for collective security, and hence the effectiveness of the League itself, was permanently damaged. Amidst the recriminations, the uncertainty over oil sanctions and the distraction of the German action in March 1936, Mussolini, using poison gas sprayed from the air, conquered Abyssinia rapidly and annexed the country in May 1936. Sanctions were withdrawn in June.

In many respects Abyssinia was a turning point. British interference had in almost every way made matters worse.

Abyssinia was not saved; Italy was estranged and increasingly turned to Germany; difficulties had been created with France; a mockery had been made of the League at a time which proved to be its last chance to be effective; collective security was dead. Moreover, Hitler had taken the measure of the other Great Powers and showed what he thought of them by the military reoccupation of the Rhineland. As Churchill pointed out, Britain would have done better to have done nothing. 'The worst type of diplomacy,' Canning had written, 'is uncertain diplomacy,' and British foreign policy had been presented as devious, selfish and unprincipled. A war against Italy would have been popular in the circumstances and almost certainly rapidly successful, for her long coastline was particularly vulnerable to the Royal Navy, the best-armed British service; Germany was not yet strong enough to intervene and the Rhineland would probably not have been reoccupied; alternatively strong Anglo-French action in March 1936 would also have given a crucial turn to events.

After a year of quiescence Hitler claimed that the Franco-Russian Pact of May 1935 was directed exclusively against Germany and was incompatible with the Treaty of Locarno, which he repudiated in March 1936 despite his promise of 1935. The German generals expected the French to call Hitler's bluff in the reoccupation of the Rhineland, but the unstable French government was not prepared to risk a general mobilisation which would have been very unpopular and merely hoped to use the affair to obtain firmer promises of support from Britain should their security be more seriously menaced. In Britain Baldwin realised that Britain could hardly act alone and public opinion tended to echo Lord Lothian's remark: 'After all, they're only going into their own back garden.' A joint confrontation would almost certainly have been effective, but with Hitler arming at a rate of £500 m. a year the balance of advantage was soon to be weighted on the German side.

The council of the League met in London and although the French contemplated sanctions Eden and Halifax successfully opposed the idea. Germany was found guilty of breaking the treaties of Versailles and Locarno but no action was taken. Hitler promised that his aim was peace, that he was satisfied with Germany's boundaries and that he was willing to sign a pact of non-aggression to last twenty-five years. When he refused to be more specific or to consider the French counter-proposals, the matter was quietly dropped. Baldwin narrowly survived a vote of confidence in the Commons, but events in Spain from July onwards tended to divide his critics.

A dictatorship that helped to discredit the monarchy had been set up in Spain by Primo de Rivera in 1923. He was overthrown in 1930 and Alphonso XIII withdrew from the country the following year. A democratic republic was set up but had little real popular support; its finances were chaotic and public order was threatened by frequent revolts. After a questionable general election in 1936, a left wing 'Popular Front' government came to power. In July the Commander in Chief in Spanish Morocco, General Franco, rebelled and crossed into Spain, reaching the suburbs of Madrid by November. By then it had become an international problem. Italy supported Franco from the outset and supplied him with arms and equipment; Germany followed suit and both countries recognised his government in November. To the fascist powers Spain was an admirable testing ground for new weapons and of the resolution of France and Britain who had proclaimed a non-interventionist pact. Stalin comforted the other side; in October he telegraphed to the Spanish communists: 'The workers of the U.S.S.R. would merely fulfil their duty in rendering the revolutionary masses of Spain every possible assistance.' In practice the republicans received relatively little help. The French also had a popular front government, which was sympathetic but feared the reaction of fascist and conservative groups if military help was sent.

Despite the public branding of both sides as fascist and communist, the war was essentially a Spanish affair. In November 1936 the Republicans rallied and there was much bitter fighting with atrocities on both sides. Catalonia resisted the Nationalists particularly fiercely. Franco's policy was to obliterate resistance by terror and the action which aroused most horror abroad was when the Basque town of Guernica, which had no military significance, and 6,000 civilian inhabitants, was obliterated by bombing. Franco did not obtain firm control of the country until 1939.

The war brought considerable controversy in Britain and profoundly disturbed the emotions of the left wing. There was no thought of appealing to the League of Nations to arbitrate, but 'non-intervention' was clearly one-sided. Attempts were made during 1937 to patrol the Spanish borders and coasts but Italy and Germany made it clear that they would not withdraw until Franco had won. Attitudes in England to some extent divided on a class basis. The lower classes and the left-wing intellectuals talked seriously about fighting for the republic and some 2,000 actually did; others contented themselves with demonstrations and raising money for 'arms for Spain'. Trades unionists in the Labour party had already become more convinced of the need for force if necessary and armaments to make its possible; the Spanish Civil War helped to convert the remainder. Conversely the government, suspicious of the republic's communist connections and anxious to avoid another quarrel with Italy, became increasingly indecisive and thus contributed in a small way to a fascist victory. A major effect of the Civil War on Britain was through the newsreels in the cinemas, which brought home to ordinary people, in the most graphic way, the mass destruction of bombing and the sufferings of civilians. It helped to produce the mood of Munich, which made peace worth almost any price.

Almost apart from the activities of the Foreign Office the service chiefs sought to build up armaments that would be comparable with those of Germany, with whom they felt war would sooner or later be inevitable. By the end of 1937 German preparedness for a land war was almost complete but the economy was geared for it in a way which could only be sustained for a limited time; Hitler observed that Germany had 'nothing further to gain from a prolonged period of peace'. Little had been done, however, to prepare for a war against England; Germany had no real battle fleet and her air force preparations were exaggerated. They were convenient to Hitler as a weapon of bluff. The R.A.F. had been improved to obtain parity with Germany from 1934 onwards; upwards of £8 m. a year was being spent on aeroplanes and armaments. The Navy was still the pampered service, securing over £10 m. a year for capital ships and armaments; the Army was the Cinderella with less than £2 m., a factor which made it difficult for Britain to intervene with any effect in Europe.

The principal champions of rearmament within the Cabinet were Chamberlain, Eden and Duff Cooper, Secretary for War 1935–37 and then First Lord of the Admiralty. Outside, Churchill, still estranged from the party, ceaselessly warned of the dangers of low armaments. It was increasingly obvious to informed observers that service plans ought not to be worked out in isolation but jealousies prevented the creation of a Ministry of Defence, which had been envisaged in the twenties. In March 1936 Sir Thomas Inskip was made Minister for the Co-ordination of Defence, with the freedom to discover service requirements but no authority over the service Ministers to enforce a co-ordinated programme. Churchill in such a position might have made something of the post despite its limitations; Inskip was ineffective.

Some important steps were taken, nevertheless; the Army was to be slightly increased and the Territorials overhauled; two new battleships and one aircraft carrier were laid down and plans made to increase cruiser strength from fifty-one to seventy. In 1935 Watson Watt had shown that radar could effectively detect bomber approach, an invention that seemed to give more point to purely defensive aeroplanes. Though the main emphasis was still on bombers, Fighter Command was set up in 1936 and gradually equipped with two new aeroplanes, the Spitfire and the Hurricane. Wellington, Hampden and Blenheim bombers were also introduced. The Cabinet approved a re-equipment programme in March 1936 which added 8,000 'planes over three years. The delay in rearming did mean that by 1939 Britain had a higher proportion of up-to-date air force equipment than any other country.

Chamberlain's 1937 Budget was the first to make serious provision for rearmament. Defence estimates were £198 m. and to meet this income tax was raised to five shillings and a 5 per cent tax levied on arms profits. Special provision was made for a £400 m. loan to meet additional expenditure. The pace was fairly slow until after Munich, but in March 1938 Trades Union leaders agreed to ease craft regulations in the engineering industry and the service Ministers were given powers to compel the production of war equipment by civilian firms. After Munich Treasury control was virtually given up and production was authorised to the limit of industrial capacity. The potential of the aircraft industry was so increased, for instance, that more aircraft were produced than had been anticipated. From 1936 onwards more Royal Ordnance Factories and private arms factories were built and a Ministry of Supply was set up in April 1939, which was principally concerned with equipping the Army. The idea of a 'limited liability' army was abandoned, military conversations were held with France and an expeditionary force of twenty-one divisions was prepared, although only four were ready when war broke out.

(e) MUNICH

Baldwin resigned at the Coronation and Neville Chamberlain stepped almost inevitably into the vacant place, at 68 the oldest man to do so for the first time since 1905. His main career had been in business and he had not entered Parliament until he was 50. As a young man, at the most formative age, he had spent an almost solitary five years trying to grow sisal in the Bahamas; they had made him courageous and determined but had given him an undue dependence on his own judgment. He had been a capable Lord Mayor of Birmingham but a failure as Director of National Service where he showed little ability in building up a new organisation from scratch amidst the jealousies and rivalries of other departments. In Parliament he had been the author of most of the creative social legislation of the inter-war period. He was a man of complete integrity but inclined to be dictatorial and absolute master of his Cabinet; he only accepted advice, however cogently argued, when it pleased him. He knew little of Europe but considered that Baldwin had neglected its problems too long; he hated the thought of war but considered that difficulties must be faced in a spirit of realism and in this he had the support of much of the country. It was his misfortune that he completely lacked a flair for public relations; his appearance was forbidding even when he wished to be amiable, his voice rasping, his impatience of criticism almost invited opposition.

It was evident to him that the League of Nations had been disregarded too often for collective security through it to have the slightest chance of success. He could seek to revive the alliance that defeated Germany in the Great War, apart from Italy where Mussolini was increasingly aligning himself with Hitler. British co-operation with France and her allies was inevitable, but with the unstable nature of French politics Chamberlain felt that there was no guarantee that the French would act rather than bluster unless their territory was invaded. France consistently allowed Britain to take the initiative, even when her own obligations, for instance to Czechoslovakia, were involved. The United States deplored German actions but kept strictly neutral and even required, since 1935, belligerent countries to pay cash for essential materials and transport them in their own ships. Like most Englishmen of his time Chamberlain profoundly distrusted Russia, where Stalin's recent purges seemed to suggest serious weakness. British service chiefs considered that Russian military effectiveness was slight and it was felt, rightly, that she would seek to communise eastern Europe as the price of her co-operation. To ally with Russia against Germany, as the Left Book Club suggested, seemed to Chamberlain almost as impracticable as to accede to Hitler's proposal that Britain should ally with Germany against Russia.

In default of reliable allies, Britain's hands were seriously tied. Those who imagined that Britain could adopt, as a power of the first rank, a strictly moral attitude towards foreign affairs, independent of power politics, were guilty of a serious illusion. This view tended to be held by the Labour party, with the rider that some of its members deprecated the arms that alone could make Britain an effective major power. As a private individual, Chamberlain deplored the brutality of Nazi Germany – though it is doubtful whether he appreciated quite how brutal it was – but he was aware of the weakness of British military preparations and, while continuing to rearm, gambled on the chance that a great war could be avoided by meeting Germany's immediate claims for revision of the Versailles territorial settlement. There was a touching belief at the time that hard facts could be changed by discussion and persuasion and Chamberlain, unlike Baldwin, considered much could be done by personal diplomacy, by appealing to the human side of the dictators. He seems to have seen it in the same light as industrial negotiations and it was no accident that his principal adviser on foreign policy was Sir Horace Wilson, the government's Chief Industrial Adviser.

This was appeasement. But appeasement or the making of unilateral concessions is not wrong in itself but wrong only when fundamental principles are surrendered or fundamental interests are prejudiced. It was here that Chamberlain erred, due to his inexperience of diplomacy and his disregarding of Foreign Office advice. Until after Munich, his policy, supported by much of the Press, particularly *The Times*, was criticised by relatively few and was popular in the country, where it was seen as the only realistic alternative to war, which, with memories of 1914–18 so strong, few liked to contemplate.

He was most influenced in the Cabinet by Simon and Hoare, both of whom had a record, as foreign secretaries, of surrendering principles to force, and by Halifax, who had learned the value of appeasement during his long negotiations with Gandhi. Halifax had enormous personal prestige which arose not from what he had done – he had not been, for instance, a markedly successful Viceroy – but from what he was: a representative of the finest qualities of the English aristocracy and a man of high moral character who seemed to radiate disinterested goodness. He had a genius for non-involvement in domestic policy and seemed to stand for great principles. His approval gave the stamp of respectability to any policy and such was the regard in which he was held, by politicians and public alike, that, though quite unsuitable, he was seriously considered as an alternative to Churchill in 1940. With this formidable support Chamberlain could largely disregard Eden, the official Foreign Secretary. Eden relied on moral disapproval rather than firm action, although in the summer of 1937 he set up anti-submarine patrols to check Italian sinkings of British, French and Russian ships taking food to the Spanish Republic, an action that was immediately effective. He believed in firmness towards the dictators but in practice he had acquiesced in the Italian conquest of Abyssinia and had discouraged the French from action in the Rhineland. His chief asset was that he was completely honourable.

With preoccupations nearer home little notice was taken

of the renewal of war between China and Japan in 1937. Shanghai was attacked, the lower Yangste valley occupied by the end of the year. Although British and American ships were attacked and the League of Nations voted in favour of sanctions on Japan, Britain was only prepared to take action if the United States would do so as well. With a highly profitable trade with Japan the United States did nothing.

Meanwhile approaches were made to Germany. At the suggestion of Ribbentrop, who, entertaining lavishly as German Ambassador in London, had gained the confidence of many important people, Sir Nevile Henderson, who favoured appeasement, became Ambassador in Berlin. He urged making direct contacts. In November 1937 Göring invited Halifax to go to Berlin in his capacity as Master of the Middleton Hunt to visit a lavish hunting exhibition he had organised. This led to a talk with Hitler at Berchtesgaden about a permanent European settlement which confirmed Chamberlain in the value of personal discussion and Hitler in the belief that Britain would do little to resist his objectives.

Halifax became Foreign Secretary, reluctantly, when Eden resigned, on 20th February, 1938. Two incidents led Eden to take this step. Roosevelt offered to convene a conference, to which Hitler and Mussolini would be invited, to improve international relations. Although it is doubtful whether much would have been achieved, such a step would have made world opinion more aware of the danger of war and greater involvement by the United States would have been invaluable. Chamberlain thought appeasement would work and turned down the offer without reference to Eden who was enthusiastic towards it. More vital was a difference of emphasis in relations with Italy. Mussolini distrusted German designs in Austria and was prepared to be conciliatory. Eden was ready to respond but felt that Chamberlain was too prone to see the Italian point of view, which came out clearly in an interview the two men had with Count Grandi, the Italian Ambassador. This led to Eden's resignation, which caused a great sensation because Hitler had inveighed against him in a speech only a few hours previously. Retrospectively, Eden was seen as the man who was prepared to face the dictators but in fact he did not have an alternative policy and merely differed from Chamberlain over details. Eden thought that the point had been reached in relations with Italy beyond which Britain could not honourably go; Chamberlain thought there was still room for manœuvre. Eden's sense of loyalty inhibited him from publicly indicting Chamberlain's policy. Public confidence was restored when Halifax took over the Foreign Office.

Hitler's objectives were now becoming clear. In November 1937 he informed his principal subordinates of his plans for armed conquest of Austria and Czechoslovakia. In February 1938 he displaced those generals who disapproved of his methods and became Commander-in-Chief himself, promoting Ribbentrop to Foreign Secretary. On 12th February the Nazi, Seyss-Inquart, was placed, through German pressure, in charge of police in Austria and Nazi activities there were legalised. Faced with Nazi-sponsored disorders Chancellor Schuschnigg declared that there would be a referendum on the country's future; he was forced to resign on 11th March, German troops crossed the frontier and two days later Austria was declared to be part of the German Reich. His action took the world by surprise; the League of Nations did nothing, although Austria was a member; Mussolini acquiesced; Chamberlain made an official protest which Hitler rebuffed, describing his action as a German domestic matter. Public opinion recalled that the completely German population of Austria had been refused union with Germany in 1919.

Churchill warned Chamberlain that Czechoslovakia, with a partly German population, would probably be next. Chamberlain did not feel that the situation had materially changed. The National Council of Labour (representatives of the T.U.C. and the Labour party) urged him to co-operate with Russia and France to resist further aggression; the Russians were ready to co-operate, but Chamberlain considered that such a move would only precipitate war. He hoped the *Anschluss* would divide Hitler and Mussolini, in view of the latter's hopes of influence in Austria, and in April he concluded an agreement recognising Abyssinia as an Italian possession as soon as Italian troops were withdrawn from Spain, a condition that was fulfilled by the end of the year. When pressed to define the circumstances in which Britain would fight, Chamberlain specified an attack on France or Belgium, threats to British liberty or independence, or possibly to help a victim of aggression. He refused to give a public pledge of support to Czechoslovakia whose independence he did not consider to be a British interest.

Although it contained the most varied population of any eastern European country, Czechoslovakia was the most democratic and the best governed of the successor states of the Austro-Hungarian Empire. She had very strong natural frontiers strengthened still further by a miniature Maginot line, behind which the Czech General Staff were confident that their army of thirty-four divisions, one of the best equipped in Europe, could hold out for six weeks, by which time it was assumed that their allies, France and Russia, would be actively supporting them. The Czechs had pacts with other countries as well and if treaties were sacred their position was impregnable. The *Anschluss*, however, had weakened their position as the Austro-Czech frontier was across relatively flat country and was not as strongly defended as the frontiers with Germany.

The problem of its national minorities was real but exaggerated. Out of fourteen million people only seven and a half million were Czechs; over three million were Germans, some concentrated in the area of the Sudeten Mountains, others scattered, but the group was invariably referred to as the Sudeten Germans. There were nearly two and a half million Slovaks and the balance of the population was made up principally by Hungarians, Poles and Ruthenes. The Czechs had not always been tactful in dealing with minority groups but a National Minorities Statute was in preparation and the Sudetens were better treated than many minorities in other states.

Several political parties represented the Sudeten interests; one was Nazi and its leader Henlein was essentially Hitler's puppet. In April he put forward as the Sudeten demands full autonomy for the German areas in Czechoslovakia and the revision of Czech foreign policy. In fulfilment of their treaty obligations the French government recognised that it might have to fight and urged Britain to co-operate. Chamberlain made an ambiguous reply which produced a very bad impression in France where it was concluded that no British assistance would be forthcoming, thus giving the French

Foreign Secretary, Bonnet, who also believed in appeasement, the chance to restrain French action. Hitler, sensing a weakening, moved troops towards the Czech frontier.

On 19th May Henlein refused to continue negotiations with the Czech government and left for Berlin; on the same day German troops clashed with Czechs on the frontier. The Czech government ordered a partial mobilisation; both France and Russia promised support, though Hungary and Poland refused passage to the latter's troops. Halifax warned Hitler that Britain was prepared to fight. Hitler was essentially an opportunist, profiting from the misjudgments and irresolution of others; for once he had misjudged the situation and withdrew in a rage, absenting himself from public life for a week. The German General Staff warned him that his army was not ready for a major war and he gave orders for his forces to be greatly enlarged. The Siegfried Line was built as a protection against France. Plans were laid for another attempt on 1st October.

During the summer the appeasers were at work. Bonnet believed that French independence could only be preserved if France abandoned her allies in eastern Europe. He hoped to confuse the issue so that the French action would not appear as a surrender to brutal and naked force. Daladier, the French Prime Minister, horrified by the thought of war, allowed Bonnet to lead him. Chamberlain was also perturbed by how near conflict had been in May and felt the Czechs should make such concessions as would satisfy Germany, lest Hitler impose his solution by force. To this end he sent the Runciman Mission to Prague to act as mediator in the negotiations between President Benes and Henlein. Neither party really wished them to succeed; both hoped that their fulure would discredit the other. Although it was fully apparent to Runciman that Henlein was merely Hitler's mouthpiece, he persuaded Benes, by the end of August, to concede almost all the Sudeten demands. In his Fourth Plan Benes promised full autonomy, though he refused to change his foreign policy. In theory a genuine agreement should have been possible. Benes had ceded so much that it was hard to justify continued Sudeten agitation.

An article in *The Times* on 7th September saved the day for Hitler. Written by Geoffrey Dawson, the Editor, a determined appeaser and known to be an intimate of Chamberlain's, its suggestion that Sudetenland should be ceded outright to Germany was assumed to reflect Chamberlain's own view. A similar article appeared in *La République*. They left Hitler in no doubt that if he pressed for it he would get more. Accordingly, even though Halifax, under pressure from Churchill and senior Foreign Office officials, warned him that Britain could not remain neutral if France was involved, Hitler authorised a Sudeten revolt on 13th September, which was suppressed by the Czechs without difficulty, and made plans for armed intervention, 'Operation Green', on 30th September.

On 13th September the disunited French Cabinet decided against ordering mobilisation and Daladier urged Chamberlain to negotiate a settlement. Alarm about German air power and the geographical difficulty of assisting the Czechs directly were valid reasons for wishing to avoid war, but were used to justify an existing policy. On the other hand there were sound military reasons for making a stand: the Germans were not yet prepared for a war on two fronts and they only had half the divisions of the French and the Czechs together; Czechoslovakia had very strong frontier defences. Moreover the Russians offered to give assistance although their offers were ignored.

The French refusal to mobilise in defence of their ally meant Britain had to take the initiative. Chamberlain was not afraid to do so though he obstinately refused to heed warnings that British policy should change direction. One of the most remarkable of these came indirectly from the permanent head of the German Foreign Office, who warned that the only way to stop Hitler was for Britain to threaten war. German business interests made the same suggestion. Chamberlain, with considerable courage and audacity, decided on a personal confrontation and flew on 15th September to meet Hitler at Berchtesgaden. The visit caught the popular imagination and it was expected that Chamberlain, who was accompanied by Sir Horace Wilson and the head of the Central European section of the Foreign Office, would take a firm attitude. The meeting convinced Chamberlain that Hitler was determined to have his own way and he accordingly had to agree to the German annexation of Sudetenland. It was clear that Hitler was sure that Britain would not fight, whatever he did. The meeting was really of greater importance than Munich for it made it clear that war was the only alternative to a complete surrender to Hitler over Czechoslovakia.

On his return Chamberlain proposed to the Cabinet the transfer of all districts with a population over 50 per cent German; on the 18th he took six hours to persuade Daladier to accept this, which he would only do if Britain guaranteed the new Czech frontiers. In Prague Benes, his Cabinet and military advisers sat for thirty-six hours deciding on what course to take. The line to Paris crossed German territory and they could not use it. Britain refused to support arbitration. The Russians offered help but some members of the Czech Cabinet were suspicious of Russian intentions and the offer was disregarded. Cajoled by the French and British envoys, Benes at last gave in. 'We had no other choice,' he said, 'because we were left alone.' The Western Powers 'had worked for the King of Prussia'.

Hitler, encouraged, raised his bid. He met the British Prime Minister at Bad Godesberg on 22nd September, ostensibly to settle details. Chamberlain thought he had won and was deeply shocked when Hitler demanded areas which contained the principal Czech economic assets, and the loss of which would make what remained an unviable state. The Führer demanded immediate German occupation of Sudetenland and refused to guarantee the new frontiers. He then unctuously agreed to extend his timetable to 1st October, the date he had secretly decided on.[1] He promised no further territorial demands.

Chamberlain was convinced Hitler would keep his word, but, before he returned to London, opinion at home was hardening. Halifax agreed with Daladier that the Czechs should be instructed to mobilise and made a tentative approach to Russia. The Cabinet rejected the Godesberg terms on 24th September and Duff Cooper, First Lord of the Admiralty, urged a general mobilisation. Public opinion as a whole became aware, suddenly, that a small democratic

[1] The discussions were regularly interrupted by couriers. As he read them, Hitler's face became contorted with rage and he would shout: 'Two more Germans killed by the Czechs; I will be avenged for every one of them. The Czechs must be annihilated.'

state was being bullied. The governments were having second thoughts, however. Chamberlain gave ambiguous answers to France on future plans and appeasement gained ground there. He warned the Czechs that there was very little the Western Powers could do to help them. Hitler refused to communicate and in a speech on 26th September offered no hope of concession. Chamberlain broadcast to the nation on the 27th warning of the imminence of war but showing scant sympathy for the Czechs. The Navy was mobilised. With the example of the Spanish Civil War in mind, a devastating air raid at an early stage was feared. Trenches were dug in Hyde Park. Civil Defence preparations were made. In Paris one-third of the population fled the city in panic. On the 28th everybody expected war before the day was out.

After Chamberlain's broadcast he received a shrewdly worded appeal from Hitler asking for his help in overcoming Czech obstinacy. Consulting only Wilson, he agreed to meet Hitler a third time. In the Commons on the 28th he made a long and despairing speech, which was dramatically interrupted by the invitation from Hitler which he had already received. As he announced he would go to Munich, the tension broke, someone shouted 'Thank God for the Prime Minister' and order papers were thrown in the air in a scene of mass hysteria. Masaryk, the Czech Ambassador, who was in the gallery, confronted Chamberlain and Halifax afterwards: 'If you have sacrificed my nation to preserve the peace of the world, I will be the first to applaud you, but, if not, gentlemen, God help your souls.' Czechoslovakia was to be condemned unheard.

With Wilson Chamberlain went to Munich confidently, but Hitler had already won and the conference was merely an empty ceremony. Chamberlain refused to collaborate with Daladier, who was well-intentioned but powerless. Mussolini played the impartial mediator, following a plan supplied from Berlin. Hitler's demands at Godesberg were accepted. Sudeten territory was to be almost immediately surrendered, further areas were to be defined by an international commission and the new frontiers were to be guaranteed. As implemented, these terms, accepted by Benes under pressure from Berlin before he went into exile, which postponed the war for eleven months, deprived Czechoslovakia of 11,000 square miles of territory with a population of nearly three million Germans and nearly a million Czechs. The areas contained the bulk of her industrial strength including 70 per cent of her iron and steel, 66 per cent of her coal and 70 per cent of her electric power supplies. She lost all her defensive fortifications. The Czech authorities complied with orders from Berlin to turn back refugees from the annexed territories. The treaties with France and Russia were forfeited. Poland and Hungary stepped in to share the spoils.

Chamberlain secured in return a personal assurance from Hitler that he would never fight England and would solve mutual problems by consultation. He prized this piece of paper highly and waved it in the air when he appeared at the window of No. 10 on his return on 1st October. 'My good friends, this is the second time that there has come back from Germany to Downing Street a peace with honour. I believe it is peace for our time.'[1] In the circumstances Chamberlain had left himself little alternative. Though he had been dominant in the Cabinet since 1931 Britain was still not fully prepared, nor was she united, for the crisis had been sprung on the country and the public had been kept in ignorance of the true nature of the German régime. Chamberlain's action reflected his own narrow vision and also the muddle in most people's minds: they wanted a peace with honour, they feared war. Most of the Dominions were firmly opposed to war on such an issue. In preserving peace Chamberlain became a national hero for a few weeks, even if many would have hesitated to endorse the view of *The Times*: 'No conqueror returning from a battlefield has come adorned with nobler laurels.'

(f) DISILLUSIONMENT

Although the general mood was one of profound relief, the wisdom of the settlement was seriously queried by a number of influential people, and many of the public had second thoughts after reading Douglas Reed's book *Disgrace Abounding*. Churchill described the tragic progression of Berchtesgaden, Bad Godesberg and Munich: '£1 was demanded at pistol's point. When it was given, £2 was demanded at

[1] See above, p. 250.

pistol's point. Finally the dictator consented to take £1 17s. 6d. . . . We have suffered a total and unmitigated defeat.' In fact the Munich settlement was worse than that offered at Godesberg, which was at least specific. Duff Cooper resigned as First Lord in protest; Eden, Cranborne and Boothby, Amery, Sandys and Macmillan among the back benchers declared that Britain should have abandoned the policy of expediency and stood firm on a matter of principle. Chamberlain regarded such displays of disloyalty as 'rocking the boat'.

Attlee condemned the agreement as a bitter humiliation: the Czechs had been 'betrayed and handed over to a ruthless despotism', but the Labour party had to bear some share of the responsibility. It had opposed rearmament; it put blind faith in the League when it was evident that that body was ineffective; it encouraged appeasement when it sought to censure a policy it rightly distrusted by means of a vote against rearmament; it gave an impression of national disunity when, for instance, the *New Statesman* on 27th August contained the words: 'the strategical value of the Bohemian frontier should not be made the occasion of a world war'.

In two respects Munich gained valuable time. By September 1939 the country was much more united; the Labour party had accepted rearmament, the appeasers had been largely discredited. The Dominions were much more convinced that here was a serious matter in which they should make common cause with the mother country. Rearmament also profited from the delay; stocks increased, a chain of radar stations was completed, the R.A.F. obtained a really effective fighter force. Anderson, formerly a senior civil servant, became Lord Privy Seal with responsibility for Civil Defence and did much invaluable work of organisation. Against these gains there were very real losses. If there had been a war in 1938 instead of 1939 the efficient Czech Army would have been available; the German army virtually doubled during the year. Though Britain had superior air defences in 1939 the Germans would have found it more difficult to have obtained the bases from which raids on England would have been possible. During the interval Russian assistance became less rather than more available through the British attitude, which also helped to undermine morale in France. Opinion in the United States was horrified by Munich, which discredited the intentions of the Western Powers in the world as a whole. In September 1938 Chamberlain was confronted by a serious dilemma: no statesman should lead into war a partly armed and partly united country, nevertheless the global balance was much more heavily tipped in Britain's favour than it was to be a year later. But Chamberlain rarely looked ahead.

British sympathisers with Hitler found the Führer's next action very hard to justify. On 7th November a young Polish Jew, mentally affected by the sufferings of his parents in Germany, fatally wounded Baron vom Rath, a junior German diplomat in Paris. When he died a fifteen-hour pogrom against the Jews took place in Germany: Jewish property was destroyed, and thousands interned in concentration camps. On 12th November a fine of around £80 m. was imposed on the Jewish community and they were excluded from the economic life of the Reich. The pogrom was so thoroughly organised that it is probable that the authorities instigated vom Rath's murder. There was little sympathy in France where anti-Semitism was strong, but considerable horror in Britain, where Baldwin emerged from his retirement to launch an appeal for funds.

Practical appeasement continued. No protest was made when the Hungarians, with German encouragement, occupied part of Czechoslovakia in November. In December Bonnet signed a Franco-German Declaration of friendship with Ribbentrop. In January Chamberlain and Halifax made a futile visit to Rome which only increased Italian contempt. In February, after the fall of Barcelona, Britain recognised Franco as ruler of Spain. Chamberlain believed friendly relations could be established. On 10th March, 1939, the Prime Minister assured Press correspondents: 'Europe is settling down to a period of tranquillity', and on the same day Hoare told his constituents that a new golden age was approaching. Five days later Hitler ended what remained of Czech independence.

Public opinion was confused during the six months after Munich, which allowed Chamberlain to pursue his own policy, although his personal unpopularity grew. There was some talk of a 'People's Front' against the government but it was frustrated from the start by jealousies among its potential supporters. Halifax urged Chamberlain to form an all-party government, or to invite Eden and Churchill to take office, but Chamberlain considered that accepting the latter proposal would be tantamount to admitting that appeasement was wrong. Many resigned themselves to despair, convinced that a war in which Britain would be defeated was the only possible outcome.

Cheated of his war by Western subservience at Munich, Hitler at once planned further moves. Hungary was tempted with the thought of further annexations and every effort was made to create coolness between the Russians and the Czechs. The residue of Czecho-Slovakia was organised in four parts with the most tenuous links; the speed with which it disintegrated even surprised Hitler. In the hope of stemming the tide, President Hacha dismissed the Ruthenian government on 6th March and on the 15th was summoned to Berlin where he was tortured and blackmailed into surrender. Slovakia and Ruthenia became theoretically independent; Hungary seized Carpatho-Russia, Bohemia became a German protectorate, which German troops, followed by the Gestapo, occupied the following day.

This swift dismemberment without warning shook Britain out of its lethargy. The Conservatives as a whole had never been happy about appeasement, which was at variance with their normal attitudes, and back bench pressure and the influence on Halifax of senior Foreign Office officials led to Chamberlain denouncing Hitler's action in a speech at Birmingham on 17th March, though principally, it was noted, as a personal affront to himself rather than an outrage on Czech independence. He was still not convinced that Britain needed to change her policy, although he was prepared to take some further precautions. £6 m. of Czech money on deposit in London was handed over to the Germans, who also obtained £10 m. of sterling assets they found in Prague and a large store of munitions. Henderson was recalled from Berlin for consultations, but a Russian proposal of a conference to resist aggression in Roumania, thought to be the next victim, was dismissed as premature.

It was not certain why Roumania was thought to be in danger; the Germans did not in fact have any plans. The

German Economic Affairs Minister had visited the country recently and made the suggestion that Germany should have a monopoly of Roumanian exports, particularly grain and oil. Possibly Chamberlain just guessed. However, he thought it sufficiently serious to seek the assistance of France, Poland and Russia on 21st March. The Poles refused to co-operate with Russia, however, only to receive territorial demands from Germany the same day.

Reappearing as a sovereign state in 1919, after an interval of 125 years, Poland had made up for her absence by displays of belligerency towards all her neighbours,[1] to such an extent that Briand had commented: 'La Pologne, c'est le rheumatisme de l'Europe.' France, however, remained a firm ally but the Poles did little else to secure themselves against the enmities which they had aroused. Compared with Czechoslovakia Poland was undemocratic, inefficient and intolerant towards her minorities.[2]   The Germans had a much better case for revision of the Versailles clauses making the completely German Danzig a Free City for Poland's benefit and creating the Polish Corridor which divided their country in order to give Poland access to the sea, than they had had over Sudetenland. It was a revision of these clauses that Germany demanded on 21st March. Moreover Colonel Beck, the Polish Foreign Minister, was a devious character who had swooped on Czechoslovakia after Munich, refused to co-operate with Russia against Germany and negotiated secretly with Hitler while imploring Western assistance.

Chamberlain originally sought Polish help in case Germany invaded Roumania; Beck made no promises but obtained a British guarantee of Polish independence on 31st March. Lithuania had ceded Memel to Germany on 22nd March under threat of immediate occupation and on 29th March the British Cabinet heard unfounded rumours of troop movements against Poland. On 6th April a reciprocal defence agreement was signed between Britain and Poland.

Chamberlain saw this as a gesture which would indicate to Hitler that he had gone far enough; he did not foresee its practical consequences. He believed war had come in 1914

---

[1] See above, p. 466.
[2] She also persecuted Jews but hers were peasants and not the distinguished and talented people who fell foul of the Nazi régime in Germany.

THE HUNT FOR SECURITY

because Grey had not made the British position clear; he would not make the same mistake. On 3rd April Lloyd George indicated clearly that he had made another: 'If war occurred tomorrow, you could not send a single battalion to Poland. . . .' Any British guarantee of Poland, even though it committed France as well, could not possibly be effective without the assistance of Russia, and in guaranteeing Poland without prior consultation with the Soviet Government, Chamberlain had unwittingly thrown away his best bargaining counter. Germany could only attack Russia through Poland and therefore Chamberlain had indirectly guaranteed Russia itself against German attack. The British action was a decisive step of incredible rashness.

Nevertheless Chamberlain made other promises equally incapable of implementation. When Mussolini annexed Albania on 7th April, an Anglo-French guarantee was given to Greece and Roumania. In May he signed with Turkey a declaration against aggression in the Mediterranean. At the end of April a limited step was taken: at the insistence of the War Minister, Hore-Belisha, and despite Liberal and Labour opposition, all men of twenty and twenty-one were to be called up for six months' training. Hitler took no notice and continued to prepare his plans to crush Poland. In May 1939 he cajoled Mussolini into a firm military alliance, the Pact of Steel.

Meanwhile there was an uncertain pause during which Britain lost her one real chance of obtaining an effective guarantee against further German aggression by dilatoriness. From the rise of Hitler onwards the Russians had had few illusions about the dangers of Nazism but hoped that they could escape from their diplomatic isolation by opposing it in concert with the Western Powers. From 1937 onwards their Foreign Secretary, Litvinov, denounced at every international meeting both fascist aggression and Western timidity, thus endearing Russia to neither side. Chamberlain was suspicious of Russian intentions; Russia in consequence became suspicious of British. Chamberlain saw little need for urgency; he doubted Russian military effectiveness and felt Russia stood more in need of British assistance than the other way about. As Halifax remarked: 'It was desirable not to estrange Russia but always to keep her in play.'

Chamberlain initially proposed on 14th April that the Russians would pledge their assistance should Poland be attacked. Litvinov had been replaced by the less conciliatory Molotov who stipulated that there must be a reciprocal arrangement. Deadlock was reached by 14th May. On 27th May negotiations for a Franco-Russo-British mutual assistance pact were begun. Negotiations were at a low level; the British and French feared that unless they were careful the Russians would involve them in a war for their own purposes, and no party hurried lest a rapid agreement would precipitate action from Hitler. Chamberlain refused to go and see Stalin, so did Halifax. On 23rd July Molotov suggested that military talks should begin before the political agreement was concluded, but the British mission did not arrive in Moscow until 11th August and the talks reached deadlock over the Polish refusal to admit the Red Army. Chamberlain saw the Russian negotiations as a means of conciliating British public opinion, and perhaps of making Hitler think twice at the same time. He still thought a bargain with Hitler was possible.

Stalin meanwhile thought that a war between Germany and Britain was inevitable and hoped to buy immunity or at least a breathing space for Russia. The Germans had asked for talks in mid-July; from 12th August onwards two sets of discussions proceeded in Moscow. A Russo-German commercial agreement was signed on 19th August and on the 23rd Ribbentrop arrived in Moscow and signed a treaty during the night. Stalin had pitched his terms as high as possible; Ribbentrop granted them all. As the price for a ten-year non-aggression pact, the Soviet government obtained a free hand in Finland, Latvia, Estonia and Bessarabia. Poland was to be partitioned. In default of a Russian alliance, Hitler imagined the Western allies would give him a free hand on his eastern frontier.

He was wrong. The British government, free of an embarrassing potential ally, restated its obligations to Poland and the determination of the country as a whole to defy Hitler grew. Hitler had long had effective control of Danzig and incidents were arranged on its frontier with Poland. Beck refused to be provoked. On 22nd August secret orders were given for an attack on Poland four days later and the British

Government, aware of the troop movements, again pledged its support. Parliament was recalled on 24th August and enacted Emergency Powers legislation. Reserves were mobilised. In a letter to Hitler Chamberlain warned him of the consequences of his action and urged negotiations. Hitler was surprised at this reaction and hesitated. In a message on the 25th he promised 'to settle all differences with Britain', but inferred that the Poles were forcing his hand. Italy refused to support him, however, and plans for an attack on the 26th were suspended.

On the 28th Chamberlain urged the Poles to open negotiations. Beck agreed but orders were given for the complete mobilisation of Polish forces on 31st August. The 29th was crucial; Hitler at last realised that Britain and France would fight but attempted to browbeat Beck into surrender without a war. Beck would only negotiate on equal terms. On the 31st Hitler gave orders for an attack on Poland at first light the following day. Mussolini offered to negotiate. On 1st September a British Note was sent to Hitler demanding he withdraw his troops. There was no time limit for a reply.

On 2nd September Daladier stood firm but Chamberlain hesitated. Sir Horace Wilson told the German Chargé d'Affaires that bygones would be bygones if the Germans withdrew. In the Commons when Chamberlain made an unsatisfactory speech, L. S. Amery called over to Greenwood, temporarily leading the Opposition: 'Speak for England, Arthur', and Greenwood did his best, deeply criticising the delay in declaring war. In private he warned Chamberlain that if war was not declared the next morning it would be impossible to hold the House. In Cabinet Chamberlain and Halifax played for time, against the unanimous opposition of their colleagues. At length an ultimatum was sent to Hitler and by 11 a.m. the two countries were at war. Chamberlain broadcast the news to the country a quarter an hour later. France and the Dominions, except Eire, followed suit.

Britain fought in defence of a principle, as Duff Cooper put it: 'that one great power should not be allowed, in disregard of treaty obligations, of the laws of nations and the decrees of morality, to dominate the continent of Europe.' The time had long gone by when this could be done except by war; Friedrich Gentz had written in 1805: 'The more vigorously and courageously injustice and force are attacked in their first appearance, the less often will it be necessary to take the field against them in battle . . .' But in the 20th Century war was such that it might prejudice the very civilisation it sought to save. To the Commons on 3rd September Chamberlain said: 'Everything I have worked for, everything I have hoped for, everything I have believed in during my public life, has crashed in ruins,' and those who heard him, contemplating the second major war in their lifetime, realised how unreal was the security they had thought so real.

INDEX OF ADMINISTRATIONS

Beside the name of each Prime Minister are references to pages where the names of important members of his administration may be found.

BIBLIOGRAPHY

There are a great number of books on this period and what a student is able to read to extend his knowledge is clearly largely determined by availability. The following books have been useful to me in writing this account and I can recommend them for further study.

GENERAL BOOKS

The Oxford History of England: Vol. XIII, Woodward, The Age of Reform; Vol. XIV, Ensor, England, 1870–1914; Vol. XV, Taylor, English History, 1914–45
The Penguin History of England: Vol. VIII, Thomson, The Nineteenth Century; Vol. IX, Thomson, The Twentieth Century

History of the English People in the Nineteenth Century, Halévy: Vol. I, *England in 1815*; Vol. II, *The Liberal Awakening, 1815-30*; Vol. III, *The Triumph of Reform, 1830-42*; Vol. IV, *Victorian Years, 1842-52*, with linking essay by R. B. McCallum, *1852-95*; Vol. V, *Imperialism and the Rise of Labour, 1895-1905*; Vol. VI, *The Rule of Democracy, 1905-14*
Cole and Postgate, *The Common People*
Gregg, *Social and Economic History of Britain*
Williamson, *A Notebook of Commonwealth History*

EARLY NINETEENTH CENTURY

Brock, *Liverpool and Liberal Toryism*
White, *Waterloo to Peterloo*
Maccoby, *English Radicalism, 1786-1832*
Leigh, *Castlereagh*
Marriott, *Castlereagh*
Petrie, *Canning*
Fay, *Huskisson and His Age*
Gash, *Mr. Secretary Peel*
Gash, *Politics In the Age of Peel*
Davis, *The Age of Grey and Peel*
Wallas, *Life of Francis Place*
Trevelyan, *Lord Grey of the Reform Bill*
Butler, *The Passing of the Great Reform Bill*
Maccoby, *English Radicalism, 1832-54*
Cecil, *Melbourne*
Finer, *Chadwick*
McCord, *The Anti-Corn Law League*
Southgate, *The Passing of the Whigs*
Read and Glasgow, *Feargus O'Connor*
McDowell, *British Conservatism*
Ashton, *The Industrial Revolution*
Ashton, *Iron and Steel in the Industrial Revolution*
Hammond, *The Rise of Modern Industry*
Hammond, *The Age of the Chartists*
Bryant, *The Age of Elegance*
Young, *Victorian England*
Fay, *The Corn Laws and Social England*
Ernle, *English Farming*
Fay, *Great Britain from Adam Smith to the Present Day*
Kitson-Clark, *The Making of Victorian England*

LATE NINETEENTH CENTURY

Longford, *Victoria, R.I.*
Cecil, *Queen Victoria and her Prime Ministers*
McCallum, *The Liberal Party from Grey to Asquith*
Tilby, *Lord John Russell*
Guedella, *Palmerston*
Southgate, *The Most English Minister*
Martin, *The Triumph of Lord Palmerston*
Woodham-Smith, *The Reason Why*
Briggs, *The Age of Improvement*
Briggs, *Victorian People*
Maccoby, *English Radicalism, 1853-86*
Smith, *The Making of the Second Reform Bill*

Strachey, *Eminent Victorians*
Morley, *Life of Gladstone*
Magnus, *Gladstone*
Eyck, *Gladstone*
Hammond and Foot, *Gladstone and Liberalism*
Hammond, *Gladstone and the Irish Nation*
Seton-Watson, *Disraeli, Gladstone and the Eastern Question*
Hanham, *Elections and Party Management; Politics in the Time of Disraeli and Gladstone*
Moneypenny and Buckle, *Life of Disraeli*
Maurois, *Disraeli*
Blake, *Disraeli*
Kennedy, *Salisbury*
Churchill, *Lord Randolph Churchill*
Curtis, *Ireland*
Taylor, *The Struggle for Mastery In Europe, 1848–1918*
Maccoby, *English Radicalism; The End?*
Williams, *Botha, Smuts and South Africa*
Garvin and Amery, *Life of Joseph Chamberlain*
Fraser, *Joseph Chamberlain*
Morton and Tate, *The British Labour Movement*
Faber, *Oxford Apostles*
Inglis, *Churches and the Working Classes in Victorian England*

TWENTIETH CENTURY

Young, *Balfour*
Jenkins, *Asquith*
Magnus, *Edward VII*
Magnus, *Kitchener*
Blake, *The Unknown Prime Minister*
Dangerfield, *The Strange Death of Liberal England*
Trevelyan, *Grey of Fallodon*
Ehrmann, *Cabinet Government and War*
Jones, *Lloyd George*
Schitt, *The Origins of the First World War* (Historical Assocn. Pamphlet)
Cruttwell, *The Great War*
Gollin, *Proconsul in Politics* (Milner)
Bruce, *The Coming of the Welfare State*
Beaverbrook, *The Decline and Fall of Lloyd George*
McKenzie, *British Political Parties*
Pelling, *Short History of the Labour Party*
Symons, *The General Strike*
Pollard, *The Development of the British Economy, 1914–50*
Harrod, *John Maynard Keynes*
Masani, *Britain in India*
Spear, *Oxford History of Modern India*
Mowat, *Britain Between the Wars*
Carr, *International Relations between the Wars*
Gathorne-Hardy, *International Affairs 1920–39*
Gilbert, *Britain and Germany between the Wars*
Williams, *A Pattern of Rulers*
Churchill, *The Gathering Storm*
Eden, *Facing the Dictators*
Feiling, *Neville Chamberlain*
Wheeler-Bennett, *Munich*
Middlemass and Barnes, *Baldwin*

INDEX

Universities, 6, 220, 223–4
Unemployment, 289, 299, 328, 367, 382, 385; the Depression and, 467–8, 485, 500, 502; Cures for, 504, 515, 517, 519, 524–7, 533–5

Venezuela, 331–2
Verona, Congress of, 54, 56, 59
Versailles, Peace of, 460–4, 491, 509, 544–5, 548, 553, 566
Victoria, Queen, 105–6, 110, 163, 174, 184, 191, 207–8, 210–12, 228, 230–1, 247, 250, 273, 277, 284–5, 307, 317, 319, 324, 335, 339, 346–7, 350–1
Vienna, Congress of, 8, 46, 51–2, 106, 248

Wales, 318, 321, 356, 371, 385, 403–4, 423, 457 468, 494, 522, 528, 534
War Debts, 456, 481, 511, 513, 516, 530–1
Webb, S. and B., 133–4, 299, 327, 330, 354, 381, 383, 448, 480, 511, 518
Wellington, 1st Duke of, 9, 18, 43,

53; as Prime Minister, 69–81; 89, 107, 112, 124, 131, 146, 212
Wesley, J., 10, 33
Wheatley, J.. 479, 486–7, 512, 534
Whig Party, 5, 9, 47, 80; and First Reform Bill, 90; 154, 166, 183, 185, 196, 197, 205, 263; Third Home Rule Bill and, 272, 284
Whitbread, S., 36, 52
Wilberforce, W., 5, 35, 91
William II, Emperor of Germany, 333–5, 338–9, 344, 361, 410–11, 418, 453–4
Wilson, Sir Henry, 407–8, 421, 450, 471–2
Wilson, Sir Horace, 554, 559, 569
Wilson, Woodrow, 447, 453, 460, 462, 464, 470
Women's Suffrage, 400–3, 428, 449, 505
Wyndham, G., 357

Yorkshire, 5, 16, 22, 81, 302
Ypres, Battles of, 423, 445

Zulus, 254, 273, 336